Good Housekeeping

COOKERY BOOK

Good Housekeeping

COOKERY BOOK

THE COOK'S
CLASSIC COMPANION

COLLINS & BROWN

First published in Great Britain in 2004
by Collins & Brown
10 Southcombe Street
London W14 0RA

An imprint of Anova Books Company Ltd

This edition published 2008 for Index Books Ltd

The Good Housekeeping website is
www.goodhousekeeping.co.uk

9 8 7 6 5 4 3 2 1

Project editor: Janet Illsley
Designer: Anne Wilson
Illustrator: Philip Bannister
Editorial team: Jenny McGlyne, Kathy Steer,
Gill Hodson, Hilary Bird
Project manager: Emily Preece-Morrison

ISBN 978 1 84340 115 5

A catalogue record for this book is available from the
British Library.

Reproduction by Anorax Imaging Ltd, England
Printed and bound by SNP Leefung Printers, China

This book can be ordered direct from the publisher.
Contact the marketing department, but try your
bookshop first.

www.anovabooks.com

NOTES

- Both metric and imperial measures are given for the recipes. Follow either set of measures, not a mixture of both, as they are not interchangeable.

- All spoon measures are level. 1 tsp = 5ml spoon; 1 tbsp = 15ml spoon.

- Ovens and grills must be preheated to the specified temperature.

- Use sea salt and freshly ground black pepper unless otherwise suggested.

- Fresh herbs should be used unless dried herbs are specified in a recipe.

- Medium eggs should be used except where otherwise specified. Free-range eggs are recommended.

- Note that certain recipes, including mayonnaise, lemon curd and some cold desserts, contain raw or lightly cooked eggs. The young, elderly, pregnant women and anyone with an immune-deficiency disease should avoid these, because of the slight risk of salmonella.

- Calorie, fat and carbohydrate counts per serving are provided for the recipes. Where a recipe serves a variable number, these counts range from a larger to a smaller figure according to the portion size, which is determined by the number you are serving.

CONTENTS

FOREWORD

I always think the test of a good cookbook is how often you turn to it for inspiration – and how messy the pages are. My favourite book lives in the kitchen, has been well-thumbed through, the pages are flecked with ingredients, and odd specks of seasoning fall out whenever I pick it up.

We know from the hundreds of readers' queries we receive every month that you're fiercely proud of the Good Housekeeping cookbooks. All the recipes have been rigorously tested in the Good Housekeeping Institute kitchens so they're guaranteed to work the first time you make them.

The publication of this new, updated edition of our classic cookbook is timely – it's 80 years since the Institute was first set up to help women around the home. Since then there's been a significant change in women's role in society, with more of us going out to work now than ever before. But knowing how to cook is still just as important as it was then. Some of the recipes have changed but the classics and ethos remain. Food fads have their moment, then pass, but knowing how to cook good food will never go out of fashion.

Lindsay Nicolson, Editor-in-Chief, *Good Housekeeping*

HERBS, SPICES AND FLAVOURINGS

HERBS

Herbs are aromatic plants grown primarily for culinary purposes, although many are also attributed with medical properties. Fresh herbs lend a superb flavour to all kinds of dishes. Their flavour is derived from essential oils found in the leaves and stems, which are released when the herb is heated, crushed or chopped. Herbs may be chopped before they are added to a dish, or used whole. The more delicate herbs, such as parsley, chervil and tarragon, should be added towards the end of cooking, while tougher varieties, such as rosemary and thyme, are added at the beginning.

Most herbs, even if they do not originate in this country, can be grown successfully in the garden or in window boxes. Some are annuals and need to be sown each year, others are perennial and grow year after year. The most popular herbs – including parsley, thyme, sage, chives, oregano, basil, coriander and dill – are available fresh from supermarkets and greengrocers all year round. They are sold in pots, bunches and small packets.

Ideally, fresh herbs should be picked just before using, or used soon after purchase. If necessary they can be stored in the fridge for 1–2 days: seal in a plastic bag enclosing plenty of air. Large bunches of herbs, such as parsley and coriander, which still have their roots intact should be stored in a jug of water with a plastic bag inverted over the leaves. Herbs can also be dried (see below) or frozen for use in soups and casseroles. To freeze, chop finely and freeze in ice cube trays.

Dried herbs work well in cooked dishes, such as casseroles, but they are generally not suitable for use in salads. Dried herbs have a stronger flavour than fresh ones and should be used more sparingly: as a general guide if substituting dried for fresh herbs, use one third of the amount specified.

Dried herbs keep best in airtight jars away from the light. Opt for wood, earthenware or dark glass containers. In a cool place, dried herbs will retain their flavour for about 6 months.

The more robust varieties of home-grown herbs can be dried successfully at home. Tie in bunches and hang in a cool airy place, covered with muslin to keep the dust off. When dry, strip the leaves carefully from the stems and leave whole for optimum flavour, rather than crumble them. Bay leaves, rosemary, marjoram and thyme are particularly suitable for drying.

HERBS AND THEIR USES

Angelica

All parts of this tall plant are used for flavouring, though only the young candied stem is available commercially. Crystallised angelica stems are used to decorate cakes, pastries and desserts. The root is good for stewing with acid fruits such as rhubarb. Angelica leaves can be chopped and used to flavour salads or fish dishes.

Basil

This popular Italian herb has a distinctive aroma and flavour. The delicate leaves are easily bruised by chopping, so it's better to tear or shred them with your fingers. Basil has a natural affinity with tomatoes, but goes well with most salads, grilled meat and green vegetables. It also forms the basis of the classic Italian sauce – pesto (page 28). This herb has a short growing period during the summer and needs plenty of sun, but it is sold fresh all year round.

Bay Leaves

Shiny and smooth, bay leaves are highly aromatic, so one or two leaves is sufficient to flavour a dish. Bay leaves are used in marinades, casseroles, soups and stocks, and to flavour infusions of milk for use in sauces such as béchamel.

Bay is one of the classic ingredients of a bouquet garni, too. A bay tree in the garden is an attractive feature and ensures a constant supply. Alternatively, you can buy sprigs, freeze them in a plastic bag and use straight from the freezer.

Borage

A distinctive herb with slightly furry leaves, bright blue flowers and a flavour reminiscent of cucumber. It is mainly used in claret cup, Pimms and other cool drinks, but can be included in salads. Borage flowers can be crystallised and used as decorations for cakes and sweets. This annual herb is easy to grow in the garden, though it isn't suitable for container growing.

Bouquet Garni

This is a small bunch of herbs, tied together with string so it can be suspended in soups, casseroles and other dishes and removed before serving. The classic ingredients are bay leaves, parsley stems and thyme sprigs, but other herbs can be added to suit a particular dish. For lamb add a rosemary sprig; for pork add a sprig each of sage and savory; for beef add a thinly pared strip of orange zest and a sprig of celery leaves; for chicken use lemon thyme and add a strip of lemon zest; for fish use lemon thyme and add a sprig of fennel.

Chervil

A delicate, sweet-flavoured herb with attractive leaves, used in a similar way to parsley. It will enhance many vegetables, especially new potatoes, as well as salads, and egg, cheese, fish and chicken dishes. Chervil is one of the classic components of the French fines herbes (see right). It is also an excellent flavouring for butter sauces, such as hollandaise, and makes a pretty garnish.

Chives

This member of the onion family has long narrow, green leaves and purple flowers. The leaves are used to flavour salads, sauces and dressings, and as a garnish. A hardy perennial, this herb is easy to grow in the garden and in containers. To use, snip chives into short lengths with scissors.

Coriander

This pungent, intensely flavoured herb is an important flavouring in many parts of the world, especially in Indian and Thai dishes. Coriander is widely available in this country – sold in pots, bunches (sometimes with the roots still attached), and packets. It resembles flat-leafed parsley, but the leaves are more rounded and less spiky.

Commercially, the plant is also grown for its seeds (see page 12), which taste quite different and are used as a spice. Aromatic coriander leaves are often used in conjunction with spices, especially in Middle Eastern, Asian and Mexican dishes, as well as salads and soups.

Curry Leaves

These shiny, spiky leaves have a fresh-tasting flavour akin to curry powder. They are used as a herb in cooking, most often added whole, but sometimes chopped first. Curry leaves often feature in curries from southern India and the fresh or dried leaves can be used sparingly to flavour soups and stews. Sold fresh in bunches, curry leaves can be frozen in a plastic bag, and added to dishes as and when required.

Dill

This fragrant hardy annual is grown for its feathery leaves (also known as dill weed) and for its seeds, which are dried and used as a spice (see page 13). Dill leaves have a slightly sharp, yet sweet flavour which complements fish and shellfish dishes perfectly and it is the classic flavouring in gravad lax (Scandinavian smoked salmon). Dill is also added to salads, omelettes, chicken dishes and used as a garnish.

Fennel

This resembles dill and is a member of the same family, but it has a sweet anise flavour, which is quite different. Both the feathery leaves and seeds are used. It is a classical flavouring for fish – especially oily fish as it counteracts the richness. Fennel also works well in marinades, soups and vegetable dishes.

Fines Herbes

This classic mixture of chopped chives, chervil, parsley and tarragon leaves is used in omelettes, fish and poultry dishes, and salads.

To prepare, mix together 1 tbsp finely chopped chives, 1 tbsp finely chopped chervil, 2 tbsp finely chopped parsley and 2 tsp finely chopped tarragon.

Lemon Balm

With their wonderful lemony scent and taste, these heart-shaped leaves complement fish, poultry and ham dishes perfectly. Lemon balm also adds flavour to punches and fruit drinks and makes an excellent herbal tea. Like mint, this herb has a tendency to take over a garden unless controlled by planting in a bottomless container sunk in the earth to contain the roots.

Lemon Grass
A tall, hard grass with pale green leaves, which have a distinctive lemony aroma and taste. Lemon grass is most often used in Thai and other South-east Asian dishes to flavour soups, chicken, fish and meat dishes; it can also be used to flavour puddings. The stems are usually bruised to release their flavour and added whole before cooking, then removed prior to serving. Alternatively, the tough outer leaves are removed and the rest is chopped or ground and used as a flavouring. Dried and powdered lemon grass are also available.

Lime Leaves, Kaffir
The leaves of the kaffir lime tree have a highly aromatic lime flavour and are frequently used in Thai and Malaysian dishes. They are available from selected supermarkets and oriental food stores, and freeze successfully.

Lovage
This herb has an intense peppery flavour, akin to celery. Lovage leaves are best used sparingly to enhance the flavour of robust soups and meat stews. A little chopped lovage will add an unusual tang to salads and cold roast beef sandwiches.

Marjoram
There are three forms of this aromatic herb: sweet marjoram, pot marjoram and wild marjoram, which is better known as oregano (see right). Pot marjoram has a more powerful flavour than sweet marjoram but it is used in a similar way – to flavour pizzas, savoury flans, sausages, marinades, stuffings and roasts, such as game and pork. It is also good with vegetables.

Mint
Many different mints are available, including peppermint, spearmint, pineapple mint, lemon mint and apple mint. Most varieties have a powerful flavour and should be used sparingly. Fresh mint

sauce or jelly is the classic accompaniment to lamb. Mint is also the perfect partner to potatoes, peas and many other vegetables. Mint leaves are used to embellish wine and fruit cups, fruit salads and other desserts. Fresh mint is widely available; it is also very easy to grow.

Mixed Herbs, Dried
Sold in jars, this is used for seasoning soups and casseroles. It is usually a combination of parsley, sage, thyme, marjoram and tarragon.

Oregano (Wild Marjoram)
Oregano and marjoram are largely interchangeable, although oregano is more aromatic and strongly flavoured. It is used with meat, sausages, soups, pizzas, pasta sauces and other Italian dishes, tomatoes, in salads, with cooked vegetables, and in egg and cheese dishes.

Parsley
Both the flat-leafed and curly-leafed varieties of this common herb are widely available. Flat-leafed parsley has a more pronounced flavour and is generally preferred. Parsley stalks are always included in a bouquet garni and chopped parsley is a classic ingredient of fines herbes (page 9). Chopped parsley leaves are used in all kind of savoury dishes, including sauces, soups, salads, stuffings and herb butters, with vegetables, chicken, ham, fish and shellfish, and as a garnish.

Rosemary
This pungent herb with its characteristic spiky leaves is the classic partner to lamb. Rosemary sprigs are usually added whole to a dish and taken out before serving for a more subtle flavour. Finely chopped leaves are used sparingly, and more often as the sole herb as they tend to overpower other herbs. Rosemary sprigs are used in marinades for meat, fish and poultry, and to flavour roast and barbecued meats. Finely chopped rosemary can be added to pizza and bread doughs, stuffings, cakes and biscuits.

Sage
This soft-leafed herb has a strong, distinctive taste. Garden sage has pale grey-green leaves, but there are many other varieties including purple sage and

variegated sage. It is the classic flavouring for roast pork, but is used to enhance other meat dishes, especially liver and sausages, casseroles, stuffings, salads, egg and cheese dishes. As it is powerful, sage should be sparingly. Melted butter flavoured with fresh sage leaves is delicious on pasta, gnocchi and vegetables.

Salad Burnet
This herb was an important flavouring in Tudor kitchens, but is much less common today. Its characteristic tooth-edged leaves have a nutty flavour with a hint of cucumber. Salad burnet is good in salads and drinks. It can also be used to flavour soups and stews.

Savory
Both summer and winter varieties of this herb are available. It has a distinctive peppery flavour with a particular affinity to beans – both fresh and dried pulses. Savory also works well in soups, and pasta, egg, tomato, vegetable and cheese dishes.

Tarragon
Of the two main species of this herb, French tarragon is far superior in flavour and texture to the Russian variety. Tarragon is a strong-flavoured herb with important culinary uses. It is a component of fines herbes (page 9) and is often added to tartare, hollandaise and béarnaise sauces. Tarragon is also used to flavour wine vinegar, marinades, fish and chicken dishes, savoury butters and sauces.

Thyme
Of the many varieties of this important herb, garden and lemon thyme are the most common. Thyme has a distinctive flavour and is one of the classic ingredients in a bouquet garni. It can be rubbed over beef and lamb before roasting, and used to flavour casseroles, soups, stuffings, bread sauce, carrots, onions and mushrooms. Lemon thyme is especially good in stuffings, and in fish dishes. Thyme is also used to flavour oils and vinegars.

AROMATICS
Garlic
Garlic is not a herb but it is an important aromatic flavouring, often used in conjunction with fresh herbs. It is the most pungent member of the onion family. There are three main varieties: white, red and pinkish-purple. Garlic is widely used to enhance the flavour of savoury dishes. Raw garlic is used in marinades, salads and dressings. On cooking the flavour of garlic becomes mellow and sweet. Choose firm garlic bulbs and pull off individual cloves as required.

SPICES
Spices are the dried parts of aromatic plants and may be the fruit, bark, seed, root or flower bud. Most come from hot countries. Once rare and expensive commodities, spices are now everyday flavouring ingredients. Most spices are sold dried, either whole or ground.

For optimum flavour, buy whole spices and grind them yourself – using a pestle and mortar, or an electric spice grinder – rather than buy ready-ground spices. If possible, grind the spice just before use. An electric coffee grinder can be used, but should then be reserved for this purpose. An electric blender is suitable for larger quantities.

Buy spices in small quantities as their flavour deteriorates relatively quickly. Keep them in small, airtight glass jars, preferably coloured, away from light as this adversely affects flavour. Discard any that are not used within a year of purchase.

DRY-FRYING SPICES
Spices are often toasted in a dry heavy-based frying pan to mellow their flavour and lose any raw taste. Spices can be dry-fried individually or as mixtures. Put the hardest ones, such as fenugreek, into the pan first and add softer ones, like coriander and cumin, after a minute or so. Stir constantly until evenly browned. Cool, then grind, or crush in a pestle and mortar and use the toasted spices as required.

SPICES AND THEIR USES
Allspice
Also called Jamaica Pepper, this is sold as small dried berries or ready ground. The whole spice is an ingredient of pickling spice. It tastes like a mixture of cloves, cinnamon and nutmeg. Allspice can be used whole in marinades, meat dishes, pickles, chutneys and with poached fish. Ground allspice is added to meat and vegetable dishes, cakes, milk puddings and fruit pies.

Aniseed (Anise)

These small seeds have a strong, distinctive flavour – used mainly to flavour cakes and biscuits, but also in salad dressings, with red cabbage, in cheese, fish and shellfish dishes. Aniseed is the main flavouring in Pernod, anisette and ouzo.

Asafoetida

This is derived from the resin of a plant native to Afghanistan and Iran. It can be bought in solid form but as it is very hard asafoetida is best bought ground, in powdered form. The flavour is pungent, so use asafoetida in very small quantities – in spicy meat, fish and vegetable dishes, and pickles.

Caraway Seeds

These small brown seeds have a sharp, liquorice-like taste that is widely appreciated in central European and Jewish cookery. Caraway seeds are primarily used for flavouring cakes, biscuits and breads; they also add flavour to sauerkraut, vegetables, cheese dishes, sausages and pork.

Cardamom

Available both as small green and large black pods containing seeds, cardamom has a strong aromatic quality and should be used sparingly. Add cardamom pods whole and remove before serving, or extract the seeds and use these whole or grind them to a powder just before use. Cardamom is a component of most curry powders. It is also used in pickles, beef and pork dishes; with sweet potato, pumpkin and roasted vegetables; to infuse custards and rice puddings; and to flavour baked apples, bread, biscuits and cakes.

Cassia

Like cinnamon, cassia is the bark of an evergreen tree, dried in the sun to form quills. Cassia has a similar taste to cinnamon and the pieces of bark are used in the same way to flavour sweet and savoury dishes.

Cayenne

This spice is made from small, hot dried red chillies. It is always sold ground as cayenne pepper and is sweet, pungent and very hot. Use it sparingly to flavour meats, barbecue sauces, eggs, fish, vegetables, cheese sauces, pastry and vegetable soups. Unlike paprika, cayenne pepper cannot be used for colouring as its flavour is too pronounced.

Celery Seeds

These have a strong taste, which resembles the vegetable. They are sold whole or ground and can be used sparingly to flavour pickles and chutneys, meat and fish dishes, vegetables and salads, bread, marinades and dressings. Celery salt is a mixture of crushed celery seeds and salt.

Chilli Powder/Chilli Seasoning

Chilli powder is a fiery hot spice used cautiously in Mexican dishes, Indian curries, pickles, chutneys, ketchups, soups, tomato dishes, casseroles, spaghetti and meat sauces. Some brands, often called mild chilli powder or chilli seasoning, are a mixture of chilli and other flavourings, such as cumin, oregano, salt and garlic; these are therefore considerably less fiery than hot chilli powder. Adjust the quantity you use accordingly.

Cinnamon

The dried, rolled bark of a tropical evergreen tree, cinnamon is available as sticks and in powdered form. It has a sweet, pungent flavour. Cinnamon sticks have a more pronounced flavour than the powder, but they are difficult to grind at home, so buy ready-ground cinnamon for use in sweet, spicy baking. Cinnamon has a particularly affinity with chocolate. Use cinnamon sticks to flavour meat casseroles, vegetable dishes, chutneys and pickles, and to infuse fruit compotes, custards, hot drinks, mulled wine and fruit punches.

Cloves

Sold whole and ground, cloves have a distinctive, pungent flavour. They are used mainly to flavour apple dishes, Christmas pudding, mincemeat, bread sauce, pumpkin, mulled wine, and to stud whole baked gammon and onions. In general, whole cloves are best removed from a dish before serving.

Coriander Seeds

These have a mild, sweet, orangey flavour and taste quite different from the herb. Sold whole or ground, coriander is an ingredient of most curry powders and pickling spice. It is a typical flavouring in many spicy Moroccan, Middle Eastern and Indian meat and vegetable dishes. It is also very good in homemade chutneys and pickles.

Cumin Seeds
Cumin has a strong, slightly bitter taste, which is improved by toasting. Sold whole as seeds, or ground, it is an ingredient of curry powders and some chilli powder mixtures. Cumin is also used to flavour pickles, chutneys, cheese dishes, soups, cabbage, rice, Middle Eastern dishes, marinades and fruit pies.

Curry Pastes
Ready-made mixtures containing spices, fresh chillies, onion, ginger and oil. Many different varieties are available, including Thai red curry paste and special Indian curry pastes.

Curry Powder
Bought curry powders are readily available, but for optimum flavour make your own. Put the following spices into an electric blender or grinder: 1 tbsp each cumin and fenugreek seeds; ½ tsp mustard seeds; 1½ tsp each black peppercorns, poppy seeds and ground ginger; 4 tbsp coriander seeds; ½ tsp hot chilli powder and 2 tbsp ground turmeric. Grind to a fine powder. Store the curry powder in an airtight container and use within 1 month.

Dill Seeds
Small, oval seeds with a flavour rather like caraway, but milder. Dill seed is used to flavour fish, pickled cucumbers, potatoes and other vegetables.

Fenugreek Seeds
Small, hard seeds with a distinctive aroma and slightly harsh, hot flavour. An ingredient of commercial curry powders, fenugreek is also used in chutneys, pickles and sauces, but rarely as the only spice.

Five-spice Powder
A powerful, pungent ground mixture of star anise, Szechuan pepper, fennel seeds, cloves and cinnamon or cassia, five-spice powder is used sparingly in Chinese cooking. It is added to Chinese red-cooked meats, roast meat and poultry, marinades and stir-fries.

Galangal
This rhizome resembles ginger, but it is lighter in colour and pink-tinged. Galangal has a wonderful aroma and flavour. It is an important ingredient in Thai and Malaysian dishes, and is used to flavour casseroles, soups and sauces. It is available fresh, dried and as a powder, called laos powder.

Garam Masala
Sold ready-prepared, this Indian spice mix is aromatic rather than hot. To make your own, grind together 10 green cardamom pods, 1 tbsp black peppercorns and 2 tsp cumin seeds.

Ginger
Ginger root has a hot, fairly sweet taste and is sold in various forms. Fresh root ginger is widely available; it is also sold dried and in dried ground form. Root ginger needs to be cooked to release its true flavour – peel, slice and use in curries, sauces, chutneys and Chinese cooking. Ground ginger is used in curries, sauces, preserves, cakes and sprinkled on to melon. Stem ginger is preserved in syrup or crystallised and used to flavour sweet dishes.

Harissa
Harissa is a hot mixture of chilli and other spices, which is used in Middle Eastern cooking. It can be bought in powder and paste form and may contain up to 20 spices. It is served with couscous and other North African dishes.

To make your own harissa: Grill 2 red peppers until softened and charred, cool, then skin, core and deseed. Put 4 deseeded and roughly chopped red chillies in a food processor with 6 peeled garlic cloves, 1 tbsp ground coriander and 1 tbsp caraway seeds. Process to a rough paste, then add the grilled peppers, 2 tsp salt and 4 tbsp olive oil, and whiz until smooth. Put the harissa into a screw-topped jar, cover with a thin layer of olive oil and store in the fridge for up to 2 weeks.

Horseradish
A root of the mustard family, horseradish has a hot, biting, pungent taste and is used raw, but sparingly. It is sold ready-grated in jars. Creamed horseradish is the classic relish for roast beef and is excellent with oily fish; it is sold in jars or you can make it.

To make horseradish cream: In a small bowl, mix together 2 tbsp grated fresh horseradish, 2 tsp lemon juice, 2 tsp sugar and a pinch of mustard powder. Fold into 150ml (¼ pint) lightly whipped double cream.

Juniper Berries

These small purple-black berries have a distinctive scent, with a hint of pine. They should be crushed before being added to a dish to release their maximum flavour. Use juniper berries with game, venison, pork, in marinades and casseroles with these ingredients, and in pâtés and sauerkraut. Juniper is also a flavouring agent in gin.

Mace

The outer covering of the nutmeg, mace is bright red when harvested and dries to a deep orange colour. It is sold as blades (useful for infusing) or ground. It has a sweeter, more delicate flavour than nutmeg but it is more expensive. Use mace in mulled wine and punches, potted meat, fish dishes, béchamel sauce, soups, meat stews, milk puddings and fruit compotes.

Mixed Spice, Ground

This is a mixture of sweet-flavoured ground spices, typically used in sweet dishes, cakes, biscuits and confectionery. It can be added sparingly to curries and spiced Middle Eastern dishes, too. Ready-ground mixed spice is sold in jars.

To make your own, grind together 2 tbsp whole cloves, 5 tsp whole allspice berries, 12cm (5 inch) cinnamon stick, 4 tbsp freshly grated nutmeg and 2 tbsp ground ginger. Store in an airtight container for up to 1 month.

Mustard Seeds

There are three different mustard plants, which produce black, brown and white (or yellow) mustard seeds. The darker seeds are more pungent than the light ones. Most ready-prepared mustards are a combination of the different seeds in varying proportions. The seeds are either left whole (as in wholegrain mustard) or ground, then mixed with liquid such as wine, vinegar or cider. English mustard is sold as a dry yellow powder, as well as ready-mixed. As a condiment, mustard is typically served with sausages, steaks, ham, gammon and cheese; it is also used as a flavouring ingredient in dressings and sauces.

Nutmeg

This seed of the nutmeg fruit has a distinctive, nutty flavour. It is sold whole or ground, but is best bought whole as the flavour of freshly grated nutmeg is far superior. Use it in creamy soups; sprinkled on buttered corn, spinach, carrots and beans; in cheese dishes; with chicken and veal; in custards, milk puddings, Christmas pudding, biscuits and cakes.

Paprika

A sweet mild spice, which is always sold ground to a red powder. It is good for adding colour to pale egg and cheese dishes. Some varieties, particularly Hungarian, are hotter than others. Paprika doesn't keep its flavour well, so buy little and often. Use it in salads, fish, meat and chicken dishes, with vegetables, on canapés and, classically, in goulash where it adds the characteristic rich red colour.

Produced from oak-smoked red peppers, smoked paprika has an intense flavour and wonderful smoky aroma. Sweet, bittersweet and hot-smoked varieties are available. Smoked paprika lends an authentic flavour to paella; it is also excellent with potatoes, fish and chicken dishes.

Pepper

This ubiquitous spice is sold in several forms: green, black and white. Green or unripe berries are picked and either dried, canned or bottled. They have a milder flavour than black or white pepper berries and are used whole as a separate spice in pâtés, with duck and other rich meat, and in sauces and casseroles. They are sometimes lightly crushed to release flavour.

Black pepper consists of berries which are picked while green and dried in the sun, which shrivels and darkens them. It has a strong, pungent, hot flavour and is best used freshly ground to season virtually all savoury dishes.

White pepper is made from the fully ripened berries and is more aromatic and less hot in flavour than black pepper. It can be interchanged with it, but its main use is in light-coloured dishes and sauces whose appearance could be marred by dark flecks.

Pickling Spice

A pungent mixture of varying spices added to the vinegar when making pickles. Varying proportions of black peppercorns, mace, red chillies, allspice, cloves, ginger, mustard seeds or coriander may be included.

To make your own pickling spice, mix together 2 tbsp mace blades, 1 tbsp allspice berries, 1 tbsp whole cloves; 6 black peppercorns, 1 cinnamon stick, and 1 bay leaf, crumbled. Store in an airtight, screw-topped jar for up to 1 month. Tie in a muslin bag to use.

Pink Peppercorns

Pink peppercorns are the dried berries of a South American shrub, which is unrelated to the pepper plant. These attractive, peppery berries are used in small quantities to flavour pâtés, poultry and game dishes. If consumed in large quantities, they are mildly toxic.

Poppy Seeds

Small hard, black seeds from the opium poppy, which have a nutty flavour and no narcotic effect. Poppy seeds are used to add flavour and enhance the appearance of breads, biscuits and cakes; dips and spreads; salads and dressings; they are also used in curry powder. Creamy-coloured poppy seeds are also available.

Saffron

The most expensive of all spices, saffron is the dried stigma of the saffron crocus flower. It has a wonderful, subtle flavour and aroma, and imparts a hint of yellow to foods it is cooked with. Powdered saffron is available, but it is the whole stigmas, called saffron strands or threads, which give the best results. A generous pinch is all that is needed to flavour and colour dishes such as bouillabaisse, chicken soup, rice, paella, fish sauces, breads and cakes.

Sesame Seeds

These small seeds have an intense, sweet, slightly burnt flavour, which is enhanced by toasting or frying in butter. Use sesame seeds in salads and dressings; to flavour mashed potato; sprinkle on to fish and chicken dishes; or use to enhance pastry, biscuits and traybakes.

Star Anise

Attractive, dried, star-shaped fruit of an evergreen tree native to China, star anise is red-brown in colour with a pungent aniseed flavour. It is used whole to flavour Chinese meat stews and steamed fish. One star anise is sufficient to flavour a large quantity. Ground star anise should be used sparingly; it is a component of five-spice powder.

Szechuan Pepper

Also called anise pepper, this hot aromatic spice is made from the dried red berries of a Chinese tree. It is one of the ingredients of five-spice powder.

Tamarind

This is the pulp that surrounds the seeds within the large pods of the Indian tamarind tree. Dark brown, with a fresh, acidic flavour, it is generally sold dried and compressed into blocks. To use, simply break off pieces and reconstitute to make tamarind juice (see below). Tamarind juice is used to add a sour flavour to chutneys, sauces and curries.

To extract tamarind juice, soak 1 tbsp dried tamarind pulp in 4 tbsp warm water for 20 minutes, then strain the liquid through a sieve, pressing hard to extract as much juice from the pulp as possible.

Ready-made tamarind paste is available in jars from larger supermarkets. Lime or lemon juice can be substituted for tamarind if necessary.

Turmeric

Turmeric resembles ginger and is a member of the same family, though it is rarely available fresh. The bright orange flesh is commonly dried, then ground and sold in powdered form. Turmeric powder has an aromatic, slightly bitter flavour and should be used sparingly in curry powder, pickles, relishes and rice dishes. Like saffron, turmeric colours the foods it is cooked with, but it has a much harsher flavour than saffron.

Vanilla

Vanilla pods are the long, thin, dried, black seed pods of a climbing orchid, which are sold whole. Natural vanilla extract is also obtainable and is preferable to the inferior synthetic vanilla essence that is widely available. You can also buy vanilla bean paste. This is pure vanilla with natural vanilla seeds in a convenient paste form.

To release the seeds from a vanilla pod, slit the pod in half lengthways, then run the point of a knife along the central core to extract the seeds.

To make vanilla sugar, simply leave a vanilla pod in a jar of golden caster sugar to impart its flavour. To flavour custards, sweet sauces, ice creams and other creamy desserts, put a whole or split pod in the milk or cream to infuse. After infusing, the vanilla pod can be rinsed, dried and used again.

FLAVOURINGS AND ESSENCES

These include seasoning ingredients such as salt and monosodium glutamate, bottled flavourings and essences, beverages, wine, liqueurs and other alcoholic drinks that have a culinary role. True essences are made by naturally extracting the flavour from the food itself; flavourings are synthetic and tend to be cheaper and more potent. Both flavourings and essences are intensely flavoured and usually only a few drops is needed in a recipe.

Almond Essence

Made from bitter almonds, this essence is used in baking, usually to reinforce the flavour of almonds in the recipe. Synthetic almond flavouring is widely available, but most larger supermarkets stock real almond essence, which is far superior.

Anchovy Essence

This strong salty essence is made from cured anchovies. It should be used sparingly.

Angostura Bitters

These are made from a secret formula which includes cloves, cinnamon, citrus peel, nutmeg, prunes, quinine and rum. Commonly used to flavour aperitifs, such as Pimms and other drinks, angostura bitters may also be added to casseroles, fruit salads, puddings and cakes.

Beer

Beer is sometimes used in meat casseroles, notably beef carbonade. Lager lends a mild flavour whereas stout and dark ale give a strong taste.

Chocolate

Chocolate is available in many different forms, from cocoa powder to bars of dark bitter, plain, milk and white chocolate. In cooking, it is important to use the right chocolate for a particular recipe. If good quality dark chocolate is called for, use one which has at least 70% cocoa solids. Avoid synthetic chocolate substitutes.

Cider

Dry or medium cider is a characteristic of the cooking of south-west England. It is used to flavour casseroles, fish dishes, pork and baked gammon.

Coffee

Coffee is frequently used as a flavouring for ice creams, desserts, cakes, pastries and biscuits, sometimes in combination with chocolate to produce a 'mocha' flavour. A bottled sweetened concentrate, described as coffee essence, is sometimes used. More often recipes call for a strong concentrate of black coffee, preferably freshly brewed from fresh coffee, or made by dissolving good quality instant coffee granules in a little hot water.

Eau-de-vie

These colourless spirits, distilled from fruit, are particularly valuable in cooking, especially for flavouring desserts. Kirsch (from cherries), framboise (from raspberries), fraise (from strawberries) and poire William (from pears) are particularly useful.

Fortified Wines

These are wines which have additional alcohol added in the form of spirit during fermentation. They include sherry, port, Madeira and Marsala. These all lend character to a wide range of dishes; Madeira and Marsala are frequently used in Spanish and Italian dishes respectively. Madeira and sherry are used to enhance the flavour of gravy.

Liqueurs

These sweetened, alcoholic, after-dinner drinks acquire their individual character from their flavourings, which may be fruit, nuts, herbs, coffee etc. They are invaluable for flavouring ice creams, sorbets, fruit salads and a host of other sweet dishes. The following are most useful in the kitchen: amaretto di Saronno (almond), Calvados (apple), crème de cassis (blackcurrant),

Cointreau (orange), Grand Marnier (orange), kahlúa (coffee), and Tia Maria (coffee). Eau-de-vie (see left) are used in the same way as liqueurs.

Orange Flower Water
This potent, colourless flavouring liquid is distilled from the flowers of the Seville orange. Orange flower water is used sparingly to flavour cakes, biscuits, pastries and desserts.

Oyster Sauce
A thick Chinese sauce, which is both sweet and salty. It is widely used in oriental dishes, especially stir-fries, and is available from supermarkets.

Rose Water
A highly fragrant rose-flavoured water, which is either distilled from rose petals or prepared from rose oil. It is used sparingly in baking and desserts, Turkish delight, and other Middle Eastern recipes.

Salt
The essential seasoning ingredient, salt is available in several different forms. Common table salt is refined rock salt, mixed with magnesium carbonate and ground finely to ensure that it flows freely. Sea salt is a fairly coarse salt, produced by natural evaporation in the sun. It is available as flakes and crystals and is considered superior to table salt. Maldon sea salt from Essex is a notable variety. Salt substitutes are available for people who want to reduce their salt intake.

Soy Sauce
A light or dark brown sauce with a salty, sweetish taste, made from soya beans which have been boiled and then fermented. Light soy sauce has a more delicate flavour and is not as salty or strong as the dark variety. Japanese soy sauce is light and refined. Soy sauce is widely used in oriental cookery and a variety of savoury dishes.

Spirits
Food can be both preserved and flavoured with alcoholic spirits. For example, fruit, such as apricots and peaches, may be preserved in brandy. Rum, brandy and whisky are added to rich fruit cakes, mincemeat and Christmas pudding. Luxury chocolate cakes are sometimes spiked with a little alcohol. Many savoury dishes are enhanced by a dash of brandy. Often this is added towards the end of cooking and flambéed to drive off the alcohol, leaving the flavour intact.

Tabasco
This fiery hot sauce is based on red chillies, spirit vinegar and salt, and prepared to a secret recipe. A dash of Tabasco may be used to add a kick to soups, casseroles, sauces, rice dishes and tomato-based drinks.

Tahini
Tahini is a creamy-textured paste made from finely ground sesame seeds. It is widely used in Middle Eastern dishes and is sold in jars in larger supermarkets and delicatessens.

Thai Fish Sauce
Known as *nam pla* in Thailand, this highly pungent sauce adds a distinctive taste to Asian dishes. It is obtainable from most supermarkets, though light soy sauce can be substituted if necessary.

Vanilla Extract
True vanilla essence is extracted from vanilla pods (see page 15); it may be sold as an essence or natural vanilla extract. Synthetic vanilla flavouring is made from an ingredient in clove oil; it is widely available but inferior. Vanilla is used to enhance many sweet dishes, sometimes to bring out the flavour of chocolate.

Wine
Apart from its role as the perfect complement to food, wine is an integral part of many recipes. It adds a real depth of flavour to casseroles, sauces and a variety of other savoury and sweet dishes. A dash of wine is ideal for deglazing after pan-frying or roasting meat and poultry; the alcohol is driven off by evaporation, but the flavour is retained. White wine gives a lighter, more subtle flavour than red wine, which works well in robust casseroles and sauces.

Worcestershire Sauce
Made from a secret recipe, this pungent sauce contains anchovies, although a vegetarian version is available. It is used to flavour sauces, meat casseroles and cheese dishes.

STOCKS
AND SAUCES

STOCKS

Well-flavoured stocks form the basis of soups, sauces, stews and many other savoury dishes. You will find an extensive range of ready-made stock products in most supermarkets and these have improved significantly in recent years, but the flavour of a good homemade stock is incomparable. Stocks are easy to make. Fishmongers are usually only too happy to let you have fish bones and trimmings; similarly poulterers and butchers will generally supply chicken carcasses and other bones. Freeze any stock which is not required for immediate use, in manageable quantities. To save freezer space, you can boil the stock to reduce by half and concentrate prior to freezing.

The characteristics of a good stock are clarity and a fine flavour. Guard against over-seasoning, as boiling concentrates the flavour and saltiness. Fat and impurities will make a stock cloudy, so these should always be removed, by skimming the surface from time to time during cooking. If possible, use a conical sieve to strain the stock and allow the liquid to drip through; avoid pressing the vegetables in the sieve or you will lose clarity.

Once strained, cool the stock quickly, ideally over a bowl of chilled water, then chill. A thin solid layer of fat will form on the surface of most stocks; this can easily be removed. Bring the stock up to the boil before use.

If you haven't the time to make your own stock, opt for one of the better ready-made alternatives. Fresh stocks available in cartons from the chilled cabinet, liquid stock concentrates and vegetable bouillon powder are preferable to powdered stock cubes. These are still inclined to be strong and salty so, if you use them, do so sparingly, or opt for a low-salt variety.

SAUCES

A certain mystique is attached to sauce-making, but all that is required is a little time, patience and your undivided attention. Essentially a sauce should complement and enhance the dish it is served with. It must never be so over-powering that it masks the intrinsic flavours of the dish.

Roux-based sauces, such as béchamel, are probably the most familiar of all. These are based on equal quantities of butter and flour which are cooked together. First the butter is melted, then the flour is mixed in and the resultant roux is cooked before the liquid is added. For a classic white béchamel sauce the roux is cooked but not coloured; for a blond sauce, such as velouté, the roux is cooked until biscuit-coloured; for a brown sauce, such as espagnole, the roux is cooked until brown.

The classic French emulsified sauces, such as hollandaise, béarnaise and beurre blanc, rely on the reduction of liquids to give an intense flavour, and the addition of either butter or eggs to enrich and thicken. These sauces are a little more difficult to make because of their tendency to separate, but using a blender or food processor simplifies the process and is relatively foolproof. Emulsified sauces are best made shortly before serving and kept warm over a pan of hot water.

Some sauces are thickened towards the end of preparation. Last-minute thickeners include arrowroot, cornflour and beurre manié (butter and flour kneaded together in equal quantities).

Other popular sauces include tomato sauces, pesto, salsa verde and classic British favourites, such as apple sauce, mint sauce and cranberry sauce. These are all included in this chapter, plus gravies, savoury butters, custard and other sweet sauces to accompany desserts.

The simplest of all sauces is a coulis – a purée of fresh or cooked fruit or vegetables, thinned to a pouring consistency if necessary. Of the puréed fresh fruit sauces, strawberry, raspberry, apricot and mango are especially popular with desserts.

Allow yourself sufficient time to make a sauce – it is invariably working in haste that results in a lumpy or curdled sauce. If a roux-based sauce becomes lumpy, simply whisk or beat vigorously; if this doesn't work, pass through a sieve, or whiz in a blender or food processor. An emulsified sauce that shows signs of curdling can often be rescued by adding an ice cube and whisking thoroughly.

Most sauces can be prepared in advance and reheated carefully when required. Cover the surface closely with damp greaseproof paper as soon as the sauce is made, to prevent a skin from forming on standing.

Vegetable Stock

225g (8oz) onions, peeled
225g (8oz) celery sticks
225g (8oz) trimmed leeks
225g (8oz) carrots, peeled
2 bay leaves
few thyme sprigs
small bunch of parsley
10 black peppercorns
½ tsp sea salt

makes 1.2 litres (2 pints)
preparation: 10 minutes
cooking time: 35 minutes
per 100ml (3½fl oz): 5 cals; trace fat;
    1g carbohydrate

1 Roughly chop the onions, celery sticks, leeks and carrots, and put them into a large pan.
2 Add 1.7 litres (3 pints) cold water, the herbs, black peppercorns and salt. Bring slowly to the boil and skim the surface. Partially cover the pan and simmer for 30 minutes; check the seasoning.
3 Strain the stock through a fine sieve into a bowl and allow to cool. Cover and keep in the fridge for up to 3 days. Use as required.

Meat Stock

450g (1lb) stewing meat, cut into pieces
450g (1lb) meat bones
1 large onion, peeled and sliced
1 large carrot, peeled and sliced
2 celery sticks, sliced
bouquet garni (2 bay leaves, few thyme
    sprigs, small bunch of parsley)
1 tsp black peppercorns
½ tsp sea salt

makes 900ml (1½ pints)
preparation: 10 minutes
cooking time: 4–5 hours
per 100ml (3½fl oz): 10 cals; 1g fat;
    1g carbohydrate

1 To impart flavour and colour, first brown the meat and bones. Put them into a roasting tin and roast at 220°C (200°C fan oven) mark 7 for 30–40 minutes until well browned, turning occasionally.
2 Put the meat and bones into a large pan with the vegetables, 2 litres (3½ pints) cold water, the bouquet garni, peppercorns and salt. Bring slowly to the boil and skim the surface. Partially cover the pan and simmer gently for 4–5 hours; check the seasoning.
3 Strain the stock through a fine sieve into a bowl and cool quickly. Cover and keep in the fridge for up to 3 days. Remove the fat layer from the surface and use the stock as required.

note: *According to the flavour required, use veal, beef, lamb or pork bones.*

Chicken Stock

225g (8oz) onions, peeled
150g (5oz) trimmed leeks
225g (8oz) celery sticks
1.6kg (3½lb) raw chicken bones
bouquet garni (2 bay leaves, few thyme
    sprigs, small bunch of parsley)
1 tsp black peppercorns
½ tsp sea salt

makes 1.2 litres (2 pints)
preparation: 10 minutes
cooking time: about 2 hours
per 100ml (3½fl oz): 10 cals; 1g fat;
    1g carbohydrate

1 Roughly chop the onions, leeks and celery sticks.
2 Put the vegetables into a large pan with the chicken bones, 3 litres (5 pints) cold water, the bouquet garni, peppercorns and salt. Bring slowly to the boil and skim the surface. Partially cover the pan and simmer gently for 2 hours; check the seasoning.
3 Strain the stock through a fine sieve into a bowl and cool quickly. Cover and keep in the fridge for up to 3 days. Remove the fat from the surface and use the stock as required.

note: *Instead of chicken bones, you can use a large boiling chicken – obtainable from selected butchers and poulterers.*

Fish Stock

900g (2lb) fish bones and trimmings
2 carrots, peeled and chopped
1 onion, peeled and chopped
2 celery sticks, sliced
bouquet garni (bay leaf, thyme and parsley)
6 white peppercorns
½ tsp sea salt

makes 900ml (1½ pints)
preparation: 10 minutes
cooking time: 35 minutes
per 100ml (3½fl oz): 5 cals; trace fat;
    1g carbohydrate

1 Wash and dry the fish trimmings and put into a large pan.
2 Add the vegetables to the pan together with 900ml (1½ pints) cold water, the bouquet garni, peppercorns and salt. Bring slowly to the boil and skim the surface. Cover and simmer gently for about 30 minutes.
3 Strain the stock through a fine sieve into a bowl and check the seasoning. Cool quickly, cover and keep in the fridge for up to 2 days. Use as required.

variation: *For an enriched court bouillon, add 150ml (¼ pint) dry white wine and 3 tbsp white wine vinegar at stage 2.*

Basic Gravy

A rich gravy is traditionally served with roast meat and poultry. If possible, make the gravy in the roasting tin while the joint (or bird) is resting. This will incorporate the meat juices that have escaped during roasting.

makes about 300ml (½ pint)
preparation: 2 minutes
cooking time: 2–3 minutes
per 100ml (3½fl oz): 10 cals; 2g fat;
    1g carbohydrate

1 Carefully pour (or skim) off the fat from a corner of the roasting tin, leaving the sediment behind. Put the tin on the hob over a medium heat and pour in 300–450ml (½–¾ pint) vegetable water, or chicken, vegetable or meat stock as appropriate.

2 Stir thoroughly, scraping up the sediment, and boil steadily until the gravy is a rich brown colour.

note: *A little gravy browning can be added to intensify the flavour and colour.*

variations
rich wine gravy: *Deglaze the roasting tin with about 150ml (¼ pint) red or white wine, or 90ml (3fl oz) fortified wine such as sherry or Madeira, and allow to bubble for a minute or two before adding the stock or water. For a sweeter flavour, add 2 tbsp redcurrant jelly with the wine.*
thick gravy: *Sprinkle 1–2 tbsp flour into the roasting tin and cook, stirring, until browned, then gradually stir in the liquid and cook, stirring for 2–3 minutes until smooth and slightly thickened.*

Béchamel Sauce

300ml (½ pint) semi-skimmed milk
1 onion slice
6 peppercorns
1 mace blade
1 bay leaf
15g (½oz) butter
15g (½oz) plain flour
salt and pepper
freshly grated nutmeg

makes 300ml (½ pint)
preparation: 5 minutes, plus infusing
cooking time: 5 minutes
per 75ml (5 tbsp): 75 cals; 4g fat;
   7g carbohydrate

1 Pour the milk into a pan. Add the onion slice, peppercorns, mace and bay leaf. Bring almost to the boil, remove from the heat, cover and leave to infuse for about 20 minutes. Strain.
2 To make the roux, melt the butter in a pan, stir in the flour and cook, stirring, for 1 minute until cooked but not coloured.

3 Remove from the heat and gradually pour on the milk, whisking constantly. Season lightly with salt, pepper and nutmeg.
4 Return to the heat and cook, stirring constantly, until the sauce is thickened and smooth. Simmer gently for 2 minutes.

variations
simple white sauce: *Omit the flavouring ingredients and infusing stage, simply stirring the cold milk into the roux.*
thick (binding) sauce: *Increase the butter and flour to 25g (1oz) each.*
cheese (Mornay) sauce: *Off the heat, stir 50g (2oz) finely grated Gruyère or mature Cheddar cheese and a large pinch of mustard powder or cayenne pepper into the finished sauce. Heat gently to melt the cheese if necessary.*
parsley sauce: *Stir in 2 tbsp chopped parsley at stage 4.*
onion (Soubise) sauce: *Sauté 1 large onion, finely diced, in a little butter over a low heat for 10–15 minutes, until softened. Stir the sautéed onion into the sauce at stage 4.*

Espagnole Sauce

25g (1oz) butter
25g (1oz) streaky bacon rashers, derinded
   and chopped
1 shallot, peeled and chopped
1 small carrot, peeled and chopped
4 tbsp chopped mushroom stalks (preferably
   brown-cap)
2–3 tbsp plain flour
450ml (¾ pint) brown meat stock
bouquet garni (bay leaf, thyme and parsley)
2 tbsp tomato purée
salt and pepper
1 tbsp sherry (optional)

makes 300ml (½ pint)
preparation: 15 minutes
cooking time: 1¼ hours
per 75ml (5 tbsp): 120 cals; 6g fat;
   4g carbohydrate

1 Melt the butter in a pan, add the bacon and fry for 2–3 minutes. Add the shallot, carrot and mushroom stalks and fry gently until softened.
2 Stir in the flour and cook, stirring, for 5 minutes or until the roux is dark brown but not scorched.
3 Remove from the heat and gradually pour in the stock, whisking constantly.
4 Return to the heat and cook, stirring, until the sauce is thickened. Add the bouquet garni, tomato purée, salt and pepper. Lower the heat, partially cover the pan and simmer very gently for about 1 hour, skimming occasionally.
5 Strain the sauce into a clean pan, then reheat and skim the surface. Check the seasoning and flavour with the sherry if using.

note: *This classic brown sauce is traditionally served with red meat and game.*

variation
demi-glace: *For a simplified version of this classic sauce, add 150ml (¼ pint) jellied meat stock to the prepared espagnole sauce and bring to the boil. Let bubble until the sauce is shiny and slightly syrupy. Whisk in a knob of butter if you like, for added gloss.*

Hollandaise

4 tbsp white wine vinegar

6 black peppercorns

1 mace blade

1 onion slice

1 bay leaf

3 egg yolks

150g (5oz) unsalted butter, at room
temperature, cut into pieces

salt and white pepper

2 tbsp single cream (optional)

lemon juice, to taste

serves 6
preparation: 20 minutes
cooking time: 2–3 minutes
per serving: 230 cals; 24g fat;
trace carbohydrate

1 Put the vinegar into a small pan with the pepper-corns, mace, onion slice and bay leaf. Bring to the boil and reduce to 1 tbsp liquid. Dip the base of the pan in cold water to stop further evaporation; set aside.

2 Put the egg yolks into a heatproof bowl with 15g (½oz) butter and a pinch of salt. Beat until well combined, then strain in the reduced vinegar.

3 Put the bowl over a pan of barely simmering water and whisk for 3–4 minutes until the mixture is pale and beginning to thicken.

4 Beat in the remaining butter, a piece at a time, until the mixture begins to thicken and emulsify. Ensure each addition of butter is incorporated before adding the next. Do not allow the mixture to overheat or the eggs will scramble and split. Remove from the heat.

5 Whisk in the cream if using. Season the sauce with salt and pepper, and add a little lemon juice to taste. Serve at once.

notes
• *Hollandaise is a wonderfully rich sauce to serve with hot or cold vegetables, such as asparagus and globe artichokes, and poached fish and shellfish.*
• *If the sauce shows signs of curdling, add an ice cube and whisk thoroughly; the hollandaise should re-combine.*
• *To make hollandaise in a food processor, melt the butter and let cool until tepid. Put the strained reduced vinegar, egg yolks and salt in the processor bowl and process for 10 seconds. With the motor running, add the melted butter in a thin steady stream through the feeder tube and process until emulsified. Finish as in stage 5, above.*

Béarnaise Sauce

4 tbsp white wine vinegar or tarragon vinegar

2 shallots, peeled and finely chopped

6 black peppercorns

few tarragon sprigs, chopped

2 egg yolks

75g (3oz) butter, at room temperature, cut
into pieces

salt and white pepper

2 tsp chopped flat-leafed parsley or chervil
(optional)

serves 4–6
preparation: 20 minutes
cooking time: 2–3 minutes
per serving: 180–120 cals; 18–12g fat;
2–1g carbohydrate

1 Put the vinegar, shallots, peppercorns and tarragon into a very small pan. Bring to the boil and reduce to 1 tbsp. Dip the base of the pan in cold water to stop further evaporation; allow to cool, then strain.

2 Beat the egg yolks and reduced vinegar together in a heatproof bowl.

3 Put the bowl over a pan of barely simmering water and whisk for 3–4 minutes until the mixture is pale and beginning to thicken.

4 Beat in the butter a piece at a time, until the mixture begins to thicken and emulsify. Ensure each addition of butter is incorporated before adding the next. Do not allow the mixture to overheat or the eggs will scramble and split. Take off the heat.

5 Season with salt and pepper to taste. Stir in the chopped herbs if using.

notes
• *If the sauce looks to be curdling, add an ice cube and whisk thoroughly; the sauce should re-combine.*
• *Serve this classic butter sauce with grilled beef and lamb steaks.*

Beurre Blanc

3 tbsp white wine vinegar

3 tbsp white wine

2 shallots, peeled and finely chopped

225g (8oz) butter, chilled and cut into
    small cubes

salt and pepper

serves 4–6

preparation: 20 minutes

cooking time: 2–3 minutes

per serving: 420–280 cals; 46–31g fat;
    2–1g carbohydrate

1 Put the vinegar, white wine and shallots into a very small pan. Bring to the boil and reduce to 1 tbsp.

2 Over a low heat, whisk in the butter, a piece at a time, until the sauce begins to thicken as the butter melts. Move pan on and off heat to avoid overheating.

3 If a smooth sauce is preferred, pass the sauce through a sieve. Season with salt and pepper to taste.

notes

• *Serve with poached or grilled fish and poultry.*

• *If the sauce splits, whisk in an ice cube.*

variations

• *Add 2 tbsp chopped herbs, such as tarragon, chives or chervil to the finished sauce.*

• *For a red wine sauce, use 6 tbsp red wine instead of the white wine and vinegar.*

Curried Coconut Sauce

2 tbsp oil

175g (6oz) onions, peeled and finely chopped

2 garlic cloves, peeled and crushed

2.5cm (1 inch) piece fresh root ginger, peeled
    and grated

3–4 tbsp mild curry paste

3 tbsp coconut milk powder

salt

serves 6

preparation: 5 minutes

cooking time: 20 minutes

per serving: 80 cals; 7g fat;
    3g carbohydrate

1 Heat the oil in a pan. Add the onions with 1 tbsp water and cook gently for 10 minutes or until softened and golden brown.

2 Add the garlic, ginger and curry paste and cook for 1–2 minutes.

3 Mix the coconut milk powder with 450ml (¾ pint) warm water, stir into the curried mixture and bring to the boil. Let bubble for 5–10 minutes. Season with salt to taste.

note: *This curried sauce is particularly good with fish and shellfish.*

Barbecue Sauce

50g (2oz) butter

1 large onion, peeled and chopped

1 tsp tomato purée

2 tbsp wine vinegar

2 tbsp Worcestershire sauce

2 tsp mustard powder

salt and pepper

serves 4

preparation: 5 minutes

cooking time: about 25 minutes

per serving: 110 cals; 10g fat;
    4g carbohydrate

1 Melt the butter in a pan, add the onion and sauté gently for 10 minutes until softened. Stir in the tomato purée and cook, stirring, for 2 minutes.

2 Mix together the wine vinegar, Worcestershire sauce, mustard powder, salt and pepper in a bowl, stir in 150ml (¼ pint) water, then add to the pan. Bring to the boil and let bubble for 10 minutes.

note: *Serve with barbecued or grilled chicken, sausages, burgers or chops.*

Creamy Mushroom and Wine Sauce

2 tbsp oil
2 shallots or 1 onion, peeled and finely diced
175g (6oz) button or cup mushrooms, sliced
150g (5oz) mixed wild mushrooms, sliced
2 garlic cloves, peeled and crushed
150ml (¼ pint) white wine
200ml (7fl oz) crème fraîche
salt and pepper
2 tsp chopped thyme

serves 6
preparation: 10 minutes
cooking time: 20 minutes
per serving: 190 cals; 18g fat;
    3g carbohydrate

1 Heat the oil in a pan, add the shallots and cook gently for 10 minutes. Add the mushrooms and garlic and cook over a high heat for 4–5 minutes until tender and all the moisture has been driven off.
2 Pour in the wine, bring to the boil and let bubble until reduced by half.
3 Add the crème fraîche, 100ml (3½fl oz) water and seasoning. Bring to the boil and bubble for 5 minutes or until the liquid is slightly thickened and syrupy. Add the chopped thyme, adjust the seasoning and serve immediately.

note: *This sauce is particularly good with pan-fried steak or chicken.*

variation: *Replace the crème fraîche with red wine for a lighter sauce.*

Bread Sauce

1 onion, peeled and quartered
4 cloves
2 bay leaves
450ml (¾ pint) milk
150g (5oz) fresh white breadcrumbs
½ tsp freshly grated nutmeg, or to taste
50g (2oz) butter
200ml (7fl oz) crème fraîche
salt and pepper

serves 8
preparation: 10 minutes
cooking time: 15 minutes
per serving: 210 cals; 16g fat;
    13g carbohydrate

1 Stud each onion quarter with a clove. Put the onion, bay leaves and milk into a pan. Heat very gently on the lowest possible heat for 15 minutes.
2 Remove the onion and bay leaves, then add the breadcrumbs, nutmeg and butter and stir to combine. Add the crème fraîche and season with salt and pepper to taste. Serve warm.

Apple Sauce

450g (1lb) cooking apples, such as Bramleys
2 tbsp sugar, or to taste
25g (1oz) butter

serves 4
preparation: 10 minutes
cooking time: 10 minutes
per serving: 110 cals; 5g fat;
    17g carbohydrate

1 Peel, core and slice the apples and put into a pan with 2–3 tbsp water. Cover and cook gently for about 10 minutes, stirring occasionally, until soft and reduced to a pulp.
2 Beat with a wooden spoon until smooth, then pass through a sieve if a smooth sauce is preferred. Stir in sugar to taste and the butter. Serve warm.

note: *This sauce is traditionally served with roast pork and goose, to cut the richness.*

Gooseberry Sauce

350g (12oz) gooseberries
25g (1oz) butter
2 tbsp sugar, or to taste
¼ tsp freshly grated nutmeg
salt and pepper

serves 4
preparation: 10 minutes
cooking time: 10 minutes
per serving: 110 cals; 5g fat;
   16g carbohydrate

1 Put the gooseberries into a pan with 150ml (¼ pint) water and cook gently for about 5 minutes, stirring occasionally, until soft and reduced to a pulp.
2 Beat with a wooden spoon until smooth, then pass through a sieve. Stir in the butter, sugar, nutmeg, salt and pepper to taste. Reheat to serve.

note: *Serve with oily fish, such as trout or mackerel.*

Cranberry Sauce

2 tbsp olive oil
450g (1lb) red onions, peeled and
   thinly sliced
grated zest and juice of 1 large orange
1 tsp coriander seeds, lightly crushed
¼ tsp ground cloves
1 bay leaf
150g (5oz) dark muscovado sugar
150ml (¼ pint) red wine
450g (1lb) cranberries

serves 8
preparation: 30 minutes, plus chilling
cooking time: 1 hour 5 minutes
per serving: 140 cals; 3g fat;
   26g carbohydrate

1 Heat the oil in a medium pan, add the onions and cook gently for 5 minutes. Add the orange zest and juice, coriander seeds, ground cloves, bay leaf, sugar and red wine. Simmer gently for 40 minutes.
2 Add the cranberries, bring back to the boil and simmer for 20 minutes. Cool and chill until required. Bring to room temperature before serving.

note: *Serve this tangy relish with the traditional Christmas turkey.*

Cumberland Sauce

finely pared zest and juice of 1 orange
finely pared zest and juice of 1 lemon
4 tbsp redcurrant jelly
1 tsp Dijon mustard
4 tbsp port
salt and pepper
pinch of ground ginger (optional)

serves 4–6
preparation: 10 minutes, plus cooling
cooking time: 10 minutes
per serving: 70–50 cals; 0g fat;
   15–10g carbohydrate

1 Cut the citrus zests into fine julienne strips and put into a small pan. Add cold water to cover and simmer for 5 minutes; drain.
2 Put the orange and lemon juices, citrus zests, redcurrant jelly and mustard into a pan and heat gently, stirring, until the sugar has dissolved. Simmer for 5 minutes, then add the port.
3 Allow to cool. Season with salt and pepper to taste, and add a little ginger if you like.

note: *Serve this sauce cold, with gammon.*

Fresh Tomato Sauce

900g (2lb) vine-ripened tomatoes,
  roughly chopped
2 tbsp extra-virgin olive oil
2 garlic cloves, peeled and crushed
grated zest of 1 lemon
1 tsp dried oregano
2 tbsp chopped basil
salt and pepper
pinch of sugar, or to taste (optional)

serves 4
preparation: 10 minutes
cooking time: about 30 minutes
per serving: 100 cals; 7g fat;
  8g carbohydrate

1 Put the tomatoes into a pan with the olive oil, garlic, lemon zest and oregano. Bring to the boil, cover and simmer gently for 20 minutes.
2 Add the chopped basil, salt and pepper to taste and a little sugar if required. Simmer, uncovered, for a further 10 minutes or until the sauce is slightly thickened. If a smooth sauce is preferred, pass through a sieve and reheat before serving.

Rich Tomato Sauce

50g (2oz) butter
1 onion, peeled and finely chopped
2 garlic cloves, peeled and finely chopped
2 x 400g cans plum tomatoes with their juice
  (see note)
3 tbsp sun-dried tomato paste
2 oregano sprigs, or 1 tsp dried
salt and pepper

serves 4–6
preparation: 10 minutes
cooking time: about 40 minutes
per serving: 150–100 cals; 11–7g fat;
  11–7g carbohydrate

1 Melt the butter in a pan, add the onion and garlic and cook gently for about 10 minutes until softened.
2 Add the tomatoes with the tomato paste and oregano. Cook, uncovered, over a low heat for 25–30 minutes, stirring occasionally, until the sauce is thick and pulpy.
3 Discard the oregano and season with salt and pepper to taste.

note: *Use full-flavoured ripe tomatoes if available: you will need 1kg (2¼lb) tomatoes, skinned, chopped and deseeded. Canned plum tomatoes are a better choice than flavourless fresh ones.*

Mint Sauce

small bunch of mint, stalks removed
1–2 tsp golden caster sugar, to taste
1–2 tbsp wine vinegar, to taste

serves 4
preparation: 10 minutes, plus standing
per serving: 10 cals; trace fat;
  2g carbohydrate

1 Finely chop the mint leaves and put into a bowl with the sugar. Stir in 1 tbsp boiling water and set aside for about 5 minutes to dissolve the sugar.
2 Add the wine vinegar to taste. Leave to stand for about 1 hour before serving.

note: *Mint sauce is the classic accompaniment to roast lamb.*

Pesto

50g (2oz) basil leaves
1–2 garlic cloves, peeled
25g (1oz) pine nuts
6 tbsp extra-virgin olive oil
salt and pepper
2 tbsp freshly grated Parmesan cheese
squeeze of lemon juice (optional)

serves 4
preparation: 10 minutes
per serving: 250 cals; 26g fat;
   1g carbohydrate

1 Roughly tear the basil and put into a mortar with the garlic, pine nuts and a little of the olive oil. Pound with a pestle to a paste. Alternatively, work in a food processor to a fairly smooth paste.

2 Gradually work in the rest of the oil and season with salt and pepper to taste. Transfer to a bowl.
3 Stir in the Parmesan, check the seasoning and add a squeeze of lemon juice if you like.
4 Store in a screw-topped jar, covered with a thin layer of oil, in the fridge for up to 3 days.

Illustrated on page 18

variations
sun-dried tomato pesto: *Replace half of the basil with 50g (2oz) sun-dried tomatoes in oil, drained and roughly chopped. Use a blender or food processor to work the ingredients together to a paste.*
coriander pesto: *Replace the basil with coriander leaves. Add 1 deseeded and chopped chilli with the garlic if you like. Omit the Parmesan.*
rocket pesto: *Replace the basil with rocket leaves. Add 1 tbsp chopped parsley at stage 3.*

Salsa Verde

small handful of parsley, about 40g (1½oz)
6 tbsp fresh white breadcrumbs
5 tbsp olive oil
1 tsp capers
1 gherkin
2 tbsp lemon juice
1 tbsp chopped chives
salt and pepper

serves 4
preparation: 5 minutes
per serving: 190 cals; 17g fat;
   8g carbohydrate

1 Put all the ingredients into a blender or food processor and process until thoroughly combined.
2 Turn into a bowl and season with salt and pepper to taste. Store in the fridge for up to 5 days.

note: *This piquant, fresh-tasting sauce is good with pork schnitzel and grilled meats.*

Flavoured Butters

These are excellent quick alternatives to sauces for serving with grilled meats, fish and all kinds of vegetables. They need to be prepared several hours in advance to allow time to chill and become firm enough to slice.

Use unsalted butter at room temperature. Beat in the flavouring(s) by hand or using a food processor. Turn on to clingfilm, shape into a log, wrap tightly and chill in the fridge for at least 1 hour. Allow about 25g (1oz) savoury butter per person.

Add the following flavourings to 125g (4oz) butter, at room temperature:
anchovy butter: Add 6 mashed anchovy fillets.
blue cheese butter: Add 50g (2oz) blue cheese.
herb butter: Add 2 tbsp chopped mixed fresh herbs, such as flat-leafed parsley, chervil and tarragon, plus a squeeze of lemon juice.
garlic butter: Add 1 crushed garlic clove and 2 tsp chopped parsley or chervil.
watercress butter: Add 50g (2oz) chopped watercress.

Fresh Vanilla Custard

600ml (1 pint) whole milk
1 vanilla pod or 1 tsp vanilla extract
6 large egg yolks
2 tbsp golden caster sugar
2 tbsp cornflour

serves 8
preparation: 20 minutes, plus cooling
cooking time: 10 minutes
per serving: 120 cals; 8g fat;
   10g carbohydrate

1 Pour the milk into a pan. Slit the vanilla pod lengthways and scrape out the seeds, adding them to the milk with the pod, or add the vanilla extract. Slowly bring to the boil. Turn off the heat immediately and set aside to infuse for 5 minutes.

2 Put the egg yolks, sugar and cornflour into a bowl and whisk together. Gradually whisk in the warm milk, leaving the vanilla pod behind if using.

3 Rinse the pan and pour the mixture back in. Heat gently, whisking or stirring constantly for 2–3 minutes or until the custard thickens – it should just coat the back of a wooden spoon in a thin layer. Serve immediately or cover the surface closely with a round of wet greaseproof paper, then cover with clingfilm and chill until needed.

note: *If prepared ahead, to serve warm, microwave on medium for 2 minutes, stir, then microwave for a further 2 minutes.*

Sabayon Sauce

75g (3oz) golden caster sugar
3 egg yolks
125ml (4fl oz) double cream
grated zest and juice of 1 lemon

serves 6–8
preparation: 15 minutes
cooking time: about 10 minutes
per serving: 170–130 cals; 12–9g fat;
   14–10g carbohydrate

1 Put the sugar and 125ml (4fl oz) water into a small pan over a low heat until dissolved. Increase the heat to high and boil for 7–8 minutes or until the syrup registers 105°C on a sugar thermometer (and looks very syrupy with large pea-size bubbles).

2 Meanwhile, whisk the egg yolks in a small bowl. Gradually pour on the hot syrup in a thin stream, whisking all the time. Continue to whisk until the mixture is thick, mousse-like and cool.

3 In a separate bowl, whisk the cream until it forms stiff peaks, then add the lemon zest and juice and whip again to soft peaks. Fold the citrus cream into the mousse mixture.

4 Cover and chill in the fridge until required. Whisk well before serving.

note: *Serve as an alternative to vanilla custard, with grilled fruit and other desserts.*

Butterscotch Sauce

50g (2oz) butter
75g (3oz) light muscovado sugar
50g (2oz) golden caster sugar
150g (5oz) golden syrup
125ml (4fl oz) double cream
few drops of vanilla extract
juice of ½ lemon

serves 8
preparation: 5 minutes
cooking time: 10 minutes
per serving: 230 cals; 12g fat;
   32g carbohydrate

1 Put the butter, sugars and golden syrup in a medium heavy-based pan over a low heat and stir occasionally until melted together and smooth. Cook gently, stirring, for 5 minutes.

2 Off the heat, slowly stir in the cream. Add the vanilla extract and lemon juice. Stir over a low heat for 1–2 minutes until smooth. Serve hot or cold.

note: *Serve poured over ice cream or with steamed or baked puddings.*

Caramel Sauce

50g (2oz) golden caster sugar
150ml (¼ pint) double cream

serves 6
preparation: 5 minutes
cooking time: 10 minutes
per serving: 150 cals; 12g fat;
  9g carbohydrate

1 Melt the sugar in a small heavy-based pan over a low heat until liquid and golden in colour. Increase the heat to medium and cook to a rich, dark caramel.
2 Immediately take off the heat and pour in the cream in a slow steady stream, taking care as the hot caramel will cause the cream to boil up in the pan.
3 Stir over a gentle heat until the caramel has melted and the sauce is smooth. Serve hot or cold.

note: *Serve poured over ice cream or with steamed or baked puddings.*

Rich Chocolate Sauce

125g (4oz) plain, dark chocolate with
  70% cocoa solids, in pieces
2 tbsp light muscovado sugar
25g (1oz) unsalted butter

serves 6
preparation: 5 minutes
cooking time: 5 minutes
per serving: 150 cals; 12g fat;
  10g carbohydrate

1 Put the chocolate into a small pan with the sugar and 150ml (¼ pint) water. Stir over a low heat until the chocolate is melted and the sugar is dissolved, then bring to the boil, stirring.
2 Let bubble for 1 minute, then remove from the heat and stir in the butter.

note: *Serve poured over ice cream, profiteroles, or steamed or baked puddings.*

variation

chocolate and Grand Marnier sauce: *Omit the sugar. Add 2 tbsp Grand Marnier (or other liqueur of your choice) to the sauce with the butter.*

Chocolate Custard Sauce

300ml (½ pint) milk
50g (2oz) plain, dark chocolate with at least
  60% cocoa solids, in pieces
1 vanilla pod, split
3 egg yolks, beaten
1 tbsp golden caster sugar

serves 4
preparation: 20 minutes, plus infusing
cooking time: 10–20 minutes
per serving: 160 cals; 10g fat;
  11g carbohydrate

1 Pour the milk into a heavy-based saucepan and add the chocolate and vanilla pod. Heat slowly until the chocolate has melted and the mixture is almost boiling. Take off the heat and set aside to infuse for about 20 minutes. Remove the vanilla pod.

2 Whisk the egg yolks and sugar together in a bowl until thick and creamy. Gradually whisk in the hot chocolate milk, then strain back into the pan.
3 Cook over a low heat, stirring constantly, for 10–20 minutes until the custard thickens enough to lightly coat the back of the wooden spoon; do not allow to boil or the custard may curdle.
4 Serve warm or, if serving cold, pour into a chilled bowl, cover with a disc of dampened greaseproof paper to prevent a skin forming and set aside to cool.

note: *It is essential to avoid overheating the custard otherwise it is liable to curdle. As a precaution, you can beat 1 tsp cornflour with the egg yolks and sugar at stage 1. This helps to stabilise the custard, but must be cooked through over gentle heat otherwise it will adversely affect the flavour.*

variation: *For an extra rich creamy custard sauce, replace half of the milk with single cream.*

Melba Sauce

225g (8oz) raspberries
2 tbsp kirsch or framboise eau-de-vie
icing sugar, to taste

serves 4–6
preparation: 5 minutes
per serving: 60–40 cals; 0g fat;
   12–8g carbohydrate

1 Put the raspberries into a blender or food processor with the kirsch and work to a purée.
2 Pass through a sieve to remove the pips and sweeten with icing sugar to taste.

note: *Serve this sauce poured over ice cream, or with meringues.*

Brandy Butter

150g (5oz) unsalted butter, at room
   temperature
150g (5oz) golden icing sugar, sifted
3 tbsp brandy

serves 8
preparation: 10 minutes, plus chilling
per serving: 230 cals; 16g fat;
   20g carbohydrate

1 Put the butter into a bowl and whisk to soften. Gradually whisk in the icing sugar, pouring in the brandy just before the final addition. Continue whisking until the mixture is pale and fluffy, then spoon into a serving dish.
2 Cover and chill until needed. Remove from the fridge 30 minutes before serving.

note: *For a light, fluffy texture, whisk the brandy butter using an electric mixer just before serving.*

Chantilly Cream

284ml carton double cream
1 tbsp golden caster sugar
finely grated zest of 1 orange (optional)

serves 8
preparation: 10 minutes, plus chilling
per serving: 180 cals; 17g fat;
   4g carbohydrate

1 Whip the cream with the sugar until it forms soft peaks. Fold in half the grated orange zest if using. Cover and chill until needed.
2 Serve the Chantilly cream sprinkled with the remaining orange zest if you like.

note: *Flavour the Chantilly cream with 2 tbsp Grand Marnier to serve with Christmas pudding.*

Crème Pâtissière

300ml (½ pint) milk
1 vanilla pod, split, or 1 tsp vanilla extract
3 egg yolks, beaten
50g (2oz) golden caster sugar
2 tbsp plain flour
2 tbsp cornflour

makes 450ml (¾ pint)
preparation: 15 minutes, plus infusing
cooking time: 5 minutes
per 75ml (5 tbsp): 120 cals; 4g fat;
   18g carbohydrate

1 Pour the milk into a heavy-based pan. Scrape the vanilla seeds into the milk and add the pod, or add the vanilla extract. Slowly bring to the boil, take off the heat and leave to infuse for 10 minutes. Discard pod.
2 Meanwhile, whisk the egg yolks and sugar together in a bowl until thick and creamy, then whisk in the flour and cornflour until smooth. Gradually whisk in the hot milk, then strain back into the pan.
3 Slowly bring to the boil, whisking constantly. Cook, stirring, for 2–3 minutes until thickened and smooth.
4 Pour into a bowl, cover the surface with a round of wet greaseproof paper and allow to cool. Use as a filling for fruit flans and other pastries.

SOUPS

There is nothing quite as comforting as a flavourful homemade soup that makes the most of seasonal ingredients. The secret of a great-tasting soup is invariably a well-flavoured homemade stock, but if you are short of time, use one of the fresh stock products available from supermarkets. Chunky hot soups are the obvious choice for winter starters and many of the recipes in this chapter are substantial enough to serve as a meal in themselves – especially if you increase the quantities and serve them with lots of warm, crusty bread. For summer starters, choose lighter soups – a chilled soup is the perfect refreshing choice for a hot summer's day. For best results, use really fresh ingredients in prime condition.

GARNISHES AND ACCOMPANIMENTS

Adding a complementary finishing touch will enhance the flavour as well as the appearance of a fresh soup. Smooth soups, in particular, benefit from a contrasting swirl of cream or crème fraîche and, perhaps, a sprinkling of pepper or paprika. A scattering of herbs, such as snipped chives or torn parsley, chervil, basil, coriander or mint, will enliven most soups.

Top robust soups with Parmesan shavings or a sprinkling of freshly grated Gruyère, Parmesan, pecorino or Cheddar. Try stirring a spoonful of pesto (page 28) into hearty vegetable potages; this also works well with tomato soups. Use classic, sun-dried tomato, coriander or rocket pesto.

Citrus butters make a tasty garnish. Simply blend a little finely grated orange, lemon or lime zest into some softened butter, form into a log, wrap in clingfilm and chill until firm. Thinly slice the butter and top each portion of soup with a few slices – it will melt deliciously into the soup as you serve it.

Croûtons

A classic garnish for soups, these are easy to make. Remove the crusts from 3 or 4 thick slices of day-old white bread, then cut into 2.5cm (1 inch) squares. Heat a 2.5cm (1 inch) depth of oil in a frying pan, then fry the bread cubes, turning constantly, until crisp and golden. Remove and drain on kitchen paper.

Use flavoured bread, such as walnut or sun-dried tomato bread, to make savoury croûtons. Toss the flavoured bread cubes in appropriate oil, such as walnut oil or sun-dried tomato oil (from a jar of sun-dried tomatoes). Put into a shallow roasting tin and bake in the oven at 200°C (180°C fan oven) mark 6 for about 15 minutes until golden; drain on kitchen paper.

For a lower calorie option, simply cut toasted chunky bread slices into cubes. Croûtons can be prepared ahead, allowed to cool, then stored in an airtight tin. To serve, warm through in the oven.

Melba Toast

This wafer-thin, brittle toast is traditionally served with soups and pâtés. Toast 3 or 4 slices of soft-grain bread lightly on both sides. Quickly cut off the crusts, split each slice horizontally in two and scrape off any doughy bits. Sprinkle with Parmesan and paprika if you like. Lay on a baking sheet and bake at 180°C (160°C fan oven) mark 4 for about 10 minutes until uniformly golden and curled. If preferred, Melba toast can be prepared ahead, allowed to cool, then stored in an airtight tin. To serve, warm through in the oven.

Bruschetta

This Italian favourite goes well with most soups. Grill thick slices of day-old rustic bread lightly on both sides. Immediately rub all over with a peeled garlic clove, drizzle with a little fruity extra-virgin olive oil and serve with the soup.

Parmesan Crisps

These complement fresh-tasting creamed soups, such as Vichyssoise (page 45) and watercress soup (page 46). Put heaped tablespoons of freshly grated Parmesan on to two baking sheets lined with baking parchment, spacing them well apart and spreading each one out slightly. Sprinkle with poppy seeds and bake at 200°C (180°C fan oven) mark 6 for 5–10 minutes until lacy and golden. Leave on the baking sheets for 2–3 minutes to firm up slightly, then transfer to a wire rack to cool.

Chicken Consommé

1.7 litres (3 pints) well-flavoured fat-free
    chicken stock
350g (12oz) lean skinless chicken breast
    fillet, minced
2 leeks, trimmed and thinly sliced
2 celery sticks, thinly sliced
2 carrots, peeled and thinly sliced
2 shallots, peeled and diced
2 egg whites, lightly whisked
2 egg shells, crushed
salt and pepper
dash of sherry or Madeira (optional)

serves 4
preparation: 30 minutes
cooking time: 1¼ hours
per serving: 20 cals; trace fat;
    1g carbohydrate

1 Heat the stock in a pan. Combine the chicken and vegetables in another large pan, then mix in the egg whites and shells.
2 Gradually whisk in the hot stock, then bring to the boil, whisking. As soon as it comes to the boil, stop whisking, lower the heat and simmer very gently for 1 hour. By this time, a crust will have formed on the surface and the stock underneath should be clear.
3 Carefully make a hole in the crust and ladle the clear stock out into a muslin-lined sieve over a large bowl. Allow to drain through slowly, then return to the cleaned pan and reheat. Check the seasoning and flavour with a little sherry or Madeira if you like.

variations
beef consommé: *Use well-flavoured fat-free beef stock and lean minced steak.*
consommé julienne: *Add thin strips of cooked vegetables, such as celery, carrot and turnip to the consommé before serving.*

French Onion Soup

75g (3oz) butter
700g (1½lb) small onions, peeled and
    finely chopped
3 garlic cloves, peeled and crushed
1 tbsp plain flour
200ml (7fl oz) dry white wine
1.5 litres (2½ pints) vegetable stock
bouquet garni (thyme sprigs, bay leaf and
    parsley sprigs)
salt and pepper

TO SERVE
1 small French stick, cut into 1cm (½ inch)
    thick slices
50g (2oz) Gruyère or Cheddar cheese, grated

serves 4–6
preparation: 30 minutes
cooking time: about 1 hour
per serving: 420–280 cals; 21–14g fat;
    44–29g carbohydrate

1 Melt the butter in a large heavy-based pan. Add the onions and cook slowly over a very low heat, stirring frequently, until very soft and golden brown; this should take at least 30 minutes. Add the garlic and flour; cook, stirring, for 1 minute.
2 Pour in the wine and let bubble until reduced by half. Add the stock, bouquet garni and seasoning. Bring to the boil and simmer gently, uncovered, for 20–30 minutes.
3 Remove the bouquet garni and let the soup cool a little. Put one third into a blender or food processor and blend until smooth, then stir this back into the soup in the pan.
4 Lightly toast the slices of French bread on both sides. Reheat the soup and adjust the seasoning.
5 Divide the soup among ovenproof soup bowls. Float 2 or 3 slices of toast on each portion and sprinkle thickly with the grated cheese. Stand the bowls under a hot grill until the cheese is melted and golden brown. Serve at once.

Thai Chicken Broth

4 boneless, skinless chicken thighs, about 300g (11oz)

1 tbsp olive oil

3 garlic cloves, peeled and chopped

2 medium red chillies, deseeded and finely diced

1 lemon grass stalk, finely sliced

5cm (2 inch) piece fresh root ginger, finely chopped

1.2 litres (2 pints) chicken stock

50g (2oz) rice noodles

8 coriander sprigs

125g (4oz) French beans, trimmed and halved

125g (4oz) beansprouts

4 spring onions, trimmed and sliced

2 tbsp Thai fish sauce

juice of ¼ lime

serves 6
preparation: 30 minutes
cooking time: 15 minutes
per serving: 130 cals; 5g fat;
    9g carbohydrate

1 Cut the chicken into cubes. Heat the olive oil in a large pan, then add the chicken pieces, garlic, chillies, lemon grass and ginger and cook for 3–5 minutes or until the chicken is opaque.

2 Add the stock, bring to the boil, then simmer for 10 minutes or until the chicken is cooked through.

3 Meanwhile, put the noodles into a heatproof bowl, pour on boiling water to cover and leave to soak for 4 minutes. Pick the leaves off the coriander and put to one side.

4 Finely chop the coriander stalks and add to the pan with the French beans. Cook for 3 minutes. Add the beansprouts and spring onions along with the Thai fish sauce and lime juice. Bring to the boil and taste for seasoning.

5 Drain the noodles and divide among four deep bowls. Ladle the broth into each bowl, making sure each serving has a share of chicken and beansprouts. Garnish with coriander leaves and serve.

Illustrated on page 32

variation: *Use fine egg noodles in place of rice noodles if you prefer.*

Cream of Jerusalem Artichoke Soup

450g (1lb) Jerusalem artichokes

50g (2oz) butter

2 shallots, peeled and diced

1 tsp mild curry paste

900ml (1½ pints) vegetable stock

150ml (¼ pint) single cream

freshly grated nutmeg, to taste

pinch of cayenne pepper

4 tbsp freshly grated Parmesan cheese

salt and pepper

TO SERVE
3–4 slices Melba toast (page 33)

serves 6
preparation: 15 minutes
cooking time: 30 minutes
per serving: 190 cals; 14g fat;
    12g carbohydrate

1 Scrub the Jerusalem artichokes thoroughly, pat dry, then slice thinly.

2 Melt the butter in a large pan, add the shallots and cook gently for 10 minutes until soft and golden.

3 Stir in the curry paste and cook for 1 minute. Add the sliced artichokes and stock; stir well. Bring to the boil, cover and simmer for about 15 minutes until the artichokes are tender.

4 Add the cream, nutmeg and cayenne to the soup. Transfer to a blender or food processor and whiz until smooth, then pass through a sieve into a clean pan.

5 Reheat the soup and stir in the grated Parmesan. Taste and adjust the seasoning. Serve at once, with the hot Melba toast.

variation: *For a less rich soup, use semi-skimmed milk rather than single cream.*

Roasted Tomato and Pepper Soup

1.4kg (3lb) full-flavoured tomatoes,
   preferably vine-ripened
2 red peppers, cored, deseeded
   and chopped
4 garlic cloves, peeled and crushed
3 small onions, peeled and thinly
   sliced
20g (³⁄₄oz) thyme sprigs
4 tbsp olive oil
4 tbsp Worcestershire sauce
4 tbsp vodka
salt and pepper
6 tbsp double cream

serves 6
preparation: 20 minutes
cooking time: about 1 hour
per serving: 240 cals; 17g fat;
   14g carbohydrate

1 Remove any green stalk heads from the tomatoes and discard. Put the tomatoes into a large roasting tin with the peppers, garlic and onions. Scatter 6 thyme sprigs on top, drizzle with the olive oil and roast at 200°C (180°C fan oven) mark 6 for 25 minutes. Turn the vegetables over and roast for a further 30–40 minutes until tender and slightly charred.

2 Put one third of the vegetables into a blender or food processor with 300ml (½ pint) boiled water. Add the Worcestershire sauce and vodka, plus plenty of salt and pepper. Whiz until smooth, then pass through a sieve into a pan.

3 Whiz the remaining vegetables with 450ml (³⁄₄ pint) boiled water, then sieve and add to the pan.

4 To serve, warm the soup thoroughly, stirring occasionally. Pour into warmed bowls, add 1 tbsp double cream to each, then drag a cocktail stick through the cream to create a swirl. Scatter a few fresh thyme leaves over the top to finish.

Spinach and Pea Soup

2 tbsp olive oil
1 onion, peeled and chopped
1 garlic clove, peeled and chopped
½ tsp ground cumin
450g (1lb) spinach leaves, stalks removed,
    shredded
225g (8oz) shelled peas, defrosted if frozen
2 tbsp chopped mint
900ml (1½ pints) vegetable stock
¼ tsp freshly grated nutmeg
salt and pepper

TO SERVE
4 tbsp extra-virgin olive oil
2 tbsp lemon juice
Parmesan cheese shavings (optional)

serves 4
preparation: 10 minutes
cooking time: 30 minutes
per serving: 300 cals; 24g fat; 10g
    carbohydrate

1 Heat the olive oil in a pan, add the onion, garlic and cumin and fry gently for about 10 minutes until the onions are softened and lightly golden.

2 Add the shredded spinach to the pan with the peas, mint and stock. Bring slowly to the boil, cover and simmer over a very gentle heat for 15 minutes.

3 Transfer the soup to a blender or food processor and whiz until very smooth. Return to the pan and heat gently until the soup just reaches the boil. Add the nutmeg and seasoning to taste.

4 To serve, whisk together the olive oil and lemon juice. Spoon the soup into warmed bowls and drizzle the lemon oil over the surface. Serve at once, topped with Parmesan shavings if you like.

variation: For a more substantial soup, add 225g (8oz) peeled diced potatoes with the onion. Increase the stock to 1.2 litres (2 pints); add to the potatoes and onion and simmer for 15 minutes before stirring in the spinach etc. Finish as above.

Beetroot Soup

750g (1lb 10oz) raw beetroot
1 tbsp olive oil
1 onion, peeled and finely chopped
275g (10oz) potatoes, peeled and
    roughly chopped
2 litres (3½ pints) hot vegetable stock
juice of 1 lemon
salt and pepper

TO SERVE
125ml (4fl oz) soured cream
25g (1oz) mixed root vegetable crisps
    (optional)
2 tbsp snipped chives

serves 8
preparation: 15 minutes
cooking time: 40–45 minutes
per serving: 290 cals; 25g fat;
    15g carbohydrate

1 Peel the beetroot and cut into 1cm (½ inch) cubes. Heat the olive oil in a large pan. Add the onion and cook for 5 minutes to soften. Add the beetroot and potatoes and cook for a further 5 minutes.

2 Add the stock and lemon juice, and bring to the boil. Season with salt and pepper, lower the heat and simmer, half-covered, for 25 minutes. Cool slightly, then whiz in a blender or food processor until smooth.

3 Pour the soup into a clean pan and reheat gently. Divide the soup among warmed bowls. Swirl 1 tbsp soured cream on each portion, scatter with a few vegetable crisps if you like, and sprinkle with snipped chives to serve.

Squash and Sweet Potato Soup

1 tbsp olive oil

1 large onion, peeled and finely chopped

1–2 red chillies, deseeded and chopped

2 tsp coriander seeds, crushed

1 butternut squash, about 750g (1lb 10oz),
   peeled, deseeded and roughly chopped

2 medium sweet potatoes, peeled and
   roughly chopped

2 tomatoes, skinned and diced

1.7 litres (3 pints) hot vegetable stock

salt and pepper

serves 8

preparation: 15 minutes

cooking time: 25 minutes

per serving: 100 cals; 2g fat;
   19g carbohydrate

1 Heat the olive oil in a large pan, add the onion and fry for about 10 minutes until soft. Add the chillies and coriander seeds to the pan and cook for 1–2 minutes.

2 Add the squash, potatoes and tomatoes and cook for 5 minutes. Add the hot stock, then cover the pan and bring to the boil. Simmer gently for 15 minutes or until the vegetables are soft.

3 Whiz the soup in batches in a blender or food processor until smooth. Adjust the seasoning and reheat to serve.

note: *Savoury cheese straws (page 70) make a delicious accompaniment to this soup.*

Cream of Mushroom Soup

15g (½oz) dried porcini mushrooms

50g (2oz) butter

1 large onion, peeled and chopped

1 garlic clove, peeled and crushed

1 tbsp chopped sage

700g (1½lb) chestnut mushrooms, or mixed
   chestnut and flat mushrooms, wiped
   and chopped

750ml (1¼ pints) vegetable stock

150ml (¼ pint) crème fraîche

salt and pepper

pinch of freshly grated nutmeg

snipped chives, to serve

serves 4–6

preparation: 15 minutes, plus soaking

cooking time: 35 minutes

per serving: 290–190 cals; 26–18g fat;
   8–5g carbohydrate

1 Put the dried mushrooms into a bowl, pour on 150ml (¼ pint) boiling water and set aside to soak for 20 minutes. Remove the porcini with a slotted spoon; strain the liquid and reserve. Chop the mushrooms and set aside.

2 Melt half the butter in a pan, add the onion, porcini, garlic and sage and fry for 10 minutes until softened and lightly golden. Add the remaining butter, then add the fresh mushrooms and increase the heat. Stir-fry for 5 minutes until the mushrooms are browned.

3 Stir in the reserved porcini liquid and stock. Bring to the boil, cover and simmer gently for 20 minutes. Transfer to a blender or food processor and whiz until smooth. Return to the pan.

4 Stir in most of the crème fraîche and salt, pepper and nutmeg to taste. Reheat the soup gently. Spoon into warmed bowls and add a swirl of crème fraîche and a sprinkling of snipped chives to each portion. Serve at once.

Carrot and Coriander Soup

40g (1½oz) butter
175g (6oz) leeks, trimmed and sliced
450g (1lb) carrots, peeled and sliced
2 tsp ground coriander
1 tsp plain flour
1.2 litres (2 pints) vegetable stock
salt and pepper
150ml (¼ pint) single cream
coriander leaves, roughly torn, to serve

serves 6
preparation: 15 minutes
cooking time: about 30 minutes
per serving: 130 cals; 11g fat;
    7g carbohydrate

1 Melt the butter in a large pan. Add the sliced leeks and carrots, stir, then cover the pan and cook gently for 7–10 minutes until the vegetables begin to soften but not colour.
2 Stir in the ground coriander and flour and cook, stirring, for 1 minute.
3 Add the stock and bring to the boil, stirring. Season, reduce the heat, cover and simmer for about 20 minutes, until the vegetables are tender.
4 Allow to cool a little, then whiz in a blender or food processor until quite smooth.
5 Return to the pan and stir in the cream. Adjust the seasoning and reheat gently; do not boil. Serve scattered with torn coriander leaves.

Minestrone with Pesto

175g (6oz) dried haricot, cannellini or
    flageolet beans, soaked overnight
salt and pepper
2.4 litres (4 pints) vegetable stock
1 dried red chilli
450g (1lb) potatoes, peeled and diced
450g (1lb) carrots, peeled and diced
2 large leeks, trimmed and thinly sliced
450g (1lb) courgettes, trimmed and diced
225g (8oz) French beans, trimmed and
    halved
425g can chopped tomatoes
125g (4oz) dried pastina (tiny soup pasta)

TO SERVE
pesto (preferably homemade, page 28)
50g (2oz) pecorino or Parmesan cheese,
    freshly grated

serves 6–8
preparation: 20 minutes, plus overnight
    soaking
cooking time: about 2–2½ hours
per serving: 400–300 cals; 13–10g fat;
    53–40g carbohydrate

1 Drain the soaked beans and put them into a large pan with enough fresh cold water to cover. Bring to the boil and boil steadily for 10 minutes, then lower the heat and simmer for 1–1½ hours or until the beans are tender, adding salt towards the end of the cooking time. Drain thoroughly.
2 Pour the stock into a large pan and add the dried chilli. Bring to the boil, then add the cooked beans, potatoes, carrots and leeks. Lower the heat, cover and simmer for 25 minutes or until the vegetables are very tender.
3 Add the courgettes, French beans, tomatoes and pasta, and season generously with salt and pepper. Re-cover and simmer for a further 10 minutes or until the pasta is just cooked.
4 Serve as a lunch or supper with plenty of good bread. Hand the pesto and grated cheese separately.

variations
• Use 2 x 400g cans beans instead of dried ones. Drain and add to the soup towards the end of stage 3 to heat through.
• For a fiery version, serve with coriander pesto flavoured with chilli (page 28).

Curried Parsnip Soup

40g (1½oz) butter
1 onion, peeled and sliced
700g (1½lb) parsnips, peeled, cored and
    finely diced
1 tsp curry powder
½ tsp ground cumin
1.2 litres (2 pints) chicken or vegetable stock
salt and pepper
150ml (¼ pint) single cream
paprika, to sprinkle

serves 6
preparation: 20 minutes
cooking time: 50 minutes
per serving: 180 cals; 11g fat;
    17g carbohydrate

1 Melt the butter in a large pan, add the onion and fry gently for 5–7 minutes. Add the parsnips and fry gently for about 3 minutes.
2 Stir in the curry powder and cumin and cook for a further 2 minutes.
3 Add the stock, season with salt and pepper and bring to the boil. Reduce the heat, cover and simmer for 35 minutes or until the vegetables are tender.
4 Allow to cool slightly, then whiz in a blender or food processor until smooth.
5 Return to the pan and adjust the seasoning. Add the cream and reheat but do not boil. Serve sprinkled with paprika.

Mexican Bean Soup

4 tbsp olive oil
1 onion, peeled and chopped
2 garlic cloves, peeled and chopped
pinch of crushed red chillies
1 tsp ground coriander
1 tsp ground cumin
½ tsp ground cinnamon
900ml (1½ pints) vegetable stock
300ml (½ pint) tomato juice
1–2 tsp chilli sauce
2 x 400g cans red kidney beans
2 tbsp chopped coriander
salt and pepper

TO SERVE
lime butter (optional, see note)
coriander leaves, roughly torn

serves 6
preparation: 15 minutes
cooking time: 25 minutes
per serving, with lime butter: 240 cals;
    16g fat; 19g carbohydrate
per serving, without lime butter: 180 cals;
    9g fat; 19g carbohydrate

1 Heat the olive oil in a large pan, add the onion, garlic, chilli and spices and fry gently for 5 minutes until lightly golden.
2 Add the stock, tomato juice, chilli sauce and beans with their liquid. Bring to the boil, cover and simmer gently for 20 minutes. Let cool slightly.
3 Whiz in a blender or food processor until very smooth, then return the soup to the pan. Stir in the chopped coriander and heat through. Season with salt and pepper to taste.
4 Spoon the soup into warmed bowls. Top each portion with a few slices of lime butter if serving, and scatter with torn coriander leaves.

note: *This soup is delicious topped with lime butter. To prepare, beat the grated zest and juice of ½ lime into 50g (2oz) softened butter and season with salt and pepper. Shape into a log, wrap in clingfilm and chill until needed. Unwrap and thinly slice to serve.*

Celery and Stilton Soup

40g (1½oz) butter
1 small onion, peeled and finely chopped
1 small leek, trimmed and finely chopped
4 celery sticks, chopped
2 tbsp plain flour
300ml (½ pint) semi-skimmed milk
600ml (1 pint) chicken stock
225g (8oz) Stilton cheese, crumbled
salt and pepper
4 bacon rashers, crisp-fried, to serve

serves 4
preparation: 20 minutes
cooking time: 35 minutes
per serving: 470 cals; 37g fat;
   14g carbohydrate

1 Melt the butter in a pan, add the onion and leek and fry for 10 minutes until soft but not browned. Add the celery and cook for a further 5 minutes. Stir in the flour and cook gently for 1 minute.

2 Gradually stir in the milk and stock. Bring to the boil, then cover and simmer for 15 minutes or until the celery is tender.

3 Gradually add the crumbled Stilton and stir until melted. Season with salt and pepper to taste and reheat gently. Ladle the soup into warmed bowls. Break the bacon into bite-sized pieces and scatter over the soup to serve.

Split Pea and Ham Soup

500g pack dried yellow split peas, soaked
   overnight
25g (1oz) butter
1 large onion, peeled and finely chopped
125g (4oz) rindless smoked streaky bacon
   rashers, roughly chopped
1 garlic clove, peeled and crushed
1.7 litres (3 pints) well-flavoured ham or
   vegetable stock
bouquet garni (parsley sprigs, thyme sprigs
   and bay leaf)
1 tsp dried oregano
salt and pepper
125g (4oz) cooked ham, chopped
cracked black pepper, to serve

serves 6
preparation: 15 minutes, plus overnight
   soaking
cooking time: 1 hour 5 minutes
per serving: 430 cals; 12g fat;
   51g carbohydrate

1 Drain the soaked split peas. Melt the butter in a large pan, add the onion, bacon and garlic, and cook over a low heat for about 10 minutes until the onion is soft.

2 Add the drained split peas to the pan with the stock. Bring to the boil and skim the surface. Add the bouquet garni and oregano, then season with salt and pepper. Cover and simmer for 45 minutes to 1 hour or until the peas are very soft.

3 Cool a little, then whiz half the soup in a blender or food processor until smooth. Return to the pan and reheat, then add the ham and check the seasoning. Sprinkle with cracked black pepper to serve.

note: *Dried peas form the base of this comforting soup. First, you need to soak them overnight in about 1 litre (1¾ pints) cold water. If you forget, put them straight into a pan with the water, bring to the boil and cook for 1–2 minutes, then leave to stand for 2 hours before using.*

Scotch Broth

1 piece of marrow bone, about 350g (12oz)

1.4kg (3lb) piece of beef skirt

300g (11oz) mixed dried pulses (pearl barley,
   red lentils, split peas, green peas etc.)
   soaked according to pack instructions

2 carrots, peeled and finely chopped

1 parsnip, peeled and finely chopped

2 onions, peeled and finely chopped

¼ white cabbage, finely chopped

1 leek, trimmed and finely chopped

salt and pepper

2 tbsp chopped parsley, to serve

serves 8

preparation: 20 minutes, plus soaking

cooking time: 2 hours

per serving: 170 cals; 1g fat;
   33g carbohydrate

1 Put the marrow bone and beef skirt into a 5.7 litre (10 pint) stock pot and add 2.7 litres (4½ pints) cold water – there should be enough to cover the meat.

2 Bring to the boil, remove the scum from the surface and discard. Turn the heat down to low, add the dried pulses and simmer, partially covered, for 1½ hours, skimming the surface occasionally.

3 Add the carrots, parsnip, onions, cabbage and leek and another 600ml (1 pint) water. Cover to bring to the boil quickly, then simmer for 30 minutes.

4 Remove the marrow bone and piece of beef from the broth. Season the broth with plenty of salt and some pepper, then stir in the chopped parsley.

note: *This is two courses in one – starter and main course. The beef is removed before the broth is served as a starter. For the next course, divide up the meat and serve it with a potato and turnip mash.*

Cock-a-Leekie

1.4kg (3lb) oven-ready chicken
2 onions, peeled and roughly chopped
2 carrots, peeled and roughly chopped
2 celery sticks, roughly chopped
1 bay leaf
25g (1oz) butter
900g (2lb) leeks, trimmed and sliced
125g (4oz) ready-to-eat pitted prunes, sliced
salt and pepper

DUMPLINGS
125g (4oz) self-raising white flour
pinch of salt
50g (2oz) shredded suet
2 tbsp chopped parsley
2 tbsp chopped thyme

TO SERVE
chopped parsley

serves 8
preparation: 20 minutes
cooking time: 1 hour 20 minutes
per serving: 290 cals; 11g fat;
   27g carbohydrate

1 Put the chicken into a pan in which it fits quite snugly. Add the chopped vegetables, bay leaf and chicken giblets (if available). Add 1.7 litres (3 pints) water, bring to the boil, reduce the heat, cover and simmer gently for 1 hour.
2 Melt the butter in a large pan, add the leeks and fry gently for 10 minutes until softened.
3 Remove the chicken from the pan; strain the stock and set aside. Strip the chicken from the bones and shred roughly. Add to the stock with the prunes and softened leeks.
4 For the dumplings, sift the flour and salt into a bowl. Stir in the suet, herbs and about 5 tbsp water to make a fairly firm dough. Lightly shape the dough into 2.5cm (1 inch) balls.
5 Bring the soup just to the boil and season well. Reduce the heat, add the dumplings and cover the pan with a lid. Simmer for about 15–20 minutes until the dumplings are light and fluffy. Serve scattered with chopped parsley.

notes
• As a main course, this soup will serve 4.
• If possible, make the stock a day ahead. Cool overnight, then remove any fat from the surface.

Curried Mussel Soup

2kg (4½lb) fresh mussels in shells, cleaned
   (see page 82)
90ml (3fl oz) dry white wine
pinch of saffron strands
450ml (¾ pint) hot fish or vegetable stock
25g (1oz) butter
4 shallots, peeled and finely chopped
1 garlic clove, peeled and crushed
1 tsp grated fresh root ginger
½ tsp ground turmeric
½ tsp garam masala
150ml (¼ pint) double cream
1 tbsp chopped parsley or chervil
1 tsp lemon juice, or to taste
pepper

serves 4
preparation: 15 minutes
cooking time: 20 minutes
per serving: 380 cals; 26g fat;
   5g carbohydrate

1 Put the mussels into a large pan with the wine. Cover with a tight-fitting lid and steam for 4–5 minutes until the shells have opened, shaking the pan frequently; discard any that remain closed.
2 Meanwhile, put the saffron strands into a bowl, pour on the hot stock and leave to infuse for about 10 minutes.
3 Strain the mussel liquor through a muslin-lined sieve and set aside. Shell the mussels, keeping eight in their shells for the garnish.
4 Melt the butter in a pan, add the shallots, garlic, ginger, turmeric and garam masala and fry gently for 5 minutes until the shallots are soft but not golden. Add the saffron stock and mussel liquor and simmer gently, uncovered, for 10 minutes.
5 Stir in the cream, shelled mussels and parsley and heat through. Add the lemon juice and season with pepper to taste. Spoon the soup into warmed bowls and top with the reserved mussels in shells. Serve with warm crusty bread.

Bouillabaisse

1kg (2¼lb) mixed fish fillets and shellfish,
  such as red mullet, John Dory, monkfish,
  red snapper, whiting, mussels in shells,
  cooked large prawns and crab claws
pinch of saffron strands
3 tbsp olive oil
1 onion, peeled and sliced
1 leek, trimmed and sliced
2 celery sticks, sliced
2 garlic cloves, peeled and crushed
400g can plum tomatoes, or skinned,
  deseeded flavourful fresh ones, chopped
bouquet garni (thyme sprigs, bay leaf and
  parsley sprigs)
1 strip of orange zest
1 tbsp sun-dried tomato paste
½ tsp fennel seeds
1.2 litres (2 pints) fish stock
salt and pepper
2 tbsp chopped parsley
1 tbsp chopped thyme

serves 4
preparation: 15 minutes
cooking time: 45 minutes
per serving: 330 cals; 13g fat;
  9g carbohydrate

1 Cut the fish fillets into bite-sized pieces.
2 Put the saffron strands into a bowl, pour on 150ml (¼ pint) boiling water and leave to soak.
3 Heat the olive oil in a large pan, add the onion, leek, celery and garlic and cook until softened. Add the tomatoes, bouquet garni, orange zest, sun-dried tomato paste and fennel seeds; cook for 1–2 minutes.
4 Add the fish stock together with the saffron and its soaking liquid. Season with pepper and a little salt and bring to the boil. Lower the heat and simmer for about 30 minutes.
5 Add the fish pieces and mussels (not the prawns or crab claws) and cook for about 5–6 minutes, until the fish is just cooked and the mussels have opened; discard any unopened ones.
6 Stir in the chopped herbs, prawns and crab claws. Heat through and serve in warmed bowls with plenty of crusty bread.

note: *This classic French fish soup originates from Marseilles. It possible, buy whole fish and fillet them yourself, using the bones and trimmings to make a flavourful stock (see page 21).*

Vichyssoise

75g (3oz) butter
2 onions, peeled and thinly sliced
450g (1lb) leeks (white part only), trimmed
  and sliced
175g (6oz) floury potatoes, peeled and diced
1 bay leaf
1.3 litres (2¼ pints) vegetable stock
300ml (½ pint) semi-skimmed milk
150ml (¼ pint) crème fraîche
salt and white pepper

TO SERVE
extra crème fraîche
snipped chives

serves 6
preparation: 15 minutes, plus optional
  chilling
cooking time: 30 minutes
per serving: 300 cals; 26g fat;
  15g carbohydrate

1 Melt the butter in a large pan and add the onions and leeks. Stir well, add 3 tbsp water, cover tightly and sweat over a gentle heat for 10 minutes until soft and golden.
2 Stir in the diced potatoes, bay leaf, stock and milk. Bring to the boil, lower the heat, cover and simmer for 20 minutes until the potatoes are tender.
3 Discard the bay leaf. Leave the soup to cool a little, then transfer to a blender or food processor and whiz until smooth. Pass through a sieve. Return to the pan if serving hot.
4 Stir in the crème fraîche and season with salt and pepper to taste. Either cool and chill (in this case, season liberally) or reheat and pour into warmed soup bowls. Serve topped with a dollop of crème fraîche and chives.

variation: *Add a bruised lemon grass stalk to the soup in place of the bay leaf to impart a delicate flavour and fragrance.*

Smoked Haddock Chowder

25g (1oz) butter

2 onions, peeled and chopped

125g (4oz) rindless smoked streaky bacon
    rashers, chopped

600ml (1 pint) whole milk

salt and pepper

225g (8oz) potatoes, peeled and cut into 1cm
    (½ inch) cubes

3 celery sticks, thinly sliced

198g can sweetcorn, drained

450g (1lb) skinless smoked haddock fillet, cut
    into 8 pieces

serves 4

preparation: 15 minutes

cooking time: 25 minutes

per serving: 490 cals; 25g fat;
    35g carbohydrate

1 Heat the butter in a large wide pan, add the onions and fry for 3 minutes. Add the bacon and cook for a further 5 minutes until it is no longer pink.

2 Add the milk and 600ml (1 pint) boiling water, then season with 1 tsp salt and plenty of pepper. Add the potatoes and celery and cook for 5 minutes.

3 Stir in the drained sweetcorn and lower in the haddock gently. Cover and cook for 10 minutes or until the fish is just cooked. Serve in individual bowls, with plenty of crusty bread.

variation: *Serve the chowder topped with croûtons (see page 33) and plenty of chopped parsley.*

Cream of Watercress Soup

250g (9oz) watercress

75g (3oz) butter

1 onion, peeled and finely chopped

700g (1½lb) potatoes, peeled and cut into
    small pieces

900ml (1½ pints) semi-skimmed milk

900ml (1½ pints) vegetable stock

284ml carton single cream

salt and pepper

serves 6

preparation: 15 minutes

cooking time: 30 minutes

per serving: 460 cals; 29g fat;
    32g carbohydrate

1 Trim the watercress and discard any coarse stalks. Set aside a few good sprigs for the garnish; roughly chop the rest.

2 Melt the butter in a large pan, add the onion and cook gently for 8–10 minutes until soft. Add the potatoes and cook for 1 minute, then pour in the milk and stock and bring to the boil. Reduce the heat and cook for 15–20 minutes until tender.

3 Take off the heat and stir in the watercress. Blend the soup in a blender or food processor in batches until smooth, then pour into a clean pan.

4 Add the cream and season with salt and pepper to taste. Heat through and serve garnished with the reserved watercress sprigs.

note: *The secret of keeping this soup's brilliant colour is to stir the leaves into the hot soup and blend straightaway – cook the watercress for too long and it will lose its vibrancy.*

Lettuce and Sorrel Soup

1 tbsp olive oil

6 spring onions, trimmed and sliced

1 garlic clove, peeled and crushed

1 tsp chopped thyme (ideally lemon thyme)

50g (2oz) long-grain rice

450g (1lb) cos lettuce, shredded

125g (4oz) sorrel, shredded

1.2 litres (2 pints) vegetable stock

2 tbsp snipped chives

pinch of freshly grated nutmeg

3 tbsp extra-virgin olive oil

salt and pepper

Parmesan cheese shavings, to serve
 (optional)

serves 4

preparation: 15 minutes

cooking time: 20–25 minutes

per serving: 240 cals; 17g fat;
 14g carbohydrate

1 Heat the 1 tbsp olive oil in a pan, add the spring onions, garlic and thyme and fry gently for 5 minutes until softened but not coloured. Add the rice and stir-fry for 1 minute.

2 Stir in the lettuce and sorrel, then pour in the stock. Bring to the boil, cover the pan and simmer gently for 15 minutes until the rice is cooked.

3 Transfer to a blender or food processor, add the chives and nutmeg and whiz until smooth. Return the soup to the pan.

4 Heat through, whisking in the extra-virgin oil and seasoning with salt and pepper to taste. Serve hot, topped with a few Parmesan shavings if you like.

variations
• For a more substantial soup, replace the rice with 225g (8oz) peeled and diced potatoes, reducing the lettuce to 225g (8oz).
• Use spinach instead of sorrel.

Gazpacho

1 medium cucumber, peeled, deseeded and
 coarsely chopped

450g (1lb) fully ripened tomatoes, skinned,
 deseeded and chopped

100g (3½oz) green pepper, cored, deseeded
 and chopped

50–100g (2–3½oz) onions, peeled and
 chopped

2 garlic cloves, peeled and chopped

3 tbsp olive oil

3 tbsp white wine vinegar

450ml (¾ pint) tomato juice

2 tbsp tomato purée

salt and pepper

TO SERVE

4 thick slices white bread, crusts removed

50g (2oz) butter

1 green pepper, cored, deseeded and
 finely diced

serves 6

preparation: 20 minutes, plus chilling

cooking time: 10 minutes

per serving: 220 cals; 14g fat;
 21g carbohydrate

1 Mix all the gazpacho ingredients together in a large bowl, seasoning with ¼ tsp salt. Purée the mixture in batches in a blender or food processor until smooth.

2 Return the soup to the bowl, cover and chill for at least 2 hours.

3 To make croûtons, cut the bread into cubes. Heat the butter in a large frying pan and sauté the bread cubes over a medium heat, stirring frequently, until golden on all sides. Remove and drain the croûtons on kitchen paper.

4 Just before serving, add a few ice cubes to the soup. Serve each portion garnished with diced green pepper and the croûtons.

note: This Spanish iced soup is wonderfully refreshing in hot weather. Drop in a few ice cubes just before serving to make it as cold as possible.

Chilled Asparagus Soup

1.1kg (2½lb) asparagus, trimmed
3 tbsp olive oil
4 large shallots, peeled and finely chopped
200g (7oz) leeks, trimmed and finely chopped
salt and pepper
chervil sprigs, to serve

serves 6
preparation: 15 minutes, plus chilling
cooking time: 25 minutes
per serving: 130 cals; 8g fat;
    9g carbohydrate

1 Cut the tips off the asparagus and set aside. Cut the stalks into 2.5cm (1 inch) lengths.

2 Heat the olive oil in a large pan, add the shallots and cook gently for 2–3 minutes. Add the leeks and cook, stirring occasionally, for about 10 minutes or until they are soft.

3 Add the asparagus stalks, 900ml (1½ pints) water and seasoning. Bring to the boil, lower the heat and simmer very gently, uncovered, for 10 minutes or until the asparagus is soft. Let cool slightly.

4 Transfer the soup to a blender or food processor and whiz until smooth. Pour into a bowl and set aside to cool.

5 Add the asparagus tips to a pan of boiling salted water and cook for 2–3 minutes until tender; drain and refresh under cold running water.

6 Add the asparagus tips to the soup, cover and chill for several hours.

7 To serve, stir about 450ml (¾ pint) iced water into the soup to obtain the required consistency. Season generously with salt and pepper. Serve in chilled soup bowls, topped with chervil.

Chilled Pea Soup with Mint Salsa

450g (1lb) fresh peas in their pods
2 tbsp olive oil
2 leeks, trimmed and sliced
1 garlic clove, peeled and crushed
175g (6oz) potato, peeled and cubed
1 litre (1¾ pints) vegetable stock
salt and pepper
150ml (¼ pint) double cream

MINT SALSA
juice of 1 lemon
25g (1oz) golden caster sugar
1 small onion, peeled and finely chopped
125g (4oz) cucumber, peeled, deseeded
    and diced
4 tbsp chopped mint

TO GARNISH
mint sprigs

serves 4
preparation: 20 minutes, plus chilling
cooking time: 35–40 minutes
per serving: 370 cals; 26g fat;
    28g carbohydrate

1 Remove the peas from their pods, reserving both peas and pods. String the pods and cut into pieces.

2 Heat the olive oil in a pan, add the leeks, garlic and pea pods and fry gently for 5 minutes. Add the potato and stock, bring to the boil, cover and simmer gently for 20 minutes.

3 Purée the soup in a blender or food processor until smooth. Pass through a fine sieve into the cleaned pan and stir in the fresh peas. Cover and cook gently for a further 10 minutes until the peas are tender.

4 Meanwhile, make the salsa. Put the lemon juice and sugar into a small pan and heat gently to dissolve. Add the onion, cucumber and a pinch of salt. Remove from the heat, stir in the mint and set aside to cool.

5 Season the soup with salt and pepper, cool, then chill for several hours.

6 To serve, stir the cream into the soup and adjust the seasoning. Divide among bowls and top with the salsa and mint, adding a few ice cubes, if you like.

note: *The pea pods add a depth of flavour and richness to the soup.*

STARTERS

The ideal starter is attractive and mouth-watering to stimulate the appetite and set the tone for the meal to follow. At the start of a meal, appetites are at their keenest and most appreciative, so a well chosen starter is important. Soups, salads, seafood, pâtés, mousses, fruit starters ... the choice is endless, but should always be made with the other courses in mind. Aim to achieve a balance of flavours, textures and colours throughout the meal and, if your main course is rich and substantial, make sure you choose a light starter.

There are no hard and fast rules but variety is the key. It is invariably best to avoid a fish or shellfish starter if your main course is fish, or a meat starter if the main dish is meat. Keep starter portions reasonably small to avoid taking the edge off the appetite.

Soups, of course, are ideal first courses as they can be prepared ahead and there are plenty to choose from in the previous chapter. Salad starters are light, simple and quick. In addition to the recipes in this chapter, you will find more potential starters in the Salads chapter – simply adjust the quantities accordingly. Warm salads are particularly tempting starters.

Most of the recipes in this chapter can be prepared well in advance – a factor which is always important when you are entertaining. If you are serving a large number of guests, opt for a starter which can be put on the table before your guests are seated. Alternatively, for an informal gathering, you might prefer to serve a selection of canapés and/or savoury finger foods with drinks rather than a sit-down starter. You'll find recipes for these – and nibbles to serve at drinks parties – towards the end of this chapter (see pages 68–75).

QUICK STARTERS

For impromptu entertaining, or if you are short of time, try one of the following simple suggestions:

Smoked Salmon

Serve thin slices of good quality smoked salmon or ready-prepared gravad lax with thinly sliced brown bread and lime or lemon wedges.

Parma Ham with Melon or Figs

Cut fragrant, ripe melon or fresh figs into wedges and drape thin slices of Parma ham on top.

Grilled Vegetables

Brush slices of courgette, peppers, aubergine, red onion etc., with olive oil and grill, turning, until tender and lightly caramelised. Drizzle with extra-virgin olive oil and serve with pesto (page 28) or aïoli (page 351).

Avocado

Halve avocados, remove the stone and spoon a little herb or raspberry vinegar flavoured vinaigrette into the cavities. Serve on a bed of salad leaves.

Shellfish Platter

Serve very fresh shellfish, such as cooked prawns in their shells, dressed crab, or raw oysters on their half-shell simply with brown bread and lemon wedges. Accompany prawns and fresh crab with good mayonnaise.

Hors d'Oeuvres

Serve a selection of ready prepared meats, such as salami, Parma ham, cured pork, roast ham, smoked chicken and bresaola (cured beef), with a simple salad and black olive garnish.

Antipasto

Buy a selection of antipasti from your local deli or supermarket and arrange on a large platter for guests to help themselves. Include Parma or Serrano ham, salami, olives, marinated artichokes, roasted peppers and anchovies. Serve with ciabatta or other rustic bread.

Tomato Bruschetta

6 ripe plum tomatoes, peeled and
  roughly diced
¼ tsp golden caster sugar
1 tbsp chopped basil, plus extra sprigs
  to garnish
4 tbsp extra-virgin olive oil
4 slices day-old ciabatta or baguette
1 garlic clove, peeled and halved
salt and pepper

serves 4
preparation: 15 minutes, plus infusing
cooking time: 1–2 minutes
per serving: 240 cals; 15g fat;
  23g carbohydrate

1 Put the tomatoes into a bowl with the sugar, chopped basil and half of the olive oil. Cover and set aside for 30 minutes to allow the flavours to mingle.

2 Toast the bread on both sides until crisp and golden, then rub all over with the cut garlic clove.
3 Spoon the tomato mixture on top of the toasted bread, pressing it firmly into the bread. Drizzle over the remaining olive oil and season generously with salt and pepper. Garnish with basil leaves to serve.

variations
bruschetta with tapenade and antipasti: *Spread the toasted bread slices with olive tapenade, then top with a selection of antipasti, such as marinated red peppers, artichokes and aubergines (available from supermarkets). Garnish with basil sprigs.*
Parma ham and asparagus bruschetta: *For the topping, toss 50g (2oz) rocket leaves in a light lemony vinaigrette. Brush 225g (8oz) trimmed asparagus with olive oil and grill for 4–5 minutes until charred and tender. Arrange the rocket on the toasted bread, then top with the asparagus, 4 slices of Parma ham and a few Parmesan shavings. Drizzle with olive oil to serve.*

Roasted Vegetable Crostini

300g pack cherry tomatoes on the vine
2 sweet romano peppers, cored, deseeded
   and sliced
2 garlic cloves, peeled and sliced
1 red onion, peeled and sliced
5 tbsp olive oil
salt and pepper
1 sfilatino, ciabatta, or baguette, sliced
1 tbsp balsamic vinegar
basil leaves, to garnish

serves 6
preparation: 10 minutes
cooking time: 30 minutes
per serving: 260 cals; 13g fat;
   31g carbohydrate

1 Divide the cherry tomatoes into 6 clusters and put them into a roasting tin with the peppers, garlic and onion. Drizzle with 2 tbsp of the olive oil and season well with salt and pepper. Bake at 220°C (200°C fan oven) mark 7 for 30 minutes.

2 Meanwhile, put the bread slices on a baking sheet and drizzle with 2 tbsp olive oil. Bake for 15 minutes or until golden.

3 Top the bread slices with the roasted vegetables. Drizzle with balsamic vinegar and the remaining olive oil, and garnish with basil to serve.

Melon with Port and Ginger Vinaigrette

1 Ogen melon
1 honeydew melon
1 charentais melon
4 balls of preserved stem ginger in syrup,
   drained, plus 1 tsp syrup from the jar
1 tbsp port
4 tbsp extra-virgin olive oil
2 tsp lemon juice
salt and pepper

serves 8
preparation: 15 minutes, plus chilling
per serving: 140 cals; 7g fat;
   17g carbohydrate

1 Halve each melon and scoop out the seeds. Cut each melon half into 4 wedges and remove the skin. Put the wedges on a tray, cover and chill until needed. (Melon is best served slightly chilled, not very cold.) Cut the stem ginger into matchstick strips.

2 For the dressing, put 1 tsp ginger syrup into a bowl with the port, olive oil and lemon juice. Season with salt and pepper and whisk well.

3 Arrange the melon wedges on a large platter, or individual plates. Scatter the ginger over and drizzle with the vinaigrette to serve.

Tomato and Mozzarella Salad

25g (1oz) pine nuts
125g pack buffalo mozzarella cheese, drained
3 ripe flavourful beef tomatoes, sliced
15 small basil leaves

DRESSING
2 tbsp balsamic vinegar
4 tbsp extra-virgin olive oil
salt and pepper

serves 4
preparation: 15 minutes
per serving: 260 cals; 24g fat;
   2g carbohydrate

1 First make the dressing. Put the balsamic vinegar and olive oil into a small bowl and whisk together. Season generously with salt and pepper to taste.

2 Put the pine nuts in a dry frying pan and toast over a moderate heat, shaking the pan, until evenly toasted. Set aside for a few minutes to cool.

3 Tear the mozzarella into bite-sized pieces. Arrange the tomatoes and mozzarella on a large plate and season with salt and pepper. Drizzle with the dressing.

4 Scatter the pine nuts and basil on top and serve with plenty of crusty bread.

Illustrated on page 50

Baked Stuffed Mushrooms

4 large cup mushrooms
3 tbsp extra-virgin olive oil
50g (2oz) rindless smoked bacon, diced
2 large garlic cloves, peeled and crushed
50g (2oz) fresh white breadcrumbs
50g (2oz) ground almonds
2 tbsp chopped basil
50g (2oz) goat's cheese, in pieces
2 tbsp single cream
1 tbsp lemon juice
salt and pepper

serves 4
preparation: 20 minutes
cooking time: 20 minutes
per serving: 290 cals; 26g fat;
   8g carbohydrate

1 Cut the stalks from the mushrooms and chop them finely, reserving the whole caps.
2 Heat 2 tbsp of the olive oil in a frying pan, add the mushroom caps, rounded-side down, and fry quickly for about 1 minute to brown. Remove with a slotted spoon and arrange, cup-side up, in a baking dish.
3 Add the chopped mushroom stalks, bacon and garlic to the frying pan and fry for 5 minutes, then transfer to a bowl. Add the breadcrumbs, ground almonds, basil, goat's cheese, cream and lemon juice. Mix well and season with salt and pepper to taste. Divide among the mushroom caps.
4 Drizzle the remaining olive oil over the stuffing and bake at 200°C (180°C fan oven) mark 6 for about 20 minutes until the stuffing is crisp and golden on top. Serve hot.

Warm Goat's Cheese Salad

4 slices goat's cheese log (with rind)
1 quantity rocket pesto (page 28)
50g (2oz) rocket leaves
1 bunch of watercress, trimmed
40g (1½oz) walnut halves, toasted

DRESSING
1 tbsp walnut oil
1 tbsp sunflower oil
1 tsp balsamic or sherry vinegar
salt and pepper

serves 4
preparation: 20 minutes
cooking time: 1–2 minutes
per serving: 520 cals; 46g fat;
   2g carbohydrate

1 For the dressing, whisk the ingredients together in a bowl, seasoning with salt and pepper to taste.
2 Lay the goat's cheese slices on a foil-lined baking sheet. Put under the grill, as close to the heat as possible, for 1–2 minutes until browned.
3 Put a slice of goat's cheese on each plate and top with a spoonful of rocket pesto. Toss the rocket and watercress leaves with the dressing and then arrange around the goat's cheese. Scatter the walnuts over the salad and serve immediately.

variation: *Use halved crottins de Chavignol (small hard goat's cheeses) instead of the log chèvre.*

Asparagus and Quail's Egg Salad

24 quail's eggs

24 asparagus spears, trimmed

salt and pepper

juice of ½ lemon

5 tbsp olive oil

4 large spring onions, trimmed and
   finely sliced

100g bag watercress, roughly chopped

few dill sprigs

few tarragon sprigs

serves 8

preparation: 30 minutes

cooking time: 2 minutes

per serving: 180 cals; 14g fat;
   3g carbohydrate

1 Add the quail's eggs to a pan of boiling water and cook for 2 minutes, then drain and plunge into cold water. Cook the asparagus in boiling salted water for 2 minutes or until just tender. Drain, plunge into cold water and set aside to cool.

2 Whisk together the lemon juice, olive oil and salt and pepper. Stir in the spring onions and set aside.

3 Peel the quail's eggs and cut in half. Put into a large bowl with the asparagus, watercress, dill and tarragon. Pour over the dressing and lightly toss all the ingredients together. Season and serve.

note: *Quail's eggs are obtainable from selected supermarkets but, if you prefer, you can replace the quail's eggs with 8 small hen's eggs. Boil for 4–6 minutes, shell and cut into quarters.*

Smoked Salmon Salad with Mustard and Dill

1 small head of fennel
110g bag baby leaf salad
75g (3oz) wild rocket leaves
400g (14oz) oak-smoked wild salmon

DRESSING
4 tbsp extra-virgin olive oil
juice of 1 lemon
½ tsp golden caster sugar
2 tsp wholegrain mustard
salt and pepper
4 tsp finely chopped dill

serves 8
preparation: 15 minutes, plus chilling
per serving: 140 cals; 9g fat;
    1g carbohydrate

1 For the dressing, combine the olive oil, lemon juice, sugar and mustard in a screw-topped jar and season with salt and pepper. Shake to combine.
2 Using a sharp knife, trim the fennel and slice very thinly. Combine with the baby leaf salad and rocket.
3 To serve, arrange 2 slices of smoked salmon on each plate to form a circle. Pile the salad leaves and fennel into the centre.
4 Add the chopped dill to the dressing and shake well to mix. Drizzle over and around the salad leaves. Serve immediately.

Grilled Stuffed Mussels

1.4kg (3lb) large fresh mussels in their shells
5 tbsp dry white wine
2 slices Parma ham, finely chopped
25g (1oz) fresh white breadcrumbs
3 tbsp chopped parsley
1 tbsp chopped oregano
1–2 garlic cloves, peeled and crushed
salt and pepper
5 tbsp olive oil
lemon wedges, to serve

serves 4–6
preparation: 15 minutes
cooking time: 5–6 minutes
per serving: 270–180 cals; 19–13g fat;
   3–2g carbohydrate

1 Clean the mussels thoroughly and remove their 'beards' (see page 82). Rinse well and discard any that do not close when tapped firmly.
2 Put the mussels into a large pan with the white wine, cover with a tight-fitting lid and put over a high heat. Steam for 3–4 minutes or until the shells open. Drain the mussels, reserving the liquid. Discard any that have not opened.
3 Remove and discard the empty half-shells. Arrange the mussels in their half-shells on sturdy baking sheets.
4 Put the Parma ham, breadcrumbs, chopped herbs and garlic in a bowl and season with salt and pepper to taste. Add half of the olive oil and moisten with a little of the reserved mussel liquor, mixing with a fork.
5 Spoon the crumb mixture on top of the mussels in their half-shells to cover them completely. Sprinkle with the remaining olive oil and grill under a medium high heat for about 2 minutes until the crumb mixture is crisp and golden. Serve hot, with lemon wedges.

variation: *Replace the Parma ham with 2 rashers of smoked bacon, finely diced. Dry-fry the bacon until beginning to crisp, then mix with the other stuffing ingredients. Continue as above and sprinkle with freshly grated Parmesan before grilling.*

Seafood Cocktail

½ iceberg lettuce, washed and shredded
175g (6oz) cooked peeled prawns or
   shrimps, flaked white crab meat or
   lobster meat, defrosted if frozen

DRESSING
2 tbsp mayonnaise
2 tbsp tomato ketchup
2 tbsp yogurt
squeeze of lemon juice, or a dash of
   Worcestershire sauce
salt and pepper

TO SERVE
cucumber slices, capers or lemon wedges

serves 4
preparation: 15 minutes
per serving: 110 cals; 7g fat;
   3g carbohydrate

1 Line four small glasses with shredded lettuce.
2 For the dressing, in a bowl, mix the mayonnaise with the tomato ketchup, yogurt and lemon juice or Worcestershire sauce. Season with salt and pepper to taste.
3 Combine the shellfish and dressing, and pile the mixture into the glasses.
4 Garnish with cucumber slices, capers or lemon wedges and serve immediately.

note: *This dish can be as simple or as exotic as you like – depending on which shellfish you choose.*

Potted Crab

250g pack unsalted butter, cut into cubes
2.5cm (1 inch) piece fresh root ginger, peeled
    and finely grated
3 spring onions, trimmed and finely sliced
350–375g (12–13oz) mixed fresh white and
    brown crab meat
juice of ½ lime
salt and pepper
6 thin lime slices
toast slices, to serve

serves 6
preparation: 30 minutes, plus chilling
cooking time: 5 minutes
per serving: 390 cals; 38g fat;
    trace carbohydrate

1 First clarify the butter. Melt it in a small pan over a low heat without stirring, then bring to the boil and let bubble for 1–2 minutes until a foam appears on the surface. Carefully skim off the foam with a slotted spoon and discard. Allow the butter to settle, then carefully pour it into a second pan, leaving the milky sediment behind (discard this sediment). Pour about 5 tbsp of the clarified butter into a small bowl and put to one side.

2 Add the grated ginger and sliced spring onions to the clarified butter remaining in the pan and cook gently for 2–3 minutes until the spring onions are soft. Leave to cool.

3 Flake the crab meat into a bowl. Add the ginger and onion butter along with the lime juice. Season with salt and pepper to taste and mix well.

4 Spoon the mixture into six 150ml (¼ pint) ramekins or pots. Smooth the surface of each and put a lime slice on top. Pour the reserved butter over to form a thin layer, then cover with clingfilm and chill until the butter is set. Take the pots out of the fridge 20 minutes before serving. Accompany with warm toast.

notes
• *Use freshly prepared crab or buy ready-dressed crab meat.*
• *These pots can be made up to 2 days in advance and kept in the fridge.*

Ceviche of Fish with Avocado Salsa

700g (1½lb) very fresh halibut fillet
    or Icelandic cod
juice of 1 large orange
juice of 6 limes

SALSA
3 large ripe tomatoes
1 large red pepper, cored, deseeded
    and finely diced
2 small red chillies, halved, deseeded
    and finely chopped
1 red onion, diced
2 Hass avocados, halved, stoned,
    peeled and diced
4 tbsp chopped coriander
2 tbsp chopped parsley
salt and pepper

serves 6
preparation: 10–15 minutes, plus at
    least 8 hours marinating
per serving: 230 cals; 12g fat;
    7g carbohydrate

1 Remove any skin and bones from the fish, cut the flesh into bite-sized pieces and put into a bowl. Pour the orange and lime juices over and turn the fish to coat thoroughly. Cover and marinate in the fridge for at least 8 hours or overnight.

2 To make the salsa, plunge the tomatoes into boiling water for 30 seconds, then refresh in cold water. Peel away the skin. Cut into quarters, deseed, then dice. Put into a bowl.

3 Add the red pepper, chillies, onion and avocados to the bowl, along with the coriander and parsley. Season with salt and pepper to taste and toss well.

4 To serve, drain the fish, then pile on to plates. Spoon the salsa over, then coarsely grind over some black pepper.

note: *The fish is marinated in lime juice long enough for the acid to cure it. If you can't get hold of halibut or Icelandic cod, substitute another firm-fleshed white fish such as turbot, monkfish, brill or scallops – just be sure that the fish is extremely fresh.*

Warm Chicken Liver and Orange Salad

4 small oranges
450g (1lb) chicken livers, trimmed
75g (3oz) pine nuts
300g (11oz) asparagus tips, trimmed
25g (1oz) butter
125g (4oz) wild rocket leaves

DRESSING
200ml (7fl oz) light olive oil
4 tbsp red wine vinegar
grated zest and juice of 2 small oranges
2 tbsp thin honey
50g (2oz) raisins
salt and pepper

serves 6
preparation: 10 minutes
cooking time: 20 minutes
per serving: 500 cals; 39g fat;
    20g carbohydrate

1 To make the dressing, whisk the olive oil, vinegar, orange zest and 6 tbsp orange juice together in a small pan. Add the honey, raisins and seasoning and bring gently to the boil. Remove from the heat and set aside.
2 For the salad, peel and segment the oranges, discarding all white pith and pips. Rinse the chicken livers and pat dry on kitchen paper.
3 Toast the pine nuts in a dry frying pan over a low heat, shaking the pan to colour evenly. Tip into a bowl to cool. Cook the asparagus in simmering salted water for 5 minutes. Drain, then dry on kitchen paper.
4 Heat the butter in a large heavy-based frying pan until foaming. Add the chicken livers and cook, turning, over a high heat for 5 minutes or until well browned. Remove from the pan and keep warm.
5 Add the dressing and remaining orange juice to the pan. Bubble for 2 minutes, scraping up the sediment.
6 Divide the livers, orange segments, asparagus and rocket among six bowls. Scatter the pine nuts on top, spoon the dressing over and serve at once.

Glazed Spare Ribs

900g (2lb) pork spare ribs
2 tbsp malt vinegar
2 tbsp sesame oil
90ml (3fl oz) rice or wine vinegar
4 tbsp dark soy sauce
2 tsp grated fresh root ginger
1 garlic clove, peeled and crushed
grated zest of 1 lime
4 tbsp muscovado or soft brown sugar
½ tsp Chinese five-spice powder
lime wedges, to serve

serves 4
preparation: 15 minutes
cooking time: 1½ hours
per serving: 330 cals; 20g fat;
    12g carbohydrate (but variable depending
    on proportion of fat on ribs)

1 Wash and dry the spare ribs and put into a pan. Cover with plenty of cold water and add the malt vinegar. Bring to the boil and simmer for 20 minutes, skimming the surface from time to time.

2 Meanwhile, put the remaining ingredients into a small pan with 90ml (3fl oz) water and bring to the boil. Simmer for 5 minutes to reduce and thicken slightly.

3 Drain the ribs and transfer to a roasting dish that will hold them in a single layer. Pour over the soy mixture and toss the ribs to coat evenly.

4 Cover loosely with foil and roast at 220°C (200°C fan oven) mark 7 for 30 minutes. Remove the foil and cook for a further 30 minutes, turning and basting the ribs every 5 minutes.

5 Let stand for 5 minutes before serving, with lime wedges. Provide finger bowls and napkins too.

variation: For glazed chicken wings, omit the parboiling stage. Roast as above, coated with the glaze, for 30–40 minutes in total or until glazed and tender.

Warm Asparagus and Herb Mousses

75g (3oz) butter
450g (1lb) thin asparagus spears
salt and pepper
3 eggs
2 egg yolks
2 tsp chopped chervil or tarragon
2 tsp chopped chives
600ml (1 pint) double cream
2 shallots, peeled and finely chopped
150ml (¼ pint) dry white wine
150ml (¼ pint) vegetable stock
chervil or tarragon sprigs, to garnish

serves 6
preparation: 20 minutes
cooking time: 30–40 minutes
per serving: 650 cals; 64g fat;
    6g carbohydrate

1 Melt 25g (1oz) of the butter and use to liberally grease six 150ml (¼ pint) ramekins. Put these in the fridge. Set aside 12 small asparagus tips for garnish; trim and roughly chop the remaining asparagus.

2 Cook the chopped asparagus in boiling salted water for 4–5 minutes until tender. Remove with a slotted spoon, refresh in iced water, then drain. Add the asparagus tips to the boiling water and cook for 1–2 minutes; drain and set aside.

3 Put the chopped asparagus into a food processor or blender with the whole eggs and extra yolks. Process until smooth, then pass through a sieve into a bowl. Stir in the herbs and 450ml (¾ pint) of the cream. Season generously with salt and pepper.

4 Divide the mixture among the ramekins. Stand in a large roasting tin containing enough boiling water to come halfway up the sides and cover the tin loosely with foil. Bake at 180°C (160°C fan oven) mark 4 for 30–40 minutes or until the mousses are just set.

5 In the meantime, melt the rest of the butter in a pan, add the shallots and cook for 10 minutes until soft. Add the wine and stock, bring to the boil and simmer for 10 minutes. Add the remaining cream and season to taste. Simmer for 10 minutes.

6 To serve, reheat the asparagus tips in the hot sauce for 1 minute. Turn the mousses out on to warmed plates. Spoon the sauce around them and garnish with the asparagus tips and herb sprigs.

Salmon and Asparagus Terrine

75g (3oz) butter, plus extra to grease
1 red chilli, deseeded and finely chopped
1 garlic clove, peeled and chopped
½ lemon grass stalk, trimmed and finely
   chopped
1kg (2¼lb) skinless salmon fillet
250g (9oz) asparagus spears, trimmed
salt and pepper
250g (9oz) smoked salmon
4 tbsp chopped dill, plus sprigs to garnish

serves 10
preparation: 40 minutes, plus infusing
   and overnight chilling
cooking time: about 1 hour
per serving: 280 cals; 19g fat;
   1g carbohydrate

1 Melt the butter in a pan over a low heat, then bring to the boil and skim off the foam. Pour into a bowl and add the chilli, garlic and lemon grass. Leave to infuse.

2 Check over the salmon and remove any residual pin bones with tweezers. Cook the asparagus in a pan of boiling salted water for 3–4 minutes. Drain and refresh under cold running water.

3 Grease a 900g (2lb) loaf tin; line with greased foil. Line the tin with three quarters of the smoked salmon. Sprinkle over 1 tbsp dill and drizzle with a little infused butter. Cut the salmon fillet in half to fit the tin.

4 Lay one piece of salmon in the tin. Sprinkle over 1 tbsp dill and drizzle with a little infused butter. Layer the asparagus on top and cover with the other piece of salmon, sprinkling each layer with dill and some infused butter, and seasoning well. Lay the remaining smoked salmon on top and cover the tin with foil.

5 Stand in a roasting tin containing enough hot water to come halfway up the sides. Bake at 180°C (160°C fan oven) mark 4 for 50–60 minutes or until a skewer inserted in the middle for 30 seconds comes out clean. Cool, weight down with 450g (1lb) weights and chill the terrine in the fridge overnight.

6 To serve, turn out the terrine and garnish with dill sprigs. Cut into slices, using a sharp knife, to serve.

Mackerel Pâté with Beetroot Salsa

1 tbsp olive oil

25g (1oz) butter

1 small onion, finely chopped

225g (8oz) cooking apples, peeled and
 chopped

4 smoked peppered mackerel fillets, about
 300g (11oz)

1 tbsp hot horseradish sauce

6 tbsp mayonnaise

1 tbsp lemon juice

salt and pepper

BEETROOT SALSA

6 tbsp walnut oil

3 tbsp lemon juice

175g (6oz) cooked beetroot (not in vinegar),
 diced

2 tbsp chopped chives

2 small green eating apples, cored and diced

serves 6
preparation: 15 minutes, plus chilling
cooking time: 15–20 minutes
per serving: 490 cals; 44g fat;
 12g carbohydrate

1 Heat the olive oil and butter in a pan, add the onion and cook for about 10 minutes until soft. Add the chopped apples, then cover and cook for about 10–15 minutes until softened. Leave to cool.

2 Remove the skin from the mackerel, then flake the flesh into a bowl. Add the apple mixture, horseradish, mayonnaise and lemon juice. Mix together and season with salt and pepper to taste. Spoon the pâté into six small bowls, coarsely grind over black pepper and chill.

3 To make the beetroot salsa, whisk together the walnut oil and lemon juice and season with salt and pepper. Put the beetroot, chives and diced apple in a bowl, add the dressing and mix well.

4 Serve the pâté with the beetroot salsa and toast fingers or warm, crusty bread.

Roasted Vegetable Terrine

600g (1lb 5oz) red peppers, cored, deseeded
   and quartered
600g (1lb 5oz) yellow peppers, cored,
   deseeded and quartered
600g (1lb 5oz) aubergines, trimmed
500g (1lb 2oz) courgettes, trimmed
4 tbsp extra-virgin olive oil
salt and pepper
250g (9oz) asparagus spears, trimmed
25g (1oz) butter
1 medium red chilli, deseeded and finely
   chopped
1 garlic clove, peeled and chopped
½ lemon grass stalk, trimmed and finely
   chopped
600ml (1 pint) red wine
11g sachet powdered gelatine (see note)
oil, to oil tin
5 tbsp chopped dill, plus extra sprigs
   to garnish

serves 8
preparation: 50 minutes, plus overnight
   chilling
cooking time: 40 minutes
per serving: 140 cals; 9g fat;
   10g carbohydrate

1 Put the peppers skin-side up on a baking sheet and grill under a high heat until charred. Tip into a large bowl, cover the bowl with clingfilm and leave to cool, then peel away the skins.
2 Slice the aubergines and courgettes lengthways into 1cm (½ inch) slices, brush with olive oil and put them in two large roasting tins. Season well with salt and pepper. Roast at 220°C (200°C fan oven) mark 7 for 30–40 minutes until soft and golden, turning from time to time.
3 Cook the asparagus in a pan of boiling salted water for 3–4 minutes until tender.
4 Melt the butter in a pan over a low heat. Add the chilli, garlic and lemon grass, then pour in the wine. Bring the mixture to the boil and let bubble until reduced to 450ml (¾ pint). Take off the heat, whisk in the gelatine and season well with salt and pepper. Keep the mixture warm, otherwise it will start to set.
5 Oil a 900g (2lb) loaf tin and line with clingfilm. Layer the vegetables in this order: half of the red peppers, aubergines, courgettes and yellow peppers, all of the asparagus, and then the remaining yellow peppers, courgettes, aubergines and red peppers, sprinkling a little dill, seasoning and wine mixture between the layers. Cover the tin with clingfilm and a baking sheet, and press down with 450g (1lb) weights. Chill the terrine overnight.
6 To serve, turn out the terrine on to a board and cut into slices, using a sharp knife. Garnish with dill sprigs.

note: *Use a sachet of Vege-Gel rather than gelatine if the terrine is to be served to vegetarians; the set will be slightly less firm.*

Smoked Salmon Pâté

250g (9oz) smoked salmon
3 tbsp half-fat fromage frais
1½ tbsp creamed horseradish
salt and white pepper
6 tbsp olive oil
1 tbsp lemon juice
120g bag baby or herb salad

TO SERVE
Melba toast (page 33)

serves 6
preparation: 15 minutes, plus chilling
per serving: 190 cals; 15g fat;
   2g carbohydrate

1 Put the salmon in a blender and whiz to chop roughly. Add the fromage frais and horseradish and pulse briefly to combine. Transfer the mixture to a bowl, season with salt and white pepper, cover and chill for 1–2 hours.
2 Put the oil and lemon juice in a screw-topped jar and season well. Shake to combine.
3 Shape the pâté using two dessertspoons by scraping a spoonful of pâté from one spoon to the other several times to form a smooth oval. Put one oval on each plate with a pile of salad and drizzle with the dressing. Serve with Melba toast.

Aubergine, Mushroom and Coriander Pâté

2 medium aubergines

3 tbsp olive oil

2 shallots, peeled and finely chopped

2–3 tsp crushed coriander seeds

225g (8oz) large flat mushrooms, finely
   chopped

3 tbsp dry white wine

4 tbsp chopped coriander, plus sprigs
   to garnish

salt and pepper

serves 4–6

preparation: 20 minutes

cooking time: 45 minutes

per serving: 130–90 cals; 11–7g fat;
   7–4g carbohydrate

1 Put the aubergines on a baking sheet and bake in the oven at 200°C (180°C fan oven) mark 6 for about 45 minutes or until they feel soft and the skins are beginning to char.

2 In the meantime, heat the olive oil in a pan, add the shallots with the coriander seeds and cook gently for about 5 minutes until softened and golden. Add the mushrooms and wine and cook over a high heat for 10 minutes or until all the liquid has evaporated, stirring occasionally.

3 Split the cooked aubergines, scoop out the flesh and chop roughly, then beat into the mushroom mixture. Stir in the chopped coriander and season well with salt and pepper.

4 Either serve warm or leave to cool, then chill. Garnish with coriander sprigs and serve with toast; toasted walnut bread goes particularly well.

variation: For a milder flavour, stir in 125g (4oz) fromage frais at stage 3.

Chunky Pâté with Port and Green Peppercorns

350g (12oz) boneless belly pork, derinded
   and roughly chopped

1 large skinless chicken breast fillet

225g (8oz) chicken livers, trimmed

1 large duck breast, skinned and chopped
   into small pieces

125g (4oz) streaky bacon, derinded and
   diced

3 tbsp port or brandy

salt and pepper

1 tbsp finely chopped rosemary

2 tbsp green peppercorns

TO FINISH

few bay leaves

few rosemary sprigs

2 tsp powdered gelatine

150ml (¼ pint) white port or sherry

serves 8

preparation: 25 minutes, plus setting

cooking time: about 1½ hours

per serving: 350 cals; 25g fat;
   1g carbohydrate

1 Coarsely mince the belly pork in a food processor, retaining some small chunks. Mince the chicken breast in the processor; repeat with the chicken livers.

2 Mix all the meats together in a large bowl with the port, 1 tsp salt, some pepper, the chopped rosemary and green peppercorns.

3 Pack the mixture into a 1.2 litre (2 pint) terrine and stand in a roasting tin containing 2.5cm (1 inch) boiling water. Cover with foil and cook at 170°C (150°C fan oven) mark 3 for 1 hour.

4 Remove the foil and arrange a few bay leaves and rosemary sprigs on top of the pâté. Cook for a further 30 minutes or until the juices run clear when the pâté is pierced in the centre with a skewer.

5 Drain the meat juices into a small bowl and leave to cool. Skim off any fat, then sprinkle over the gelatine and leave until softened. Stand the bowl in a pan of gently simmering water until the gelatine is dissolved. Stir in the port. Make up to 450ml (¾ pint) with water, if necessary.

6 Pour the jellied liquid over the pâté and chill until it has set. Store the pâté in the fridge for up to 2 days. Serve with crusty bread.

Chicken Liver Pâté

700g (1½lb) chicken livers
75g (3oz) butter
1 onion, peeled and finely chopped
1 large garlic clove, peeled and crushed
1 tbsp double cream
2 tbsp tomato purée
3 tbsp dry sherry or brandy
4 bay leaves, to garnish (optional)

serves 4
preparation: 15 minutes, plus chilling
cooking time: 10 minutes
per serving: 420 cals; 28g fat;
   6g carbohydrate

1 Trim away any sinews and fat from the chicken livers, then rinse and pat dry on kitchen paper. Melt the butter in a frying pan over a low heat, then increase the heat to medium and fry the chicken livers for about 5 minutes until they change colour; do not overcook or they will toughen.
2 Reduce the heat and add the onion and garlic. Cover the pan and cook the mixture for 5 minutes. Tip the contents of the pan into a bowl and cool.
3 Add the cream, tomato purée and sherry. Transfer the mixture to a food processor or blender and whiz until smooth.
4 Pack the pâté into four 150ml (¼ pint) individual dishes and cool until firm. Top with bay leaves, if you like. Chill the pâté for at least 2 hours or overnight.
5 Serve the chicken liver pâté with hot toast fingers or French bread.

variation: *Pack the pâté into a 450g (1lb) loaf tin. After chilling, cut it into chunky slices to serve.*

Smooth Pork Pâté with Brandy

50g (2oz) piece pancetta or smoked
   bacon, diced
125g (4oz) unsalted butter
1 small onion, peeled and grated
1 garlic clove, peeled and crushed
125g (4oz) chicken livers, trimmed and diced
1 tsp chopped thyme
4 tbsp brandy
½ tsp ground mixed spice
pinch of cayenne pepper
25g (1oz) fresh white breadcrumbs
salt and pepper
225g (8oz) cooked pork, diced
4–6 bay leaves

serves 4
preparation: 20 minutes, plus chilling
cooking time: 15 minutes
per serving: 490 cals; 37g fat;
   6g carbohydrate

1 Preheat a heavy-based frying pan, add the pancetta and cook, stirring, over a high heat until it is browned and has released some fat.
2 Add 25g (1oz) of the unsalted butter to the pan. When it has melted, add the onion and garlic, and fry for 5 minutes until golden. Add the chicken livers and thyme and stir-fry for 2 minutes until browned.
3 Lower the heat and stir in the brandy, mixed spice and cayenne. Cover and simmer gently for about 5 minutes. Remove the pan from the heat and set aside to cool.
4 Transfer the cooled mixture to a food processor, add the breadcrumbs and seasoning, and whiz until fairly smooth. Add the pork, pulse briefly to combine, then spoon into one large or four small pâté dishes. Smooth the surface.
5 Melt the remaining butter, cool slightly, then pour over the pâté. Leave until the butter is almost set, then press in the bay leaves. Chill for several hours.
6 Serve the pâté with toast or bread.

DIPS

Serve these dips with warm pitta bread fingers, corn chips, breadsticks or an assortment of crudités (vegetable sticks), such as strips of celery, fennel, cucumber, courgette, peppers and carrots, blanched asparagus tips and cauliflower florets, and cherry or baby plum tomatoes.

Tzatziki

1 cucumber
300ml (½ pint) Greek-style yogurt
2 tsp olive oil
2 tbsp chopped mint
1 large garlic clove, peeled and crushed
salt and pepper

serves 8
preparation: 10 minutes
per serving: 50 cals; 4g fat;
    1g carbohydrate

1 Halve, deseed and dice the cucumber and put into a bowl.
2 Add the yogurt and olive oil. Stir in the chopped mint and garlic, and season with salt and pepper to taste. Cover and chill in the fridge until ready to serve.
3 Serve with warm pitta bread and vegetable sticks.

Hummus

400g can chickpeas, drained and rinsed
juice of 1 lemon
4 tbsp tahini paste
1 garlic clove, peeled and crushed
5 tbsp extra-virgin olive oil
salt and pepper

serves 6
preparation: 15 minutes
per serving: 170 cals; 14g fat;
    7g carbohydrate

1 Put the chickpeas, lemon juice, tahini paste, garlic and olive oil in a blender or food processor. Season generously with salt and pepper, then whiz to a paste.
2 Spoon the hummus into a bowl, then cover and chill until needed.
3 Serve with warm pitta bread or toasted flatbreads.

Taramasalata

100g (3½oz) country-style bread, crusts
    removed
75g (3oz) smoked cod roe
2 tbsp lemon juice
100ml (3½fl oz) light olive oil
pepper

serves 6
preparation: 15 minutes
per serving: 180 cals; 15g fat;
    7g carbohydrate

1 Put the bread into a bowl, cover with cold water and leave to soak for 10 minutes. Drain and squeeze out most of the water.
2 Soak the smoked cod roe in cold water to cover for 10 minutes, then drain and remove the skin.
3 Put the roe in a blender or food processor with the bread and whiz for 30 seconds. With the motor running, add the lemon juice and olive oil and whiz briefly to combine. Season with pepper to taste.
4 Spoon into a bowl, cover and chill until needed. Serve with warm pitta or toasted flatbreads.

Blue Cheese Dip

150ml (¼ pint) soured cream
1 garlic clove, peeled and crushed
175g (6oz) blue Stilton cheese
juice of 1 lemon
salt and pepper
snipped chives, to garnish

serves 6–8
preparation: 5 minutes
per serving: 170–130 cals; 15–12g fat;
    1g carbohydrate

1 Put all of the ingredients in a blender or food processor and work to a smooth paste.
2 Transfer to a serving dish and chill until required. Check the seasoning, sprinkle with chives and serve with a selection of vegetable sticks.

variation: *Use dolcelatte instead of Stilton cheese.*

Guacamole

2 ripe avocados
2 small tomatoes, deseeded and chopped
juice of 2 limes
2 tbsp extra-virgin olive oil
2 tbsp chopped coriander
salt and pepper

serves 6
preparation: 10 minutes
per serving: 160 cals; 16g fat;
    2g carbohydrate

1 Cut the avocados in half, remove the stone and peel away the skin. Tip the flesh into a bowl and mash with a fork.
2 Quickly add the tomatoes, lime juice, olive oil and chopped coriander. Mix well and season with salt and pepper to taste. Cover and chill until ready to serve.
3 Serve the guacamole with tortilla chips or warm pitta bread and vegetable sticks.

Tapenade

3 tbsp capers, rinsed and drained
75g (3oz) pitted black olives
50g can anchovy fillets in oil, drained
100ml (3½fl oz) olive oil
2 tbsp brandy
pepper

serves 4–6
preparation: 5 minutes
per serving: 270–180 cals; 26–18g fat;
    trace carbohydrate

1 Put the capers in a blender or food processor with the olives and anchovies. Process briefly to chop.
2 With the motor running, add the olive oil in a steady stream. Stir in the brandy and season with pepper to taste. Transfer to a serving bowl.
3 Serve the tapenade with raw vegetable sticks and/or grilled vegetables and toasted French bread.

CANAPÉS AND NIBBLES

Canapés are perfect for drinks parties as they can be made ahead and simply warmed through prior to serving. Similarly dips and savoury finger foods, such as spiced nuts and marinated olives, can be prepared in advance, or bought from your deli or supermarket. Extend your selection with a few simple savouries, such as mini pretzels, grissini or breadsticks with Parma ham wrapped around the top, and thin slices of French bread spread with tapenade and topped with goat's cheese. Homemade canapés are easy to make, especially if you use ready-prepared bases, such as ready-rolled puff pastry and croustades, available from larger supermarkets and delicatessens.

Allow about 10 canapés per person, with nuts, olives, dips and 'dunks' as extras. A colourful platter of crudités and a selection of dips always looks attractive.

Lemon Chilli Olives

½ lemon, preferably unwaxed
300g jar green olives
2 tsp fennel seeds
3 small dried chillies
about 450ml (¾ pint) olive oil

makes one 600ml (1 pint) jar
preparation: 15 minutes, plus marinating
per jar: 300 cals; 34g fat; 0g carbohydrate

1 Cut the lemon half into very thin wedges and remove the pips.
2 Put the olives, lemon, fennel seeds and chillies in a bowl and mix together.
3 Spoon into a 600ml (1 pint) sterilised jar (see page 534), pour in enough olive oil to cover the olives, then seal the jar, label and leave to marinate in a cool place for 3–4 days. Use within 1 month.

Peppadew Olives

230g jar stuffed green olives, drained
375g jar mild peppadew sweet peppers, drained
basil leaves, to garnish

serves 8
preparation: 10 minutes
per serving: 35 cals; 3g fat; 2g carbohydrate

1 Push a cocktail stick through each olive, then push the olives into the peppadew shells.
2 Just before serving, put a basil leaf into each pepper shell to garnish.

note: *A relatively new item in stores, peppadew peppers have a sweet-sour flavour with a mildly hot kick and they contrast perfectly with the olives.*

Red Pepper Croûtes

1 thin French stick
olive oil, to brush
4 marinated red pepper pieces (from a jar)
125ml (4fl oz) pesto (page 28)
24 pine nuts, to garnish

makes 24
preparation: 20 minutes
cooking time: 15–20 minutes
per croûte: 80 cals; 4g fat; 9g carbohydrate

1 Slice the French stick into 24 rounds. Brush both sides of the bread slices with olive oil and lay on a baking sheet. Bake at 200°C (180°C fan oven) mark 6 for 15–20 minutes.
2 Meanwhile, cut each marinated red pepper piece into 6 strips. Spread 1 tsp pesto on each croûte, then top with a pepper strip and a pine nut. Serve hot.

Maple Salted Nuts

2 tbsp light muscovado sugar
100ml (3½fl oz) maple syrup
4 tbsp sunflower oil
3 tbsp sea salt
200g (7oz) whole almonds, with skins left on
250g (9oz) lightly salted peanuts, with skins
  left on
100g (3½oz) pecan halves

makes 550g (1¼lb)
preparation: 15 minutes
cooking time: 20 minutes
per 25g (1oz) serving: 190 cals; 16g fat;
  6g carbohydrate

1 Put the muscovado sugar, maple syrup, oil and 2·tbsp of the sea salt into a roasting tin. Stir thoroughly to combine.
2 Add the almonds, peanuts and pecans and stir well to coat the nuts in the mixture. Roast at 200°C (180°C fan oven) mark 6 for 15–20 minutes, stirring occasionally, until the nuts are golden brown.
3 Remove from the oven and sprinkle with the remaining sea salt. Tip the nuts on to baking parchment and leave to cool.
4 Store the maple salted nuts in an airtight container for up to 1 month.

note: *These nuts are an ideal food gift.*

Cheese Palmiers

2 x 375g packs puff pastry
flour, to dust
50g (2oz) Parmesan cheese, freshly grated
paprika, to dust
sesame seeds, to sprinkle

makes 48
preparation: 20 minutes
cooking time: 14–16 minutes
per serving: 60 cals; 4g fat;
   6g carbohydrate

1 Roll out one packet of pastry on a lightly floured surface to a rectangle, 30 x 25cm (12 x 10 inches). Sprinkle evenly with a little of the cheese and paprika.
2 Fold the longer sides of the dough halfway towards the centre, sprinkle with cheese and paprika, then fold again, so that these sides meet in the middle. Sprinkle with paprika, then fold in half again, concealing the first folds; press down lightly to adhere.
3 Cut across the roll into 24 equal-sized pieces. Lay the palmiers, cut-side down, on a large dampened baking sheet. Flatten them slightly with a palette knife or the palm of your hand, then sprinkle with sesame seeds. Repeat with the other pack of pastry.
4 Bake, one sheet at a time, at 220°C (200°C fan oven) mark 7 for about 8 minutes until golden. Carefully turn the palmiers over and bake for a further 6–8 minutes until crisp and golden. Transfer to wire racks and leave to cool.

Cheese Straws

200g (7oz) self-raising flour, plus extra to dust
pinch of cayenne pepper
125g (4oz) unsalted butter, chilled and diced
125g (4oz) Parmesan cheese, finely grated
2 medium eggs, one separated
1 tsp ready-made English mustard
sesame and poppy seeds, to sprinkle

makes about 24
preparation: 20 minutes, plus chilling
cooking time: 20 minutes
per cheese straw: 95 cals; 7g fat;
   6g carbohydrate

1 Put the flour, cayenne and butter in a food processor and pulse until the mixture resembles breadcrumbs. Add the Parmesan and pulse to mix together.
2 Put the whole egg in a bowl with the other egg yolk. Add the mustard and mix together. Pour into the food processor and whiz to bring the mixture together.
3 Tip the dough on to a board and knead lightly for 30 seconds. Wrap in clingfilm and chill for 30 minutes.
4 On a lightly floured surface, roll out the pastry to a 23 x 30cm (9 x 12 inch) rectangle. Cut into 24 straws and carefully twist each one twice. Lay the cheese straws on two greased baking sheets.
5 Beat the reserved egg white with a fork until frothy. Brush the egg white over the cheese straws, then sprinkle sesame and poppy seeds over them.
6 Bake at 180°C (160°C fan oven) mark 4 for 18–20 minutes or until golden. Cool on the baking sheet for 5 minutes, then transfer to a wire rack to cool.
7 Serve the cheese straws as an appetiser with drinks, or as an accompaniment to soups.

Falafel with Minted Yogurt Dip

225g (8oz) dried chickpeas, soaked overnight

1 tbsp tahini paste

1 garlic clove, peeled and crushed

1 tsp sea salt

1 tsp ground turmeric

1 tsp ground cumin

¼ tsp cayenne pepper

2 tbsp chopped coriander

1 tbsp chopped mint

1 tbsp lemon juice

seasoned flour, to dust

oil, to shallow-fry

YOGURT DIP

150ml (¼ pint) Greek-style yogurt

1–2 garlic cloves, peeled and crushed

1 tbsp olive oil

2 tbsp chopped mint

salt and pepper

makes about 24

preparation: 20–25 minutes, plus overnight
   soaking and standing

cooking time: 8–10 minutes

per falafel: 70 cals; 5g fat;
   5g carbohydrate

1 Drain the soaked chickpeas. Put into a food processor and process to a fairly smooth paste.

2 Transfer to a bowl and add the tahini paste, garlic, salt, spices, herbs and lemon juice. Stir well, then cover and leave to stand for at least 30 minutes to allow the flavours to develop.

3 Meanwhile, mix all the ingredients for the yogurt dip together in a bowl and season with salt and pepper to taste. Cover and set aside until required.

4 With floured hands, shape the chickpea mixture into 2.5cm (1 inch) balls. Flatten slightly and dust with the seasoned flour.

5 Heat a 1cm (½ inch) depth of oil in a frying pan. When hot, fry the patties in batches for 1–2 minutes on each side until evenly browned. Drain on crumpled kitchen paper and keep warm while cooking the rest.

6 Serve the falafel warm or cool, with the yogurt dip and some warm pitta bread.

notes
• *Falafel are always made with dried chickpeas, which need to be soaked, but not pre-cooked.*
• *For optimum flavour, prepare the mixture well in advance to the end of stage 2.*

Deep-fried Potato Skins with Chilli Salsa

8 potatoes, each about 125g (4oz)

2 tbsp oil

salt and pepper

oil, to deep-fry

CHILLI SALSA

350g (12oz) ripe tomatoes, diced

2 spring onions, trimmed and finely chopped

1 tbsp chilli sauce

SOURED CREAM AND CHIVE DIP

150ml (¼ pint) soured cream

2 tbsp chopped chives

serves 3–4

preparation: 15 minutes

cooking time: 1 hour

per serving: 280–210 cals; 16–12g fat;
   30–22g carbohydrate

1 Scrub the potatoes and pat dry with kitchen paper. Push a skewer through each one, then brush with the oil and sprinkle with salt. Put directly on to the oven shelf and bake at 200°C (180°C fan oven) mark 6 for 45–55 minutes or until the potatoes feel soft when gently squeezed.

2 Meanwhile, make the dips. Mix the ingredients for the chilli salsa together in a bowl and check the seasoning. Mix the soured cream with the chives and season with salt and pepper to taste. Cover both dips with clingfilm and chill.

3 Halve the baked potatoes lengthways and carefully scoop out the flesh, leaving a layer of potato about 1cm (½ inch) thick on the skin. Cut each potato skin in half lengthways.

4 Heat the oil in a deep-fryer or deep pan to 190°C, or until a cube of bread dropped into the oil browns within 30 seconds. Deep-fry the potato skins, a few at a time, for ½–1 minute until crisp. Remove and drain on kitchen paper.

5 Once all the potato skins are fried, sprinkle them with a little salt. Serve immediately, with the dips.

Chicken Satay Skewers

1 tbsp coriander seeds

1 tbsp cumin seeds

2 tsp ground turmeric

4 garlic cloves, peeled and roughly chopped

grated zest and juice of 1 lemon

2 bird's eye chillies, deseeded and finely
    chopped

3 tbsp oil

salt

4 boneless, skinless chicken breasts, about
    550g (1¼lb)

SATAY SAUCE

200g (7oz) salted peanuts

1 tbsp molasses sugar

½ lemon grass stalk, trimmed and chopped

2 tbsp dark soy sauce

juice of ½ lime

200ml pack coconut cream

TO SERVE

½ cucumber, sliced thinly lengthways

makes 24

preparation: 30 minutes, plus marinating

cooking time: 10 minutes

per bite: 60 cals; 8g fat; 2g carbohydrate

1 Pre-soak 24 bamboo skewers, each about 15cm (6 inches) long, in cold water for 30 minutes or so.

2 Put the coriander, cumin and turmeric in a dry frying pan and heat for 30 seconds, shaking the pan constantly.

3 Tip the spices into a mini processor and add the chopped garlic, lemon zest and juice, chillies, 1 tbsp of the oil and 1 tsp salt. Whiz for 1–2 minutes.

4 Cut the chicken into finger-length strips. Put the spice paste in a large, shallow dish, add the chicken and toss to coat. Cover and leave to marinate in the fridge for at least 20 minutes, or up to 24 hours.

5 To make the satay sauce, put the peanuts, sugar, lemon grass, soy sauce, lime juice and coconut cream into a food processor and add 2 tbsp water. Whiz to make a thick, chunky sauce, and spoon into a dish.

6 Thread the marinated chicken strips on to the soaked bamboo skewers. Place on the grill rack and drizzle with the remaining oil. Grill under a medium-high heat for about 4–5 minutes on each side until the chicken is cooked through.

7 Serve the skewers with the satay sauce and cucumber slices.

note: An ideal prepare ahead recipe – marinate the chicken for as long as possible, for optimum flavour.

Beef and Parma Ham Bites

350g (12oz) fillet steak, about 2cm
    (¾ inch) thick

salt and pepper

olive oil, to brush

6 slices Parma ham

48 basil leaves

24 sun-blush tomatoes

makes 24

preparation: 15 minutes

cooking time: about 12 minutes

per bite: 30 cals; 1g fat; trace carbohydrate

1 Season the steak all over with salt and pepper. Brush a griddle pan with a little olive oil, then heat over a medium-high heat. Add the steak and cook for 3 minutes on each side. Leave to rest for 5 minutes.

2 Cut each slice of Parma ham lengthways into 4 strips. Slice the steak into 4 lengths, then cut each into 6 pieces. Put a small basil leaf on top of each piece of steak, then wrap a strip of Parma ham around the steak.

3 Place the mini steaks on a lightly oiled baking sheet and roast at 200°C (180°C fan oven) mark 6 for 5–7 minutes until just cooked through.

4 Meanwhile, push a basil leaf and one of the sun-blush tomatoes on to a cocktail stick and repeat until you have 24 assembled sticks. Take the baking sheet out of the oven and push one of the cocktail sticks halfway into each piece of beef, making sure the sharp end of the stick doesn't protrude. Serve at once, on warmed platters.

note: Prepare to the end of stage 2 well in advance for convenience, and chill until ready to cook.

Mini Koftas

1 small onion, peeled and quartered
1 garlic clove, peeled
2.5cm (1 inch) fresh root ginger, peeled and
    roughly chopped
1 tsp ground cumin
1 tsp ground coriander
3 tbsp oil
450g (1lb) lean beef mince
3 tbsp chopped coriander
salt and pepper
1 small egg, beaten
flour, to dust

RAITA
300ml (½ pint) Greek-style yogurt
5cm (2 inch) piece cucumber, grated
3 tbsp chopped coriander

makes about 50
preparation: 20 minutes, plus standing
cooking time: about 15 minutes
per kofta: 30 cals; 2g fat;
    trace carbohydrate

1 To make the raita, stir the ingredients together in a bowl and season with salt and pepper to taste. Cover and leave to stand for 30 minutes.

2 To make the koftas, put the onion, garlic and ginger in a blender or food processor and chop finely. Add the spices and process until evenly mixed.

3 Heat 1 tbsp oil in a frying pan, add the onion paste and cook over a medium heat for 2–3 minutes, stirring. Leave to cool.

4 Put the beef mince in a bowl and break it up with a fork. Add the chopped coriander, seasoning and cooled onion paste, and mix thoroughly. Add just sufficient beaten egg to bind – not too much or the mixture will be too sticky to shape.

5 Using lightly floured hands, shape the mixture into bite-sized balls. Heat the remaining oil in a large frying pan. Fry the koftas in batches for about 5 minutes, shaking the pan, until evenly browned and cooked through. Drain on kitchen paper.

6 Skewer the koftas on to wooden cocktail sticks. Serve hot, with the raita.

note: For convenience, prepare the koftas well in advance and freeze. Defrost overnight at room temperature and reheat at 200°C (180°C fan oven) mark 6 for about 10 minutes.

Garlic Prawns with Spiced Yogurt Dip

700g (1½lb) raw tiger prawns, peeled and
    deveined (see page 80)
1 tbsp oil
2.5cm (1 inch) piece fresh root ginger, peeled
    and finely chopped
3 garlic cloves, peeled and crushed
1 tbsp light soy sauce
juice of ½ lime

SPICED YOGURT DIP
5 tbsp thick yogurt
5 tbsp double cream
2 tbsp mango chutney
1 tbsp chopped coriander

makes 25–30
preparation: 20 minutes, plus marinating
cooking time: 15 minutes
per bite: 40–30 cals; 2g fat;
    1g carbohydrate

1 Put the prawns into a bowl with the oil, ginger, garlic, soy sauce and 1 tbsp lime juice. Cover and leave to marinate in a cool place for at least 2 hours, preferably overnight in the fridge.

2 For the dip, mix together the yogurt, cream, mango chutney and coriander.

3 Thread the prawns on to pre-soaked bamboo skewers (see note).

4 Grill the prawns for 2–3 minutes, turning once. Serve warm or cold, with the dip.

note: Pre-soak the bamboo skewers in cold water for about 30 minutes to prevent them from burning during cooking.

Smoked Salmon and Dill Roulades

300g (11oz) smoked rainbow trout fillets
grated zest and juice of 1 lemon
5 tbsp horseradish sauce
125g (4oz) cream cheese
salt and pepper
150ml (¼ pint) double cream, lightly whipped
450g (1lb) thinly sliced smoked salmon
4 tbsp chopped dill
salad leaves, to serve

makes 50–60
preparation: 30 minutes, plus chilling
per bite: 50–40 cals; 3g fat;
    trace carbohydrate

1 Put the smoked trout into a food processor with the lemon zest, horseradish and cream cheese. Pulse until the mixture is just smooth.
2 Transfer the mixture a bowl. Add 2 tbsp lemon juice and season with salt and pepper. Fold in the whipped cream.
3 Fit a large piping bag with a 2cm (¾ inch) plain nozzle and fill with the smoked trout mixture.
4 Cut 12cm (5 inch) wide strips of smoked salmon and lay each one on a piece of clingfilm; pipe the trout mixture along the length of each strip. Carefully roll the smoked salmon around the filling to enclose it, using the clingfilm to help. Put on a tray, cover loosely with clingfilm and chill in the fridge for at least 1 hour.
5 To serve, cut the salmon on the diagonal into 2.5cm (1 inch) lengths, using a very sharp knife. Dip the ends into the chopped dill. Serve on a bed of salad leaves.

note: *If the roulades are too soft to cut, firm up in the freezer for 10–15 minutes.*

Shellfish Mini Tartlets

PASTRY
350g (12oz) plain flour, plus extra to dust
175g (6oz) butter
75g (3oz) Parmesan cheese, freshly grated
2 eggs, lightly beaten

FILLING
1 egg, beaten
pinch of saffron strands
150ml (¼ pint) double cream
3 tbsp chopped chives
salt and pepper
225g (8oz) cooked peeled prawns, roughly
    chopped, or white crab meat, flaked

TO GARNISH
snipped chives

makes 60
preparation: 50 minutes, plus chilling
cooking time: 20 minutes
per mini tartlet: 70 cals; 4g fat;
    5g carbohydrate

1 To make the pastry, put the flour, butter and cheese into a food processor and whiz until the mixture resembles fine crumbs. Add the eggs and 3 tbsp iced water. Pulse until the dough comes together in a ball. Wrap in clingfilm and chill for 30 minutes.
2 Roll out the pastry thinly on a lightly floured surface. Stamp out rounds with a 5cm (2 inch) plain cutter and use to line 60 mini tartlet tins. Prick the bases well and chill for 30 minutes.
3 Bake the tartlet cases at 200°C (180°C fan oven) mark 6 for 10 minutes or until golden.
4 Meanwhile, prepare the filling. Whisk together the egg, saffron, cream and chives, and season with salt and pepper.
5 Divide the shellfish among the pastry cases and top each with a teaspoonful of the saffron cream. Bake for 5–10 minutes. Serve immediately, garnished with chives.

note: *Prepare ahead and freeze for convenience. Defrost overnight at cool room temperature. Reheat at 200°C (180°C fan oven) mark 6 for 5–10 minutes.*

SHELLFISH

Shellfish are prized for their delicate flavours and textures, especially the excellent species which are caught off our coastline – including lobsters, crabs and scallops. Shellfish can be divided into three main categories: crustaceans, molluscs and cephalopods. Crustaceans – lobsters, crabs, crayfish, prawns, shrimps etc. – have hard external skeletons, which are segmented to allow for movement. Molluscs live inside one or two hard shells (valves). Cockles, winkles and whelks are univalves. The bivalves include mussels, clams, oysters and scallops. Cephalopods, namely squid, octopus and cuttlefish, belong to the mollusc family, but they do not have external shells; the clear plastic-like quill inside squid is effectively an internal shell.

CHOOSING SHELLFISH

Always buy shellfish from a reputable fishmonger or supermarket fresh fish counter with a high turnover and prepare within 24 hours. Most seafood from supermarkets has been previously frozen, so don't re-freeze it. It is unwise to gather shellfish yourself, unless you are sure the area is free from pollution; molluscs are particularly susceptible to pollution and can carry diseases.

When choosing molluscs, select those with tightly closed, undamaged shells. Mussels, clams, scallops and oysters that are sold fresh are still alive and an open shell may indicate that the shellfish is far from fresh. A sharp tap on the shell should persuade it to close up if it's alive, if not avoid or discard it. Similarly univalves should withdraw back into their shell when prodded.

When buying cooked shellfish, such as lobster, crab and prawns, make sure the shells are intact. Lobsters and crabs should feel heavy for their size and have a fresh aroma. Any sign of an unpleasant smell is an indication that the shellfish is past its best. When choosing cephalopods, such as squid and octopus, look for those with firm flesh and a pleasant smell of the sea.

GUIDE TO SHELLFISH VARIETIES

Cockle: *May–December*
These molluscs are invariably sold cooked and shelled, and they are typically eaten plain or with vinegar. To prepare fresh cockles, wash thoroughly, then soak in cold water for 2–3 hours. Steam or cook in a little boiling water for 5 minutes until the shells open; discard any that remain closed. Shell, then cook for a further 4 minutes. Serve with lemon juice or vinegar, butter and pepper.

Clam: *All year, best in autumn*
There are many varieties of this bivalve, varying considerably in size, from the smaller carpet shell and manilla clam to the American hard-shell clam or quahog, which grows up to 12cm (5 inches). These varieties are cream or brown coloured, whereas the venus shell is creamy red or pink and grows to 7.5cm (3 inches). Clams are sold live in their shells and smaller ones are eaten raw; larger ones are cooked before they are eaten. To open if eating raw, protect your hand with a thick cloth or glove and prise open the shell at the hinge, using a clam knife (as for oysters, page 81). Otherwise cook and shell clams (as for mussels, page 78). Clams are available frozen, canned and smoked.

Crab: *April–December*
There are many different species of this crustacean. All are encased in a hard shell, which is shed periodically to allow the crab to grow. The

common brown crab is the variety most often sold here; it has a brownish-red shell and grows to a width of about 20cm (8 inches). Other varieties include the spider crab, rock crab, green-shelled shore crab, southern stone crab with its huge claws, and the soft-shelled American blue crab. Crabs are usually sold cooked.

If you are able to buy a live crab from your fishmonger, choose one that seems really lively, making sure all its legs are intact. To cook, put into a large pan of cold salted water, cover with a tight-fitting lid and bring slowly to the boil. Boil steadily, allowing 15 minutes for the first 450g (1lb) and a further 5 minutes for each additional 450g (1lb). To extract the meat from a cooked crab refer to the step-by-step instructions on pages 80–1. There are two types of meat in a crab: the delicate, creamy white meat in the claws and legs, and the stronger brown meat which is found in the body shell. Crab meat is also available frozen and canned.

Crawfish: *April–October*
Also known as the spiny lobster, this resembles a lobster, but without the big claws, and it is prepared and cooked in the same way (see right).

Crayfish: *All year*
This freshwater crustacean looks like a miniature lobster and varies in colour from dark purple to black. Crayfish are sold both live and ready cooked. To prepare live ones, plunge into a pan of boiling water, cover tightly and cook for about 5 minutes until pinkish-red. Drain and, when cool enough to handle, remove the bitter-tasting dark intestinal tube from under the tail, using a pointed knife. Small crayfish can be used to garnish fish dishes or in soups; larger ones are best served cold with a salad or hot with a creamy sauce.

Cuttlefish: *All year*
This cephalopod resembles a squid, but is less widely availabe. Prepare and cook it as for squid (see right).

Dublin Bay Prawn (Scampi): *April–November*
This pink crustacean grows up to 25cm (10 inches) in length and is known by various names including

Norway lobster, langoustine (in France) and cigale (in Spain). Here the whole creature is usually called a Dublin Bay Prawn, whereas the peeled, uncooked tail meat is generally referred to as scampi. It can be served whole, as for lobster, or the uncooked tail meat can be coated in egg and breadcrumbs, deep-fried until golden and served with tartare sauce.

Lobster: *April–November*
The lobster is regarded as the most delectable of all shellfish; it is also the most expensive, partly because these shellfish are caught in special pots off the coast and it takes 7 years for one to reach a marketable size. The European lobster is deemed to have a better flavour than the American lobster. Live lobsters are dark blue in colour and turn bright pink when cooked. Most lobsters, however, are sold ready-cooked.

If you are able to buy a live lobster from your fishmonger, choose one that has all claws and legs intact. To cook a live lobster, put into a pan of cold salted water, cover with a tight-fitting lid and bring slowly to the boil. Boil steadily, allowing 10 minutes for the first 450g (1lb) and a further 5 minutes for each additional 450g (1lb). Leave to cool in the liquid. To extract the meat from a cooked lobster refer to the step-by-step instructions on page 80. Ready-dressed lobster is available from most fishmongers and fresh fish counters of larger supermarkets. The fine, delicate flavour of lobster is best appreciated if it is served with a simple accompaniment, such as good mayonnaise or a warm butter sauce.

Mussel: *September–March*
Mussels are bivalves with blue-black to golden tortoiseshell-coloured shells. They cling to rocks or the sea-bed and take about 2 years to reach maturity. Mussels are either sold by weight or volume: 1.2 litres (2 pints) of mussels is roughly equivalent to 900g (2lb). Do not buy mussels with cracked or open shells. To prepare mussels, see page 82. To cook mussels simply, put into a large pan with a cupful of water or white wine, flavoured with a little chopped shallot and herbs. Cover tightly and steam for 3–5 minutes until the shells open, shaking the pan frequently. Discard any that do not open.

Octopus: *May–December*

Octopus vary enormously in size and can grow up to 3 metres (10 feet). Small specimens are better for eating as large ones are usually tough. To prepare an octopus, hold the head firmly and cut through the flesh below the eyes, severing the head from the tentacles. Pull out and discard the soft body contents. Rinse the body and tentacles, then beat with a wooden mallet to tenderise. Blanch in boiling water for 5 minutes, then drain and cut into manageable pieces when cool enough to handle. All but the smallest specimens then need long, slow braising or stewing to tenderise.

Oyster: *September–April*

Oysters are farmed extensively in oyster beds around our coast and the native English oyster is considered to be one of the best. Other varieties include the European oyster, American blue point, larger Portuguese oyster and giant Pacific oyster. With the exception of the large varieties, oysters are considered at their best eaten raw. Allow about 6 oysters per person and open or 'shuck' them just before serving (see page 81). Season lightly with salt and cayenne pepper or a little Tabasco and serve the oysters on their cupped half-shell on a bed of crushed ice. Accompany with lemon wedges and brown bread. Frozen and smoked oysters are also available. Oysters are also used sparingly to enhance the flavour of a variety of cooked dishes.

Prawn: *All year*

Probably the best known of all shellfish, prawns are available in a variety of sizes, from the ubiquitous common prawn to the Mediterranean jumbo prawns and king prawns, which come from various different seas. There are several varieties of king prawn, which can be up to 20cm (8 inches) long. Most fresh prawns are sold ready-cooked, but raw prawns – especially king prawns and tiger prawns – are increasingly available from good fishmongers and supermarket fish counters. Buy fresh ones if possible, as these tend to have a superior flavour and texture. To prepare fresh prawns, see page 80. Cook just until they turn pink and opaque; this will take 3–8 minutes depending on size. Do not overcook or they will toughen. Heat ready-cooked prawns through for a few minutes only.

Scallop: *September–March*

Two varieties of this pretty, ribbed-shelled mollusc are caught around the British coast: the larger great scallop and the small pink shelled Queen scallop. Scallops are sold fresh, both in the shell and ready-shelled; they are also available frozen. To prepare scallops, see page 82. Scallops may be pan-fried, lightly poached or grilled, but care must be taken to avoid overcooking or their delicate texture will be ruined.

Shrimp: *February–October*

The smallest of the crustaceans, these are greyish-brown when alive and pink or brown when cooked, depending on the variety. Fresh shrimps are invariably sold cooked, either peeled or whole, and have a delicate flavour; frozen and canned shrimps are also available. To prepare cooked fresh shrimps, simply pull off the heads and peel away the shell. (Note that in North America the term shrimp is used to describe our prawns.)

Squid: *All year*

Several varieties of squid are caught around our coast and these vary considerably in size. They are often sold ready-cleaned, either as whole tubes or sliced into rings. To prepare whole squid, see pages 82–3. Small squid can be sautéed, poached, grilled or deep-fried; larger ones generally require stewing. In the Mediterranean, squid are sometimes cooked in their ink, in which case the ink sac needs to be removed intact and reserved.

Whelk: *February–August*

These grey or brown molluscs are generally sold cooked and shelled. Usually eaten plain or with lemon juice or vinegar. Prepare fresh whelks as for winkles (below), increasing the cooking time to 15–20 minutes. Use a skewer to extract the meat.

Winkle: *September–April*

Gathered from rock pools, these tiny molluscs are usually sold cooked, with or without shells. To prepare raw winkles, wash thoroughly, then soak in cold water for 2–3 hours. Steam or cook in boiling water for 5–10 minutes. A long pin is required to extract the flesh from the shell. Serve with lemon juice, butter and pepper.

PREPARATION TECHNIQUES

TO PREPARE LARGE PRAWNS (RAW OR COOKED)

1 Grip the head between your thumb and forefinger and hold the tail shell with the other hand. Gently pull the head from the body to detach it.

2 Peel off the body shell and the legs, leaving the tail end intact if you like.

3 Make a shallow cut down the back of the prawn and carefully prise out the bitter-tasting dark intestinal vein that runs along the length with a sharp knife.

TO PREPARE A COOKED LOBSTER

1 Twist off the claws and legs as close to the body as possible. Crack open the large claws using the back of a heavy knife, being careful not to crush the meat inside. Reserve the smaller claws to use as a garnish.

2 Put the lobster, back upwards, on a flat surface. Using a sharp knife, split the lobster cleanly in two, piercing through the 'cross' at the centre of the head.

3 Remove and discard the intestinal vein from the tail, the stomach (which lies near the head) and the inedible gills or 'dead man's fingers'.

4 Using a teaspoon, scoop out the edible soft grey liver (tomalley) and red roe (if any). Carefully lift the tail meat from the shell, pulling it out in one piece.

5 Using a skewer, carefully remove the meat from the legs. Scrub the body shell under cold running water and dry well if the lobster meat is to be served in it.

TO PREPARE A COOKED CRAB

Aim to keep the brown body meat, which is mostly liver, separate from the delicate flaky white meat and the creamy body meat.

1 Lay the crab on a board, with its back down, and twist off the legs and claws as close to the body as possible.

2 Bend each claw backwards at the joint until it snaps in half, then crack open with a rolling pin or hammer; avoid crushing the flesh or shattering the shell. Ease the white meat out of the claws and discard any membrane. Crack the larger legs open and extract the meat, using a thin skewer to get any awkward bits. Keep the small legs to use as a garnish, if wished.

3 Put the crab on its back with the tail flap pointing towards you. Twist off this flap, then hold the crab shell firmly and press the body section upwards with your thumbs until it comes away. If it won't move, use the point of a rigid knife to ease it away.

4 Pull the inedible feathery gills or 'dead man's fingers' away from

the body section and discard. Using a heavy knife, cut the body in half. Prise out the white meat from the crevices with a skewer.

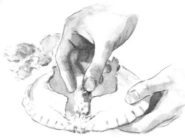

5 Using a teaspoon, loosen the creamy brown meat from the main shell and scoop it out into a bowl. If the crab is female, extract the coral roe too. Remove and discard the stomach bag, which you will find between the eyes. (If this breaks make sure you remove all the greenish or grey-white matter.)

note: *To prepare the shell for serving if required, tap just inside the natural line of the shell, using a hammer, until the inner shell breaks away smoothly. Scrub the shell under cold running water, then pat dry with kitchen paper.*

TO OPEN OR 'SHUCK' OYSTERS

1 Hold the oyster in a cloth on a surface with the flatter shell up and the hinge pointing towards you. Grip the oyster knife firmly and insert into the small gap in the hinge. Twist the knife from side to side to work the shells apart.

2 Slide the blade of the knife along the inside of the upper shell to sever the muscle that holds the shells together.

3 Lift off the top shell, taking care to avoid spilling any of the juice. Clean away any pieces of broken shell from the lower shell.

4 Carefully run the blade of the knife under the oyster to loosen it from the shell.

TO CLEAN MUSSELS

1 Rinse the mussels under cold running water to help rid them of any grit and sand. Scrub the mussel shells thoroughly, using a small stiff brush to remove any grit and barnacles.

2 Pull away the hairy 'beard', which protrudes from one side of the shell.

3 Tap any open mussels sharply with the back of the knife or on the surface. If they refuse to close, throw them away. Rinse the mussels again under cold running water before cooking.

TO PREPARE SCALLOPS

1 Scrub the shells under cold running water. Discard any that do not close when tapped sharply with the back of a knife. Hold, rounded-side down, in the palm of your hand, and insert the point of a sturdy knife between the shells close to the hinge. Twist and work the knife to prise the shells apart, then cut round the top shell to sever the muscle and allow the shells to be parted.

2 Push the top shell back until the hinge snaps. Rinse the scallop (still attached to the lower shell), under cold running water.

3 Using a small knife, cut away and discard the soft grey, fringe-like membrane.

4 Carefully slide the knife under the black thread on the side of the scallop. Gently pull it off with the attached black intestinal bag. Ease the scallop free from the bottom shell.

5 If required, separate the roe or 'coral' from the white scallop meat. Halve or slice the meat into rounds if required.

note: *If the rounded scallop shells are to be used as dishes, scrub them thoroughly.*

TO CLEAN SQUID

1 Hold the squid body pouch in one hand and grasp the head just below the eyes with the other hand. Pull apart gently but firmly, to separate the tentacles. Cut the tentacles away from the head just below the eyes. Discard the head.

2 Remove the almost transparent 'quill' and any soft innards from the body pouch; discard.

3 Peel off the thin layer of dark skin that covers the body and discard. Rinse the tentacles and the squid pouch thoroughly.

4 The cleaned squid pouch may now be sliced into rings. Or, cut open to give large pieces and score using a small sharp knife.

Classic Dressed Crab

1 medium crab, about 900g (2lb), cleaned
   (see pages 80–1)
1 tbsp lemon juice
salt and pepper
2 tbsp fresh white breadcrumbs
1 egg, hard-boiled
1 tbsp chopped parsley
salad leaves, to serve

serves 2
preparation: 30 minutes
per serving: 180 cals; 8g fat;
   5g carbohydrate

1 Flake the white crab meat into a bowl, removing any shell or membrane, then add 1 tsp lemon juice and season to taste. Mix lightly with a fork.
2 Pound the brown crab meat in another bowl and work in the breadcrumbs and remaining lemon juice. Season with salt and pepper to taste.
3 Using a small spoon, put the white crab meat into the cleaned crab shell, arranging it down either side and piling it up well. Spoon the brown meat into the middle between the sections of white meat.
4 Chop the egg white; press the yolk through a sieve. To garnish the crab, spoon lines of chopped parsley, sieved egg yolk and chopped egg white along the 'joins' between the white and brown crab meat. Serve on a bed of salad leaves, with brown bread and butter.

Crab Gratin

1 medium crab, about 900g (2lb), cleaned
   (see pages 80–1)
50g (2oz) fresh white breadcrumbs
100g (3½oz) Cheddar cheese, grated
¼ tsp mustard powder
½ tsp cayenne pepper
salt and pepper
few drops of Worcestershire sauce
about 3 tbsp single cream
1 bunch of watercress, tough stalks removed

serves 4
preparation: 10 minutes
cooking time: 20 minutes
per serving: 230 cals; 14g fat;
   7g carbohydrate

1 In a bowl, combine the crab meat, breadcrumbs, cheese, mustard, cayenne, ½ tsp pepper and the Worcestershire sauce. Add enough single cream to mix the ingredients together and give a fairly soft consistency. Check the seasoning.
2 Spoon the mixture into the cleaned crab shell and bake in the oven at 200°C (180°C fan oven) mark 6 for about 20 minutes.
3 Put the crab shell and claws on a bed of watercress and serve.

Lobster with Basil Mayonnaise

4 cooked lobsters, about 450g (1lb) each

BASIL MAYONNAISE

150ml (¼ pint) mayonnaise (see note)

1½ tsp lemon juice

15g (½oz) basil leaves, chopped

TOMATO COMPOTE

2 tbsp olive oil

1 shallot, peeled and finely chopped

350g (12oz) plum tomatoes, skinned and
   roughly chopped

1 tbsp sugar

2 tsp balsamic vinegar

salt and pepper

TO SERVE

50g (2oz) rocket leaves

serves 4

preparation: 30 minutes

cooking time: 8 minutes

per serving: 540 cals; 40g fat;
   8g carbohydrate

1 Flavour the mayonnaise with the lemon juice and basil; check the seasoning, cover and chill.

2 To make the tomato compote, heat the olive oil in a pan, add the shallot and cook gently until softened. Add the tomatoes, sugar and balsamic vinegar. Stir well, increase the heat and cook for 3 minutes. Using a slotted spoon, transfer the tomatoes to a bowl. Let the liquid bubble until reduced and slightly syrupy; add to the tomatoes. Season with salt and pepper to taste and leave to cool.

3 Lay the lobsters, back upwards, on a board. Using a sharp knife, split each lobster lengthways cleanly in two, piercing through the cross at the centre of the head, then prepare them according to the step-by-step instructions on page 80. Reserve the smaller claws (and legs if you wish) for the garnish. Cut the tail meat into thick slices.

4 Arrange the lobster and rocket leaves on plates, with the claws and legs to one side. Add a spoonful each of the basil mayonnaise and tomato compote. Equip everyone with a lobster pick or fine skewer, to extract the leg meat.

note: *Ideally use homemade mayonnaise (see page 351), or a good quality ready-made version.*

Lobster Thermidor

4 cooked lobsters, about 450g (1lb) each

25g (1oz) butter

1 shallot, peeled and finely chopped

150ml (¼ pint) dry white wine

300ml (½ pint) béchamel sauce (page 22)

1½ tbsp chopped parsley

2 tsp chopped tarragon

6 tbsp freshly grated Parmesan cheese

pinch of mustard powder

salt

pinch of paprika

serves 4

preparation: 30 minutes

cooking time: about 15 minutes

per serving: 400 cals; 19g fat;
   8g carbohydrate

1 Lay the lobsters, back upwards, on a board. Using a sharp knife, split each lobster lengthways cleanly in two, piercing through the cross at the centre of the head, then prepare them according to the step-by-step instructions on page 80. Cut the tail meat into thick slices.

2 Melt the butter in a pan, add the shallot and fry gently for 5 minutes to soften. Add the wine and let bubble until reduced by half. Add the béchamel sauce and simmer until reduced to a creamy consistency.

3 Add the lobster meat with the herbs, 4 tbsp of the Parmesan, and mustard, salt and paprika to taste.

4 Spoon the mixture into the cleaned shells, sprinkle with the remaining cheese and pop under a hot grill briefly, to brown the top. Serve at once.

Prawn and Pak Choi Stir-fry

250g pack medium egg noodles

200g (7oz) pak choi

1 bunch of spring onions, trimmed

1 tbsp sunflower oil or sesame oil

1 garlic clove, peeled and sliced

1 tsp grated fresh root ginger

250g (9oz) peeled raw tiger prawns,
    defrosted if frozen

160g jar Chinese yellow bean stir-fry sauce

serves 4

preparation: 10 minutes

cooking time: 5 minutes

per serving: 340 cals; 6g fat;
    50g carbohydrate

1 Put the egg noodles into a large heatproof bowl, pour over plenty of boiling water and leave to soak for 4 minutes. Meanwhile, cut the pak choi leaves from the white stems and set aside. Cut the white stems into thick slices. Cut each spring onion into 4 pieces. Drain the noodles and set aside.

2 Heat a wok, add the oil, then stir-fry the garlic and ginger for 30 seconds. Add the spring onions and prawns and cook for 2 minutes.

3 Add the chopped white pak choi stems and the yellow bean sauce. Fill the empty sauce jar with boiling water and pour this into the wok too.

4 Add the egg noodles and continue to cook for 1 minute, tossing every now and then to heat through. Finally, add the green pak choi leaves and cook briefly until just wilted. Serve at once.

Prawns Fried in Garlic

50g (2oz) unsalted butter

2 tbsp olive oil

12 raw Dublin Bay prawns in shell

3 garlic cloves, peeled and crushed

4 tbsp brandy

salt and pepper

flat-leafed parsley sprigs, to garnish

lemon wedges, to serve

serves 2

preparation: 10 minutes

cooking time: 5 minutes

per serving: 580 cals; 36g fat;
   3g carbohydrate

1 Heat the butter with the olive oil in a large heavy-based frying pan.

2 Add the prawns and garlic and fry over a high heat for about 5 minutes, tossing the prawns constantly, until the shells have turned pink.

3 Sprinkle the brandy over the prawns and let bubble rapidly to reduce right down. Season with salt and pepper to taste.

4 Serve immediately, garnished with parsley and accompanied by lemon wedges and plenty of crusty bread. Remember to provide everyone with finger bowls and napkins.

Prawn Madras with Coconut Chutney

MADRAS PASTE

2.5cm (1 inch) piece root ginger, peeled
   and finely chopped

1 small onion, peeled and finely chopped

2 garlic cloves, peeled and crushed

juice of ½ lemon

1 tbsp cumin seeds

1 tbsp coriander seeds

1 tsp cayenne pepper

2 tsp ground turmeric

2 tsp garam masala

salt

COCONUT CHUTNEY

1 tbsp groundnut oil

1 tbsp black mustard seeds

125g (4oz) desiccated coconut

1 onion, peeled and grated

1 red chilli, deseeded and diced

CURRY

2 tbsp groundnut oil

1 onion, peeled and finely sliced

1 green chilli, deseeded and finely chopped

600ml (1 pint) vegetable stock

450g (1lb) raw king prawns, peeled and
   deveined (see page 80)

2 bay leaves

coriander leaves, to garnish

serves 4

preparation: 10 minutes

cooking time: 25 minutes

per serving: 430 cals; 31g fat;
   13g carbohydrate

1 To make the madras paste, put all the ingredients into a food processor, together with 1 tsp salt and 2 tbsp water, and whiz until smooth. Set aside one third of the curry paste; freeze the rest for later use (see note).

2 To make the coconut chutney, heat the oil in a pan and add the mustard seeds. Cover the pan with a lid and cook over a medium heat until the seeds pop – you'll hear them jumping against the lid. Add the rest of the chutney ingredients and cook for 3–4 minutes to toast the coconut. Set aside.

3 To make the curry, heat the oil in a pan, add the onion and fry for 10 minutes until soft and golden. Add the madras paste and chopped green chilli, and cook for 5 minutes. Add the stock and bring to the boil.

4 Turn the heat down to a simmer and add the king prawns and bay leaves. Cook for 3–5 minutes or until the prawns turn pink and are cooked through. Garnish with coriander leaves and serve with the coconut chutney and basmati rice.

Illustrated on page 76

note: *Freeze the rest of the curry paste in two portions and use within 3 months. Defrost at cool room temperature for about 1 hour.*

Saffron and Lime Prawns

32 raw tiger prawns in shells
finely grated zest and juice of 1 lime
large pinch of saffron strands
1 garlic clove, peeled and crushed
2 small red chillies, deseeded and finely diced
5 tbsp extra-virgin olive oil
lime wedges, to serve

serves 4, or 8 as a starter
preparation: 10 minutes, plus marinating
cooking time: 4 minutes
per serving: 320 cals; 18g fat;
   2g carbohydrate

1 Pre-soak eight bamboo skewers in cold water for 30 minutes. Peel and devein the prawns (see page 80).
2 For the marinade, put the lime zest and juice into a small pan and heat gently. Take off the heat, add the saffron and leave to infuse for 5 minutes. Stir in the garlic and chillies and add the olive oil. Pour into a screw-topped jar, secure the lid and shake well.
3 Put the prawns in a shallow dish and pour on the marinade. Cover and leave to marinate in a cool place for at least 1 hour. Thread 4 prawns on to each skewer.
4 Lay the skewers on the grill rack and cook under a hot grill for 2–3 minutes on each side until the prawns just turn pink. Serve with lime wedges and bread.

Creamy Grilled Oysters

12 fresh oysters, shucked (see page 81)
2 shallots, peeled and finely chopped
300ml (½ pint) single cream
4 sun-dried tomatoes in oil, drained
1 tbsp chopped chervil, plus sprigs to garnish
2 tbsp dried breadcrumbs
2 tbsp freshly grated Parmesan cheese
pinch of cayenne pepper
salt

serves 4
preparation: 10 minutes
cooking time: 1 minute
per serving: 240 cals; 19g fat;
   11g carbohydrate

1 Discard the flatter half of each oyster shell and strain the juices into a small pan. Put the oysters in their cleaned shells into a gratin dish.
2 Add the shallots and cream to the juices in the pan and bring to the boil, reduce by half and strain through a fine sieve into a bowl. Leave to cool.
3 Chop the sun-dried tomatoes and stir into the cream with the chervil. Spoon a little over each oyster.
4 Mix the breadcrumbs with the Parmesan, cayenne and a little salt, and scatter over the top of the oysters. Put under a hot grill for 30 seconds to 1 minute until bubbling and golden. Serve at once, garnished with chervil sprigs.

Mussels in White Wine

1kg (2¼lb) fresh mussels in shells, cleaned
   (see page 82)
25g (1oz) unsalted butter
2 shallots, peeled and finely chopped
2 garlic cloves, peeled and finely chopped
few parsley stalks
150ml (¼ pint) dry white wine
1–2 tbsp chopped parsley
4 tbsp double cream
pepper

serves 2, or 4 as a starter
preparation: 10 minutes
cooking time: 10 minutes
per serving: 410 cals; 28g fat;
   5g carbohydrate

1 Heat the butter in a pan large enough to hold the mussels, add the shallots and garlic and fry gently for about 5 minutes to soften. Add the parsley stalks and wine; bring to the boil.
2 Add the mussels to the pan, cover with a tight-fitting lid and cook over a medium heat, shaking the pan occasionally, until the shells open; about 4–5 minutes. Discard the parsley stalks and any mussels that have refused to open.
3 Strain the cooking liquid through a muslin-lined sieve into a small pan. Add the chopped parsley, cream and pepper to taste; bring just to the boil.
4 Transfer the mussels to warmed serving bowls and pour over the sauce. Serve immediately.

Mussels with Tomato and Harissa

2kg (4½lb) fresh mussels in shells, cleaned
(see page 82)

3 tbsp olive oil

3 large shallots, peeled and finely chopped

4 garlic cloves, peeled and crushed

1.1kg (2½lb) ripe, flavourful tomatoes,
skinned, deseeded and chopped

2 celery sticks, chopped

300ml (½ pint) white wine

4 tsp balsamic vinegar

2 tbsp harissa (see note)

2 bay leaves

4 tbsp chopped flat-leafed parsley

serves 4, or 8 as a starter
preparation: 30 minutes
cooking time: 50 minutes
per serving: 330 cals; 17g fat;
12g carbohydrate

1 Heat the olive oil in a very large pan (big enough to take the mussels). Add the chopped shallots and cook gently for 5–10 minutes or until soft and transparent. Add the garlic and cook for 2–3 minutes.

2 Add the tomatoes, celery, wine, balsamic vinegar, harissa and bay leaves. Bring to the boil, lower the heat slightly and bubble gently for 20–30 minutes or until reduced by half.

3 Add the mussels to the pan, cover with a tight-fitting lid, bring to the boil and cook for 4–5 minutes or until the mussels have opened; discard any that do not open.

4 Spoon the mussels, along with some of the cooking liquid, into warmed deep soup bowls for serving. Scatter with chopped parsley and serve with warm crusty bread.

note: *If harissa is unobtainable, fry 2 large, finely chopped red chillies with the shallots at stage 1.*

Deep-fried Scampi

225g (8oz) raw scampi, defrosted if frozen

125g (4oz) plain flour

salt and pepper

1 tbsp extra-virgin olive oil

1 egg, separated

2–3 tbsp mixed milk and water

sunflower oil, to deep-fry

tartare sauce (page 351) or tomato sauce
(page 27), to serve

serves 2
preparation: 20 minutes
cooking time: 10 minutes
per serving: 480 cals; 28g fat;
42g carbohydrate

1 If using fresh scampi, prepare as for large prawns (see page 80). If using frozen, drain well on kitchen paper after defrosting.

2 Season 25g (1oz) flour with salt and pepper. Dip the scampi into the seasoned flour to coat, shaking to remove excess.

3 Mix the rest of the flour and a pinch of salt with the olive oil, egg yolk and enough milk and water to give a thick batter that will coat the back of the spoon; beat until smooth. Just before cooking, whisk the egg white until stiff and fold it into the batter, using a large metal spoon.

4 Heat the oil in a deep-fryer or deep pan to 190°C, or until a cube of bread dropped into the oil browns within 20–30 seconds.

5 Deep-fry the scampi, a few at a time, for 3–4 minutes until golden brown on the outside and cooked through. Remove with a slotted spoon, drain on kitchen paper and keep warm on a baking tray in a low oven while you deep-fry the remainder. Serve the scampi with tartare sauce or tomato sauce.

Scampi Provençale

3 tbsp olive oil

4 shallots, peeled and finely chopped

3 garlic cloves, peeled and crushed

1 tbsp sun-dried tomato paste

150ml (¼ pint) white wine

700g (1½lb) ripe, flavourful tomatoes,
   skinned, deseeded and roughly chopped

bouquet garni

salt and pepper

700g (1½lb) peeled and deveined raw
   scampi or tiger prawns

torn parsley, to garnish

serves 4

preparation: 25 minutes

cooking time: 20 minutes

per serving: 300 cals; 12g fat;
   12g carbohydrate

1 Heat the olive oil in a large frying pan, add the shallots and cook for 1–2 minutes. Add the garlic and cook for 30 seconds, then stir in the tomato paste and cook for 1 minute. Pour in the wine, bring to the boil and let bubble for about 10 minutes until well reduced and syrupy.

2 Add the chopped tomatoes and bouquet garni and season with salt and pepper to taste. Bring to the boil and simmer gently for 5 minutes or until pulpy.

3 Add the raw scampi or tiger prawns to the hot sauce and simmer gently, stirring, for 2–3 minutes until the shellfish are pink and just cooked through to the centre. Discard the bouquet garni.

4 Scatter over torn parsley and serve immediately, with rice and a leafy salad.

Seared Scallops with Roasted Plum Tomatoes

16 large fresh scallops, shelled (see page 82)

6 tbsp extra-virgin olive oil

2 garlic cloves

2 tbsp chopped thyme or parsley

coarse sea salt and pepper

6 large ripe, flavourful tomatoes (preferably
   plum), halved lengthways

3 rosemary sprigs

juice of 1 small lemon

serves 4

preparation: 15 minutes

cooking time: about 45 minutes

per serving: 410 cals; 16g fat;
   3g carbohydrate

1 Rinse the scallops and pat dry with kitchen paper. Put into a bowl with 3 tbsp olive oil. Add the garlic, thyme or parsley and seasoning; mix well. Cover and chill while preparing the tomatoes.

2 Put the tomatoes, cut-side up, in one layer in a shallow baking tin. Add the rosemary and season liberally with sea salt. Drizzle over the remaining olive oil. Roast at 180°C (160°C fan oven) mark 4 for about 45 minutes until tender but still holding their shape.

3 About 10 minutes before the tomatoes will be ready, preheat a large, dry (not oiled) cast-iron griddle pan over a high heat for about 5 minutes. Lower the heat to medium.

4 Add the scallops to the pan in one layer, and allow to sizzle undisturbed for 1½ minutes. Turn and cook the other side for 1–1½ minutes. (You may need to cook the scallops in two batches.)

5 Put the roasted tomatoes on warmed serving plates with the scallops and rosemary sprigs.

6 Tip the oil from the tomatoes into the griddle pan and add the lemon juice. Stir well and scrape up the sediment from the bottom of the pan. Trickle the juices over the scallops and roasted plum tomatoes. Serve immediately.

Seafood Gumbo

125g (4oz) butter

50g (2oz) plain flour

1–2 tbsp Cajun spice

1 onion, peeled and chopped

1 green pepper, cored, deseeded and
   chopped

5 spring onions, trimmed and sliced

1 tbsp chopped parsley

1 garlic clove, peeled and crushed

1 beef tomato, chopped

125g (4oz) garlic sausage, finely sliced

75g (3oz) American easy-cook rice

1.2 litres (2 pints) vegetable stock

450g (1lb) okra, trimmed and sliced

1 bay leaf

1 thyme sprig

salt and pepper

¼ tsp cayenne pepper

juice of ½ lemon

4 cloves

575g (1¼lb) frozen mixed seafood
   (containing mussels, squid and prawns),
   defrosted and drained

serves 4
preparation: 10 minutes
cooking time: 25 minutes
per serving: 620 cals; 38g fat;
   35g carbohydrate

1 Heat the butter in a large heavy-based pan. Add the flour and Cajun spice and cook, stirring, for 1–2 minutes or until golden brown.

2 Add the onion, green pepper, spring onions, parsley and garlic. Cook, stirring occasionally, for about 5 minutes.

3 Add the tomato, garlic sausage and rice and stir well to combine. Add the stock, okra, bay leaf, thyme, 2 tsp salt, cayenne, lemon juice, cloves and some black pepper. Bring to the boil and simmer, covered, for 12 minutes or until the rice is tender.

4 Add the seafood and cook for 2 minutes to heat through. Serve in deep bowls.

note: *Based on a Creole dish, this is halfway between a soup and a stew. Okra is an essential ingredient as it lends a characteristic silky texture.*

Fried Squid with Chilli Dipping Sauce

700g (1½lb) squid, cleaned (see pages 82–3)

4 tbsp plain flour

1 tbsp salt

2 tsp chilli powder

1 tsp white pepper

½ tsp Chinese five-spice powder

oil, to deep-fry

CHILLI DIPPING SAUCE
50g (2oz) golden caster sugar
90ml (3fl oz) rice or white wine vinegar
1 tsp crushed dried chillies
½ tsp salt

serves 4
preparation: 20 minutes
cooking time: 5–6 minutes
per serving: 390 cals; 22g fat;
   20g carbohydrate

1 First make the chilli dipping sauce. Put all the ingredients into a small pan and heat gently to dissolve the sugar. Remove from the heat and set aside to cool.

2 Put the cleaned squid on a board and slice along the length of the body; lay out flat and cut into thin strips. Halve the tentacles, if large.

3 Mix together the flour, salt, chilli powder, pepper and five-spice powder in a shallow bowl. Add the squid and toss until evenly coated.

4 Heat a 5cm (2 inch) depth of oil in a wok or deep pan until it registers 180°C on a thermometer, or until a cube of bread dropped into the oil browns within 40 seconds.

5 Deep-fry the squid in batches for 2–3 minutes until crisp and golden. Drain on kitchen paper and serve piping hot, accompanied by the chilli dipping sauce.

FISH

Fish is classified into two main categories: white fish or demersal, which have their oil concentrated in the liver; and oily fish or pelagic, where the oil is dispersed throughout the flesh. There are two types of white fish: round species, such as cod, and flat species, such as plaice. White fish have a more delicate flavour and texture than oily fish.

Fish is tasty, satisfying and highly nutritious. It is high in protein and rich in B vitamins, minerals and natural oils. White fish are low in calories, while oil-rich fish are an important source of vitamins A and D, and omega-3 fatty acids that help to lower blood cholesterol levels.

Some fish are available fresh all year round, others have a close period when they cannot be fished, which is usually the spawning time. General availability is given in the individual entries (see pages 95–8), but it can vary depending on the region and weather conditions. There is increasing concern about the impact of over-fishing, in the North Sea in particular. Stocks of favourite fish, including cod, haddock, skate and tuna, have been depleted in recent years and consumers are being encouraged to buy farmed fish and less vulnerable species, such as hoki, witch and tilapia.

In addition to fresh fish, some varieties are sold preserved by salting, marinating or smoking. There are two methods of smoking fish: hot and cold. Most cold smoked fish, like kippers, have a strong smoky flavour and must be cooked before they are eaten. The most notable exception is salmon, which is cold-smoked for a long time and eaten raw. Hot-smoked fish, such as trout, doesn't need further cooking. Both hot and cold-smoked mackerel are available, though the former is more common.

BUYING FISH

Freshness is of prime importance when it comes to choosing and buying fish. Whole fish must have bright eyes, shiny, moist, firm skin and vivid pink or red gills. The fish should feel stiff to the touch and smell like a whiff of sea air. Fillets, steaks and cutlets must have translucent flesh and show no signs of discoloration. Smoked fish should appear glossy with a fresh smoky aroma. Ideally fish should be cooked on the day you purchase it, but it can be stored, well wrapped, in the fridge for up to 24 hours. If you are buying frozen fish make sure it is frozen hard with no sign of partial thawing, freezer burn or damaged packaging. Frozen fish is best thawed in the fridge overnight before cooking.

PREPARING FISH

Preparing fresh fish isn't difficult – refer to the illustrated step-by-step guide on the following pages. Alternatively, your supplier should be willing to prepare the fish for you according to how you intend to cook it. Ask for heads, bones and trimmings to make into stock, either for your chosen recipe, or to freeze for future use. Prepare and cook fish as soon as possible after purchase. Note that once fish has been cut into fillets, cutlets or steaks it is liable to deteriorate more rapidly.

COOKING FISH

Fish is relatively quick to cook – whichever method you use. To check when fish is cooked, insert a thin skewer into the thickest part of the flesh. It should pass through easily and the flesh should begin to flake. White fish loses its translucency when it is cooked, turning white and opaque.

Baking

This is suitable for most whole fish, steaks, cutlets and fillets. Put the fish into an ovenproof dish, season with salt and pepper, then add herbs, a knob of butter and a little stock or white wine. Or wrap the fish in greased foil with herbs, seasoning, lemon slices and a knob of butter or little liquid. Bake at 180°C (160°C fan oven) mark 4, allowing 30–40 minutes for large whole fish; 15–25 minutes for steaks, cutlets and small fish.

Barbecuing

This is suitable for many types of fish, especially firm-textured varieties and oily fish including trout, red mullet and sardines. Special fish-shaped racks can be used to prevent whole fish from breaking up; or fish can be threaded on to long skewers.

Braising

Cooking fish on a bed of sautéed vegetables in a sealed pan is another good method, especially suited to firm, meaty fish, such as monkfish or tuna. Lay the fish on top of the vegetables, add some stock, court bouillon or wine, cover and cook for 10–20 minutes over a low heat or in the oven at 180°C (160°C fan oven) mark 4.

Cooking 'en Papillote'

Small whole fish, cutlets and fillets cook well in a sealed paper or foil parcel with flavourings such as herbs, spices, a flavoured butter or citrus juice.

Deep-frying

Small whole fish, such as whitebait and squid, as well as cutlets and fillets are suited to deep-frying. Normally the fish is first coated with seasoned flour, beaten egg and breadcrumbs, or batter, which forms a crisp, protective coating.

To make a suitable coating batter, sift 125g (4oz) plain flour with a large pinch of salt into a bowl, add 1 egg, then gradually beat in 150ml (¼ pint) milk, or milk and water mixed, until smooth.

Heat the oil in a deep-fryer to 190°C, dip the fish into the batter, or flour, egg and breadcrumbs, then lower into the oil in the basket and deep-fry for 4–5 minutes until the batter is crisp and golden brown and the fish is cooked. Drain on kitchen paper.

Griddle Cooking

Cooking fish on a ridged cast-iron or non-stick griddle pan is an excellent quick method. It's best applied to firmer fish, such as monkfish, tuna, swordfish and squid, which will hold together over the high heat. This method produces attractive criss-cross markings on the fish.

Grilling

This method is ideal for cooking small whole fish, thin fillets and thicker cuts. Make 2 or 3 slashes through the skin on each side of whole fish to allow the heat to penetrate through to the flesh. Brush with oil or melted butter and grill under a medium heat, basting frequently and turning thicker cuts halfway through. Allow 4–5 minutes for thin fillets; 8–10 minutes for thicker cuts and small whole fish.

Pan-frying

A good technique for small oily fish, such as sardines, herring and red mullet, all of which need the merest lick of oil or butter. White fish should be coated in seasoned flour or egg and breadcrumbs before shallow-frying in a little hot oil, clarified butter, or oil and butter. Allow 3–4 minutes for small whole fish, fillets and steaks, 8–10 minutes for larger cuts, turning halfway through.

Poaching

This method is perfect for larger whole fish such as salmon and sea bass, as well as smaller whole fish, cutlets and fillets. The fish is gently cooked in a court bouillon, flavoured broth or milk. Heat the liquid in a shallow pan, or fish kettle if cooking large whole fish, then add the fish and simmer very gently, until just cooked. Cooking times vary considerably, depending on size and thickness. The cooking liquor can be used to make a sauce.

To poach a whole salmon to serve cold: Put the cleaned fish into a fish kettle, add sufficient court bouillon to cover, put on a tight-fitting lid and slowly bring to a simmer; simmer for about 2 minutes, then turn off the heat and leave the fish to cool completely; it will slowly cook in the residual heat.

Microwave Cooking

This is ideal for small whole fish, and fish fillets and steaks of uniform thickness. Cook in a covered container with a little butter or liquid and season after cooking. Cooking time is determined by the thickness of the fish and quantity. For example, 450g (1lb) fillets would take about 4–5 minutes, plus 2 minutes standing time.

Steaming

A simple, healthy technique, suitable for whole fish, steaks and fillets. The fish cooks in its own juices so much of the original flavour is retained. Season the fish, put in the steamer over boiling water and cover with a tight-fitting lid. Allow 5–10 minutes for fillets; 15–20 minutes for steaks and whole fish.

GUIDE TO FISH VARIETIES

FLAT WHITE FISH

Brill: *June–February*
A grey-yellow delicately flavoured fish, resembling turbot but smaller. Sold whole or as fillets. Suitable for grilling, baking and poaching.

Dab: *September–May*
Small white-fleshed member of the plaice family, weighing from 225–700g (8oz–1½lb). Sold whole and as fillets. Suitable for grilling, baking and poaching. Smaller dab are suitable for grilling and frying whole.

Flounder: *March–November*
This fish resembles plaice, but doesn't have such a good flavour and texture. Sold whole and as fillets, flounder is cooked like plaice.

Halibut: *June–March*
Very large flat fish with marbled olive skin, halibut is prized for its fine flavoured flesh. Sold as fillets or steaks; cook as for turbot or cod.

Plaice: *May February*
Popular variety with brown skin and orange spots on the upperside, creamy-white skin underneath and soft, white delicately flavoured flesh. Sold whole or as fillets; suitable for most cooking methods, including steaming, frying, baking and grilling.

Skate: *May–February*
Ray-shaped fish, blue-grey on the upperside, greyish-white underneath. Only the wings are sold for cooking. They may be fried, grilled or poached.

Sole: *May–February*
This name is applied to several species, including Dover sole, lemon sole and witch or Torbay sole. The Dover sole is one of the finest flat fish. It has dark brown skin and pale, firm flesh with a delicious flavour. Lemon sole is lighter in colour, slightly longer and its head is more pointed than Dover sole. Witch is shaped like Dover sole, but it has slightly pinkish skin and its flesh tastes more like that of lemon sole. Sold whole or as fillets; sole can be grilled, fried, baked or steamed.

Turbot: *April–February*
Diamond-shaped fish with very small scales, dappled brown skin on the upperside and creamy-white skin underneath. Turbot has delicious, creamy-white flesh and it is considered to be the finest of the flat fish. Usually sold as steaks, which can be grilled, baked or poached.

ROUND WHITE FISH

Bass: *August–March*
Silvery blue-grey fish, with a white or yellowish belly and delicate white or pale pink flesh, weighing up to 4.5kg (10lb). Sold whole or as steaks or fillets. Small whole fish are suitable for grilling; steaks and fillets are usually poached or baked.

Bream (Sea), Red: *June–February*
Red-backed fish with a silvery belly, red fins and firm, delicately flavoured white flesh. It is usually sold whole and may be stuffed and baked, poached or braised. Fillets are best fried or grilled.

Bream, Emperor: *All year*
Family of exotic species, also known collectively as emperors. Species include *capitaine rouge*, *capitaine blanc* and *lascar*. Cook as for sea bream.

Cod: *June–February*
Familiar, large olive-brown fish with white underside and close-textured white flesh. Usually sold as steaks or fillets, though smaller cod may be sold whole. With the depletion of North Sea stocks, consumers are being urged to buy Icelandic or Norwegian cod instead. Suitable for most cooking methods, including poaching, frying, baking and grilling. Smoked cod, salt cod and cod's roe are also available.

Coley (Saithe): *August–February*
Blue-black fish with pinkish-grey flesh, which turns white when cooked. Sold as fillets. Cook as for cod, with some liquid as the flesh is inclined to be dry.

Conger Eel: *March–October*
Dark grey fish, with silver underside and fairly tough, full-flavoured white flesh. Best steamed or boiled.

Groupers: *All year; fresh or frozen*
Exotic family of fish varying enormously in size, usually grey-brown skinned, but the red grouper is considered to be one of the best. Groupers resemble snappers in flavour and texture. They are sold whole and as steaks and fillets; cook as for red snapper.

Gurnard, Red: *July–February*
Small, red fish with distinctive bony head and pectoral fins. Sold whole or as fillets. Best baked, grilled or poached.

Haddock: *May–February*
Grey-skinned fish with firm white flesh, suited to most cooking methods. Usually sold as fillets or steaks. Smoked haddock is also widely available. Haddock is typically cold-smoked until it is pale yellow; a bright yellow-orange colour indicates that the smoked fish has been artificially dyed as well. Finnan haddock are split, lightly salted and smoked. Arbroath smokies are hot-smoked small whole haddock, which don't need further cooking.

Hake: *June–March*
Member of the cod family and similar in shape, but with a closer-textured white flesh and a finer flavour. Sold whole, and as steaks, cutlets and fillets. Cook as for cod.

Hoki: *All year; fresh or frozen*
This large firm-textured fish from New Zealand has white, moist flesh, with few bones. It is similar to cod and haddock and can be cooked in the same way. Hoki is available as frozen fillets and steaks all year round.

Huss (Rock Salmon): *All year*
Also known as dogfish, this long, pointed fish has light brown skin, a cream-coloured belly and firm, white flesh. Sold as fillets or cutlets. Best fried or used in soups and stews.

Jacks: *All year; fresh or frozen*
Diverse tropical family, which includes the superior pompano with its silky skin and sweet, white flesh. Other jacks include horse mackerel, yellowtail and runners. Sold whole or as steaks or fillets. Cook in the same way as sea bream.

John Dory: *All year*
Ugly olive-brown fish with a flattened body and a large head. John Dory has firm-textured white flesh, which has a good flavour. Can be poached or baked whole, or filleted and cooked like sole.

Monkfish (Angler Fish): *All year*
Round fish with a large, ugly head. Only the tail is eaten; this may be sold whole or filleted; the tough outer skin must be removed. Monkfish has firm, white 'meaty' flesh with an excellent texture and flavour. It is suited to most cooking methods, especially baking, braising, grilling and pan-frying.

Mullet, Grey: *September–February*
Similar to sea bass but with an inferior flavour and texture, grey mullet is sold whole or as fillets. It is suitable for baking, grilling, steaming or poaching.

Mullet, Red: *May–November*
Unrelated to the grey mullet, this small bright red fish has firm flesh with a unique, delicate flavour. Sold whole and suitable for pan-frying, grilling, barbecuing and baking.

Parrotfish: *All year; fresh or frozen*
Tropical fish with brilliant blue skin and a beak-like snout. Usually sold whole, parrotfish are best steamed or poached.

Pollack: *May–September*
Member of the cod family with coarser grey flesh which turns white on cooking. Sold and cooked in the same way as cod.

Redfish (Ocean Perch): *All year*
Large fish with a flattened round body and bright orange-red skin. The flesh is white and has a good flavour. Sold whole or as fillets, which can be cooked as for bream.

Rockfish (Catfish): *February–July*
Blue-grey fish with firm, pink-tinged, strongly flavoured flesh. Sold as fillets, portions and cutlets; best used in soups and stews.

Snappers: *All year; fresh or frozen*
Tropical family with distinctive red or pink skin, which includes red snapper, *bourgeois, job gris*

and *therese*. These fish have delicious white flesh. Snappers are usually sold whole, but steaks and fillets are also available. Bake or braise whole fish; grill or steam portions.

Whiting: *June–February*
Fairly small fish with an olive-green back and cream-coloured belly. The flesh is soft and white with a delicate flavour. Sold whole or as fillets; best poached, steamed or pan-fried.

OILY FISH
Anchovy: *All year*
Small round fish with a strong flavour, usually filleted and cured, by salting or brining. Cured anchovies are typically used to enhance pizzas, canapés etc. Fresh anchovies are sometimes obtainable, and delicious.

Herring: *May–December*
Fairly small, round fish with creamy-coloured flesh that has a distinctive flavour. Sold whole or filleted. Usually grilled, fried or stuffed and baked. Cured herrings are also available, including salted herrings, herrings preserved in vinegar (rollmops), and smoked herrings in a variety of forms. Buckling are hot-smoked and ready to eat; bloaters, kippers and red herring are all cold-smoked.

Mackerel: *All year*
A long, slender round fish with blue black markings on its back, cream-coloured flesh and a very distinctive flavour. Sold whole and can be cooked whole or filleted – by baking, grilling or frying. Both hot- and cold-smoked mackerel are available too.

Sardine: *November–February*
Sardines are strictly immature pilchards. Most are sold canned in olive oil or tomato sauce, but fresh sardines are increasingly available in this country. These are delicious grilled, fried or baked.

Smelt: *November–February*
Small round, silvery fish, similar in flavour to trout. Can be deep-fried or baked.

Sprat: *October; March*
Small member of the herring family. Clean through the gills, then grill or fry.

Swordfish: *All year; fresh or frozen*
A long sword-like nose gives this fish its name. It has firm, close-textured white flesh, not unlike tuna in flavour and texture. Sold as steaks, which are best braised, pan-fried or griddle-cooked.

Tuna: *All year; fresh or frozen*
Large, round fish with dark blue back, and silvery grey sides and belly. The meaty flesh is deep reddish-pink and is sold in steaks or slices. Braise, poach, grill or pan-fry. Canned tuna is popular.

Whitebait: *All year, best February–June*
Tiny silvery young of the sprat or herring, whitebait are eaten whole. They are typically coated in flour and deep-fried.

FRESHWATER FISH
Salmon and trout are by far the most popular freshwater fish, but other less familiar species are available. These fish must be cleaned and scaled soon after they are caught.

Carp: *All year; best June–March*
Carp fished from its natural muddy water habitat needs to be soaked in cold water for 3–4 hours and rinsed well before cooking. Not surprisingly, carp farmed in clean water tastes better. Sold whole; suitable for baking, poaching or braising.

Char: *All year*
Related to the salmon trout, this fish has firm white to pink flesh. Cook as for salmon trout.

Eel: *All year; best September–December*
Long, snake-like fish with shiny, dark skin and dense, fatty flesh. Eels must be eaten very fresh and are therefore often sold live: to kill, pierce the spinal cord, then remove the skin. Eels are also sold as fillets, and jellied. Fresh eels are best sautéed or stewed.

Grayling: *All year*
A silvery member of the trout family, with a scent of thyme and firm, white flesh. Cook as for trout.

Perch: *June–March*
This large fish has fine-flavoured firm, white flesh, but it is bony. Best poached or fried.

Pike: *June–March*

Sharp-nosed fish with large jaws and sharp teeth. The flesh is quite dry, but has a good flavour. Perch should be soaked in cold water for a few hours prior to poaching or baking.

Salmon: *All year*

Strictly a saltwater fish, which travels up rivers to spawn, salmon has bright, silvery scales, red gills and deep pink flesh, which turns pale pink when cooked. Fresh 'wild' Scottish salmon is regarded as the best; this is in season from February to August. Farmed Scottish salmon is always available, so too is imported salmon. Sold whole, and as steaks and fillets. Whole salmon are best baked or poached; steaks and cutlets can be grilled, pan-fried, poached or baked. Smoked salmon is, of course, widely available; Scottish smoked salmon is considered to be the finest.

Trout, Salmon: *All year; best March–July*

This is a trout which has spent a season or longer in the sea, feeding on crustaceans, so that its flesh acquires a flavour and colour rather like that of salmon, though in texture it is slightly coarser and less succulent. Prepare and cook as for salmon.

Trout, Rainbow: *All year*

Reared on trout farms, this green-gold fish with pink or white delicately flavoured flesh is the most common trout. It is sold and usually cooked whole – either baked, grilled or fried. Smoked trout is widely available; this is invariably hot-smoked rainbow trout.

Trout, River: *All year; best March–September*

Also known as brown trout, this is considered to have a superior flavour to rainbow trout, but it is not widely available.

PREPARATION TECHNIQUES

Most fish is cleaned before it is sold; ie its scales, fins and entrails are removed. If not ask your fishmonger to do this or clean the fish yourself.

SCALING FISH

Hold the fish firmly by the tail and, using the back of a knife or a fish scaler, scrape off the scales from tail to head – the opposite way to the direction the scales lie.

GUTTING FISH

1 To gut round fish, such as sardines or trout, slit open along the belly from the gills to the tail vent, using a sharp knife.

2 Carefully loosen the soft innards from the belly and behind

the gills with your fingers, pull them out and discard.

3 Rinse thoroughly under cold running water to remove all traces of blood.

note: *To remove the entrails from flat fish, such as sole and plaice, open the cavity which lies behind the gills and clean out the entrails in the same way; rinse thoroughly.*

SKINNING FISH

If you intend to cook flat fish whole, remove the dark skin only; the white skin will help keep the fish in one piece during cooking. Flat fish that are to be filleted should be skinned completely. Round fish and very large flat fish, such as turbot and halibut, are easier to skin after they have been filleted or cooked.

TO SKIN FLAT FISH

1 Lay the fish on a board, dark side uppermost. Make an incision across the skin where the tail joins the body. Starting at the cut, use the point of the knife to lift a flap of skin away from the flesh until you can get a firm grip on it.

2 Grasping the flap of skin with salted fingers and holding down the tail in the other hand, pull the skin cleanly away in one piece. Turn the fish over and remove the white skin in same way, if wished.

BONING AND FILLETING

A sharp filleting knife with a long flexible blade is essential. Flat fish yield 4 fillets, which are skinned before filleting if required. Round fish yield 2 fillets and are skinned after filleting.

TO FILLET FLAT FISH

1 Lay the fish on a board with the tail pointing towards you and the eyes facing up. With the tip of the filleting knife, cut from head to tail along the backbone.

2 At the head end, insert the knife blade between the flesh and bones. Aiming to skim the blade over the bones, cut down along the flesh. When the head end of the fillet is detached, lift it and continue cutting until you have removed the fillet.

3 Remove the second fillet from this side in the same way.

4 Turn the fish over. Cut 2 fillets from this side, leaving a skeleton.

TO FILLET ROUND FISH

1 Lay the fish on its side, tail towards you. Cut along the backbone from head to tail, then cut through behind the gills to separate the fillet from the head.

2 Starting at the head end, insert the knife between flesh and bones.

Aiming to skim the knife over the bones, detach the fillet. Holding the fish by the exposed bones, cut the other fillet from the ribs.

3 Check over the fillets with your fingers for any small bones; remove these with tweezers.

4 To skin fillets, lay skin-side down, tail towards you. Make a cut at the tail end so the fillet can be lifted slightly from the skin. With salted fingers, press on the exposed skin to hold it down. Insert the knife at an angle below the fillet and cut away from you to separate it from the skin.

TO BONE LARGE ROUND FISH

1 Cut off the head and tail (or leave on if preferred). Extend

the cut along the belly (used for gutting) right to the tail.

2 Open the fish out and lay it on its side. Cut the rib bones free from the flesh on the upperside.

3 Turn the fish over and repeat on the other side, working through to the backbone, being careful not to cut through the flesh.

4 With scissors, cut through the backbone as close to the head as possible. Hold the backbone at the head end and carefully pull it free. Snip it at the tail end so you can remove it completely. Check for any remaining bones, removing small ones with tweezers.

TO BONE SMALL ROUND FISH

To remove the backbones from small fish, such as sardines, make sure the cut along the belly (used for gutting) extends along to the tail (see Gutting Fish, page 98).

1 Put the fish, slit-side down, on a board and open it out. Press firmly along the length of the backbone with your thumbs to loosen it from the flesh.

2 Turn the fish over and pull out the backbone through the slit in the belly. Use scissors to snip the end of the backbone free inside the fish if necessary.

Navarin of Cod

175g (6oz) podded broad beans

25g (1oz) butter

2 tbsp sunflower oil

1 onion, peeled and sliced

225g (8oz) baby carrots, scrubbed and
    trimmed

225g (8oz) courgettes, trimmed and cut into
    2cm (¾ inch) chunks

1 garlic clove, peeled and crushed

1.1kg (2½lb) thick chunky cod fillet, skinned

salt and pepper

4 tbsp plain flour

150ml (¼ pint) dry white wine

300ml (½ pint) fish stock

1 tbsp lemon juice

3 tbsp double cream

2 tbsp chopped parsley

serves 6

preparation: 15 minutes

cooking time: 25 minutes

per serving: 340 cals; 13g fat;
    16g carbohydrate

1 If the broad beans are large, blanch them in a pan of boiling water for 1–2 minutes, then drain and refresh in cold water.

2 Heat half the butter and half the oil in a large sauté pan. Add the onion, carrots, courgettes and garlic, and cook gently until softened and just beginning to brown. Remove from the pan and set aside.

3 Season the fish with salt and pepper, then dust lightly with the flour. Heat the remaining butter and oil in the pan, add the fish and brown on all sides. Remove from the pan and set aside.

4 Add the wine to the hot pan, stirring and scraping up any sediment from the bottom. Simmer for 1–2 minutes, then return the carrots, courgettes, onion, garlic and fish to the pan. Add the broad beans and stock. Bring to a simmer, then cover the pan and simmer gently for about 10 minutes or until the fish is opaque and flakes easily.

5 Stir in the lemon juice, cream and parsley. Divide among six bowls, grind over some coarse black pepper and serve with buttered baby new potatoes.

variation: *For a special dish, use monkfish fillet in place of cod. You'll also need to cook it for slightly longer at stage 4 – around 15 minutes.*

Cod Fillets with a Herby Cheese Crust

4 long skinless cod fillets, about 175g
    (6oz) each

plain flour, to coat

salt and pepper

50g (2oz) fresh white breadcrumbs

50g (2oz) pecorino or Parmesan cheese,
    freshly grated

2 tbsp chopped parsley

2 tbsp chopped chervil or dill

1 large egg, beaten

oil, to oil grill pan

serves 4

preparation: 30 minutes, plus chilling

cooking time: 15 minutes

per serving: 260 cals; 7g fat;
    11g carbohydrate

1 Season the fish with salt and pepper and toss in flour to coat, shaking off excess.

2 Mix the breadcrumbs with the cheese, herbs and seasoning.

3 Dip the floured cod fillets into the beaten egg, then immediately roll in the breadcrumb mixture to coat thoroughly. Twist as if into a knot, put on a baking sheet, cover lightly and chill for 1 hour.

4 Put the fish in a lightly oiled grill pan and cook under a medium-hot grill for 12–14 minutes or until cooked through, turning halfway through. Serve with tomatoes and peas.

Baked Spiced Fish Steaks

4 large white fish fillets, such as cod,
  haddock or hoki, about 175g (6oz) each

SPICE MIXTURE
3 garlic cloves, peeled and crushed
grated zest and juice of 1 lemon
grated zest of 1 lime
2 tbsp chopped coriander
2 tbsp chopped parsley
large pinch of powdered saffron
large pinch of ground turmeric
1 tsp ground cumin
½ tsp ground cinnamon
1–2 tsp hot chilli sauce
2 tsp muscovado sugar
1 tbsp sweet paprika
4 tbsp olive oil
salt and pepper

serves 4
preparation: 15 minutes, plus marinating
cooking time: 10–15 minutes
per serving: 260 cals; 14g fat;
  3g carbohydrate

1 Combine all the ingredients for the spice mixture in a bowl, seasoning with plenty of salt and pepper. Whisk together with a fork.

2 Spoon the spice mixture evenly over the fish fillets and rub it well in, making sure that each piece is completely coated. Leave to marinate in a cool place for 30 minutes to 1 hour, no longer or the acid in the marinade will begin to 'cook' the fish.

3 Wrap each fish fillet in a piece of foil and put on a baking sheet. Bake at 200°C (180°C fan oven) mark 6 for about 10–15 minutes until the fish flakes easily when tested with a fork.

4 Unwrap and lift each fish fillet on to a warmed plate. Pour the liquid from each parcel over the fish. Serve straightaway, with herbed bulgur wheat salad (page 359), or other salad and rice.

note: *The cooking time will depend on the thickness of the fillets. Chunky cod fillets, for example, will take longer than thinner, more delicate fillets.*

Sole Florentine

25g (1oz) butter, plus extra to grease
1 garlic clove, peeled and crushed
6 tomatoes, skinned and thickly sliced
900g (2lb) spinach leaves, stalks removed
salt and pepper
pinch of freshly grated nutmeg
8–12 single sole fillets
300ml (½ pint) hot cheese sauce (page 22)
1 tbsp dried breadcrumbs
1 tbsp freshly grated Parmesan cheese

serves 4
preparation: 30 minutes
cooking time: 10–15 minutes
per serving: 370 cals; 18g fat;
  16g carbohydrate

1 Melt 15g (½oz) butter in a frying pan, add the garlic and tomatoes and fry for 1 minute. Transfer to a buttered ovenproof dish and spread out evenly.

2 Put the spinach in a large pan with just the water clinging to the leaves after washing. Cover and cook for 5 minutes, shaking the pan frequently. Drain well, squeezing out excess moisture. Chop the spinach roughly, then return to the pan.

3 Add the remaining butter and season with salt, pepper and nutmeg. Cook, stirring, for 1 minute. Spread the spinach over the tomatoes.

4 Lay the sole fillets on a board, skinned-side up. Season, then roll up from the tail end. Lay on top of the spinach. Pour on the hot cheese sauce and top with the breadcrumbs and Parmesan. Bake at 180°C (160°C fan oven) mark 4 for 10–15 minutes until golden and bubbling. If necessary, pop under the grill to brown the topping before serving.

Dover Sole with Parsley Butter

2 Dover soles, about 275g (10oz) each,
  gutted and descaled
3 tbsp plain flour
salt and pepper
2 tbsp sunflower oil
25g (1oz) unsalted butter
2 tbsp chopped flat-leafed parsley
juice of ½ lemon
lemon wedges, to serve

serves 2
preparation: 5 minutes
cooking time: 20 minutes
per serving: 450 cals; 25g fat;
  16g carbohydrate

1 Rinse the fish under cold water, then gently pat them dry with kitchen paper. Put the flour on a large plate and season with salt and pepper. Dip the fish into the seasoned flour, to coat both sides, gently shaking off excess.

2 Heat 1 tbsp of the oil in a large sauté pan or frying pan and fry one fish for 4–5 minutes on each side until golden. Transfer to a warmed plate and keep warm in a low oven. Add the remaining oil to the pan and cook the other fish in the same way; put on a plate in the oven to keep warm.

3 Add the butter to the pan and melt. Turn up the heat slightly until it turns golden, then take off the heat. Add the parsley and lemon juice, then season well. Put one fish on each warmed dinner plate and pour over the parsley butter. Serve with lemon wedges.

Skate with Black Butter and Rocket Mash

6 skate wings, about 175g (6oz) each
125g (4oz) plain flour, to dust
salt and pepper
125g (4oz) butter

ROCKET MASH
1.8kg (4lb) floury potatoes, such as Maris
    Piper, peeled and cut into chunks
3 garlic cloves, peeled
200ml carton crème fraîche
100g (3½oz) rocket leaves

BLACK BUTTER
175g (6oz) butter
30 caper berries
6 tbsp white wine vinegar

TO SERVE
handful of rocket leaves
lemon wedges

serves 6
preparation: 40 minutes
cooking time: 40 minutes
per serving: 830 cals; 56g fat;
    6g carbohydrate

1 For the rocket mash, put the potatoes and garlic into a large pan of cold salted water. Cover, bring to the boil and cook for 15 minutes or until tender.

2 Meanwhile, trim the skate wings if necessary. Put the flour on a plate and season well with salt and pepper. Dip each skate wing in the seasoned flour to cover both sides evenly and shake off excess.

3 Melt the 125g (4oz) butter in a large frying pan over a low heat, then fry the skate over a medium heat, in two or three batches, for 5 minutes on each side, taking care that the butter doesn't burn. Put the skate wings on a baking sheet and keep them warm in a low oven while you cook the rest. Don't throw away the butter in the frying pan when you have finished.

4 Drain the potatoes and garlic, then return to the pan. Add the crème fraîche and mash until smooth. Season well with salt and pepper. Chop the rocket leaves and stir into the mash. Put the lid on to keep the potatoes warm.

5 For the black butter, add the butter to the frying pan and melt over a low heat. Add the caper berries and wine vinegar, and stir until heated through. Season well with salt and pepper.

6 Transfer the skate wings to warmed plates, drizzle with the black butter and top with rocket leaves. Serve with lemon wedges and the rocket mash.

Braised Monkfish in Parma Ham with Lentils

1kg (2¼lb) monkfish tail, filleted and skinned
1 tbsp chopped marjoram
salt and pepper
1 small lemon, peel and pith removed,
    thinly sliced
4–6 thin slices Parma ham
3 tbsp olive oil
1 small onion, peeled and finely diced
1 carrot, peeled and finely diced
1 celery stick, finely diced
1 garlic clove, peeled and finely chopped
350g (12oz) Puy lentils
150ml (¼ pint) red wine
2 tbsp chopped coriander

serves 4–6
preparation: 15 minutes, plus marinating
cooking time: 40 minutes
per serving: 610–410 cals; 15–10g fat;
    47–31g carbohydrate

1 Lay the fish, cut-side up, on a board and sprinkle with the marjoram. Season with salt and pepper. Lay the lemon slices over one fillet, then sandwich together with the other monkfish fillet.

2 Wrap the fish in the Parma ham, making sure it is completely covered. Tie at 5cm (2 inch) intervals with fine cotton string. Cover and leave in a cool place for 1–2 hours to allow the flavours to develop.

3 Heat 2 tbsp olive oil in a medium pan, then add the onion, carrot, celery and garlic. Cook, stirring, for about 8 minutes until golden. Stir in the lentils and wine. Add sufficient water to cover, bring to the boil and cook for 10 minutes.

4 Heat the remaining oil in a large frying pan. Add the monkfish parcel and fry, turning, until the Parma ham is browned all over. Carefully take out the fish parcel and transfer the lentils to the frying pan. Put the fish on top, partially burying it in the lentils. Cover and cook on a medium-low heat for 20 minutes or until the juices from the fish run clear, when tested with a knife.

5 Remove the string and cut the fish into thick slices. Serve on the lentils, sprinkled with the coriander.

Swordfish with Green Beans and Pistachios

4 swordfish steaks, about 175g (6oz) each

juice of ½ lemon

125ml (4fl oz) extra-virgin olive oil, plus
    extra to drizzle

3 large ripe tomatoes, cut into wedges

1–2 tbsp chopped oregano

1 garlic clove, peeled and crushed

salt and pepper

250g (9oz) fine green beans, trimmed

100g (3½oz) shelled pistachio nuts

serves 4

preparation: 15 minutes, plus marinating

cooking time: 12 minutes

per serving: 670 cals; 49g fat;
    7g carbohydrate

1 Lay the swordfish steaks in a shallow dish. Mix the lemon juice with 2 tbsp of the olive oil and drizzle over the swordfish. Turn to coat, then cover and leave to marinate in the fridge for at least 30 minutes.

2 Put the tomato wedges into a large bowl, add the oregano, the remaining olive oil and the garlic and season with salt and pepper.

3 Cook the beans in a large pan of salted water for 3–5 minutes or until tender. Drain well and add to the tomatoes. Add the pistachio nuts and toss together.

4 Preheat a non-stick frying pan or griddle pan. Lift the swordfish out of the marinade, season generously with salt and pepper and place in the pan. Cook over a medium heat for 3–4 minutes on each side.

5 Lift a swordfish steak on to each warmed plate, spoon the green beans alongside and drizzle with a little olive oil to serve.

Mediterranean Fish Stew

2 tbsp olive oil

1 small Spanish onion, peeled and finely
    chopped

1–2 garlic cloves, peeled and chopped

2 tsp tomato purée

pinch of powdered saffron

1 large potato, about 250g (9oz), peeled

750ml (1¼ pints) well-flavoured fish stock

½ head fennel, trimmed and thinly sliced

3 tomatoes, skinned, deseeded and sliced

225g (8oz) cod fillet, skinned

225g (8oz) monkfish fillet, skinned

4 tsp plain flour

¼ tsp cayenne pepper

salt and pepper

125g (4oz) peeled raw tiger prawns, deveined

1 tbsp brandy (optional)

1–2 tbsp roughly chopped flat-leafed parsley

TO SERVE

25g (1oz) ciabatta croûtes

3 tbsp rouille paste or garlic mayonnaise

4 tbsp freshly grated Parmesan cheese

serves 4

preparation: 30 minutes

cooking time: 40 minutes

per serving: 430 cals; 21g fat;
    23g carbohydrate

1 Heat the olive oil in a large pan, add the onion and cook gently for 10 minutes or until soft. Add the garlic, tomato purée and saffron, and cook for 2 minutes.

2 Cut the potato into large chunks and add to the pan with the fish stock. Bring to the boil, then lower the heat and simmer for 15 minutes. Add the fennel and tomatoes and cook for a further 5 minutes.

3 Meanwhile, cut the cod and monkfish into 4cm (1½ inch) chunks. Put the flour and cayenne into a large plastic bag and season with salt and pepper. Add the cod and monkfish and toss together until the pieces are completely coated. Tip them into a sieve, shaking away any excess flour.

4 Add the fish to the simmering stew and poach gently for 3 minutes until it is cooked. Don't allow it to boil or the fish will break up. Add the prawns and cook for 2 minutes or until pink.

5 If using brandy, pour it into a warm ladle, then ignite it with a taper. When the flames have died down a little, pour the brandy into the stew. Season with salt and pepper to taste and add the chopped parsley.

6 Serve the stew in warmed bowls. Spread the croûtes with rouille or garlic mayonnaise, top with Parmesan and serve alongside for guests to add to their portion.

Illustrated on page 92

Pan-fried Red Mullet with Citrus and Basil

4 red mullet, about 225g (8oz) each, filleted

6 tbsp olive oil

10 peppercorns, crushed

2 oranges

1 lemon

salt and pepper

2 tbsp plain flour

15g (½oz) butter

2 anchovy fillets

15g (½oz) shredded basil

serves 4

preparation: 10 minutes, plus marinating

cooking time: 10 minutes

per serving: 390 cals; 28g fat;

   10g carbohydrate

1 Lay the fish fillets in a shallow dish, drizzle over the olive oil and sprinkle with the peppercorns. Peel 1 orange, removing all white pith, then slice thinly. Lay the orange slices over the fish. Cover and leave to marinate in the fridge for 4 hours.

2 Remove the skin and white pith from one half of the lemon, then slice thinly and reserve for the garnish. Squeeze the juice from the other half.

3 Lift the fish out of the dish, reserving the marinade, and pat dry on kitchen paper. Season with salt and pepper, then dust lightly with flour.

4 Heat 3 tbsp of the marinade in a sauté pan or frying pan. Add the fish fillets and fry for 2 minutes on each side. Remove and set aside. Discard the oil remaining in the pan.

5 Melt the butter in the pan and add the remaining marinade. Add the anchovy fillets and crush until dissolved. Add the lemon juice and the juice from the other orange. Season and cook until slightly reduced. Lastly, stir in the shredded basil. Pour over the fish and garnish with the reserved lemon slices. Serve at once, with steamed couscous or rice and a salad.

variation: *Use sole fillets instead of red mullet.*

Spicy Tuna with Raita

4 tuna steaks, about 150g (5oz) each

2 tbsp tomato purée

1 tbsp oil, plus extra to brush

1 tbsp lemon juice

1 tsp grated fresh root ginger

1 garlic clove, peeled and crushed

1 tsp ground cumin

2 tsp ground coriander

1 tsp chilli powder

salt and pepper

RAITA

150ml (¼ pint) Greek-style yogurt

1 tbsp chopped mint

50g (2oz) peeled cucumber, deseeded
   and grated

pinch of sugar

serves 4

preparation: 20 minutes, plus marinating

cooking time: 5 minutes, plus resting

per serving: 290 cals; 13g fat;

   3g carbohydrate

1 Rinse the tuna steaks, pat dry with kitchen paper and put them into a shallow dish. Mix the tomato purée with the oil, lemon juice, ginger, garlic, cumin, coriander, chilli powder and 1 tsp salt. Spread this mixture all over the tuna steaks, cover and leave to marinate in a cool place for 2 hours.

2 Meanwhile, make the raita. Combine all of the ingredients in a bowl and season with salt and pepper to taste; set aside.

3 Brush a griddle or heavy-based frying pan with a little oil and put over a high heat. When hot, add the tuna steaks and cook for 2–3 minutes, then turn and cook the other side for 2 minutes. Remove from the pan and leave to rest in a warm place for 5 minutes.

4 Put the tuna steaks on warmed serving plates, add a dollop of raita and serve with a mixed salad.

Red Thai Seafood Curry

1 tbsp oil
3 tbsp Thai red curry paste
450g (1lb) monkfish tail, filleted and sliced
    into rounds
350g (12oz) peeled large raw prawns,
    deveined
400ml can half-fat coconut milk
200ml (7fl oz) fish stock
juice of 1 lime
1–2 tbsp Thai fish sauce
125g (4oz) mangetout, trimmed and
    sliced lengthways
3 tbsp torn coriander
salt and pepper

serves 4
preparation: 15 minutes
cooking time: 8–10 minutes
per serving: 350 cals; 19g fat;
    5g carbohydrate

1 Heat the oil in a large non-stick sauté pan or wok. Add the Thai red curry paste and cook, stirring, for 1–2 minutes.
2 Add the monkfish and prawns and stir well to coat in the curry paste. Add the coconut milk, stock, lime juice and fish sauce. Stir all the ingredients together and bring just to the boil.
3 Add the mangetout and simmer for 5 minutes or until both mangetout and fish are tender. Stir in the coriander and season with salt and pepper to taste. Serve with plain boiled rice.

notes
• This quantity of monkfish should yield about 350g (12oz) filleted weight.
• If you can't find half-fat coconut milk, use half a can of full-fat coconut milk and make up the difference with water or stock.

Sea Bass with Saffron and Orange Sauce

75g (3oz) butter, plus extra to grease
1 large sea bass, about 1.4kg (3lb)
salt and pepper
handful of mixed herb sprigs, such as
    tarragon, parsley, chervil, plus extra
    to garnish

SAFFRON AND ORANGE SAUCE
½ tsp saffron strands
1 tsp cornflour
300ml (½ pint) double cream
finely grated zest of 1 orange

serves 6
preparation: 25 minutes
cooking time: 40 minutes
per serving: 520 cals; 38g fat;
    2g carbohydrate

1 Line a roasting tin large enough to hold the fish with a lightly buttered sheet of foil. Rub the fish inside and out with salt and pepper and put in the foil-lined tin. Tuck the herbs into the cavity and dot the butter over the fish.
2 Cover the sea bass with foil and bake at 220°C (200°C fan oven) mark 7 for 40 minutes or until the thickest part flakes easily when tested with a knife.
3 Meanwhile make the sauce. Crumble the saffron into a bowl, add 2 tbsp hot water and set aside. Blend the cornflour with a little cold water in a small pan, then stir in the cream, orange zest and a little seasoning. Add the saffron and liquid to the pan and cook, stirring, until slightly thickened. Simmer gently for 3 minutes.
4 Carefully lift the cooked sea bass on to a board and peel away the skin from the upper surface, then turn the bass on to a warmed serving platter. Remove the skin from the other side. Garnish the fish lavishly with herbs and serve with the warm saffron and orange sauce.

note: If the bass won't fit comfortably in the tin, cut off the head and bake it beside the fish. Reposition the head as you serve the fish.

variation: Use a sea trout instead of bass.

Deep-fried Whitebait

700g (1½lb) whitebait
4 tbsp plain flour
salt and pepper
oil, to deep-fry

LIME AND BASIL MAYONNAISE
150ml (¼ pint) mayonnaise (see note)
grated zest of 1 lime
1 tbsp chopped basil

TO SERVE
lime or lemon wedges

serves 4
preparation: 5 minutes
cooking time: about 15 minutes
per serving: 800 cals; 77g fat;
  5g carbohydrate

1 Rinse the whitebait and pat thoroughly dry with kitchen paper.
2 For the flavoured mayonnaise, mix the ingredients together in a bowl and season with salt and pepper.
3 Put the flour into a large plastic bag and season with salt and pepper to taste. Add the whitebait and toss to coat in the seasoned flour.
4 Heat the oil in a deep-fryer to 190°C. Deep-fry the whitebait in the hot oil in batches for about 3 minutes or until golden brown. Drain on crumpled kitchen paper and keep hot in a low oven while cooking the rest of the fish.
5 Serve the hot whitebait with lime or lemon wedges and the flavoured mayonnaise.

note: *Use either homemade mayonnaise (see page 351) or a good, thick ready-made alternative.*

Grilled Herrings with Spinach and Nut Stuffing

4 herrings, about 225g (8oz) each, cleaned
  and boned

STUFFING
25g (1oz) butter
1 onion, peeled and finely chopped
25g (1oz) blanched almonds or pine nuts,
  roughly chopped
125g (4oz) young spinach leaves, stalks
  removed
25g (1oz) medium oatmeal
75g (3oz) mature Cheddar cheese, grated
salt and pepper

TO FINISH
2 tsp balsamic or wine vinegar
lemon wedges, to serve

serves 4
preparation: 15 minutes
cooking time: about 15 minutes
per serving: 430 cals; 30g fat;
  9g carbohydrate

1 Rinse the herrings inside and out, and pat dry with kitchen paper.
2 To make the stuffing, melt the butter in a frying pan, add the onion and nuts and fry for 3 minutes. Stir in the spinach and cook until just wilted. Remove from the heat and stir in the oatmeal. Cool slightly, then add the cheese and a little seasoning.
3 Score the herrings several times on each side. Sprinkle the balsamic vinegar inside the cavities and over the skins.
4 Spoon the prepared stuffing into the cavities and secure the opening with wooden cocktail sticks.
5 Line the grill pan with lightly oiled foil and put the herrings in the pan. Grill under a medium heat for about 15 minutes, turning halfway through cooking.
6 Transfer the herrings to warmed plates and serve with lemon wedges and a tomato salad.

note: *If fresh spinach isn't available, use 50g (2oz) frozen, thawing it thoroughly and squeezing out all excess moisture.*

Oatmeal and Dill Crusted Herrings

4 herrings, about 225g (8oz) each, filleted
1 tbsp olive oil
3–4 tbsp pinhead oatmeal
1 tsp dill seed
finely grated zest and juice of 1 lemon
salt and pepper
½ cucumber, peeled
1 little gem lettuce
50g (2oz) butter
2 tbsp finely chopped dill
dill sprigs, to garnish

serves 4
preparation: 10 minutes
cooking time: 5–6 minutes
per serving: 560 cals; 45g fat;
   9g carbohydrate

1 Rinse the herrings and pat dry with kitchen paper, then smear the fleshy surface of each fillet with olive oil. Line the grill pan with foil and put the fish, flesh-side up, on the grill rack.

2 Mix the oatmeal with the dill seed, lemon zest and seasoning. Sprinkle the mixture evenly over the herring fillets. Pat down lightly to give a good coating and grill under a medium-high heat for 4–5 minutes, without turning.

3 In the meantime, halve the cucumber lengthways and scoop out the seeds, using a teaspoon. Cut the cucumber and lettuce crossways into 1cm (½ inch) thick slices.

4 Melt the butter in a frying pan and add the lemon juice. Add the cucumber and lettuce and cook, stirring, until the lettuce wilts. Add the chopped dill and season with salt and pepper to taste.

5 Transfer the grilled herrings to warmed plates and spoon the lettuce and cucumber alongside. Garnish with dill to serve.

variation: *Use mackerel or trout fillets instead of herring fillets.*

Sardines with Herbs

900g (2lb) sardines (at least 12), gutted
125ml (4fl oz) olive oil
3 tbsp lemon juice
2 tsp grated lemon zest
4 tbsp chopped mixed herbs, such as
   parsley, chervil and thyme
salt and pepper

serves 4
preparation: 10–30 minutes
cooking time: about 10 minutes
per serving: 340 cals; 25g fat;
   0g carbohydrate

1 If preferred, bone the sardines (see page 100), leaving the heads and tails intact. Rinse the sardines and pat dry with kitchen paper

2 In a bowl, mix together the olive oil, lemon juice, lemon zest, herbs and seasoning.

3 Lay the sardines on a grill rack, drizzle the herb dressing over them and grill under a medium-high heat for 5–7 minutes each side, basting frequently with the dressing. Serve hot or cold, accompanied by plenty of crusty bread.

Japanese-style Salmon

575g (1¼lb) piece salmon fillet, with skin
4 tbsp dark soy sauce
4 tbsp mirin
2 tbsp sake
2cm (¾ inch) piece fresh root ginger, peeled
    and cut into slivers, plus extra to garnish
1–2 tbsp oil

serves 2
preparation: 5 minutes, plus marinating
cooking time: 5 minutes
per serving: 500 cals; 33g fat;
    0g carbohydrate

1 Cut the salmon fillet widthways into 4 equal pieces. Put the soy sauce, mirin, sake and ginger slivers into a shallow bowl and mix together.
2 Add the salmon, turn to coat and leave to marinate in a cool place for 20 minutes.
3 Heat the oil in a non-stick frying pan until very hot. Add the salmon and fry, turning occasionally, for about 5 minutes or until crisp all over. Transfer to warmed plates and top with ginger slivers to garnish. Serve with plain boiled rice.

Salmon Kedgeree

75g (3oz) split green lentils
50g (2oz) butter
700g (1½lb) onions, peeled and sliced
2 tsp garam masala
1 garlic clove, peeled and crushed
750ml (1¼ pints) vegetable stock
225g (8oz) basmati rice
1 green chilli, deseeded and finely chopped
salt and pepper
350g (12oz) salmon fillet, skinned
coriander sprigs, to garnish

serves 4
preparation: 15 minutes, plus soaking
cooking time: 50 minutes
per serving: 540 cals; 21g fat;
    62g carbohydrate

1 Put the lentils into a bowl, pour on 300ml (½ pint) boiling water to cover and leave to soak for about 15 minutes, then drain.
2 Melt the butter in a flameproof casserole over a low heat. Add the onions and cook for 5 minutes or until softened and transluscent. Remove a third of the onions and put them to one side. Increase the heat to medium and continue to cook the remaining onions for 10 minutes or until caramelised. Remove and reserve for the garnish.
3 Return the transluscent onions to the casserole, add the garam masala and garlic, and cook, stirring, for 1 minute. Add the drained lentils and the stock, and bring to the boil. Lower the heat, cover and cook for 15 minutes.
4 Add the rice and green chilli, and season with salt and pepper. Bring to the boil, cover and simmer for 5 minutes.
5 Put the salmon fillet on top of the rice. Cover the casserole and cook gently for 15 minutes or until the rice is cooked, the stock is absorbed and the salmon turns opaque.
6 Lift off the salmon and divide it into flakes. Return the salmon to the casserole, and fork it through the rice. Serve the kedgeree garnished with the reserved caramelised onions and coriander sprigs.

Herby Salmon Fish Cakes

900g (2lb) floury potatoes, such as Maris
   Piper, peeled and quartered

salt and pepper

900g (2lb) salmon fillets

juice of 1 lemon

4 tbsp mayonnaise

pinch of cayenne pepper

2 tbsp freshly chopped herbs, such as
   tarragon, basil or parsley

2 tbsp chilli oil

serves 4

preparation: 20 minutes, plus chilling

cooking time: 45 minutes

per serving: 730 cals; 46g fat;
   36g carbohydrate

1 Put the potatoes into a large pan of cold salted water. Cover, bring to the boil and cook for about 20 minutes or until tender. Drain well, put the pan back on the heat to dry the potatoes, then mash well.

2 Meanwhile, put the salmon fillets and half the lemon juice into a pan with 600ml (1 pint) cold water. Cover and bring just to the boil, then lower the heat and simmer for 1 minute. Turn off the heat and leave the fish to cool in the liquid for 20–30 minutes; it will finish cooking in the residual heat.

3 Drain the salmon and remove the skin. Flake the flesh and add to the mashed potato with the remaining lemon juice, mayonnaise, cayenne and chopped herbs. Season generously and mix well.

4 Line a large baking sheet with a non-stick Teflon liner. Put a 7.5cm (3 inch) plain metal ring on the tray and fill with an eighth of the mixture. Lift off, and repeat to make 8 cakes in total. Chill in the fridge for about 2 hours to firm up before cooking.

5 Drizzle the fish cakes with chilli oil and bake at 200ºC (180ºC fan oven) mark 6 for 25 minutes or until golden. Serve with a green vegetable or salad.

note: *Baking rather than frying or grilling fish cakes means you won't need to turn them, so even if they are crumbly they won't disintegrate during cooking.*

Grilled Salmon Fillets with Caper and Lemon Butter Sauce

4 salmon fillets, with skin, about 175g
   (6oz) each
salt and pepper
1 tbsp oil

CAPER AND LEMON BUTTER SAUCE
125g (4oz) butter
4 tsp lemon juice
2 tsp white wine vinegar
2 large egg yolks
1–2 tbsp capers, rinsed and chopped

serves 4
preparation: 15 minutes
cooking time: 5–6 minutes
per serving: 640 cals; 55g fat;
   trace carbohydrate

1 First make the sauce. Slowly melt the butter in a pan over a low heat. Pour the lemon juice and vinegar into another pan and bring to the boil.
2 Meanwhile, whiz the egg yolks in a blender or food processor for 10 seconds, then with the motor running, add the hot vinegar mixture. Increase the heat under the butter and quickly bring to the boil. Again with the motor running, trickle the hot butter on to the egg mixture. When it is all incorporated the sauce should be the thickness of lightly whipped cream. Spoon it into a small bowl and fold in the capers to taste. Set aside.
3 Meanwhile, season the salmon and put skin-side down on a foil-lined grill pan. Brush with the oil and grill under a medium heat for about 1 minute. Turn skin-side up and grill under a high heat for a further 4–5 minutes until the skin is crisp and golden and the salmon is just cooked through. Lift on to warmed serving plates and top with the butter sauce.

variation: *Omit the capers and flavour the butter sauce with 2 tsp chopped tarragon.*

Salmon en Papillote with Lime Butter Sauce

75g (3oz) unsalted butter
4 salmon steaks, about 175g (6oz) each
salt and pepper
15g (½oz) fresh root ginger, peeled and
   cut into julienne strips
grated zest of 1 lime
juice of 2 limes
4 spring onions, trimmed and chopped
pinch of sugar
3 tbsp dry sherry
3 tbsp double cream

serves 4
preparation: 20 minutes
cooking time: 12–15 minutes
per serving: 530 cals; 42g fat;
   3g carbohydrate

1 Cut four baking parchment or greaseproof paper rectangles, measuring about 30 x 20cm (12 x 8 inches). Using 25g (1oz) of the butter, grease the paper.

2 Put a salmon steak on one half of each paper rectangle. Season with salt and pepper. Scatter the ginger and lime zest on top, then sprinkle with the juice of 1 lime. Fold the other half of the paper over the top, brushing the edges together. Make small overlapping folds along the edges to seal. Put on a baking sheet and set aside.
3 To make the sauce, heat 15g (½oz) butter in a small pan, add the spring onions and cook until softened. Add the remaining lime juice, sugar and sherry. Increase the heat and boil steadily until the liquid is reduced by half.
4 Bake the fish papillotes at 200°C (180°C fan oven) mark 6 for 12–15 minutes; the parcels will puff up.
5 Add the cream to the sauce and allow to bubble for a few seconds. Gradually whisk in the remaining butter, a piece at a time, taking the pan off the heat occasionally to prevent the sauce from splitting. The sauce should be smooth and slightly thickened. Season with salt and pepper to taste.
6 Transfer the papillotes to warmed plates, allowing guests to open their own parcels and savour the aroma. Serve the sauce separately.

Whole Baked Salmon

1 whole salmon, about 2.5kg (5½lb),
   filleted in two, skin left on
1 fennel bulb, quartered and cored
1 tbsp olive oil, plus extra to brush
1 organic lemon, very thinly sliced
handful of dill sprigs
4 tbsp white wine
salt and pepper

DILL AND CAPER MAYONAISSE
300ml (½ pint) mayonnaise (page 351)
4 tbsp chopped dill
1 tbsp roughly chopped capers

serves 8
preparation: 30 minutes
cooking time: 50 minutes
per serving: 800 cals; 66g fat;
   1g carbohydrate

1 Check the salmon for any small bones and remove with tweezers.

2 Cut the fennel into very thin slices. Heat the olive oil in a large pan, add the fennel and cook gently for 10 minutes or until softened, then leave to cool.

3 Brush a large piece of foil with oil and put on a baking sheet. Lay one salmon fillet, skin-side down, on the foil. Top with the fennel, lemon slices and dill, spoon over the wine and season with pepper.

4 Place the second salmon fillet on top, skin-side up. Score the skin with a sharp knife and brush with a little oil. Scrunch the foil up loosely around the fish, leaving the skin exposed. Bake at 190°C (170°C fan oven) mark 5 for 30–40 minutes until the flesh is opaque and firm to the touch.

5 For the flavoured mayonnaise, add the chopped dill and capers to the mayonnaise, stir to mix and check the seasoning.

6 Serve the salmon whole, either hot or cold, sprinkled with black pepper. Accompany with the mayonnaise, minted new potatoes and rocket leaves. For a buffet, ease portions apart with forks along score lines to serve.

Salmon with Pesto en Croûte

¼ filleted whole salmon, about 500g
   (1lb 2oz), skinned
85g pack Parma ham
375g pack ready-rolled puff pastry
flour, to dust
1 medium egg, lightly beaten

PESTO
2 garlic cloves, peeled and roughly chopped
pinch of salt
40g (1½oz) pine nuts
20g pack basil leaves
2 tbsp olive oil
15g (½oz) Parmesan cheese, freshly grated

TO GARNISH
basil sprigs
lemon slices

serves 5
preparation: 25–30 minutes
cooking time: 40–45 minutes
per serving: 620 cals; 44g fat;
   28g carbohydrate

1 First make the pesto. Whiz the garlic in a mini food processor with the salt, pine nuts, basil, olive oil and Parmesan until fairly smooth. Tip into a bowl, cover and chill until needed.

2 Spread the pesto over the salmon fillet, then wrap in the slices of Parma ham to cover completely. Wrap in clingfilm and chill.

3 Cut one third off the pastry. Roll out this smaller piece on a lightly floured surface to a 3mm (⅛ inch) thickness and 1cm (½ inch) larger than the salmon all round. Prick with a fork and transfer to a lined baking sheet (preferably with a Teflon liner). Bake at 220°C (200°C fan oven) mark 7 for 10–12 minutes or until golden and crisp. Set aside to cool.

4 Lower the oven setting to 200°C (180°C fan oven) mark 6. Roll out the remaining pastry on a lightly floured surface to a 3mm (⅛ inch) thickness, about 5cm (2 inches) larger all round than the salmon. Dust a lattice cutter with flour, then roll firmly over the pastry sheet once. Gently ease the lattices open with a sharp knife, keeping the sheet intact.

5 Lay the salmon on top of the cooled baked pastry base. Cover the salmon with the lattice pastry and tuck the ends underneath. Seal the edges and trim off any excess pastry. Brush with beaten egg and bake for 30–35 minutes until the pastry is crisp and golden. Garnish with basil and lemon slices to serve.

Trout with Almonds

4 trout, gutted, with heads and tails intact
salt and pepper
2 tbsp plain flour
65g (2½oz) butter
50g (2oz) flaked almonds
juice of ½ lemon, or to taste
1–2 tbsp chopped parsley

serves 4
preparation: 5 minutes
cooking time: 10–15 minutes
per serving: 450 cals; 28g fat;
   6g carbohydrate

1 Rinse the trout and pat dry with kitchen paper. Dust the fish with seasoned flour to coat lightly. Melt 50g (2oz) of the butter in a large frying pan. Fry the trout, two at a time, for 5–7 minutes on each side, turning once, until golden on both sides and cooked.

2 Remove the fish from the pan, drain on kitchen paper and put on a warmed platter; keep warm. Wipe out the pan.

3 Melt the remaining butter in the pan and fry the almonds until lightly browned. Add the lemon juice and spoon over the trout. Scatter with chopped parsley and serve immediately.

Marinated Mackerel

4 mackerel, about 350g (12oz) each, cleaned

3 onions, peeled, 1 finely chopped,
    2 finely sliced

salt and pepper

3 garlic cloves, peeled and crushed

2 lemons, 1 thinly sliced, 1 squeezed
    to extract the juice

3 tbsp olive oil

1 red pepper, cored, deseeded and
    finely sliced into rings

5 black peppercorns

2 bay leaves

150ml (¼ pint) white wine vinegar

serves 4
preparation: 20 minutes, plus marinating
cooking time: 25 minutes
per serving: 560 cals; 39g fat;
    12g carbohydrate

1 Rinse the mackerel and pat dry with kitchen paper. Put into a large, shallow container and sprinkle inside and out with the chopped onion, a little salt and one third of the garlic. Scatter over the lemon slices, pour over the lemon juice and season generously with pepper. Cover and leave to marinate in the fridge for at least 2 hours.

2 Heat 1 tbsp of the olive oil in a frying pan, add the sliced onions and fry over a low heat for 5 minutes to soften, stirring regularly. Add the remaining garlic and the red pepper and cook for a further 3 minutes.

3 Add the peppercorns, bay leaves, wine vinegar and 150ml (¼ pint) water. Bring to the boil, then lower the heat and simmer for about 10 minutes until the liquid is reduced by one third. Set aside.

4 Drain the mackerel. Heat the remaining 2 tbsp of oil in a large heavy-based frying pan. Add the mackerel and fry for 8–10 minutes, turning as needed, until the fish is tender and lightly browned.

5 Return the mackerel to a shallow dish and pour over the vinegar and pepper mixture. Serve warm, or cool and chill.

note: *This dish is best prepared a day ahead to allow the flavours to mingle. To serve warm the next day, microwave on high for about 3 minutes.*

Salt-crusted Trout with Tarragon Sauce

about 900g (2lb) sea salt

6–8 garlic cloves (unpeeled)

6 tbsp chopped tarragon

6 trout, gutted, with heads and tails intact

TARRAGON SAUCE

500ml carton crème fraîche

1 tsp Dijon mustard

1 garlic clove, peeled and crushed

salt and pepper

2 tbsp chopped tarragon

TO SERVE

lemon wedges

serves 6
preparation: 10 minutes
cooking time: 20 minutes
per serving: 550 cals; 41g fat;
    2g carbohydrate

1 Line a roasting tin with foil and add enough salt to make a 1cm (½ inch) layer. Scatter the garlic and about half the tarragon over the salt, then place the fish on top. Press the trout down into the salt, scatter over the remaining tarragon, then cover completely with the remaining salt. Bake at 220°C (fan oven 200°C) mark 7 for about 20 minutes.

2 Meanwhile, prepare the sauce. To serve warm, combine the ingredients except the tarragon in a pan, bring to the boil and simmer for a few minutes, adding the tarragon just before serving. To serve cold, simply mix all the ingredients together in a bowl.

3 Remove the fish from the oven and crack the salt crust open. Carefully lift out the trout on to a board and peel away the skin. Serve with lemon wedges and the tarragon sauce.

note: *Baking fish in a salt crust is a great way to seal in the natural flavours and keep the fish moist. You can serve the fish cold if you like, but the salt and skin must be removed before chilling, otherwise the fish will taste salty.*

Smoked Fish Pie

450g (1lb) smoked haddock fillet, skinned
200ml carton crème fraîche
15g (½oz) plain flour
20g pack flat-leafed parsley, chopped
salt and pepper
375g pack ready-rolled puff pastry

serves 4
preparation: 10 minutes
cooking time: 30 minutes
per serving: 640 cals; 43g fat;
    39g carbohydrate

1 Preheat a large shallow baking tray in the oven set at 230°C (210°C fan oven) mark 8. Check over the smoked haddock for small bones, removing any with tweezers, then cut the fish into small chunks.

2 Reserve 1 tsp crème fraîche. Put the rest into a bowl with the fish, flour and parsley. Mix together, seasoning with plenty of black pepper and a little salt.

3 Unroll the pastry on to a second baking tray and brush the edges with water. Spoon the fish mixture evenly over half of the pastry, leaving a border along the wet edges. Fold the pastry to make an envelope, press the edges together and crimp to seal.

4 Mix the reserved crème fraîche with 1 tsp water and brush over the pastry to glaze. Slash the pastry diagonally with a sharp knife to allow steam to escape.

5 Slide the baking tray on top of the hot one in the oven. Bake for 30 minutes or until piping hot and golden brown.

Fritto Misto

75g (3oz) plain flour
salt and pepper
1 litre (1¾ pints) fresh mussels in shells,
    cleaned (see page 82)
250ml (8fl oz) dry white wine
1 small shallot, peeled and finely chopped
few parsley sprigs
175g (6oz) squid, cleaned (see pages 82-3)
175g (6oz) small sole or red mullet fillets,
    skinned
175g (6oz) medium raw prawns, peeled and
    deveined (see page 80)
175g (6oz) whitebait
oil, to deep-fry
lemon wedges, to serve

serves 6
preparation: 20 minutes
cooking time: 15 minutes
per serving: 380 cals; 26g fat;
    12g carbohydrate

1 To make the batter, pour 200ml (7fl oz) water into a shallow bowl. Sift in the flour and a pinch of salt and whisk until smooth.

2 Put the mussels into a large pan with the white wine, chopped shallot and parsley. Cover tightly and steam over a medium high heat for 3–5 minutes until the shells open, shaking the pan frequently. Shell the mussels, discarding any that do not open.

3 Cut the squid pouches into thick rings; leave the tentacles whole. Slice the fish fillets. Dry all of the seafood well on kitchen paper.

4 Heat the oil in a deep-fryer to 180°C, or until a cube of bread dropped in browns within 40 seconds. Dip the squid into the batter to coat, then deep-fry for 2–3 minutes until golden and crisp. Remove with a slotted spoon and drain on kitchen paper. Keep warm in a low oven with the door ajar.

5 Repeat with rest of the seafood in turn, frying the fish fillets for 3 minutes; prawns for 4–5 minutes; whitebait for 3–4 minutes; mussels for 2–3 minutes. Toss all the seafood together and season with salt and pepper. Serve immediately, with lemon wedges.

POULTRY
AND GAME

Domesticated birds which are bred for the table – including chicken, turkey, duckling, guinea fowl and goose - are classified as poultry, while game refers to wild animals or birds that are hunted for food. Nowadays, this strict distinction doesn't apply, because many types of game, including rabbit, pheasant, pigeon and quail, are farmed. Most game is protected by law and can only be hunted at certain times of the year (see individual entries); quail is now a protected species that cannot be hunted.

Chicken, in particular, has become increasingly popular in recent years as a less expensive and healthier option to red meat. From a nutritional angle, it is an excellent food – high in protein and vitamins, yet low in fat (once the skin has been removed). Most supermarkets and butchers offer a wide range of chicken and other poultry, plus a selection of game.

CHOOSING POULTRY

Whichever type of bird you are buying, freshness is of the utmost importance, so check the 'use-by' date. Look for a bird with a good plump breast and a firm unblemished skin. If you are buying from a farm, refuse a bird that's been carelessly plucked and singed. A young chicken will have a pliable breastbone, and a young duckling a pliable beak. Regulations for poultry labelling are complex, but the following information is a guide:

Organic chickens and other organic birds are allowed to roam free, are reared without drugs, and eat feed that is mainly organic. There's also a limit to the number of birds that can be reared in one space. All this helps to make a good, well-flavoured bird. Organic chickens cost around twice as much as intensively reared birds, but they invariably have a superior flavour and texture.

Free-range birds are raised predominantly on a grain diet and allowed access to open air runs, though they do not necessarily get as much exercise as organic chickens. Drugs may be used routinely. Free-range birds are usually tastier than intensively reared chickens, but less so than organic birds.

Intensively reared poultry, as the description suggests, is raised in overcrowded huts. As the birds cannot move around easily, they end up fatter. The use of drugs and undesirable farming practices, such as beak trimming, are routine.

HANDLING AND STORING POULTRY

All poultry contains low levels of salmonella and campylobacter, and these bacteria can cause food poisoning if they multiply. It is therefore important that poultry is handled and stored hygienically. Always get poultry home and into a fridge as soon as possible after buying. If the bird contains giblets take them out and store in a separate container, since these will deteriorate most rapidly. Wash your hands before and after handling poultry, and never use the same utensils for preparing raw poultry and cooked foods.

Ensure poultry is cooked thoroughly. To test, pierce the thickest part of the thigh with a skewer. Only if the juices run clear – not at all pink – is the poultry cooked. Chill leftover meat as soon as possible and eat within 2 days.

FROZEN POULTRY

Frozen poultry can be kept in the freezer for up to 3 months. Check that it is well wrapped to prevent the skin from being damaged by freezer burn. Defrost poultry at cool room temperature rather than in the fridge and make sure you allow sufficient time. A large turkey, weighing 6.8–9kg (15–20lb) for example, will take 24–30 hours to defrost thoroughly at cool room temperature. Even a 3.6–5kg (8–11lb) turkey will take 18–20 hours. It is essential that frozen poultry is fully defrosted before cooking. Check that there are no ice crystals in the body cavity. A fully defrosted bird will be flexible, too – try moving the leg joints. Once fully thawed, poultry can be stored in the fridge for a short time but it should be cooked within 24 hours.

CHICKEN

Oven-ready chickens are sold completely eviscerated, both fresh and frozen, with or without giblets. They range in weight from 1.4–3.2kg (3–7lb). Pre-basted birds are also available. Apart from roasting, oven-ready chickens can be poached, braised or pot-roasted. You need to allow approximately 350g (12oz) per person.

Corn-fed chickens have a distinctive yellow colour and characteristic flavour, acquired because they are reared on a diet of maize. Cook as for oven-ready chickens.

Poussins are 4–6 week-old chickens, weighing 450–700g (1–1½lb). One poussin serves 1–2. These are very tender birds and can be stuffed and roasted; or spatchcocked (split and flattened), then grilled or barbecued.

Spring chickens are young 12 week-old birds, weighing about 1.1kg (2½lb); one spring chicken will serve 2–3. Cook these tender birds as for oven-ready chickens.

Boiling fowl are at least 18 months old and weigh 1.8–3.2kg (4–7lb). These older birds are tougher, but full-flavoured and ideal for making stock. They are rarely available these days.

Chicken portions are available in various forms, boneless or whole, with or without skin. Apart from chicken quarters, breasts, thighs and drumsticks, boneless, skinless chicken thighs and chicken breast fillets are useful cuts. Other convenient products include chicken mince, crumb-coated chicken steaks and goujons – thin strips of breast meat suitable for stir-frying or coating in egg and breadcrumbs and deep-frying.

Skinned and flattened chicken breast fillets are described as escalopes. Breast fillets sold with the wing bone still attached are called suprêmes. Allow approximately 150g (5oz) boneless chicken per person, or about 225g (8oz) on the bone.

TURKEY

Turkeys are available all year round, whole or as a boneless roast, but of course they are synonymous with Christmas.

Oven-ready turkeys are available fresh or frozen. Most turkeys on sale are in the size range 2.3–9kg (5–20lb), although larger birds are obtainable. If possible, buy a fresh rather than a frozen turkey, as the flavour is superior and less water is lost during cooking. Free-range bronze turkeys are particularly tasty. Self-basting turkeys, which have butter or another basting ingredient injected under the skin, are also available.

Turkey portions are also readily available, including turkey steaks, escalopes (cut from the breast) and turkey mince. Similar cuts of chicken and turkey are interchangeable, so if a recipe calls for tender chicken breast meat, turkey fillet or escalopes can be substituted. Slow-cooked curries, casseroles and stews containing chicken drumsticks or thighs could be made with turkey leg meat instead.

GUINEA FOWL

These are lean golden birds with a superb flavour. They taste a little more gamey than chicken, and are cooked in the same way. Guinea fowl usually weigh around 1.4kg (3lb), which is sufficient to serve 4 people.

DUCKLING

Whole ducklings are sold fresh and frozen, and duckling portions are widely available. Oven-ready ducklings range from 1.4–2.7kg (3–6lb). Duck is much fattier than chicken or turkey, with a higher proportion of bone to meat, so you need to allow at least 450g (1lb) per person. The fat is concentrated in a layer under the skin and must be rendered during roasting otherwise the meat would be too fatty to eat.

Duckling breasts are fine flavoured and meaty with a good layer of fat, which should be cooked until crisp. They usually weigh around 175–200g (6–7oz) each, making a generous serving for one. If you buy the larger 350g (12oz) magret size, one duck breast should serve 2. Unless cooked in a casserole, duckling breasts are at their best served with the upper fat layer crisp and browned and the meat slightly pink inside.

GOOSE

The main season for goose is September to December, but frozen oven-ready goose is increasingly available at other times of the year, notably Easter. Geese range in weight from 3.6–6.3kg (8–14lb). As a rough guide, a 5.4kg (12lb) bird will serve 10. The most extravagant of all poultry birds, goose is richer and fattier than duck and has a fine flavour if properly cooked. It is almost always roasted whole, to render the fat from under the skin. Goose fat, itself, is regarded as something of a delicacy and is excellent for roasting potatoes.

GAME

Fresh wild game is only available during the hunting season, but farmed varieties are usually obtainable all year round from specialist suppliers and some supermarkets. Farmed game is usually milder than its hunted counterpart. Most game needs to be hung to develop its flavour and tenderise the flesh. Furred game includes venison, wild boar, rabbit and hare. The most common game birds are described below. Young game birds are suitable for roasting, but older birds are best casseroled.

GAME BIRDS

Pheasant *October 1st–February 1st*

Young pheasant is regarded by some as the best of all game birds. A brace of pheasants (one male and one female) garnished with the tail feathers makes a spectacular centrepiece. The hen pheasant is smaller than the cock pheasant and has more tender flesh. Only young pheasant is suitable for roasting; young and older pheasants make good casseroles.

Grouse *August 12th–December 10th*

Grouse are quite small, and one bird serves 1–2. The young birds are best for eating; these are distinguished by the soft, downy feathers under their wings. Ptarmigan and capercaillie are members of the grouse family, though they are considered inferior to the red grouse.

Quail *Available all year*

This is a protected species, which is now widely farmed and available from supermarkets. Quail are tiny birds; as a main course you'll need to serve 2 per person. Quail have a mild flavour and are best roasted – whole or spatchcocked, or split and grilled or pan-fried.

Wild Duck *September 1st–January 31st*

Wild duck has a stronger, more gamey flavour than its farm-reared counterpart. It can be prepared and cooked in the same way. Note that wild duck may taste unpleasantly fishy if it has been living by the coast and feeding on fish.

Woodcock *October 1st–January 31st*

These small birds are generally roasted whole (undrawn) and served on toast.

Wood Pigeon *Available all year*

Wild pigeon has a very strong flavour and is best casseroled as it needs long slow cooking to tenderise the flesh. Farmed pigeon is a rich, dark well-flavoured meat, which can be roasted.

FURRED GAME

Rabbit and Hare

Although these belong to the same family, they taste quite different. Rabbit, especially farmed rabbit, has a mild flavour, resembling that of chicken. Hare has strong gamey flesh. As a rough guide an average rabbit weighing 1.1–2kg (2½–4½lb) will serve 2–3; a hare weighing 2.7–3.6kg (6–8lb) will serve 6–8. The saddle of both animals can be roasted; other cuts are best casseroled. Very young hares (leverets) may be roasted whole.

Venison

Venison is a lean, dark, close-textured meat with a good flavour. The meat from the roe deer is considered superior to that from fallow and red deer. Farmed venison is now widely available; it has a milder flavour and is invariably more tender than wild venison.

Loin, saddle, fillet and leg are prime venison cuts for roasting; escalopes and medallions (cut from the boned loin or the haunch) are suitable for pan-frying; while shoulder, neck and breast cuts are best reserved for casseroles. All venison benefits from being marinated before cooking; strong-flavoured red wine marinades spiced with juniper berries work well.

PREPARATION TECHNIQUES

TRUSSING POULTRY

Trussing keeps the bird in a neat compact shape for even roasting, holds in the stuffing and makes carving easier. You will need a trussing needle threaded with fine cotton string and a few thin skewers. Remove the giblets from the cavity (if present). Lift up the loose skin at the neck end and fill the cavity with the cold stuffing.

1 Lay the bird breast-side down on a board. Lift up the neck flap over the stuffing and up on to the back, then bring the wing tips round on top so that they hold it in position.

2 Use the trussing needle and a long length of string to oversew the neck flap to the bird, enclosing the stuffing.

3 Push the needle into the second joint of one wing, into the body and out through the same joint on the other side.

4 Insert the needle in the first joint of the wing and push it through the back of the body, catching the wing tips and neck skin, and out through the opposite side. You should be back near to where you started. Cut the string and tie the ends together.

5 Tuck in the parson's nose and secure it with a skewer. Take a length of string and loop it around each side of the skewer, then tie the legs together and secure them with a double knot.

SPATCHCOCKING A POUSSIN

The bird is split and flattened so that it can be baked, grilled or barbecued quickly and evenly. This technique is applied to small game birds.

1 Using poultry shears, cut down one side of the backbone.

2 Cut down the other side of the backbone, then remove it. Snip the wishbone in half.

3 Open out the bird on a board and press down hard on the breastbone with the heel of your

hand to break the bone and
flatten the bird.

4 Thread two fine wooden or
metal skewers crossways
through each poussin to hold it
in a flat position. Each skewer
should pass through one wing
and out through the leg on the
opposite side.

2 Turn the bird over and cut
through the skin where the thigh
joins the body. Cut right down
between the ball and socket joint,
being careful to keep the oyster
meat attached to the thigh.
Repeat with the other leg.

JOINTING POULTRY

All chickens and turkeys are
treated in much the same way,
size being the only difference.

5 Repeat on the other side.
Then cut right the way through
the ribcage, parallel to the
backbone on both sides. Pull
the back section away.

3 If liked, separate the thighs
from the drumsticks by cutting
through at the joints. Trim off the
bone end from the drumsticks.

1 Put the bird breast-side
down and, with the tip of a
knife, cut round the two
portions of oyster meat (which
lie against the backbone) so
they remain attached to the
thigh joint.

4 Turn the chicken over again, so
it is breast-side down. Using
poultry shears, cut firmly through
the back into the body cavity
between the backbone and one
shoulder blade, leaving the wing
attached to the breast.

6 Turn the breast with the
wings still attached, skin-side
up. Remove the wing portions
by cutting through at a slight
diagonal so that some breast is
attached to the wing. Cut the
breast into two or four portions.

ROASTING CHICKEN

Remove the giblets if there are any and reserve for making gravy. If you're stuffing a whole bird, put the stuffing in the neck end only, just before cooking. Don't stuff the body cavity as this would slow down the heat penetration, increasing the chance of an undercooked result, with potential health risks. Don't pack the stuffing in too tightly, as it will expand on cooking and you don't want the skin to split or the stuffing to ooze out. Cook any excess stuffing separately in a small dish.

If you don't want stuffing, put half a lemon, a few fresh herbs and a few peeled garlic cloves into the body cavity to impart flavour.

At this stage, it's a good idea to truss the bird so that it keeps its shape (see page 126). Or simply fold the wings under the body, then tie the legs together with a piece of string or secure with a skewer or cocktail sticks.

Weigh the bird and calculate the cooking time, allowing 20 minutes per 450g (1lb) plus 20 minutes. Put the bird into a roasting tin, season with salt and pepper and smear the breast with butter or oil, or cover with a few rashers of fatty bacon. Roast in a preheated oven at 190°C (170°C fan oven) mark 5 for the calculated time or until the juices run clear when the thickest part of the thigh is pierced with a skewer or fork. Baste with the accumulated juices from time to time during roasting to keep the meat moist. If the breast shows signs of browning too quickly, cover it with a piece of foil.

Chicken portions can be roasted at the same temperature and will take about 30–45 minutes depending on size. Poussins will take 45 minutes to 1 hour, depending on size. Like a whole chicken, the juices will run clear when a poussin is cooked.

ROASTING TURKEY

Allow at least 275g (10oz) per person (see the chart below). Like chickens, turkeys should be stuffed in the neck end only to ensure rapid heat penetration through the body cavity.

With a small sharp knife, cut out the wishbone to ease carving. Stuff and truss the bird just before cooking (see page 126). Weigh the stuffed bird and calculate the cooking time; allow for 20 minutes' resting before carving. Season the turkey, then smear with butter or oil.

Put the turkey straight into a deep roasting tin and cover loosely with a tent of foil, or wrap in buttered muslin (see recipe, page 152). Roast in a preheated oven at 190°C (170°C fan oven) mark 5 for the time suggested (in the chart below), basting frequently to keep the bird moist. Fold back the foil 45 minutes before the end of the calculated time to allow the breast to brown and crisp. Test by inserting a skewer in the thickest part of the thigh; the juices should run clear, not at all pink.

Once the turkey is cooked, leave it to rest, covered with foil, in a warm place for 20–30 minutes. This allows the juices to seep back into the meat, making the bird easier to carve and the flesh more succulent to eat. To make carving easier, first remove the legs, then slice the breast meat, using a long, sawing movement.

ROASTING DUCKLING

Weigh the duckling and calculate the cooking time, allowing 15 minutes per 450g (1lb), plus 15 minutes. Stuffing is best cooked separately. Prick the skin and rub with salt. Put the duck on a trivet in a roasting tin and roast uncovered at 200°C (180°C fan oven) mark 6 for the calculated time.

TURKEY ROASTING TIMES

OVEN-READY WEIGHT	NUMBER OF SERVINGS	COOKING TIME FOIL-WRAPPED
2.3–3.6kg (5–8lb)	6–10	2–3 hours
3.6–5kg (8–11lb)	10–15	3–3¼ hours
5–6.8kg (11–15lb)	15–20	3¼–4 hours
6.8–9kg (15–20lb)	20–30	4–5½ hours

ROASTING GOOSE

Remove the fat from the goose cavity. If required, stuff the bird at the neck end only, with a sage and onion or fruity stuffing (see page 131) just before cooking, then truss the bird. Weigh the bird and calculate the cooking time, allowing 15 minutes per 450g (1lb), plus 15 minutes. Put the bird into a roasting tin, thoroughly prick the skin with a fork, rub with oil and sprinkle generously with salt. Cover the breast with foil and roast at 200°C (180°C fan oven) mark 6 for the calculated time, basting regularly and removing the foil for the last 30 minutes to brown the breast.

ROASTING GAME BIRDS

The rules for roasting are much the same for all game birds – keep the breast moist with streaky bacon rashers and cook at a fairly high temperature. Large birds are carved in the same way as chicken; smaller ones, such as partridge, can be cut in half; and the smallest of all, for instance quail, can be served whole – allowing two birds per person.

ROASTING GAME BIRDS

BIRD	ROASTING TEMP/TIME
Grouse	200°C (180°C fan oven) mark 6 for 35–40 mins
Partridge	200°C (180°C fan oven) mark 6 for 40 mins
Pheasant	200°C (180°C fan oven) mark 6 for 50 mins
Quail	190°C (170°C fan oven) mark 5 for 15–20 mins
Woodcock	190°C (170°C fan oven) mark 5 for 15–20 mins
Wood Pigeon	230°C (210°C fan oven) mark 8 for 15–20 mins
Wild Duck (Mallard)	220°C (200°C fan oven) mark 7 for about 30 mins

1 Wash the bird inside and out and dry on kitchen paper. If it is to be stuffed, put the stuffing in the neck end only. Pull the skin over the stuffing and truss the bird neatly to keep it in good shape. If you are not using stuffing, put half an onion or an apple inside the body cavity and season well. Lean birds benefit from a little butter flavoured with lemon zest or herbs inside the cavity.

2 Lay the streaky bacon rashers over the breast or smear with softened butter. Have the bird at room temperature before roasting. Calculate the cooking time (see chart, below left). Baste frequently with butter and cover towards the end of the cooking time if the breast is browning too quickly.

3 Serve garnished with watercress sprigs. Accompany with thin gravy, bread sauce (page 25), game chips and vegetables.

note: To make game chips, peel potatoes and cut into wafer-thin slices. Deep-fry in hot oil until crisp and golden. Drain on kitchen paper.

GRAVY

Use poultry giblets to make a well-flavoured stock if they are available, or use a good homemade or ready-prepared chicken stock. Boil the stock down to reduce until thick and syrupy. To impart character, include a little mashed roast garlic (cooked with the bird); a splash of wine (then reduced to evaporate the alcohol); or fragrant herbs like thyme, bay and tarragon.

Roast duck and turkey both have a stronger flavour than chicken, so they can take a more robust gravy. A spoonful or two of cranberry sauce or redcurrant jelly adds a pleasant fruitiness, while a little orange zest or balsamic vinegar can help to offset the richness of duck. You may prefer to use medium dry sherry or Madeira rather than wine in a duck gravy. Aromatic spices, such as cinnamon sticks or cardamom pods, can be simmered in the gravy to lend flavour then removed before serving.

STUFFINGS

A moist, tasty stuffing will enhance the flavour of poultry and game birds; it will also improve their appearance by helping to plump the bird into a neat shape. Boned joints of meat, whole boned fish and vegetables, such as peppers, aubergines and large tomatoes, lend themselves perfectly to stuffing, too.

Most stuffings are based on breadcrumbs, rice, sausage meat, oatmeal or suet, with added flavouring ingredients and beaten egg or other liquid to bind the stuffing together. If required, the dry ingredients can be mixed together in advance, but the liquid should be added shortly before use. Stuff the bird (or meat or fish) just before cooking, and weigh after stuffing in order to calculate the cooking time.

When stuffing poultry, stuff the neck end only to ensure sufficient heat penetration through to the body cavity. The stuffing swells during cooking as it absorbs juices from the meat, poultry or fish, so don't pack it in too tightly or it may spill out. Cook any surplus stuffing in a separate baking dish.

Herb and Lemon Stuffing

40g (1½oz) butter
1 small onion, peeled and chopped
1 garlic clove, peeled and crushed
75g (3oz) white breadcrumbs
2 tbsp chopped flat-leafed parsley
2 tbsp chopped tarragon or thyme
finely grated zest and juice of 1 small lemon
1 medium egg yolk
salt and pepper

serves 4
preparation: 10 minutes, plus cooling
cooking time: 10 minutes
per serving: 150 cals; 10g fat;
   12g carbohydrate

1 Melt the butter in a small pan, add the onion and garlic and fry gently for 7–10 minutes to soften. Tip into a bowl and leave to cool.
2 Add the breadcrumbs, chopped herbs, lemon zest and juice, then stir in the egg yolk to bind the stuffing. Season well with salt and pepper.

notes
• *This stuffing is sufficient for a 1.4kg (3lb) oven-ready chicken.*
• *Keep the spent lemon halves to put into the cavity of the bird for flavour.*

Spicy Sausage Stuffing

350g (12oz) spicy Italian-style pork sausages
125g (4oz) butter
2 onions, peeled and chopped
225g (8oz) oatmeal
1 tsp finely chopped thyme
salt and pepper

serves 8–10
preparation: 10 minutes, plus cooling
cooking time: 10 minutes
per serving: 400–320 cals; 29–23g fat;
   28–22g carbohydrate

1 Skin the sausages and break up the sausage meat in a bowl.
2 Melt the butter in a pan, add the onions and cook gently for 7–10 minutes until soft and golden, then mix in the oatmeal and thyme. Leave to cool.
3 Add the mixture to the sausage meat and mix well, seasoning generously with salt and pepper.

note: *This stuffing is sufficient for a 4.5kg (10lb) oven-ready turkey.*

variation: *Shape the mixture into small balls. Heat a little oil in a baking tin. Add the sausage balls and bake at 180°C (160°C fan oven) mark 4 for about 45 minutes until cooked through, turning occasionally.*

Sage and Onion Stuffing

1 tbsp oil
75g (3oz) onion, peeled and chopped
125g (4oz) pork sausage meat
1 tbsp finely chopped sage
salt and pepper

serves 4–6
preparation: 10 minutes, plus cooling
cooking time: 10 minutes
per serving: 150–100 cals; 13–9g fat;
    4–3g carbohydrate

1 Heat the oil in a pan, add the onion and cook gently for 7–10 minutes until soft and golden. Turn into a bowl and leave to cool.
2 Add the sausage meat and sage to the cooled onion mixture and season with salt and pepper.

note: *This stuffing is sufficient for a 1.4kg (3lb) oven-ready chicken.*

Mushroom and Cashew Nut Stuffing

50g (2oz) butter
2 onions, peeled and finely chopped
450g (1lb) brown-cap mushrooms, roughly chopped
4 tbsp chopped parsley
75g (3oz) salted cashew nuts, toasted and roughly chopped
125g (4oz) fresh white breadcrumbs
2 large eggs, beaten
salt and pepper

serves 10
preparation: 15 minutes, plus cooling
cooking time: 15 minutes
per serving: 140 cals; 9g fat;
    11g carbohydrate

1 Melt the butter in a pan, add the onions and cook gently for 7–10 minutes until soft and golden. Add the mushrooms and fry briskly for 4–5 minutes until softened and the moisture has evaporated. Turn into a bowl.
2 Mix in the chopped parsley, cashew nuts and breadcrumbs. Leave to cool.
3 Add the beaten eggs and mix well to bind the stuffing, seasoning with salt and pepper.

note: *This stuffing is sufficient for a 4.5kg (10lb) oven-ready turkey.*

Fruity Celery Stuffing

25g (1oz) butter
125g (4oz) celery, finely sliced
125g (4oz) ready-to-eat dried apricots, finely chopped
175g (6oz) fresh breadcrumbs
1 tbsp chopped sage
¼ tsp ground mixed spice
1 egg
1 tbsp Dijon mustard
salt and pepper

serves 10
preparation: 10 minutes, plus cooling
cooking time: 5 minutes
per serving: 90 cals; 3g fat;
    13g carbohydrate

1 Melt the butter in a pan, add the celery and fry gently for 5 minutes. Turn into a bowl and add the apricots, breadcrumbs, sage and spice. Stir well and leave to cool.
2 In another bowl, beat the egg with the mustard, then add to the stuffing and mix thoroughly to bind, seasoning generously with salt and pepper. If the stuffing is too dry, moisten with a little stock.

note: *This stuffing is sufficient for a 4.5kg (10lb) oven-ready turkey.*

Classic Roast Chicken

1.4kg (3lb) organic or free-range chicken

salt and pepper

2 garlic cloves

4 parsley sprigs

4 tarragon sprigs

herb and lemon stuffing (page 130)

2 bay leaves

50g (2oz) butter, cut into cubes

GRAVY

200ml (7fl oz) white wine

1 tbsp Dijon mustard

450ml (¾ pint) hot chicken stock

beurre manié: 25g (1oz) butter mixed with
    25g (1oz) plain flour

serves 4

preparation: 30 minutes

cooking time: 1 hour 20 minutes

per serving: 510 cals; 30g fat;
    17g carbohydrate

1 Place the chicken on a board and put 1 tsp each sea salt and coarsely ground pepper, the garlic cloves and half the parsley and tarragon sprigs inside the cavity (with the spent lemon halves from the stuffing).
2 Turn the chicken round, so the parson's nose is facing away from you. Lift up the loose skin at the neck end and fill the cavity with the cold stuffing. Turn the chicken on its breast, lift up the neck flap and pull it over the stuffing to cover. Rest the wing tips across it and secure the flap with trussing string or a skewer. Truss the chicken (see page 126).
3 Put the chicken on a roasting rack, standing in a roasting tin. Season with 1 tsp each salt and pepper, the remaining parsley and tarragon sprigs, and the bay leaves. Dot the cubed butter over the breast.
4 Roast at 190°C (170°C fan oven) mark 5 for about 1 hour 20 minutes, or allowing 20 minutes per 450g (1lb) plus 20 minutes, basting with the cooking juices halfway through. Test by inserting a thin skewer into the thickest part of the thigh; the juices must run clear.
5 Put the chicken on a carving plate, cover with foil and leave to rest in a warm place. Tip off the fat in the roasting tin, leaving about 3 tbsp. Put the roasting tin directly on the hob over a low heat. Pour in the wine and boil for 2 minutes, then add the mustard and stock. Bring to the boil, then gradually whisk in small knobs of the beurre manié to make a smooth, slightly thickened gravy. Season to taste. Carve the chicken and the stuffing and serve with the gravy.

Mediterranean Roast Chicken

900g (2lb) floury potatoes, such as Maris
    Piper, halved or quartered if large

salt and pepper

125g (4oz) butter, softened

4 tbsp roughly chopped sage leaves, stalks
    reserved, plus extra leaves

4 tbsp roughly chopped thyme, stalks
    reserved, plus extra sprigs

1.4kg (3lb) organic or free-range chicken

juice of 1 unwaxed lemon, spent halves
    reserved

2 fennel bulbs, cut into wedges

1 red onion, peeled and cut into wedges

serves 4

preparation: 40 minutes

cooking time: about 1¼ –1½ hours

per serving: 600 cals; 33g fat;
    44g carbohydrate

1 Add the potatoes to a large pan of cold salted water, bring to the boil and cook for 5 minutes.
2 Meanwhile, put the butter into a bowl and mix in the chopped sage and thyme. Season well.
3 Put the chicken on a board and push the lemon halves and herb stalks into the cavity. Ease your fingers under the breast skin at the neck end to loosen it, then push most of the herb butter under the skin.
4 Season the chicken, put into a roasting tin and pour the lemon juice over. Top with sage and thyme sprigs and the remaining butter. Drain the potatoes and shake in a colander to roughen the edges. Put the potatoes, fennel and red onion around the chicken.
5 Roast at 190°C (170°C fan oven) mark 5 for 1 hour 20 minutes, or allowing 20 minutes per 450g (1lb) plus 20 minutes, basting several times, until the juices run clear. Carve chicken and serve with the vegetables.

Illustrated on page 122

Spiced Roasted Chicken with Garlic, Peppers and Potatoes

900g (2lb) floury potatoes, such as Maris
    Piper, halved or quartered if large
salt and pepper
1.4kg (3lb) organic or free-range chicken
1 orange, cut into wedges
1 small onion, peeled and halved
1 head of garlic (unpeeled)
2 red peppers, cored, deseeded and cut
    into eighths
75g (3oz) pine nuts

SPICE MIX
2 tbsp sweet paprika
1 tbsp ground coriander
1 tsp ground ginger
1 tsp ground cinnamon
large pinch of saffron strands, crushed
2 garlic cloves, peeled and crushed
juice of ½ orange
2 tbsp olive oil

serves 4
preparation: 30 minutes
cooking time: about 1½ hours
per serving: 540 cals; 23g fat;
    48g carbohydrate

1 Add the potatoes to a large pan of cold salted water and bring to the boil. Cook for 5 minutes.
2 Meanwhile, prepare the spice mix. Put the paprika, coriander, ginger, cinnamon, saffron, garlic, orange juice and olive oil into a bowl. Add ½ tsp each of salt and coarsely ground black pepper and mix well.
3 Put the chicken into a roasting tin and push the orange wedges and onion inside the cavity. Season well, then the rub spice mix all over the chicken.
4 Drain the potatoes and shake in a colander to roughen up the edges. Put them around the chicken. Add the head of garlic and red peppers.
5 Roast at 190°C (170°C fan oven) mark 5 for 1 hour 20 minutes, or allowing 20 minutes per 450g (1lb) plus 20 minutes. About 10 minutes before the end of cooking, sprinkle the pine nuts over. Continue to cook until the chicken juices run clear when the thickest part of the thigh is pierced with a skewer. Carve the chicken and serve with the garlic and vegetables.

Chicken in a Pot

2 tbsp oil
1 large onion, peeled and cut into wedges
2 rindless streaky bacon rashers, chopped
1.6kg (3½lb) organic or free-range chicken
6 medium carrots, peeled
2 small turnips, peeled and cut into wedges
1 garlic clove, peeled and crushed
bouquet garni (1 bay leaf, few parsley and
    thyme sprigs)
600ml (1 pint) hot chicken stock
100ml (3½fl oz) dry white wine
salt and pepper
12 button mushrooms
3 tbsp chopped flat-leafed parsley

serves 6
preparation: 20 minutes
cooking time: 1 hour 40 minutes
per serving: 470 cals; 34g fat;
    10g carbohydrate

1 Heat the oil in a flameproof casserole, then add the onion and bacon and fry for 5 minutes until golden. Remove and set aside.
2 Add the whole chicken to the casserole and fry for 10 minutes, turning carefully to brown all over. Remove and set aside.
3 Add the carrots, turnips and garlic to the casserole and fry for 5 minutes.
4 Return the bacon and onion, then put the chicken back in. Add the bouquet garni, stock and wine. Season with salt and pepper. Bring to a simmer, then cover and cook in the oven at 200°C (180°C fan oven) mark 6 for 30 minutes.
5 Remove the casserole from the oven and add the mushrooms. Baste the chicken, then re-cover and cook for a further 50 minutes.
6 Stir in the chopped parsley. Lift out the chicken, carve and serve with the vegetables, cooking liquid and mashed potatoes.

Baked Couscous with Spiced Chicken

12 boneless, skinless chicken thighs

salt and pepper

3 tbsp medium-hot curry powder

2 tbsp paprika

1 tsp ground cinnamon

10 garlic cloves, peeled and crushed

6 tbsp olive oil

450g (1lb) couscous

600ml (1 pint) hot chicken or vegetable stock

50g (2oz) sultanas

75g (3oz) butter, diced

5 tbsp coriander leaves, roughly torn

serves 6

preparation: 15 minutes, plus marinating

cooking time: 25–30 minutes

per serving: 630 cals; 30g fat;
   63g carbohydrate

1 Put the chicken thighs into an ovenproof dish and season generously with salt and pepper. Mix the curry powder, paprika, cinnamon, garlic and olive oil together. Spoon over the chicken and turn to coat all over. Cover and leave to marinate in the fridge for at least 30 minutes, preferably overnight.

2 Put the couscous into an ovenproof serving dish, pour on the stock and add 1 tsp salt. Stir and leave for 5 minutes to allow the stock to be absorbed.

3 Bake the chicken thighs at 200°C (180°C fan oven) mark 6 for 5 minutes. Meanwhile, add the sultanas to the couscous and dot the butter over the top. Cover the dish with foil and bake on the shelf below the chicken for a further 20–25 minutes until the chicken is cooked right through.

4 Add the spicy baked chicken thighs and juices to the couscous and toss gently to mix. Scatter the coriander leaves over to serve.

Chicken Baked in a Lemon Vinaigrette

2 lemons

175g (6oz) shallots or onions, peeled and
   thickly sliced

6 chicken suprêmes or 12 boneless thighs,
   with skin

salt and pepper

2 tbsp balsamic vinegar

2 tbsp sherry vinegar

4 tbsp thin honey

150ml (¼ pint) olive oil

serves 6

preparation: 10 minutes

cooking time: 40 minutes

per serving: 420 cals; 28g fat;
   10g carbohydrate

1 Grate the zest and squeeze the juice of 1 lemon; set aside. Thinly slice the other lemon. Scatter the lemon slices and shallots over the base of a small roasting tin (see note). Lay the chicken on top and season generously with salt and pepper.

2 Whisk the grated lemon zest and juice, vinegars, honey and olive oil together in a bowl. Pour this lemon vinaigrette over the chicken.

3 Bake at 200°C (180°C fan oven) mark 6, basting regularly, for 35 minutes or until the chicken is golden and cooked through. Transfer the chicken to a serving dish and keep warm.

4 Put the roasting tin with its juices on the hob over a medium heat. Bring to the boil and let bubble for 2–3 minutes or until syrupy. Spoon the liquor over the chicken to serve.

note: *The roasting tin should be just large enough to hold the chicken comfortably in a single layer.*

Chicken Drumsticks in a Barbecue Sauce

450g (1lb) tiny potatoes, scrubbed clean

salt

8 chicken drumsticks, skinned

125ml (4fl oz) tomato ketchup

2 tbsp muscovado sugar

1 tbsp mild mustard

2 tbsp Worcestershire sauce

1 garlic clove, peeled and crushed

2 onions, peeled and sliced into thick rings

2 tbsp oil

serves 4

preparation: about 15 minutes

cooking time: 40–50 minutes

per serving: 410 cals; 13g fat;
   40g carbohydrate

1 Add the potatoes to a pan of cold salted water, bring to the boil and cook for 5 minutes.

2 Make 2–3 deep cuts in each chicken drumstick, using a sharp knife.

3 In a large bowl, mix together the tomato ketchup, sugar, mustard, Worcestershire sauce and garlic. Add the chicken and onions, and stir until well coated.

4 Drain the potatoes thoroughly. Heat the oil in a roasting tin on the hob, tip in the potatoes and shake the tin to ensure the potatoes are well coated in oil. Turn off the heat, add the chicken drumsticks and onion rings with the sauce and toss well.

5 Bake at 220°C (200°C fan oven) mark 7 for 40–50 minutes or until the chicken drumsticks are cooked through and the potatoes are tender, turning from time to time to ensure even browning.

Mustard Chicken Wings with Thyme

12 large chicken wings

4 tbsp thick honey

grated zest and juice of 2 unwaxed lemons

4 tbsp Dijon mustard

4 tbsp olive oil

handful of thyme leaves, roughly chopped

salt and pepper

serves 6

preparation: 5 minutes, plus marinating

cooking time: 40 minutes

per serving: 340 cals; 23g fat;
  4g carbohydrate

1 Lay the chicken wings in a shallow dish. Mix the honey, lemon zest and juice, mustard, olive oil and thyme together and pour over the wings. Cover and leave the chicken to marinate in the fridge for at least 20 minutes.

2 Put the chicken wings together with the marinade into a roasting tin and season well with salt and pepper. Roast at 200°C (180°C fan oven) mark 6 for 40 minutes or until the juices run clear, turning and basting halfway through the cooking time.

note: *Roasted cherry tomatoes are an excellent accompaniment.*

Chicken Breasts Stuffed with Mushrooms

2 tbsp olive oil

1 shallot, peeled and very finely chopped

125g (4oz) small open cup mushrooms, finely
  chopped

40g (1½oz) mild creamy goat's cheese

2 thin slices Parma ham, finely chopped

3 tbsp chopped parsley

salt and pepper

125g (4oz) butter, softened

2 tbsp chopped basil

squeeze of lemon juice

6 chicken breast fillets, with skin

serves 6

preparation: 25 minutes, plus chilling

cooking time: 25–30 minutes

per serving: 560 cals; 50g fat;
  1g carbohydrate

1 Heat the olive oil in a heavy-based frying pan, add the shallot and cook gently until softened but not browned. Add the mushrooms and cook until well reduced and softened. Remove from the heat and let cool slightly.

2 Add the goat's cheese, Parma ham and half of the parsley. Mix well and season generously with salt and pepper. Leave to cool completely.

3 Meanwhile, beat 75g (3oz) of the butter with the remaining parsley, basil, lemon juice and seasoning. Transfer the herb butter to a sheet of greaseproof paper and shape into a cylinder. Wrap in the paper and chill until firm.

4 When the stuffing is cold, carefully loosen the skin from each chicken breast, keeping it attached along one long side. Carefully spoon the stuffing under the skin and secure by pushing a fine wooden skewer through the skin and breast along the open side. Lay the chicken in a roasting tin, skin-side uppermost.

5 Melt the remaining butter and brush over the chicken. Season with salt and pepper. Roast at 200°C (180°C fan oven) mark 6 for 25–30 minutes or until the chicken is cooked through.

6 Cut the herb butter into thin slices. Serve the chicken breasts on warmed plates, topped with slices of herb butter.

Chicken Fillets with Fennel

50g (2oz) butter
175g (6oz) fennel, cut into fine strips
4 chicken breast fillets, with skin
1 onion, peeled and roughly chopped
2 garlic cloves, peeled and crushed
150ml (¼ pint) white wine
300ml (½ pint) chicken stock
150ml (¼ pint) double cream
salt and pepper
1 tbsp chopped tarragon
1 tbsp chopped chives

serves 4
preparation: 5 minutes
cooking time: 20 minutes
per serving: 640 cals; 55g fat;
    5g carbohydrate

1 Heat 25g (1oz) butter in a frying pan. Add the fennel and stir-fry for 2–3 minutes, then remove from the pan and set aside. Add the chicken, skin-side down, and cook for 3 minutes; turn and cook on the other side for 2 minutes.
2 Transfer the chicken, skin-side up, to a baking sheet and bake at 200°C (180°C fan oven) mark 6 for 10–15 minutes or until the chicken is cooked through.
3 Meanwhile, melt the remaining butter in the pan, add the onion and garlic and fry, stirring, for 5 minutes. Pour in the wine, stock and cream. Bring to the boil and let bubble for 10 minutes or until syrupy. Season well with salt and pepper, then stir in the chopped tarragon and chives, and stir-fried fennel.
4 Transfer the chicken to warmed plates, pour on the fennel sauce and serve.

Tandoori Chicken

4 chicken breast fillets, about 600g (1¼lb)
4 tbsp groundnut oil, plus extra to oil
2 x 150ml cartons natural yogurt
juice of ½ lemon

TANDOORI PASTE
24 garlic cloves, about 125g (4oz), peeled
    and crushed
5cm (2 inch) piece fresh root ginger, peeled
    and chopped
3 tbsp coriander seeds
3 tbsp cumin seeds
3 tbsp fenugreek seeds (or powder)
3 tbsp paprika
3 red chillies, deseeded and chopped
3 tsp English mustard
2 tbsp tomato purée

CUCUMBER RAITA
½ cucumber
150ml carton natural yogurt
salt and pepper

serves 4
preparation: 45 minutes, plus marinating
cooking time: 20 minutes
per serving: 360 cals; 20g fat;
    10g carbohydrate

1 First prepare the tandoori paste. Put all of the ingredients into a mini processor with 1 tsp salt and 8 tbsp water, then whiz to a paste. Set aside one third of the tandoori paste; freeze the rest for later use (see note).
2 Cut the chicken fillets into long strips, about 2.5cm (1 inch) wide. In a large bowl, mix the portion of tandoori paste with 2 tbsp of the oil, the yogurt and lemon juice. Add the chicken to the mixture and stir well to coat. Cover the bowl and leave to marinate in the fridge for at least 4 hours, preferably overnight.
3 Transfer the chicken to an oiled roasting tin, spoon over any remaining marinade from the bowl and drizzle with the rest of the oil. Bake at 220°C (200°C fan oven) mark 7 for 20 minutes or until the chicken is cooked through.
4 Meanwhile, prepare the raita. Grate the cucumber or cut into fine strips and put into a bowl. Add the yogurt, stir to mix and season with salt and pepper to taste. Cover and chill.
5 Serve the tandoori chicken with the cucumber raita, a mixed salad and warm naan bread.

note: *Freeze the rest of the tandoori paste in two portions and use within 3 months. Defrost at cool room temperature for about 1 hour.*

Chicken Tarragon Burgers

2 shallots, peeled and finely chopped
225g (8oz) chicken mince
25g (1oz) fresh white breadcrumbs
15ml (1 tbsp) chopped tarragon
1 egg yolk
salt and pepper
oil, to brush

ROQUEFORT BUTTER
50g (2oz) Roquefort cheese
25g (1oz) unsalted butter, softened

serves 2
preparation: 30 minutes, plus chilling
cooking time: 12 minutes
per serving: 270 cals; 14g fat;
   10g carbohydrate

1 First make the Roquefort butter. Beat the cheese and butter together until evenly blended, then season with pepper to taste. Shape into a cylinder on a sheet of greaseproof paper and wrap tightly. Chill until firm.

2 Put the shallots, chicken mince, breadcrumbs, tarragon and egg yolk into a bowl. Mix well, then beat in about 5 tbsp cold water to bind the mixture. Season well with salt and pepper.

3 Lightly oil a foil-lined baking sheet. Divide the chicken mixture into 4 portions, shape into burgers and place on the foil. Using the back of a wet spoon, flatten each portion to a thickness of 2.5cm (1 inch). Cover and chill for 30 minutes.

4 Grill the chicken burgers under a medium-high heat for 5–6 minutes on each side or until cooked through, brushing occasionally with oil.

5 Serve topped with slices of Roquefort butter, a salad and chips or paprika-flavoured crisps.

Deep-fried Chicken Drumsticks

16 chicken drumsticks

1 onion, peeled and finely chopped

3 garlic cloves, peeled and crushed

2 tbsp white wine vinegar

6 tbsp chicken seasoning

salt and pepper

oil, to deep-fry

125g (4oz) plain flour

2 limes, cut into wedges, to serve (optional)

serves 8

preparation: 20 minutes, plus marinating

cooking time: 30 minutes

per serving: 400 cals; 28g fat;
   9g carbohydrate

1 Dip your fingers in salt to get a good grip, then pull the skin off the chicken drumsticks. Pierce each drumstick several times with a sharp knife.

2 Put the onion, garlic, vinegar, 4 tbsp chicken seasoning and 1 tbsp coarsely ground black pepper into a sealable plastic container (large enough to take the chicken). Mix well, then add the drumsticks.

3 Seal, then shake the container to coat the chicken in the seasoning. Put the covered container in the fridge and leave to marinate for at least 4 hours, preferably overnight.

4 Heat the oil in a deep-fryer or deep heavy pan to 170°C, or until a cube of bread dropped in browns in 10 seconds.

5 On a large plate, mix the remaining 2 tbsp chicken seasoning with the flour. Press the chicken drumsticks into the seasoned flour, turning them to coat evenly. Deep-fry the coated drumsticks, a few at a time, for 5 minutes, then drain on kitchen paper and transfer to a baking sheet.

6 Bake the drumsticks in the oven at 180°C (160°C fan oven) mark 4 for 12–15 minutes or until cooked through. Sprinkle the drumsticks with salt and serve them hot or cold with the lime wedges, if you like.

Grilled Spicy Chicken

4 skinless chicken breast fillets

1 tbsp coriander seeds, crushed

1 tsp ground cumin

2 tsp mild curry paste

1 garlic clove, peeled and crushed

450ml (¾ pint) yogurt

salt and pepper

3 tbsp chopped coriander

serves 4

preparation: 10 minutes, plus marinating

cooking time: 20 minutes

per serving: 250 cals; 9g fat;
   9g carbohydrate

1 Prick the chicken breasts all over with a fork and flatten them slightly.

2 Mix the crushed coriander seeds with the ground cumin, curry paste, garlic and yogurt in a large shallow dish. Season with salt and pepper, and stir in the chopped coriander.

3 Add the chicken and turn to coat with the spiced mixture. Cover and leave to marinate in the fridge for at least 30 minutes, preferably overnight.

4 Transfer the chicken to the grill rack and grill under a high heat, turning occasionally, for about 20 minutes or until cooked through. Serve straightaway, with rice and a mixed salad.

Grilled Chicken with Pesto Butter

4 chicken breast fillets, suprêmes or
    quarters, with skin
salt and pepper
75g (3oz) butter, softened
3 tbsp pesto
lemon juice, to sprinkle

serves 4
preparation: 10 minutes
cooking time: 20–30 minutes
per serving: 540 cals; 47g fat;
    trace carbohydrate

1 Make 3–4 deep cuts on each side of the chicken breasts. If using portions, make several cuts on the skin side. Season well with salt and pepper.
2 Put the butter into a bowl and gradually work in the pesto. Spread half of the pesto butter over the chicken skin and sprinkle with a little lemon juice.
3 Lay the chicken breasts on the grill rack and grill under a medium-high heat for about 10 minutes. Turn the portions over, spread with the remaining pesto butter and sprinkle with a little more lemon juice. Grill for about 10 minutes until cooked through. (Some portions may take longer.)
4 Serve the grilled chicken with any accumulated pan juices poured over.

Coq au Vin

1 bottle full-bodied white wine, such as
    Burgundy or Chardonnay
4 tbsp brandy
2 bouquet garni (bay leaves, parsley and
    thyme sprigs)
1 garlic clove, peeled and bruised
flour, to coat
salt and pepper
1.4kg (3lb) organic or free-range chicken,
    jointed, or 2 boneless breasts, halved,
    plus 2 drumsticks and 2 thighs
125g (4oz) butter
125g (4oz) rindless unsmoked bacon, cut
    into strips
225g (8oz) baby onions
225g (8oz) brown-cap mushrooms, halved,
    or quartered if large

BEURRE MANIÉ
25g (1oz) butter mixed with 25g (1oz) plain
    flour

serves 4–6
preparation: 45 minutes
cooking time: 45 minutes
per serving: 760–510 cals; 52–34g fat;
    13–8g carbohydrate

1 Pour the wine and brandy into a saucepan and add 1 bouquet garni and the garlic. Bring to the boil and simmer until reduced by half. Allow to cool.
2 Season the flour with salt and pepper and use to lightly coat the chicken joints. Melt half of the butter in a large frying pan. When foaming, add the chicken joints and brown all over (in batches if necessary); transfer to a flameproof casserole. Add the bacon to the frying pan and fry until golden. Remove with a slotted spoon and add to the chicken.
3 Strain the cooled reduced wine mixture over the chicken and add the other bouquet garni. Bring to the boil, cover and cook in the oven at 180°C (160°C fan oven) mark 4 for 30 minutes.
4 Meanwhile, peel the baby onions, but leave the root ends intact. Melt the remaining butter in a frying pan and fry the onions until tender and lightly browned. Add the mushrooms and fry until softened.
5 Add the mushrooms and onions to the casserole, cover and cook for a further 10 minutes or until the chicken is tender. Lift out the chicken and vegetables with a slotted spoon and put into a warmed serving dish; cover and keep warm.
6 Bring the cooking liquid in the casserole to the boil. Whisk in the beurre manié, a piece at a time, until the sauce is shiny and syrupy. Check the seasoning.
7 Pour the sauce over the chicken. Serve with buttered noodles or rice.

variation: *Use a bottle of full-bodied red, rather than white wine.*

Creamy Mustard and Tarragon Chicken

3 tbsp oil
1 onion, peeled and chopped
1 garlic clove, peeled and crushed
2 leeks, trimmed and sliced
4 carrots, peeled and roughly diced
4 boneless, skinless chicken thighs
4 chicken drumsticks, skin removed
1 tbsp plain flour
300ml (½ pint) cider
300ml (½ pint) chicken stock
4 tbsp Dijon mustard
salt and pepper
200ml carton crème fraîche
4 tbsp chopped tarragon

serves 4
preparation: 20 minutes
cooking time: 40 minutes
per serving: 540 cals; 36g fat;
    18g carbohydrate

1 Heat 1 tbsp oil in a large flameproof casserole or pan. Add the onion and cook over a medium heat for 4–5 minutes. Add the garlic and cook for 1 minute.
2 Add the leeks and carrots, cover and cook for about 5 minutes until the vegetables soften slightly.
3 Meanwhile, heat the remaining oil in a large non-stick frying pan and brown the chicken pieces all over in batches. Set aside.
4 Sprinkle the flour over the vegetables, stir and cook for 1 minute. Stir in the cider, stock and mustard, and season well with salt and pepper. Add the browned chicken pieces, then cover and bring to the boil. Reduce the heat and simmer for 20–25 minutes or until the chicken is tender.
5 Stir in the crème fraîche and tarragon and heat through for a couple of minutes.

note: *Skinned chicken breasts or even skinned rabbit portions can be used in place of the chicken thighs and drumsticks.*

Chicken Casserole

1 tbsp olive oil
1kg (2¼lb) chicken pieces, such as thighs
    and drumsticks
salt and pepper
1 onion, peeled and finely sliced
2 garlic cloves, peeled and crushed
2 celery sticks, thickly sliced
2 carrots, peeled and cut into 2cm (¾ inch)
    chunks
2 leeks, trimmed and cut into 2cm (¾ inch)
    chunks
600g (1¼lb) potatoes, peeled and cut into
    large chunks
1 tbsp plain flour
600ml (1 pint) hot chicken stock
2 rosemary sprigs
½ lemon

serves 4
preparation: 25 minutes
cooking time: 45–50 minutes
per serving: 380 cals; 14g fat;
    31g carbohydrate

1 Heat the olive oil in a large flameproof casserole. Season the chicken pieces with salt and pepper and add to the casserole. Cook over a medium heat for 10 minutes until browned all over, stirring occasionally. Remove with a slotted spoon and set aside. Drain off all but 1 tbsp of the fat from the casserole.
2 Add the onion, garlic, celery, carrots, leeks and potatoes to the casserole and cook, stirring, for 5–10 minutes. Stir in the flour and cook for 2 minutes.
3 Pour in the stock, return the chicken to the casserole and season well. Add the rosemary sprigs, squeeze over the juice from the lemon and add the spent lemon half to the casserole. Cover and bring to a simmer.
4 Cook in the oven at 180°C (160°C fan oven) mark 4 for 25–30 minutes until the chicken is cooked through and the sauce is thickened.

variation

Spanish chicken: *Add 1 tbsp tomato purée and 3 tbsp harissa paste with the flour. Add a 400g can chopped tomatoes after the stock. Once cooked, stir in 2 tbsp chopped parsley.*

Spicy Caribbean Chicken

1kg (2¼lb) skinless chicken thighs and
  drumsticks
1 onion, peeled and sliced
1 garlic clove, peeled and sliced
2 tbsp chicken seasoning
2 tbsp ground coriander
2 tbsp ground cumin
1 tbsp paprika
1 hot red chilli, deseeded and chopped
juice of ½ lemon
2 tbsp soy sauce
8 thyme sprigs, plus extra to garnish
2 tbsp sunflower oil
2 tbsp light muscovado sugar
500g (1lb 2oz) potatoes, peeled and cut into
  5cm (2 inch) pieces
600ml (1 pint) chicken stock

serves 5
preparation: 20 minutes, plus marinating
cooking time: 50 minutes
per serving: 400 cals; 14g fat;
  31g carbohydrate

1 Pierce each chicken piece several times with a skewer, then put into a shallow, sealable plastic container. Sprinkle over the onion, garlic, chicken seasoning, coriander, cumin, paprika, chilli, lemon juice, soy sauce and thyme. Stir well to combine, then seal and leave to marinate in the fridge for at least 30 minutes, preferably overnight.

2 Heat the oil and sugar in a large heavy-based flameproof casserole over a medium heat until the sugar dissolves and turns a dark golden brown. (Be careful not to overcook or the mixture will blacken and taste burnt.)

3 Immediately add the chicken pieces, reserving the marinade and onion slices. Cook over a medium heat for 5 minutes, turning as necessary.

4 Add the potatoes, onion and marinade and cook over a low heat for 10 minutes, turning occasionally.

5 Pour in the stock, bring to a simmer, then cover and cook for 25 minutes. Remove the lid and cook for a further 10 minutes until the chicken and potatoes are tender and the liquid has reduced slightly. Garnish with thyme sprigs and serve.

variation: *Replace the potatoes with 350g (12oz) American easy-cook rice and 2 x 300g cans black-eyed beans, drained. Add the rice to the casserole at stage 5, before you add the stock. Stir to combine, then add the stock with 300ml (½ pint) water. Simmer, covered, for 20 minutes or until the rice is tender and most of the liquid has been absorbed, then add the black-eyed beans. Cook for a further 5 minutes until the beans are warmed through and all the liquid has been absorbed.*

Chicken Tikka Masala

2 tbsp oil
1 onion, peeled and finely sliced
2 garlic cloves, peeled and crushed
6 skinless chicken thigh fillets, cut into strips
2 tbsp tikka masala curry paste
200g can chopped tomatoes
450ml (¾ pint) hot vegetable stock
225g (8oz) baby leaf spinach

serves 4
preparation: 15 minutes
cooking time: 25 minutes
per serving: 270 cals; 14g fat;
  10g carbohydrate

1 Heat the oil in a large pan, add the onion and fry over a medium heat for 5–7 minutes until golden. Add the garlic and chicken and stir-fry for about 5 minutes until golden.

2 Stir in the tikka masala curry paste, then add the chopped tomatoes and stock. Bring to the boil, then cover and simmer on a low heat for 15 minutes or until the chicken is cooked through.

3 Add the spinach to the curry, stir and cook until the leaves have just wilted. Serve with plain boiled rice, mango chutney and poppadoms.

Thai Red Chicken Curry

4 chicken breast fillets, about 600g (1¼lb)

1 tbsp oil

3 tbsp Thai red curry paste

400ml can coconut milk

300ml (½ pint) hot chicken or vegetable
   stock

juice of 1 lime

200g pack mixed baby corn and mangetout

2 tbsp chopped coriander

serves 4

preparation: 10 minutes

cooking time: 10 minutes

per serving: 410 cals; 28g fat;
   5g carbohydrate

1 Cut the chicken fillets crossways into 1cm (½ inch) thick slices. Heat the oil in a wok or large sauté pan. Add the red curry paste and cook, stirring, for about 2 minutes.

2 Add the chicken and stir-fry over a medium-high heat until evenly browned.

3 Add the coconut milk, stock, lime juice and baby corn. Bring to the boil, then add the mangetout. Reduce the heat and simmer for 4–5 minutes until the chicken is cooked. Scatter the coriander over the curry and serve.

Normandy Chicken

50g (2oz) butter

1.4kg (3lb) organic or free-range chicken,
   jointed, or 2 boneless breasts, halved,
   plus 2 drumsticks and 2 thighs

6 shallots, peeled and halved

2 celery sticks, thickly sliced

250ml (8fl oz) dry cider

150ml (¼ pint) chicken stock

salt and pepper

2 small red apples, cored and sliced
   into wedges

2 tbsp plain flour

5 tbsp crème fraîche

flat-leafed parsley, to garnish

serves 4

preparation: 15 minutes

cooking time: 40–50 minutes

per serving: 350 cals; 23g fat;
   18g carbohydrate

1 Heat 25g (1oz) butter in a large frying pan over a low heat. Add half the chicken joints, skin-side down, increase the heat to high and brown evenly on all sides. Remove and set aside, while you brown the remaining pieces.

2 Melt half the remaining butter in a large flameproof casserole over a low heat. Add the shallots and celery and cook over a low heat for 5 minutes. Put the chicken joints on top of the vegetables, placing the breasts on top of the legs.

3 Pour the cider and stock over the chicken, season with salt and pepper and bring to the boil. Cover and simmer for 20 minutes or until the juices run clear when the thickest piece of chicken is pierced with a sharp knife.

4 Meanwhile, heat the remaining butter in a clean frying pan until it is foaming and beginning to turn slightly brown. Add the apple wedges and fry until lightly coloured; keep warm on a low heat.

5 Using a slotted spoon, transfer the chicken joints and vegetables to the frying pan with the apple. Cover the pan and keep warm.

6 Mix the flour with the crème fraîche to form a smooth paste and whisk this into the bubbling liquid in the casserole. Bring to the boil and simmer for 3–4 minutes until thickened and smooth. Spoon the sauce over the chicken and serve garnished with parsley.

variation: *For a flavour boost, add a handful of tarragon leaves or 2 tbsp Dijon mustard to the crème fraîche at stage 6.*

Chicken and Mushroom Pies

350g (12oz) boneless, skinless chicken thighs
2 tbsp olive oil
1 leek, about 200g (7oz), trimmed and finely
    sliced
2–3 garlic cloves, peeled and crushed
200g (7oz) chestnut mushrooms, sliced
142ml carton double cream
2 tbsp chopped thyme
salt and pepper
500g pack puff pastry
plain flour, to dust
1 medium egg, beaten

serves 4
preparation: 20 minutes, plus chilling
cooking time: about 1 hour
per serving: 830 cals; 59g fat;
    49g carbohydrate

1 Cut the chicken into 2.5cm (1 inch) cubes. Heat the olive oil in a pan, add the leek and fry over a medium heat for 5 minutes. Add the garlic and cook for 1 minute.

2 Add the chicken and cook for 8–10 minutes. Add the mushrooms and cook for another 5 minutes or until all the juices have evaporated.

3 Pour the cream into the pan, bring to the boil and let bubble for 5 minutes to reduce and thicken. Add the thyme and season well with salt and pepper. Tip the mixture into a bowl and leave to cool.

4 Roll out the pastry on a floured surface to a 33cm (13 inch) square, then cut into 4 squares.

5 Brush the edges of one pastry square with water, then spoon a quarter of the chicken mixture into the middle. Bring the corners of the pastry up over the filling to meet in the middle and make a parcel. Crimp the edges to seal the parcel, leaving a small hole in the middle. Repeat to make the other 3 pies.

6 Brush the pies with beaten egg and lift on to a baking sheet. Leave to rest in the fridge for 20 minutes before cooking.

7 Bake the pies at 200°C (180°C fan oven) mark 6 for 30–40 minutes.

Chicken Enchiladas

450g (1lb) skinless chicken breast fillets, cut
    into strips
1 tsp dried oregano
1 tsp cumin seeds
salt and pepper
5 tbsp olive oil, plus extra to oil
2 onions, peeled and finely chopped
125g (4oz) celery, cut into strips
2 garlic cloves, peeled and crushed
50g (2oz) sun-dried tomatoes in oil, drained
    and roughly chopped
225g (8oz) brown-cap mushrooms, chopped
250g (9oz) Cheddar cheese, grated
2 tbsp chopped coriander
2 tbsp lemon juice
6–8 flour tortillas
salsa verde (page 28), to serve

serves 4–6
preparation: 30 minutes
cooking time: 50 minutes
per serving: 820–550 cals; 48–32g fat;
    50–34g carbohydrate

1 Put the chicken strips into a bowl and add the oregano, cumin seeds and salt and pepper. Toss to coat the chicken.

2 Heat half the olive oil in a large frying pan. Add the onions, celery and garlic and cook gently for 5–7 minutes. Add the sun-dried tomatoes and mushrooms, and cook for a further 2–3 minutes. Remove from the pan and set aside.

3 Add the remaining oil to the pan and stir-fry the chicken in batches for 2–3 minutes. Add the chicken to the mushroom mixture, with two thirds of the cheese, the chopped coriander and lemon juice. Mix well and season with salt and pepper to taste.

4 Divide the chicken mixture between the tortillas and roll up to enclose the filling. Put, seam-side down, in an oiled baking dish, then sprinkle with the remaining cheese.

5 Bake in the oven at 180°C (160°C fan oven) mark 4 for 25–30 minutes or until golden and bubbling. Spoon the salsa verde over the enchiladas to serve.

Poussin and Vegetable Casserole

3 poussins, about 450g (1lb) each

75g (3oz) butter

2 shallots, peeled and finely chopped

1 small garlic clove, peeled and chopped

grated zest and juice of ½ lemon

salt and pepper

450ml (¾ pint) chicken stock

10–12 bulbous spring onions, trimmed

2 x 170g packs mixed baby carrots and
   French beans

100g (3½oz) asparagus tips

150g (5oz) baby button mushrooms

2 tbsp plain flour

3 tbsp crème fraîche

1 tbsp chopped tarragon

serves 6

preparation: 30 minutes

cooking time: 1 hour

per serving: 390 cals; 28g fat;
   9g carbohydrate

1 Put the poussins on a board with the backbone uppermost. Using poultry shears, cut the carcass on either side of the backbone, then remove the backbone and set aside. Cut the birds completely in half through the breastbone.

2 Heat 25g (1oz) of the butter in a large flameproof casserole and brown the poussin halves, skin-side down, in batches, for about 3 minutes. Turn and brown lightly on the other side. Remove and set aside. Brown the backbones in the casserole; set aside.

3 Lower heat, add 15g (½oz) butter to the casserole and cook the shallots and garlic for 5 minutes or until soft. Add the poussins, skin-side up, the backbones, lemon zest and seasoning. Pour in the stock and bring to the boil, then cover and simmer for 5 minutes.

4 Transfer to the oven at 180°C (160°C fan oven) mark 4 and cook for 25–30 minutes or until the poussins are ready; keep warm. Discard the bones.

5 Meanwhile, add the spring onions to a pan of boiling water and bubble for 2 minutes, then add the carrots and bubble for a further 2 minutes. Finally, add the beans and asparagus and bubble for 1 minute. Drain the vegetables, then refresh in icy cold water.

6 Heat 15g (½oz) butter in a small frying pan, add the mushrooms and fry quickly. Take off the heat, add the remaining butter, then stir in the flour. Strain the stock from the poussins and slowly blend in, then bring the sauce to the boil and simmer for 2 minutes.

7 Stir in the crème fraîche, lemon juice and tarragon and adjust the seasoning. Drain the vegetables, add to the sauce and bring to the boil, then pour over the poussins. Bring to the boil, cover and return to the oven for 5–10 minutes to warm through.

Moroccan Spiced Poussins

6 poussins, about 450g (1lb) each
3 tbsp cumin seeds
1½ tbsp coriander seeds
1 tbsp black peppercorns
1½ tbsp sweet paprika
grated zest and juice of 2 lemons
6 tbsp olive oil
2–3 onions, about 350g (12oz) in total, peeled
    and finely sliced
300ml (½ pint) hot chicken or vegetable
    stock
salt and pepper
coriander sprigs, to garnish

serves 6
preparation: 25 minutes, plus marinating
cooking time: about 1¼ hours
per serving: 500 cals; 38g fat;
    5g carbohydrate

1 Find a large, shallow, sealable plastic container that will hold the poussins in a single layer. Put the cumin seeds, coriander seeds and peppercorns into a spice grinder or coffee grinder and whiz to a powder. Tip into the container and add the paprika, lemon zest and juice, and olive oil. Mix well.

2 Add the poussins and onions and mix everything together. Cover and leave to marinate in the fridge for at least 4 hours, preferably overnight.

3 Transfer the poussins, onions and marinade to a roasting tin and add the hot stock. Season with salt and pepper. Cover with foil and bake at 200°C (180°C fan oven) mark 6 for 50 minutes.

4 Remove the foil and roast for a further 20 minutes or until the poussins are golden and the juices run clear when the thighs are pierced.

5 Garnish with coriander and serve with saffron couscous (page 311) and courgettes.

Pan-fried Guinea Fowl with Red Wine Sauce

25g (1oz) butter
1 tbsp oil
6 guinea fowl suprêmes or chicken
    suprêmes, with skin, each about 150g
    (5oz)
175g (6oz) rindless streaky bacon, chopped
225g (8oz) button mushrooms
225g (8oz) baby onions, peeled
6 tbsp brandy
350ml (12fl oz) red wine, such as Cabernet
    Sauvignon
750ml (1¼ pints) chicken stock
2 tbsp redcurrant jelly
salt and pepper

serves 6
preparation: 10 minutes
cooking time: 25–30 minutes
per serving: 410 cals; 31g fat;
    7g carbohydrate

1 Heat the butter and oil in a heavy-based frying pan. Add the guinea fowl, skin-side down, and cook over a high heat for 3 minutes until deep golden brown. Turn and seal the other side for 2–3 minutes. Transfer the guinea fowl to an ovenproof dish and finish cooking in the oven at 150°C (130°C fan oven) mark 2, while you make the sauce.

2 Add the bacon, mushrooms and baby onions to the frying pan. Cook for 4–5 minutes or until golden; remove the bacon and mushrooms and set aside.

3 Add the brandy, red wine, stock and redcurrant jelly to the pan. Bring to the boil and leave to bubble rapidly for about 15 minutes or until the sauce is well reduced and syrupy.

4 Return the guinea fowl to the pan with the bacon and mushrooms. Bring to a simmer and check the seasoning. Serve at once, with a root vegetable purée or creamy mashed potatoes and a green vegetable.

Roast Guinea Fowl

1 guinea fowl
3 bay leaves
5 thyme sprigs
1 tbsp black peppercorns, lightly crushed
2 unwaxed lemons, one quartered
25g (1oz) butter
150ml (¼ pint) hot chicken stock
2 tbsp redcurrant jelly
100ml (3½fl oz) dry white wine
salt and pepper

serves 4
preparation: 20 minutes, plus marinating
cooking time: 1 hour 10 minutes
per serving: 390 cals; 25g fat;
   5g carbohydrate

1 Put the guinea fowl into a bowl and add the bay leaves, thyme and peppercorns. Add the grated zest and juice from the whole lemon. Cover and leave to marinate in a cool place for 1 hour.

2 Put the bird into a roasting tin, breast-side down, and put the lemon quarters and the butter into the cavity. Pour the stock over the bird and roast at 200°C (180°C fan oven) mark 6 for 50 minutes.

3 Turn the guinea fowl on to the backbone, and roast for a further 20 minutes or until the juices run clear when a thigh is pierced with a skewer.

4 Put the guinea fowl on a board, cover with foil and leave to rest while you make the gravy.

5 Put the roasting tin on the hob over a medium-high heat and add the redcurrant jelly, wine and 3 tbsp water, scraping up the sediment from the bottom. Simmer for 3–5 minutes, then season well.

6 Carve the guinea fowl and serve with the gravy and a selection of vegetables, including roast potatoes.

Roast Goose with Wild Rice and Cranberry Stuffing

5kg (11lb) goose, with giblets
salt and pepper
25g (1oz) butter, plus extra to grease
3 red-skinned apples
4 sage sprigs, plus extra to garnish
2 tbsp golden caster sugar

GRAVY
15g (½oz) butter
1 onion, peeled and cut into quarters
1 celery stick, sliced
1 tsp black peppercorns
2 bay leaves
bouquet garni (parsley and thyme sprigs)
2 tbsp plain flour
150ml (¼ pint) red wine
2 tbsp redcurrant jelly

STUFFING
125g (4oz) wild rice
225g (8oz) rindless streaky bacon, cut into
    short strips
2 red onions, about 225g (8oz), peeled and
    finely chopped
75g (3oz) dried cranberries
1 medium egg, beaten

serves 6
preparation: 45 minutes, plus cooling
cooking time: about 5 hours, plus resting
per serving: 730 cals; 43g fat;
    41g carbohydrate

1 To make stock for the gravy, put the giblets, except the liver, into a large pan with the butter. Add the onion and celery and cook, stirring occasionally, until golden. Add 1.7 litres (3 pints) cold water and bring slowly to the boil, skimming the surface. Add the peppercorns and herbs. Simmer, partly covered, for 1–2 hours or until well flavoured. Strain the stock and set aside; there should be about 600ml (1 pint).

2 To make the stuffing, put the wild rice into a pan, add 900ml (1½ pints) cold water and ¼ tsp salt, and bring to the boil. Simmer, partially covered, for 45 minutes or until the rice is cooked. Drain and cool.

3 Dry-fry the bacon in a large frying pan until lightly browned. Remove with a slotted spoon and put into a bowl. (If you want to use the goose liver, cook it in the same pan for 2–3 minutes, cool, chop finely, then add

to the bacon.) Add the onions to the frying pan and cook gently until softened. Add the cranberries and cook for 1–2 minutes, then add the mixture to the bacon and leave to cool. Add the cooked rice and egg, season with salt and pepper, then stir thoroughly to combine.

4 To make the goose easier to carve, remove the wishbone from the neck by lifting the flap and cutting around the bone with a small knife, then take out. Using your fingers, ease the skin away from the flesh to make room for the stuffing, Put the goose on a tray in the sink and pour a generous amount of just-boiled water over it. Pat dry with kitchen paper.

5 Pack the neck of the goose with half of the stuffing and secure the opening with skewers, or using a trussing needle threaded with fine string. Wrap the remaining stuffing in a buttered sheet of foil. Season the goose cavity, then put in one whole apple and the sage sprigs.

6 Stand the goose on a rack placed in a roasting tin and season generously with salt and pepper. Roast at 230°C (210°C fan oven) mark 8 for 30 minutes, basting occasionally with the fat that is rendered, then remove and reserve the excess fat.

7 Lower the oven setting to 190°C (170°C fan oven) mark 5 and cook for a further 2½ hours, removing the excess fat every 20 minutes. About 30 minutes before the end of the cooking time, put the parcel of stuffing into the oven. To test whether the goose is cooked, pierce the thigh with a skewer – if it's cooked, the juices will run clear.

8 Remove the goose from the oven and put on a board. Cover with foil and leave to rest in a warm place for at least 20 minutes. Meanwhile, cut the other 2 apples into thick wedges, removing the cores. Heat the butter in a heavy-based frying pan until it is no longer foaming. Add the apple wedges with the sugar and stir-fry over a high heat for 4–5 minutes until caramelised; set aside.

9 To make the gravy, drain off all but 3 tbsp fat from the roasting tin. Add the flour and stir to make a smooth paste. Add the wine and boil for 5 minutes, then stir in the stock and redcurrant jelly. Bring to the boil and simmer for 5 minutes. Strain before serving.

10 Carve the goose and serve garnished with sage, and accompanied by the stuffing and apples.

note: *Keep the excess goose fat in the fridge – it's perfect for roasting potatoes.*

Roast Turkey Breast with Sausage, Apple and Cranberry Stuffing

1.4kg (3lb) turkey breast joint

salt and pepper

3 tbsp olive oil

1–2 tsp chicken seasoning

1 red eating apple, cored and sliced into
    rounds

4–5 bay leaf sprigs

STUFFING

50g (2oz) butter

1 onion, peeled and chopped

1 garlic clove, peeled and crushed

75g (3oz) dried cranberries

2 tbsp chopped flat-leafed parsley

4 Lincolnshire sausages, about 275g (10oz),
    skinned and broken up

1 red eating apple, peeled, cored and
    chopped

GRAVY

1 tbsp plain flour

2 tbsp cranberry jelly

300ml (½ pint) dry cider

600ml (1 pint) hot chicken stock

serves 8
preparation: 20 minutes, plus soaking
cooking time: about 1¾ hours, plus resting
per serving: 450 cals; 21g fat;
    19g carbohydrate

1 Put three or four wooden skewers in a bowl of water to soak for 30 minutes.

2 Next, make the stuffing. Melt the butter in a pan, add the onion and sauté for 5 minutes or until softened. Add the garlic and cook for 1 minute. Tip into a bowl and allow to cool slightly, then add the cranberries, parsley, sausage meat and apple. Season well with salt and pepper and mix to combine.

3 Put the turkey joint on a board, skin-side down. Cut down the middle along the length of the joint, to just over three-quarters of the way through. Season well. Spoon the stuffing inside, then push back together. Secure with string and skewers.

4 Weigh the joint and calculate the cooking time, allowing 20 minutes per 450g (1lb), plus 20 minutes. Put the joint into a roasting tin, skin-side up, drizzle with the olive oil and sprinkle with chicken seasoning. Cover with foil and roast at 200°C (180°C fan oven) mark 6.

5 About 30 minutes before the end of the cooking time, remove the foil and push the apple slices and bay leaf sprigs under the string. Roast, uncovered, for the final 30 minutes or until cooked through – the juices should run clear when the meat is pierced in the thickest part with a skewer.

6 Lift the meat on to a warmed plate, cover with foil and leave to rest in a warm place while you prepare the gravy. Drain off all but 1 tbsp fat from the roasting tin. Sprinkle in the flour, stir and put the roasting tin on the hob over a medium heat. Cook for 1 minute, scraping up the sediment from the base of the tin. Stir in the cranberry jelly and cider, bring to the boil and bubble until the liquid has reduced by half. Add the hot stock and cook for about 5 minutes until slightly thickened.

7 Remove the skewers from the turkey, then carve the meat and stuffing into slices. Serve with the gravy, green beans and sweet potatoes.

Roast Turkey with Parsley, Sage and Thyme

6.3kg (14lb) turkey

salt and pepper

3 tbsp chicken seasoning

2 small red onions, peeled and halved

1 garlic clove, peeled

1 lemon, halved

6 thyme sprigs

4 sage sprigs

4 flat-leafed parsley sprigs

STUFFING

2 tbsp olive oil

1 large onion, peeled and finely
  chopped

2 garlic cloves, peeled and crushed

75g (3oz) fresh white breadcrumbs

50g (2oz) pistachio nuts, chopped

finely grated zest of 1 lemon

2 tbsp chopped flat-leafed parsley

2 tbsp chopped sage

1 medium egg, lightly beaten

juice of ½ lemon

TO COOK THE TURKEY

250g pack butter

60cm (24 inch) square of muslin

12 sage leaves

10 thyme sprigs

2 lemons, cut into wedges

4 small red onions, peeled and cut into
  wedges

4 garlic cloves

TO SERVE

rich wine gravy (page 21)

bread sauce (page 25)

rosemary bacon rolls and sausages
  (see right)

serves 16

preparation: 40 minutes, plus cooling

cooking time: about 3¾ hours, plus resting

per serving: 300 cals; 15g fat;
  4g carbohydrate

1 First make the stuffing. Heat the olive oil in a pan and fry the onion and garlic gently for 5 minutes to soften without browning. Remove from the heat and set aside to cool. Put the breadcrumbs, pistachios, lemon zest, parsley, sage and egg into a bowl, then sprinkle with the lemon juice. Add the onion mixture, then season with salt and pepper. Stir well to bind the ingredients together. Let the stuffing cool completely.

2 Stand the turkey upright on a board with the parson's nose facing upwards. Sprinkle 2 tsp sea salt, 1 tsp coarsely ground black pepper and 1 tbsp chicken seasoning into the cavity, then add the onions, garlic, lemon, thyme, sage and parsley.

3 Sit the turkey with the parson's nose facing away from you. Lift up the loose skin at the neck end with one hand and, using the other hand, insert the cold stuffing. Turn the turkey on to its breast, lift the neck flap up and over the stuffing to cover it, and rest the wing tips across it to secure.

4 Use a trussing needle and and a 2 metre (6½ feet) length of string to oversew the neck flap to the turkey, enclosing the stuffing. Push the needle into one wing and through to the other, pulling it tight. Tuck in the parson's nose and secure it with a skewer. Bring the string up and under the leg, and wrap it tightly around the loop of the skewer. Tie the legs together and secure them with a double knot.

5 When ready to cook, melt the butter in a pan and pour into a roasting tin. Cool slightly then immerse the muslin in the butter, stretching it out, with the edges overhanging the tin. Put the turkey in the middle, sprinkle it with the remaining chicken seasoning, then season with pepper. Scatter the sage and thyme across the turkey and arrange the lemons, onions and garlic around it. Wrap the turkey in the muslin and turn it over so it's sitting breast-side down in the tin.

6 Roast the turkey in the oven at 200°C (180°C fan oven) mark 6 for 3 hours 40 minutes, or allowing 15 minutes for each 450g (1lb), including the weight of the stuffing. After 1 hour 50 minutes, turn the turkey over so it's breast-side up and continue roasting for the remaining 1 hour 50 minutes, or until the juices run clear when a knife is inserted into the thickest part of the thigh. Remove the turkey from the tin, unwrap and put it on a serving dish. Cover with foil and rest for 20 minutes before carving. Reserve the pan juices for the gravy.

7 Carve the turkey and stuffing and serve with the accompaniments, gravy and vegetables.

note: *Preparing and stuffing a turkey the night before will enhance the flavour and save time on the day.*

rosemary bacon rolls and sausages: *Cut about 10 maple-smoked rindless bacon rashers in half. Use the back of a knife to stretch each rasher slightly, then roll up into bacon rolls. Put into a small roasting tin with 20 cocktail sausages and scatter with 4 rosemary sprigs. Cover and chill overnight. Roast at 200°C (180°C fan oven) mark 6 for 30 minutes until cooked through and browned.*

Turkey, Pepper and Haricot Bean Casserole

350g (12oz) dried haricot beans, soaked in
   cold water overnight

2 large onions, peeled

2 small carrots, peeled and cut into chunks

bouquet garni (bay leaf, parsley and thyme)

1 tbsp olive oil

2 red chillies, deseeded and chopped

2 garlic cloves, peeled and crushed

350g (12oz) lean turkey meat, cut into
   bite-sized pieces

1 large red pepper, cored, deseeded and
   finely diced

1 large orange pepper, cored, deseeded
   and finely diced

2 courgettes, trimmed and finely diced

salt and pepper

400g can chopped tomatoes

1 tbsp sun-dried tomato paste

large handful of basil leaves

serves 6

preparation: 20 minutes, plus overnight
   soaking

cooking time: 1 hour 20 minutes

per serving: 310 cals; 5g fat;
   41g carbohydrate

1 Drain the soaked haricot beans, put them into a large flameproof casserole and cover with fresh water. Quarter one onion and add to the casserole with the carrots and bouquet garni. Bring to the boil, then cover, lower the heat and simmer for 45 minutes or until the beans are tender. Drain the haricot beans, reserving 150ml (¼ pint) of the cooking liquid; discard the flavouring vegetables. Set the beans aside.

2 Finely slice the other onion. Heat the olive oil in the clean casserole, add the onion and cook gently for 5 minutes. Add the chillies and garlic and cook for 1 minute until softened.

3 Add the turkey and stir-fry for 5 minutes, then add the peppers and courgettes. Season well. Cover the casserole and cook for 5 minutes until the vegetables are slightly softened.

4 Add the tomatoes and sun-dried tomato paste, cover and bring to the boil. Add the haricot beans and reserved cooking liquid. Stir and season well with salt and pepper, then cover and simmer for 15 minutes. Stir in the basil leaves just before serving.

Turkey Curry

2 tbsp oil

1 large onion, peeled and chopped

2 garlic cloves, peeled and finely chopped

1 tsp ground turmeric

½ tsp chilli powder

1½ tsp ground cumin

1½ tsp ground coriander

400g can chopped tomatoes

salt

600g (1¼lb) cooked turkey

1 tsp garam masala

150ml (¼ pint) thick yogurt

serves 4

preparation: 15 minutes

cooking time: 35 minutes

per serving: 330 cals; 12g fat;
   8g carbohydrate

1 Heat the oil in a heavy-based pan, add the onion and garlic and fry gently until softened and golden. Add the turmeric, chilli powder, cumin and coriander, and cook, stirring, for 1 minute.

2 Add the tomatoes and salt. Bring to the boil, cover and simmer for 20 minutes.

3 Remove any skin from the turkey, then cut into chunks. Add to the pan with the garam masala and 4 tbsp yogurt. Cover and cook gently for 10 minutes, then stir in the remaining yogurt. Serve with rice.

note: *This is an ideal recipe for using up the leftover Christmas turkey.*

variations

• *For a more intense flavour, fry 1 tsp black mustard seeds with the spices.*

• *Scatter over 2–3 tbsp chopped coriander to serve.*

Roast Duck with Orange

2 large oranges

1 oven-ready duckling, about 2.3kg (5lb),
    preferably with giblets

2 large thyme sprigs

4 tbsp oil

salt and pepper

2 shallots, peeled and chopped

1 tsp plain flour

600ml (1 pint) chicken stock

25g (1oz) golden caster sugar

2 tbsp red wine vinegar

100ml (3½fl oz) unsweetened fresh orange
    juice

100ml (3½fl oz) fruity German white wine

2 tbsp Grand Marnier or other orange liqueur
    (optional)

1 tbsp lemon juice

serves 4

preparation: 30 minutes

cooking time: 1¼–1½ hours, plus resting

per serving: 630 cals; 47g fat;
    17g carbohydrate

1 Pare the zest from the oranges with a zester. Add the zest of one orange to a pan of cold water, bring to the boil, drain and set aside. Segment both oranges, discarding all pith.

2 Remove the giblets from the duckling, if applicable. Put the thyme and unblanched orange zest into the cavity. Rub the skin with 2 tbsp oil and sprinkle with salt and pepper.

3 Put the duckling, breast-side up, on a rack over a roasting tin. Roast at 200°C (180°C fan oven) mark 6 for 1¼–1½ hours until just cooked, basting regularly and turning the duckling breast-side down after 30 minutes. About 10 minutes before the end of the cooking time, turn breast-side up.

4 Meanwhile, heat the remaining oil in a heavy-based pan. Add the chopped giblets if using and brown well. Add the shallots and fry until softened. Add the flour; cook, stirring, for 1 minute. Stir in the stock, bring to the boil and bubble until reduced by half; strain.

5 Put the sugar and vinegar into a heavy-based pan and dissolve over a low heat. Increase the heat and cook to a dark caramel. Carefully pour in the orange juice, stirring.

6 Lift the duckling on to a warmed platter, cover with foil and leave to rest in a warm place. Meanwhile, skim off all fat from the roasting tin, leaving about 2 tbsp sediment. Add the wine, stirring to deglaze, and bubble for 5 minutes until syrupy. Add the stock and caramel orange mixture, bubble until syrupy, then add the blanched orange zest and orange segments. Add the liqueur if using, and lemon juice.

7 Carve the duck and serve with the orange sauce and vegetables of your choice.

Duck Breast with Beetroot and Red Onion Relish

3 oranges

4 tbsp oil

450g (1lb) red onions, peeled and
    thinly sliced

4 duck breasts, about 175g (6oz) each

salt and pepper

300ml (½ pint) red wine

2.5cm (1 inch) piece fresh root ginger,
    peeled and grated

1½ tsp light muscovado sugar

200ml (7fl oz) port

175g (6oz) cooked beetroot, sliced

serves 4

preparation: 15 minutes

cooking time: 30 minutes, plus resting

per serving: 780 cals; 57g fat;
    26g carbohydrate

1 Grate the zest and squeeze the juice of 2 oranges; slice the other orange.

2 Heat the oil in a heavy-based frying pan, add the onions and cook gently, stirring frequently, for 15–20 minutes, until soft and caramelised.

3 Meanwhile, lightly score the duck fat with a sharp knife and rub a little salt into the cuts. Put the duck breasts, skin-side up, into a roasting tin and tuck the orange slices in between. Roast at 200°C (180°C fan oven) mark 6 for about 15 minutes.

4 Add the wine and orange juice to the onions. Bring to the boil and let bubble for about 5 minutes until the liquid is totally reduced. Add the grated ginger, orange zest, sugar and port, bring to the boil and bubble for 5 minutes or until syrupy. Add the beetroot and warm through. Season with salt and pepper to taste.

5 Let the duck rest in a warm place for 5 minutes. Serve with the roasted orange slices, and beetroot and red onion relish.

Glazed Duck with Rosemary and Garlic

4 duck breasts, about 175g (6oz) each
finely grated zest and juice of 1 lemon
1 garlic clove, peeled and crushed
salt and pepper
125g (4oz) shallots
225g (8oz) leeks (preferably baby ones),
    trimmed
225g (8oz) small carrots, peeled and halved
    lengthways
450g (1lb) new potatoes, scrubbed and
    halved
2 tbsp olive oil
2 tbsp chopped rosemary, plus extra sprigs
    to garnish
4 tsp thin honey

serves 4
preparation: 20 minutes, plus marinating
cooking time: 50 minutes–1 hour
per serving: 660 cals; 47g fat;
    29g carbohydrate

1 Score the fat of the duck breasts with a sharp knife. Put the grated lemon zest and juice, garlic, salt and pepper into a shallow dish. Add the duck breasts in a single layer, turn to coat in the mixture and leave to marinate in a cool place for 1 hour to allow the flavours to mingle.

2 Meanwhile, immerse the shallots in a pan of boiling water for 5 minutes, then drain and peel away the skins. Halve the shallots if large. If using regular leeks, cut into 7.5cm (3 inch) pieces.

3 Put the shallots, leeks, carrots and potatoes into a large roasting tin. Add the olive oil, toss to coat, then sprinkle with sea salt and chopped rosemary. Roast at 220°C (200°C fan oven) mark 7 for 30 minutes.

4 Lay the duck breasts on a roasting rack, smear the skin with the honey and season well with sea salt. Remove roasting tin from oven, turn the vegetables and drain off any oil. Lay the duck breasts on the rack over the vegetables and roast for 20–25 minutes until browned and tender, and the vegetables are tender and a little charred. Serve garnished with rosemary.

Spiced Duck with Port and Berry Sauce

6 duck breasts, about 225g (8oz) each
salt and pepper
¼ tsp ground allspice
½ tsp ground cinnamon

PORT AND BERRY SAUCE
4 tsp oil
175g (6oz) onion, peeled and roughly
    chopped
3 tbsp golden caster sugar
3 tbsp red wine vinegar
150ml (¼ pint) port
450ml (¾ pint) red wine
450ml (¾ pint) chicken stock
1 cinnamon stick
1 bay leaf
1 clove
175g (6oz) frozen mixed berries, such as
    redcurrants, blackcurrants, raspberries
    and cranberries, defrosted and drained

serves 6
preparation: 15 minutes
cooking time: 1 hour, plus resting
per serving: 800 cals; 61g fat;
    14g carbohydrate

1 Score the fat of the duck breasts using a sharp knife; set aside.

2 To make the sauce, heat the oil in a pan, add the onion and cook gently for 10 minutes or until soft. Add the sugar and cook over a high heat until golden. Add the vinegar and bubble until totally reduced. Add the port, bubble and reduce by one third, then add the red wine and reduce by half. Add the stock, cinnamon, bay leaf and clove. Bring to the boil and bubble for 25 minutes or until reduced by half. Strain and set aside.

3 When ready to cook the duck, heat a heavy-based frying pan until hot. Add the duck breasts, skin-side down, and cook for 5–7 minutes until the skin is well browned. Transfer the duck breasts to a roasting tin, turning them skin-side up. Season with salt, pepper, allspice and cinnamon.

4 Cook at 220°C (200°C fan oven) mark 7 allowing 10 minutes for rare; 15 minutes for medium rare; or 20 minutes for well done. Leave to rest in a warm place for 5 minutes.

5 Pour off the fat from the roasting tin, then add any meat juices to the sauce. Bring to the boil and add the berries. Check the seasoning.

6 Carve the duck breasts into slices and serve on a pool of the berry sauce.

Roast Quail in Red Peppers

4 quails

salt and pepper

4 tbsp olive oil

2 large red peppers, halved lengthways,
   cored and deseeded

4 slices Parma ham

125ml (4fl oz) chicken stock

2 tbsp balsamic vinegar

TO SERVE

soft herb polenta (page 311)

serves 4

preparation: 20 minutes

cooking time: 35–40 minutes

per serving (without polenta): 480 cals;
   35g fat; 3g carbohydrate

1 Season the quails inside and out with salt and pepper, rubbing well into the skin. Heat the olive oil in a heavy-based frying pan and quickly fry the quails over a high heat until browned on all sides; remove with a slotted spoon.

2 Fry the pepper halves in the oil remaining in the pan until slightly softened. Line each pepper cavity with a slice of Parma ham and sit a quail in each one. Put into a flameproof casserole and sprinkle with half of the stock and vinegar.

3 Bake at 200°C (180°C fan oven) mark 6, basting regularly, for 25–30 minutes or until the quails are cooked. Lift on to a warmed plate; keep warm.

4 Put the casserole over a high heat and add the remaining stock and vinegar, stirring to deglaze. Bubble until reduced and slightly syrupy. Pour over the quails and serve, with piping hot herb polenta.

Pigeon on Crisp Polenta with Tomato Salsa

4 wood pigeons, plucked and drawn

25g (1oz) butter

1 garlic clove, peeled and crushed

4 chicken livers, trimmed

pinch of powdered mace

salt and pepper

oil, to brush

TOMATO SALSA

4 large ripe tomatoes, skinned, deseeded
   and diced

2 garlic cloves, peeled and finely chopped

4 tbsp chopped mixed herbs, such as basil,
   oregano and parsley

5 tbsp olive oil

TO SERVE

fried herb polenta (page 311)

herb sprigs, to garnish

serves 4

preparation: 40 minutes

cooking time: 25 minutes

per serving: 980 cals; 62g fat;
   36g carbohydrate

1 Mix together the ingredients for the tomato salsa in a bowl and season with salt and pepper to taste.

2 Cut the legs from the pigeons and set aside. Using a sharp knife, cut down the breastbone on each side and ease off the pigeon breasts; cover and set aside.

3 Melt the butter in a frying pan, add the garlic and fry gently for 2 minutes until golden. Add the chicken livers and cook over a high heat for 5 minutes until browned on the outside, but still pink in the middle. Season with the mace, salt and pepper. Transfer to a bowl and set aside.

4 Lay the pigeon legs on the grill rack, brush with oil and grill under a medium-high heat for 2 minutes. Turn the legs over. Add the pigeon breasts to the rack, skin-side up, brush with oil and grill for 4 minutes. Turn the pigeon legs and breasts and cook for a further 2 minutes.

5 Meanwhile, warm the tomato salsa. Mash the chicken livers and spread on the hot fried polenta slices. Put on warmed plates and top with the pigeon. Garnish with herbs and serve with the tomato salsa.

Pot-roasted Pheasant with Red Cabbage

25g (1oz) butter

1 tbsp oil

2 oven-ready young pheasants, halved

2 onions, peeled and sliced

450g (1lb) red cabbage, cored and finely
    shredded

1 tsp cornflour

250ml (8fl oz) red wine

2 tbsp redcurrant jelly

1 tbsp balsamic vinegar

salt and pepper

4 rindless smoked streaky bacon rashers,
    halved

serves 4

preparation: 20 minutes

cooking time: 40 minutes

per serving: 570 cals; 31g fat;
    15g carbohydrate

1 Melt the butter with the oil in a large flameproof casserole. Add the pheasant halves and brown on all sides, then remove and set aside. Add the onions and cabbage to the casserole, and fry for 5 minutes, stirring frequently, until softened.

2 Blend the cornflour with a little water. Add to the casserole with the wine, redcurrant jelly, vinegar and seasoning. Bring to the boil, stirring.

3 Arrange the pheasant halves, skin-side up, on the cabbage. Lay the halved bacon rashers on top. Cover the casserole and cook at 200°C (180°C fan oven) mark 6 for 30 minutes or until tender (older pheasants would take an extra 10–20 minutes).

4 Serve the pot-roasted pheasant and red cabbage with the cooking juices spooned over.

variation: *Instead of the pheasants, use oven-ready pigeons; put an onion wedge inside each bird before browning to impart extra flavour.*

Pheasant with Smoked Bacon and Mushrooms

15g (½oz) dried porcini or mixed dried
    mushrooms, rinsed

2 garlic cloves, peeled and crushed

2 oven-ready young pheasants

25g (1oz) butter

10 juniper berries, lightly crushed

1 small onion, peeled and finely chopped

125g (4oz) rindless smoked bacon, diced

2 tsp plain flour

300ml (½ pint) red wine

150ml (¼ pint) chicken or pheasant stock

175g (6oz) chestnut mushrooms, halved

2 tbsp redcurrant jelly

salt and pepper

TO GARNISH

125g (4oz) ready-made puff pastry

1 tbsp finely chopped rosemary

beaten egg yolk, to glaze

serves 4

preparation: 35 minutes

cooking time: about 50 minutes

per serving: 780 cals; 42g fat;
    25g carbohydrate

1 Soak the dried mushrooms in 300ml (½ pint) warm water for 20 minutes; drain.

2 Meanwhile, for the garnish, roll out the puff pastry to a 5mm (¼ inch) thickness. Sprinkle with rosemary, then roll out to a 3mm (⅛ inch) thickness. Cut out small triangles and put on a dampened baking sheet. Brush with egg and bake at 220°C (200°C fan oven) mark 7 for about 8 minutes until puffed and golden; set aside.

3 Spread the garlic over the pheasants. Melt the butter in a frying pan and sear the pheasants on all sides. Drain and put into a large casserole dish; add the juniper berries.

4 Add the onion and bacon to the frying pan and fry gently for 10 minutes. Stir in the flour, then the wine and stock. Bring to the boil and pour over the pheasants. Cover and bake at 200°C (180°C fan oven) mark 6 for 25 minutes.

5 Tuck the fresh and dried mushrooms around the pheasants in the casserole. Return to the oven and cook, uncovered, for a further 20–25 minutes until the pheasants are tender.

6 Transfer the pheasants and mushrooms to a warmed platter, using a slotted spoon; keep warm. Add the redcurrant jelly to the cooking juices and heat until melted; check the seasoning. Garnish the pheasant with the pastries and serve with the sauce.

Pheasant Casserole with Cider and Apples

2 large oven-ready pheasants

salt and pepper

2 tbsp plain flour, plus extra to dust

4 crisp eating apples, such as Granny Smiths

1 tbsp lemon juice

50g (2oz) butter

4 rindless streaky bacon rashers, halved

2 onions, peeled and chopped

2 celery sticks, chopped

1 tbsp dried juniper berries, lightly crushed

2.5cm (1 inch) piece fresh root ginger, peeled
    and finely chopped

300ml (½ pint) pheasant or chicken stock

750–900ml (1¼–1½ pints) dry cider

150ml (¼ pint) double cream

serves 6–8

preparation: 50 minutes

cooking time: 1¾ hours

per serving: 670–500 cals; 40–31g fat;
    20–15g carbohydrate

1 Cut each pheasant into 4 portions, season with salt and pepper, and dust with flour. Quarter, core and cut the apples into wedges, then toss in the lemon juice.

2 Melt the butter in a large flameproof casserole and brown the pheasant portions, in batches, over a high heat until deep golden brown on all sides. Remove with a slotted spoon and set aside.

3 Add the bacon to the casserole and fry for 2–3 minutes until golden. Add the onions, celery, apples, juniper and ginger, and cook for 8–10 minutes. Stir in the flour and cook, stirring, for 2 minutes, then add the stock and cider and bring to the boil, stirring.

4 Return the pheasant to the casserole and bring to a simmer. Cover and cook at 170°C (150°C fan oven) mark 3 for 45 minutes to 1 hour, or until the pheasant is tender (timing depends on age).

5 Lift out the pheasant and put into a warmed dish; keep warm. Strain the sauce through a sieve and return to the casserole. Stir in the cream, bring to the boil and let bubble for 10 minutes or until syrupy. Return the pheasant to the sauce and check the seasoning before serving.

Rabbit Casserole with Red Wine and Sherry

1.4kg (3lb) rabbit joints

4 garlic cloves, peeled and crushed

2 thyme sprigs

2 bay leaves

600ml (1 pint) red wine

salt and pepper

2 tbsp plain flour, plus extra to dust

4 tbsp olive oil

75g (3oz) rindless streaky bacon, diced

350g (12oz) onions, peeled and roughly
    chopped

350g (12oz) carrots, peeled and chopped

350g (12oz) fennel, roughly chopped

2 celery sticks, roughly chopped

150ml (¼ pint) medium dry sherry

600ml (1 pint) chicken stock

1 tbsp redcurrant jelly

serves 6

preparation: 40 minutes, plus marinating

cooking time: about 1½ hours

per serving: 460 cals; 23g fat;
    14g carbohydrate

1 Put the rabbit joints into a large bowl with the garlic, thyme, bay leaves and red wine. Cover and leave to marinate in the fridge for at least 6 hours, preferably overnight.

2 Drain the rabbit, reserving the marinade. Pat dry, season with salt and pepper and dust lightly with flour. Heat the olive oil in a large flameproof casserole. Brown the rabbit joints, in batches on all sides, over a high heat. Remove and set aside.

3 Add the bacon and fry for 2–3 minutes. Add the vegetables and cook gently for 10 minutes or until softened and beginning to colour. Stir in the flour and cook for 2 minutes.

4 Return the rabbit to the casserole, and add the reserved marinade, sherry and stock. Bring to the boil, cover and cook at 170°C (150°C fan oven) mark 3 for 1–1½ hours until the rabbit is tender.

5 Transfer the rabbit to a warmed dish, using a slotted spoon; keep warm. Strain the sauce through a sieve, pressing as much of the vegetable mixture through as possible; pour back into the casserole. Add the redcurrant jelly and bubble for 5–10 minutes until syrupy; adjust the seasoning.

6 Return the rabbit to the casserole and simmer for 5 minutes before serving.

Rabbit Casserole with Grainy Mustard

4–6 rabbit joints, about 700–900g (1½–2lb)
  in total
salt and pepper
2 tbsp plain flour, plus extra to dust
2 tbsp oil
15g (½oz) butter
2 garlic cloves, peeled and crushed
300g (10oz) shallots, peeled and halved
  if large
225g (8oz) carrots, peeled and thickly sliced
150ml (¼ pint) white wine
300ml (½ pint) chicken stock
3–4 tbsp wholegrain mustard
4 tbsp crème fraîche
chopped herbs, to garnish

serves 4
preparation: 15 minutes
cooking time: 1–1½ hours
per serving: 410 cals; 24g fat;
  16g carbohydrate

1 Season the rabbit joints with salt and pepper and toss in flour to coat lightly, shaking off excess.

2 Heat the oil and butter in a large flameproof casserole and brown the rabbit joints on all sides over a high heat, in batches if necessary. Remove and set aside.

3 Reduce the heat and add the garlic, shallots and carrots to the casserole; cook for 5 minutes. Stir in the flour and cook for 2 minutes.

4 Add the wine, stock and mustard, stir well and bring to the boil. Return the rabbit to the casserole, then put the lid on and cook in the oven at 170°C (150°C fan oven) mark 3 for 1–1½ hours until the rabbit is very tender.

5 Transfer the rabbit and vegetables to a warmed serving dish, using a slotted spoon; keep warm.

6 If necessary, put the casserole over a high heat for a few minutes to reduce the sauce a little. Stir in the crème fraîche and check the seasoning. Pour the creamy mustard sauce over the rabbit and garnish with herbs to serve.

Roast Venison with Mustard and Mushrooms

600g (1¼lb) piece loin of venison, about 6cm
  (2½ inches) in diameter
1 tbsp wholegrain mustard
2 small onions, peeled and thinly sliced
350g (12oz) small shiitake or brown-cap
  mushrooms
150ml (¼ pint) olive oil
1 tbsp chopped thyme
1 tbsp chopped parsley
5 tsp balsamic vinegar
salt and pepper
lemon juice, to taste

serves 4
preparation: 15 minutes
cooking time: 25 minutes
per serving: 600 cals; 42g fat;
  6g carbohydrate

1 Rub the venison with the mustard and put into a roasting tin. Scatter the onions and mushrooms around the meat and drizzle over half of the olive oil. Roast at 230°C (210°C fan oven) mark 8, allowing 30–35 minutes for medium-rare; 40 minutes for well-done meat.

2 Scatter the chopped thyme and parsley on a board. Roll the hot venison in the chopped herbs to coat and put on a warmed serving platter with the mushrooms and onions. Cover with foil and leave to rest in a warm place while preparing the dressing.

3 Add the remaining olive oil and the balsamic vinegar to the roasting tin and warm on the hob, stirring. Season with salt and pepper and add lemon juice to taste.

4 Carve the venison into thick slices and serve with the hot dressing.

Venison Stew

900g (2lb) stewing venison, trimmed

2 onions, peeled, one sliced, one diced

1 tsp black peppercorns, crushed

6 juniper berries, crushed

1 tbsp chopped thyme, plus sprigs
    to garnish

300ml (½ pint) red wine

100ml (3½fl oz) olive oil

4 tbsp sunflower oil

200g (7oz) pancetta or bacon lardons

1 garlic clove, peeled and crushed

2 tbsp plain flour

300ml (½ pint) beef stock

1 bay leaf

1 strip of finely pared orange zest

salt and pepper

350g (12oz) shallots

25g (1oz) butter

1 tsp golden caster sugar

225g (8oz) vacuum-packed chestnuts

75g (3oz) dried cranberries

serves 6

preparation: 1 hour, plus 1–2 days marinating

cooking time: about 2¼ hours

per serving: 730 cals; 47g fat;
    31g carbohydrate

1 Cut the venison into 4cm (1½ inch) cubes and put into a large bowl with the sliced onion, peppercorns, juniper berries, thyme, red wine and olive oil. Mix well, then cover and marinate in the fridge for 24–48 hours.

2 Drain the venison and pat dry with kitchen paper, reserving the marinade but discarding the onion. Heat 2 tbsp sunflower oil in a flameproof casserole and brown the venison in batches over a high heat.

3 Fry the pancetta in the casserole for 5 minutes or until browned; remove and set aside with the venison. Add the remaining oil to the casserole, then add the chopped onion and garlic, and cook over a medium heat for 10 minutes or until softened and golden. Stir in the flour, cook for a minute, then add the reserved marinade. Bring to the boil, stirring, and allow to bubble for 2–3 minutes.

4 Return the venison to the casserole, together with any juices and the pancetta. Add the stock, bay leaf, orange zest and salt and pepper. Bring to a simmer, cover and simmer for 5 minutes, then transfer to the oven and cook at 170°C (150°C fan oven) mark 3 for 1¼ hours or until the venison is tender.

5 Meanwhile, add the shallots to a pan of cold water, bring to the boil and simmer for 3–4 minutes. Drain, cool slightly, then peel.

6 Heat the butter in a frying pan. Add the shallots with the sugar, then cover and cook for 15–20 minutes or until they are caramelised and soft to the centre. Add the chestnuts and cranberries, stir and cook for a further 2–3 minutes.

7 Add the shallot mixture to the casserole and return to the oven for 15 minutes. Garnish with thyme and serve with creamy mash.

Pan-fried Venison with Blueberry Sauce

15g (½oz) butter

1 tbsp oil

6 venison steaks, 125–175g (4–6oz) each

BLUEBERRY SAUCE

225g (8oz) blueberries

150ml (¼ pint) dry white wine

2 tsp golden caster sugar, or to taste

4 tbsp freshly squeezed orange juice

1 tbsp wine vinegar

salt and pepper

25g (1oz) unsalted butter, diced

serves 6

preparation: 15 minutes

cooking time: about 15 minutes

per serving: 360 cals; 16g fat;
    7g carbohydrate

1 To make the sauce, put three quarters of the blueberries into a heavy-based pan with the white wine and sugar. Bring to the boil, then cover and simmer for 10 minutes, until soft, stirring occasionally. Leave to cool slightly.

2 Press the stewed blueberries through a sieve and return to the pan. Add the orange juice, wine vinegar and seasoning to taste. Bring to the boil and simmer, stirring, until reduced and thickened slightly. Whisk in the unsalted butter, a piece at a time.

3 Heat the butter and oil in a large frying pan and pan-fry the venison steaks over a high heat for 3–4 minutes each side, until cooked to your liking.

4 Add the sauce and reserved blueberries to the venison and heat through. Serve at once.

MEAT

Meat is a valuable source of high quality protein, B vitamins and iron, and has an important role in a healthy balanced diet. However, it is also a source of saturated fatty acids, which are associated with raised blood cholesterol levels – a risk factor in coronary heart disease. For this reason, it is wise to avoid eating too much red meat, perhaps limiting it to a maximum of three main meals per week.

In this country beef, lamb and pork are the most popular red meats, while veal is eaten to a much lesser extent. The flavour and texture of meat is determined by the breed of the animal, its environment, and feed. Meat from cattle raised on lush pastures will taste far superior to that from corn-fed animals. Organic meat is derived from animals that have been reared on a natural diet, and is therefore an endorsement of quality. With the exception of veal, meat is hung before it is sold to improve the texture and develop flavour. The most expensive cuts – suitable for roasting, grilling and frying – are from those parts of the animal that are least exercised – rump, tenderloin, etc. Cheaper, tougher cuts from those parts of the animal that move the most need slow, gentle cooking with liquid to tenderise them. If you are looking to cut down on red meat, make a little go further by serving it with lots of vegetables or by combining it with pulses in casseroles and stews.

CHOOSING MEAT

Always buy your meat from a reliable source. Quality butchers and supermarkets sell a wide range of cuts and a helpful butcher should be able to offer you advice, and be willing to bone meat, cut steaks to a certain thickness, and prepare meat in other ways to your specific requirements.

Meat should look and smell fresh, but colour is not an obvious indicator. Bright red, for example, doesn't necessarily indicate quality. Instead look for a good clear colour, which will darken naturally on exposure to the air. A greyish tinge is a bad sign.

A little fat is essential to prevent meat drying out during cooking, but look for relatively lean cuts without too much visible fat. Any fat should be creamy white. With the exception of some specialist breeds, such as Jersey and Guernsey beef, creamy yellow fat suggests that the meat is probably past its prime. Look for a smooth outer layer of fat, if appropriate to the cut, and a fine marbling of fat distributed throughout the meat; this will keep it moist during cooking and add flavour.

Always choose a neat, fairly well trimmed piece of meat. Splinters of bone and ragged edges indicate poor butchery. Cuts should be trimmed of sinew. Joints and steaks should be of uniform thickness so that they cook evenly. Offal should look fresh and moist, and it should not smell.

STORING MEAT

Once you've made your purchase, get the meat home and into the fridge as soon as possible. It should be stored in the coolest part of the fridge, loosely wrapped and well away from cooked foods to prevent cross-contamination.

If you've bought pre-packed meat from a supermarket, stick to the 'use-by' date. Offal, minced meat and small cuts of veal are best eaten on the day of purchase. Larger joints, chops and steaks will keep in the fridge for 2–3 days.

If meat is past its best, the fat will begin to turn rancid. 'Off' or bad meat will have an unpleasant smell, slimy surface and possibly a greenish tinge. Because of the risk of food poisoning, it's not worth the risk if you have any doubt about freshness.

A GUIDE TO MEAT CUTS

Cuts of meat and terms used to describe them vary enormously across Britain and throughout Europe and the United States. Some butchers and supermarkets in this country now stock a good range of continental cuts. If you are unsure of a particular description it's best to ask.

BEEF

Considering the wide range of different cuts available from good butchers and supermarkets, and the different cooking options, beef is wonderfully versatile. The quality of beef is determined by its age, breed and feeding. Aberdeen Angus is one of the recognised quality breeds in this country, producing meat with a superb flavour and close-grained texture. We recommend that you buy organic beef whenever possible, and particularly in the case of grilled, barbecued, pan-fried and roasted meat which is to be served rare, or medium-rare.

Topside is a very lean cut with little fat, so it is usually sold with a layer of fat tied around it. This cut is primarily used for roasting and braising. Topside is also sold sliced for making beef roulades.

Rib is traditionally sold as a large roasting joint on the bone, though it is also sold boned and rolled – sometimes described as rib eye. Rib has more fat than topside, but its flavour is superb and considered by many to be the finest of the roasting joints. Entrecôte is literally the meat between the ribs, or rib steaks, though a slice cut from the sirloin or rump is sometimes sold by this name.

Sirloin is another tender beef cut, sold boned and rolled for roasting, or cut into sirloin steaks. Porterhouse steak is cut from the thick end of the sirloin and can weigh as much as 700g (1½lb). Large T-bone steaks, which include the bone, are also cut from the sirloin. Minute steak is very thin steak cut from the upper part of the sirloin. Strips of sirloin are suitable for stir-frying.

Fillet or tenderloin is the small eye of meat beneath the backbone under the sirloin. It has little fat and can be cooked in a large piece or as steaks. Fillet is regarded as the ultimate joint for roasting and Beef Wellington. It is expensive, but very lean and tender. Fillet is best served rare. Chateaubriand is a thick slice or steak cut from the middle of the fillet that serves two. Tornedos or filet mignon steaks are also cut from the fillet.

Rump steak is a popular lean tender cut from the hind quarter. Suitable for grilling and frying.

Flash-fry steaks are cut from the thick flank, topside or silverside. These steaks are beaten and passed between spiked rollers to make them tender.

Silverside is another lean, boneless joint from the hind quarter sold for roasting, though it can be

dry and tough if cooked in this way. Traditionally it is salted and boiled. Uncooked salted beef is an unpalatable shade of grey, but it soon becomes pink when cooked.

Brisket comes from the shoulder. It has a good flavour but is inclined to be fatty. Commonly sold boned and rolled, it may also be salted. Brisket is best braised or pot roasted, but it can be roasted.

Chuck and blade steak is lean meat from the shoulder, which is usually sold sliced or cubed for braising, stewing and pie fillings. Look for some marbling of fat throughout.

Thick flank (top rump) is a lean cut from the top of the leg for pot roasting and braising. If thinly sliced it can be fried.

Thin flank is suitable for braising and stewing.

Neck and clod are economical cuts, used for stewing or mince.

Shin and leg are relatively lean cuts with lots of connective tissue in need of slow, moist cooking, such as stewing or casseroling.

VEAL

Veal comes from young calves so it is a very tender, lean meat. The palest (and most desired by some) comes from baby milk-fed calves. As the animals get older their diet is supplemented with grass and the meat darkens. The consumption of veal is regarded by some as inhumane. If you eat veal, buy it from a butcher who uses a reliable supplier. Despite its tenderness, veal does not roast well because it is so lean that it tends to become dry.

Leg is a prime cut, sold in slices as escalopes.

Fillet is the most expensive cut, generally sold in a piece for roasting. Follow recipes carefully, basting as suggested, because it tends to dry out. If possible, ask your butcher to lard it for you, or marinate for about 1 hour before cooking.

Osso buco or knuckle is an Italian cut, used to make the Italian speciality of the same name.

Loin is sold as entrecôte steak, or as a rolled cut for roasting.

Breast is usually the cheapest cut. Sold boned and rolled and sometimes ready stuffed for roasting.

Pie veal is sold ready chopped and needs long slow cooking.

Calf's liver and kidney are considered to be superior to that from other animals. Calf's liver is mild and tender, and is usually sliced and pan-fried.

LAMB

Home-produced lamb is at its best in spring, and is largely farmed in the hilly areas of Wales, Scotland and the north of England. Succulent and lean, British meat is considered to be excellent, but there is a good supply of lamb all year round, largely owing to imported supplies from New Zealand. There is a wide variety of cuts to choose from.

Leg of lamb is one of the leanest cuts and the most popular choice for roasting. It is traditionally sold with the bone in, either whole or as a half leg – fillet end or knuckle/shank end. Boned and rolled leg is also widely available. After boning it can also be 'butterflied' – flattened for grilling or barbecuing – so that it cooks quickly and easily. Leg steaks are prime cuts for grilling and pan-frying.

Shoulder is sold whole or as a half shoulder – blade or knuckle end – for roasting. Chops or steaks can also be cut from the shoulder for grilling or braising.

Loin comprises both chump and loin chops. Chump chops have a small round bone in the centre, and loin chops a small T bone. Loin steaks are boneless loin chops. The whole loin can also be roasted in one piece, on or off the bone.

Saddle of lamb or double loin is a very large joint for roasting, comprising of the whole loin from both sides of the lamb. It is sometimes sold sliced into butterfly or Barnsley chops.

Fillet of lamb is also cut from the loin; it is very lean and can be roasted or cooked en croûte.

Rack of lamb is also known as best end of neck. It is sold as a whole roasting joint consisting of 6–8 chops or cutlets. Usually chined by the butcher to make serving easier, the tips of the cutlet bones are then scraped of all fat and meat to look neat. This cut is used for 'crown roast' and 'guard of honour'.

Lamb cutlets are popular for grilling and frying. Boned and rolled cutlets are called noisettes; these neat lean portions are excellent grilled or pan-fried.

Scrag and middle neck are sold as neck cuts on the bone for stewing and braising in dishes such as Lancashire hotpot. The main eye of the middle is sold as neck fillet for grilling and frying.

Breast of lamb is an inexpensive cut, generally sold ready boned and rolled. It is tender enough to roast, but because it contains a lot of connective tissue, it is best cooked slowly and thoroughly. If braised, it must be well trimmed as it is a fatty cut.

Lamb's liver is suitable for pan-frying or braising. To tone down the strong flavour, soak it in milk for 1 hour before cooking, if you like.

Lamb's kidney is darker than calf's and smaller. It is best quickly fried or grilled.

PORK

Pork must be well cooked to prevent the risk of infection by trichinosis. It should never be served rare or medium. Part of the attraction of roast pork is the crackling. For good, crisp crackling score the rind, pat it dry, then rub it with oil and a generous amount of salt. Don't baste the rind as it cooks or it will not crisp. For moist methods of cooking, like stews and casseroles, the rind is best removed.

Loin consists of the hind loin, which is a prime joint for roasting, and the foreloin, which is the rib end. The hind loin contains the tenderloin, which is often sold separately. Loin of pork generally has a good layer of crackling and is a popular joint for roasting – either on the bone or boned, stuffed and rolled. It may also be cut into loin chops, which sometimes have the kidney attached. Loin steaks are simply boned loin chops.

Tenderloin or pork fillet is a versatile lean cut, weighing about 350g (12oz), taken from under the lower backbone. It can be split longthways, stuffed, tied and baked. Cubed fillet can be made into kebabs. Thinly sliced pork tenderloin is perfect for pan-frying. Escalopes are thin, batted-out slices cut across the grain from the fillet or the leg.

Leg is usually sold divided into the fillet end and the knuckle or shank end. Both joints are good for roasting. The fillet end is sometimes cut into leg steaks for grilling or frying.

Shoulder or handspring is another suitable joint for roasting, or using diced in pie fillings, curries and casseroles.

Spare ribs are cut from the belly or the ribs. Spare rib chops can be casseroled or braised, while trimmed American or Chinese spare ribs are less meaty and are typically cooked in barbecue sauce.

Belly is a long thin cut, streaked with fat. It may also be sold as a boned and rolled joint.

Pig's liver has a very strong flavour, which can be toned down slightly by soaking in milk for 1–2 hours before cooking. It is really only suitable for inclusion in pâtés and terrines – mixed with other meats and well flavoured with herbs and spices.

BACON, GAMMON AND HAM

Bacon is fresh pork that has been preserved by curing with dry salt, a brine solution, or a mixture of salt, sugar, seasonings and preservatives, which colour and flavour the meat. Bacon may be smoked after curing. Unsmoked bacon is sometimes called green bacon. Always check whether a recipe states smoked or unsmoked bacon. Smoked bacon will lend a smoky flavour and in some dishes this may be too strong.

Gammon is the name given to the whole hind leg from a side of bacon after it has been cured. Uncooked gammon is sold as boneless joints or steaks. When cooked and eaten cold, gammon is often called ham.

Strictly by definition, ham is the hind leg of a pig cut from the whole side, then cured and matured separately. Hams may be salted, or salted and smoked to cure them. Hams are usually sold ready cooked; if not you will need to cook them as you would a bacon joint. Some of the best known cures are York, Suffolk, Honey roast, Cumberland and Virginia. Some hams, such as the famous Italian Parma ham, French Bayonne and Spanish Serrano are eaten raw.

Back bacon is usually sold as lean rashers and chops for frying or grilling.

Streaky bacon comes from the fattier chest meat and is commonly sold as rashers for frying or grilling. Throughcut (middle) rashers are the back and streaky joined together. Lardons are small cubes of bacon used to flavour a variety of dishes. Pancetta, an Italian type of bacon is used in a similar way; it is available smoked and unsmoked. Always drain grilled or fried bacon on kitchen paper after cooking.

Collar of bacon is taken from the shoulder, then boned and rolled. This is a good joint for boiling or braising; it usually needs to be pre-soaked.

Forehock of bacon is an inexpensive cut, sold bone in or boned and rolled. It has a good flavour and is fairly lean. Use in pot roasts, braise with lentils and vegetables or simmer it gently.

Gammon is sold raw as a whole or half gammon, or more commonly as smaller cuts, which are known as middle, corner and gammon hock. Most are sold boned, ready to boil, braise or bake. Gammon steaks and rashers are cut after boning and are suitable for grilling or frying.

To cook bacon and gammon joints you will need to soak large smoked joints overnight in cold water before cooking, changing the water frequently, in order to remove excess salt. Green or mild cure joints need only 4–6 hours' soaking or none at all – ask your butcher's advice. Simmer the joint in water, with a few vegetables added for extra flavour, allowing 20 minutes per 450g (1lb) plus 20 minutes. For joints over 4.5kg (10lb) allow 15–20 minutes per 450g (1lb) plus 15 minutes.

MARINATING MEAT

A good marinade makes all the difference to meat. Usually based on oil or wine or something acidic, like fruit juice or yogurt, a marinade will tenderise tougher cuts and lend a subtle aroma and flavour. Oil- and wine-based marinades tend to permeate the meat adding moisture to dry cuts, while yogurt will tenderise and form a soft crust on the food as it cooks. Aromatics like lemon zest, thyme, bay, garlic and onion add fragrance as well as flavour.

Put the meat into a shallow non-metallic dish and pour over the marinade. Leave in a cool place for at least 1 hour but preferably overnight. When ready to cook, brush or strain off excess marinade and cook as directed in the recipe. If you are cooking on a barbecue or under the grill, baste the meat frequently with the marinade as it cooks.

COOKING METHODS

To get the most from a cut of meat you need to cook it appropriately. Lean, fine-grained cuts respond well to quick cooking methods, while tougher cuts with more connective tissue need long, slow cooking to make them tender.

Stewing and Casseroling

These cooking methods are almost identical except that strictly, a stew is cooked on the hob while a casserole is cooked in the oven. For a good colour, brown the meat thoroughly, in batches if necessary, before adding any liquid. Skim excess fat off the stew or casserole before serving. The most effective way of removing fat is to prepare the dish ahead and allow it to cool completely until the fat solidifies on the surface; it can then be removed easily.

Choose a good heavy-based pan or casserole to prevent the contents burning or sticking to the bottom and make sure that it has a tight-fitting lid so that the liquid will not evaporate too rapidly. Keep the liquid at a gentle simmer just below boiling point; if it boils the meat is likely to be tough. All the less tender, more economical cuts of meat can be used. Any meat labelled 'stewing' will take longer to cook than meat labelled 'braising'.

Most stews and casseroles freeze very well. If a dish is to be frozen, use aromatics, such as garlic, sparingly as their flavour tends to be more pronounced after thawing. On reheating defrosted casseroles, you may find it is necessary to add a little more stock.

Braising

Braising is similar to stewing and casseroling but generally involves less liquid and slightly more tender cuts are used. The browned meat is set on a bed of vegetables with sufficient liquid to create steam, covered tightly and cooked very gently. Check supermarket labels or ask your butcher for advice on suitable cuts for braising.

Boiling

This is a misnomer since boiling produces tough and tasteless meat. Meat for 'boiling' is usually salted and must be soaked overnight in several changes of cold water before cooking. Cover the meat with fresh cold water and bring to a simmer. Cover with a tightly fitting lid and simmer gently for about 25 minutes per 450g (1lb) plus 30 minutes for large joints; 1½ hours minimum for small joints; do not boil. Add vegetables, spices and herbs to the cooking liquid if you intend using it as stock. Using a pressure cooker will reduce the cooking time significantly; refer to the manufacturer's handbook, but in general allow about two thirds of the cooking time.

Frying, Grilling and Barbecuing

These methods are only suitable for tender cuts. Marinating the meat before cooking helps to add flavour and keeps it moist. Ensure that the frying pan, grill or barbecue is hot before you begin cooking so that the meat is sealed and browned. If cooking thicker pieces, or pork or sausages, which must be cooked right through, reduce the heat once the meat has browned or if barbecuing move it further away from the heat source.

Frying requires a good heavy-based pan and a fat or oil that can withstand the high temperature: olive or vegetable oil; clarified butter rather than pure butter; dripping; some vegetable margarines (not low-fat types that contain water and splatter). **Stir-frying** requires meat to be cut into small even-sized pieces across the grain. A marinade of soy sauce, garlic and a dash of dry sherry will ensure that the meat is tasty and tender unless an alternative is suggested in the recipe. Heat a little vegetable oil in a preheated wok or deep-sided frying pan until very hot. Add the meat, drained of marinade, and keep turning and stirring as it cooks. **Cooking steaks** to perfection is a little difficult whichever cooking method you use. Professional chefs determine when a steak is cooked as required by pressing it with their fingertips – the less the degree of resistance, the rarer the meat. For inexperienced cooks, the most reliable way is to cut the steak open and look at it. Timing depends on thickness rather than the size of the piece of meat. As a rough guide, a 2cm (¾ inch) thick steak will take about 2½ minutes' grilling or frying on each side for rare; 3–4 minutes each side for medium; 6 minutes for well-done meats.

Roasting

Only good quality tender joints are suitable for roasting. Opinions on temperatures and timings differ but roasting at a constant high temperature of 230°C (210°C fan oven) mark 8, is only suitable for prime cuts, such as beef fillet.

However you decide to cook your roast, it's important to weigh the joint and bring it to room temperature before cooking. Put the meat, fat-side up, on a roasting rack and smear with mustard or stud with slivers of garlic. Pork should be rubbed with oil and salt to make a nice crisp crackling. With the exception of pork with crackling, baste all roasts frequently during cooking to keep them moist; if the joint is very lean, add moisture in the form of dripping or oil.

Refer to the chart (overleaf) for suggested roasting times. Most joints benefit from being put into a hot oven at 230°C (210°C fan oven) mark 8 for the first 20 minutes or so; this gives the meat a blast of heat, sealing in juices and keeping the joint succulent. After this initial period, the oven temperature is usually lowered.

Use a meat thermometer to check that the joint is cooked. Or insert a skewer into the thickest part, press the surface hard and watch the colour of the juices: slightly red for rare meat; pink for medium; for well done meat the juices should run clear.

CARVING MEAT

Whichever joint of meat you are carving, a good-sized, really sharp knife is essential. A proper carving fork with two long prongs and a finger guard helps keep the meat firmly in place.

Leave the joint to stand, loosely covered with foil, on an edged dish in a warm place for 5–15 minutes before you start carving. This allows the meat to 'relax' and makes it much easier to slice. Add any juices that collect in the dish to the gravy.

Always put the joint on a firm, flat, non-slip surface. A board is ideal, but some people prefer to use a spiked metal dish. Remove any string or skewers which will get in the way as you carve. Before starting to carve, loosen the cooked meat from any outer, exposed bones. Cut across the grain of the meat, which usually means cutting at a right angle to the main bone. Simply lay boned and rolled joints on their side and carve through.

To carve a leg of lamb, put the joint on a board with the meatier side uppermost and the carving fork firmly in the knuckle end to steady it. Cut a narrow wedge-shaped piece of meat from the top (middle) of the joint, cutting right down to the bone. Carve slices from either side of the first cut, gradually slanting the knife as you go to get larger slices. Turn the joint over, cut off the fat then carve slices along the joint.

To carve a shoulder of lamb, hold at the shank end with the crisp skin uppermost. Cut a wedge-shaped slice through the middle of the joint in the angle between shoulder blade and leg bone. Carve slices from each side of the cut until the shoulder and shank bones are reached. Turn the joint over and carve horizontal slices from the underside.

If roasting a pork loin, ask the butcher to chine the bone. When you come to carving, sever the chined bone from the rib bones. Cut the crackling off, then divide into portions. Cut down between the rib bones to divide the joint into chops, or cut along the length of the joint between the meat and rib bones then carve off slices without bone.

To carve a leg of pork (shank end), remove some crackling. Cut thin slices down to, and around the bone. When the shank bone is reached, carve at an angle over the top of the bone. Turn the joint over and cut down towards the thin end of the bone at an angle.

To carve a leg of pork (fillet end), carve slices through to the bone on either side of it.

ROASTING MEAT

MEAT	COOKING TIME AT 180°C (160°C FAN OVEN) MARK 4	INTERNAL TEMPERATURE
Beef		
Rare	20 mins per 450g (1lb), plus 20 mins	60°C
Medium	25 mins per 450g (1lb), plus 25 mins	70°C
Well Done	30 mins per 450g (1lb), plus 30 mins	80°C
Veal		
Well Done	25 mins per 450g (1lb), plus 25 mins	70°C
Lamb		
Medium	25 mins per 450g (1lb), plus 25 mins	70–75°C
Well done	30 mins per 450g (1lb), plus 30 mins	75–80°C
Pork		
Well done	35 minutes per 450g (1lb), plus 35 mins	80–85°C

Classic Roast Beef with Yorkshire Puddings

1 boned and rolled rib, sirloin, rump or
   topside of beef joint, about 1.8kg (4lb)
1 tbsp plain flour
1 tbsp mustard powder
salt and pepper

YORKSHIRE PUDDING
125g (4oz) plain flour
½ tsp salt
300ml (½ pint) milk
2 eggs

GRAVY
150ml (¼ pint) red wine
600ml (1 pint) beef stock

serves 8
preparation: 20 minutes
cooking time: about 1½ hours, plus resting
per serving: 320 cals; 11g fat;
   16g carbohydrate

1 Put the beef in a roasting tin, with the thickest part of the fat uppermost. Mix the flour with the mustard powder and seasoning. Rub the mixture over the joint.

2 Position the roasting tin so that the joint is in the middle of the oven and roast at 230°C (210°C fan oven) mark 8 for 30 minutes.

3 Baste the beef and lower the oven setting to 190°C (170°C fan oven) mark 5. Cook for a further 1 hour, approximately, basting occasionally.

4 Meanwhile, make the Yorkshire pudding batter. Sift the flour and salt into a bowl. Mix in half the milk, then add the eggs and season with pepper. Beat until smooth, then whisk in the rest of the milk.

5 Put the beef on a carving dish, cover loosely with foil and leave to rest in a warm place. Increase the oven setting to 220°C (200°C fan oven) mark 7.

6 Pour off about 3 tbsp fat from the roasting tin and use to grease 8–12 individual Yorkshire pudding tins. Heat in the oven for 5 minutes or until the fat is almost smoking. Pour the Yorkshire batter into the tins. Bake for 15–20 minutes until well risen, golden and crisp.

7 Meanwhile, make the gravy. Skim off any remaining fat from the sediment in the roasting tin. Add the wine and boil on the hob until syrupy. Pour in the stock and, again, boil until syrupy; there should be about 450ml (¾ pint) gravy; adjust the seasoning.

8 Carve the beef into slices. Serve with the gravy, Yorkshire puddings and vegetables of your choice.

Stuffed Topside of Beef

1.4kg (3lb) topside or top rump of beef joint
1 tbsp balsamic vinegar
2 tbsp white wine vinegar
3 tbsp olive oil
3 tbsp chopped marjoram or thyme
salt and pepper
2 red peppers, cored, quartered and deseeded
75g (3oz) spinach, cooked and well drained
75g (3oz) pitted black olives
50g (2oz) smoked ham
75g (3oz) raisins or sultanas

serves 6
preparation: 35 minutes, plus marinating
cooking time: 1–1¼ hours, plus resting
per serving: 310 cals; 14g fat;
   10g carbohydrate

1 Make a deep incision along the beef and put into a dish. Combine the vinegars, olive oil, marjoram and some pepper. Pour over the beef and into the pocket. Marinate in a cool place for 4–6 hours, or overnight.

2 Grill the peppers, skin-side up, under a hot grill until the skins are charred. Cool in a covered bowl, then remove the skins.

3 Squeeze excess water from the spinach, then chop and put into a bowl with the olives, ham and raisins. Mix well and season with salt and pepper.

4 Line the pocket of the beef with the peppers, reserving 2 pepper quarters for the gravy. Spoon the spinach mixture into the pocket and spread evenly. Reshape the meat and tie at intervals with string.

5 Put the beef joint into a roasting tin (just large enough to hold it). Pour the marinade over and roast at 190°C (170°C fan oven) mark 5 for 1 hour for rare beef, or 1¼ hours for medium rare, basting from time to time. Transfer the beef to a warmed platter, cover with foil and leave to rest in a warm place while you make the gravy.

6 Skim off the excess fat from the roasting tin. Bring the pan juices to the boil and add 125 ml (4fl oz) water; let bubble for 2–3 minutes. Finely chop the remaining pepper pieces and add to the gravy.

7 Carve the beef into slices and serve with gravy and vegetables of your choice.

Fillet of Beef en Croûte with Red Wine Sauce

1–1.4kg (2¼–3lb) piece fillet of beef, trimmed
salt and pepper
50g (2oz) butter
2 shallots, peeled and chopped
15g (½oz) dried porcini, soaked in 100ml
    (3½fl oz) boiling water for 20 minutes
2 garlic cloves, chopped
225g (8oz) flat mushrooms, finely chopped
2 tsp chopped thyme
175g (6oz) chicken liver pâté
175g (6oz) Parma ham
375g pack ready-rolled puff pastry
flour, to dust
1 medium egg, beaten

RED WINE SAUCE
2 tbsp olive oil
350g (12oz) shallots, peeled and finely
    chopped
3 garlic cloves, peeled and chopped
3 tbsp tomato purée
2 tbsp balsamic vinegar
200ml (7fl oz) red wine
600ml (1 pint) beef stock

serves 6–8
preparation: 1 hour, plus soaking
cooking time: about 1½ hours, plus resting
per serving: 850–640 cals; 51–38g fat;
    38–28g carbohydrate

1 Season the beef all over with salt and pepper. Melt 25g (1oz) butter in a large frying pan. When it is foaming, put the beef in the pan and brown it all over for 4–5 minutes, taking care not to burn the butter. Transfer to a plate and leave to cool.

2 Melt the remaining butter in a pan, add the shallots and cook for 1 minute. Drain the porcini, reserving the liquor, then chop and add to the pan with the garlic, reserved liquor and fresh mushrooms. Increase the heat and cook until the liquid has evaporated, then season with salt and pepper and add the chopped thyme. Leave to cool.

3 Put the pâté into a bowl and beat until smooth. Add the mushroom mixture and stir well until thoroughly combined. Check the seasoning. Put the cold beef on a board and spread half the mushroom mixture evenly over it, using a palette knife.

4 Lay half the Parma ham on a sheet of clingfilm, overlapping the slices. Invert the mushroom-topped beef on top. Spread the remaining mushroom mixture over the beef, then cover with the rest of the Parma ham slices, also overlapping, to enclose the beef completely. Wrap in clingfilm and chill.

5 To make the sauce, heat the olive oil in a pan, add the shallots and cook until soft. Add the garlic and tomato purée, cook for 1 minute, then add the balsamic vinegar. Bubble until the liquid has almost totally reduced, then add the red wine and reduce by half. Pour in the stock and bubble until reduced by one third. Set aside.

6 Cut off one third of the pastry and roll it out on a lightly floured surface to a 3mm (⅛ inch) thickness, 2.5cm (1 inch) larger all round than the beef. Prick well with a fork, transfer to a baking sheet and bake at 220°C (200°C fan oven) mark 7 for 12–15 minutes until brown and crisp. Cool on a wire rack, then trim to the size of the beef and place on a baking sheet. Unwrap the beef, brush with beaten egg and place on the cooked pastry.

7 Roll out the remaining puff pastry to a 25 x 30cm (10 x 12 inch) rectangle. Roll over a lattice pastry cutter and gently ease the lattice open, keeping it intact. Cover the beef with the lattice, tuck the ends under and seal the edges. Brush with beaten egg, then bake for 40 minutes for rare to medium rare, or 45 minutes for medium.

8 Leave the beef to stand for 10 minutes before carving. In the meantime, reheat the red wine sauce. Cut the beef into slices and serve with the sauce.

Fillet of Beef with Mushrooms and Chestnuts

1kg (2¼lb) piece fillet of beef, trimmed

400ml (14fl oz) red wine

50ml (2fl oz) Madeira

2 tbsp balsamic vinegar

5 large shallots, peeled and sliced

1 bay leaf

1 thyme sprig, plus extra to garnish

100g (3½oz) butter

350ml (12fl oz) beef or veal stock

2 tbsp mixed peppercorns, crushed

1 tbsp oil

1 medium shallot, peeled and finely chopped

450g (1lb) mixed wild mushrooms, cleaned,
   trimmed and sliced (if large)

200g (7oz) cooked and peeled whole
   chestnuts, halved

3 tbsp finely chopped flat-leafed parsley

salt and pepper

serves 6

preparation: 20 minutes, plus marinating

cooking time: 45 minutes, plus resting

per serving: 530 cals; 28g fat;
   20g carbohydrate

1 Put the beef into a bowl and add the wine, Madeira, vinegar, sliced shallots, bay leaf and thyme. Cover and leave to marinate in a cool place for 2–3 hours. Remove the shallots and beef with a slotted spoon; reserve the liquid. Pat the beef dry with kitchen paper.

2 Melt 25g (1oz) of the butter in a pan and gently fry the sliced shallots until soft. Add the marinade, bring to the boil and boil until reduced to one third. Add the stock and boil to reduce to one third again. Discard the bay leaf and thyme. Set the sauce aside.

3 Roll the beef in the crushed peppercorns to coat. Heat the oil in a heavy-based frying pan, add the beef and brown all over on a high heat. Transfer the beef to a roasting tin and roast at 200°C (180°C fan oven) mark 6 for 25 minutes (for medium rare). Lift the meat on to a board, cover with foil and rest for 10 minutes.

4 Melt 25g (1oz) butter in the frying pan (used for the meat) and cook the chopped shallot until it is soft. Add the mushrooms and sauté until the liquid has evaporated. Stir in the chestnuts and parsley, and season with salt and pepper. Cover and set aside.

5 Gently reheat the sauce over a very low heat and whisk in the remaining butter, a piece at a time. Carve the beef into slices and serve with the mushrooms, chestnuts and Madeira sauce. Garnish with thyme.

Grilled Steaks with Shallots and Wine

50g (2oz) chilled butter, cubed

225g (8oz) shallots, peeled and chopped

350ml (12fl oz) red wine, such as Bordeaux

4 sirloin or rump steaks, about 175–200g
   (6–7oz) each

2 tbsp oil

8 slices French bread

2–3 tsp Dijon mustard

2 tbsp chopped parsley

serves 4

preparation: 15 minutes

cooking time: 4–12 minutes

per serving: 540 cals; 26g fat;
   30g carbohydrate

1 Melt 15g (½oz) of the butter in a pan, add the shallots and sauté for 5 minutes until slightly softened. Add the red wine and bring to the boil. Simmer until the wine is reduced by half and the shallots are soft.

2 Smear the steaks on both sides with the oil. Cook on a preheated griddle pan or on the grill rack under a high heat, as close to the heat as possible, turning the steaks every 2 minutes. Allow 4 minutes (one turn) for rare steaks; 8 minutes (three turns) for medium. For well-done steaks allow 12 minutes, increasing the time between turns to 3 minutes. Season the steaks with salt and pepper as you make the final turn.

3 Meanwhile, beat the remaining butter into the sauce, a piece at a time, making sure each one is absorbed before adding the next. This will thicken the sauce and make it glossy.

4 Transfer the steaks to warmed plates and keep warm. Press the bread slices on to the grill pan or griddle to soak up the juices, then spread each lightly with Dijon mustard. Put 2 slices beside each steak. Pour the sauce over the steaks and sprinkle with chopped parsley to serve.

Steak au Poivre

2 tbsp black or green peppercorns
4 rump or sirloin steaks, 200g (7oz) each
25g (1oz) butter
1 tbsp oil
salt
2 tbsp brandy
150ml (¼ pint) double cream or crème fraîche

serves 4
preparation: 10 minutes
cooking time: 4–12 minutes
per serving: 480 cals; 35g fat;
    1g carbohydrate

1 Crush the peppercorns coarsely using a pestle and mortar, or rolling pin. Scatter the peppercorns on a board, lay the steaks on top and press hard to encrust the surface of the meat; repeat with the other side.
2 Heat the butter and oil in a frying pan and quickly sear the steaks over a high heat. Lower the heat to medium and cook for a further 3–12 minutes, according to taste, turning every 2 minutes (see grilled steaks with shallots and wine, left). Season with salt.
3 Remove steaks from the pan; keep warm. Add the brandy to the pan, take off the heat and set alight. When the flame dies, stir in the cream, season and reheat gently. Pour the sauce over the steaks to serve.

Steaks on Ciabatta with Herb Dressing

2 tbsp oil
4 fillet steaks, about 150g (5oz) each
2 large tomatoes, sliced
salt and pepper
8 slices toasted ciabatta
1 quantity herb dressing (page 351)

serves 4
preparation: 15 minutes
cooking time: 10–15 minutes
per serving: 800 cals; 49g fat;
    40g carbohydrate

1 Heat 1 tbsp oil in a heavy-based frying pan and fry the steaks for 3 minutes each side for medium rare, 4–5 minutes for medium. Remove when cooked to your taste, put to one side and keep warm.
2 Wipe out the pan, add the remaining oil and fry the tomatoes quickly on both sides, then season with salt and pepper to taste.
3 Put a slice of toasted ciabatta on each warmed plate, add a fillet steak and spoon the pan-fried tomatoes on top. Drizzle with the herb dressing and top with a second slice of toasted ciabatta.

Boeuf Stroganoff

700g (1½lb) rump or fillet steak, trimmed
50g (2oz) unsalted butter or 4 tbsp olive oil
1 onion, peeled and thinly sliced
225g (8oz) brown-cap mushrooms, sliced
3 tbsp brandy
1 tsp French mustard
200ml (7fl oz) crème fraîche
100ml (3½fl oz) double cream
3 tbsp chopped parsley
salt and pepper

serves 4
preparation: 10 minutes
cooking time: about 20 minutes
per serving: 640 cals; 51g fat;
    6g carbohydrate

1 Cut the steak into 5mm (¼ inch) wide strips, about 5cm (2 inches) long.
2 Heat half of the butter or olive oil in a large heavy-based frying pan, add the onion and fry gently for 10 minutes or until softened and golden; remove with a slotted spoon and set aside. Add the mushrooms to the pan and sauté for 2–3 minutes until golden brown; remove and put to one side.
3 Increase the heat and quickly fry the meat, in two or three batches, for 2–3 minutes, stirring constantly to ensure even browning. Add the brandy and let bubble to reduce.
4 Return all the meat, onion and mushrooms to the pan. Lower the heat and stir in the mustard, crème fraîche and cream. Heat through, stir in most of the parsley and season with salt and pepper to taste. Serve with rice or noodles and scatter with the remaining parsley.

Steak and Boursin Parcels

4 fillet steaks, about 125g (4oz) each

salt and pepper

½ tbsp olive oil

375g pack puff pastry

flour, to dust

150g pack Boursin (soft herb cheese), sliced
   into 4 rounds

4 rosemary sprigs

1 medium egg, lightly beaten, to glaze

serves 4

preparation: 20 minutes, plus cooling

cooking time: 25–30 minutes

per serving: 680 cals; 47g fat;
   32g carbohydrate

1 Season the steaks all over with salt and pepper. Heat the olive oil in a large heavy-based pan and brown the steaks on each side for 1 minute. Transfer to a plate and leave to cool.

2 Roll out the puff pastry on a lightly floured surface to a 35cm (14 inch) square. Cut a 3mm (⅛ inch) strip from each edge of the square and set aside. Cut the pastry square into quarters.

3 Put a Boursin round in the centre of one square of pastry, then top with a steak. Season well with salt and pepper. Brush the pastry edges with water, then bring the corners up over the filling to meet in the middle and make a parcel. Crimp the edges to seal the parcel. Repeat to make the other 3 parcels.

4 Turn the parcels over and top each with a rosemary sprig. Cut each strip of reserved pastry in half and brush with water. Lay 2 pastry strips, damp-side down, across the rosemary sprig to form a cross and wrap around each parcel. Brush the parcels with beaten egg and put on to a baking sheet with the seams underneath. Chill for 10 minutes.

5 Bake the steak parcels at 220°C (200°C fan oven) mark 7 for 25 minutes until the pastry is golden; the steak will be medium rare. For well-done steaks, cook for a further 5 minutes.

Teriyaki Beef Stir-fry

450g (1lb) piece fillet of beef
225g (8oz) carrots, peeled
½ cucumber, deseeded
4–6 spring onions, trimmed
2 tbsp vegetable or groundnut oil

TERIYAKI MARINADE
4 tbsp Japanese soy sauce (Kikkoman)
4 tbsp mirin or medium sherry
1 garlic clove, peeled and finely chopped
2.5cm (1 inch) piece fresh root ginger, peeled
   and finely chopped

TO SERVE
a little wasabe paste (optional)

serves 4
preparation: 20 minutes, plus marinating
cooking time: 5 minutes
per serving: 250 cals; 12g fat;
   6g carbohydrate

1 Slice the beef as thinly as possible, then cut into 1cm (½ inch) wide strips. Mix the ingredients for the marinade together in a bowl, add the beef and turn to coat. Cover and leave to marinate in a cool place for at least 30 minutes, preferably overnight.

2 Cut the carrots and cucumber into thin matchstick strips. Thinly slice the spring onions on the diagonal. Drain the meat, reserving any marinade.

3 Heat the oil in a preheated wok or large frying pan until it is smoking. Add the vegetables and fry over a high heat for 2 minutes until the edges are well browned; remove and set aside.

4 Add the beef to the wok and stir-fry over a very high heat for 2 minutes.

5 Return the vegetables to the wok and add the reserved marinade. Stir-fry briefly until heated through. Serve immediately with noodles tossed in a little sesame oil and a tiny bit of wasabi paste.

Thai Beef Curry

450g (1lb) sirloin steak
4 cloves
1 tsp coriander seeds
1 tsp cumin seeds
seeds from 3 cardamom pods
2 garlic cloves, peeled and roughly chopped
2.5cm (1 inch) piece fresh root ginger, peeled
   and roughly chopped
1 small onion, peeled and roughly chopped
2 tbsp sunflower oil
1 tbsp sesame oil
1 tbsp Thai red curry paste
1 tsp ground turmeric
225g (8oz) potatoes, peeled and quartered
4 tomatoes, quartered
1 tsp sugar
1 tbsp light soy sauce
300ml (½ pint) coconut milk
150ml (¼ pint) beef stock
4 red chillies, bruised
50g (2oz) cashew nuts

serves 4
preparation: 30 minutes
cooking time: 40–45 minutes
per serving: 500 cals; 34g fat;
   22g carbohydrate

1 Cut the sirloin steak into 3cm (1¼ inch) cubes.

2 Put the cloves, coriander, cumin and cardamom seeds into a small heavy-based frying pan over a high heat for 1–2 minutes until the spices release their aroma. Leave to cool slightly, then grind to a powder in a spice grinder or blender.

3 Purée the garlic, ginger and onion in a blender or food processor to form a smooth paste. Heat the two oils together in a deep frying pan. Add the onion purée with the curry paste and stir-fry for 5 minutes, then add the roasted ground spices and turmeric and fry for a further 5 minutes.

4 Add the beef to the pan and fry for 5 minutes until browned on all sides. Add the remaining ingredients, except the cashew nuts. Bring to the boil, then lower the heat, cover and simmer gently for 20–25 minutes until the beef is tender and the potatoes are cooked.

5 Stir in the cashew nuts and serve the curry with plain boiled rice or noodles and stir-fried vegetables.

Spiced Silverside

1.8kg (4lb) piece boned salted silverside
1 onion, peeled and sliced
4 carrots, peeled and sliced
1 small turnip, peeled and sliced
1–2 celery sticks, chopped
8 cloves
125g (4oz) light muscovado sugar
½ tsp mustard powder
1 tsp ground cinnamon
juice of 1 orange

serves 6
preparation: 20 minutes, plus soaking
cooking time: 4–5 hours
per serving: 200 cals; 6g fat;
    10g carbohydrate

1 Soak the piece of meat in cold water to cover for several hours or overnight.

2 Rinse the silverside and put into a large heavy-based pan with the vegetables. Add sufficient water to cover the meat and bring slowly to the boil. Skim off any scum, cover with a lid and simmer for 3–4 hours until tender. Leave to cool in the liquid.

3 Drain the meat well, then put into a roasting tin and press the cloves into the fat. Mix together the sugar, mustard, cinnamon and orange juice and spread over the meat.

4 Bake in the oven at 180°C (160°C fan oven) mark 4 for 45 minutes to 1 hour, basting from time to time. Serve hot or cold.

note: *If the meat is to be served cold, you may prefer to press it after cooking. Put into a casserole or foil-lined tin in which it fits snugly. Spoon a little of the liquid over the meat, cover with a board or plate and put a heavy weight on top. Leave in a cold place for several hours.*

Carbonnade de Boeuf

1.4kg (3lb) chuck steak, trimmed
50g (2oz) beef dripping
700g (1½lb) onions, peeled, halved and
    thinly sliced
4 garlic cloves, peeled and crushed
2 tbsp light muscovado sugar
3 tbsp plain flour
600ml (1 pint) light ale
300ml (½ pint) beef stock
1 bay leaf
2 large thyme sprigs
salt and pepper
2 tbsp wine or cider vinegar
chopped parsley, to garnish

serves 6
preparation: 35 minutes
cooking time: about 2½ hours
per serving: 490 cals; 19g fat;
    24g carbohydrate

1 Cut the meat into fairly large pieces, roughly 5cm (2 inches) square and 1cm (½ inch) thick. Heat the beef dripping in a large heavy-based frying pan and brown the meat in batches over a high heat. Transfer to a large casserole, using a slotted spoon.

2 Add the onions to the pan and cook gently for 10 minutes, stirring until they begin to soften. Add the garlic and sugar, mix well and cook for 10 minutes or until they begin to brown and caramelise.

3 Stir in the flour, then gradually add the beer, stirring. Bring to the boil, scraping up any sediment from the bottom of the pan, then pour over the beef in the casserole.

4 Add the stock, herbs and plenty of pepper; stir lightly to mix. Bring to a simmer, then cover tightly and cook in the oven at 150°C (130°C fan oven) mark 2 for about 2 hours.

5 Stir in the vinegar and cook for a further 30 minutes or until the meat is very tender. Check the seasoning. Serve garnished with chopped parsley.

variation: *For a darker stew, use half light ale and half stout.*

Beef Braised in Red Wine

1.5–1.6kg (3–3½lb) piece topside or top rump
   of beef
2 onions, peeled and chopped
2 carrots, peeled and chopped
2 celery sticks, chopped
2 bay leaves
2 large rosemary sprigs, plus extra to garnish
6 peppercorns
2 allspice berries, crushed
1 bottle full-bodied red wine, such as
   Burgundy or Barolo
2 tbsp olive oil
2 tbsp sun-dried tomato paste
300–600 ml (½–1 pint) beef stock
salt and pepper
few sun-dried tomatoes, roughly chopped
   (optional)

serves 8
preparation: 30 minutes, plus overnight
   marinating
cooking time: 2½–3 hours
per serving: 250 cals; 10g fat;
   6g carbohydrate

1 Put the piece of meat into a large bowl with the vegetables, bay leaves, rosemary sprigs, peppercorns and crushed allspice berries. Pour in the red wine, turn the meat, then cover the bowl and leave to marinate in the fridge overnight.

2 Take out the meat and pat dry. Strain the marinade, reserving the vegetables, herbs and spices.

3 Heat the olive oil in a deep flameproof casserole (just large enough to hold the meat and vegetables) and brown the meat on all sides. Stir in the vegetables, with the herbs and spices.

4 Pour over the reserved marinade and stir in the tomato paste. Add enough stock to just cover the meat and vegetables. Bring to a simmer, lower the heat and cover lightly. Cook at 170°C (150°C fan oven) mark 3 for 2½–3 hours until the meat is very tender, turning the beef every 30 minutes and topping up the liquid with extra stock if necessary.

5 Using a slotted spoon, lift out the meat and put into a covered dish; keep warm. Discard the bay leaves and rosemary sprigs, then pour the sauce and vegetables into a blender or food processor and whiz until smooth. Adjust the seasoning and reheat, adding the sun-dried tomatoes if using. The sauce should be quite thick; if not, boil to reduce.

6 To serve, carve the meat into thin slices and arrange on warmed serving plates. Garnish with rosemary and serve with the sauce and creamy mash.

Boeuf Bourguignonne

1kg (2¼lb) topside, rump or lean braising
   steak
50g (2oz) butter
2 tbsp oil
125g (4oz) bacon lardons
1 garlic clove, peeled and crushed
3 tbsp plain flour
salt and pepper
bouquet garni
150ml (¼ pint) beef stock
300ml (½ pint) Burgundy or other full-bodied
   red wine
12 baby onions, peeled
175g (6oz) button mushrooms
chopped parsley, to garnish

serves 6
preparation: 30 minutes
cooking time: 3 hours
per serving: 470 cals; 27g fat;
   14g carbohydrate

1 Cut the meat into 3cm (1¼ inch) cubes.
2 Melt half of the butter with 1 tbsp oil in a large flameproof casserole. Add the bacon and brown quickly, then remove with a slotted spoon.
3 Reheat the fat in the casserole and brown the meat in batches. Return the bacon to the casserole and add the garlic. Sprinkle in the flour and stir well.
4 Add salt and pepper, the bouquet garni, stock and wine. Bring to the boil, stirring, then cover and cook in the oven at 170°C (150°C fan oven) mark 3 for about 2½ hours.
5 Meanwhile, heat the remaining butter and oil in a frying pan and fry the onions until glazed and golden brown. Remove with a slotted spoon and set aside. Sauté the mushrooms in the pan for 2–3 minutes until slightly softened.
6 Add the sautéed mushrooms and onions to the casserole and cook for a further 30 minutes. Discard the bouquet garni, check the seasoning and serve sprinkled with chopped parsley.

Peppered Winter Stew

900g (2lb) stewing venison, beef or lamb
salt and pepper
25g (1oz) plain flour
5 tbsp oil
225g (8oz) baby onions or shallots, peeled
225g (8oz) onions, peeled and finely chopped
4 garlic cloves, peeled and crushed
2 tbsp tomato purée
125ml (4fl oz) red wine vinegar
1 bottle full-bodied red wine
2 tbsp redcurrant jelly
4–6 thyme sprigs, plus extra to garnish
4 bay leaves
6 cloves
600–900ml (1–1½ pints) beef stock
900g (2lb) mixed root vegetables, such as
   carrots, parsnips, turnips and celeriac,
   peeled

serves 6
preparation: 30 minutes
cooking time: about 2¼ hours
per serving: 450 cals; 19g fat;
   24g carbohydrate

1 Cut the meat into 4cm (1½ inch) cubes and toss in the seasoned flour. Heat 3 tbsp oil in a large deep flameproof casserole and quickly brown the meat on all sides, in batches. Remove and set aside.
2 Heat the remaining oil in the casserole and fry the whole baby onions for 5 minutes or until golden. Remove with a slotted spoon.
3 Add the chopped onion and garlic to the casserole. Cook, stirring, for 5–7 minutes or until starting to soften and turn golden. Add the tomato purée and cook for a further 2 minutes. Add the wine vinegar and red wine and bring to the boil. Let bubble for about 10 minutes.
4 Add the redcurrant jelly, thyme, bay leaves, cloves and 1 tbsp coarsely ground pepper. Return the meat to the casserole and pour in enough stock to barely cover it. Bring to a simmer, cover and cook in the oven at 180°C (160°C fan oven) mark 4 for 1–1½ hours.
5 Meanwhile cut the vegetables into 4cm (1½ inch) chunks; cut the carrots smaller.
6 Remove the meat from casserole with a slotted spoon. Strain the liquid through a fine sieve, pushing through the residue, and return to the casserole. Add the meat, root vegetables and browned baby onions. Bring to a simmer, cover and cook in the oven for a further 45–50 minutes or until the vegetables and meat are very tender. Serve garnished with thyme.

Beef, Mushroom and Red Wine Casserole

800g (1¾lb) braising steak

1 tbsp steak seasoning

3 tbsp oil

25g (1oz) butter

200g (7oz) bacon lardons

350g (12oz) onions, peeled and sliced

1 large garlic clove, peeled and crushed

350g (12oz) small carrots, peeled and halved
    lengthways

1 tbsp tomato purée

1 tbsp plain flour

225ml (8fl oz) red wine

300ml (½ pint) beef stock

bouquet garni (sprig each of thyme and
    parsley, bay leaf and strip of orange zest)

6 juniper berries, crushed or chopped

salt and pepper

225g (8oz) shiitake, large flat or chestnut
    mushrooms

chopped parsley, to garnish

serves 4

preparation: 20 minutes

cooking time: about 1¾ hours

per serving: 690 cals; 44g fat;
    16g carbohydrate

1 Cut the steak into 4cm (1½ inch) cubes and toss in the steak seasoning. Heat 2 tbsp oil in a large flameproof casserole, then add the butter. When it is foaming, brown the beef in batches over a high heat on all sides, then set aside.

2 Fry the bacon in the casserole until it is golden. Add the onions, garlic and carrots and cook over a medium heat until lightly browned.

3 Stir in the tomato purée, then sprinkle in the flour and cook for 1–2 minutes, stirring. Stir in the red wine and bring to the boil. Let bubble for 2–3 minutes.

4 Return the beef to the casserole, and pour in enough stock to barely cover it. Tuck the bouquet garni into the casserole, add the juniper berries and season with salt and pepper. Bring to the boil, then cover and cook in the oven at 170°C (150°C fan oven) mark 3 for 1 hour or until tender.

5 Meanwhile, heat the remaining oil in a large frying pan, add the mushrooms and stir-fry until just cooked. When the beef is tender, remove the bouquet garni and add the mushrooms to the casserole. Serve scattered with chopped parsley.

Beef Goulash

1kg (2¼lb) stewing steak

2 tbsp plain flour

salt and pepper

3 tbsp oil

700g (1½lb) onions, peeled and chopped

225g (8oz) pancetta cubes or bacon lardons

2 garlic cloves, peeled and crushed

4 tbsp paprika

2 tsp dried mixed herbs

400g can peeled plum tomatoes

300ml (½ pint) beef stock

150ml (¼ pint) soured cream

chopped parsley, to garnish

serves 6

preparation: 30 minutes

cooking time: 2–2½ hours

per serving: 540 cals; 34g fat;
    16g carbohydrate

1 Cut the beef into 3cm (1¼ inch) cubes. Season the flour with salt and pepper and toss the beef cubes in it to coat.

2 Heat 1 tbsp oil in a deep flameproof casserole. Add the onions and fry gently for 5–7 minutes until starting to soften and turn golden; remove. Add the pancetta to the casserole and fry over a high heat until crispy; remove. Heat the remaining oil in the casserole and quickly fry the meat in small batches until browned on all sides.

3 Return the onions and pancetta to the casserole. Stir in the garlic and paprika, and cook, stirring, for 1 minute.

4 Add the herbs, tomatoes and stock. Bring to a simmer, cover tightly and cook in the oven at 170°C (150°C fan oven) mark 3 for 1½–2 hours or until tender. Check after 1 hour, adding a little extra liquid if necessary.

5 Check the seasoning, then stir in the soured cream. Garnish with parsley and serve with noodles.

Chilli con Carne

2 tbsp sunflower oil

1 onion, peeled and roughly chopped

2 garlic cloves, peeled and crushed

1 red pepper, cored, deseeded and chopped

450g (1lb) beef mince

1 tsp chilli powder

1 tsp chilli flakes

1 tsp ground cumin

1 tsp ground coriander

300ml (½ pint) red wine

1 tbsp Worcestershire sauce

400g can chopped tomatoes

salt and pepper

400g can kidney beans, rinsed and drained

grated cheese, to sprinkle

guacamole (page 67) or soured cream, to
    serve

serves 6
preparation: 10 minutes
cooking time: about 1 hour
per serving (without guacamole): 270 cals;
    12g fat; 13g carbohydrate

1 Heat the oil in a large frying pan, add the onion, garlic and red pepper, and cook gently for 5 minutes.
2 Add the beef mince to the pan, stirring to break it up, and cook over a high heat for 5 minutes or until well browned.
3 Stir in the chilli powder and flakes, cumin and coriander, then cook for 2 minutes. Add the red wine and simmer for 2 minutes.
4 Stir in the Worcestershire sauce and chopped tomatoes, and season with salt and pepper, then cook for 30 minutes. Add the kidney beans to the mixture and cook for a further 20 minutes.
5 Serve the chilli with rice, or piled on top of baked potatoes. Sprinkle with the grated cheese and serve with guacamole or soured cream.

notes
• This chilli is fairly mild, but it can easily be made hotter by adding more chilli powder and flakes.
• The flavour is improved if the chilli con carne is prepared a day ahead.

Italian Meatballs in Tomato Sauce

2 tbsp olive oil

350g (12oz) onions, peeled and chopped

3 garlic cloves, peeled and crushed

2 x 400g cans chopped tomatoes

1 tsp salt

1 tbsp cider vinegar

½ tsp ground cinnamon

450g (1lb) lean beef mince

2 tbsp chopped basil

1 tsp dried oregano

75g (3oz) fresh breadcrumbs

1 egg, plus 1 egg yolk, beaten

2 tbsp chopped parsley, plus extra to garnish

3 tbsp freshly grated Parmesan cheese

salt and pepper

12 thin smoked streaky bacon rashers,
    about 200g (7oz)

serves 4
preparation: 20 minutes
cooking time: 1¼ hours
per serving: 580 cals; 37g fat;
    22g carbohydrate

1 Heat the olive oil in a shallow flameproof casserole, add the onions with two-thirds of the garlic and fry gently until beginning to soften, about 5–7 minutes. Add the tomatoes, salt, cider vinegar and cinnamon. Bring to the boil, cover and simmer for 20 minutes.
2 Put the beef mince in a bowl with the basil, oregano, breadcrumbs, remaining garlic, egg, egg yolk, parsley and 1 tbsp Parmesan. Season with salt and pepper. Work the ingredients together with your hands until evenly mixed.
3 Shape the mixture into 12 even-sized balls, with dampened hands, then wrap a bacon rasher around each one.
4 Put the meatballs in the casserole on top of the tomato sauce. Cover and cook at 180°C (160°C fan oven) mark 4 for about 45 minutes or until piping hot and cooked through.
5 Scatter with the remaining Parmesan and plenty of chopped parsley. Serve with rice.

Beef Roulades with Tomato and Herb Sauce

12 very thin slices frying steak, about 450g
(1lb) in total
18 slices Parma ham, about 175g (6oz)
salt and pepper
olive oil, to fry

STUFFING

75g (3oz) pine nuts, toasted and chopped
50g (2oz) Parmesan cheese, freshly grated
4 garlic cloves, peeled and crushed
6 tbsp chopped parsley

TOMATO AND HERB SAUCE

2 tbsp olive oil
225g (8oz) shallots, peeled and chopped
2 garlic cloves, peeled and crushed
4 tbsp white wine
2 x 400g cans chopped tomatoes
3 tbsp chopped basil or parsley
pinch of sugar

serves 6
preparation: 25 minutes
cooking time: 25 minutes
per serving: 380 cals; 25g fat;
    8g carbohydrate

1 First make the stuffing. In a bowl, mix together the pine nuts, Parmesan, garlic and parsley. Season with salt and pepper to taste.

2 Lay the steak slices on a board. Put a slice of Parma ham on each steak and spread with a thin layer of the stuffing. Roll up and secure with a wooden cocktail stick. Chill the roulades in the fridge while preparing the sauce.

3 For the sauce, heat the olive oil in a pan, add the shallots and fry gently for 6–7 minutes. Add the garlic and cook, stirring, for 1–2 minutes. Add the wine, tomatoes, basil and sugar. Bring to the boil and simmer, uncovered, for 15 minutes. Season with salt and pepper to taste.

4 Heat a thin film of olive oil in a large frying pan. When hot, add the beef roulades and fry, turning carefully, over a medium-high heat for 2–3 minutes or until browned all over.

5 Serve immediately, with the tomato sauce.

note: *You may find it necessary to fry the roulades in two batches. If so, keep the first batch warm in a low oven while you cook the rest.*

Cottage Pie

1 tbsp oil
450g (1lb) onions, peeled and chopped
450g (1lb) beef mince
1 tbsp tomato purée
1 tbsp plain flour
1 tbsp Worcestershire sauce
450ml (¾ pint) beef stock
salt and pepper
700g (1½lb) potatoes, peeled and cut into
    large chunks
450g (1lb) parsnips, peeled and quartered
25g (1oz) butter
4 tbsp milk

serves 4
preparation: 15 minutes
cooking time: about 2 hours
per serving: 470 cals; 16g fat;
    56g carbohydrate

1 Heat the oil in a flameproof casserole, add the onions and fry gently for 10 minutes or until softened.

2 Add the beef and cook on a higher heat, stirring, for about 15 minutes until the mince is well browned.

3 Stir in the tomato purée and cook for 30 seconds. Stir in the flour, then add the Worcestershire sauce and stock. Bring to the boil and season generously.

4 Cover and cook in the oven at 170°C (150°C fan oven) mark 3 for about 45 minutes or until the mince is very tender. Cool slightly, then skim off any fat from the surface. Increase the oven temperature to 220°C (200°C fan oven) mark 7.

5 Meanwhile, put the potatoes and parsnips into a large pan of salted water. Bring to the boil and cook for about 20–25 minutes until very soft. Drain and put back into the pan over a low heat to dry off. Mash until smooth, and then beat in the butter and milk. Season with salt and pepper to taste.

6 Put the beef mixture into a 1.7 litre (3 pint) dish and spoon the mash on top. Stand the dish on a baking tray and bake for 25–30 minutes or until piping hot and the topping is golden brown.

variation: *To make individual pies, use four 450ml (¾ pint) shallow ovenproof dishes.*

American-style Hamburger

1kg (2¼lb) extra-lean beef mince
2 tbsp steak seasoning
salt and pepper
sunflower oil, to brush

TO SERVE
6 large soft traditional rolls
6 thin-cut slices havarti or raclette cheese
4 small cocktail gherkins, sliced lengthways
1–2 tsp American-style mustard
6 tbsp mayonnaise
6 lettuce leaves such as frisée or batavia
4 large vine-ripened tomatoes, sliced
1 large shallot, peeled and sliced into rings

serves 6
preparation: 20 minutes, plus chilling
cooking time: 15 minutes
per serving: 650 cals; 30g fat;
   51g carbohydrate

1 Tip the beef mince into a large bowl and add the steak seasoning, 2 tsp salt and plenty of pepper. Mix the ingredients together thoroughly, with clean hands.
2 Press the mixture into six lightly oiled 10cm (4 inch) rösti rings on a foil-lined baking sheet, or use your hands to shape the mixture into 6 patties. Cover with clingfilm and chill for at least 1 hour.
3 Heat a large griddle pan. Cut the rolls in half and toast, cut-side down, on the griddle until golden.
4 Lightly oil the griddle pan. Ease the burgers out of the moulds and brush lightly with oil. Cook the burgers over a medium heat for about 3 minutes, then carefully turn, using a palette knife. Put a cheese slice and a few gherkin slices on each and cook for a further 3 minutes.
5 Spread the toasted side of the rolls with a little mustard and the mayonnaise. Put the bases on warmed plates and cover with the lettuce, tomato and shallot. Put the burgers on top and sandwich together with the tops of the rolls. Serve straightaway.

Steak and Onion Puff Pie

3 tbsp oil
2 onions, peeled and sliced
900g (2lb) casserole beef, cut into cubes
3 tbsp plain flour, plus extra to dust
500ml (16fl oz) hot beef stock
2 rosemary sprigs, bruised
salt and pepper
500g pack puff pastry
beaten egg, to glaze

serves 4
preparation: 20 minutes, plus chilling
cooking time: 2½ hours
per serving: 1080 cals; 67g fat;
   67g carbohydrate

1 Heat 1 tbsp oil in a flameproof casserole and sauté the onions for 10 minutes or until golden. Lift out with a slotted spoon, and put them to one side.

2 In the same casserole over a high heat, sear the beef in batches, turning until browned all over, and using the rest of the oil as necessary. Lift out the meat with a slotted spoon and set aside.

3 Sprinkle the flour into the casserole and cook for 1–2 minutes to brown. Return the onions and beef, add the hot stock and rosemary, and season well with salt and pepper. Cover and bring to a simmer, then cook in the oven at 170°C (150°C fan oven) mark 3 for 1½ hours or until the meat is tender.

4 About 30 minutes before the end of the cooking time, roll out the puff pastry on a lightly floured surface until about 5cm (2 inches) larger all round than a deep 1.2 litre (2 pint) pie dish. Put the pastry on a baking sheet and chill for 30 minutes.

5 Remove the casserole from the oven and increase the temperature to 220°C (200°C fan oven) mark 7. Transfer the beef mixture to the pie dish. Brush the rim of the dish with water, then lift the pastry lid over the filling and press the edge down lightly on to the rim to seal. Lightly score the top with a small, sharp knife and brush with beaten egg.

6 Stand the pie dish on the baking sheet and bake in the oven for 30 minutes or until the pastry is crisp and golden brown.

variation: *To make individual steak pies, use four 300ml (½ pint) pie dishes and bake for 25 minutes.*

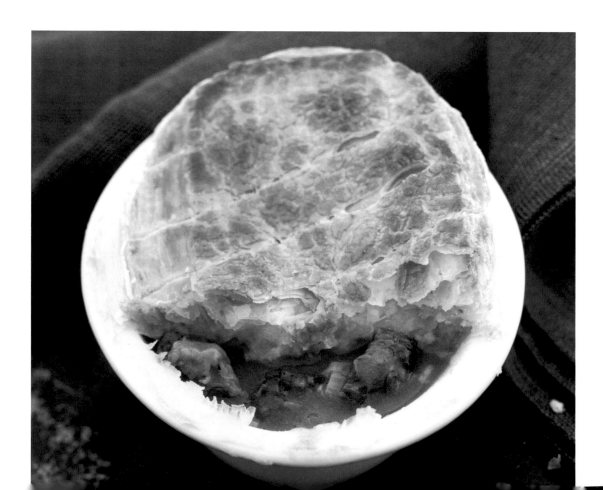

Steak and Kidney Pudding

700g (1½lb) braising or stewing steak, trimmed

225g (8oz) ox kidney, trimmed and core removed

4 tbsp plain flour

salt and pepper

3 tbsp oil

2 small onions, peeled and chopped

450ml (¾ pint) beef stock

6 tbsp port

225g (8oz) mushrooms, halved if large

8 canned smoked oysters (optional)

PASTRY

300g (11oz) self-raising flour

½ tsp salt

150g (5oz) suet

flour, to dust

serves 6
preparation: 35 minutes
cooking time: about 3½ hours
per serving: 690 cals; 36g fat;
   54g carbohydrate

1 Cut the steak into 2cm (¾ inch) pieces. Cut the kidney into 1cm (½ inch) chunks. Season the flour with salt and pepper and use to coat the meat.

2 Heat the oil in a large frying pan and fry the steak in batches until browned on all sides. Transfer to a flameproof casserole, using a slotted spoon. Brown the kidney in the frying pan, then add to the steak in the casserole.

3 Add the onions to the frying pan and fry gently for 10 minutes or until soft. Add to the meat with the stock, port and seasoning. Bring to a simmer, cover and simmer gently for 1¼ hours.

4 To make the pastry, sift the flour and salt into a bowl and stir in the suet. Add enough water – about 175ml (6fl oz) – to mix to a soft dough. Roll out a scant three quarters of the dough on a lightly floured surface and use to line a 1.7 litre (3 pint) pudding basin.

5 Stir the mushrooms into the meat, with the oysters if using. Turn into the lined basin. Brush the top edge of the pastry with water. Roll out the remainder to make a lid and lay over the pudding, pressing the edges together to seal.

6 Cover the basin with a pleated, double layer of greaseproof paper, securing under the rim with string. Cover with foil and put in a steamer or on an upturned saucer in a large saucepan. Pour in enough hot water to come halfway up side of the basin. Cover and steam for 2 hours, checking the water level occasionally and topping up with more boiling water as necessary.

7 Remove the foil and paper and loosen the edges of the pudding. Invert on to a warmed plate and serve.

Cornish Pasties

450g (1lb) stewing steak, trimmed

175g (6oz) potato, peeled and diced

175g (6oz) swede, peeled and diced

1 onion, peeled and chopped

1 tbsp chopped thyme

1 tbsp chopped parsley

1 tbsp Worcestershire sauce

salt and pepper

shortcrust pastry (page 269), made with 500g (1lb 2oz) plain flour, plus flour to dust

25g (1oz) butter

1 egg, beaten, to glaze

serves 6
preparation: 30 minutes
cooking time: 1¼ hours
per serving: 640 cals; 36g fat;
   59g carbohydrate

1 Cut the meat into very small pieces and put into a bowl with the potato, swede and onion. Add the chopped herbs, Worcestershire sauce and seasoning, then mix well.

2 Divide the pastry into six and roll out each piece thinly on a lightly floured surface to a 20cm (8 inch) round. Spoon the filling on to one half of each round and top with a small knob of butter.

3 Brush the edges of the pastry with water, then fold the uncovered side over to make pasties. Press the edges firmly together to seal and crimp them. Make a slit in the top of each pasty. Put on a baking sheet.

4 Brush the pastry with beaten egg to glaze and bake the pasties at 220°C (200°C fan oven) mark 7 for 15 minutes. Reduce the oven setting to 170°C (150°C fan oven) mark 3 and bake for a further 1 hour to cook the filling. Serve the pasties warm or cold.

Veal Tonnato

1 boned loin of veal, about 900g (2lb)

salt and pepper

225g (8oz) frozen leaf spinach, defrosted

1 tbsp extra-virgin olive oil

finely grated zest of 1 lemon

6–8 thin slices Parma ham

300ml (½ pint) dry white wine

1 carrot, peeled and sliced

1 celery stick, sliced

1 onion, peeled and quartered

2 bay leaves

4–6 juniper berries, crushed

DRESSING

200g can tuna chunks in oil, drained

4 anchovy fillets in oil, drained

300ml (½ pint) good thick mayonnaise

3 tbsp chopped basil

1 tbsp capers in brine, rinsed, drained and
   roughly chopped

TO GARNISH

black olives

serves 6–8

preparation: 30 minutes, plus chilling

cooking time: 1¼–1½ hours

per serving: 730–550 cals; 56–42g fat;
   4–3g carbohydrate

1 Lay the meat on a clean surface and season the inside of the flap (where the bones meet). Squeeze the spinach to remove as much moisture as possible, then toss in the olive oil, lemon zest and seasoning to taste. Spread this over the meat, bringing the flap over the spinach to cover.

2 Carefully wrap the meat in the Parma ham and tie at intervals with string.

3 Put the veal into a heavy flameproof casserole. Add the wine, carrot, celery, onion, bay leaves, juniper berries and seasoning. Add enough water to just cover the veal and bring slowly to the boil. Lower the heat and barely simmer for 1¼–1½ hours until tender. Leave the veal to cool in the liquid.

4 When completely cold, take out the veal, drain and pat dry. Strain and reserve the liquid. Cover the veal and chill.

5 To make the dressing, mash the tuna and anchovy fillets together or pound with a pestle and mortar. Stir in the mayonnaise, basil and capers. Thin to a pouring consistency with a little of the reserved liquid and check the seasoning.

6 To serve, thinly slice the veal and arrange on a serving platter. Spoon the dressing over the meat and scatter with black olives to garnish.

Saltimbocca alla Romana

8 veal escalopes, about 125g (4oz) each

1–2 tbsp lemon juice

pepper

8 sage leaves, plus extra to garnish

8 thin slices Parma ham

50g (2oz) butter

1 tbsp oil

2 tbsp Marsala

serves 8

preparation: 10 minutes

cooking time: about 10 minutes

per serving: 220 cals; 11g fat;
   trace carbohydrate

1 Put the veal escalopes between two sheets of greaseproof paper and pound with a rolling pin to flatten. Sprinkle with lemon juice and pepper.

2 Put a sage leaf on each escalope and cover with a slice of Parma ham. Roll up and secure with a wooden cocktail stick.

3 Heat the butter and oil in a frying pan, add the veal rolls and fry gently until golden brown. Stir in the Marsala, bring to simmering point, then cover the pan and simmer gently for about 8–10 minutes.

4 Serve the veal rolls with the pan juices poured over, and garnished with sage.

Veal Schnitzel with Salsa Verde

4 veal escalopes, about 100g (3½oz) each
175g (6oz) dried breadcrumbs
125g (4oz) ground almonds
salt and pepper
flour, to coat
1 egg, beaten
6 tbsp oil

TO SERVE
salsa verde (page 28)
lemon wedges

serves 4
preparation: 30 minutes
cooking time: 15 minutes
per serving (without salsa verde): 650 cals;
    41g fat; 39g carbohydrate

1 Lay the veal escalopes between two pieces of greaseproof paper and beat with a rolling pin to flatten. If too large for the frying pan, cut in half.
2 Mix the dried breadcrumbs and ground almonds together on a plate. Season the veal, then coat lightly with flour. Dip each piece in beaten egg, then into the breadcrumb mixture to coat, patting to adhere.
3 Fry the veal in three batches. Heat 2 tbsp oil in a large heavy-based frying pan, add one third of the veal and fry for 1–2 minutes on each side until deep golden brown. Transfer to a heatproof plate and keep warm in a low oven. Wipe out the frying pan with kitchen paper and cook the rest of the veal in the same way, using fresh oil for each batch.
4 Serve the schnitzel as soon as it is all cooked, with the salsa verde and lemon wedges.

Basil and Citrus Veal Escalopes

4 veal escalopes, about 100g (3½oz) each
25g (1oz) butter
1 tbsp olive oil
125ml (4fl oz) freshly squeezed orange juice
2 tbsp lemon juice
15g (½oz) basil leaves, shredded
salt and pepper

serves 4
preparation: 10 minutes
cooking time: 5 minutes
per serving: 250 cals; 12g fat;
    3g carbohydrate

1 Place the veal escalopes between two sheets of greaseproof paper and pound with a rolling pin until about 3mm (1/8 inch) thick. If very large, cut them into manageable neat pieces.
2 Heat the butter and olive oil in a heavy-based frying pan or sauté pan. Fry the veal, in two batches if necessary, for 1 minute on each side. Add the orange and lemon juices and let bubble for a few seconds, turning the veal in the juice.
3 Add the shredded basil and season with salt and pepper to taste. Serve at once, with noodles.

Roast Leg of Lamb with Rosemary and Garlic

1.7kg (3¾lb) leg of lamb

50g can anchovy fillets in oil, drained,
   reserving 1 tbsp oil

2 rosemary stems, separated into small
   sprigs

2 garlic cloves, peeled and sliced

salt and pepper

150ml (¼ pint) red wine

serves 6

preparation: 20 minutes

cooking time: about 1 hour 40 minutes,
   plus resting

per serving: 270 cals; 11g fat;
   0g carbohydrate

1 Put the lamb on a board and make small incisions all over the skin. Roll up the anchovy fillets and insert these into alternate slits. Push a tiny sprig of rosemary and a slice of garlic into each of the other slits.

2 Put the lamb into a roasting tin and drizzle with the reserved anchovy oil. Season with salt and pepper. Roast at 200°C (180°C fan oven) mark 6, allowing 20 minutes per 450g (1lb), plus 20 minutes.

3 Lift the lamb on to a warmed plate, cover with foil and rest in a warm place for about 15 minutes. Drain off the fat from the roasting tin, then add the red wine to the remaining juices. Bring to the boil on the hob, stirring to deglaze. Add any juices from the lamb and season with salt and pepper to taste.

4 Carve the lamb and serve with the gravy, and vegetables of your choice.

Roast Shoulder of Lamb with a Fruity Stuffing

50g (2oz) ready-to-eat pitted prunes

25g (1oz) ready-to-eat dried figs

25g (1oz) ready-to-eat dried apricots

300ml (½ pint) apple juice

25g (1oz) butter

125g (4oz) onion, peeled and chopped

125g (4oz) celery, roughly chopped

25g (1oz) walnuts, roughly chopped

50g (2oz) fresh breadcrumbs

½ tsp ground allspice

2 tbsp chopped parsley

1 egg yolk

salt and pepper

1.4kg (3lb) boned shoulder of lamb

2 tbsp oil

2–3 rosemary sprigs

4 garlic bulbs

350g (12oz) shallots or baby onions, peeled

450ml (¾ pint) lamb stock or water

150ml (¼ pint) dry white wine

serves 6–8

preparation: 35 minutes, plus overnight
   soaking

cooking time: about 2 hours, plus resting

per serving: 610–460 cals;
   34–25g fat; 24–18g carbohydrate

1 Roughly chop the dried fruit and soak in the apple juice overnight.

2 Melt the butter in a frying pan, add the chopped onion and celery and cook for 5–7 minutes until softened. Turn into a bowl and leave to cool.

3 Drain the fruits, reserving the liquid, and add them to the cooled mixture with the walnuts, breadcrumbs, allspice, parsley and egg yolk. Season generously and mix well.

4 Stuff the bone cavity of the lamb with the fruit mixture and sew or secure with wooden cocktail sticks. Season the meat with salt and pepper.

5 Heat the oil in a roasting tin and brown the lamb on all sides. Put the rosemary sprigs under the lamb and add the garlic bulbs and shallots to the tin. Roast at 200°C (180°C fan oven) mark 6 for about 1½ hours for pink lamb, 1¾ hours for well-done meat, basting the lamb and turning the shallots and garlic bulbs occasionally.

6 Put the lamb on a warmed platter with the shallots and 3 garlic bulbs. Loosely cover with foil and leave to rest in a warm place.

7 Skim off the fat from the roasting tin. Crush the remaining garlic bulb to extract the pulp and add to the roasting tin with the fruit liquid, stock and wine. Boil for 5–10 minutes or until syrupy. Check the seasoning and strain into a warmed sauceboat.

8 Carve the lamb and serve with the shallots, garlic, gravy and vegetables of your choice.

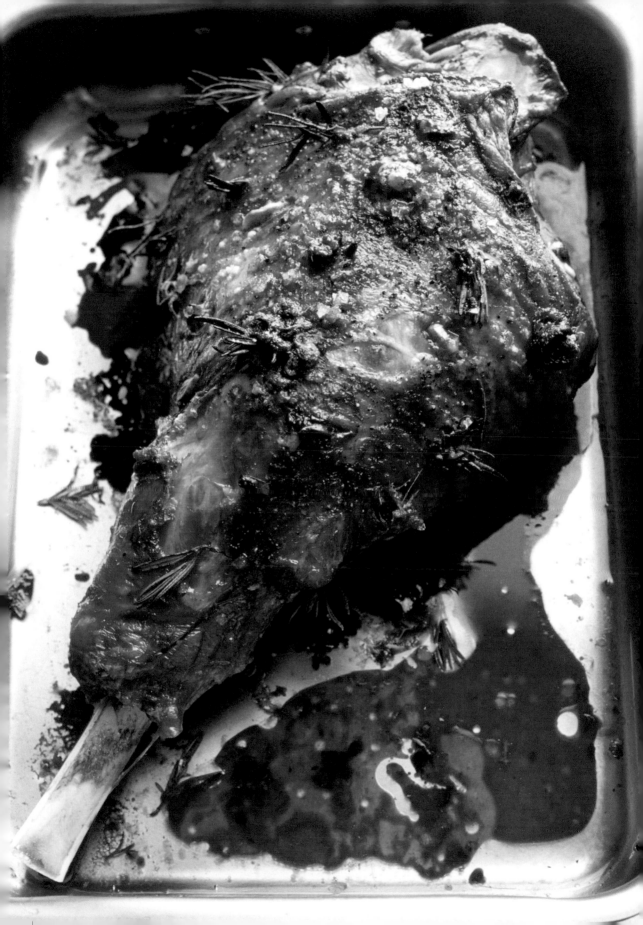

Herb-crusted Rack of Lamb

1 onion, peeled and sliced
1kg (2¼lb) potatoes, peeled and thinly
 sliced
2 garlic cloves, peeled and sliced
butter, to grease
salt and pepper
300ml (½ pint) hot vegetable stock
2 French-trimmed racks of lamb, each
 with 8 cutlets
3 tbsp grainy French mustard
75g (3oz) fresh breadcrumbs
2 tsp chopped rosemary, plus 1 long stem
4 tbsp chopped flat-leafed parsley
6 tbsp olive oil

serves 4
preparation: 25 minutes
cooking time: about 1¾ hours, plus resting
per serving: 590 cals; 30g fat;
 56g carbohydrate

1 Put the onion into a pan of cold water, bring to the boil and simmer for 2 minutes, then drain.

2 Layer the potatoes, onion and garlic in a greased 1.5 litre (2½ pint) roasting tin, starting and ending with potatoes. Season with salt and pepper and add the hot stock. Bake at 200°C (180°C fan oven) mark 6 for 1 hour or until the potatoes are tender, basting every 20 minutes.

3 Season the lamb with salt and pepper and spread the mustard over the meaty side.

4 Put the breadcrumbs in a bowl. Add the chopped rosemary, parsley, olive oil and seasoning; mix well. Press the mixture on to the mustard-coated surface of the lamb. Stand the lamb racks on a wire rack, resting on the rosemary stem.

5 Increase the oven temperature to 220°C (200°C fan oven) mark 7. Sit the rack holding the lamb on top of the potatoes and cook in the oven for 40 minutes for rare, 50 minutes for medium-rare lamb. Cover with foil and leave to rest for 10 minutes before serving.

Roast Lamb with Mushroom and Garlic Stuffing

225g (8oz) brown-cap mushrooms
6 large garlic cloves, peeled
4 tbsp olive oil
1 leek, trimmed and chopped
3 tbsp chopped oregano
salt and pepper
2.3kg (5lb) boned leg of lamb
3–4 tbsp redcurrant jelly
2 tsp wine vinegar
150ml (¼ pint) red wine
300ml (½ pint) lamb stock
herb sprigs, to garnish

serves 8
preparation: 20 minutes, plus cooling
cooking time: 2½–3 hours, plus resting
per serving: 500 cals; 39g fat;
 6g carbohydrate

1 Put the mushrooms and garlic into a food processor and whiz briefly until finely chopped. Heat the olive oil in a frying pan. Add the mushrooms, garlic and leek and fry for about 10 minutes until the juices have evaporated and the mixture is the consistency of a thick paste. Stir in the oregano and season with salt and pepper. Leave to cool.

2 Open out the boned lamb and pack the mushroom and garlic stuffing down the centre. Fold the meat over the stuffing to enclose and tie at intervals with cotton string. Put the lamb, joined-side down, into a roasting tin.

3 Roast the lamb at 180°C (160°C fan oven) mark 4 for 25 minutes per 450g (1lb) plus 25 minutes for medium; 30 minutes per 450g (1lb) plus 30 minutes for well done.

4 Meanwhile, melt the redcurrant jelly in a small pan with the wine vinegar. Thirty minutes before the end of the roasting time, brush the lamb with the redcurrant glaze. Repeat several times before the end of the cooking time.

5 Lift the lamb on to a warmed serving platter and leave to rest in a warm place while you prepare the gravy. Drain off the fat from the roasting tin and stir in the red wine and stock. Bring to the boil and boil until slightly reduced. Strain the gravy, if preferred, into a warmed sauceboat.

6 Remove the string from the lamb. Surround with herbs and serve accompanied by the gravy, and vegetables of your choice.

variation: *Whole roasted garlic bulbs make an attractive and delicious garnish. Roast them in their skins around the meat in the roasting tin.*

Crown Roast of Lamb

2 French-trimmed racks of lamb, each with
  6 cutlets
40g (1½oz) butter
1 large onion, peeled and chopped
4 celery sticks, chopped
1 large eating apple
50g (2oz) ready-to-eat dried apricots,
  chopped
150g (5oz) fresh breadcrumbs
2 tbsp chopped parsley
finely grated zest of ½ large lemon
5 tsp lemon juice
1 egg, beaten
salt and pepper
1–2 tbsp olive oil
1 tbsp plain flour
300ml (½ pint) lamb stock

serves 6
preparation: 30 minutes
cooking time: about 1 hour
per serving: 500 cals; 27g fat;
  23g carbohydrate

1 Bend the lamb racks around, fat-side inwards, and sew together using cotton string to form a crown.
2 Melt the butter in a pan, add the onion and celery and cook gently for 5–7 minutes until softened. Meanwhile, peel, core and chop the apple. Add to the pan and cook for a further 2–3 minutes until golden brown. Turn into a bowl and leave to cool.
3 Stir in the apricots, breadcrumbs, parsley, lemon zest and juice, egg and seasoning. Allow to cool.
4 Fill the centre of the crown with the stuffing. Put into a small roasting tin and spoon over the olive oil. Cover the exposed bones with foil. Roast at 200°C (180°C fan oven) mark 6 for about 1 hour, basting occasionally and covering with foil if necessary to avoid over-browning.
5 Remove the foil and transfer the crown roast to a warmed serving dish; keep warm. Drain off as much fat as possible from the roasting tin, add the flour and blend well. Cook for 1–2 minutes, stirring, then stir in the stock and cook for 2–3 minutes. Season with salt and pepper to taste and serve with the joint.

variation

Guard of Honour: *This is also prepared from two French-trimmed racks of lamb. Interlace the bones, fat-side outwards, to form an arch. Fill the cavity with the stuffing (as above) and secure with string.*

Minted Lamb Chops with Pea Purée

2 tbsp golden caster sugar, plus a pinch
50ml (2fl oz) white wine vinegar
1 tbsp roughly chopped mint
50g (2oz) butter
125g (4oz) onion, peeled and finely chopped
350g (12oz) frozen peas
150ml (¼ pint) double cream
salt and pepper
4 lamb chops, about 175g (6oz) each

serves 4
preparation: 15 minutes, plus cooling
cooking time: 30 minutes
per serving: 520 cals; 38g fat;
  19g carbohydrate

1 Put the 2 tbsp caster sugar and the wine vinegar into a small pan and dissolve over a low heat, then bring to the boil and boil for 2–3 minutes. Turn into a bowl, cool, then stir in the mint.
2 Melt 25g (1oz) butter in a pan, add the onion and cook for 5–7 minutes or until softened and beginning to colour.
3 Add the peas, cream, pinch of sugar, salt, pepper and 150ml (¼ pint) water. Bring to the boil and simmer for 5–10 minutes or until the peas are tender and the liquid has reduced by half. Transfer to a food processor and process to a rough purée. Check the seasoning. Return to the pan.
4 Melt the remaining butter in a large frying pan. When it is hot and sizzling, add the lamb chops and fry for about 5 minutes on each side or until tender and well browned. Meanwhile, reheat the pea purée over a low heat.
5 Add the mint sauce to the lamb and swirl to mix with the pan juices. Serve the lamb chops with the pan juices poured over, accompanied by the pea purée.

Crisp Crumbed Lamb Cutlets

75g (3oz) breadcrumbs, made from
   one-day old bread
40g (1½oz) Parma ham, finely chopped
3 tbsp freshly grated Parmesan cheese
8 lamb cutlets, well-trimmed, or
   2 French-trimmed racks of lamb, about
   350g (12oz) each, divided into cutlets
salt and pepper
2 eggs, beaten
3 tbsp oil
3 large garlic cloves, peeled

serves 4
preparation time: 20 minutes
cooking time: 10 minutes
per serving: 520 cals; 32g fat;
   9g carbohydrate

1 Mix together the breadcrumbs, Parma ham and Parmesan, spread out on a large plate and set aside.
2 Season the lamb with salt and pepper, and brush lightly with beaten egg. Press the lamb into the breadcrumbs to coat evenly, but lightly.
3 Heat the oil in a large non-stick frying pan, add the garlic cloves and heat gently until golden brown, then discard the garlic.
4 Fry the lamb in the garlic-infused oil over a low to medium heat for 4–5 minutes on each side until deep golden brown and crisp. Turn and fry the fat edge for 1–2 minutes.
5 Serve the cutlets with a tomato relish, new potatoes and a salad or green vegetable.

Lamb Chops with Ginger and Coriander

5cm (2 inch) piece fresh root ginger, peeled
   and roughly chopped
2 garlic cloves, peeled
2 tbsp thin honey
2 tbsp freshly squeezed orange juice
1 tsp Chinese five-spice powder
125g (4oz) butter, softened
4 lamb chops, about 175g (6oz) each
salt and pepper
2 tbsp white wine vinegar
2 tbsp dry sherry
2 tbsp chopped coriander

serves 4
preparation: 5 minutes
cooking time: about 10 minutes
per serving: 420 cals; 34g fat;
   6g carbohydrate

1 Put the ginger and garlic into a food processor with the honey and orange juice; process until finely chopped. Add the five-spice powder and softened butter and process again until evenly mixed.
2 Season the lamb chops with salt and pepper. Heat half of the spiced butter in a frying pan. Add the chops and fry for about 5 minutes on each side until tender and well browned; transfer to a warmed plate and keep warm.
3 Add the remaining spiced butter, wine vinegar and sherry to the pan. Bring to the boil, then add the chopped coriander.
4 Serve the chops straightaway, with the sauce.

Lamb Steaks with Aubergine and Mint Pesto

4 lamb leg steaks
1 medium aubergine, trimmed
olive oil, to brush
salt and pepper
balsamic vinegar, to sprinkle

MINT PESTO
50g (2oz) unblanched almonds
25g (1oz) mint leaves
25g (1oz) parsley leaves
250ml (8fl oz) extra-virgin olive oil
75g (3oz) Parmesan cheese, freshly grated
1 tsp lemon juice

serves 4
preparation: 20 minutes
cooking time: 8 minutes
per serving: 940 cals; 84g fat;
   3g carbohydrate

1 First make the mint pesto. Spread the almonds on a baking tray and roast at 180°C (160°C fan oven) mark 4 until well browned. Cool, then put into a food processor with the mint and parsley. Whiz until roughly chopped, adding a little olive oil. Stir in the remaining oil, Parmesan and lemon juice.

2 Slice the aubergine to give 8 good slices. Brush these, and the lamb steaks with olive oil. Season well with salt and pepper.

3 Put the lamb steaks and aubergines on a grill rack or preheated griddle pan and cook for 3–5 minutes on each side.

4 Serve the lamb steaks on the aubergine slices. Sprinkle with a little balsamic vinegar and drizzle with the mint pesto. Serve with roasted tomatoes, topped with any remaining pesto.

Lamb Noisettes with Tarragon Sauce

2 tbsp olive oil
8 lamb noisettes, about 125g (4oz) each
175g (6oz) onion, peeled and finely chopped
1 tbsp tarragon vinegar
150ml (¼ pint) white wine
150ml (¼ pint) double cream
300ml (½ pint) lamb or chicken stock
salt and pepper
1 tbsp chopped tarragon, plus extra sprigs
   to garnish

serves 4
preparation: 25 minutes
cooking time: 25 minutes
per serving: 650 cals; 46g fat;
   5g carbohydrate

1 Heat 1 tbsp olive oil in a frying pan and brown the lamb noisettes, in batches, for 2 minutes on each side or until the fat is crisp.

2 Put the lamb noisettes in a roasting tin and cook at 200°C (180°C fan oven) mark 6 for 10 minutes for medium-rare; 15 minutes for well done.

3 Meanwhile, heat the remaining oil in the frying pan, add the onion and cook for 5–7 minutes until softened but not coloured. Add the tarragon vinegar and wine, bring to the boil and bubble for 2 minutes. Add the cream and stock; let bubble for 10 minutes or until syrupy. Check the seasoning.

4 Remove the string from the lamb. Add the chopped tarragon and roasting juices to the sauce and warm through.

5 Serve the lamb with the sauce poured over, garnished with tarragon sprigs.

Moroccan Lamb Kebabs

3 garlic cloves, peeled and roughly chopped

1 onion, peeled and roughly chopped

½ tsp ground coriander

½ tsp ground cumin

½ tsp sweet paprika

½ tsp ground ginger

1kg (2¼lb) lamb mince

3 tbsp chopped mint

3 tbsp chopped coriander

salt and pepper

12 large vine leaves (preserved in brine)

olive oil, to brush

serves 6

preparation: 30 minutes, plus soaking

cooking time: about 15 minutes

per serving: 300 cals; 17g fat;

   2g carbohydrate

1 Pre-soak 6 long wooden kebab skewers in cold water for 30 minutes (to stop them burning under the grill). Put the garlic, onion and spices in a food processor and whiz to form a paste. Add the minced lamb and herbs and pulse until well mixed. Season with salt and pepper.

2 Divide the mixture into 12 portions, then with wet hands, roll into long sausage shapes. Rinse and dry the vine leaves on kitchen paper. Wrap each kebab in a vine leaf and skewer lengthways through the middle, putting two on each skewer. Brush generously with olive oil and place side by side across the grill rack.

3 Grill the kebabs under a medium-high heat for about 15 minutes, turning frequently, until cooked through. Serve at once, with warm pitta bread, tzatziki (page 66) and a tomato salad.

Navarin of Lamb with Spring Vegetables

900g (2lb) boned shoulder of lamb

3 tbsp olive oil

1 onion, peeled and roughly chopped

1 carrot, peeled and roughly chopped

125g (4oz) celery, roughly chopped

2 garlic cloves, peeled and crushed

1 tbsp plain flour

2 tbsp sun-dried tomato paste

150ml (¼ pint) dry white wine

1 litre (1¾ pints) lamb or chicken stock

3 thyme sprigs, plus extra to garnish

2 bay leaves

125g (4oz) baby carrots, scraped

125g (4oz) baby turnips, peeled

175g (6oz) new potatoes

1 tbsp golden caster sugar

25g (1oz) butter

salt and pepper

125g (4oz) French beans, trimmed

125g (4oz) asparagus spears, trimmed

serves 6

preparation: 40 minutes

cooking time: 1½ hours

per serving: 420 cals; 24g fat;

   17g carbohydrate

1 Cut the lamb into 5cm (2 inch) cubes. Heat the olive oil in a large flameproof casserole. Brown the lamb in batches on all sides over a high heat; remove with a slotted spoon.

2 Add the onion, carrot and celery to the casserole and cook, stirring, for 10 minutes until softened and golden. Add the garlic, flour and tomato paste. Cook, stirring, for 2 minutes.

3 Add the wine, bring to the boil and bubble to reduce by half. Add the lamb, stock and herbs and bring to the boil. Cover tightly and cook in the oven at 150°C (130°C fan oven) mark 2 for 1 hour.

4 Towards the end of the cooking time, put the baby carrots, turnips and new potatoes into a frying pan with the sugar, butter and 300ml (½ pint) water. Bring to the boil and simmer for 15 minutes or until the water has evaporated and the vegetables are tender and glazed. If necessary, add more hot water and cook for a little longer.

5 Meanwhile, lift out the lamb and set aside; discard the herbs. Tip the stock and flavouring vegetables into a food processor and whiz until smooth. Return to the casserole with the lamb and simmer for 5 minutes. If necessary, thin the sauce with a little water and adjust the seasoning.

6 Meanwhile, bring a pan of salted water to the boil. Cook the French beans for 2 minutes, then add the asparagus and cook for a further 3 minutes. Drain and add to the lamb with the glazed vegetables. Toss to mix and serve garnished with thyme.

Moussaka

1kg (2¼lb) aubergines, trimmed
5 tbsp olive oil
salt and pepper
450g (1lb) onions, peeled and finely sliced
3 garlic cloves, peeled and crushed
700g (1½lb) lamb mince
2 tbsp sun-dried tomato paste
400g can chopped tomatoes
1 cinnamon stick, slightly crushed
2 bay leaves
1 tbsp chopped oregano, plus extra sprigs
   to garnish

TOPPING
200g carton Greek-style yogurt
1 large egg
50g (2oz) Parmesan cheese, freshly grated
freshly grated nutmeg
75g (3oz) feta cheese, roughly crumbled

serves 6
preparation: 20 minutes
cooking time: 1 hour 20 minutes, plus
   standing
per serving: 470 cals; 31g fat;
   12g carbohydrate

1 Cut the aubergines into 5mm (¼ inch) thick slices, brush both sides with a little olive oil and lay on four baking sheets. Season with salt and pepper. Roast at 200°C (180°C fan oven) mark 6 for 35–40 minutes, turning halfway through.

2 Meanwhile, heat the rest of the olive oil in a large pan. Add the onions and cook over a low heat for about 10 minutes until soft. Add the garlic and cook for 2 minutes. Tip into a bowl and set aside while you cook the mince.

3 Put the mince in the pan and brown, stirring, over a high heat. Return the onions and garlic to the pan. Add the tomato paste, chopped tomatoes, cinnamon, bay leaves and oregano. Bring to a simmer and add seasoning. Simmer, half-covered, for 20 minutes.

4 To make the topping, put the yogurt, egg and half the grated Parmesan into a bowl and season with salt, pepper and a little nutmeg. Mix together, using a balloon whisk, until combined.

5 Spoon half the lamb mixture into a 2 litre (3½ pint) ovenproof dish. Cover with half the aubergine slices, overlapping them as necessary. Season well and repeat the layers, finishing with aubergine slices.

6 Scatter the crumbled feta on top, then pour the yogurt mixture over and sprinkle with the remaining Parmesan. Bake for 35–40 minutes until golden brown. Leave the moussaka to stand for 10–15 minutes before serving, garnished with oregano and accompanied by a green salad.

Braised Lamb Shanks with Cannellini Beans

3 tbsp olive oil
6 lamb shanks
1 large onion, peeled and chopped
3 carrots, peeled and sliced
3 celery sticks, sliced
2 garlic cloves, peeled and crushed
2 x 400g cans chopped tomatoes
125ml (4fl oz) balsamic vinegar
salt and pepper
2 bay leaves
2 x 410g cans cannellini beans, drained
   and rinsed

serves 6
preparation: 15 minutes
cooking time: about 3 hours
per serving: 490 cals; 25g fat;
   20g carbohydrate

1 Heat the olive oil in a large flameproof casserole and brown the lamb shanks, in two batches, all over. Remove and set aside.

2 Add the onion, carrots, celery and garlic to the casserole and cook gently until softened and just beginning to colour.

3 Return the lamb to the casserole and add the chopped tomatoes and balsamic vinegar, giving the mixture a good stir. Season with salt and pepper and add the bay leaves. Bring to a simmer, cover and cook on the hob for 5 minutes.

4 Transfer to the oven and cook at 170°C (150°C fan oven) mark 3 for 1½–2 hours or until the lamb shanks are nearly tender.

4 Remove the casserole from the oven and add the cannellini beans. Cover and return to the oven for a further 30 minutes. Serve with some crusty bread – ciabatta would be perfect.

Lamb and Leek Hotpot

50g (2oz) butter
400g (14oz) small or medium leeks,
    trimmed and sliced
1 onion, peeled and chopped
800g (1¾lb) boneless lamb, cubed
1 tbsp plain flour
1 tbsp olive oil
2 garlic cloves, peeled and crushed
salt and pepper
800g (1¾lb) waxy potatoes, such as Desirée,
    peeled and sliced
3 tbsp chopped parsley
1 tsp chopped thyme
300ml (½ pint) lamb stock
142ml carton double cream

serves 6
preparation: 20 minutes
cooking time: 2¾–3 hours
per serving: 530 cals; 33g fat;
    27g carbohydrate

1 Melt half of the butter in a 3.5 litre (6 pint) flame-proof casserole. Add the leeks and onion, stirring to coat with the butter. Cover the casserole and cook over a low heat for 10 minutes.

2 Meanwhile, toss the lamb in the flour to coat lightly. Lift out the leeks and onion using a slotted spoon and set aside. Add the olive oil to the casserole and heat it, then brown the meat in batches with the garlic and plenty of salt and pepper. Remove from the heat, take out the meat and set aside.

3 Layer half the potatoes in the bottom of the casserole and season with salt and pepper. Add the meat, then spoon the leek mixture over. Arrange the remaining potatoes on top in an overlapping layer, sprinkle with the herbs, then pour in the stock.

4 Return the casserole to the heat and bring to a simmer. Cover and place on a low shelf in the oven at 170°C (150°C fan oven) mark 3. Cook for about 1 hour 50 minutes.

5 Remove the lid, dot the potatoes with the rest of the butter and add the cream. Cook the hotpot, uncovered, for a further 30–40 minutes until the potatoes are golden brown.

Lamb Meatballs with Dill Sauce

6 spring onions
175g (6oz) unsmoked rindless streaky bacon,
    roughly chopped
1 garlic clove, peeled
pinch of ground cinnamon
700g (1½lb) lean lamb mince
salt and pepper
3 tbsp olive oil
450ml (¾ pint) dry white wine
4 tbsp chopped dill, plus extra sprigs
    to garnish
300ml (½ pint) double cream
2 egg yolks

serves 6
preparation: 30 minutes
cooking time: 1 hour 10 minutes
per serving: 640 cals; 54g fat;
    2g carbohydrate

1 Put the spring onions, bacon, garlic and cinnamon into a food processor and blend until almost smooth. Add the lamb mince and season with plenty of salt and pepper. Process until well mixed and smooth.

2 With wet hands, shape the mixture into 30–36 even-sized balls.

3 Heat the olive oil in a large frying pan and brown the meatballs in batches, then transfer to a shallow ovenproof dish. Pour the wine into the frying pan and bring to the boil, scraping up any sediment from the bottom. Pour over the meatballs, cover and bake at 180°C (160°C fan oven) mark 4 for 1 hour.

4 Pour the cooking liquid into a pan; cover the meatballs and keep warm. Bring the liquid to the boil and boil rapidly until reduced to 300ml (½ pint). Lower the heat and stir in the chopped dill, cream and egg yolks. Stir over a gentle heat for about 10 minutes or until slightly thickened; do not allow to boil. Taste and adjust the seasoning.

5 Put the meatballs on warmed plates and spoon the sauce over them. Garnish with dill and serve with new potatoes or buttered noodles.

Lamb Tagine

1.4kg (3lb) boneless leg or shoulder of lamb

2 tsp ground ginger

2 tsp ground coriander

½ tsp saffron strands

5 tbsp olive oil

salt and pepper

275g (10oz) baby onions or shallots

1 garlic clove, peeled and crushed

1 tbsp plain flour

1 tbsp sun-dried tomato paste

450ml (¾ pint) lamb or chicken stock

150ml (¼ pint) sherry

2 tbsp chopped coriander, plus extra
    to garnish

2 tbsp chopped parsley

1 bay leaf

1 cinnamon stick

75 g (3 oz) pitted dates

1 tbsp thin honey

serves 8

preparation: 20 minutes, plus marinating

cooking time: about 1¾ hours

per serving: 420 cals; 24g fat;
    12g carbohydrate

1 Cut the lamb into 4cm (1½ inch) cubes. Put into a bowl with the ground spices, saffron and 1 tbsp olive oil. Season with salt and pepper, then cover and leave to marinate in the fridge for at least 4 hours, preferably overnight.

2 Immerse the onions or shallots in boiling water for 2 minutes, then drain. Refresh in cold water, drain and peel. Put to one side.

3 Heat 1 tbsp olive oil in a heavy-based flameproof casserole and brown the lamb in batches, using more oil as necessary. Add the garlic and stir for 1 minute.

4 Return the lamb to the casserole. Stir in the flour and tomato paste, then add the onions, stock, sherry, herbs and cinnamon stick. Season with salt and pepper. Bring to a simmer, then cover and cook in the oven at 180°C (160°C fan oven) mark 4 for 1¼ hours, stirring occasionally.

5 Discard the cinnamon and bay leaf. Add the dates and honey to the casserole and return to the oven for 15–20 minutes. Scatter with chopped coriander to garnish and serve with couscous.

Lamb and Pumpkin Curry

800g (1¾lb) boneless lamb

450g (1lb) pumpkin, peeled and deseeded

1 medium aubergine, trimmed

5 tbsp olive oil

3 large red onions, peeled and sliced

2 garlic cloves, peeled and crushed

2.5cm (1 inch) piece fresh root ginger, grated

1 red chilli, sliced into rounds

4 tbsp red balti curry paste

400ml can coconut milk

450ml (¾ pint) hot lamb stock

salt and pepper

ONION AND CORIANDER SALSA

1 onion, peeled and sliced

juice of 1 lime

4 tbsp chopped coriander, plus sprigs to
    garnish

serves 4–6

preparation: 30 minutes

cooking time: 1¼ hours

per serving: 740–490 cals; 54–36g fat;
    17–12g carbohydrate

1 Cut the lamb into 2.5cm (1 inch) cubes. Cut the pumpkin and aubergine into 2.5cm (1 inch) pieces and set aside.

2 Heat 2 tbsp olive oil in a large pan and fry the onions over a medium heat for 5–10 minutes until lightly coloured. Add the garlic and ginger and cook for 1 minute. Remove with a slotted spoon and put to one side.

3 Heat the remaining oil in the pan and brown the lamb in batches over a high heat, on all sides. Add the pumpkin and aubergine and cook for 5 minutes. Return the onions to the pan and stir well.

4 Add the red chilli and curry paste and cook, stirring, for 1 minute, then pour in the coconut milk and stock. Season with salt and pepper. Cover, bring to the boil, then lower the heat and cook gently on the hob for 1 hour or until the lamb is tender.

5 Meanwhile, put the salsa ingredients in a bowl, add a pinch of salt and and toss well; chill until needed.

6 Spoon the curry into warmed dishes, garnish with coriander and serve with the salsa and basmati rice.

Illustrated on page 164

Lamb Korma

KORMA PASTE

3 tbsp ground cinnamon

36 green cardamoms

30 cloves

18 bay leaves

1 tbsp fennel seeds

CURRY

700g (1½lb) boneless lamb

150ml carton yogurt

1 tbsp golden caster sugar

3 tbsp groundnut oil

1 tsp ground turmeric

2 tsp ground coriander

1 small onion, peeled and finely chopped

4 garlic cloves, peeled and crushed

1cm (½ inch) piece fresh root ginger, finely
    chopped

50g (2oz) ground almonds

142ml carton double cream

large pinch of powdered saffron

salt and pepper

RED ONION AND TOMATO SALSA

1 red onion, peeled and finely sliced

1 tomato, deseeded and diced

1 tbsp chopped mint, plus extra to garnish

juice of ½ lime

serves 4

preparation: 20 minutes, plus marinating

cooking time: 2 hours

per serving: 660 cals; 49g fat;

    15g carbohydrate

1 To prepare the korma paste, put all of the paste ingredients into a mini processor or spice grinder, add 1 tsp salt, and whiz to a powder. Tip the powder into a bowl and add 4 tbsp water, stirring well to make a paste. Set aside one-third of the paste; freeze the rest for later use (see note).

2 To make the curry, cut the lamb into 2.5cm (1 inch) pieces. In a large bowl, mix the portion of korma paste with the yogurt and sugar, then add the lamb and toss well. Cover and leave to marinate in the fridge for at least 4 hours, preferably overnight.

3 Heat the oil in a flameproof casserole, add the turmeric and coriander and fry for 30 seconds. Add the onion and cook, stirring, for 10 minutes until softened and golden. Add the garlic and ginger and cook for 1–2 minutes. Add the lamb, stir well, then cover and cook in the oven at 190°C (170°C fan oven) mark 5 for 20 minutes.

4 Meanwhile, make the salsa. Toss all the ingredients together in a small bowl and season well with salt; chill until ready to serve.

5 Take the casserole out of the oven and lower the oven setting to 170°C (150°C fan oven) mark 3. Add the ground almonds, cream, saffron and 100ml (3½fl oz) water. Season well with salt and pepper, and stir together. Cover and cook for 1½ hours or until the meat is tender.

6 Serve the lamb korma in warmed deep bowls, garnished with mint and accompanied by the salsa and warm naan bread.

note: *Freeze the rest of the korma paste in two portions and use within 3 months. Defrost at cool room temperature for about 1 hour.*

Honey Roast Pork with Potatoes and Apples

1kg (2¼lb) loin of pork, with crackling and
    4 bones (see note)
salt and pepper
4 tbsp olive oil
25g (1oz) butter
700g (1½lb) Charlotte potatoes, scrubbed
    and halved lengthways
1 large onion, peeled and cut into 8 wedges
1 tbsp thin honey
1 tbsp wholegrain mustard
2 Cox's apples, cored and each cut into
    6 wedges
12 sage leaves
175ml (6fl oz) dry cider

serves 4
preparation: 20 minutes
cooking time: about 1¾ hours, plus resting
per serving: 770 cals; 34g fat;
    45g carbohydrate

1 Put the pork on a board and use a Stanley knife or very sharp knife to score the skin into thin strips, cutting about halfway into the fat underneath the skin. Rub 1 tsp salt and 2 tbsp olive oil over the skin and season the pork well with pepper.

2 Put the meat on a rack, skin-side up, over a large roasting tin. (If you don't have a rack, you can simply put the pork in the tin.) Roast it on a high oven shelf at 240°C (220°C fan oven) mark 9 for 25 minutes, then lower the oven setting to 190°C (170°C fan oven) mark 5 and roast for a further 15 minutes.

3 Add the remaining oil and the butter to the roasting tin. Scatter the potatoes and onion around the meat, and season them with salt and pepper. Continue to roast the meat and vegetables for 45 minutes.

4 Mix the honey with the mustard, and brush it over the meat. Add the apple wedges and the sage leaves to the tin and roast for a further 15 minutes.

5 Remove the pork from the tin and wrap in foil, then leave it to rest in a warm place. Transfer the potatoes, onions and apples to a serving dish and keep warm in the switched-off oven.

6 Put the roasting tin on the hob over a low heat, then add the cider, stirring well, to make a thin gravy. Season with salt and pepper to taste.

7 Remove the foil from the pork, and cut the meat away from the bone. Cut between each bone. Pull the crackling away from the meat and cut it into strips. Carve the joint, giving each person some meat and crackling. Serve with the cider gravy and the roast potatoes, onion and apples.

note: *For really crisp crackling, leave the joint uncovered in the fridge overnight to dry out the skin, before scoring the fat with a Stanley knife and rubbing a little oil and salt into it.*

Roast Pork with Apple Sauce

1.4kg (3lb) loin of pork, with bone, chined
    (ie backbone removed for ease of carving)
salt and pepper
oil, to baste

TO SERVE
apple sauce (page 25)

serves 6
preparation: 10 minutes, plus standing
cooking time: about 1½ hours, plus resting
per serving (without apple sauce): 340 cals;
    24g fat; 0g carbohydrate

1 To prepare the pork for crisp crackling, score the rind with a Stanley knife or very sharp knife, rub with salt and leave for 5–10 minutes, then pat dry with kitchen paper. Smear liberally with oil and rub with a little more salt.

2 Put the pork into a roasting tin and roast at 230°C (210°C fan oven) mark 8 for 10–15 minutes, then lower the oven setting to 200°C (180°C fan oven) mark 6 and roast for a further 1¼ hours or until the pork is cooked through.

3 Transfer the pork joint to a warmed platter, cover loosely with foil and leave to rest in a warm place for 10–15 minutes.

4 To serve, remove the crackling with a sharp knife and cut into pieces with kitchen scissors. Carve the pork into thin slices and arrange on the platter with the crackling. Serve with the warm apple sauce, roast potatoes and seasonal vegetables.

Stuffed Pork Tenderloins

25g (1oz) butter
1 onion, peeled and finely chopped
1 tbsp chopped thyme
grated zest of ½ orange
50g (2oz) fresh white breadcrumbs
salt and pepper
2 pork fillets (tenderloins)
2 tbsp olive oil
200ml (7fl oz) hot chicken stock
50ml (2fl oz) red wine

serves 6
preparation: 25 minutes
cooking time: 1 hour, plus resting
per serving: 280 cals; 16g fat;
    7g carbohydrate

1 Melt the butter in a pan, add the onion and cook for 3–4 minutes until softened. Add the thyme and orange zest and cook for a further 1 minute. Add the breadcrumbs, stir and season with salt and pepper. Allow to cool.

2 Trim any fat from the pork, then cut each fillet lengthways down the middle, almost but not quite through. Season well, then open out and spoon half the breadcrumb mixture along each fillet. Bring the sides over the filling to enclose and carefully tie with string at intervals to secure.

3 Heat the olive oil in a heavy-based roasting tin on the hob, add the pork fillets and brown all over, then transfer to the oven and roast at 190°C (170°C fan oven) mark 5 for 40–45 minutes until cooked through.

4 Lift the pork on to a warmed plate, cover with foil and leave to rest. Add the stock and red wine to the roasting tin and bring to the boil, scraping up the sediment from the bottom. Season with salt and pepper to taste and simmer for 5–6 minutes until syrupy. Slice the pork and serve with the sauce, mashed potato and carrots.

Pork Steaks with Sage and Parma Ham

4 pork shoulder steaks, about 150g (5oz),
    each, halved if large
4 thin slices Parma ham or pancetta
6 sage leaves
pepper
1 tbsp oil
150ml (¼ pint) pure unsweetened apple juice
50g (2oz) chilled butter, diced
squeeze of lemon juice

serves 4
preparation: 5 minutes
cooking time: 10 minutes
per serving: 380 cals; 25g fat;
    4g carbohydrate

1 Put the pork steaks on a board. Lay a slice of Parma ham or pancetta and a sage leaf on each pork steak, then secure to the meat with a wooden cocktail stick. Season with pepper.

2 Heat the oil in a large heavy-based frying pan and fry the pork for about 3–4 minutes on each side until golden brown.

3 Pour in the apple juice, stirring and scraping up the sediment from the bottom of the pan. Let the liquid bubble until reduced by half. Lift the pork out on to a warmed plate.

4 Return the pan to the heat, add the butter and swirl until melted into the pan juices. Add lemon juice to taste and pour over the pork to serve. Serve with curly kale or cabbage and parsnips.

variation: Use white wine instead of apple juice.

Pork with Pease Pudding

1.8kg (4lb) piece salt pork or gammon
225g (8oz) baby onions, peeled
350g (12oz) small carrots, peeled
350g (12oz) baby turnips, peeled
2 celery sticks, roughly chopped
2 bay leaves
salt and pepper

PEASE PUDDING
225g (8oz) split yellow peas, soaked
    overnight
2 tsp chopped thyme
2 tsp chopped mint
1 tsp golden caster sugar
25g (1oz) butter
1 egg yolk
olive oil, to oil and drizzle
extra herbs, to sprinkle

serves 6
preparation: 30 minutes, plus overnight
    soaking
cooking time: about 1¾ hours
per serving: 430 cals; 15g fat;
    29g carbohydrate

1 To prepare the pease pudding, drain the soaked split peas and turn on to a pudding cloth or large square of muslin. Sprinkle with the herbs, sugar and salt and pepper, then bring the edges of the cloth up over the top and secure with string, allowing plenty of room for the peas to expand.

2 Put the meat into a large heavy-based pan and cover with water. Bring to the boil and skim off any scum, using a slotted spoon. Add the pudding bag to the pan, securing the string to the pan handle.

3 Put the vegetables into the pan around the meat, with the bay leaves and seasoning. Simmer gently, allowing 25 minutes per 450g (1lb) pork.

4 Remove the pease pudding bag from the pan and drain thoroughly. Tip into a bowl and mash well, beating in the butter and egg yolk. When light and fluffy, put spoonfuls on to a lightly oiled baking sheet. Drizzle with oil, seasoning and extra chopped herbs, and grill under a medium-high heat until coloured.

5 Lift the meat out of the pan and carve into slices. Drain the vegetables, reserving the cooking liquor. Arrange the meat on warmed serving plates with the pease pudding and vegetables. Serve the cooking liquor as gravy.

note: *If you prefer less soft vegetables, add to the pan 30 minutes from the end of the cooking time.*

variation: *Use green split peas or red lentils instead of the yellow split peas.*

Pan-fried Pork with Rosemary

400g (14oz) pork fillet (tenderloin)
50g (2oz) butter
300ml (½ pint) medium dry white wine
4 tsp finely chopped rosemary
salt and pepper

serves 4
preparation: 10 minutes
cooking time: 7 minutes
per serving: 260 cals; 17g fat;
    trace carbohydrate

1 Put the pork fillet between two sheets of greaseproof paper and beat with a rolling pin to flatten. Cut into thick diagonal slices.

2 Melt the butter in a large heavy-based frying pan, add the pork and cook over a high heat until golden brown and cooked through. Remove from the pan; keep warm.

3 Add the wine to the pan, bring to the boil and bubble for 2–3 minutes or until reduced by at least half. Add the chopped rosemary.

4 Return the pork to the pan and toss to combine with the sauce. Season with salt and pepper to taste. Serve with pasta and baby spinach.

Pork and Vegetable Stir-fry

450g (1lb) pork fillet (tenderloin)
2 tbsp dry sherry
2 tbsp light soy sauce
2 garlic cloves, peeled and crushed
5cm (2 inch) piece fresh root ginger, grated
1 tsp cornflour
1 tbsp groundnut oil
1 large carrot, peeled and cut into fine
    matchsticks
225g (8oz) broccoli, broken into small florets
8 spring onions, trimmed and finely shredded
150g (5oz) beansprouts
salt and pepper

serves 4
preparation: 15 minutes, plus marinating
cooking time: 15 minutes
per serving: 250 cals; 12g fat;
    6g carbohydrate

1 Trim any fat off the pork and cut the meat into thin slices. Put 1 tbsp sherry, 1 tbsp soy sauce, the garlic, ginger and cornflour into a large bowl and mix well to make a marinade. Add the pork and toss well, then set aside for 15 minutes.

2 Heat a non-stick wok until very hot, then add the groundnut oil. Stir-fry the pork slices in two batches until browned; remove and set aside.

3 Reheat the wok, then add the carrot and broccoli, and stir-fry for 5 minutes. Add the remaining sherry and soy sauce together with 4 tbsp cold water, and bring just to the boil. Add the cooked pork and stir-fry for 2–3 minutes to heat through.

4 Add the spring onions and beansprouts and stir-fry for 1 minute. Season with salt and pepper to taste, and serve with plain boiled rice or egg noodles.

Pan-fried Pork Escalopes with Apple Salsa

2 small pork fillets (tenderloins),
    about 450g (1lb) in total
175g (6oz) dried breadcrumbs
125g (4oz) ground almonds
salt and pepper
flour, to coat
1 egg, beaten
6 tbsp oil

APPLE SALSA
2 crisp eating apples
2 tsp lemon juice
2 tsp chopped sage
4 tbsp crème fraîche

TO SERVE
lemon wedges

serves 4
preparation: 30 minutes
cooking time: 15 minutes
per serving: 790 cals; 53g fat;
    45g carbohydrate

1 First make the salsa. Peel, core and grate the apples. Put into a bowl, add the other ingredients and mix well. Season with salt and pepper to taste.

2 Slice the pork very thinly on the diagonal. Lay the slices between two pieces of greaseproof paper and beat with a rolling pin to flatten.

3 Mix together the breadcrumbs and ground almonds on a plate. Season the pork, then coat lightly with flour. Dip each piece in beaten egg, then into the breadcrumb mixture to coat, patting to adhere.

4 Fry the pork in three batches. Heat 2 tbsp oil in a large heavy-based frying pan, add a third of the pork and fry for 1–2 minutes on each side until deep golden brown. Transfer to a heatproof plate and keep warm in a low oven. Wipe out the frying pan with kitchen paper and cook the rest of the pork in the same way, using fresh oil for each batch.

5 Serve the pork escalopes straightaway, with lemon wedges and the apple salsa.

Sweet and Spicy Pork with Pineapple

425g can pineapple pieces in natural juice

4 pork shoulder steaks

2 garlic cloves, peeled and crushed

1 tbsp mild curry paste

2 tbsp lemon juice

2 tbsp mango chutney

chopped parsley, to garnish

serves 6

preparation: 5 minutes

cooking time: 35 minutes

per serving: 200 cals; 8g fat;

   13g carbohydrate

1 Drain and roughly chop the pineapple pieces, reserving the juice.

2 Heat a non-stick frying pan and dry-fry the pork steaks over a high heat for 2 minutes each side until golden brown. Transfer to a small ovenproof dish just large enough to hold the pork steaks in one layer.

3 Add the garlic and curry paste to the pan and fry gently for 30 seconds. Stir in the pineapple and juice, lemon juice and mango chutney. Bring to the boil and bubble to reduce slightly, then pour over the pork.

4 Bake at 200°C (180°C fan oven) mark 6 for about 25 minutes, basting the pork steaks occasionally. Scatter with chopped parsley to serve.

variation: *Use 700g (1½lb) pork fillet (tenderloin). Fry in 1 tbsp oil at stage 2, turning to brown all over.*

Pork and Bean Hotpot

1.4kg (3lb) boned shoulder of pork, trimmed

6 garlic cloves, peeled and crushed

7 tbsp oil

2 tbsp red wine vinegar

4 tbsp light muscovado sugar

few drops of chilli sauce

salt and pepper

2 tsp dried thyme

1 tbsp dried oregano

450g (1lb) onions, peeled and sliced

2 tbsp sun-dried tomato paste

150ml (¼ pint) vegetable stock

2 x 400g cans chopped tomatoes

300ml (½ pint) red wine

4 bay leaves

2 x 400g cans haricot or flageolet beans,
   drained

25g (1oz) butter

125g (4oz) fresh white breadcrumbs,
   preferably ciabatta or French bread

125g (4oz) Gruyère cheese, grated

serves 8

preparation: 20 minutes, plus marinating

cooking time: 2¼ hours

per serving: 800 cals; 50g fat;

   35g carbohydrate

1 Cut the pork into 2.5cm (1 inch) chunks and put into a bowl with the garlic, 2 tbsp oil, the wine vinegar, sugar, chilli sauce, salt, pepper, thyme and 2 tsp oregano. Stir well, cover and leave to marinate in the fridge for at least 8 hours.

2 Drain the pork, saving the marinade. Heat 3 tbsp oil in a large flameproof casserole and brown the pork, in batches, on all sides. Remove with a slotted spoon and set aside.

3 Heat the remaining oil in the casserole. Add the onions and fry over a medium-high heat for about 10 minutes until soft and lightly caramelised. Add the tomato paste and cook for 1 minute.

4 Return the pork to the casserole and add the stock, tomatoes, wine, bay leaves and reserved marinade. Bring to the boil, then cover and cook at 180°C (160°C fan oven) mark 4 for 2 hours or until the pork is very tender, adding the beans 20 minutes before the end.

5 Raise the oven setting to 200°C (180°C fan oven) mark 6 and move the pork to the lowest shelf. Melt the butter in a roasting tin, add the breadcrumbs, remaining oregano and seasoning, and toss to mix. Put the roasting tin on the top shelf of the oven for 10 minutes to brown. Serve the hotpot sprinkled with the crumb mixture and grated cheese.

Ribs and Beans in a Sticky Barbecue Sauce

8 meaty pork spare ribs

salt and pepper

1 large onion, peeled and chopped

2 large garlic cloves, peeled and chopped

4 tbsp light muscovado sugar

1 tbsp French mustard

4 tbsp sun-dried tomato paste

150g (5oz) passata

4 tbsp malt vinegar

4 tbsp tomato ketchup

2 tbsp Worcestershire sauce

568ml can dry cider

2 x 410g cans black-eyed beans, drained

4 tbsp chopped parsley

serves 4

preparation: 10 minutes

cooking time: 1¼ hours

per serving: 620 cals; 25g fat;
    53g carbohydrate

1 Trim the spare ribs of excess fat if necessary and season with salt and pepper.

2 Put the onion, garlic, sugar, mustard, tomato paste, passata, vinegar, ketchup and Worcestershire sauce in a large roasting tin and stir well.

3 Add the spare ribs and stir to coat in the sauce. Cook in the oven at 210°C (190°C fan oven) mark 6½ for 30 minutes, then turn the ribs over and cook for a further 30 minutes until they are crisp and brown.

4 Add the cider and stir to mix well with the sauce, scraping up the sediment from the bottom of the pan. Add the black-eyed beans, stir and return to the oven for a further 15 minutes. Scatter with the chopped parsley to serve.

variation: *Use canned haricot or pinto beans instead of black-eyed beans.*

Cajun Pork

1kg (2¼lb) boned shoulder of pork, trimmed
4 green chillies, deseeded and finely
   chopped
4 garlic cloves, peeled and crushed
¼ tsp cayenne pepper
1 tbsp Cajun seasoning
450g (1lb) onions, peeled
1 large red pepper, cored and deseeded
1 large yellow pepper, cored and deseeded
4 tbsp oil
400g can chopped tomatoes
150ml (¼ pint) chicken stock
2–3 thyme sprigs
salt and pepper
coriander sprigs, to garnish

serves 6
preparation: 50 minutes, plus marinating
cooking time: 1½ hours
per serving: 370 cals; 21g fat;
   10g carbohydrate

1 Cut the pork into 2.5cm (1 inch) cubes and put into a bowl with the chillies, garlic, cayenne and Cajun seasoning. Mix well, cover and leave to marinate in a cool place for at least 4 hours, preferably overnight.
2 Cut each onion into 6 or 8 wedges; cut the sweet peppers into 2.5cm (1 inch) cubes.
3 Heat the oil in a large flameproof casserole and fry the pork in batches until deep brown all over; remove with a slotted spoon and set aside.
4 Add the onions to the casserole and cook over a medium heat for 5–7 minutes until softened. Add the peppers and cook for 1–2 minutes.
5 Return the pork to the casserole and add the tomatoes, stock and thyme. Bring to the boil and season with salt and pepper. Cover and cook in the oven at 180°C (160°C fan oven) mark 4 for 1¼ hours or until tender. Check the seasoning.
5 Serve garnished with coriander and accompanied by couscous or rice.

Mustard Pork Casserole with Cherry Tomatoes

700g (1½lb) boned shoulder of pork, trimmed
6 tbsp oil
2 tsp finely chopped rosemary
25g (1oz) butter
450g (1lb) medium onions, peeled and
   quartered
3 garlic cloves, peeled and crushed
4 tbsp sun-dried tomato paste
100ml (3½fl oz) dry sherry
2 tsp plain flour
450ml (¾ pint) chicken stock
2 tsp dark soy sauce
salt and pepper
450g (1lb) small dark flat mushrooms
3 tbsp wholegrain mustard
250g (9oz) cherry tomatoes

serves 4
preparation: 30 minutes, plus marinating
cooking time: about 1¼ hours
per serving: 600 cals; 39g fat;
   16g carbohydrate

1 Cut the pork into 2.5cm (1 inch) chunks and put into a bowl. Add 2 tbsp oil and the rosemary. Cover and set aside to marinate in a cool place for 2 hours.
2 Heat the butter in a flameproof casserole and fry the pork in batches to a rich golden brown. Remove with a slotted spoon and set aside.
3 Lower the heat, add the onions to the casserole and cook for 5–7 minutes or until slightly softened and golden. Add the garlic and tomato paste and fry for 2–3 minutes. Pour in the sherry and bring to the boil. Bubble to reduce by half.
4 Stir in the flour, then pour in the stock, stirring. Bring to the boil. Return the pork to the casserole and add the soy sauce and seasoning. Simmer for 5 minutes, then cover tightly and cook at 180°C (160°C fan oven) mark 4 for 1–1¼ hours until tender.
5 In the meantime, heat the remaining oil in a large frying pan. Add the mushrooms and fry briskly for 3–4 minutes. Season with salt and pepper and add to the casserole 10 minutes before the end of the cooking time.
6 Stir in the mustard, return to a simmer on the hob, then add the cherry tomatoes. Heat through for about 2–3 minutes, then serve.

Cider Pork Casserole with Spring Vegetables

1kg (2¼lb) boned shoulder of pork, trimmed

3 tbsp oil

200g (7oz) onions, peeled and chopped

1 tbsp plain flour

275ml can dry cider

300ml (½ pint) chicken stock

salt and pepper

225g (8oz) crisp eating apples

1–2 tsp cider vinegar, to taste

125g (4oz) French beans

125g (4oz) asparagus tips

125g (4oz) mangetout

6–8 spring onions, trimmed and
  sliced diagonally

serves 6

preparation: 30 minutes

cooking time: 1½ hours

per serving: 370 cals; 19g fat;
  12g carbohydrate

1 Cut the pork into 2.5cm (1 inch) cubes. Heat half the oil in a large flameproof casserole and fry the pork in batches over a high heat until browned; remove and put to one side.

2 Lower the heat, add the onions to the casserole and cook gently for 5–6 minutes. Stir in the flour, cook for 1 minute, then pour in the cider, stirring until smooth. Bring to the boil and let bubble until reduced by two thirds.

3 Return the pork to the casserole, and add the stock and seasoning. Bring to the boil, then cover and cook in the oven at 180°C (160°C fan oven) mark 4 for 1¼ hours or until the pork is tender.

4 In the meantime, quarter and core the apples, then cut into wedges. Heat the remaining oil in a frying pan and fry the apples until light golden brown. Remove and add to the casserole 5 minutes before the end of the cooking time. Add the cider vinegar and adjust the seasoning.

5 Meanwhile, cut the vegetables diagonally into short lengths and cook separately in boiling salted water for 2–3 minutes until just tender. Drain and season with salt and pepper. Add to the pork before serving.

Spiced Meatballs in Tomato Sauce

MEATBALLS

350g (12oz) boned shoulder of pork

175g (6oz) belly of pork

175g (6oz) piece unsmoked gammon

2 garlic cloves, peeled

1 tsp coarse sea salt

1 tsp sugar

1 tbsp coarsely crushed black pepper

1 tsp fennel seeds

¼ tsp dried chilli flakes

TO SERVE

2 tbsp oil

tomato sauce (page 27)

freshly grated Parmesan cheese

serves 4

preparation: 30 minutes, plus optional
  chilling

cooking time: 20–25 minutes

per serving: 530 cals; 38g fat;
  9g carbohydrate

1 Trim both cuts of pork and the gammon of any skin or connective tissue, then cut into rough chunks.

2 Put the meat into a food processor, add all the remaining meatball ingredients and process until smooth. At this stage the mixture is ready to use, but you can cover the bowl and leave it to mature in the fridge overnight if preferred.

3 With wet hands, shape the mixture into small even-sized balls.

4 Heat the oil in a large frying pan and fry the meatballs, in batches if necessary, until evenly browned. Pour the tomato sauce over them, bring to the boil and simmer gently for 10–15 minutes.

5 Serve the meatballs on a bed of noodles, topped with Parmesan cheese.

variation: For a quicker version, replace the meats with 450g (1lb) pork mince and 225g (8oz) diced unsmoked streaky bacon.

Cumberland Glazed Baked Gammon

4.5kg (10lb) smoked gammon joint,
   on the bone
2 celery sticks, roughly chopped
1 onion, peeled and quartered
1 carrot, peeled and roughly chopped
1 tsp black peppercorns
1 tbsp cloves
75g (3oz) redcurrant sprigs

CUMBERLAND GLAZE
grated zest and juice of ½ lemon
grated zest and juice of ½ orange
4 tbsp redcurrant jelly
1 tsp Dijon mustard
2 tbsp port
salt and pepper

serves 16
preparation: 30 minutes
cooking time: 3½–4¼ hours
per 125g (4oz) gammon serving: 230 cals;
   7g fat; 6g carbohydrate

1 Put the gammon into a large pan. Add the celery, onion, carrot and peppercorns. Cover the meat and vegetables with cold water and bring to the boil. Simmer, covered, for 2¾ hours–3½ hours, or allowing 15–20 minutes per 450g (1lb) plus 15 minutes. Lift the gammon out of the pan.

2 Meanwhile, make the glaze. Heat the lemon and orange zests and juices, redcurrant jelly, mustard and port in a pan to dissolve the jelly. Bring to the boil and bubble for 5 minutes until syrupy. Season with salt and pepper to taste.

3 Remove the gammon rind and score the fat in a diamond pattern. Put the gammon into a roasting tin, then stud the fat with cloves. Spoon the glaze evenly over the gammon joint.

4 Roast the gammon at 200°C (180°C fan oven) mark 6 for 40 minutes, basting the meat with any juices. Add the redcurrant sprigs 10 minutes before the end of the cooking time. Serve the gammon hot or cold, carved into thin slices.

Gammon with Parsley Mash

1.4kg (3lb) gammon knuckle
1 onion, quartered
1 carrot, peeled and cut into chunks
1 celery stick, thickly sliced
1 tsp black peppercorns
2 bay leaves
700g (1½lb) white potatoes, cut into large
   chunks
salt and pepper
6–8 tbsp milk
40g (1½oz) butter
1 tbsp chopped parsley
1 Savoy cabbage, cut into wedges

serves 4
preparation: 20 minutes
cooking time: about 1¾ hours, plus resting
per serving: 790 cals; 27g fat;
   43g carbohydrate

1 Put the gammon knuckle into a deep pan, add the onion, carrot, celery, peppercorns and bay leaves and cover with cold water. Bring very slowly to the boil – this should take 20–30 minutes. Skim, then simmer very gently, covered with a lid, for 1½ hours or until the meat is cooked through and tender.

2 Allow the gammon to rest in the liquid in the pan for 15 minutes.

3 Meanwhile, add the potatoes to a pan of cold salted water, bring to the boil and simmer for about 15 minutes until soft. Drain and put back into the pan over a low heat to dry off. Take off the heat and mash the potatoes. Put the pan back over a low heat, push the mashed potatoes to one side and add the milk and 25g (1oz) butter. Warm through, then beat into the mash until fluffy, adding more milk if necessary. Season and add the chopped parsley.

4 Bring a large pan of salted water to the boil, add the cabbage and return to the boil. Immediately drain and dry on kitchen paper, then melt the remaining butter and brush over the cabbage. Heat a griddle or frying pan, add the cabbage and fry until beginning to brown – about 5 minutes.

5 Lift the gammon from the cooking liquid, then remove the skin and slice. Serve with the mashed potatoes, cabbage and a little liquid from the pan.

Gammon Steaks with Mustard and Dill Sauce

4 gammon steaks
150ml (¼ pint) dry vermouth
1 tbsp Dijon mustard
1 tbsp wholegrain mustard
125ml (4fl oz) double cream
2 tsp chopped dill
salt and pepper

serves 4
preparation: 10 minutes
cooking time: 6–8 minutes
per serving: 400 cals; 23g fat;
   2g carbohydrate

1 Grill the gammon steaks under a medium-high heat for 3–4 minutes each side until cooked through.
2 Meanwhile, pour the vermouth into a medium pan, bring to the boil and bubble to reduce by half. Stir in the mustards and let bubble for 1 minute, then pour in the cream and cook for 1 minute. Stir in the chopped dill and season with salt and pepper to taste.
3 Transfer the gammon steaks to warmed serving plates and pour on the mustard and dill sauce. Serve with crunchy green cabbage and mashed potatoes.

note: *If you find gammon steaks are a little too salty, pre-soak them in cold water to cover for 30 minutes. Drain and pat dry before cooking.*

Chorizo Sausage Pan-fry

450g (1lb) potatoes, peeled
2 tbsp olive oil
300g (11oz) piece chorizo sausage, skinned
2 red onions, peeled and sliced
1 tsp paprika
1 red pepper, cored, deseeded and sliced
250g pack cherry tomatoes
100ml (3½fl oz) dry sherry
2 tbsp chopped flat-leafed parsley

serves 4
preparation: 10 minutes
cooking time: 30 minutes
per serving: 430 cals; 24g fat;
   30g carbohydrate

1 Cut the potatoes into 2.5cm (1 inch) cubes. Heat the oil in a large heavy-based frying pan and fry the potatoes for 7–10 minutes until lightly browned, turning often. Meanwhile, cut the chorizo into chunky slices.
2 Reduce the heat, add the onions and continue to cook for 10 minutes, stirring from time to time until they have softened but not browned.
3 Add the chorizo to the pan with the paprika and red pepper. Cook for 5 minutes, stirring occasionally.
4 Add the cherry tomatoes and sherry. Toss to mix and cook for 5 minutes, until the sherry has reduced down and the tomatoes have softened and warmed through. Scatter with the chopped parsley and serve.

Illustrated right

Sausage Hash Browns

700g (1½lb) medium potatoes (unpeeled)
salt
50g (2oz) butter
1 small onion, peeled and chopped
450g (1lb) pork sausages
2 red onions, peeled and cut into rings
sunflower oil, to brush
450g (1lb) small vine-ripened tomatoes

serves 4
preparation: 15 minutes
cooking time: 35 minutes
per serving: 740 cals; 51g fat;
   56g carbohydrate

1 Add the potatoes to a pan of cold salted water, bring to the boil and par-boil for 10 minutes. Drain, then cut into 2.5cm (1 inch) cubes.
2 Heat the butter in a large heavy-based frying pan. Add the chopped onion and fry for 1 minute. Add the potatoes and fry over a medium heat for 25 minutes or until crisp and brown, turning frequently.
3 Meanwhile, grill the sausages under a medium-high heat for about 20 minutes until browned and cooked through to the centre, turning from time to time. Halfway through cooking, brush the onion rings with oil and add to the grill pan with the tomatoes. Grill until softened and lightly caramelised.
4 Serve the sausages on top of the hash brown potatoes, with the onion rings and tomatoes.

Italian Sausage Stew

25g (1oz) dried porcini mushrooms
300g (11oz) whole rustic Italian salami
   sausages, such as salami Milano
2 tbsp olive oil
1 onion, peeled and sliced
2 garlic cloves, peeled and chopped
1 small chilli, chopped
1 tender rosemary stem, plus sprigs
   to garnish
400g can chopped tomatoes
200ml (7fl oz) red wine
salt and pepper

CHEESY POLENTA
175g (6oz) instant polenta
50g (2oz) butter
50g (2oz) Parmesan cheese, grated,
   plus shavings to serve (optional)
75g (3oz) fontina cheese, cubed

serves 4
preparation: 10 minutes, plus soaking
cooking time: 15 minutes
per serving: 780 cals; 48g fat;
   47g carbohydrate

1 Put the dried mushrooms into a small bowl, pour on 100ml (3½fl oz) boiling water and leave to soak for 20 minutes or soften in the microwave on high for 3½ minutes and set aside to cool. Cut the salami into 1cm (½ inch) slices and put aside.

2 Heat the olive oil in a pan, add the onion, garlic and chilli and gently fry for 5 minutes. Meanwhile, strip the leaves from the rosemary stem and add them to the pan, stirring.

3 Add the salami and fry for 2 minutes on each side or until browned. Drain and chop the mushrooms and add them to the pan. Stir in the chopped tomatoes and red wine, then season with pepper. Simmer uncovered for 5 minutes.

4 Meanwhile, make the polenta. Put 750ml (1¼ pints) boiling water and 1 tsp salt into a heavy-based pan. Return to the boil, sprinkle in the polenta, stirring, and cook according to the pack instructions. Add the butter, Parmesan and fontina and mix well.

5 Serve the sausage stew accompanied by the polenta, topped with Parmesan shavings and garnished with rosemary.

Toad in the Hole

125g (4oz) plain flour, sifted
2 large eggs, lightly beaten
150ml (¼ pint) semi-skimmed milk
salt and pepper
2 tbsp oil
4 good quality sausages

serves 2
preparation: 10 minutes
cooking time: 25–30 minutes
per serving: 680 cals; 41g fat;
   58g carbohydrate

1 Put the flour into a bowl, make a well in the centre and pour in the eggs and milk. Whisk the batter thoroughly and season it well with salt and pepper.

2 Divide the oil and sausages between two 600ml (1 pint) shallow ovenproof dishes and cook at 220°C (200°C fan oven) mark 7 for 10 minutes, turning once or twice.

3 Divide the batter between the dishes and continue to cook for 15–20 minutes or until the batter is puffy and a rich golden colour all over. Serve immediately, with steamed carrots and broccoli or green beans.

Braised Oxtail

2 oxtails, about 1.6kg (3½lb) in total, trimmed

2 tbsp plain flour

salt and pepper

4 tbsp oil

2 large onions, peeled and sliced

900ml (1½ pints) beef stock

150ml (¼ pint) red wine

1 tbsp tomato purée

finely grated zest of ½ lemon

2 bay leaves

2 medium carrots, peeled and chopped

450g (1lb) parsnips, peeled and chopped

chopped parsley, to garnish

serves 6

preparation: 20 minutes

cooking time: about 4 hours

per serving: 580 cals; 33g fat;
    20g carbohydrate

1 Cut the oxtails into large pieces. Season the flour with salt and pepper and use to coat the pieces. Heat the oil in a large flameproof casserole and brown the oxtail pieces, a few at a time. Remove from the casserole with a slotted spoon and set aside.

2 Add the onions to the casserole and fry over a medium heat for about 10 minutes until softened and lightly browned. Stir in any remaining flour.

3 Stir in the stock, red wine, tomato purée, lemon zest and bay leaves. Season with salt and pepper. Bring to the boil, then return the oxtail and lower the heat. Cover and simmer very gently for 2 hours.

4 Skim off the fat from the surface, then stir in the carrots and parsnips. Re-cover the casserole and simmer very gently for a further 2 hours until the oxtail is very tender.

5 Skim off all fat from the surface, then check the seasoning. Serve scattered with chopped parsley.

Pressed Ox Tongue

1.6–1.8kg (3½lb–4lb) pickled ox tongue

1 onion, peeled and thickly sliced

1 carrot, peeled and thickly sliced

4 celery sticks, thickly sliced

2 tbsp wine vinegar

2 bay leaves

12 black peppercorns

1 tsp powdered gelatine

serves 10–12

preparation: 20 minutes, plus overnight
    soaking and overnight chilling

cooking time: about 4¼ hours

per serving: 500–420 cals; 41–34g fat;
    trace carbohydrate

1 A day in advance of cooking, scrub and rinse the tongue under cold water. Put into a large bowl, cover with cold water and leave to soak overnight.

2 Drain the tongue, then roll into a neat shape and secure with a skewer. Wrap in a single thickness of muslin, tying the ends together. Put the tongue into a large pan. Cover with cold water, bring to the boil and boil for 1 minute. Drain, rinse with cold water, then return to the pan and cover with fresh water. Add the vegetables to the pan with the wine vinegar, bay leaves and peppercorns. Bring to the boil, cover and simmer gently for about 4 hours.

3 Lift the tongue on to a large plate, reserving the cooking liquid. Unwrap, ease out the skewer and use it to pierce the thickest piece; if it slips in easily, the tongue is cooked. If not, simmer for a little longer.

4 Put the tongue into a colander and rinse with cold water until cool enough to handle; this will help to loosen the skin. Using a sharp knife, make a shallow slit along the underside. Peel the skin off in strips, starting from the tip end. Ease out the bones and gristle lying at the base.

5 Tightly curl the warm tongue and put it into a 15cm (6 inch) deep-sided soufflé dish or non-stick cake tin into which it fits tightly.

6 Strain the cooking liquid, measure 600ml (1 pint) and pour into a pan. Boil rapidly to reduce to 150ml (¼ pint). Meanwhile, put 2 tbsp water into a small bowl and sprinkle on the gelatine. Leave to soak for 10 minutes, then add to the stock and stir gently to dissolve. Leave to cool.

7 Gently pour the cooled stock over the tongue. Put a small plate that will just fit inside the soufflé dish on top of the tongue. Put weights on top of the plate and chill overnight.

8 Lift the weights off the tongue and then ease off the plate. To release the tongue, run a blunt-edged knife around the inside of the dish, then immerse the base and sides in hot water for a few seconds only. Invert on to a serving plate, shaking to release the tongue. Slice the tongue thinly to serve.

Lancashire Tripe and Onions

450g (1lb) dressed tripe, washed
225g (8oz) shallots, peeled
600ml (1 pint) milk
salt and pepper
pinch of freshly grated nutmeg
1 bay leaf
25g (1oz) butter
3 tbsp plain flour
chopped parsley, to garnish

serves 4
preparation: 20 minutes
cooking time: about 2¼ hours
per serving: 240 cals; 10g fat;
   20g carbohydrate

1 Put the tripe into a pan and cover with cold water. Bring to the boil, then drain and rinse under cold running water. Cut into 2.5cm (1 inch) pieces.
2 Put the tripe, shallots, milk, seasoning, nutmeg and bay leaf into the rinsed-out pan. Bring to the boil, cover and simmer for about 2 hours until tender. Strain and reserve 600ml (1 pint) of the liquid. Discard the bay leaf.
3 Melt the butter in a pan, stir in the flour and cook gently for 1 minute, stirring. Remove the pan from the heat and gradually stir in the reserved cooking liquid. Bring to the boil and continue to cook, stirring, until the sauce thickens.
4 Add the tripe and shallots and reheat. Check the seasoning and sprinkle with chopped parsley to serve.

Calf's Liver with Sage Butter

75g (3oz) butter
8 sage leaves, shredded, plus extra sprigs
   to garnish
2 red onions, peeled and sliced
1 tbsp lemon juice
2 tsp balsamic vinegar
8 thin slices calf's liver, about 450g (1lb)
   in total
salt and pepper

serves 4
preparation: 20 minutes, plus standing
cooking time: 25 minutes
per serving: 340 cals; 24g fat;
   8g carbohydrate

1 First clarify the butter. Slowly melt the butter in a small pan, then allow to settle for 5 minutes. Spoon off the golden butter into a bowl, leaving the white milky residue behind. Pour off this residue, wipe out the pan, then return the clarified butter. Stir in half of the shredded sage and heat until almost boiling. Turn off the heat and leave to stand for at least 10 minutes.
2 Strain the butter into a frying pan, to remove the sage, and put over a medium heat. Toss the onions in the lemon juice, then add to the hot pan and cook gently, stirring frequently, for about 20 minutes until very soft and caramelised. Stir in the balsamic vinegar and the remaining shredded sage. Lift the onions out on to a plate, with a slotted spoon.
3 Increase the heat. When the pan is very hot, fry the calf's liver, in two batches, for 1 minute on each side. Return the onions to the pan with all the liver and reheat gently. Taste and adjust the seasoning. Serve immediately, garnished with sage.

Calf's Liver with Black Pudding and Bacon

4 smoked streaky bacon rashers, derinded

1 eating apple

700g (1½lb) calf's liver

1 tbsp oil

25g (1oz) butter

125g (4oz) black pudding, sliced

150ml (¼ pint) double cream

125ml (4fl oz) medium cider

4 tsp chopped sage, plus extra sprigs
    to garnish

salt and pepper

serves 4

preparation: 15 minutes

cooking time: 8 minutes

per serving: 720 cals; 55g fat;
    14g carbohydrate

1 Stretch each bacon rasher with the back of a knife, then cut in half. Cut the apple into 8 wedges, cutting away the core. Trim the calf's liver and cut into slightly smaller pieces.

2 Heat the oil with the butter in a large frying pan. Add the apple wedges and fry gently for 2 minutes; remove with a slotted spoon.

3 Wrap an apple wedge in each bacon strip and secure with a wooden cocktail stick. Return to the pan and fry for 2 minutes, turning frequently. Add the black pudding and cook for 1 minute on each side.

4 Remove the bacon rolls and black pudding from the pan with a slotted spoon and keep warm. Add the liver to the pan and cook for 30 seconds on each side; remove and set aside.

5 Add the cream, cider and chopped sage to the pan and season with salt and pepper. Bring to the boil. Return the liver to the pan, lower the heat and simmer for 1 minute to heat through; do not overcook.

6 Arrange the liver, bacon rolls and black pudding on warmed plates and pour over the sauce. Serve at once, garnished with sage.

variation: *Instead of the black pudding, use a quartered lamb's kidney.*

Sautéed Lamb's Kidneys and Baby Onions

8 lamb's kidneys

225g (8oz) baby onions, peeled

25g (1oz) unsalted butter

3 tbsp balsamic vinegar

1 tbsp plain flour

300ml (½ pint) well-flavoured lamb stock

3 tbsp Madeira

salt and pepper

chopped parsley, to garnish

serves 4

preparation: 10 minutes

cooking time: 30 minutes

per serving: 180 cals; 8g fat;
    8g carbohydrate

1 Halve the lamb's kidneys horizontally and snip out the white cores with kitchen scissors. Add the baby onions to a pan of boiling water and blanch for 3–5 minutes; drain well.

2 Melt the butter in a sauté pan, add the onions and cook gently for 10–15 minutes until soft and browned. Increase the heat and add the lamb's kidneys, stirring and turning them for about 2 minutes until browned. Lift the kidneys and onions out on to a plate.

3 Deglaze the pan with the balsamic vinegar, scraping up any sediment from the bottom of the pan, and allow almost all of the liquid to evaporate. Sprinkle in the flour and cook, stirring, over a medium heat until it begins to colour. Whisk in the stock and Madeira. Bring the sauce to the boil, then turn down the heat and simmer until reduced and slightly syrupy. Check the seasoning.

4 Return the kidneys and baby onions to the sauce and reheat gently for 5 minutes. Scatter with plenty of chopped parsley and serve with noodles or rice.

VEGETARIAN

The number of vegetarians in this country has more than doubled over the last decade – 7% of the population is now vegetarian, while the proportion is 12% amongst 15–24 year olds, indicating that the upward trend is set to continue. In addition, many of us who are happy to eat meat consume far less than we used to – choosing instead to eat vegetarian dishes on a regular basis.

A vegetarian is someone who avoids eating meat, poultry and fish, though some non-meat eaters will eat fish. Many vegetarians also avoid gelatine, animal fats such as lard and suet, and animal rennet in non-vegetarian cheeses. However, the majority of vegetarians eat dairy produce, including milk, vegetarian cheeses and free-range eggs. Vegans follow a more restrictive diet, which also excludes all dairy products, eggs, and even foods like honey.

The ever-increasing variety of fresh vegetables, fruits, nuts, seeds, spices and herbs makes it easy to cook a wide range of tasty, nutritious vegetarian meals. To make shopping easier, many products suitable for vegetarians are now endorsed and easy to identify – including invaluable ingredients, such as vegetarian cheeses, vegetarian stocks, cooking oils and fats, and free-range eggs, which are now widely available.

As with any kind of diet, variety is all important. Provided a vegetarian diet includes a good range of cereals and grains, pulses, nuts and seeds, fruit and vegetables, dairy and/or soya products, it should be nutritionally sound. A small quantity of plant oils, margarine or butter is needed to provide essential fatty acids and vitamins.

VEGETARIAN INGREDIENTS

Certain ingredients are particularly significant in a vegetarian diet. These include rice, grains, pasta, eggs, cheese, vegetables, fruit and nuts, all of which are featured in subsequent chapters. Pulses and other vegetarian products are detailed here.

Pulses

The term pulse is used to describe all of the various beans, peas and lentils that have been preserved by drying. They are highly nutritious, especially when eaten with grains, such as couscous, pasta, rice or bread. Pulses should be stored in airtight containers in a cool, dry cupboard. They keep well, but after about 6 months their skins start to toughen and they take progressively longer to cook the longer they are stored.

The weight of dried beans approximately doubles during soaking and cooking, so if a recipe calls for 225g (8oz) cooked beans, you would need to start with 125g (4oz) dried weight. Once cooked, pulses keep well in the fridge for 2–3 days.

With the exception of lentils and split peas, pulses need to be soaked overnight in plenty of cold water. The following day, drain off the water prior to cooking.

Cooking pulses is quite a lengthy process. For some pulses, notably red kidney beans, aduki beans, black-eyed beans, black beans and borlotti beans, it is essential to cover with plenty of fresh cold water, bring to the boil and boil vigorously for 10 minutes to destroy any toxins present on the skins. Although pre-boiling isn't mandatory for other dried pulses, it does no harm and saves the need to remember which ones require it.

After the initial fast-boiling, lower the heat, cover and simmer until tender. To enhance the flavour, a bouquet garni, a few bay leaves and/or 1 or 2 garlic cloves can be added to the cooking water. Salt should only be added 10–15 minutes before the end of the cooking time; if added at the start, it will toughen the skins.

The cooking time is determined by the type of pulse, soaking time and, above all, by the length of time it has been stored. As an approximate guide: lentils take 30–45 minutes; split peas require 45–60 minutes; aduki, black-eyed, borlotti, pinto flageolet and haricot beans need 1–1½ hours;

black beans, butter beans and red kidney beans take 1½–2 hours; chickpeas require 2–3 hours; while soya beans need 3–4 hours. (Note that soya beans must always be pre-boiled for 1 hour, to destroy a substance they contain which prevents the body from absorbing protein.)

Canned pulses are a convenient, quick alternative to cooking your own and most supermarkets stock a wide range. A 400g can is roughly equivalent to 75g (3oz) dried beans and contains about 150ml (¼ pint) liquid.

Seeds

Seeds are an excellent, highly nutritious vegetarian ingredient, adding texture, flavour and interest to a variety of foods, including breads, cakes and salads. Sunflower seeds, poppy seeds, sesame seeds and pumpkin seeds are especially popular. To enhance their flavour, toast in a dry frying pan for a few minutes, shaking the pan constantly.

Sprouted Beans and Seeds

These are rich in nutrients and lend a nutty taste and crunchy texture to salads and stir-fries. Fresh beansprouts are available from most supermarkets. Many beans and seeds can be sprouted at home, though it is important to buy ones which are specifically produced for sprouting – from a healthfood shop or other reliable source. Mung beans, aduki beans, alfalfa seeds and fenugreek are all suitable.

Vegetarian Cheeses

Some vegetarians prefer to avoid cheeses which have been produced by the traditional method, because it uses animal-derived rennet. Most supermarkets and cheese shops now stock an excellent range of vegetarian cheeses, produced using vegetarian rennet.

Tofu

Also known as bean curd, tofu is made from pressed soya beans in a process akin to cheese-making. It is highly nutritious, but avoided by many vegetarians because it is virtually tasteless. However, it readily absorbs other flavours on marinating and is worth experimenting with.

Tofu is sold as a chilled product and should be stored in the fridge. Once the packet is opened, the tofu should be kept immersed in a bowl of water in the fridge and eaten within 4 days.

Firm tofu is usually cut into chunks, then immersed in tasty marinades and dressings prior to grilling, stir-frying, deep-frying, adding to stews, or tossing raw into salads. It can also be chopped and made into burgers and nut roasts.

Smoked tofu has more flavour than firm tofu; it is used in the same way.

Silken tofu is softer and creamier than firm tofu and is useful for sauces and dressings.

Textured Vegetable Protein (TVP)

This forms the bulk of most ready-prepared vegetarian burgers, sausages and mince. It is made from a mixture of soya flour, flavourings and liquid, which is cooked, then extruded under pressure and cut into chunks or small pieces to resemble mince. Unlike tofu, it has a slightly chewy meat-like texture, which makes it unappealing to some vegetarians. TVP can be included in stews, pies, curries and other dishes, rather as meat would be used by non-vegetarians.

Quorn

Quorn is a vegetarian product derived from a distant relative of the mushroom. Although it is not suitable for vegans because it contains egg albumen, quorn is a good source of complete protein for vegetarians. It has a texture rather like chicken, which some find off-putting, but it is worth trying. Like tofu, quorn has a bland flavour and benefits from being marinated before cooking. Available from the chilled cabinet, quorn should be kept in the fridge and used within 3 days.

Gelazone and Agar-agar

Ordinary gelatine is derived from beef bones and is therefore unsuitable for vegetarians. Alternative gelling agents include gelazone and agar-agar, which is derived from seaweed. Both are sold in powdered form and used in a similar way to powdered gelatine, although agar-agar only dissolves when it is boiled. A slightly softer set may be obtained with vegetarian gelatine.

Grilled Vegetables with Walnut Sauce

2 large carrots, peeled
1 fennel bulb
225g (8oz) sweet potatoes
225g (8oz) Jerusalem artichokes, scrubbed
225g (8oz) thick asparagus spears
8 baby leeks
4–6 tbsp olive oil
salt and pepper

WALNUT SAUCE
50g (2oz) day-old bread, crusts removed
75g (3oz) walnuts, toasted
2 garlic cloves, peeled and chopped
1 tbsp red wine vinegar
2 tbsp chopped parsley
90ml (3fl oz) olive oil
50ml (2fl oz) walnut oil

serves 4
preparation: 25 minutes
cooking time: 15–20 minutes
per serving: 670 cals; 57g fat;
    35g carbohydrate

1 First prepare the walnut sauce. Crumble the bread into a bowl, add 2 tbsp water, then squeeze dry. Put the bread into a food processor with the toasted walnuts, garlic, wine vinegar and parsley; blend until fairly smooth. Add the olive and walnut oils and process briefly to form a thick sauce. Season with salt and pepper to taste and transfer to a serving dish.
2 Prepare the vegetables. Cut the carrots into 5mm (¼ inch) slices; thinly slice the fennel lengthways; peel and thinly slice the sweet potatoes; thinly slice the Jerusalem artichokes. Trim the asparagus and leeks, but leave whole.
3 Baste the vegetables with olive oil and grill in batches under a medium-high heat, turning once, for 2–6 minutes each side until charred and tender (see note); keep warm in a low oven while grilling the rest.
4 Transfer all the grilled vegetables to a warmed serving platter and season with a little salt and pepper. Serve accompanied by the walnut sauce and plenty of warm crusty bread.

note: *The root vegetables take longest to cook through, while the asparagus and leeks only need a short time under the grill.*

Nutty Bean Burgers

2 tbsp olive oil
1 small onion, peeled and chopped
1 garlic clove, peeled and crushed
2 tsp chopped thyme
400g can red kidney beans, drained
400g can butter beans, drained
50g (2oz) chopped mixed nuts
40g (1½oz) fresh white breadcrumbs
1 tbsp dark soy sauce
1 tbsp lemon juice
salt and pepper
oil, to shallow-fry

TO SERVE
6 soft burger buns, split
selection of relishes

serves 6
preparation: 20 minutes, plus standing
cooking time: 25 minutes
per serving: 450 cals; 13g fat;
    70g carbohydrate

1 Heat the olive oil in a frying pan, add the onion, garlic and thyme, and fry for 10 minutes until softened and golden.
2 Rinse the canned beans, drain well and add to the pan. Fry gently for a further 5 minutes, then transfer to a food processor and process briefly to form a rough paste; turn into a bowl.
3 Add the nuts, breadcrumbs, soy sauce and lemon juice, stir until evenly combined and season generously with salt and pepper. Cover and set aside for several hours to allow the flavours to develop.
4 Divide the bean mixture into 6 equal portions and shape into burgers.
5 Heat a little oil in a heavy-based frying pan and fry the burgers in batches for 2–3 minutes on each side until golden and cooked through. Drain on kitchen paper and keep warm while frying the rest.
6 Serve in burger buns, with your favourite relishes and a mixed salad.

Stir-fried Mushrooms and Beans with Noodles

25g (1oz) butter

1 tbsp olive oil

1–2 garlic cloves, peeled and crushed

1 lemon grass stalk, finely chopped

1 medium red chilli, deseeded and chopped

250g (9oz) fine green beans, trimmed

250g pack dried egg noodles

150g (5oz) shiitake mushrooms, trimmed

150g (5oz) oyster mushrooms, halved if large

4 tbsp roughly chopped coriander, plus extra
   leaves to garnish

salt and pepper

1 lemon, cut into wedges, to serve

serves 4

preparation: 15 minutes

cooking time: 15 minutes

per serving: 320 cals; 10g fat;
   50g carbohydrate

1 Put the butter and oil in a wok or large frying pan and heat gently to melt the butter. Add the crushed garlic, chopped lemon grass and chilli and stir-fry for around 30 seconds.

2 Put the green beans into a steamer over a large pan of boiling water, cover and steam for 5 minutes. Remove the steamer from the pan, then use the water to cook the egg noodles, according to the pack instructions. Drain well.

3 Add the green beans and both types of mushroom to the wok or frying pan and stir-fry for 3–4 minutes. Add the egg noodles and chopped coriander and toss everything together. Season with salt and pepper to taste.

4 Serve in warmed bowls, garnished with coriander and with lemon wedges on the side.

Spicy Vegetable Kebabs

12 baby onions

salt and pepper

12 new potatoes

12 button mushrooms

2 courgettes, trimmed

2 garlic cloves, peeled and crushed

1 tsp ground coriander

1 tsp ground turmeric

½ tsp ground cumin

1 tbsp sun-dried tomato paste

1 tsp chilli sauce

juice of ½ lemon

4 tbsp olive oil

295g pack smoked tofu

YOGURT SAUCE

225g (8oz) Greek-style yogurt

1 garlic clove, peeled and crushed

2 tbsp chopped coriander

TO SERVE

lemon wedges

serves 6

preparation: 30 minutes, plus marinating

cooking time: 8–10 minutes

per serving: 420 cals; 21g fat;
   34g carbohydrate

1 Blanch the baby onions in a pan of salted boiling water for 3 minutes; drain, refresh in cold water and peel away the skins.

2 Put the potatoes into a pan of cold salted water, bring to the boil and par-boil for 8 minutes; drain and refresh under cold water.

3 Blanch the button mushrooms in boiling water for 1 minute; drain and refresh under cold water. Cut each courgette into 6 chunky slices and blanch for 1 minute; drain and refresh.

4 Mix the garlic, spices, ½ tsp salt, pepper, tomato paste, chilli sauce, lemon juice and olive oil together in a shallow dish. Add the well-drained vegetables and tofu and toss to coat. Cover and leave to marinate in a cool place for several hours or overnight.

5 Cut the tofu into 2.5cm (1 inch) cubes. Thread the tofu and vegetables on to 6 metal kebab skewers alternating them. Lay the kebabs on a rack set over the grill pan and grill under a medium-high heat for 8–10 minutes or until the vegetables are evenly charred and cooked through, turning frequently and basting with the marinade.

6 Meanwhile, in a small bowl, mix together the ingredients for the yogurt sauce, seasoning with salt and pepper to taste.

7 Serve the vegetable kebabs with the yogurt sauce and lemon wedges.

Stir-fried Vegetables with Tofu

275g pack tofu, drained

2 tbsp hoisin sauce

2 tbsp dark soy sauce

2 tbsp sherry vinegar

1 tbsp chilli sauce

1 tbsp thin honey

2 tsp sesame oil

3 tbsp sunflower oil

2 carrots, peeled and thinly sliced

175g (6oz) broccoli, cut into small florets

125g (4oz) shiitake mushrooms, halved

1 leek, trimmed and sliced

4 spring onions, trimmed and sliced

125g (4oz) mangetout, trimmed and halved

toasted sesame seeds, to sprinkle

serves 4

preparation: 20 minutes

cooking time: 30 minutes

per serving: 470 cals; 25g fat;
    30g carbohydrate

1 Cut the tofu into 2.5cm (1 inch) cubes and put into a shallow roasting dish.

2 For the glaze, combine the hoisin sauce, soy sauce, sherry vinegar, chilli sauce, honey and sesame oil in a bowl. Pour two-thirds of this mixture over the tofu and toss to coat. Bake on the top shelf of the oven at 230°C (210°C fan oven) mark 8 for 20 minutes, stirring halfway through.

3 Heat the sunflower oil in a preheated wok or large frying pan. Add the carrots, broccoli and mushrooms and stir-fry for 3 minutes. Add the leek, spring onions and mangetout and stir-fry for a further 2 minutes.

4 Stir 3 tbsp water into the remaining glaze and add to the wok. Cook gently for 3–4 minutes until the vegetables are tender. Stir in the roasted tofu and serve at once, sprinkled with the sesame seeds.

variation: *Omit the tofu and serve the stir-fried vegetables simply with rice or noodles.*

Spring Vegetable Stew

225g (8oz) new potatoes, scrubbed

salt and pepper

75g (3oz) unsalted butter

4 shallots, peeled and thinly sliced

1 garlic clove, peeled and crushed

2 tsp chopped thyme

1 tsp grated lime zest

6 baby leeks, trimmed and sliced into 5cm
    (2 inch) lengths

125g (4oz) baby carrots, scrubbed

125g (4oz) podded peas

125g (4oz) podded broad beans

300ml (½ pint) vegetable stock

1 little gem lettuce, shredded

4 tbsp chopped herbs, such as chervil,
    chives, mint and parsley

serves 4

preparation: 30 minutes

cooking time: 25–30 minutes

per serving: 270 cals; 17g fat;
    23g carbohydrate

1 Put the potatoes into a saucepan with plenty of cold water to cover. Add a little salt, bring to the boil, cover and par-boil for 5 minutes. Drain and refresh under cold water.

2 Meanwhile, melt half the butter in a large sauté pan, add the shallots, garlic, thyme and lime zest, and fry gently for 5 minutes until softened and lightly golden. Add the leeks and carrots and sauté for a further 5 minutes.

3 Stir in the potatoes, peas and broad beans, then pour in the stock. Bring to the boil, cover and simmer gently for 10 minutes. Remove the lid and cook, uncovered, for a further 5–8 minutes until all the vegetables are tender.

4 Add the shredded lettuce to the stew with the chopped herbs and remaining butter. Heat through until the butter is melted. Check the seasoning and serve at once.

Mediterranean Vegetable Couscous with Feta

2 red onions, peeled and roughly chopped

2 courgettes, trimmed and roughly chopped

1 aubergine, trimmed and roughly chopped

2 red peppers, cored, deseeded and roughly
   chopped

2 garlic cloves, peeled and sliced

4 tbsp olive oil

salt and pepper

350g (12oz) tomatoes, halved

225g (8oz) couscous

300ml (½ pint) hot vegetable stock

4 tbsp roughly chopped flat-leafed parsley

2 tbsp balsamic vinegar

200g (7oz) feta cheese, cubed

serves 4

preparation: 20 minutes, plus soaking

cooking time: 1 hour

per serving: 580 cals; 25g fat;
   73g carbohydrate

1 Put the red onions, courgettes, aubergine, red peppers and garlic into a roasting tin and drizzle with the olive oil. Season with salt and pepper, then toss together and roast at 200°C (180°C fan oven) mark 6 for 30 minutes.

2 Add the tomatoes to the tin. Toss together and roast for a further 30 minutes.

3 Meanwhile, put the couscous into a large bowl. Pour in the stock, stir and cover. Set aside to soak for 10 minutes.

4 Fluff up the warm couscous with a fork, then add the chopped parsley, balsamic vinegar, and roasted vegetables. Toss together, then spoon into warmed bowls, scatter over the feta cheese and serve.

Spiced Bean and Pumpkin Stew

700g (1½lb) sweet potatoes, peeled

700g (1½lb) pumpkin, peeled and deseeded

3 tbsp olive oil

2 small onions, peeled and sliced

2 garlic cloves, peeled and crushed

1 tbsp sweet paprika

1 small dried red chilli, deseeded and finely
   chopped

125g (4oz) okra, trimmed

500g carton passata

salt and pepper

400g can haricot or cannellini beans, drained

serves 4

preparation: 20 minutes

cooking time: 30 minutes

per serving: 250 cals; 8g fat;
   42g carbohydrate

1 Cut the sweet potatoes into 2.5cm (1 inch) cubes. Cut the pumpkin into 4cm (1½ inch) chunks.

2 Heat the olive oil in a large heavy-based pan, add the onions and garlic, and cook over a low heat for about 5 minutes. Stir in the paprika and chilli, and cook for 2 minutes.

3 Add the sweet potatoes, pumpkin, okra, passata and 900ml (1½ pints) water. Season generously with salt and pepper. Cover, bring to the boil and simmer for 20 minutes or until the vegetables are just tender.

4 Add the haricot beans and cook for 3 minutes to warm through. Serve with crusty bread.

Split Pea Roti

125g (4oz) yellow split peas, soaked
  in cold water overnight
¼ tsp ground turmeric
1 tsp ground cumin
1 garlic clove, peeled and finely sliced
1½ tsp salt
225g (8oz) plain flour, sifted, plus extra
  to dust
1½ tsp baking powder
1 tbsp vegetable oil, plus extra to fry
125–150ml (4–5fl oz) milk

serves 4
preparation: 25 minutes, plus
  overnight soaking and resting
cooking time: 40 minutes
per serving: 170 cals; 3g fat;
  32g carbohydrate

1 Drain the split peas and put into a small pan with the turmeric, cumin, garlic and 1 tsp salt. Add 200ml (7fl oz) cold water, bring to the boil and simmer for 30 minutes or until the peas are soft, adding a little more water if necessary. Set aside to cool.
2 Sift the flour, baking powder and remaining salt into a large bowl. Make a well in the centre, add the oil and gradually mix in enough milk to form a soft dough. Transfer to a lightly floured surface and knead until smooth. Cover with a damp tea-towel and leave to rest for 30 minutes.
3 Whiz the cooled peas in a food processor or blender until smooth, adding 1 tbsp water.
4 Divide the dough into eight. On a lightly floured surface, roll out each piece to a 20cm (8 inch) round. Divide the pea mixture between 4 rounds, placing it in the centre, then top with the other rounds and press the edges together to seal.
5 Heat a large heavy-based frying pan until really hot. Brush each roti with a little oil and fry one or two at a time, for 1 minute on each side or until lightly brown. Keep warm while you cook the rest. Serve with a vegetable curry (below).

Illustrated with Vegetable Curry on page 222

Vegetable Curry

150g (5oz) potato, peeled
150g (5oz) carrots, peeled
125g (4oz) aubergine, trimmed
3 tbsp vegetable oil
1 onion, peeled and finely sliced
4 garlic cloves, peeled and crushed
2.5cm (1 inch) piece fresh root ginger, peeled
  and grated
3 tbsp medium curry powder
6 curry leaves
900ml (1½ pints) vegetable stock
pinch of powdered saffron
salt and pepper
150g (5oz) green beans, trimmed
75g (3oz) frozen peas
3 tbsp chopped coriander leaves

serves 4
preparation: 20 minutes
cooking time: 30 minutes
per serving: 190 cals; 11g fat;
  19g carbohydrate

1 Cut the potato into 1cm (½ inch) cubes. Cut the carrots into 5mm (¼ inch) dice. Cut the aubergine into 2cm (¾ inch) long sticks, 5mm (¼ inch) wide.
2 Heat the oil in a large heavy-based pan. Add the onion and fry over a low heat for 5–10 minutes until softened and golden. Add the garlic, ginger, curry powder and curry leaves and fry for a further 1 minute.
3 Add the potato and aubergine to the pan and fry, stirring, for 2 minutes. Add the carrots, stock, saffron, 1 tsp salt and plenty of black pepper. Cover and cook for 10 minutes until the vegetables are almost tender.
4 Add the beans and peas to the pan and cook for a further 4 minutes.
5 Transfer to a serving dish, scatter with coriander and serve with roti (see above).

Illustrated on page 222

Squash and Chickpea Balti

1 large onion, peeled and chopped

4 garlic cloves, peeled and chopped

4 red chillies, deseeded and chopped

2 tsp grated fresh root ginger

4 tbsp sunflower oil

2 tsp ground coriander

1 tsp each ground cinnamon, paprika,
   fenugreek, turmeric and mustard powder

½ tsp ground cumin

3 cardamom pods, bruised

450g (1lb) ripe tomatoes, chopped

350g (12oz) peeled potatoes

350g (12oz) peeled, deseeded butternut
   squash

2 tbsp lemon juice

400g can chickpeas, drained

225g (8oz) French beans, halved

salt and pepper

coriander leaves, to garnish

serves 6
preparation: 30 minutes
cooking time: 1¼ hours
per serving: 220 cals; 11g fat;
   27g carbohydrate

1 Put the onion, garlic, chillies and ginger into a food processor and blend until fairly smooth.

2 Heat the oil in a saucepan, add the onion mixture and fry gently for 10 minutes until lightly golden, then stir in the spices. Add the tomatoes and cook for a further 5 minutes.

3 Cut the potatoes and squash into 2.5cm (1 inch) cubes and add to the pan with the lemon juice, chickpeas and 450ml (¾ pint) water. Bring to the boil, partially cover and simmer for 30–45 minutes until the potatoes are tender.

4 Add the French beans and cook for a further 5–10 minutes. Season with salt and pepper to taste.

5 Scatter over the coriander and serve with naan bread and poppadoms.

Roasted Ratatouille with Herb Dumplings

1 large red onion, peeled and sliced

2 garlic cloves, peeled and crushed

2 courgettes, trimmed and sliced

1 medium aubergine, trimmed and diced

2 red peppers, halved, deseeded and cut
   into chunky slices

4 tbsp olive oil

salt and pepper

2 x 400g cans chopped tomatoes

good pinch of golden caster sugar

DUMPLINGS

125g (4oz) self-raising flour, plus extra
   to dust

50g (2oz) vegetable suet

1 tbsp chopped parsley

1 tsp thyme leaves

1 litre (1¾ pints) hot vegetable stock

serves 4
preparation: 25 minutes
cooking time: 1–1¼ hours
per serving: 410 cals; 25g fat;
   41g carbohydrate

1 Put the onion, garlic, courgettes, aubergine and peppers into a roasting tin and mix them all together. Drizzle with olive oil and season well with salt and pepper. Roast at 200°C (180°C fan oven) mark 6 for 40–50 minutes.

2 Add the tomatoes and sugar and stir thoroughly. Return to the oven for 15–20 minutes.

3 Meanwhile, make the herbed dumplings. Put the flour, vegetable suet, parsley and thyme leaves into a bowl and season well with salt and pepper. Add 6–7 tbsp cold water and mix everything together with a knife. Dust your hands with a little flour and shape the mixture into 4 dumplings.

4 Bring the stock to the boil in a medium pan, then reduce the heat. Add the dumplings and poach gently for 5 minutes, turning once with a slotted spoon.

5 Divide the ratatouille among four ovenproof serving dishes and put a dumpling into each dish. Stand the dishes on a baking tray and put into the oven for 10 minutes until the dumplings are lightly browned. Allow to stand for 3 minutes before serving.

Aubergine and Red Pepper Moussaka

450g (1lb) potatoes, peeled

salt and pepper

1 aubergine, trimmed and sliced into rounds

1 large red onion, peeled and cut into wedges

2 red peppers, cored, deseeded and sliced

4 tbsp olive oil

2 tbsp chopped thyme

225g (8oz) tomatoes, thickly sliced

2 garlic cloves, peeled and sliced

250g carton passata

2 x 125g cartons soft goat's cheese

2 x 150ml cartons natural yogurt

3 medium eggs

25g (1oz) Parmesan cheese, freshly grated

serves 6

preparation: 45 minutes

cooking time: 1½ hours

per serving: 340 cals; 21g fat;
   23g carbohydrate

1 Cut the potatoes lengthways into 5mm (¼ inch) slices. Add to a pan of cold salted water, bring to the boil and par-boil for 5 minutes. Drain well.

2 Put the potatoes into a large roasting tin with the aubergine, onion and peppers. Drizzle with the olive oil, add the thyme and toss to mix. Season generously with salt and pepper. Roast at 230°C (210°C fan oven) mark 8 for 30 minutes, stirring occasionally.

3 Add the tomatoes and garlic to the tin and roast for a further 15 minutes. Remove from the oven and lower the setting to 200°C (180°C fan oven) mark 6.

4 Spread half of the vegetables in a 1.7 litre (3 pint) ovenproof dish, then cover with half of the passata. Spoon the goat's cheese evenly on top. Layer the rest of the roasted vegetables over the cheese and cover with the passata.

5 Lightly whisk the yogurt, eggs and Parmesan together in a bowl and season generously. Pour on top of the moussaka, then bake for 45 minutes until golden and bubbling.

Mozzarella, Tomato and Aubergine Layer

6 large aubergines, about 2kg (4½lb)
   in total, trimmed

8–10 tbsp olive oil, plus extra to brush

2 garlic cloves, peeled and crushed

400g can chopped tomatoes

2 x 200g packs smoked mozzarella cheese,
   sliced (see note)

20 basil sprigs

salt and pepper

100g (3½oz) Parmesan cheese, freshly
   grated

serves 6

preparation: 20 minutes

cooking time: 44–55 minutes

per serving: 490 cals; 38g fat;
   9g carbohydrate

1 Slice the aubergines lengthways into 5mm (¼ inch) thick slices. Place in a single layer on lightly oiled non-stick baking sheets and brush lightly with olive oil. Scatter the crushed garlic on top. Bake at 230°C (210°C fan oven) mark 8 for 10–15 minutes until softened and golden brown.

2 Meanwhile, tip the canned tomatoes and their juice into a blender or food processor and whiz for 1–2 seconds to make a chunky passata; avoid making the sauce too smooth.

3 Lower the oven setting to 180°C (160°C fan oven) mark 4. Cover the bottom of a 3 litre (5 pint) shallow ovenproof dish with a quarter of the passata and arrange one third of the garlic-roasted aubergines in the dish. Cover with another layer of passata, then arrange half of the mozzarella and basil on top, seasoning well as you do so.

4 Repeat these layers, then finish with a layer of aubergines and the remaining passata. Sprinkle the grated Parmesan evenly over the surface and bake for 35–40 minutes until bubbling and golden brown.

notes
• If smoked mozzarella is unavailable, use ordinary buffalo mozzarella instead.
• If obtainable, use ready-made chunky passata rather than blend the tomatoes yourself.

Boston Baked Beans

225g (8oz) dried black-eyed beans, soaked
   overnight in cold water
2 tbsp olive oil
1 large onion, peeled and chopped
1 large garlic clove, peeled and finely
   chopped
600ml (1 pint) dry cider
150g (5oz) passata
2 tbsp tomato paste (preferably sun-dried)
1 tbsp black treacle
1 tbsp demerara sugar
1 tsp French mustard
sea salt and pepper
parsley sprigs, to garnish

serves 4
preparation: 10 minutes, plus overnight
   soaking
cooking time: 2–2½ hours
per serving: 310 cals; 8g fat;
   45g carbohydrate

1 Drain the beans, rinse under cold running water, then put into a large pan. Cover with plenty of fresh cold water, bring to the boil and boil steadily for 10 minutes. Remove any scum from the surface with a slotted spoon. Lower the heat, cover and simmer for a further 20 minutes.

2 Heat the olive oil in another pan, add the onion and garlic, and fry gently until tender. Add the cider, passata, tomato paste, black treacle, demerara sugar and mustard. Bring to the boil.

3 Drain the beans and transfer to a casserole. Stir in the tomato mixture. Cover and cook in the oven at 170°C (150°C fan oven) mark 3 for 1½–2 hours or until the beans are tender. Check and stir the beans occasionally during cooking and add a little extra cider or water if necessary to prevent them drying out; the finished sauce should be thick and syrupy.

4 Season with salt and pepper to taste. Serve garnished with parsley and accompanied by hot crusty garlic bread or jacket potatoes and a salad.

variation: *Use haricot beans instead of black-eyed beans, adjusting the cooking time accordingly.*

White Nut Roast

225g (8oz) mixed white nuts, such as
   brazil, macadamia, pine nuts and
   blanched almonds
40g (1½oz) butter, plus extra to grease
1 onion, peeled and finely chopped
1 garlic clove, peeled and crushed
125g (4oz) fresh white breadcrumbs
grated zest and juice of ½ lemon
75g (3oz) sage Derby or Parmesan cheese,
   freshly grated
125g (4oz) canned peeled chestnuts,
   roughly chopped
½ x 390g can artichoke hearts,
   roughly chopped
salt and pepper
1 medium egg, lightly beaten
2 tsp chopped thyme, plus extra sprigs
2 tsp chopped sage, plus extra sprigs
2 tsp chopped parsley, plus extra sprigs

serves 8
preparation: 20 minutes, plus chilling
cooking time: 1–1¼ hours
per serving: 340 cals; 26g fat;
   16g carbohydrate

1 Whiz the nuts together in a food processor until ground; set aside.

2 Melt the butter in a pan and cook the onion and garlic for 5–7 minutes or until softened. Put into a large bowl and set aside to cool.

3 Add the ground nuts, breadcrumbs, lemon zest and juice, grated cheese, chestnuts and artichoke hearts. Season with plenty of salt and pepper and mix in the beaten egg to bind the ingredients together. Stir in the chopped herbs.

4 Put the mixture on to a large buttered piece of foil and shape into a fat sausage, packing tightly. Scatter over the extra herb sprigs and wrap in the foil. Cool, cover and chill for at least 2 hours or overnight, or freeze until needed.

5 Cook on an upturned Swiss roll tin at 200°C (180°C fan oven) mark 6 for 35 minutes (or 45 minutes from frozen), then unwrap the foil slightly and cook the nut roast for a further 15 minutes until turning golden.

Savoury Vegetarian Crumble

25g (1oz) butter or margarine
225g (8oz) baby onions, peeled
1 garlic clove, peeled and crushed
2 tbsp chopped sage
225g (8oz) carrots, peeled and chopped
225g (8oz) peeled, deseeded butternut
    squash, cut into cubes
400g can chopped tomatoes
225g (8oz) broccoli florets
300ml (½ pint) double cream
200ml (7fl oz) milk
salt and pepper

CRUMBLE TOPPING
175g (6oz) plain wholemeal flour
75g (3oz) butter or margarine, diced
50g (2oz) walnuts, finely chopped
25g (1oz) Cheddar cheese, grated

serves 4–6
preparation: 45 minutes
cooking time: 35–40 minutes
per serving: 860–580 cals; 68–45g fat;
    50–33g carbohydrate

1 Melt the butter in a frying pan, add the onions, garlic and sage, and fry gently for 10 minutes until softened. Add the carrots and squash and fry for a further 10 minutes. Add the tomatoes, cover and simmer for 15 minutes until the vegetables begin to soften. Leave to cool slightly.

2 Meanwhile, prepare the crumble topping. Sift the flour and a pinch of salt into a bowl, then rub in the butter until the mixture resembles fine breadcrumbs. Stir in the walnuts and cheese. Set aside.

3 Add the broccoli, cream and milk to the vegetable mixture and season well with salt and pepper. Spoon into a 2 litre (3½ pint) pie dish and scatter over the crumble topping. Cover with foil and bake at 190°C (170°C fan oven) mark 5 for 20 minutes.

4 Remove the foil and return to the oven for a further 15–20 minutes until bubbling and golden on top. Serve with a green vegetable.

Leek, Mushroom and Artichoke Croûte

3 tbsp olive oil
2 garlic cloves, peeled and crushed
125g (4oz) shiitake mushrooms, sliced
1 tbsp balsamic vinegar
50g (2oz) whole cooked chestnuts, roughly
    chopped
5 thyme sprigs, leaves only
400g can artichoke hearts, drained and
    quartered
350g (12oz) leeks, trimmed and sliced
375g pack ready-rolled puff pastry
flour, to dust
salt and pepper
butter, to grease
1 egg, lightly beaten, to glaze

TO SERVE
cranberry sauce (page 26)

serves 8
preparation: 30 minutes, plus overnight
    chilling
cooking time: 30–35 minutes
per serving: 270 cals; 19g fat;
    22g carbohydrate

1 Heat 2 tbsp olive oil in a large pan and fry the garlic for 1 minute. Add the mushrooms and cook, stirring, over a low heat for 3 minutes to soften. Add the balsamic vinegar, chestnuts, ½ tsp thyme leaves and the artichoke hearts, then cook for 1 minute.

2 Heat the remaining 1 tbsp oil in a clean pan, add the leeks and cook for 4 minutes to soften slightly. Turn into a bowl and cool for 5 minutes.

3 Unroll the pastry on a lightly floured surface and sprinkle with the remaining thyme. Roll lightly to imbed the leaves in the pastry, then flip over so the herbs are on the underside. Roll the pastry lightly to a 38 x 25cm (15 x 10 inch) rectangle. Using a sharp knife, cut the pastry in half lengthways to give two long thin oblongs.

4 Spoon half the mushroom mixture down the centre of each piece of pastry. Top with the leeks and season with salt and pepper. Brush the pastry edges with water, then fold each side of the pastry up over the filling and seal. Cut both rolls in half and put, seam-side down, on a greased baking sheet. Cover and chill overnight or freeze.

5 To cook, brush the pastry with egg to glaze. Bake at 200°C (180°C fan oven) mark 6 for 20 minutes (25 minutes from frozen) until the pastry is golden. Serve with cranberry sauce.

Easy Leek Pie

PASTRY

275g (10oz) plain flour, plus extra to dust
1 tsp English mustard powder
175g (6oz) cold butter, cut into cubes
½ tsp salt
50g (2oz) mature Cheddar cheese, grated
2 medium egg yolks, lightly beaten

FILLING

900g (2lb) leeks, trimmed
2 medium red onions, peeled
juice of ½ lemon
5 thyme sprigs, leaves only
salt and pepper
4 tbsp olive oil

TO GLAZE

1 small egg, lightly beaten

serves 6
preparation: 15 minutes
cooking time: 1 hour
per serving: 540 cals; 38g fat;
   42g carbohydrate

1 To make the pastry, put the flour, mustard, butter and salt into a food processor. Pulse until the mixture forms crumbs, then add the cheese, egg yolks and 2–3 tbsp cold water. Process briefly until the mixture comes together. Form into a ball, wrap in clingfilm and put in the freezer for 10 minutes.

2 Cut the leeks into 1cm (½ inch) slices, then wash and drain. Put the leeks into a microwave-proof bowl. Add 3 tbsp water, cover with clingfilm, pierce the top and microwave on high for 8 minutes. (Alternatively, cook the leeks with the water in a small covered pan over a low heat until softened.) Drain in a colander, then set aside.

3 Cut each onion into 8 wedges, put into the bowl and toss in the lemon juice. Cover, pierce as before and microwave on high for 5 minutes. (Alternatively, gently cook the onions with the lemon juice in a small covered pan until softened.)

4 Roll out the pastry on a lightly floured large sheet of baking parchment to a 38cm (15 inch) round. Lift the paper and pastry on to a large baking sheet.

5 Put the onions and leeks in the centre of the pastry, leaving a 7.5cm (3 inch) border all round. Sprinkle the thyme leaves over the vegetables, season with salt and pepper, and drizzle with the olive oil.

6 Lift the pastry edges up and fold them over the vegetables at the edge. Brush the pastry rim with beaten egg and bake at 200°C (180°C fan oven) mark 6 for 50 minutes or until the pastry is golden and the vegetables are tender.

Baked Stuffed Tomatoes

50g (2oz) long-grain rice
4 large beef tomatoes, about 225g (8oz) each
2 tbsp pesto
50g (2oz) mozzarella cheese, shredded
25g (1oz) Parmesan cheese, freshly grated
salt and pepper
basil leaves, to garnish

serves 4
preparation: 20 minutes
cooking time: 30 minutes
per serving: 190 cals; 9g fat;
   17g carbohydrate

1 Cook the rice according to the pack instructions; drain and set aside.

2 Meanwhile, cut a thin sliver from the base of each tomato so that it will sit flat. Cut a slightly thicker slice from the top of each one, then scoop out the seeds and pulp, taking care to avoid cutting through the skins; discard the seeds.

3 Finely chop the tomato pulp and stir into the rice with the pesto, mozzarella and half of the Parmesan. Season with salt and pepper to taste.

4 Spoon the rice mixture into the tomato shells and scatter over the remaining Parmesan. Put into a small roasting dish and bake at 220°C (200°C fan oven) mark 7 for 20 minutes until bubbling and golden. Garnish with basil and serve hot or warm, with a green salad and crusty bread.

Spicy Bean and Tomato Fajitas

2 tbsp sunflower oil

1 medium onion, peeled and sliced

2 garlic cloves, peeled and crushed

½ tsp hot chilli powder

1 tsp ground coriander

1 tsp ground cumin

1 tbsp tomato purée

400g can chopped tomatoes

220g can red kidney beans, drained and
　　rinsed

300g can borlotti beans, drained and rinsed

300g can flageolet beans, drained and rinsed

150ml (¼ pint) hot vegetable stock

salt and pepper

2 ripe avocados, quartered, peeled and
　　chopped

juice of ½ lime

1 tbsp chopped coriander, plus sprigs
　　to garnish

pack of 8 ready-made flour tortillas

142ml carton soured cream

lime wedges, to serve

serves 4

preparation: 15 minutes

cooking time: 23 minutes

per serving: 620 cals; 28g fat;
　　74g carbohydrate

1 Heat the oil in a large pan, add the onion and cook gently for 5 minutes. Add the garlic and spices and cook for a further 2 minutes.

2 Add the tomato purée and cook for 1 minute, then add the tomatoes, beans and hot stock. Season well with salt and pepper, bring to the boil and simmer for 15 minutes, stirring occasionally.

3 Put the avocado into a bowl, add the lime juice and the chopped coriander and mash together. Season well with salt and pepper.

4 Warm the tortillas: either wrap them in foil and heat in the oven at 180°C (160°C fan oven) mark 4 for 10 minutes or put on a plate and microwave on high for 45 seconds.

5 Spoon the beans down the centre of each tortilla. Fold up one edge to keep the filling inside, then wrap the two sides in so they overlap. Dollop on the avocado and top with soured cream. Garnish with coriander sprigs and serve with lime wedges.

Chestnut Mushroom Gratin

700g (1½lb) small sweet potatoes, peeled
　　and cut in half

50g (2oz) butter

700g (1½lb) chestnut mushrooms, quartered

150ml (¼ pint) dry white wine

100ml (3½fl oz) crème fraîche

1 tsp chopped thyme

salt and pepper

3 tbsp fresh white breadcrumbs

5 tbsp freshly grated Parmesan cheese

serves 4

preparation: 15 minutes

cooking time: 35 minutes

per serving: 410 cals; 25g fat;
　　41g carbohydrate

1 Cook the sweet potatoes in boiling salted water 15–20 minutes until just tender, drain. Leave to cool, then cut into 5mm (¼ inch) slices; set aside.

2 Melt half the butter in a large frying pan. When it is foaming, add half the mushrooms and fry over a high heat for 2–3 minutes, then remove from the pan and set aside. Fry the rest of the mushrooms in the remaining butter.

3 Add the wine to the pan, bring to the boil and leave to bubble until reduced by half, then add the crème fraîche and let bubble for 2–3 minutes. Return the mushrooms to the pan, add the chopped thyme and season with salt and pepper. Mix well, then transfer to a 1.4 litre (2½ pint) ovenproof dish.

4 Arrange the sweet potatoes around the edge in an overlapping layer. Mix together the breadcrumbs and Parmesan and scatter over the potatoes. Bake at 190°C (170°C fan oven) mark 5 for 15 minutes or until thoroughly hot. Serve with a green salad.

CHEESE
AND EGGS

These nutritious dairy foods have a wide range of culinary uses. Keep a supply of eggs and cheese in the fridge and you will always have a quick and easy lunch, supper or snack to hand. Both ingredients are rich sources of high quality protein, vitamins A and D; in addition, eggs provide vitamin B12 and cheese is rich in calcium, which is so vital for strong bones and teeth.

CHEESE

For culinary purposes, cheeses can be categorised as follows: hard cheeses, such as Parmesan and pecorino; semi-hard cheeses, such as Cheddar, Gruyère and Stilton; soft ripened cheeses, such as Brie and Camembert; and fresh soft cheeses, like mozzarella, mascarpone and soft goat's cheeses. Most cheeses, including the popular hard cheeses – Cheddar, Stilton and Parmesan – have a high fat content and should be consumed in moderate quantities, although low-fat varieties are available.

In the cheese-making process, rennet (or a vegetarian alternative) is used to curdle milk and separate it into firm curds and liquid whey. The curds are then processed, shaped and matured as necessary to create a wide range of cheeses. The method varies according to the type of cheese. Very hard cheeses, such as Parmesan, take up to 3 years to develop their full flavour, while soft cheeses, like Brie, are ready to eat within a month or two. Fresh soft goat's cheeses, mozzarella and cream cheeses are not matured in this way.

BUYING AND STORING CHEESE

Probably the best place to buy cheese is from a specialist cheese shop if you are lucky enough to have access to one, otherwise many supermarkets have a fresh cheese counter offering a good variety of farmhouse and factory-made cheeses.

Try and taste first before you commit to buying a cheese, as artisan cheeses will vary within, as well as across, varieties – some cheeses differ according to the time of year and certain varieties are seasonal. Once you have made your choice, make sure the cheese is freshly sliced to your requirements. Buy only as much or as little as you think you need – central heating and refrigeration will dry out the cheese once you get it home.

The best way to store cheese is wrapped in wax paper in the lower (least cold) part of the fridge. Put the wrapped cheese in an unsealed plastic food bag or cheese box in the fridge. If you have a whole, rinded cheese, cover the cut surface with clingfilm.

To enjoy cheese at its best, you should always remove it from the fridge at least 2 hours before serving to bring it to room temperature. Loosen the wrapping and remove it just before serving. Provide at least two knives for cutting, so there is a separate one for blue cheese.

SELECTING FOR A CHEESEBOARD

Selecting cheeses for a cheeseboard is a matter of satisfying everyone's taste, so a range of flavours from mild to strong, and a variety of textures, is important. Think about shapes and colours, too. If you are serving four cheeses, choose one hard, one soft, one blue and one goat's cheese. If you are buying from a specialist cheese shop or a supermarket cheese counter, ask to try a piece first so you know what you are getting and can balance the flavours. It is a question of quality rather than quantity, as a few excellent cheeses are more appealing than five or six with competing flavours.

To accompany your cheeses, choose crisp apples, juicy pears, grapes or figs. Very mild, soft goat's cheeses can be eaten with strawberries; slightly harder ones go well with cherry tomatoes or olives. Salad leaves should be bitter – try some chicory, frisée or rocket. Walnuts and celery are excellent with blue cheese. Oatcakes, wheat wafers and digestive biscuits go well with most cheeses, and if you want to serve bread make sure it is fresh and crusty. Butter should be unsalted.

As for when you serve cheese, rounding off the meal with the cheeseboard is the norm in this country, but the French custom of moving from main course to cheese course is worth considering. It enables you to savour the cheeses before you are too full to enjoy them, and you can carry on with the same wine.

TYPES OF CHEESE

Semi-hard and hard cheeses are produced by removing as much of the whey as possible from the curds, then moulding and ripening the cheese. Hard cheeses undergo a further process which involves heating the curd so that it shrinks and hardens. Semi-hard cheeses include Cheddar and Edam, while the most familiar hard cheeses are Parmesan and pecorino.

Vegetarian cheeses produced using vegetarian rennet are becoming increasingly available from supermarkets and specialist cheese shops.

Soft cheeses are generally made by coagulating milk with rennet; the addition of a starter ensures a clean, acidic flavour. Some varieties of soft cheese, such as Brie, Camembert and the blue-veined cheeses are mould-ripened. It is these cheeses that are susceptible to listeria contamination.

Fresh cheeses are soft and light, with a refreshing tang. There are many different types of fresh cheeses, with different fat contents, depending on whether they are made from whole or skimmed milk. These cheeses have a relatively short shelf life.

Cream cheese is a fresh, bland cheese made from pasteurised milk. Its fat content varies, depending on the type. Cream cheese has many uses, including cheesecakes and dips.

Fromage frais is a soft cheese produced from skimmed milk and rennet. The curd is stirred and the whey drained off. Fromage frais can be used as an alternative to cream.

Curd cheese has a clean, acidic flavour and a soft, slightly granular texture. It is made solely by the action of lactic acid; rennet is not used. There are several varieties of this soft, fresh cheese, including quark, which has a very low-fat content.

Cottage cheese is made from the curds of skimmed milk, which are heated to make them firm and dense. The resulting curd cheese is then broken up and finished with a little cream. Cottage cheese is low in fat.

Goat's cheeses are increasingly popular, as reflected in the infinite variety now available, most of which are simply termed chèvres. British-made goat's cheeses are now widely produced, in response to the demand. Young, soft ·goat's cheese is rindless with a mild, clean flavour – ideal for recipes using soft cheeses. Harder, rinded varieties are often sliced and grilled, then served on salads or bread.

POPULAR CHEESE VARIETIES

Unless otherwise stated, the following cheeses are made from cow's milk.

Banon

This French goat's milk cheese is traditionally made as a small cylinder. It is often sold wrapped in chestnut leaves.

Beaufort

A hard cheese, rather like Gruyère, with a smooth texture and a nutty, sweet favour, best served cut into very thin slices.

Beenleigh Blue

A seasonal sheep's milk cheese from Devon, this variety is available from August to January. It is steely blue, with a pronounced flavour and a strong spicy after-taste.

Bel Paese

This is the trade name for a soft Italian cheese with a mild flavour.

Bleu de Bresse
A French blue cheese, comparatively mild in flavour, with a creamy texture.

Boursin
This is the brand name of a French cream cheese. The most familiar Boursin is flavoured with garlic and herbs; others are rolled in crushed peppercorns or herbs.

Brie
A popular soft, unpressed French cheese with a smooth, creamy texture and a white, bloomy rind. It has a very subtle flavour with a slight mushroom aroma and a hint of ammonia. Brie de Meaux is especially rich, creamy and robustly flavoured and is one of the best varieties. Somerset Brie is a mild-tasting cheese.

Caerphilly
A hard, lightly pressed Welsh cheese made from skimmed milk. Ivory white in colour, it has a fresh, salty, lemony taste and a flaky texture. It is named after the Glamorgan village of Caerphilly and was originally produced in the early 19th century.

Cambazola
Also known as Blue Brie, this German soft blue cheese with its thick, smooth, white rind was created in the 1970's. It is a combination of Camembert and Gorgonzola, and has a smooth, rich, creamy consistency and a mildly spicy, sweet-sour taste.

Camembert
This popular soft, unpressed cheese from Normandy has a bloomy rind, a velvety texture and a taste of wild mushrooms. It is sold in a small, wooden box, originally created so the cheese could be transported outside its region of origin. The recipe for Camembert dates back to the French Revolution.

Cashel Blue
This blue cheese was first made 10 years ago in Tipperary. When young, it is firm and tangy, with a slight hint of tarragon; when mature, it becomes spicier and creamier. Cashel Blue is delicious spread thickly on warm walnut bread.

Cantal
A hard, pressed French cheese with a greyish rind and a supple, light-yellow interior. It is made in the form of a large cylinder and tastes a little like a mild English Cheddar.

Chaource
A goat's cheese from Burgundy with a fine, distinctive flavour, which develops over a short period to a tangy, fruity ripeness.

Cheddar
Perhaps the most popular of hard English cheeses, Cheddar originates from the town of Cheddar in the Mendip Hills in Somerset and is now made worldwide. Young Cheddar has a mild, nutty smell and a rich, sweet taste, and it is pale in colour. As it matures, the cheese acquires a nutty, deep flavour and a more intense colour. Cheddar is traditionally made from unpasteurised milk and wrapped in cloth. Among the finest farmhouse varieties are Montgomery's and Keen's from Somerset, and Quicke's from Devon.

Cheshire
A hard, pressed English cheese which comes in three different colours: white, blue and red, which is stained with a vegetable dye. Blue Cheshire is rich in flavour; white and red Cheshires are mild, salty, moist and crumbly. Cheshire is one of the oldest British cheeses.

Comté
This French cheese is similar to Gruyère and takes its name from the Franche-Comté region, where it is made. It is a hard, pressed cheese produced in large, flat wheels and has a greyish rind. Comté has a dense, firm texture and a smooth, fruity flavour.

Cornish Yarg
A moist, crumbly, white hard cheese, which is wrapped in nettles, giving it a distinct flavour. It is based on a 17th century recipe and was first produced in 1983 by a couple called Gray, who created its rustic name by reversing their surname.

Crottin de Chavignol
A small, cylindrical French goat's cheese aged for a few months to give a dry texture and strong taste.

Danish Blue
Ever-popular blue cheese from Denmark with blue-green veining, a creamy texture and a sharp taste.

Derby
A hard, pressed English cheese with a mild flavour and dense texture. Sage Derby is flavoured with sage leaves, which give it a distinctive mottled green appearance.

Dolcelatte
This is the commercial name for a factory-made Gorgonzola. Dolcelatte means 'sweet milk'. It has a mild, spicy flavour and can be used in salad dressings and pasta sauces.

Dorset Blue Vinny
This hard blue cheese has a dry texture and a low-fat content. When mature, the cheese has a grassy flavour with a sharp tang. Vinny is the old English word for veining.

Double Gloucester
This large, round, hard, pressed English cheese is made from whole milk. It ranges from pale to deep red-orange in colour, depending on the addition of a vegetable dye called annatto. Double Gloucester is smooth, with a rich, buttery flavour and a flaky texture. Single Gloucester is made from partly skimmed milk and is lighter and more crumbly.

Edam
Generally made from semi-skimmed milk, this semi-hard, pressed Dutch cheese has a low fat content. Edam is shaped into rounds and coated in red wax for export. The texture is firm and springy and the flavour is mild. Some imitations can be bland and rubbery.

Emmental
A hard, cooked, pressed Swiss cheese, produced in enormous wheels. It has a mild, fruity, sweet taste and characteristic large holes or 'eyes'. Emmental is now made in France and Germany, as well as Switzerland.

Feta
This soft, unpressed fresh Greek cheese was originally made by shepherds to preserve milk. Feta can be made from sheep, goat or cow's milk, or a combination of all three. It is a pure white rindless cheese, made in rectangular blocks and stored in brine, where it will keep almost indefinitely. Feta has a slightly sharp, salty taste and is excellent in salads and pastries.

Fontina
A hard, cooked, pressed Italian cheese with tiny holes, a sweet, nutty flavour and a smooth texture. Fontina is an excellent melting cheese and is perfect for fondues. The Swiss version is good as a table cheese.

Fourme d'Ambert
Distinctive blue French cheese formed into a tall cylinder shape. It has a whitish-red mould covering the rind. The cheese has a rounded flavour with a pungent after-taste.

Gorgonzola
This creamy textured Italian blue cheese from Lombardy is one of the oldest and best blue cheeses in the world. There are two styles: *dolce*, a soft and smelly blue cheese (see Dolcelatte), and *naturale*, an aged version with a firmer texture and a stronger flavour. Gorgonzola is ideal with ripe pears, which cut the richness, and it is used in dressings and pasta sauces.

Gouda
A hard, pressed Dutch cheese, with a compact, creamy texture and a yellow wax coating. The flavour is mild, even bland, when the cheese is young, but aged Gouda has a sweet, caramel-like intensity. Mature Gouda is coated in black wax. Gouda can be grated and used in cheese sauces and fondues.

Gruyère
This semi-hard cooked, pressed Swiss cheese has an earthy, nutty flavour, a smooth, dense texture and tiny holes. Gruyère is an excellent cooking cheese and is widely used in sauces, gratins, soups and Swiss fondues.

Halloumi
A traditional Cypriot sheep's milk cheese flavoured with shreds of mint, halloumi has a milky, slightly

salty taste and a rubbery texture. This cheese only really comes into its own when it is cooked. Slices of halloumi are delicious pan-fried or grilled and eaten with salads.

Jarlsberg
A popular mild cheese from Norway, similar to Emmental and with a nutty flavour.

Lancashire
A hard English cheese with a sharp, peppery taste and a firm texture.

Manchego
A hard ewe's milk cheese from Spain with a high fat content. It is rich and creamy with a wax-coated rind, a nutty, caramel flavour and small, irregular 'eyes'. To qualify for the Manchego label, the cheese must be made with milk produced in the La Mancha region of Spain.

Mozzarella
Traditionally made from buffalo milk, but also sometimes from cow's milk, this Italian cheese is valued for its delicate, soft texture. Mozzarella is formed into small balls and should be stored in its own whey, or water in the fridge, to keep it moist. Older mozzarella, sold in blocks, is inclined to be rubbery, but melts to form the characteristic elastic, stringy pizza topping.

Mascarpone
Although technically not a cheese as it is made from matured cream, mascarpone is often described as a curd cheese. It makes a good alternative to cream and is the main ingredient in tiramisu.

Maytag Blue
An American blue cheese with a peppery flavour and a very creamy, spreadable texture. It is produced in Iowa and is very popular in the States.

Monterey Jack
This American cheese originates from Monterey in California. It is a soft, white, rindless cheese and often has chopped jalapeno peppers added to it during production. Monterey Jack is matured for only 1 week; Dry Jack is a harder cheese, which is matured for 7–10 months.

Munster
A small, cylindrical soft unpressed cheese made in the Alsace region of France, with a washed orange-red rind and a highly pungent smell. Munster cheeses are shaped into flat discs and sold in boxes.

Neufchâtel
A soft French cheese from Normandy with a delicate taste and a mould-ripened rind. It is often sold in the shape of a small heart.

Parmesan (Parmigiano-reggiano)
This renowned hard, cooked, pressed Italian cheese has a distinctive flavour, which sharpens with age. It is one of the *grana* variety – the collective name for Italian grating cheeses. Older, harder Parmesan is best reserved for grating on to pasta, risottos and other dishes. Younger Parmesan is pale and crumbly; it makes a good table cheese. Tubs of dry, ready-grated Parmesan are a poor substitute for the real thing. *Grana Padano* is a cheaper version of true Parmesan.

Pecorino
This hard, cooked, pressed Italian cheese is made from sheep's milk and pressed into large cylinders. Pecorino, like Parmesan, is a *grana* cheese with a granular texture. It has an excellent sharp, pungent, salty flavour. There are many different varieties, but Pecorino Romano is one of the best.

Pont l'Evêque
A soft, pressed French cheese with a reddish rind, made in small squares and sold boxed. Pont l'Evêque is supple with a subtle flavour and a strong smell.

Port-Salut
This soft, pressed French cheese has a thin washed orange rind and a creamy yellow interior. It has a mild, sweet-sour flavour and a smooth, velvety texture. Originally made by the Trappist monks of Notre Dame du Port-du-Salut, this is now one of the most popular of French cheeses.

Provolone
A hard Italian cheese, which comes in a huge variety of shapes and sizes. It has a sharp flavour,

a yellowish rind and a firm, pale yellow interior. There are two main types: *dolce*, which is young and mild-tasting, and *piccante*, which has a sharper, saltier taste and can be grated over pasta.

Raclette
A semi-soft cheese common to Savoie in France and the Canton of Valais in Switzerland. Raclette is a melting cheese which, when heated to boiling point, becomes nutty, sweet and slightly fruity in flavour. It is excellent on baked potatoes.

Roquefort
This highly popular blue French cheese is made from ewe's milk. It has been produced and then matured in the cool, damp limestone caves of Cambalou for over 2,000 years. Roquefort has a crumbly, moist, creamy texture and a strong, salty, sharp flavour. It takes 4.5 litres (7½ pints) of milk to produce just 1kg (2¼lb) Roquefort, which explains why it is expensive.

Reblochon
A soft, lightly pressed French cheese with a washed pinkish white rind, which is sold in a small disc, usually boxed. Reblochon is creamy and fresh-tasting, with a complex taste and a hint of apple in the aroma.

Red Leicester
An English hard cheese with a bright orange rind, a dense, flaky texture and a slightly sweet, nutty flavour. The cheese gets its colour from the natural red dye, annatto. An ancient cheese, it was produced as early as the 18th century. It is particularly good in a cheese sauce.

Ricotta
A soft, moist, white unripened Italian cheese made from cow's or sheep's whey and mixed with whole milk. Low in fat and mild in flavour, it is often used in ravioli and other stuffed pasta, desserts and sweet pastries, or eaten with fresh fruit. There are many different varieties of ricotta from the different regions of Italy.

Saint-Nectaire
From the Auvergne, this semi-soft, pressed French cheese has a smooth, reddish rind and a pale interior with tiny holes. Saint-Nectaire has a mild, earthy flavour and a grassy aroma.

Shropshire Blue
An orange-coloured, semi-hard blue cheese with a creamy, crumbly texture and a good flavour. There is a hint of caramel in the flavour, which contrasts with the sharp taste of the blue mould.

Stilton
One of Britain's favourite cheeses, this has a very creamy, firm texture, a strong, tangy flavour, and blue-green veining. In the early 1900's, Stilton makers formed an association to protect the cheese – even now, Stilton can only be produced in Nottinghamshire, Derbyshire and Leicestershire, to a certain recipe. Stilton makes a good creamy salad dressing and a tasty soup. It is traditionally served at the end of a meal with a glass of port, but the custom of pouring port into the centre of the cheese tends to rot it.

Stinking Bishop
Produced in Gloucestershire, this orange-rinded, smooth-textured cheese resembles a Munster. As its name suggests, it has a pungent flavour.

Taleggio
This semi-soft, pressed Italian cheese is shaped into squares. Taleggio has a rough rose-grey rind, a soft, cream-coloured interior and a sweet aroma reminiscent of almonds.

Tomme de Savoie
A soft, pressed French cheese with a rough grey rind and a yellow interior. It has a supple texture and a nutty taste.

Vacherin
Produced in France and Switzerland, this seasonal cheese has a sweet, nutty flavour and a buttery, runny texture.

Wensleydale
This hard, pressed English cheese from the Yorkshire Dales is based on an 11th century recipe created by Cistercian monks. It has a moist, crumbly texture and a sweet, fresh flavour. Wensleydale is traditionally eaten with apple pie.

EGGS

Eggs are a concentrated source of protein and vitamins, including A, B12, D, E and K; they also contain iron. The average egg contains only 80–90 calories, so they are not particularly high in calories, but they are relatively high in cholesterol and, for this reason, it is recommended that egg consumption is restricted to three or four per week. Apart from being a wonderfully useful fast food, eggs have special culinary properties. They are invaluable for thickening, binding, emulsifying, raising and glazing.

BUYING AND STORING EGGS

Most supermarkets stock a range of eggs produced by different farming methods, including organic eggs, free-range eggs, eggs from grain-only fed hens and barn eggs. Free-range eggs are produced by hens which have easy access to open pasture and are fed a natural cereal diet. However, the majority of eggs sold in this country are still produced by 'battery hens', which are raised by intensive farming methods. There is no intrinsic difference in flavour or value between white or brown eggs.

Always refer to the 'use-by' date on the pack. The familiar lion – displayed on egg boxes – is a symbol of quality. Never buy cracked or damaged eggs; open the box before buying and check that all of the eggs are sound.

Store eggs in the fridge, pointed-end down to centre the yolk within the white. Before use, check the 'use-by' date stamped on each egg and bring to room temperature.

Eggs are now graded into four categories according to weight: very large, large, medium and small. It is important to use the correct size of egg for a recipe. Unless otherwise stated, medium eggs should be used for Good Housekeeping recipes.

Any general culinary reference to eggs implies hens' eggs, though other types are available. Quail's eggs are tiny and attractively speckled; they are usually soft-boiled for 1–2 minutes and often used as a garnish. Duck, goose and turkey eggs are larger and richer than hens' eggs. These are particularly vulnerable to salmonella and should be cooked thoroughly.

EGG SAFETY

Eggs are susceptible to salmonella, one of the bacteria responsible for food poisoning. This is because their shells are porous and can absorb the bacteria if they come into contact with it. Thorough cooking will destroy salmonella, so it isn't generally a problem. However, raw or lightly cooked eggs are used in many classic recipes, including mayonnaise, cold soufflés, meringues, ice creams and sorbets, lemon curd and scrambled eggs. Although the risk is small, those who are particularly vulnerable – including the young, the elderly, pregnant women and anyone with an immune-deficiency disease – should avoid eating raw or lightly cooked eggs.

COOKING WITH EGGS

The unique culinary properties of eggs are rather taken for granted. In addition to being simply poached, fried, baked, boiled, scrambled or turned into tasty omelettes, eggs are used to lighten soufflés and cakes; thicken mousses; bind stuffings, set baked custards; glaze pastry and breads; and emulsify sauces and dressings, such as hollandaise and mayonnaise.

The capacity of egg white, in particular, to incorporate air and dramatically increase in volume on whisking gives soufflés, meringues and whisked cakes their characteristic, light airy texture.

To Separate an Egg

Many recipes call for separated eggs. To do this, crack the egg against the rim of a clean, dry bowl and open the two halves with your thumbs, allowing some of the white to run out into the bowl. Carefully pass the egg yolk back and forth between the two half shells without breaking it, allowing the rest of the egg white to fall into the bowl. Put the separated yolk into another container. Don't let the yolk break and mingle with the white, because egg whites will not whisk satisfactorily if even a trace of yolk is present.

If you are separating several eggs, it is worth transferring the separated whites to another bowl, so that if you do happen to break a yolk only one egg white will be spoiled.

To Whisk Egg Whites

Use a large balloon whisk or a' hand-held electric whisk, rather than a food processor with a whisk attachment, which rarely gives maximum volume. Make sure the bowl and whisk are scrupulously clean and dry. Any trace of grease, water or egg yolk will adversely affect the whisking and result in a poor volume.

Whisk the egg whites until they stand in soft peaks (or as specified in the recipe). Do not over-whisk or you will have dry powdery whites which will be impossible to fold into a mixture evenly.

Fold in egg whites as soon as you have whisked them; if left to stand they will lose volume and collapse. Make sure the mixture you are folding into is neither too hot or too cold, otherwise much of the volume of the whisked egg whites will be lost. To lighten 'or let down' the mixture, quickly fold in a spoonful of whisked egg white, then lightly fold in the rest of the whites, using a large metal spoon and a cutting and folding action.

Baked Eggs

Put a knob of butter into each ramekin and heat in the oven until melted. Break a large egg into each ramekin and bake at 170°C (150°C fan oven) mark 3 for 10 minutes.

Boiled Eggs

Boiling is a misnomer, since steady boiling results in rubbery egg white. Simply lower the egg(s) into a small pan of simmering water, using a spoon, making sure there is sufficient water to cover the egg. If the egg cracks, add a little salt or vinegar to coagulate the white and stop it all running out.

For soft-boiled eggs, allow 3½–5 minutes, according to size and whether you prefer a very soft or slightly firmer set.

Eggs mollet are soft-boiled eggs with firm whites. To cook these, simmer for about 6 minutes, plunge into cold water and peel.

For lightly set coddled eggs, put into a pan of boiling water, cover with a lid, take off the heat and leave to stand in a warm place for 8–10 minutes.

For hard-boiled eggs, allow 10–12 minutes. Once cooked, drain and cool quickly under cold running water, then crack the shell to prevent a black rim forming around the yolk. When ready to serve, crack the shell all over and peel.

Poached Eggs

To poach an egg, take a wide shallow pan and two-thirds fill it with boiling water, adding 1 tbsp vinegar to each 600ml (1 pint) water. Carefully break an egg into a saucer, make a whirlpool with a large spoon in the boiling water and lower the egg into the water. Reduce the heat and cook gently for 3 minutes or until the white is just set and the yolk soft. Using a slotted spoon, lift the egg out of the pan and put it into a shallow dish of warm water. Repeat with the remaining eggs.

Alternatively, cook the eggs in an egg poacher. Half-fill the lower container with water, put a small knob of butter into each cup and bring the water to the boil. Break an egg into each cup and cook gently until set, about 3 minutes.

Fried Eggs

Heat a little butter or oil in a frying pan. Break each egg separately into a cup and add to the hot fat. Fry over a medium heat until lightly set, spooning the hot fat on top of the yolk as it cooks. If preferred, the eggs can be fried on both sides.

Scrambled Eggs

Beat the eggs well with plenty of seasoning. Melt a knob of butter in a heavy non-stick saucepan and add the eggs. Stir over a very gentle heat until just beginning to thicken. Add another knob of butter and continue stirring over the heat until the eggs start to scramble. Take off the heat and continue to stir; the eggs will continue to cook in the residual heat without turning rubbery. (Allow 25g/1oz butter to 4 eggs, adding half at each stage.)

Omelettes

An omelette must be served as soon as it is cooked so have warmed plates ready. Use a good heavy-based non-stick omelette pan or frying pan. For a two or three egg omelette you will need an 18–20cm (7–8 inch) pan; for a larger six egg quantity use a 23–25cm (9–10 inch) pan.

Lightly beat the eggs in a bowl with 1–2 tbsp water, using a fork or balloon whisk. Heat a large knob of butter in the pan, then pour in the eggs. Stir with a fork or wooden spatula until the mixture is three-quarters set to ensure an even, creamy texture, then cook without stirring, for a further 30 seconds or so until set; do not overcook.

Classic French Omelette

2–3 medium eggs
salt and pepper
1 tbsp milk or water
25g (1oz) unsalted butter, to fry

serves 1
preparation: 5 minutes
cooking time: about 2 minutes
per serving: 300 cals; 28g fat;
    0g carbohydrate

1 Whisk the eggs in a bowl – just enough to break them down; over-beating spoils the texture of the omelette. Season with salt and pepper and add the milk or water.
2 Heat the butter in an 18cm (7 inch) omelette pan or non-stick frying pan until it is foaming, but not brown.
3 Add the beaten eggs. Stir gently with a fork or wooden spatula, drawing the mixture from the sides to the centre as it sets and letting the liquid egg in the centre run to the sides. When set, stop stirring and cook for a further 30 seconds or until the omelette is golden brown underneath and still creamy on top; don't overcook.
4 If you are making a filled omelette (see right), add the filling at this point.
5 Tilt the pan away from you slightly and use a palette knife to fold over a third of the omelette to the centre, then fold over the opposite third. Slide the omelette out on to a warmed plate, letting it flip over so that the folded sides are underneath. Serve immediately, with a salad and warm bread.

omelette variations and fillings

herb: *Add 1 tsp each finely chopped chervil, chives and tarragon, or 1 tbsp chopped parsley, to the beaten egg mixture before cooking.*
tomato: *Fry 2 skinned and chopped tomatoes in a little butter for 5 minutes or until soft and pulpy. Put in the centre of the omelette before folding.*
cheese: *Grate 40g (1½oz) Gruyère or Cheddar cheese. Sprinkle half on the omelette before folding. Sprinkle the rest over the finished omelette.*
mushroom: *Thickly slice 50g (2oz) mushrooms (preferably wild) and cook in butter until soft. Put in the centre of the omelette before folding.*
goat's cheese: *Soften about 25g (1oz) mild goat's cheese and blend with a little crème fraîche. Season with salt and pepper and put in the centre of the omelette before folding.*
smoked salmon: *Toss 25g (1oz) chopped smoked salmon with a little chopped dill and 1–2 tbsp crème fraîche. Scatter over the omelette before folding.*

Mushroom Soufflé Omelette

50g (2oz) small chestnut mushrooms, sliced
3 tbsp crème fraîche
2 medium eggs, separated
salt and pepper
15g (½oz) butter
5 chives, roughly chopped

serves 1
preparation: 5 minutes
cooking time: 7 minutes
per serving: 480 cals; 44g fat;
    1g carbohydrate

1 Heat a small non-stick frying pan for 30 seconds. Add the mushrooms and cook, stirring, for 3 minutes to brown slightly, then stir in the crème fraîche and turn off the heat.
2 Lightly beat the egg yolks in a bowl, add 2 tbsp cold water and season with salt and pepper.
3 In a separate bowl, whisk the egg whites until stiff but not dry, then gently fold into the egg yolks. Be careful not to overmix.
4 Heat an 18cm (7 inch) non-stick frying pan and melt the butter in it. Add the egg mixture, tilting the pan in all directions to cover the base. Cook over a medium heat for 3 minutes or until the underside is golden brown.
5 Gently reheat the mushrooms and add the chives. Put the pan under a medium-hot grill for 1 minute, or until the surface of the omelette is just firm and puffy. Tip the mushroom mixture on top. Run a spatula around and underneath the omelette to loosen it, then carefully fold it and turn on to a plate.

Spanish Omelette

900g (2lb) potatoes, peeled and left whole
salt and pepper
3–4 tbsp vegetable oil
1 onion, peeled and finely sliced
8 medium eggs
3 tbsp chopped flat-leafed parsley
3 streaky bacon rashers

serves 4
preparation: 15 minutes
cooking time: 30–45 minutes
per serving: 530 cals; 32g fat;
    38g carbohydrate

1 Add the potatoes to a pan of cold salted water, bring to the boil and simmer for 15–20 minutes until almost cooked. Drain and leave until cool enough to handle, then slice thickly.

2 Heat 1 tbsp oil in an 18cm (7 inch) non-stick frying pan (suitable for use under the grill). Add the onion and fry gently for 7–10 minutes until softened; remove and set aside.

3 Lightly beat the eggs in a bowl and season well with salt and pepper.

4 Heat the rest of the oil in the frying pan, then layer the potato slices, onion and 2 tbsp chopped parsley in the pan. Pour in the beaten eggs and cook for 5–10 minutes until the omelette is firm underneath. Meanwhile, grill the bacon until golden and crisp, then break into pieces.

5 Put the omelette in the pan under the grill for 2–3 minutes until the top is just set. Scatter the bacon and remaining chopped parsley over the surface. Serve cut into wedges, with a green salad.

Courgette and Parmesan Frittata

40g (1½oz) butter
1 small onion, peeled and finely chopped
225g (8oz) courgettes, trimmed and
    finely sliced
6 medium eggs, beaten
salt and pepper
25g (1oz) Parmesan cheese, freshly grated,
    plus shavings to garnish

serves 4
preparation: 10 minutes
cooking time: 12 minutes
per serving: 260 cals; 20g fat;
    4g carbohydrate

1 Melt 25g (1oz) butter in an 18cm (7 inch) non-stick frying pan and cook the onion for about 10 minutes until softened. Add the courgettes and fry gently for 5 minutes or until they begin to soften.

2 Meanwhile, beat the eggs in a bowl and season well with salt and pepper.

3 Add the remaining butter to the pan and heat, then pour in the eggs. Cook for 2–3 minutes or until golden underneath and cooked round the edges.

4 Sprinkle the grated cheese over the frittata and grill under a medium-high heat for 1–2 minutes or until just set. Scatter with Parmesan shavings, cut into quarters and serve, with crusty bread.

variation

cherry tomato and rocket frittata: *Replace the courgettes with 175g (6oz) vine-ripened cherry tomatoes, frying them for 1 minute only, until they begin to soften. Immediately after pouring in the eggs, scatter 25g (1oz) rocket leaves over the surface. Continue as above.*

Eggs Benedict

hollandaise sauce (page 23), freshly prepared
4 medium eggs
4 slices ham, or 150g (5oz) bacon rashers
4 English muffins
chopped parsley, to sprinkle (optional)

serves 4
preparation: 10 minutes
cooking time: about 5 minutes
per serving: 390 cals; 46g fat;
   30g carbohydrate

1 Prepare the hollandaise sauce just before serving and set aside. Poach the eggs gently for 3 minutes or until the white is just set and the yolk soft (see instructions on page 248).
2 Meanwhile, warm the ham in the microwave on medium for 1 minute (or in a warm oven). If using bacon rashers, cook under the grill. Split the muffins and lightly toast them.
3 Place a slice of ham on each muffin base and top with a poached egg. Spoon the hollandaise on top of the egg and sprinkle with chopped parsley if you like. Put the other muffin half on top and serve at once.

Poached Eggs on Mushroom Bruschetta

4 thick slices country bread, such as
   pugliese
2 garlic cloves, peeled and halved
50g (2oz) butter
450g (1lb) field mushrooms, thinly sliced
2 tsp chopped thyme
4 large eggs
salt and pepper

serves 4
preparation: 10 minutes
cooking time: about 10 minutes
per serving: 290 cals; 18g fat;
   19g carbohydrate

1 Grill the bread on both sides until golden, then immediately rub all over with the cut garlic cloves; keep warm in a low oven.
2 Melt the butter in a large frying pan and stir-fry the mushrooms with the thyme over a high heat for 4–5 minutes until golden and beginning to release their juices. Cover and keep warm.
3 Poach the eggs gently for 3 minutes or until the white is just set and the yolk soft (see instructions on page 248).
4 Put a slice of garlic bread on each warmed serving plate. Spoon on the stir-fried mushrooms and pan juices, then top each serving with a poached egg. Season with salt and pepper and serve at once.

Scrambled Eggs with Smoked Salmon, Chives and Asparagus

125g (4oz) asparagus tips
salt and pepper
6 medium eggs
25g (1oz) butter
50g (2oz) crème fraîche
1 tbsp chopped chives
125g (4oz) smoked salmon, cut into strips
warm buttered toast, to serve

serves 2
preparation: 15 minutes
cooking time: 5 minutes
per serving (without toast): 560 cals;
   43g fat; 2g carbohydrate

1 Add the asparagus tips to a pan of lightly salted boiling water and blanch for 2 minutes. Drain, refresh under cold water and pat dry. Cut the asparagus into 2.5cm (1 inch) lengths.
2 Beat the eggs together thoroughly in a bowl and season with a little salt and plenty of black pepper.
3 Melt the butter in a non-stick saucepan over a low heat and add the eggs, stirring with a fork. Cook for about 1 minute until the eggs are just starting to set, then stir in the crème fraîche and chives.
4 When the eggs are scrambled to a creamy consistency, fold in the blanched asparagus and smoked salmon.
5 Serve the scrambled eggs on warm buttered toast.

Spinach Baked Eggs with Mushrooms

3 tbsp olive oil

125g (4oz) chestnut mushrooms, quartered

225g bag washed baby leaf spinach

salt and pepper

2 large eggs

4 tbsp double cream

serves 2

preparation: 5 minutes

cooking time: 13 minutes

per serving: 440 cals; 42g fat;
    35g carbohydrate

1 Heat the olive oil in a large frying pan, add the mushrooms and stir-fry for 30 seconds, then add the spinach and stir-fry until wilted. Season with salt and pepper and divide between two 600ml (1 pint) ovenproof dishes.

2 Carefully break an egg into the centre of each dish and spoon the cream over the top. Season well.

3 Bake at 200°C (180°C fan oven) mark 6 for about 12 minutes or until the eggs are just set. (Remember that they will continue to cook a little once they're out of the oven.) Serve immediately.

Illustrated on page 240

Vegetarian Scotch Eggs

2 x 420g cans chickpeas, drained

2 garlic cloves, peeled and crushed

1–2 red chillies, deseeded and finely
    chopped

4 spring onions, trimmed and roughly
    chopped

2 tomatoes, preferably plum, deseeded
    and finely chopped

125g (4oz) pitted black olives, roughly
    chopped

4 tbsp chopped parsley

salt and pepper

6 medium eggs, hard-boiled and shelled

1 egg, beaten

75g (3oz) fresh white breadcrumbs

oil, to deep-fry

aïoli (page 351), to serve

serves 6

preparation: 30 minutes, plus chilling

cooking time: 15 minutes

per serving (without aïoli): 400 cals; 28g fat;
    21g carbohydrate

1 Put the chickpeas into a food processor with the crushed garlic and process for 1 minute or until roughly chopped. Transfer to a bowl and add the chillies, spring onions, tomatoes, olives and chopped parsley. Season generously with salt and pepper and mix thoroughly.

2 Divide the mixture into 6 equal portions. Shape each into a flat cake and mould around a hard-boiled egg, as evenly as possible. Brush with beaten egg and roll in the breadcrumbs to coat thoroughly. Chill, uncovered, for 3–4 hours or overnight.

3 Heat the oil in a deep-fryer or large deep heavy pan to 160°C, or until a cube of bread dropped in begins to sizzle. Cook the eggs in batches. Gently lower each egg into the oil and deep-fry for 7–8 minutes or until golden brown. Remove and drain on kitchen paper.

4 Serve the Scotch eggs warm, with the aïoli.

note: Make sure the shelled eggs are dry to ensure the coating will adhere.

variation

Scotch eggs: *Instead of the chickpea mixture, dust the hard-boiled eggs with flour, then wrap in sausage meat, as in stage 2 and continue as above. You will need about 350g (12oz) sausage meat. Serve with plain mayonnaise.*

Egg and Bacon Tarts

500g pack shortcrust pastry
6 smoked streaky bacon rashers
6 medium eggs
3 tbsp chopped flat-leafed parsley
salt and pepper

serves 6
preparation: 20 minutes, plus chilling
cooking time: 25 minutes
per serving: 500 cals; 35g fat;
    33g carbohydrate

1 Preheat two baking sheets in the oven at 200°C (180°C fan oven) mark 6. Divide the pastry into six equal pieces, then roll out and use to line individual 10cm (4 inch) fluted flan tins. Prick the bases all over with a fork, line with greaseproof paper, fill with baking beans and chill for 10 minutes.
2 Put the tart tins on to the preheated baking sheets and bake blind for 10 minutes. Remove the paper and beans and cook for a further 5 minutes or until the pastry bases are dry. Remove the cases from the oven. Increase the oven temperature to 220°C (200°C fan oven) mark 7.
3 Put a rasher of raw bacon across the base of each tart. One at a time, crack the eggs into a cup and tip one into each tart case. Scatter the chopped parsley over the top, then season with salt and pepper and bake for 10 minutes or until the egg white has set.

Savoury Pancakes

125g (4oz) plain flour
pinch of salt
1 medium egg
about 300ml (½ pint) milk
1 tbsp oil
a little oil, to fry

makes 8
preparation: 10 minutes, plus standing
cooking time: 15–20 minutes
per pancake: 110 cals; 5g fat;
    14g carbohydrate

1 Sift the flour and salt into a bowl and make a well in the centre. Break the egg into the well and add a little of the milk. Mix the liquid ingredients together, then gradually beat in the flour until smooth.
2 Beat in the oil and the remaining milk; the batter should be the consistency of thin cream. (Alternatively, mix in a blender.) Cover the batter and leave to stand in the fridge for about 20 minutes.
3 Heat a pancake pan. When hot, brush with the minimum of oil. Add a little extra milk to the batter if it is too thick. Pour a small amount of batter into the pan and swirl around until it is evenly and thinly spread over the bottom of the pan.
4 Cook over a medium high heat for about 1 minute or until the edges are curling away from the pan and the underside is golden. Flip the pancake over using a palette knife and cook for 30 seconds–1 minute.
5 Turn the pancake out on to a sheet of greaseproof paper. Loosely fold a clean tea-towel over the top; keep warm. Repeat until all the pancake batter has been used, lightly oiling the pan in between and stacking the pancakes as they are cooked.

note: *Freeze pancakes interleaved with non-stick baking parchment. Defrost, then reheat wrapped in foil in a moderate oven.*

variations
wholewheat pancakes: *Use a mixture of half white, half wholemeal flour.*
buckwheat pancakes: *Use a mixture of half white, half buckwheat flour.*
herb pancakes: *Add 1 tbsp chopped parsley and 2 tsp chopped chives to the batter at stage 2.*

fillings
Almost any mixture of cooked vegetables, fish or chicken, flavoured with herbs and moistened with a little béchamel sauce, soured cream or cream cheese can be used. Try the following:
• *Chicken and sautéed mushrooms in béchamel.*
• *Smoked haddock and chopped hard-boiled egg with soured cream.*
• *Ratatouille.*
• *Sautéed spinach, pine nuts and feta cheese.*

Rösti Potatoes with Fried Eggs

900g (2lb) red potatoes, scrubbed and
    left whole
salt and pepper
40g (1½oz) butter
4 large eggs

serves 4
preparation: 20 minutes, plus cooling
cooking time: 35–40 minutes
per serving: 330 cals; 15g fat;
    39g carbohydrate

1 Put the potatoes into a pan of cold, well salted water. Cover, bring to the boil and par-boil for 5–8 minutes. Drain and leave to cool for 15 minutes.

2 Peel the potatoes and coarsely grate them lengthways to give long strands. Divide into eight portions and shape into mounds.

3 Melt half the butter in a large non-stick frying pan. Once it is bubbling and beginning to brown, put four of the potato mounds in the pan, spacing them well apart, and flatten them a little.

4 Fry slowly for about 6–7 minutes until golden brown, then turn them over and brown the second side for 6–7 minutes. Transfer the rösti to a warmed baking tray and keep warm in a low oven at 150°C (130°C fan oven) mark 2 while you fry the rest.

5 Just before serving, carefully break the eggs into the hot pan and fry for about 2 minutes until the white is set and the yolk is still soft. Season with salt and pepper and serve at once, with the rösti.

Carrot Roulade with Watercress Filling

2 tbsp freshly grated Parmesan cheese

1 tbsp chopped coriander, plus 12 extra
    whole leaves

125g (4oz) butter

700g (1½lb) carrots, peeled and finely grated

6 medium eggs, separated

salt and pepper

WATERCRESS FILLING

6 medium eggs, hard-boiled and shelled

1 bunch of watercress, stalks removed

200g (7oz) good quality mayonnaise

serves 6

preparation: 15 minutes, plus chilling

cooking time: 20 minutes

per serving: 640 cals; 59g fat;
    9g carbohydrate

1 Line a 33 x 23cm (13 x 9 inch) Swiss roll tin with baking parchment. Sprinkle the Parmesan over the paper, then scatter the whole coriander leaves on top.

2 Melt the butter in a frying pan. Add the carrots and cook gently for 10 minutes or until soft. Drain well, tip into a bowl and beat in the egg yolks. Season well.

3 Whisk the egg whites in a clean bowl until stiff, then fold into the mixture with the chopped coriander. Spoon into the prepared tin and spread evenly. Bake at 200°C (180°C fan oven) mark 6 for 10–12 minutes or until golden brown and springy to the touch.

4 For the filling, chop the eggs, and finely chop the watercress. Put both into a bowl with the mayonnaise and mix well, seasoning with salt and pepper to taste.

5 Turn the roulade out on to a sheet of greaseproof paper and spread with the filling, leaving a 1cm (½ inch) border. Beginning from a short side and using the greaseproof paper to help, roll up. Trim the edges to neaten. Chill until ready to serve, then cut into slices.

Cheese Soufflé

25g (1oz) butter, plus extra to grease
1 tbsp freshly grated Parmesan cheese
200ml (7fl oz) milk
few onion and carrot slices
1 bay leaf
6 black peppercorns
2 tbsp plain flour
2 tsp Dijon mustard
salt and pepper
large pinch of cayenne pepper
4 large eggs, separated, plus 1 egg white
75g (3oz) Gruyère or mature Cheddar cheese,
   finely grated

serves 4
preparation: 20 minutes, plus infusing
cooking time: 30 minutes
per serving: 280 cals; 20g fat;
   8g carbohydrate

1 Butter a 1.3 litre (2¼ pint) soufflé dish and sprinkle the Parmesan over the bottom and sides to coat evenly. Put the milk into a pan with the onion and carrot slices, bay leaf and peppercorns. Bring slowly to the boil, remove from the heat, cover and leave to infuse for 30 minutes; strain.

2 Melt the butter in a pan and stir in the flour and mustard. Season with salt, pepper and cayenne, and cook for 1 minute, stirring. Remove from the heat and gradually stir in the milk. Bring to the boil slowly and cook, stirring, until the sauce thickens. Leave to cool slightly, then beat in the egg yolks, one at a time. Stir in all but 1 tbsp of the cheese.

3 Using a balloon whisk or electric hand-held mixer, whisk the 5 egg whites in a bowl until they stand in soft peaks.

4 Mix one large spoonful of egg white into the sauce to lighten it. Gently pour the sauce over the remaining egg whites and carefully fold the ingredients together, using a metal spoon; do not over-mix.

5 Pour the soufflé mixture gently into the prepared dish; it should come about three-quarters of the way up the side of the dish.

6 Sprinkle with the reserved cheese and run a knife around the edge of the mixture. Stand the dish on a baking sheet and bake at 180°C (160°C fan oven) mark 4 for 30 minutes or until golden brown, well risen and just firm to the touch. Serve at once. There should be a hint of softness in the centre of the soufflé.

notes
• *Use a proper straight-sided soufflé dish to obtain the best rise.*
• *Running a knife around the edge before baking helps to achieve the classic 'hat' effect.*
• *If necessary, the soufflé can be prepared ahead to the end of stage 2 and left to stand for several hours before completing.*

variations
blue cheese: *Use a semi-hard blue cheese, such as Stilton or Wensleydale, instead of Cheddar.*
mushroom: *Replace the cheese with 125g (4oz) mushrooms (preferably field or wild ones), chopped and sautéed in butter.*
smoked haddock: *Replace the cheese with 75g (3oz) cooked smoked haddock, finely flaked.*

Cheese and Onion Potato Soufflé

700g (1½lb) floury potatoes, peeled and
   cut into chunks
1 onion, peeled and finely chopped
salt and pepper
15g (½oz) butter, plus extra to grease
15g (½oz) plain flour
300ml (½ pint) milk
100g (3½oz) Parmesan cheese, freshly
   grated, plus extra to finish
3 medium eggs, separated
1 tbsp Dijon mustard

serves 8
preparation: 30 minutes
cooking time: about 1 hour
per serving: 200 cals; 9g fat;
   19g carbohydrate

1 Put the potatoes and onion into a pan of cold salted water. Cover, bring to the boil and simmer, partly covered, for 15–20 minutes until tender. Drain, tip back into the pan and put over a low heat to dry a little. Mash well, seasoning with salt and pepper to taste. Cool a little.

2 Meanwhile, make the sauce. Melt the butter in a pan, stir in the flour and cook for 1 minute. Gradually stir in the milk and cook, stirring, over a low heat for 5–10 minutes until thickened. Stir in the grated Parmesan and season well with salt and pepper. Set aside to cool a little.

3 Add the cheese sauce, egg yolks and mustard to the mashed potato and mix everything together. Check the seasoning.

4 In a clean, grease-free bowl, whisk the egg whites until they stand in stiff peaks, then gently fold into the potato mixture.

5 Spoon the mixture into a buttered 1.2 litre (2 pint) soufflé dish. Stand on a baking sheet and grate over a little more Parmesan. Bake at 200°C (180°C fan oven) mark 6 for 40 minutes until risen and golden. Serve immediately.

Cheese, Potato and Parsnip Rösti

350g (12oz) waxy potatoes
225g (8oz) parsnip
1 onion, peeled and sliced
1 garlic clove, peeled and crushed
1 tbsp chopped sage
salt and pepper
1 egg, lightly beaten
2 tbsp sunflower oil
175g (6oz) fontina or Cheddar cheese, grated

serves 4
preparation: 10 minutes
cooking time: 20 minutes
per serving: 370 cals; 24g fat;
   25g carbohydrate

1 Peel the potatoes and parsnip, and grate using the medium grater attachment of a food processor; squeeze out excess liquid.

2 Put the grated vegetables, onion, garlic and chopped sage into a large bowl. Mix well and season generously with salt and pepper. Add the beaten egg and stir until evenly combined.

3 Heat the oil in a large non-stick frying pan. When hot, spread half of the vegetable mixture over the bottom of the pan. Scatter over the cheese, then top with the remaining vegetable mixture, spreading it flat.

4 Cook over a low heat for about 10 minutes until golden underneath. Carefully slip the rösti out on to a large plate and flip back into the pan. Cook for a further 10 minutes until the underside is browned and the vegetables are cooked through.

5 Serve immediately, cut into wedges, as a lunch or light supper with a leafy salad.

variation: For a more substantial meal, top with poached eggs and grilled tomatoes.

Toasted Cheese Sandwich

50g (2oz) mature Cheddar cheese,
  finely grated
2 tbsp mayonnaise
pinch of English mustard powder
salt and pepper
2 slices white country-style bread
2 tbsp good quality chutney

serves 1
preparation: 5 minutes
cooking time: 5 minutes
per serving: 700 cals; 43g fat;
  60g carbohydrate

1 Mix together the grated cheese, mayonnaise and mustard, and season well with salt and pepper.
2 Spread the mixture over one slice of bread and place under a hot grill for 1–2 minutes until the cheese is bubbling and golden.
3 Spread the chutney over the second slice of bread and sandwich together with the toasted cheese.
4 Grill the sandwich to toast on each side, then cut in half and serve.

Welsh Rarebit

225g (8oz) Cheddar cheese, grated
25g (1oz) butter
1 tsp English mustard
4 tbsp brown ale
salt and pepper
4 slices white bread, crusts removed

serves 4
preparation: 5 minutes
cooking time: 6–8 minutes
per serving: 380 cals; 25g fat;
  21g carbohydrate

1 Put the cheese, butter, mustard and beer into a heavy-based pan over a low heat and stir occasionally until the cheese is melted and the mixture is smooth and creamy. Season with salt and pepper to taste.
2 Toast the bread under the grill on one side only. Turn the slices over and spread the cheese mixture on the untoasted side. Put under the grill for 1 minute or until golden and bubbling, then serve.

Croque Monsieur

4 slices white bread
softened butter to spread, plus extra to fry
a little Dijon mustard
4 slices ham
125g (4oz) Gruyère cheese, sliced

serves 4
preparation: 5 minutes
cooking time: 6 minutes
per serving: 560 cals; 31g fat;
  39g carbohydrate

1 Spread both sides of each bread slice with butter, then spread mustard on one side of 2 slices.
2 Lay the ham slices on the mustard-spread surfaces, cover with the cheese, then top with the other bread slices – to make 2 sandwiches.
3 Heat a griddle pan and fry the sandwiches over a high heat for 2–3 minutes on each side until the bread is golden and crisp, and the cheese starts to melt, adding a little extra butter to the griddle if necessary.
4 Cut each sandwich in half and serve.

Macaroni Cheese

225g (8oz) short-cut macaroni

salt and pepper

50g (2oz) butter or margarine

50g (2oz) plain flour

900ml (1½ pints) milk

½ tsp grated nutmeg or mustard powder

225g (8oz) mature Cheddar cheese, grated

3 tbsp fresh white or wholemeal
   breadcrumbs

serves 4–6

preparation: 10 minutes

cooking time: 15 minutes

per serving: 680–460 cals; 34–23g fat;
   67–45g carbohydrate

1 Cook the macaroni in a large pan of boiling salted water until *al dente*.

2 Meanwhile, melt the butter in a pan, stir in the flour and cook, stirring, for 1 minute. Remove from the heat and gradually stir in the milk. Bring to the boil and cook, stirring, until the sauce thickens. Remove from the heat. Season with salt and pepper, and add the nutmeg or mustard.

3 Drain the macaroni and add to the sauce, together with three quarters of the cheese. Mix well, then turn into an ovenproof dish.

4 Preheat the grill to high. Sprinkle the breadcrumbs and remaining cheese over the macaroni. Put under the grill for 2–3 minutes until golden brown on top and bubbling. Serve immediately.

Cheese Fondue

1 large garlic clove, peeled and halved

2 tsp cornflour

3 tbsp kirsch

200ml (7fl oz) dry white wine

1 tbsp lemon juice

200g (7oz) Gruyère cheese, grated

200g (7oz) Emmental cheese, grated

pepper

bite-sized chunks of crusty bread, to serve

serves 4

preparation: 10 minutes

cooking time: about 10 minutes

per serving (without bread): 460 cals;
   32g fat; 6g carbohydrate

1 Rub the halved garlic clove around the inside of the fondue pan (or heavy-based pan). Blend the cornflour to a smooth paste with the kirsch.

2 Put the wine, lemon juice and cheeses in the pan with the blended cornflour and slowly bring to the boil over a very low heat, stirring all the time. Simmer gently for 3–4 minutes, stirring frequently. Season with pepper to taste.

3 Set the pan over the fondue burner (or over a heated serving tray) at the table. Serve with plenty of chunks of crusty bread – for dipping into the fondue using long-handled forks.

Glamorgan Sausages

150g (5oz) Caerphilly cheese, grated

200g (7oz) fresh white breadcrumbs

3 spring onions, trimmed and finely chopped

1 tbsp chopped flat-leafed parsley

4 thyme sprigs, leaves only

salt and pepper

3 large eggs, one separated

a little vegetable oil, to fry

serves 4

preparation: 25 minutes

cooking time: 15 minutes

per serving: 380 cals, 24g fat;
   25g carbohydrate

1 Mix the cheese with 150g (5oz) breadcrumbs, the spring onions and herbs in a large bowl. Season well.

2 Add the whole eggs plus the extra yolk and mix well to combine. Cover and chill for 5 minutes.

3 Lightly beat the egg white in a shallow bowl. Tip the rest of the breadcrumbs on to a large plate.

4 Take 2 tbsp of the mixture and shape into a small sausage, about 4cm (1½ inches) long. Roll first in the egg white, then in the breadcrumbs to coat. Repeat to make 12 sausages in total.

5 Heat 2 tsp oil in a large heavy-based pan until hot and fry the sausages in two batches for 6–8 minutes, turning until golden all over. Keep warm in a low oven while cooking the rest. Serve with a chutney.

Potato Gnocchi with Pumpkin Sauce

500g (1lb 2oz) waxy potatoes, scrubbed
salt and pepper
250g (9oz) '00' pasta flour, plus extra to dust
large pinch of freshly grated nutmeg
1 large egg
175g (6oz) Parmesan cheese, freshly grated
1 tbsp chopped parsley or sage

PUMPKIN SAUCE
3 tbsp olive oil
1 small onion, peeled and sliced
130g pack diced pancetta
500g (1lb 2oz) pumpkin, peeled, deseeded
　　and cut into 2.5cm (1 inch) cubes

serves 4
preparation: 1 hour
cooking time: about 1 hour
per serving: 740 cals, 38g fat;
　　71g carbohydrate

1 Put the potatoes into a large pan of salted water. Bring to the boil and cook for 20 minutes or until just tender. Drain and cool slightly, then peel. Press the potatoes through a ricer, or mash until very smooth.

2 Put the flour on a large board and make a wide well in the centre. Tip the mashed potato into the well and season with 1 tsp salt, plenty of pepper and the nutmeg. Add the egg and sprinkle with 75g (3oz) Parmesan. Using your fingers, draw the flour into the well and mix the ingredients together thoroughly to form a dough. Knead until smooth.

3 Divide the dough into eight. Roll each piece into a sausage, 30cm (12 inches) long and 1cm (½ inch) thick, then cut into 2cm (¾ inch) lengths. Dust each piece with a little flour, then use your thumb to press it against a coarse grater, rolling it briefly to make a textured curl. Put the gnocchi on a tray in one layer.

4 To make the pumpkin sauce, heat the oil in a heavy-based pan and sauté the onion for 5 minutes. Add the pancetta and fry for 5 minutes, then add the pumpkin. Season well and add 450ml (¾ pint) water. Cover and simmer, stirring occasionally, for 30 minutes until reduced to a thick sauce.

5 Meanwhile, bring a large pan of salted water to the boil and cook the gnocchi in batches. Add to the pan, return to the boil and, once the gnocchi have risen to the surface, cook them for 3 minutes. Drain and tip them into the pumpkin sauce. Add the parsley or sage and remaining Parmesan, stir and serve at once.

Spinach and Ricotta Gnocchi

15g (½oz) butter
1 large garlic clove, peeled and crushed
450g (1lb) frozen leaf spinach, defrosted
100g (3½oz) ricotta cheese
3 tbsp plain flour, plus extra to dust
3 medium egg yolks
75g (3oz) Parmesan cheese, freshly grated
large pinch of freshly grated nutmeg
salt and pepper

SAGE BUTTER
125g (4oz) unsalted butter
2 tbsp chopped sage

serves 4
preparation: 20 minutes
cooking time: about 10 minutes
per serving: 500 cals; 43g fat;
　　11g carbohydrate

1 Melt the butter in a small pan and gently fry the garlic until softened but not golden; set aside.

2 Squeeze out all excess liquid from the spinach, then chop finely. Put into a bowl with the garlic, ricotta, flour, egg yolks, Parmesan, nutmeg, salt and pepper, and beat until evenly combined.

3 Using 2 tablespoons, shape the ricotta mixture into gnocchi by passing a little of the mixture from one spoon to the other. Put on a plate, liberally dusted with flour. Repeat to make 20 gnocchi.

4 Bring a large saucepan containing at least 2.5 litres (4 pints) lightly salted water to the boil. Lower the heat so the water is at a steady simmer.

5 Meanwhile for the sage butter, melt the butter in a pan, add the sage and heat until foaming; keep warm.

6 Cook the gnocchi in batches. Lower into the water, return to a simmer and cook for 3 minutes or until the gnocchi float to the surface. Remove with a slotted spoon and drain on kitchen paper; keep warm. Repeat with the remaining gnocchi. Serve at once in warmed bowls drizzled with the sage butter.

variation: *Spoon the cooked gnocchi into individual gratin dishes. Pour on hot tomato sauce (page 27), top with shredded mozzarella and grill until bubbling.*

PASTRY-MAKING, TARTS, PIES AND PIZZAS

The art of successful pastry-making lies in measuring the ingredients accurately, using the correct proportion of fat to flour, and light, careful handling. With the exceptions of choux pastry and hot water crust pastry, everything needs to be kept cool when making pastry – the work surface, equipment, ingredients and your hands. It is also important to 'rest' pastry before baking, otherwise it is liable to shrink during cooking. Pastries which are handled a great deal, such as puff, must be rested before and after shaping. Most pastries are rested in the fridge and need to be well wrapped in clingfilm to prevent them from drying out.

The main types of pastry are short pastries, of which shortcrust is the most familiar, and flaked pastries, such as puff. Other pastries include hot water crust, suet crust, choux pastry and filo pastry. Sweetened versions of short pastries are often used for sweet tarts.

If you haven't the time or inclination to make your own pastry, buy a pack of ready-made chilled fresh or frozen pastry from the supermarket. Sweet shortcrust pastry is available as well as standard shortcrust. Ready-made puff pastry is so quick to use and successful that you may well prefer to buy it, as the alternative of making your own is very time-comsuming.

Packets of ready-made filo sheets are widely available and give excellent results. Note that the size of filo sheets varies considerably between brands – check whether the recipe states a specific size before buying. It is essential to keep filo sheets covered as you work to prevent them from drying out and becoming brittle.

PASTRY INGREDIENTS

For most pastries, plain flour works best, as it gives a light, crisp result. Self-raising flour would produce a soft spongy pastry. Wholemeal flour gives a heavier dough, which is more difficult to roll. For wholemeal pastry, it is therefore preferable to use half wholemeal and half white flour. Puff pastry is usually made with strong plain (bread) flour as this contains extra gluten to strengthen the dough, enabling it to withstand intensive rolling and folding. A little lemon juice is usually added to puff pastry to soften the gluten and make the dough more elastic.

Traditionally shortcrust pastry is made with a mixture of lard (for shortness) and either butter or margarine (for flavour). However, it is now more often made with a mixture of white vegetable fat and butter or margarine, or all butter for a rich flavour. If margarine is preferred, it should be the hard, block type rather than soft-tub margarine.

Care must be taken when adding the liquid to a pastry dough: too much will result in a tough end result; too little will produce a crumbly pastry, which is difficult to handle. Use chilled water and add just enough to bind the dough. Egg yolks are often used to enrich pastry.

MIXING PASTRY BY HAND

Shortcrust and similar pastries involve rubbing the fat into the flour. To do this, cut the fat into the small pieces, then add to the flour and salt and mix briefly with a round-bladed knife, to coat the pieces with flour. Then, using your fingertips, pick up a small amount of the mixture at a time and rub the fat and flour together to break the fat down into tiny pieces. Do this as lightly and quickly as possible until the mixture resembles fine crumbs; avoid using the palm of your hands.

When you are ready to add the liquid, sprinkle this evenly over the surface; uneven addition may cause blistering once the pastry is cooked. Use a round-bladed knife to mix in the liquid. You may need a little more or less than the quantity stated in the recipe because the absorbency of flours varies. For this reason, don't add it all at once. Collect the dough with your hands and knead lightly for a few seconds until you have a smooth ball.

MIXING PASTRY IN A FOOD PROCESSOR

Short pastries can be made very successfully and quickly in a food processor. To ensure that the dough is not over-worked, use the pulse button or operate the processor in short bursts. Avoid making too large a quantity at one time or the result will be disappointing.

ROLLING OUT PASTRY

To reduce the risk of shrinkage during baking, wrap the pastry in clingfilm to prevent it drying out and rest in the fridge for 20 minutes before rolling out. Lightly dust the work surface and rolling pin – never the pastry – with flour to prevent sticking. Roll the dough lightly and evenly in one direction only – until thin. Always roll away from you, using light, firm strokes and rotate the pastry frequently to keep an even shape and thickness.

Avoid over-rolling, pulling or stretching the dough as you roll it, otherwise it will shrink badly during cooking. The usual thickness for rolling out pastries is 3mm (⅛ inch), although puff pastry is sometimes rolled out to a 5mm (¼ inch) thickness, depending on the use.

SHAPING AND GLAZING

Pastry is most often used to line tart tins and cover pies (see right). It can also be folded around fillings to form pasties, or wrapped around whole boned fish or meat, as in salmon or beef en croûte.

Glazing pastry seals the surface and gives pies an attractive sheen. Brush the pastry with egg glaze (egg yolk beaten with a little water), or with beaten whole egg. Alternatively, for a less shiny finish, brush with milk.

Part-baked pastry cases are sometimes glazed, then baked for a little longer to seal before filling. Glaze the surface of pies before positioning pastry leaves or cut-out decorations, then brush the decorations with more glaze.

PASTRY QUANTITIES

Where a recipe specifies a weight of pastry, this generally refers to the weight of flour in the recipe rather than the combined weight of the ingredients. For example, if a pie or tart recipe calls for 225g (8oz) shortcrust pastry, you will need this amount of flour and 110g (4oz) fat, as the correct proportion of flour to fat is 2:1.

Recipes for the basic pastries are provided on the following pages. If your pie or tart(s) requires more (or less) than the basic recipe quantity, simply increase (or decrease) the pastry ingredients in proportion, remembering to adjust the liquid quantity accordingly.

When buying chilled or frozen ready-made pastry, it is important to note that the weight specified on the pack is the combined weight of the ingredients, not the flour weight. As a guide, a 375g (13oz) pack of ready-made shortcrust pastry is roughly equivalent to homemade pastry made with 225g (8oz) flour.

Quantity Guide for Tarts

Tart tins, including individual ones, vary in depth and this obviously affects the quantity of pastry required to line them. Therefore the following chart is an approximate guide only. For a deep tart tin, allow extra pastry.

TART TIN SIZE	PASTRY (FLOUR WEIGHT)
18cm (7 inch)	125g (4oz)
20cm (8 inch)	175g (6oz)
23cm (9 inch)	200g (7oz)
25cm (10 inch)	225g (8oz)
four 10cm (4 inch) individual	150g (5oz)
six 7.5cm (3 inch) individual	150g (5oz)

PASTRY TECHNIQUES

LINING A TART CASE

1 Roll out the pastry on a lightly floured surface until it is 5–7.5cm (2–3 inches) larger all round than the tart tin, depending on the depth of the tin. Lift the pastry on the rolling pin and carefully unroll it over the tin.

2 Lift the edges of the pastry so that it falls down into the tart tin, then gently press the pastry against the side of the tin so that there are no gaps.

3 Turn any surplus pastry outwards over the rim. Roll the rolling pin over the top of the tin, pressing down to cut away the excess pastry. (Alternatively, leave the edges overhanging and trim with a sharp knife after baking.) Rest the tart case in the fridge for 20–30 minutes before baking.

BAKING BLIND

If a recipe instructs you to 'bake blind' you need to bake, or part-bake the pastry case without its filling. The pastry may be partially cooked before filling, or completely cooked if the filling does not require baking.

1 Prick the pastry base with a fork, to prevent air bubbles forming, then line with a large piece of greaseproof paper.

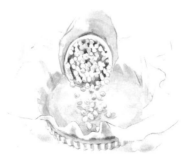

2 Fill the paper with a single layer of ceramic baking beans or dried pulses to weight the dough.

3 Bake the tart case at the temperature suggested in the recipe for 10–15 minutes or until the pastry looks set, then lift out

the greaseproof paper and beans. Bake the tart case for a further 5 minutes until the base is firm to the touch and lightly coloured; or a further 15 minutes until crisp and golden brown if the pastry case requires complete baking.

COVERING A PIE DISH

Use the inverted pie dish as a guide to the size and shape you need to roll the pastry out to.

1 Roll out the pastry on a lightly floured surface until it is about 5cm (2 inches) larger all round than the pie dish.

Put the pie dish upside-down on the pastry and cut off a 2.5cm (1 inch) strip from around the edge. Turn the pie dish the right way up and brush the rim with water. Position the pastry strip on the rim; brush with water.

2 Fill the pie dish generously so that the surface of the filling is slightly rounded; put a pie funnel in the middle if there isn't quite enough filling to do this. Use the rolling pin to help lift the pastry lid into position. Press the edges together to seal.

PASTRY FINISHES

4 Using a sharp knife, held at an angle away from the pie dish, trim off excess pastry. Make a hole in the top of the pie to allow steam to escape.

5 Knock up the pastry edge by tapping the blunt edge of a knife horizontally against the rim; this helps to seal the edge and stops the filling leaking out.

Fluted or scalloped edge
Press your thumb on the rim of the pastry and at the same time gently draw back the floured blade of a round-bladed knife about 1cm (½ inch) towards the centre. Repeat at 2.5cm (1 inch) intervals around the edge of the pie to create a decorative finish.

Crimped edge
Push your forefinger into the rim of the pastry and, using the thumb and forefinger of the other hand, gently pinch the pastry so that it is pushed up by this action. Repeat all around the edge of the pie.

Forked edge
Simply press all around the edge of the pie with the back of a floured fork.

Pastry leaves
Cut neat strips from the pastry trimmings, then cut these on the diagonal into diamonds, to shape leaves. Use the back of the knife to mark veins and pinch one end to form a stem.

Pastry cut-out decorations
Gather the pastry trimmings, knead lightly and re-roll out on a lightly floured surface. Use small cutters to stamp out decorative shapes, such as stars, hearts or leaves. For a festive pie, cut out holly leaves and roll small balls to represent berries.

Glazing
Brush the pastry with egg glaze before positioning the decorations to make sure they stick, and again afterwards for a shiny finish.

Shortcrust Pastry

This is the most widely used pastry. The proportion of flour to fat is 2:1. The choice of fat is largely a matter of taste – butter gives a rich pastry, but using half white vegetable fat improves the texture.

225g (8oz) plain flour, plus extra to dust
pinch of salt
110g (4oz) butter, or half white vegetable fat
    and half butter, cut into pieces

makes a '225g (8oz) quantity'
preparation: 10 minutes, plus resting
per 25g (1oz): 110 cals; 6g fat;
    12g carbohydrate

1 Sift the flour and salt into a bowl, add the fat and mix lightly.
2 Using your fingertips, rub the fat into the flour until the mixture resembles fine breadcrumbs.
3 Sprinkle 3–4 tbsp cold water evenly over the surface and stir with a round-bladed knife until the mixture begins to stick together in large lumps. If the dough seems dry, add a little extra water. With one hand, collect the dough together to form a ball.
4 Knead lightly on a lightly floured surface for a few seconds to form a smooth, firm dough; do not over-work. Wrap in clingfilm and leave to rest in the fridge for 30 minutes before rolling out.

notes
• *To make the pastry in a food processor, put the flour and salt in the processor bowl with the butter. Whiz until the mixture resembles fine crumbs, then add the water. Process briefly, using the pulse button, until the mixture just comes together in a ball. Continue from stage 4.*
• *Shortcrust pastry can be stored in the fridge for up to 3 days, or frozen.*

variations
wholemeal pastry: *Replace half of the white flour with wholemeal flour. A little extra water may be needed to mix the dough.*
nut pastry: *Replace 50g (2oz) of the flour with finely chopped or ground walnuts, hazelnuts or almonds, adding them to the rubbed-in mixture just before the cold water.*
cheese pastry: *Stir in 3–4 tbsp freshly grated Parmesan or 75g (3oz) finely grated Cheddar cheese and a small pinch of mustard powder before adding the water.*
herb pastry: *Stir in 3 tbsp finely chopped herbs, such as parsley, sage, thyme or rosemary, before adding the water.*
olive pastry: *Stir in 4 tbsp finely chopped pitted black olives, at stage 2.*
poppy seed pastry: *Add 15g (½oz) poppy seeds before adding the water.*

Sweet Tart Pastry

This is an enriched sweetened version of shortcrust pastry, used for sweet tarts and pies (see pages 400–414). It is quick to make, and relatively easy to roll out and shape.

225g (8oz) plain flour
pinch of salt
150g (5oz) butter, cut into pieces
2 tbsp caster sugar
1 egg yolk

makes a '225g (8oz) quantity'
preparation: 10 minutes, plus resting
per 25g (1oz): 110 cals; 7g fat;
    11g carbohydrate

1 Sift the flour and salt into a large bowl and rub in the butter using your fingertips until the mixture resembles breadcrumbs. Stir in the sugar.
2 Mix the egg yolk with 3 tbsp cold water, then add to the dry ingredients and mix with a round-bladed knife to a dough.
3 Knead gently until just smooth. Wrap the pastry in clingfilm and leave to rest in the fridge for 30 minutes before rolling out.

notes
• *To save time, use a food processor to incorporate the butter into the flour, then add the sugar and pulse to mix. Tip into a bowl and continue as above.*
• *Tart pastry can be stored in the fridge for up to 3 days, or frozen.*

Pâte Brisée

This tart pastry is an enriched smooth, pliable dough, which is rolled out thinly and used for savoury tarts.

110g (4oz) plain flour, plus extra to dust
50g (2oz) unsalted butter, at room
   temperature, cut into pieces
1 egg yolk
pinch of salt

makes a '110g (4oz) quantity'
preparation: 10 minutes, plus resting
per 25g (1oz): 120 cals; 7g fat;
   12g carbohydrate

1 Sift the flour into a mound on a clean surface and make a large well in the centre.
2 Put the butter into the well with the egg yolk, salt and 1½ tbsp cold water.
3 Using the fingertips and a 'pecking' motion, work the butter, egg yolk, salt and water together until the mixture resembles scrambled eggs.
4 Gradually work in the flour, using your fingertips, until the dough forms large clumps. Add a little extra cold water if the dough looks too dry.
5 Transfer the dough to a lightly floured clean surface. Gently push the dough away from you, using the heel of your hand to push it across the surface. Scrape the dough together with a dough scraper or palette knife. Repeat until the dough is smooth and pliable, like putty.
6 Gather up the dough and lightly knead together to form a ball. Wrap tightly in clingfilm and chill for at least 30 minutes to relax the pastry and prevent shrinkage. Allow the pastry to return to cool room temperature before rolling out to make it easier to handle.

notes
• *To make the pastry in a food processor, sift the flour and salt on to a sheet of greaseproof paper. Put the butter and egg yolk in the processor and blend until smooth. Shoot in the flour and work until just combined. Continue from stage 5.*
• *Tart pastry can be stored in the fridge for up to 3 days, or frozen.*

Pâte Sucrée

This is a sweetened version of rich tart pastry, used for sweet tarts (see pages 400–414).

110g (4oz) plain flour
pinch of salt
50g (2oz) unsalted butter, at room
   temperature, cut into pieces
2 egg yolks
50g (2oz) caster sugar

makes a '110g (4oz) quantity'
preparation: 10 minutes, plus resting
per 25g (1oz): 110 cals; 6g fat;
   14g carbohydrate

1 Sift the flour and salt into a mound on a clean surface. Make a large well in the centre and add the butter, egg yolks and sugar.
2 Using the fingertips of one hand, work the sugar, butter and egg yolks together until well blended.
3 Gradually work in all the flour to bind the mixture together.
4 Knead the dough gently on a lightly floured clean surface until smooth, then wrap in clingfilm and leave to rest in the fridge for at least 30 minutes before rolling out.

note: *This pastry can be stored in the fridge for up to 3 days, or frozen.*

Rough Puff Pastry

Rough puff pastry isn't too time-consuming to make and gives excellent results. It has the buttery flakiness of puff pastry, although it won't rise as much.

225g (8oz) plain flour, plus extra to dust
pinch of salt
175g (6oz) butter, chilled
1 tsp lemon juice

makes a '225g (8oz) quantity'
preparation: 25 minutes, plus resting
per 25g (1oz): 100 cals; 7g fat;
   9g carbohydrate

1 Sift the flour and salt together into a bowl. Cut the butter into 2cm (¾ inch) cubes and add to the flour. Mix lightly to coat the pieces of butter with flour.
2 Using a round-bladed knife, stir in 100ml (3½fl oz) chilled water together with the lemon juice to make a soft elastic dough. If the pastry is too dry, add a little extra water.
3 Turn out on to a lightly floured work surface and lightly knead the dough until smooth.
4 Roll the pastry out to a neat oblong, measuring 30 x 10cm (12 x 4 inches).
5 Fold the bottom third up and the top third down, then give the pastry a quarter turn, so that the folded edges are at the sides. Press the edges with a rolling pin to seal. Wrap in clingfilm and leave to rest in the fridge for 15 minutes.
6 Put the pastry on a lightly floured surface with the folded edges to the sides. Repeat the rolling, folding and turning sequence four more times. Wrap in clingfilm and leave to rest in the fridge for 30 minutes before rolling out.
7 Shape the rough puff pastry as required, then rest in the fridge for 30 minutes before baking.

Puff Pastry

This is the richest of all pastries, and requires patience, practice and very light handling. If possible, it should be made the day before it is to be used. It is not practical to make less than a 450g (1lb) flour weight quantity.

   Good quality ready-made puff pastry is available fresh and frozen, so use this for convenience if you prefer. Two 375g (13oz) packs would be roughly equivalent to this homemade quantity.

450g (1lb) strong plain (bread) flour,
   plus extra to dust
pinch of salt
450g (1lb) butter, chilled
1 tbsp lemon juice

makes a '450g (1lb) quantity'
preparation: 40 minutes, plus resting
per 25g (1oz): 100 cals; 8g fat;
   7g carbohydrate

1 Sift the flour and salt together into a bowl. Cut off 50g (2oz) of the butter and flatten the remaining large block with a rolling pin to a slab, about 2cm (¾ inch) thick; set aside.
2 Cut the 50g (2oz) butter into small pieces and rub into the flour, using your fingertips.
3 Using a round-bladed knife, stir in the lemon juice and enough chilled water to make a soft elastic dough; you will need about 300ml (½ pint).
4 Turn out on to a lightly floured surface and quickly knead the dough until smooth. Cut a cross through half of the depth, then open out to form a star.
5 Roll out, keeping the centre four times as thick as the flaps. Put the slab of butter in the centre of the dough. Fold the flaps over the dough, envelope-style.
6 Press gently with a rolling pin and roll out to a rectangle, measuring 40 x 20cm (16 x 8 inches).
7 Fold the bottom third up and the top third down, keeping the edges straight. Wrap in clingfilm and leave to rest in the fridge for 30 minutes.
8 Put the pastry on a lightly floured surface with the folded edges to the sides. Repeat the rolling, folding, resting and turning sequence five times.
9 Shape the puff pastry as required, then rest in the fridge for about 30 minutes before baking.

Suet Crust Pastry

This pastry is used for sweet and savoury steamed puddings, and dumplings. It has a light, spongy texture provided it is handled gently, and cooked by steaming or simmering. Vegetarian suet can be used.

300g (11oz) self-raising flour
½ tsp salt
150g (5oz) shredded suet

makes a '300g (11oz) quantity'
preparation: 10 minutes
per 25g (1oz): 90 cals; 5g fat;
   10g carbohydrate

1 Sift the flour and salt into a bowl, add the shredded suet and stir to mix.
2 Using a round-bladed knife, mix in enough cold water to make a soft dough; you will need about 175ml (6fl oz). If the dough seems too dry, add a little extra liquid.
3 Knead very lightly until smooth. Use as required.

note: *For instructions on lining a pudding basin with suet crust pastry, see steak and kidney pudding (page 187).*

Hot Water Crust Pastry

This firm-textured pastry is used for raised pies. It must be shaped soon after making, while is still pliable. Any pastry not in use must be kept covered with a damp tea-towel in a warm place (if exposed to air it will become dry and impossible to use).

300g (11oz) plain flour
¼ tsp salt
65g (2½oz) white vegetable fat

makes a '300g (11oz) quantity'
preparation: 10 minutes, plus resting
per 25g (1oz): 80 cals; 3g fat;
   10g carbohydrate

1 Sift the flour and salt into a bowl and make a well in the middle.
2 Put the fat and 150ml (¼ pint) water in a small pan and heat slowly until the fat melts, then increase the heat and bring to the boil.
3 Pour the hot liquid into the flour well. Gradually lap the flour into the liquid, then beat together.
4 Lightly knead against the side of the bowl until smooth. Wrap the dough in a tea-towel and leave to rest in a warm place for 20 minutes. Use the pastry while it is still warm.

note: *For instructions on shaping hot water crust pastry, see raised game pie (page 285).*

Choux Pastry

This light, airy, crisp pastry is used for sweet and savoury choux puffs, éclairs, profiteroles and gougère. It can either be spooned or piped into shape, usually directly on to a dampened baking sheet.

65g (2½oz) plain flour
pinch of salt
50g (2oz) butter
2 medium eggs, lightly beaten

makes a '2–egg quantity'
preparation: 10 minutes
per 25g (1oz): 50 cals; 4g fat;
   3g carbohydrate

1 Sift the flour and salt on to a generous sheet of greaseproof paper.
2 Pour 150ml (¼ pint) cold water into a medium pan, add the butter and melt over a low heat. Increase the heat and bring to a rolling boil.
3 Take off the heat, immediately tip in all of the flour and beat vigorously, using a wooden spoon. Continue beating until the mixture is smooth and leaves the sides of the pan to form a ball; do not over-beat. Leave to cool slightly, for 1–2 minutes.
4 Gradually add the eggs, beating well between each addition, adding just enough to give a smooth dropping consistency. The choux pastry should be smooth and shiny. Use as required.

PIZZAS

Pizzas are surprisingly easy to make and you can create all kinds of different toppings. For a really authentic flavour and texture, make your own pizza dough, using fast-action dried yeast or fresh yeast. This is easy to do – you just need to allow sufficient time for the dough to rise. Alternatively, if you are very short of time, you can use ready-made pizza bases, or a pizza base mix. A 155g pack of pizza base mix is roughly equivalent to the basic recipe quantity below. Bake the pizzas on a pizza stone if you have one, otherwise a preheated baking sheet will give a lovely crisp result.

Pizza Base Dough

225g (8oz) strong plain (bread) flour, plus
   extra to dust
½ tsp sea salt
½ tsp fast-action dried yeast
1 tbsp extra-virgin olive oil, plus extra to oil

makes 1 large or 2 small pizza bases
preparation: 5 minutes, plus rising
per 25g (1oz): 60 cals; 1g fat;
   11g carbohydrate

1 Sift the flour and salt into a bowl and stir in the dried yeast. Make a well in the centre and gradually work in 150ml (¼ pint) warm water and the olive oil to form a soft dough.

2 Turn the pizza dough on to a lightly floured surface and knead well for 8–10 minutes until smooth and elastic. (Alternatively, use a large food mixer fitted with a dough hook.)
3 Put into an oiled bowl, turn the dough once to coat the surface with oil and cover the bowl with clingfilm. Leave to rise in a warm place for about 1 hour until doubled in size.
4 Knock back the dough and shape as required.

note: *If preferred, use 15g (½oz) fresh yeast instead of fast-action dried yeast. Mix with 2 tbsp of the flour, a pinch of sugar and the warm water. Leave in a warm place for 10 minutes until frothy, then add to the rest of the flour and salt. Mix to a dough and continue as above.*

Mozzarella and Tomato Pizza

1½ x quantity pizza base dough (above)
flour, to dust
1 tbsp olive oil
½ x 400g can chopped tomatoes
125g (4oz) mozzarella cheese, sliced
50g (2oz) Parmesan cheese
8 black olives, pitted and halved
salt and pepper
handful of roughly chopped basil leaves
   (optional)

serves 4
preparation: 20 minutes, plus rising
cooking time: 20 minutes
per serving: 520 cals; 21g fat;
   65g carbohydrate

1 Make the pizza dough and leave to rise for 1 hour or until doubled in size.
2 Put a lightly floured pizza stone or a large baking sheet into the oven at 230°C (210°C fan oven) mark 8 to preheat.
3 Turn the pizza dough on to a lightly floured surface and punch down to knock out the air. Roll out to a large rectangle and put on the hot pizza stone or baking sheet. Spoon over the tomatoes, top with mozzarella and grate over the Parmesan. Add the olives and season with salt and pepper.
4 Bake in the top of the oven for 20 minutes or until the pizza is golden and the cheeses have melted. Take out of the oven and leave to stand for a few minutes. Scatter with the basil if using, cut into quarters and serve.

Illustrated on page 264

Parma Ham, Rocket and Tomato Pizza

1 quantity pizza base dough (page 273)

flour, to dust

400g can chopped tomatoes

2 garlic cloves, peeled and crushed

grated zest of ½ lemon

3 tbsp extra-virgin olive oil

2 tbsp chopped basil

pinch of caster sugar

salt and pepper

6 slices Parma ham

50g (2oz) rocket leaves

25g (1oz) Parmesan cheese shavings

serves 2–4

preparation time: 15 minutes, plus rising

cooking time: 35–40 minutes

per serving: 780–390 cals; 35–18g fat;
    93–46g carbohydrate

1 Make the pizza dough and leave to rise for 1 hour or until doubled in size.

2 Meanwhile, put the chopped tomatoes, garlic, lemon zest, 2 tbsp olive oil, the basil, sugar, salt and pepper into a pan and bring to the boil. Cover and simmer gently for 15 minutes, then cook uncovered for a further 10 minutes until reduced and thickened. Leave to cool.

3 Put a lightly floured pizza stone or a large baking sheet into the oven at 230°C (210°C fan oven) mark 8 to preheat. On a well floured surface, knock back the pizza dough and roll it out thinly to a 30–35cm (12–14 inch) round, according to preferred thickness. Transfer to a cold baking sheet.

4 Spread the tomato sauce over the dough, almost to the edges. Slide on to the hot pizza stone or baking sheet and bake on the top shelf of the oven for 10–15 minutes or until the dough is crisp and golden.

5 Meanwhile, toss the rocket in the remaining 1 tbsp olive oil. On removing the pizza from the oven, immediately top with the slices of Parma ham, rocket, salt and pepper, and finally the Parmesan shavings. Serve immediately.

Four Cheese Pizza with Sun-dried Tomatoes

1 quantity pizza base dough (page 273)

flour, to dust

50g (2oz) drained sun-dried tomatoes in oil,
    sliced

125g (4oz) mozzarella cheese, grated

125g (4oz) dolcelatte cheese, diced

125g (4oz) mascarpone

50g (2oz) Parmesan cheese, freshly grated

1 tsp dried oregano

salt and pepper

serves 4

preparation: 20 minutes, plus rising

cooking time: 10–15 minutes

per serving: 620 cals; 39g fat;
    44g carbohydrate

1 Make the pizza dough and leave to rise for 1 hour or until doubled in size.

2 Put a lightly floured pizza stone or a large baking sheet into the oven at 230°C (210°C fan oven) mark 8 to preheat. Knock back the risen dough and divide into four.

3 On a well floured surface, roll out each piece to a thin 18cm (7 inch) round. Top with the sun-dried tomatoes and cheeses, then sprinkle with the oregano and seasoning.

4 Remove the heated pizza stone or baking sheet from the oven and carefully lift the pizzas on to it. Bake in the oven for 10–15 minutes until bubbling and golden. Serve at once.

note: *You will need a large baking sheet to take all 4 pizzas; alternatively, you may prefer to cook them in two batches.*

Asparagus, Mushroom and Tomato Pizza

1 quantity pizza base dough (page 273)

flour, to dust

2 tbsp olive oil

225g (8oz) firm tomatoes, thickly sliced

150g (5oz) asparagus tips, blanched

100g (3½oz) large flat mushrooms,
    roughly chopped

1 tbsp chopped tarragon or parsley

salt and pepper

150g pack mozzarella cheese, drained
    and sliced

serves 4

preparation: 20 minutes, plus rising

cooking time: 18–20 minutes

per serving: 410 cals; 19g fat;
    45g carbohydrate

1 Make the pizza dough and leave to rise for 1 hour or until doubled in size.

2 Put a lightly floured pizza stone or a large baking sheet into the oven at 200°C (180°C fan oven) mark 6 to preheat.

3 Knock back the pizza dough and roll out thinly on a well floured surface to a 30cm (12 inch) round. Lift on to a cold baking sheet and brush with 1 tbsp olive oil. Scatter over the tomatoes, asparagus, mushrooms and chopped tarragon. Season with salt and pepper.

4 Arrange the mozzarella slices on top, season with pepper and drizzle with the remaining olive oil.

5 Remove the heated pizza stone or baking sheet from the oven and carefully slide the pizza on to it. Bake for 18–20 minutes or until the cheese is golden brown. Serve the pizza cut into wedges, with a salad.

Pizza with Spinach and Pine Nuts

1 quantity pizza base dough (page 273)

flour, to dust

3 tbsp olive oil, plus extra to drizzle

1 large onion, peeled and thinly sliced

2 garlic cloves, peeled and crushed

450g (1lb) frozen leaf spinach, defrosted
    and drained

salt and pepper

25g (1oz) raisins (optional)

2 tbsp sun-dried tomato paste

125g (4oz) feta cheese

150g (5oz) mascarpone

15g (½oz) pine nuts

serves 3–4

preparation: 20 minutes, plus rising

cooking time: about 15 minutes

per serving: 975–650 cals; 61–41g fat;
    83–55g carbohydrate

1 Make the pizza dough and leave to rise for 1 hour or until doubled in size.

2 Put two baking sheets in the oven at 230°C (210°C fan oven) mark 8 to preheat. Heat 2 tbsp olive oil in a frying pan, add the onion and garlic and fry gently for 10 minutes until softened.

3 Squeeze out excess water from the spinach and chop finely, then mix with the onion, remaining olive oil, seasoning, and raisins if using.

4 Knock back the risen dough and divide in half. Roll out each piece on a lightly floured surface to a 23cm (9 inch) round and put on cool baking sheets. Spread each one with sun-dried tomato paste and top with the spinach mixture.

5 Cream the feta cheese and mascarpone together in a bowl, then dot over the pizza. Scatter the pine nuts on top.

6 Slide the pizzas on to the heated baking sheets (see note) and bake for 15 minutes or until melted and bubbling. Serve at once.

note: *Cook the pizzas on different oven shelves, transposing them halfway through baking to ensure even cooking.*

Roasted Onion and Olive Calzone

1 quantity pizza base dough (page 273)

flour, to dust

FILLING

4 red onions, peeled and cut into wedges

1 garlic clove, peeled and crushed

1 tsp chopped rosemary

1 tsp grated lemon zest

4 tbsp olive oil

125g (4oz) ricotta cheese

125g (4oz) fontina or mozzarella cheese,
    diced

2 tbsp olive paste

salt and pepper

serves 4

preparation: 40 minutes, plus rising

cooking time: 45 minutes, plus standing

per serving: 530 cals; 28g fat;
    55g carbohydrate

1 Make the pizza base dough and leave to rise for 1 hour or until doubled in size.

2 Meanwhile, make the filling. Put the onions into a roasting tin with the garlic, rosemary and lemon zest. Add the olive oil and toss well. Roast at 200°C (180°C fan oven) mark 6 for 30 minutes, stirring occasionally until the onions are softened and browned. Turn into a bowl and leave to cool.

3 Add the ricotta to the cooled filling with the fontina and olive paste and mix well. Preheat a baking sheet on the top shelf of the oven at 230°C (210°C fan oven) mark 8.

4 Knock back the risen dough and divide into four. Keeping the other pieces covered with clingfilm, roll out one portion on a well floured surface to a 20cm (8 inch) round. Transfer to a well floured board.

5 Spoon a quarter of the onion mixture on to one half of the dough and dampen the edges with a little water. Fold over the other half of the dough and press the edges together well to seal. Repeat to make 4 calzone in total.

6 Transfer the calzone to the preheated baking sheet on the top shelf of the oven and bake for 15 minutes until puffed up slightly and golden. Leave to stand for 5 minutes, then serve with a tomato salad.

Sausage Rolls

450g (1lb) pack puff pastry

450g (1lb) pork sausage meat

flour, to dust

milk, to brush

beaten egg, to glaze

makes 28

preparation: 25 minutes

cooking time: 30 minutes

per sausage roll: 110 cals; 7g fat;
    8g carbohydrate

1 Roll out half of the puff pastry on a lightly floured surface to an oblong, 40 x 20cm (16 x 8 inches); cut lengthways into 2 strips.

2 Divide the sausage meat into four, dust with flour and form 2 portions into rolls, the length of the pastry. Lay a sausage meat roll on each strip of pastry.

3 Brush the pastry edges with a little milk, fold one side of the pastry over and press the long edges together to seal. Repeat with the remaining pastry and sausage meat. Trim the ends.

4 Brush the pastry with egg to glaze and cut each roll into 5cm (2 inch) lengths. Make 2 or 3 slits in the top of each one.

5 Transfer to a baking sheet and bake at 220°C (200°C fan oven) mark 7 for 15 minutes. Lower the oven setting to 180°C (160°C fan oven) mark 4 and bake for a further 15 minutes. Transfer to a wire rack. Serve hot or cold.

Moroccan Goat's Cheese Parcels

125g (4oz) spinach leaves
2 tbsp sunflower oil
1 onion, peeled and finely chopped
1 large garlic clove, peeled and chopped
250g (9oz) soft goat's cheese
salt and pepper
270g pack filo pastry
50g (2oz) butter, melted
sesame seeds, to sprinkle
rocket leaves, to garnish

serves 6
preparation: 45 minutes, plus resting
cooking time: 15–20 minutes
per serving: 320 cals; 19g fat;
    28g carbohydrate

1 Plunge the spinach into a pan of boiling water, bring back to the boil and bubble for 1 minute, then drain and run under cold water. Once cold, squeeze out all excess liquid and chop finely. Put to one side.

2 Heat the oil in a pan, add the onion and garlic and cook for 7–10 minutes until softened and translucent, then allow to cool.

3 Put the spinach, onion mixture and goat's cheese into a bowl and mix well, seasoning generously with salt and pepper.

4 Cut the filo pastry into 24 x 12cm (5 inch) squares. Brush one square with melted butter, cover with a second square and brush with more melted butter. Put to one side and cover with a damp cloth to prevent the pastry drying out. Repeat with the remaining filo squares, making 12 sets in total.

5 Put a dessertspoonful of the filling in the centre of each square and draw up the corners to meet in the middle over the filling. Press the edges together to seal and form a square parcel. Brush the pastry with a little more butter, sprinkle with sesame seeds and put in the fridge to rest for 20 minutes.

6 Bake the filo parcels at 220°C (200°C fan oven) mark 7 for about 8–10 minutes or until the pastry is crisp and brown at the edges. Arrange on serving plates and garnish with rocket to serve.

Red Onion and Parmesan Tarts

PASTRY

225g (8oz) plain flour, sifted, plus extra
    to dust

100g (3½oz) unsalted butter, chilled
    and diced

pinch of salt

1 medium egg yolk

FILLING

4 medium red onions, peeled

1 tbsp lemon juice

15g (½oz) butter

1 tbsp olive oil

200ml carton crème fraîche

1 tbsp chopped thyme, plus extra sprigs to
    garnish

salt and pepper

50g (2oz) Parmesan cheese, freshly grated

serves 6
preparation: 40 minutes, plus resting
cooking time: 30 minutes
per serving: 500 cals; 36g fat;
    38g carbohydrate

1 To make the pastry, put the flour and butter into a food processor and whiz until the mixture resembles breadcrumbs. Tip into a bowl and add the salt, egg yolk and 7 tsp cold water. Mix well and bring the dough together with your hands. Wrap in clingfilm and rest in the fridge for 15 minutes.

2 To make the filling, cut the onions into fine wedges and toss in the lemon juice. Melt the butter with the olive oil in a frying pan. Add the onions and sauté gently for 15 minutes. Put to one side.

3 Divide the pastry into six. Roll out each piece on a lightly floured surface and use to line six greased 11cm (4½ inch) loose-based individual tart tins. Prick the bases with a fork. Put on a lipped baking sheet, cover with clingfilm and leave to rest in the fridge for 20 minutes.

4 Line the tart tins with greaseproof paper and baking beans and bake at 200°C (180°C fan oven) mark 6 for 10–15 minutes. Remove the paper and beans and return to the oven for 5 minutes to dry the pastry bases.

5 Increase the oven temperature to 230°C (210°C fan oven) mark 8. Mix the crème fraîche and thyme together in a bowl and season with salt and pepper.

6 Divide half the onions among the pastry cases, spoon over half the crème fraîche and sprinkle with half the Parmesan. Top with the rest of the onions, crème fraîche and Parmesan. Bake for 5–10 minutes or until golden. Serve garnished with thyme.

Tomato Tarts with Feta Cheese

150g (5oz) sheet ready-rolled puff pastry

300g (11oz) plum tomatoes, thinly sliced

pinch of caster sugar

salt and pepper

150g (5oz) feta cheese, crumbled

1 tbsp chopped thyme

1 tbsp extra-virgin olive oil

serves 4
preparation: 10 minutes
cooking time: 15–20 minutes
per serving: 280 cals; 20g fat;
    17g carbohydrate

1 Cut the puff pastry into 4 rectangles and lay on a baking sheet. Arrange the tomatoes on top, leaving a 1cm (½ inch) border at the edges. Sprinkle over the caster sugar and season well with salt and pepper. Scatter the feta and thyme on top and drizzle with the olive oil.

2 Bake the tarts at 200°C (180°C fan oven) mark 6 for 15–20 minutes or until the pastry is golden brown and risen around the filling. Serve warm, or allow to cool, then wrap and take on a picnic.

note: *If you have time, sprinkle the sliced tomatoes with a little salt and leave for 30 minutes to draw out some of the juice before draining and using them. This will make the pastry crisper.*

Spinach, Smoked Salmon and Crème Fraîche Tart

PASTRY
225g (8oz) plain flour, plus extra to dust
75g (3oz) butter, cut into pieces
pinch of salt

FILLING
125g (4oz) spinach leaves
200ml carton crème fraîche
2 medium eggs, beaten
100g (3½oz) smoked salmon trimmings,
   roughly chopped
salt and pepper
25g (1oz) Parmesan cheese

serves 4
preparation: 25 minutes, plus resting
cooking time: 45 minutes
per serving: 610 cals; 43g fat;
   41g carbohydrate

1 Whiz the pastry ingredients together in a food processor until the mixture resembles breadcrumbs. Add 3–4 tbsp cold water and whiz briefly to combine.
2 Knead gently and roll out on a lightly floured surface until large enough to line a 23cm (9 inch) fluted tart tin. Press the pastry into the tin, prick the base and chill for 30 minutes. Meanwhile, put a baking sheet in the oven at 200°C (180°C fan oven) mark 6 to preheat.
3 Line the pastry case with greaseproof paper and baking beans. Bake blind on the hot baking sheet for 10 minutes. Remove the paper and beans, and bake for a further 10 minutes until the pastry base is dry.
4 Meanwhile, wilt the spinach leaves in a pan with a little boiling water for 1 minute. Refresh under cold water, drain well and pat dry with kitchen paper.
5 Put the spinach in a large bowl and add the crème fraîche, eggs, smoked salmon and seasoning. Stir well, then spoon into the pastry case. Grate the Parmesan over and bake for 25 minutes until set and golden.

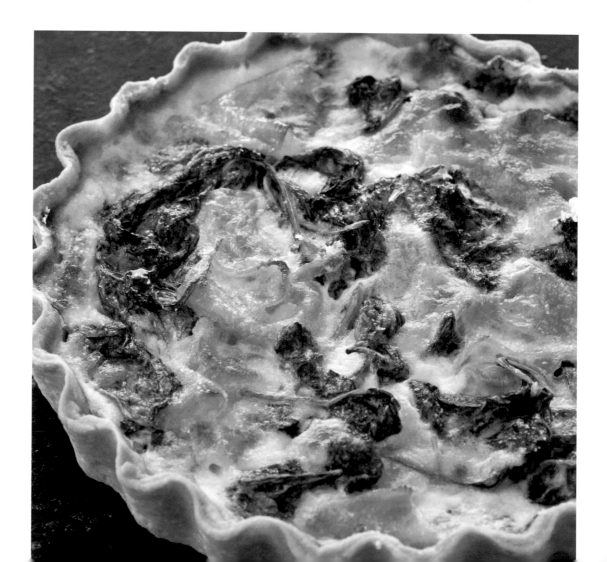

Quiche Lorraine

PASTRY

200g (7oz) plain flour, plus extra to dust

pinch of salt

100g (3½oz) butter, diced

1 egg

FILLING

5 medium eggs, lightly beaten

225g (8oz) streaky bacon (preferably in one
    piece), derinded and cut into strips

40g (1½oz) butter

125g (4oz) shallots or onions, peeled and
    finely chopped

400ml (14fl oz) crème fraîche

100g (3½oz) Gruyère cheese, grated

salt and pepper

serves 6–8

preparation: 35 minutes, plus resting

cooking time: 55 minutes

per serving: 860–650 cals; 72–54g fat;
    29–22g carbohydrate

1 To make the pastry, put the flour, salt and butter into a food processor. Whiz until the mixture resembles fine crumbs, then add the egg and 1 tbsp cold water. Process until the dough just comes together in a ball. Turn on to a lightly floured surface and knead lightly until smooth. Wrap and chill for at least 30 minutes.

2 Roll out the pastry on a lightly floured surface and use it to line a 23cm (9 inch), 3cm (1¼ inch) deep, loose-based tart tin. Chill for 20 minutes.

3 Prick the base, then line with greaseproof paper and baking beans. Bake blind at 200°C (180°C fan oven) mark 6 for 10 minutes. Remove the paper and beans and bake for a further 10 minutes until the pastry is golden. Brush with a little of the beaten egg and return to the oven for 5 minutes, to seal. Lower the oven setting to 190°C (170°C fan oven) mark 5.

4 Put the bacon into a pan and add cold water to cover. Bring to the boil, then drain and pat dry. Melt the butter in a frying pan, add the shallots and cook for 1 minute. Add the bacon and cook, stirring, until browned. Drain, then put into the pastry case.

5 Beat the eggs with the crème fraîche, cheese and seasoning, then pour over the bacon and shallots in the pastry case. Bake for 30 minutes or until golden and set. Leave to stand for 10 minutes before serving.

Mediterranean Quiche

1 quantity shortcrust pastry (page 269)

flour, to dust

FILLING

3 tbsp olive oil

1 red onion, peeled and thinly sliced

1 large red or yellow pepper, cored,
    deseeded and thinly sliced

1 small courgette, trimmed and sliced

1 garlic clove, peeled and crushed

1 tbsp chopped thyme

2 tsp dried oregano

225g (8oz) ricotta cheese

25g (1oz) Parmesan cheese, freshly grated

2 medium eggs

150ml (¼ pint) double cream

salt and pepper

25g (1oz) pitted black olives

serves 4–6

preparation: 25 minutes, plus resting

cooking time: 45 minutes

per serving: 840–560 cals; 63–42g fat;
    51–34g carbohydrate

1 Roll out the pastry on a lightly floured surface and use to line a 25cm (10 inch) loose-based tart tin. Rest in the fridge for 20 minutes.

2 Prick the base, then line with greaseproof paper and baking beans. Bake blind at 200°C (180°C fan oven) mark 6 for 10 minutes, then remove the paper and beans and bake for a further 10 minutes until the pastry is golden. Lower the oven setting to 190°C (170°C fan oven) mark 5.

3 Meanwhile, heat the olive oil in a large frying pan, add the vegetables, garlic and thyme and stir-fry over a high heat for 5–6 minutes until lightly golden. Drain on kitchen paper.

4 In a bowl, beat the ricotta, Parmesan and eggs together until evenly blended, then stir in the cream; season generously with salt and pepper.

5 Spoon the vegetables into the pastry case and scatter the olives over them. Pour the ricotta mixture on top and bake for 25 minutes or until risen and firm. Leave to stand for 10 minutes. Serve warm or cold, with a tomato and basil salad.

Courgette Puff Pie

450g (1lb) courgettes, trimmed and sliced
3 tbsp olive oil
375g pack ready-rolled puff pastry
flour, to dust
2 medium eggs
2 tbsp crème fraîche
75g (3oz) Gruyère cheese, grated
2 garlic cloves, peeled and crushed
4 tbsp chopped parsley
salt and pepper
50g (2oz) fresh white breadcrumbs

serves 4
preparation: 25 minutes, plus resting
cooking time: 40 minutes
per serving: 650 cals; 47g fat;
    43g carbohydrate

1 Put the courgettes on a large baking sheet and drizzle with the olive oil. Roast at 200°C (180°C fan oven) mark 6 for 8 minutes. Transfer the courgettes to a sheet of greaseproof paper.

2 Roll out the pastry on a lightly floured surface to a 30cm (12 inch) square. Lift on to the baking sheet.

3 Crack one egg into a bowl, add the crème fraîche and whisk lightly. Add 50g (2oz) of the cheese, along with the garlic and parsley. Season with salt and pepper and mix together until well combined.

4 Arrange the courgettes on top of the pastry, leaving a clear margin at the edge and pour the egg and crème fraîche mixture over them. Scatter the breadcrumbs and remaining cheese over the filling.

5 Lift the pastry sides up and over the edge of the filling to create a thick pastry rim. Chill for 10 minutes. Beat the remaining egg and brush over the pastry. Bake for 30 minutes or until the pastry is crisp and golden brown.

Cheese and Chive Tart

PASTRY
200g (7oz) plain flour, plus extra to dust
100g (3½oz) butter, chilled and cubed
pinch of salt
pinch of cayenne pepper
25g (1oz) Parmesan or Cheddar cheese,
    grated
1 large egg, beaten

FILLING
3 large eggs, lightly whisked
125g (4oz) creamy goat's cheese
100ml (3½fl oz) crème fraîche
2 tbsp chopped chives
pepper
pinch of freshly grated nutmeg
250g (9oz) firm goat's cheese, rind removed

serves 6–8
preparation: 15–20 minutes, plus resting
cooking time: 55 minutes, plus standing
per serving: 510–380 cals; 37–28g fat;
    27–20g carbohydrate

1 To make the pastry, put the flour, butter, salt and cayenne into a food processor and whiz until the mixture resembles breadcrumbs. Add the cheese and egg, and whiz briefly until combined, adding a little cold water if needed. Turn out the dough, knead lightly, then wrap in clingfilm and chill for 20 minutes.

2 Roll out the pastry on a lightly floured surface until large enough to line a 23cm (9 inch), 2.5cm (1 inch) deep, loose-based tart tin. Press the pastry into the tin, prick the base with a fork and rest in the fridge for 30 minutes.

3 Line the pastry case with greaseproof paper and baking beans, and bake blind at 200°C (180°C fan oven) mark 6 for 15 minutes. Remove the paper and beans and bake for a further 5–10 minutes or until cooked in the centre. Brush the inside of the pastry case with a little of the whisked egg, then return to the oven for 1 minute. Remove and set aside. Reduce the oven temperature to 180°C (160°C fan oven) mark 4.

4 Mix the remaining eggs with the creamy goat's cheese, crème fraîche and chives, and season with pepper and nutmeg. Crumble the firm goat's cheese into the egg mixture and pour the filling into the pastry case. Bake for 25–30 minutes or until just set.

5 Leave to stand for 15 minutes, then serve warm, with a mixed leaf salad.

Smoked Ham, Leek and Mushroom Pie

PASTRY

300g (11oz) butter, at room temperature

1 medium egg, plus 2 egg yolks

550g (1¼lb) plain flour, sifted, plus extra
to dust

½ tsp salt

FILLING

50g (2oz) butter

450g (1lb) leeks, trimmed and thinly sliced

225g (8oz) chestnut mushrooms, sliced

125g (4oz) Gruyère cheese, grated

50g (2oz) Parmesan cheese, grated

salt and pepper

225g (8oz) sliced oak smoked cooked ham,
diced

4 tbsp wholegrain mustard

200ml carton fromage frais

1 medium egg, beaten to glaze

serves 8
preparation: 40 minutes, plus resting
cooking time: 45–55 minutes
per serving: 750 cals; 48g fat;
57g carbohydrate

1 To make the pastry, put the butter, egg and extra yolks into a food processor and whiz until pale; don't worry if the mixture looks curdled. Add the flour and salt and pulse until the mixture just begins to come together. Add 2–3 tbsp iced water, whiz for 1 second, then tip into a bowl and bring the dough together with your hands. Divide into two pieces, one slightly larger than the other. Wrap and chill for 30 minutes.

2 Roll out the smaller piece of pastry to a 28 x 23cm (11 x 9 inch) rectangle on a sheet of greaseproof paper. Slide the dough on to a baking sheet. Prick all over with a fork and bake at 200°C (180°C fan oven) mark 6 for 10–15 minutes. Leave to cool.

3 To make the filling, melt the butter in a frying pan, add the leeks and mushrooms and cook for about 10 minutes until soft; cool slightly. Stir in the cheeses and season well. Spread half of the mixture over the cooked pastry base, leaving a 1cm (½ inch) border around the edges. Scatter the diced ham on top.

4 Mix the mustard with the fromage frais, season with salt and pepper to taste, then spread evenly over the ham. Top with the remaining leek and mushroom mixture. Lightly brush the pastry edges with water.

5 Roll out the larger piece of dough on a large sheet of greaseproof paper and loosen it from the paper with a palette knife. Position over the pie, then carefully slide the paper out leaving the pastry covering the filling. Press the edges together to seal, then trim and crimp, reserving the trimmings.

6 Roll out the reserved trimmings and cut out leaves or diamonds. Brush with a little water and arrange down the middle of the pie. Brush all over the surface of the pie with beaten egg, then bake for 35 minutes until the pastry is golden and crisp. Serve warm.

Tuna and Egg Pie

50g (2oz) butter

50g (2oz) plain flour, plus extra to dust

600ml (1 pint) hot vegetable stock

salt and pepper

2 tbsp chopped flat-leafed parsley

4 medium eggs, hard-boiled and roughly
chopped

400g can tuna in sunflower oil, drained
and flaked

500g pack puff pastry

a little milk, to glaze

serves 4
preparation: 30 minutes, plus chilling
cooking time: 40 minutes
per serving: 760 cals; 47g fat;
51g carbohydrate

1 Melt the butter in a pan and stir in the flour. Cook for 1 minute, stirring continuously. Gradually add the hot stock, stirring all the time, and cook for a further 5 minutes until thickened. Season well with salt and pepper and stir in the chopped parsley. Pour into a large shallow container and cool. Add the chopped eggs and tuna to the sauce, then chill for 20 minutes.

2 Cut the pastry in half. Roll out one piece on a lightly floured surface to a 28 x 20cm (11 x 8 inch) rectangle. Put on a lightly dampened baking sheet.

3 Spoon the filling on top of the pastry, leaving a 1cm (½ inch) border. Brush the edges with water. Roll out the other piece of pastry until 1cm (½ inch) larger all round than the first piece. Lift over the filling and press the edges together with a fork to seal. Trim off any excess pastry, then brush the top with milk and bake at 220°C (200°C fan oven) mark 7 for 30 minutes until golden and risen. Serve with mashed potato and peas.

Raised Game Pie

HOT WATER CRUST PASTRY

300g (11oz) plain flour

¼ tsp salt

65g (2½oz) white vegetable fat

FILLING

225g (8oz) rabbit joints, skinned and boned

225g (8oz) shoulder of venison

1.2 litres (2 pints) game or poultry stock

225g (8oz) pork sausage meat

½ onion, peeled and finely chopped

2 garlic cloves, peeled and crushed

4 tbsp Madeira

½ tsp ground mace

salt and pepper

125g (4oz) ready-to-eat dried apricots, sliced

4 ready-to-eat dried prunes, sliced

2 boneless skinless pheasant or chicken
    breasts, about 225g (8oz) in total

8 large sage leaves

beaten egg, to glaze

1 tsp powdered gelatine

serves 8–10

preparation: 1½ hours, plus cooling
    and chilling

cooking time: about 2 hours

per serving: 470–370 cals; 22–18g fat;
    40–32g carbohydrate

1 For the filling, cut the rabbit and venison into small pieces and put into a pan with the stock. Bring to a simmer, cover and cook for 25 minutes or until tender; remove with a slotted spoon and allow to cool; set aside. Boil the stock to reduce to 150ml (¼ pint).

2 Line the bottom of a 25 x 7.5cm (10 x 3 inch) loose-sided oblong raised pie mould with baking parchment. In a bowl, mix together the cooled meats, sausage meat, onion, garlic, Madeira, mace and seasoning. Cover and chill.

3 To make the pastry, sift the flour and salt into a bowl and make a well in the centre. Slowly heat the fat and 150ml (¼ pint) water together in a small pan until the fat melts, then bring to the boil and pour into the well. Gradually lap the flour into the liquid, then beat together. Lightly knead against the side of the bowl until smooth. Wrap the dough in a tea-towel and set aside to rest; use within 20 minutes while still warm.

4 Roll out three quarters of the pastry to a 40 x 23cm (16 x 9 inch) oblong; keep the rest well wrapped. Using the rolling pin, lift the pastry into the tin. Ease it into the corners and press evenly on to the sides of the tin. Trim off the excess. Line the base with greaseproof paper and baking beans. Bake blind at 200°C (180°C fan oven) mark 6 for 15–20 minutes, until golden and set. Remove the paper and beans; leave to cool.

5 Spoon half of the meat mixture into the pastry case and scatter over half of the dried fruit. Lay the pheasant or chicken breasts end to end on top and dot with the sage leaves. Scatter over the rest of the fruit and top with the rest of the meat mixture.

6 Roll out the remaining pastry to an oblong for the lid. Put in position and press the edges together to seal; trim and flute the edges. Make 3 holes in the pie lid, well apart. Brush with beaten egg to glaze. Cut decorative shapes from the pastry trimmings and arrange on top of the pie; glaze with beaten egg.

7 Stand the pie tin on a lipped baking sheet. Bake at 200°C (180°C fan oven) mark 6 for 20 minutes. Lower the oven setting to 180°C (160°C fan oven) mark 4 and cook for a further 1¼ hours, covering the top lightly with foil if necessary to prevent over-browning. Ease away the sides of the tin and bake for a further 20 minutes to brown the sides. Cool.

8 Soak the gelatine in 4 tsp water. Meanwhile, heat the reserved stock. Gradually add to the softened gelatine, stirring to dissolve; cool until on the point of setting. Put the pie on a lipped plate, easing it off the base. Slowly pour in the jellied stock through the holes. Cover loosely and chill for several hours, or overnight before serving.

PASTA

Endlessly versatile, inexpensive and quick to cook, pasta is incredibly popular. It is primarily a carbohydrate food, but it also provides protein, useful vitamins and some minerals. Certain types of pasta, notably those made with eggs, may contain as much as 13 per cent protein. Contrary to popular belief, pasta isn't particularly high in calories – it's the rich, creamy accompanying sauces that give some pasta dishes a high-calorie value.

FRESH PASTA

Pasta is surprisingly easy and very satisfying to make. Good homemade pasta has an excellent light texture and incomparable flavour – almost melting in the mouth. You need very little basic equipment – a rolling pin, metal pastry cutters, a sharp knife and a pastry wheel will suffice – but, if you intend to make pasta regularly, it is worth buying a pasta machine to take all the hard work out of rolling and cutting the dough.

Pasta dough can either be made by hand, in a food processor with a dough attachment, or in a large mixer with a dough hook. Initially it is probably best to make it by hand to learn how the dough should feel at each stage. The more you make fresh pasta the easier it will be to judge the correct texture of the dough – it should be soft, not at all sticky, and with a good elasticity.

The best type of flour to use for making pasta is '00' or 'farino tipo 00'. This very fine-textured soft wheat flour is available from larger supermarkets and delicatessens. Once you have mastered the basic pasta recipe, try making flavoured pastas; these are just as easy and taste especially good.

If you want to buy fresh pasta rather than make your own, find a good Italian delicatessen where it is freshly prepared on the premises. Commercially produced fresh pasta can be stodgy and disappointing – quite unlike homemade pasta.

DRIED PASTA

Dried pasta is available in an extensive range of shapes, sizes and flavours. The best are made from 100 per cent durum wheat (*pasta di semola grano duro*); some varieties include eggs (*all'uova*). With the exception of ravioli, dried pasta is suitable for all of the recipes in this chapter.

The choice of pasta is largely a matter of personal taste, but you will find that some shapes are more suited to particular sauces than others. Smooth-textured, slippery sauces are generally better served with long, fine pastas, such as spaghetti or linguine, whereas chunky sauces are better with short-shaped varieties. Shapes such as conchiglie (shells) and penne are ideal because they hold the sauce.

The names of shapes often vary from one region of Italy to another, and new ones are constantly being introduced. Note that the suffix gives an indication of the size of the pasta. *Oni* suggests large, as in conchiglioni (large shells); *-ette* or *-etti* denotes small, as in spaghetti and cappelletti (small hats); while *-ine* or *-ini* means tiny, as in pastina (tiny soup pasta) and spaghettini, the finer version of spaghetti.

QUANTITIES

It is difficult to give specific quantity guidelines for pasta, because there are so many factors, including the nature of the sauce and whether you are serving the pasta as a starter, lunch or main meal. Individual appetites for pasta seem to vary enormously too. As a very approximate guide, allow about 100–125g (3½–4oz) uncooked weight per person.

COOKING PASTA

All pasta should be cooked until *al dente* – tender yet firm to the bite, definitely not soft, and without a hard, uncooked centre. It is essential to cook pasta in plenty of fast-boiling water. If there is too little water, the pasta will cook unevenly and become stodgy. Allow 4 litres (7 pints) water and 1 tbsp salt to 500g (1lb 2oz) pasta. There's no need to add any oil. Bring the salted water to the boil in a large pan. Add the pasta to the fast-boiling water and stir once to prevent sticking. Cook until *al dente*.

Fresh pasta needs only the briefest of cooking, so watch it carefully. Fresh tagliatelle or spaghetti will only take about 1–2 minutes to cook. Stuffed pasta shapes such as ravioli or tortelloni need about 3 minutes to cook the filling through. Most dried pasta takes around 8–12 minutes. Use the pack instructions as a guideline, but the only way to determine when pasta is cooked is by tasting. Avoid overcooking at all costs.

As soon as the pasta is cooked, drain it in a colander or large strainer, then immediately add to the sauce, or it may start to stick together. When combining pasta with an oily sauce, hold back a few tablespoons of the cooking water; this helps to make a glossy coating sauce.

SERVING PASTA
Pasta quickly loses its heat once drained, so have warmed serving plates or bowls ready. Toss the pasta with the sauce, butter or olive oil as soon as it is cooked then transfer to the serving bowls. If Parmesan is the finishing touch, either grate it over the finished dish or shave off thin flakes, using a swivel potato peeler.

Basic Pasta Dough

225g (8oz) '00' pasta flour, plus extra to dust
1 tsp salt
2 medium eggs, plus 1 egg yolk, beaten
1 tbsp extra-virgin olive oil
1–2 tbsp cold water

serves 4
preparation: 5 minutes, plus resting
cooking time: 1–2 minutes
per serving: 280 cals, 9g fat;
   42g carbohydrate

1 Sift the flour and salt into a mound on a clean surface. Make a well in the centre and add the eggs, egg yolk, olive oil and 1 tbsp water.
2 Gently beat the eggs together with a fork, then gradually work in the flour, adding a little extra water if needed to form a soft but not sticky dough.
3 Transfer to a lightly floured surface and knead for about 5 minutes until firm, smooth and elastic.
4 Form the dough into a flattish ball, wrap in clingfilm and leave to rest for at least 30 minutes.

note: *To make pasta in a food processor, sift the flour and salt into the bowl and add the eggs, egg yolk, olive oil and 1 tbsp water (together with any flavourings). Whiz until the dough just begins to come together, adding the extra water if necessary to form a soft but not sticky dough. Wrap in clingfilm and rest (as above).*

variations
Flavoured pastas are easy to make and have a delicious flavour. Vegetable purées and flavoured pastes, such as sun-dried tomato and olive, make vibrant coloured pastas – note that some of the colour will be lost during cooking, without detriment to the flavour.
herb pasta: *Sift the flour and salt into the bowl and stir in 3 tbsp freshly chopped mixed herbs, such as basil, marjoram and parsley. Continue as for the basic pasta dough.*
olive pasta: *Beat the eggs with 2 tbsp black olive paste before adding to the flour. Reduce the water to about 2 tsp.*
sun-dried tomato pasta: *Beat the eggs with 2 tbsp sun-dried tomato paste before adding to the flour. Reduce the water to about 2 tsp.*
spinach pasta: *Blanch 50g (2oz) spinach leaves in a little boiling water until just wilted. Refresh under cold running water, then drain thoroughly and squeeze out all excess water. Finely chop the spinach and add to the flour and salt, together with the remaining ingredients. Continue as for the basic pasta dough.*

ROLLING OUT PASTA DOUGH

Most pasta machines work in the same way and this method should therefore apply, but do refer to the manufacturer's instructions for your particular model.

Divide the rested dough into 4 equal pieces; re-wrap all except one piece of dough in clingfilm to prevent it from drying out.

1 Knead the piece of dough until soft, then flatten so that it will fit through the pasta machine. With the rollers set furthest apart, pass the pasta through.

2 Fold the strip of dough in three, rotate and pass through the machine on this widest setting once more. The dough should now be smooth and of an even thickness.

3 Continue to pass the pasta through the machine in this way, narrowing the roller setting by one notch each time, and flouring the dough a little if it starts to feel sticky. Guide the dough through the machine with your hands; don't pull or the dough may tear.

4 Pass the dough just once through the penultimate setting to form a long thin sheet of silky pasta. For spaghetti and tagliatelle, this setting is generally used. For filled pastas, such as ravioli, the pasta should be rolled to the finest setting. Repeat the process with the remaining dough to form 4 thin sheets.

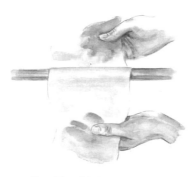

5 If making filled pasta, the dough should be used straightaway, while it is a little sticky – to help the ravioli, etc. adhere. Otherwise, drape the sheet of pasta over a narrow wooden pole or pasta dryer and leave for 3–5 minutes to dry slightly; this makes it easier to cut the pasta and prevents the strands from sticking together. Alternatively, lay pasta on a clean tea-towel to dry for 5–10 minutes.

note: *If you do not have a pasta machine you can roll the dough out very thinly by hand on a clean surface. Keep lifting and rotating the dough as you roll to prevent it from sticking.*

SHAPING PASTA

For lasagne, simply trim the pasta sheets to neaten and cut into lengths according to the size of your lasagne dish. For instructions on shaping ravioli see recipe on page 301.

Shaping Noodles

If using a pasta machine, fit the tagliatelle or linguine cutters, as required.

Pass one sheet of dough through the cutters and collect them over your hand. Hang the noodles over a wooden pole or pasta dryer for up to 5 minutes to dry out. Repeat with the remaining pasta sheets. Take the noodles a handful at a time and curl them directly on to a well floured tea-towel to form nests. The noodles are now ready to cook.

note: *If you are not using a pasta machine, you can shape noodles by hand. Flour the dough and roll up loosely, then cut into slices; the thickness depends on the noodles required. For linguine, cut 5mm (¼ inch) slices; for tagliatelle, cut 8mm (⅓ inch) slices; for broad pappardelle noodles, cut 2cm (¾ inch) slices. Unravel and allow to dry (as above).*

Creamy Parma Ham and Artichoke Tagliatelle

500g (1lb 2oz) dried tagliatelle

salt and pepper

280g jar roasted artichoke hearts, drained

80g pack Parma ham (6 slices)

500ml carton crème fraîche

2 tbsp chopped sage leaves, plus extra
   leaves to garnish

40g (1½oz) Parmesan cheese, freshly shaved

serves 4

preparation: 5 minutes

cooking time: 10 minutes

per serving: 1000 cals, 58g fat;
   97g carbohydrate

1 Cook the tagliatelle in a large pan of salted water until *al dente*.

2 Meanwhile, cut the artichoke hearts in half. Tear the Parma ham into strips.

3 Drain the tagliatelle, reserving about 4 tbsp of the cooking water, then put the pasta back into the pan.

4 Add the crème fraîche, artichoke hearts, Parma ham and chopped sage and stir everything together, thinning the sauce with the reserved cooking water. Season well with salt and pepper.

5 Serve the pasta straightaway in warmed bowls, sprinkled with the Parmesan shavings and garnished with sage leaves.

Spaghetti alla Carbonara

2 tbsp olive oil

25g (1oz) butter

125–150g (4–5oz) smoked pancetta (see
   note), derinded and cut into strips

1 garlic clove, peeled and halved

3 medium eggs

2 tbsp chopped parsley

2 tbsp dry white wine

40g (1½oz) Parmesan cheese, grated

40g (1½oz) pecorino cheese, grated

salt and pepper

400g (14oz) dried spaghetti

serves 4–6

preparation: 10 minutes

cooking time: 10 minutes

per serving: 750–500 cals; 38–25g fat;
   74–49g carbohydrate

1 Heat the olive oil and butter in a heavy-based pan. Add the pancetta and garlic and cook over a medium heat for 3–4 minutes until the pancetta begins to crisp. Turn off the heat; discard the garlic.

2 Meanwhile, in a bowl, beat the eggs with the chopped parsley, white wine and half of each of the cheeses. Season with salt and pepper.

3 Cook the spaghetti in a large pan of boiling salted water until *al dente*.

4 When the spaghetti is almost cooked, gently reheat the pancetta in the pan.

5 Drain the spaghetti thoroughly, then return to the pan. Immediately add the egg mixture together with the pancetta. Take the pan off the heat and toss well; the eggs will cook in the residual heat to form a light creamy sauce. Add the remaining cheeses, toss lightly and serve.

notes

• *If smoked pancetta is unobtainable, use smoked bacon instead, increasing the quantity to 175–225g (6–8oz).*

• *If pecorino is unobtainable, simply double the quantity of Parmesan.*

Penne with Tomato, Chilli and Basil Sauce

2 tbsp olive oil

1 small onion, peeled and finely chopped

2 garlic cloves, peeled and crushed

2 red chillies, deseeded and finely chopped

200ml (7fl oz) red wine

1kg (2¼lb) ripe plum tomatoes, chopped

salt and pepper

500g (1lb 2oz) dried penne

10 basil leaves, torn

150g (5oz) pecorino or Parmesan cheese,
   freshly shaved, to serve

serves 6

preparation: 20 minutes

cooking time: about 1 hour

per serving: 460 cals, 10g fat;
   69g carbohydrate

1 Heat the olive oil in a large pan, add the onion and cook over a low heat for about 10 minutes until soft.

2 Add the garlic and chillies to the pan and cook for 2 minutes. Add the red wine, bring to the boil and bubble for 1–2 minutes.

3 Add the tomatoes and bring to the boil, then turn down the heat to a low simmer. Continue to cook, stirring occasionally, until the tomatoes have reduced to a thick sauce; this will take about 50 minutes. Season with salt and pepper to taste.

4 Ten minutes before the sauce will be ready, cook the pasta in a large pan of boiling salted water until *al dente*. Drain the pasta well, adding a little of the cooking water to the tomato sauce to thin it.

5 Return the pasta to the pan, then add the tomato sauce and torn basil. Toss to mix and serve scattered with pecorino or Parmesan shavings.

Pasta with Aubergine and Mozzarella

1 large aubergine, trimmed and cut
   into cubes

7 tbsp olive oil

1 garlic clove, peeled and crushed

1 small red chilli, finely chopped

100g (3½oz) cherry tomatoes, halved

300ml (½ pint) passata or passata rustica

2 tbsp roughly torn basil

salt and pepper

1 quantity fresh herb pasta noodles (page
   288), or 500g (1lb 2oz) dried tagliatelle

100g (3½oz) mozzarella cheese, chopped

25g (1oz) Parmesan cheese, freshly grated

serves 4

preparation: 20 minutes

cooking time: 35–40 minutes

per serving: 760 cals, 33g fat;
   98g carbohydrate

1 Put the aubergine cubes in a roasting tin, drizzle with 3 tbsp olive oil and roast at 200°C (180°C fan oven) mark 6 for 20 minutes.

2 Heat 2 tbsp olive oil in a pan, add the garlic and chilli, and cook, stirring, for 1 minute. Add the cherry tomatoes, passata, basil and seasoning, and simmer for 10 minutes. Add the aubergine to the sauce and continue to cook for 5 minutes.

3 Bring a large pan of cold salted water to the boil. Add the pasta and cook until *al dente*; fresh pasta will only take 1–2 minutes. Drain well and return to the pan. Drizzle with the remaining 2 tbsp olive oil and season with salt and pepper.

4 Add the cheeses to the aubergine sauce and stir to melt together. Add the sauce to the pasta and toss well. Serve immediately.

note: *Use smoked mozzarella cheese if available.*

Fettuccine with Gorgonzola and Spinach

350g (12oz) young leaf spinach, trimmed

400g (14oz) dried fettuccine, tagliatelle or
long fusilli

salt and pepper

225g (8oz) Gorgonzola cheese, diced

90ml (3fl oz) milk

25g (1oz) butter

freshly grated nutmeg, to taste

serves 4–6

preparation: 15 minutes

cooking time: 10 minutes

per serving: 630–420 cals; 26–18g fat;
77–51g carbohydrate

1 Put the spinach into a pan, with just the water clinging to the leaves after washing, and cook, stirring, over a medium-high heat for 2–3 minutes until wilted. Drain well in a colander or sieve, pressing out any excess liquid.

2 Cook the pasta in a large pan of boiling salted water until *al dente*.

3 Meanwhile, put the Gorgonzola into a clean pan with the milk and butter. Heat gently, stirring, until melted to a creamy sauce. Stir in the drained spinach. Season to taste with pepper; salt shouldn't be needed.

4 Drain the pasta thoroughly and add to the sauce. Toss well to mix. Serve at once, sprinkled with a little freshly grated nutmeg.

variations

• *For a milder alternative, use dolcelatte rather than Gorgonzola cheese.*

• *Add 125g (4oz) diced cooked smoked ham to the sauce with the wilted spinach.*

Tagliatelle with Summer Vegetables and Herbs

25g (1oz) mixed herbs, such as basil, chervil,
chives and parsley, roughly chopped

1 tsp dried oregano

125ml (4fl oz) extra-virgin olive oil

700g (1½lb) mixed summer vegetables
(sliced courgettes, asparagus tips, French
beans, shelled broad beans and/or peas,
scraped and halved baby carrots)

salt and pepper

2 shallots, peeled and finely chopped

1 garlic clove, peeled and crushed

1 quantity fresh tagliatelle (page 288), or
400g (14oz) dried tagliatelle

6 tbsp single cream

Parmesan cheese shavings, to serve

serves 4–6

preparation: 25 minutes, plus infusing

cooking time: 10 minutes

per serving: 680–420 cals; 33–22g fat;
84–35g carbohydrate

1 Put the fresh herbs and dried oregano into a bowl. Add all but 2 tbsp of the olive oil. Stir well and set aside for a few hours if possible, to infuse.

2 Blanch all the summer vegetables separately in a large pan of lightly salted boiling water for 1–3 minutes depending on size and the vegetable (see note). Drain and immediately refresh under cold running water. Pat dry with a tea-towel.

3 Heat the remaining olive oil in a large frying pan, add the shallots and garlic and sauté gently for about 7 minutes until softened. Add the vegetables to the pan, stir-fry over a gentle heat to heat through, then add the herb mixture.

4 Meanwhile cook the tagliatelle in a large pan of boiling salted water until *al dente*; fresh pasta will only take 1–2 minutes.

5 Drain the pasta, reserving 4 tbsp of the cooking water. Add the pasta and reserved water to the frying pan and toss with the vegetables and sauce. Stir in the cream and heat through briefly. Serve at once, seasoned with salt and pepper, and scattered liberally with Parmesan shavings.

note: *The vegetables are listed in order of blanching time required: courgette slices take the shortest time; baby carrots the longest.*

Spaghetti with Courgettes

4 courgettes, trimmed
6 tbsp olive oil
400g (14oz) dried spaghetti
salt and pepper
75g (3oz) Parmesan cheese, freshly grated

serves 4
preparation: 10 minutes
cooking time: 15 minutes
per serving: 620 cals, 28g fat;
   76g carbohydrate

1 Using a sharp knife, cut the courgettes into very fine slices. Heat 2 tbsp olive oil in a large frying pan and fry the courgette slices in batches until golden, adding more oil to the pan when necessary. Drain on kitchen paper and set aside while cooking the rest.

2 Meanwhile, cook the spaghetti in a large pan of boiling salted water until *al dente*.

3 Drain the spaghetti well, add 1 tbsp olive oil and season generously. Toss the courgettes with the pasta, then divide among warmed bowls. Sprinkle with the Parmesan and serve at once.

Tuna Pasta

225g can tuna steak in olive oil
1 onion, peeled and finely sliced
1 garlic clove, peeled and chopped
2 x 400g cans chopped tomatoes
salt and pepper
500g (1lb 2oz) dried penne or other pasta
50g can anchovy fillets in oil, drained and
   chopped
2 tbsp small capers
2 tbsp basil leaves, roughly torn (optional)

serves 4
preparation: 10 minutes
cooking time: 30 minutes
per serving: 650 cals, 16g fat;
   102g carbohydrate

1 Drain the oil from the tuna into a pan and put the tuna to one side.

2 Heat the tuna oil, add the onion and fry over a low heat for about 10 minutes until softened. Add the garlic and cook for 1 minute.

3 Add the tomatoes and stir well. Season generously with salt and pepper, then simmer over a medium heat for 15 minutes to reduce and thicken the sauce.

4 Meanwhile, cook the pasta in a large pan of boiling salted water until *al dente*.

5 Flake the tuna and add to the tomato sauce with the anchovies, capers and basil leaves if using. Stir to mix well.

6 Drain the pasta well, return to the pan and add the tuna sauce. Toss everything together to mix and serve immediately in warmed bowls.

Pasta with Salmon and Dill

300g (10oz) fresh salmon fillet, skinned
125g (4oz) smoked salmon trimmings
40g (1½oz) butter
1 onion, peeled and chopped
250ml (8fl oz) dry white wine
2 tbsp wholegrain mustard
400g (14oz) dried tagliatelle or linguine
salt and pepper
300ml (½ pint) extra-thick double cream
30–45ml (2–3 tbsp) chopped dill

serves 4–6
preparation: 15 minutes
cooking time: 18–20 minutes
per serving: 970–650 cals; 56–38g fat;
   80–53g carbohydrate

1 Cut the fresh salmon fillet into 2.5cm (1 inch) cubes. Cut the smoked salmon trimmings into strips.

2 Melt the butter in a large frying pan. Add the onion and cook over a medium heat for 7–10 minutes until softened and golden. Stir in the wine and mustard and bring to the boil. Cook for 5–7 minutes until reduced by about half.

3 Meanwhile, cook the pasta in a large pan of boiling salted water until *al dente*.

4 Stir the cream into the sauce and leave to bubble for 1 minute, then lower the heat. Add the fresh salmon pieces and cook gently for 2–3 minutes until firm. Stir in the chopped dill and season with pepper. Remove from the heat.

5 Drain the cooked pasta and toss with the sauce and smoked salmon strips. Serve at once.

Pasta with Anchovies, Tomatoes and Olives

50g can anchovy fillets in oil
2 garlic cloves, peeled and crushed
4 sun-dried tomatoes, drained and
    roughly chopped
400g can chopped tomatoes
salt and pepper
500g (1lb 2oz) dried spaghetti
200g (7oz) black olives, pitted and
    roughly chopped
2 tbsp capers, drained
2–3 tbsp chopped flat-leafed parsley

serves 4
preparation: 15 minutes
cooking time: 20–25 minutes
per serving: 620 cals, 18g fat;
    96g carbohydrate

1 Drain the oil from the anchovies into a large pan. Heat the oil, then add the garlic and cook for 1 minute. Add the anchovies and sun-dried tomatoes and cook, stirring, for a further 1 minute. Add the canned tomatoes and bring to the boil. Season well with salt and pepper and simmer for 10–15 minutes.
2 Meanwhile, cook the spaghetti in a large pan of boiling salted water until *al dente*.
3 Stir the olives and capers into the tomato sauce. Drain the spaghetti thoroughly, reserving about 4 tbsp of the cooking water, then return to the pan.
4 Add the tomato sauce and chopped parsley to the pasta and toss well to mix, thinning the sauce with the reserved cooking water, if necessary. Serve at once.

Spaghetti with Mussels

1kg (2lb) fresh mussels in shells
1kg (2lb) ripe, flavourful tomatoes, quartered
1 onion, peeled and chopped
4 garlic cloves, peeled
6 basil leaves
150ml (¼ pint) white wine
400g (14oz) dried spaghetti
salt and pepper
2 tbsp olive oil
2 red chillies, halved, deseeded and chopped
basil leaves, to garnish

serves 4
preparation: 20 minutes
cooking time: 35 minutes
per serving: 540 cals; 11g fat;
    85g carbohydrate

1 Put the mussels into a large pan with a cupful of water. Cover with a tight-fitting lid and steam for about 3–4 minutes, shaking the pan occasionally, until the mussels open. Transfer to a bowl with a slotted spoon, discarding any unopened ones.

2 Strain the cooking juices through a muslin-lined sieve and set aside.

3 Put the tomatoes and onion into a shallow pan. Crush two of the garlic cloves and add them to the pan with the basil. Bring to the boil, then lower the heat and simmer for about 20 minutes until the tomatoes begin to disintegrate.

4 Press through a nylon sieve or mouli into a clean pan. Pour in the reserved mussel liquid and wine. Bring to the boil and let bubble until reduced by half.

5 Cook the spaghetti in a large pan of boiling salted water until *al dente*.

6 Meanwhile, heat the olive oil in another pan. Chop the other garlic cloves, and add them to the pan with the chillies. Cook until golden, then stir in the tomato sauce and mussels. Cover and simmer for 2–3 minutes until heated through. Season with salt and pepper to taste.

7 Drain the spaghetti, holding back 2 tbsp liquid. Toss the spaghetti with the mussel sauce. Serve immediately, garnished with basil leaves.

Spiced Pork and Lemon Pasta

8 thick pork sausages
500g (1lb 2oz) dried pasta shells or other
    shapes
salt and pepper
100ml (3½fl oz) dry white wine
grated zest of 1 lemon
juice of ½ lemon
large pinch of dried chilli flakes
300ml (10fl oz) half-fat crème fraîche
2 tbsp chopped flat-leafed parsley
25g (1oz) Parmesan cheese, freshly grated

serves 4
preparation: 10 minutes
cooking time: 12 minutes
per serving: 950 cals; 48g fat;
    104g carbohydrate

1 Remove the skin from the sausages and pinch the meat into small pieces. Heat a non-stick frying pan over a medium heat. When hot, add the sausage meat and cook for 5 minutes, stirring occasionally, until cooked through and browned.

2 Meanwhile, cook the pasta in a large pan of boiling salted water until *al dente*.

3 Add the wine to the sausage meat, bring to the boil and let bubble, stirring, for 2–3 minutes until the liquid has reduced right down. Add the lemon zest and juice, chilli flakes and crème fraîche. Season well with salt and pepper. Continue to cook for 3–4 minutes until reduced and thickened slightly.

4 Drain the pasta and divide it among four warmed bowls. Stir the chopped parsley into the sauce and spoon over the pasta. Sprinkle the Parmesan on top and serve, with garlic bread or focaccia.

Illustrated left

Spaghetti Bolognese

BOLOGNESE SAUCE

2 tbsp olive oil

1 onion, peeled and finely chopped

2 garlic cloves, peeled and crushed

450g (1lb) extra-lean beef mince

2 tbsp sun-dried tomato paste

300ml (½ pint) red wine

400g can chopped tomatoes

125g (4oz) chestnut mushrooms, sliced

2 tbsp Worcestershire sauce

salt and pepper

TO SERVE

500g (1lb 2oz) dried spaghetti

50g (2oz) Parmesan cheese, freshly grated

serves 6

preparation: 15 minutes

cooking time: 40 minutes

per serving: 510 cals; 12g fat;
    67g carbohydrate

1 To make the bolognese sauce, heat the olive oil in a large pan, add the onion and fry over a medium heat for 10 minutes until softened and golden. Add the garlic and cook for 1 minute.

2 Add the beef mince and brown evenly, using a wooden spoon to break up the pieces. Stir in the tomato paste and the red wine, cover and bring to the boil. Add the tomatoes, mushrooms and Worcestershire sauce and season well with salt and pepper. Bring back to the boil, lower the heat and simmer for 20 minutes.

3 Cook the spaghetti in a large pan of boiling salted water until *al dente*. Drain the pasta well, then return to the pan. Add the bolognese sauce and toss to mix together. Check the seasoning.

4 Divide among warmed plates and sprinkle with the Parmesan to serve.

variation: *Add 125g (4oz) chopped rindless smoked streaky bacon with the mince, brown, then stir in 200g (7oz) chopped chicken livers. Cook for 3 minutes before adding the tomato paste, then continue as above.*

Greek Pasta Bake

2 tbsp vegetable oil

1 onion, peeled and finely chopped

2 garlic cloves, peeled and crushed

450g (1lb) extra-lean lamb mince

2 tbsp tomato purée

400g can chopped tomatoes

2 bay leaves

150ml (¼ pint) hot beef stock

salt and pepper

SAUCE

15g (½oz) butter

15g (½oz) plain flour

300ml (½ pint) milk

1 egg, beaten

350g (12oz) dried macaroni

50g (2oz) Cheddar cheese, grated

serves 4

preparation: 10 minutes

cooking time: about 1½ hours

per serving: 720 cals, 28g fat;
    79g carbohydrate

1 Heat the oil in a large pan, add the onion and garlic and cook for 5 minutes to soften. Add the lamb mince and stir-fry over a high heat for 3–4 minutes until browned all over.

2 Stir in the tomato purée and cook for 1–2 minutes. Stir in the chopped tomatoes, bay leaves and hot stock and season with salt and pepper. Bring to the boil, lower the heat and cook for 35–40 minutes.

3 Meanwhile, make the sauce. Melt the butter in a small pan, then stir in the flour and cook over a medium heat for 1–2 minutes. Gradually add the milk over the heat, stirring constantly. Turn the heat down to low and cook, stirring, for 4–5 minutes. Remove from the heat and cool slightly. Stir in the beaten egg and season generously with salt and pepper. Put to one side.

4 Cook the macaroni in a large pan of boiling salted water until *al dente*.

5 Drain the pasta well and spoon half into a 2 litre (3½ pint) ovenproof dish. Spoon the meat mixture over, then top with the remaining macaroni. Pour the sauce evenly over the top and scatter with the grated cheese. Bake at 180°C (160°C fan oven) mark 4 for 25–30 minutes. Serve with a green salad.

Lasagne

1 quantity bolognese sauce (see left)

butter, to grease

350g (12oz) fresh lasagne, or 225g (8oz)
    'no need to pre-cook' dried lasagne
    (12–15 sheets)

1 quantity béchamel sauce (page 22)

3 tbsp freshly grated Parmesan cheese

serves 6

preparation: about 1 hour

cooking time: 45 minutes

per serving: 380 cals; 14g fat;
    37g carbohydrate

1 Spoon one third of the bolognese sauce over the base of a greased 2.3 litre (4 pint) ovenproof dish. Cover with a layer of lasagne sheets, then a layer of béchamel sauce.

2 Repeat these layers twice more, finishing with a layer of béchamel sauce to cover the lasagne completely.

3 Sprinkle the Parmesan cheese over the top and stand the dish on a baking sheet. Bake at 180°C (160°C fan oven) mark 4 for 45 minutes or until well browned and bubbling.

note: If using 'no need to pre-cook' dried lasagne, add a little extra stock or water to the sauce.

Roasted Vegetable Lasagne

1 large red pepper, halved, cored and
    deseeded

1 large yellow pepper, halved, cored and
    deseeded

2 courgettes, trimmed

2 red onions, peeled and cut into wedges

2 large garlic cloves, peeled and chopped

3 tbsp olive oil

salt and pepper

225g (8oz) cherry tomatoes

400g can artichokes, drained and quartered

3 tbsp tomato purée

40g (1½oz) each pitted black and green
    olives (optional)

7–8 sheets 'no need to pre-cook' lasagne

200g (7oz) mozzarella cheese, coarsely
    grated

SAUCE

900ml (1½ pints) milk

1 bay leaf

pinch of freshly grated nutmeg

3 peppercorns, crushed

50g (2oz) butter

50g (2oz) plain flour

40g (1½oz) pecorino cheese, grated

4 tsp chopped basil

serves 4

preparation: 30 minutes, plus infusing

cooking time: 1½ hours

per serving: 720 cals; 41g fat;
    59g carbohydrate

1 Cut the peppers and courgettes into 5cm (2 inch) pieces and put into a large roasting tin with the onion wedges. Sprinkle with the chopped garlic, drizzle with the olive oil and season well with salt and pepper. Stir together, then roast at 220°C (200°C fan oven) mark 7 for 30 minutes, stirring from time to time.

2 Meanwhile, make the sauce. Put the milk into a pan with the bay leaf, nutmeg and peppercorns. Bring to the boil, turn off the heat and set aside to infuse for 15 minutes, then strain.

3 Melt the butter in another pan, stir in the flour and cook for 1 minute. Gradually add the strained milk to the pan, whisking until smooth. Bring the sauce to the boil, stirring, and cook for 2 minutes until thickened.

4 Stir in the grated cheese, chopped basil and salt and pepper to taste. Cover the surface with a wet disc of greaseproof paper and set aside.

5 Take the roasting tin out of the oven, add the cherry tomatoes and artichokes and toss to mix. Roast for a further 20 minutes until the vegetables are slightly charred at the edges. Remove from the oven and stir in the tomato purée, and olives if using.

6 Lower the oven setting to 200°C (180°C fan oven) mark 6. Spread half of the roasted vegetables in the bottom of a 2.6 litre (4½ pint) ovenproof dish. Cover with a layer of lasagne sheets, then half of the sauce and mozzarella. Repeat these layers, finishing with mozzarella. Bake for 35–40 minutes or until bubbling and golden at the edges.

Butternut Squash and Spinach Lasagne

ROASTED SQUASH

1 butternut squash
2 tbsp olive oil
1 medium onion, peeled and sliced
salt and pepper

SAUCE

25g (1oz) butter
25g (1oz) plain flour
600ml (1 pint) milk

TO ASSEMBLE

225g bag baby leaf spinach
250g carton ricotta cheese
1 tsp freshly grated nutmeg
6 'no need to pre-cook' lasagne sheets,
    about 100g (3½oz)
50g (2oz) pecorino or Parmesan cheese,
    freshly grated

serves 6
preparation: 30 minutes
cooking time: about 1 hour
per serving: 320 cals; 17g fat;
    30g carbohydrate

1 Peel, halve and deseed the butternut squash, then cut into 3cm (1¼ inch) cubes. Put into a large roasting tin with the olive oil, onion and 1 tbsp water. Toss everything together and season well with salt and pepper. Roast at 200°C (180°C fan oven) mark 6 for 25 minutes, tossing halfway through.
2 To make the sauce, melt the butter in a pan, then stir in the flour and cook over a medium heat for 1–2 minutes. Gradually add the milk over the heat, stirring constantly. Reduce the heat to a simmer and cook, stirring, for 5 minutes or until the sauce has thickened.
3 Heat 1 tbsp water in another pan. Add the spinach, cover and cook until the leaves are just wilted. Season generously.
4 Crumble the ricotta into the sauce and add the nutmeg. Mix together thoroughly and season with salt and pepper to taste.
5 Spoon the squash and onion mixture into a 1.7 litre (3 pint) ovenproof dish. Layer the spinach on top, then cover with a third of the sauce, then the lasagne. Spoon the remaining sauce on top, season and sprinkle with the grated cheese. Bake for 30–35 minutes or until the cheese topping is golden and the pasta is cooked.

Illustrated on page 286

Mushroom and Pasta Gratin

225g (8oz) dried pasta shells
salt and pepper
25g (1oz) butter
450g (1lb) button mushrooms, halved,
    or quartered if large
90ml (3fl oz) brandy (optional)
1 tbsp chopped tarragon
1 tbsp chopped chives
a little olive oil
300ml (½ pint) double cream
50g (2oz) Parmesan cheese, freshly grated

serves 4
preparation: 10 minutes
cooking time: 30–35 minutes
per serving: 690 cals; 49g fat;
    44g carbohydrate

1 Cook the pasta in a large pan of boiling salted water until *al dente*.
2 Meanwhile, melt the butter in a large frying pan, add the mushrooms and stir-fry for 4–5 minutes until golden. Add the brandy if using and boil rapidly until only 2 tbsp liquid remains. Stir in the chopped herbs and remove from the heat.
3 Drain the pasta and immediately refresh under cold running water. Drain well, return to the pan and toss with a little olive oil to prevent sticking. Add the mushrooms, toss well together, then transfer to a lightly oiled gratin dish.
4 Mix the cream with half of the Parmesan and pour over the pasta. Sprinkle the remaining cheese on top and bake at 190°C (170°C fan oven) mark 5 for 20–25 minutes until bubbling and golden.

Goat's Cheese Ravioli

2 x quantity basic pasta dough (page 288)
semolina flour, to dust
1 medium egg, beaten, to brush

FILLING
5 tbsp chopped basil
2 tbsp chopped parsley
3 tsp chopped lemon thyme
450g (1lb) soft goat's cheese
1 medium egg
75g (3oz) Parmesan cheese, finely grated
salt and pepper

HERB OIL
6 tbsp extra-virgin olive oil
5 tbsp chopped basil, plus small leaves to
   garnish

serves 6
preparation: 2 hours, plus resting
cooking time: 6 minutes
per serving: 720 cals; 42g fat
   57g carbohydrate

1 Wrap the pasta dough in clingfilm and leave to rest for 30 minutes–1 hour while you make the filling.

2 For the filling, mix the chopped herbs together. In a bowl, beat the goat's cheese and egg together until smooth, then fold in the herbs and grated Parmesan. Season with salt and pepper. Cover and chill.

3 Divide the dough into 4 portions. Roll out one using a pasta machine to the penultimate setting (see page 289) to form a long thin sheet of pasta. Lay on a clean surface dusted with semolina flour, cut in two and cover with a damp cloth. Repeat with other portions.

4 Dust the surface again with semolina flour. Brush one sheet of pasta with the beaten egg. Top with heaped teaspoons of filling, set 1cm (½ inch) apart. Cover this with a second pasta sheet. Starting at the middle, use your finger to press down gently around the mounds of filling to expel any air trapped inside. Cut around each mound with a pastry wheel.

5 Repeat with the remaining pasta and filling to make about 30 ravioli in total. Lay them on trays dusted liberally with semolina flour and leave for 30 minutes to dry. Don't refrigerate or the pasta will become sticky.

6 Bring a large pan of salted water to the boil. Add the ravioli and cook for 3 minutes or until *al dente*. Meanwhile, mix the olive oil with the chopped basil and season with salt and pepper. Drain the ravioli and divide among warmed plates. Drizzle with the herb oil, scatter with basil leaves and serve immediately.

RICE AND GRAINS

Rice and grains are staple foods in many countries. Apart from being an important source of energy, they also provide useful amounts of protein, fibre, B vitamins, calcium and iron. There are many varieties of rice, each with its own characteristics. Some cook to a separate firm texture, some to a creamy consistency, while others cook to a sticky mass. Using the correct type of rice for a particular dish is important.

Brown rice is the whole rice grain with only the tough outer husk removed. Like other unrefined grains, it is richer in fibre, protein and B vitamins than refined rice. Because the bran is retained, brown rice has a good chewy texture and nutty flavour, and it takes longer to cook than white rice.

Long-grain white rice is the most common general purpose rice and there are many varieties, including Patna and Carolina. Once cooked the rice grains should be separate, dry and fluffy.

Easy-cook rice is long-grain rice that has been especially steam-treated to harden the grain. This process prevents the cooked rice grains from sticking together.

Arborio rice is the classic Italian risotto rice with plump medium grains. It has the capacity to absorb plenty of liquid during cooking without turning mushy. Once cooked, arborio has a wonderfully creamy texture, while still retaining a slight bite. Carnaroli is another excellent variety of Italian risotto rice.

Basmati rice is a superior variety of long-grain rice, originating from the foothills of the Himalayas. It has a characteristic, subtle fragrance and, once cooked, the grains are light, very fluffy, and quite separate. It is the perfect accompaniment to Indian curries. White basmati rice is widely available, but brown basmati is also obtainable.

Red Camargue rice from the south of France is an attractive russet colour, with a flavour and texture similar to that of brown rice. It is available from larger supermarkets and delicatessens.

Thai fragrant rice as the name suggests, has a distinctive mild aroma when cooked, and is available from larger supermarkets. Perfectly cooked Thai fragrant, or jasmine rice as it is also called, has a soft, light, fluffy texture and is perfect with Thai dishes.

Glutinous rice or sticky rice is another Asian variety. This short-medium grained rice cooks to a sticky mass, rather than separate grains and is used in sweet and savoury dishes. It is an essential ingredient in Japanese sushi.

Pudding rice is a short-grained rice used for milk puddings and rice desserts. The grains swell and absorb a lot of liquid during cooking, clinging together to give a rich creamy consistency.

Wild rice is not as the name suggests a rice at all, but the seed of an aquatic grass. It is dark brown in colour, highly nutritious and has a good bite and nutty flavour. As it is a little expensive, wild rice is typically mixed with other grains or rice – to delicious effect.

COOKING RICE

Some of the speciality rices are cooked in specific ways: liquid is added gradually to arborio when making a risotto, for example; pudding rice is usually baked slowly in the oven; glutinous rice is steamed; but in general all long-grain varieties can be cooked in the same way – either by the absorption method or by boiling in plenty of water. In general, the absorption method works better. Always check the pack instructions for suggested cooking times and methods.

Most rice is bought pre-packed and does not require washing, but if you do buy it loose, wash thoroughly. With some varieties, such as basmati, rinsing is advisable to remove excess starch. To rinse rice, put it into a sieve and hold under cold running water until the water runs clear, picking out any tiny bits of grit. Don't wash risotto rice, as it is the starch that lends the essential creamy texture.

To cook rice by the absorption method, measure it in a measuring jug and note the volume. Tip the rice into a heavy-based pan and add twice its volume of cold water. Add salt, bring to the boil, cover with a tight-fitting lid and turn the heat down to low. Cook until the water is absorbed and the rice is tender – allow 15–20 minutes for white rice, 40–45 minutes for brown rice. Don't lift the pan lid during cooking.

Alternatively, simply add rice to a large pan of fast boiling salted water, return to the boil, stir once and cook, uncovered, until tender. White rice generally takes 10–12 minutes; brown rice usually cooks in 35–40 minutes. Drain the rice in a sieve and rinse with a kettleful of boiling water.

To impart extra flavour, cook rice with herbs or spices. For saffron rice, add a large pinch of saffron strands or powdered saffron to the cooking water. For spiced rice, add a cinnamon stick, 1 clove, a blade of mace and a bay leaf to the pan; discard the spices once the rice is cooked. For herb-flavoured rice, add 1–2 tbsp chopped parsley, coriander, thyme or mixed herbs to the cooking liquid. Rice can also be cooked in stock rather than water for extra flavour.

GRAINS

Grains such as wheat, barley, corn, oats and rye are the edible seeds of different grasses and are familiar sold ground into different flours. Many of these grains are also available in other forms.

Buckwheat is sold as a grain, although it is actually the seed of a plant related to rhubarb. It is processed into groats, which are often toasted, and milled into flour, which is grey in colour.

Bulgur wheat is partially processed cracked wheat which readily absorbs moisture and cooks quickly. It has a mild, nutty taste and is used extensively in Middle Eastern cooking. Also known as pourgouri, bulghul and cracked wheat.

Couscous is a form of processed semolina grains, pale yellow in colour, with a soft texture and mild flavour. It is a staple food in north African countries.

Millet grains and flakes are available. Golden in colour, they have a chewy texture that works well in salads.

Polenta is fine ground cornmeal, which forms the basis of the traditional Italian accompaniment of the same name.

Pearl barley is the polished barley grain, which is typically added to soups and stews.

Basic Pilau Rice

50g (2oz) butter
225g (8oz) long-grain white rice
750ml (1¼ pints) chicken stock
salt and pepper
generous knob of butter, to serve

serves 4
preparation: 5 minutes
cooking time: 20 minutes, plus standing
per serving: 320 cals; 13g fat;
    45g carbohydrate

1 Melt the butter in a pan, add the rice and fry gently for 3–4 minutes until translucent.
2 Slowly pour in the stock, season, stir and cover with a tight-fitting lid. Leave, undisturbed, over a very low heat for about 15 minutes until the water has been absorbed and the rice is just tender.
3 Remove the lid and cover the surface of the rice with a clean cloth. Replace the lid and leave to stand in a warm place for about 15 minutes to dry the rice before serving.
4 Fork through and add a knob of butter to serve.

Special Fried Rice

225g (8oz) long-grain white rice
salt and pepper
75g (3oz) beansprouts
1–2 tbsp oil
1 carrot, peeled and coarsely grated
1 garlic clove, peeled and crushed
75g (3oz) frozen peas
50g (2oz) cooked peeled prawns
4 tsp light soy sauce
4–6 spring onions, trimmed and thinly sliced
1 tsp sesame oil

serves 4
preparation: 15 minutes, plus cooling
cooking time: about 20 minutes
per serving: 300 cals; 7g fat;
    50g carbohydrate

1 Cook the rice in plenty of boiling salted water until almost tender, then drain and rinse with boiling water. Spread out on a tray and leave to cool. Meanwhile, soak the beansprouts in cold water for 10 minutes, then drain.

2 Heat the oil in a preheated wok or large deep frying pan. Add the grated carrot and garlic and stir-fry for 2 minutes. Add the peas and beansprouts and stir-fry for 1 minute.

3 Add the rice and stir-fry for 1 minute, then add the prawns and soy sauce. Stir-fry for a further 2 minutes or until the prawns are heated through. Check the seasoning and stir in the spring onions.

4 Sprinkle with the sesame oil just before serving.

Thai Fried Rice with Cashews

225g (8oz) Thai fragrant rice
2 tbsp sunflower oil
2 medium eggs
pepper
1 tbsp sesame oil
2 green chillies, deseeded and sliced
5mm (¼ inch) piece fresh root ginger, peeled
    and finely chopped
150g (5oz) cashew nuts
1 garlic clove, peeled and crushed
150g (5oz) sugar snaps or mangetout
150g (5oz) baby corn, halved crossways
1 bunch of spring onions, trimmed and thinly
    sliced diagonally
4 tbsp light soy sauce
2 tbsp chopped coriander
juice of 1 lime
Thai sweet chilli dipping sauce, to serve

serves 4
preparation: 20 minutes
cooking time: 20 minutes
per serving: 590 cals, 31g fat;
    61g carbohydrate

1 Put the Thai fragrant rice into a large pan, add 600ml (1 pint) water, cover and bring to the boil. Reduce the heat and simmer for 10 minutes or until the rice is cooked and all the water has been absorbed. Fluff up with a fork.

2 Meanwhile, heat 1 tbsp sunflower oil in a non-stick frying pan, about 25cm (10 inches) in diameter. Beat the eggs with a little pepper.

3 Pour half the beaten eggs into the pan and swirl around to cover the bottom in a thin layer. Cook for 1–2 minutes until set. Turn the omelette over and cook for a further 1 minute or until golden. Remove and set aside. Add the rest of the oil to the pan and cook the remaining egg in the same way. Roll up the omelettes and slice thinly; keep warm.

4 Heat the sesame oil in a preheated wok or large frying pan. Add the chillies, ginger and cashew nuts and stir-fry for 2 minutes. Add the garlic, sugar snaps, baby corn and half the spring onions. Cook, stirring, for 3 minutes.

5 Add the cooked rice and soy sauce and mix well to heat through. Stir in the chopped coriander and lime juice. Serve in warmed bowls, topped with the omelette slivers and remaining spring onions. Serve with sweet chilli sauce.

Illustrated on page 302

Risotto Milanese

50g (2oz) butter

1 onion, peeled and finely chopped

150ml (¼ pint) dry white wine

300g (11oz) arborio rice

1 litre (1¾ pints) chicken stock

large pinch of saffron strands

50g (2oz) Parmesan cheese, freshly grated,
   plus extra to serve

salt and pepper

serves 4

preparation: 15 minutes

cooking time: about 30 minutes

per serving: 460 cals; 15g fat;
   64g carbohydrate

1 Melt half the butter in a heavy-based pan. Add the onion and cook gently for 5 minutes to soften. Add the wine and boil rapidly until almost totally reduced.

2 Add the rice and cook, stirring, for 1 minute until all the grains are coated with the butter and glossy.

3 At the same time heat the stock in a separate pan to a steady, low simmer.

4 Add the saffron and a ladleful of the stock to the rice and simmer, stirring, until absorbed. Continue adding the stock, a ladleful at a time, until the rice is tender but still has some bite to it. (Adding the stock slowly in this way helps to release the starch and make the risotto creamy.) It takes about 20 minutes; you may not need to add all of the stock.

5 Add the remaining butter and grated Parmesan. Season with salt and pepper to taste and serve at once, with extra Parmesan.

Risotto with Pancetta and Broad Beans

225g (8oz) podded fresh broad beans

salt and pepper

50g (2oz) unsalted butter

1 tsp olive oil

125g (4oz) pancetta, cut into small strips

1 onion, peeled and very finely chopped

about 1 litre (1¾ pints) vegetable stock

225g (8oz) arborio or carnaroli rice

150ml (¼ pint) dry white wine

2 tbsp chopped flat-leafed parsley

1 tbsp chopped tarragon

freshly grated Parmesan cheese, to serve

serves 2–3

preparation: 15 minutes

cooking time: 35 minutes

per serving: 1060–700 cals, 53–36g fat;
   105–70g carbohydrate

1 Add the broad beans to a pan of lightly salted boiling water and cook for about 4 minutes until just tender. Drain and refresh under cold running water, then slip the beans out of their skins. Put to one side.

2 Melt half the butter with the olive oil in a large pan. Add the pancetta and cook until golden, then add the onion and cook gently for 5 minutes or until softened and translucent, stirring from time to time. Meanwhile, bring the stock to a low simmer in another pan.

3 Add the rice to the onion and stir well to ensure all the grains are coated in butter. Pour in the wine and continue to stir over a low heat as it evaporates.

4 Start adding the hot stock, a ladleful at a time, stirring as you go and waiting for the liquid to be absorbed before adding more. This will probably take about 20 minutes but begin tasting a few minutes before. The risotto should have a dense, creamy consistency but the individual grains of rice should be distinct and firm to the bite.

5 Remove from the heat and gently stir in the broad beans and remaining butter. Season with pepper and a little salt if needed, then stir in the chopped herbs. Serve straightaway, topped with plenty of Parmesan.

Wild Mushroom Risotto

6 tbsp olive oil

2 shallots, peeled and finely chopped

2 garlic cloves, peeled and finely chopped

2 tsp chopped thyme, plus sprigs to garnish

1 tsp grated lemon zest

350g (12oz) arborio rice

150ml (¼ pint) dry white wine

900ml (1½ pints) vegetable stock

450g (1lb) mixed fresh mushrooms, such as
    oyster, shiitake and ceps, sliced if large

1 tbsp chopped flat-leafed parsley

salt and pepper

serves 4

preparation: 10 minutes

cooking time: 30 minutes

per serving: 530 cals; 21g fat;
    72g carbohydrate

1 Heat half the oil in a heavy-based pan. Add the shallots, garlic, thyme and lemon zest, and fry gently for 5 minutes or until the shallots are softened. Add the rice and stir for 1 minute until the grains are glossy.

2 Add the wine, bring to the boil and let bubble until it has almost totally evaporated. Meanwhile, heat the stock in a separate pan to a steady low simmer.

3 Gradually add the stock to the rice, a ladleful at a time, stirring with each addition and allowing it to be absorbed before adding more. Continue adding the stock slowly until the rice is tender. This will take about 20 minutes, but start tasting a few minutes earlier.

4 About 5 minutes before the rice will be ready, heat the remaining oil in a large frying pan and stir-fry the mushrooms over a high heat for 4 5 minutes. Add to the rice with the parsley. The risotto should still be moist; if necessary add a little more stock. Check the seasoning and serve at once, garnished with thyme.

Seafood Paella

3 tbsp olive oil

2 garlic cloves, peeled and crushed

1 onion, peeled and finely chopped

2 tsp paprika

1 green pepper, cored, deseeded and cut
  into strips

1 tsp saffron strands

200ml (7fl oz) passata

300g (11oz) arborio rice

1 litre (1¾ pints) hot fish stock

225g (8oz) prepared squid, sliced into rings
  (see pages 82–3)

450g (1lb) mussels in their shells, cleaned
  (see page 82)

225g (8oz) raw tiger prawns, in shells

salt and pepper

1 lemon, cut into wedges, to garnish

serves 4

preparation: 20 minutes

cooking time: 30 minutes

per serving: 480 cals; 12g fat;
  66g carbohydrate

1 Heat the olive oil in a paella pan or large deep heavy-based frying pan. Add the garlic and onion and fry gently for 5 minutes to soften. Add the paprika and green pepper and cook, stirring, for 2 minutes.

2 Stir in the saffron and passata and cook for a couple of minutes until bubbling. Then add the rice and stir for a minute or two until the grains are translucent. Pour in one third of the hot stock, bring to a simmer and cook for 5 minutes until most of the liquid is absorbed. Add half of the remaining stock and cook, stirring, for a further 5 minutes.

3 Add the squid, mussels and prawns and stir to mix with the rice. Pour in the remaining hot stock and cook for a further 10 minutes, stirring occasionally, until almost all the liquid is absorbed and the shellfish are cooked. The mussels should be open; discard any that remain closed.

4 Check the seasoning and serve garnished with lemon wedges.

note: *There are many different recipes for paella – this simple version is typical of the southern coast of Spain. Rice and saffron are essential ingredients, but otherwise paella can be vegetarian, based on fish or meat, or a combination of seafood and chicken.*

Curried Coconut Vegetable Rice

1 large aubergine, about 300g (11oz),
  trimmed

1 large butternut squash, about 500g
  (1lb 2oz), peeled and deseeded

250g (9oz) dwarf green beans, trimmed

100ml (3½fl oz) vegetable oil

1 large onion, peeled and chopped

1 tbsp black mustard seeds

3 tbsp korma curry paste

350g (12oz) basmati rice

salt and pepper

400ml can coconut milk

200g (7oz) baby spinach leaves

serves 6

preparation: 15 minutes

cooking time: 30 minutes plus standing

per serving: 540 cals, 28g fat;
  63g carbohydrate

1 Cut the aubergine and butternut squash into 2cm (¾ inch) cubes. Slice the green beans into 2cm (¾ inch) pieces.

2 Heat the oil in a large pan. Add the onion and cook for about 5 minutes until light golden. Add the mustard seeds and cook, stirring, until they begin to pop. Stir in the curry paste and cook for 1 minute.

3 Add the aubergine and cook, stirring, for 5 minutes. Add the butternut squash, beans, rice and 2 tsp salt, mixing well. Pour in the coconut milk and add 600ml (1 pint) water. Bring to the boil, cover and simmer for 15–18 minutes.

4 When the rice and vegetables are cooked, remove the lid and put the spinach leaves on top. Cover and leave off the heat for 5 minutes. Gently stir the wilted spinach through the rice, check the seasoning and serve immediately.

Spanish Spicy Chicken

1½ tsp ground turmeric
1.2 litres (2 pints) hot chicken stock
4 boneless, skinless chicken thighs
2 tbsp vegetable oil
1 onion, peeled and chopped
1 red pepper, cored, deseeded and sliced
50g (2oz) chorizo sausage, diced
2 garlic cloves, peeled and crushed
300g (11oz) long-grain rice
125g (4oz) frozen peas
salt and pepper
3 tbsp chopped flat-leafed parsley

serves 4
preparation: 25 minutes, plus infusing
cooking time: 50 minutes
per serving: 500 cals, 13g fat;
   68g carbohydrate

1 Add the turmeric to the hot stock and leave to infuse for 5 minutes. Meanwhile, cut each chicken thigh into 4 or 5 pieces. Heat the oil in a very large deep heavy-based frying pan. Add the chicken and fry, stirring occasionally, for 10 minutes or until golden. Remove from the pan and set aside.

2 Add the onion to the pan and cook over a medium heat for 5 minutes until softened. Add the red pepper and chorizo and cook for 5 minutes, then add the garlic and cook for a further 1 minute.

3 Return the chicken to the pan, add the rice and mix together. Add a third of the stock and bring to a simmer, then stir until all the liquid has been absorbed.

4 Add the remaining stock and peas. Bring to the boil, then lower the heat and cook, uncovered, for 15–20 minutes until all the liquid is absorbed. Five minutes before the end of the cooking time, season well and add the parsley. Serve with crusty bread.

Saffron Couscous

225g (8oz) couscous
75g (3oz) raisins
large pinch of saffron strands
salt and pepper
250ml (8fl oz) hot vegetable stock
25g (1oz) flaked almonds, toasted

serves 6
preparation: 10 minutes, plus standing
per serving: 180 cals, 3g fat;
   37g carbohydrate

1 Put the couscous and raisins into a large bowl. Add the saffron, ½ tsp salt and plenty of pepper. Pour the hot stock over the couscous, stir, then cover and leave to stand for 10 minutes to allow the couscous to swell and absorb the liquid.
2 Add the toasted almonds and fork through the couscous. Serve at once.

variation: *Use toasted pine nuts in place of the flaked almonds.*

Parmesan Polenta

600ml (1 pint) milk
2 garlic cloves, peeled and crushed
150g (5oz) instant polenta
salt and pepper
75g (3oz) Parmesan cheese, freshly grated
25g (1oz) butter

serves 6
preparation: 10 minutes
cooking time: 10 minutes
per serving: 180 cals, 8g fat;
   19g carbohydrate

1 Put the milk into a large pan, add 600ml (1 pint) water and the crushed garlic and bring to the boil. Add the polenta and 1 tsp salt, whisking constantly, then cook, stirring continuously, for about 5 minutes until all the liquid has been absorbed and the polenta is cooked.
2 Remove the pan from the heat, continuing to stir all the time, then add the Parmesan and butter. Season to taste with pepper and serve.

Fried Herb Polenta

175g (6oz) coarse polenta
salt and pepper
2 tbsp chopped sage
1 tbsp chopped rosemary
50g (2oz) unsalted butter, to fry

serves 4
preparation: 15 minutes, plus cooling
cooking time: 25 minutes
per serving: 250 cals; 11g fat;
   34g carbohydrate

1 Bring 900ml (1½ pints) water to the boil in a large pan with a good pinch of salt added. Sprinkle in the polenta, whisking constantly.
2 Lower the heat and simmer, stirring frequently, for 20 minutes or until the polenta leaves the sides of the pan; it will be very thick. Stir in the herbs and plenty of salt and pepper.
3 Turn out on to a board and shape the polenta into a thick oblong mound. Leave for about 1 hour until set, then cut into slices.
4 Melt the butter in a frying pan. When foaming, fry the polenta slices on both sides until golden. Serve with meat, poultry or vegetarian dishes.

note: *If preferred use instant polenta and follow the pack instructions.*

variation
soft herb polenta: *Serve at the end of stage 2, as you would mashed potato.*

VEGETABLES

Vegetables are highly nutritious. In particular, they are an excellent source of vitamins and minerals. Low in fat and cholesterol, yet high in fibre, they are also an important source of roughage. Starchy varieties, such as potatoes are also a good source of energy, but most vegetables are low in calories. Many varieties provide some protein too.

Most supermarkets now stock a wide range of organic vegetables – grown without the use of pesticides and artificial fertilisers – although they do tend to be more expensive.

Vegetables can be classified into categories:-

Brassicas otherwise known as the cabbage family, includes broccoli, brussels sprouts, cauliflower and curly kale, as well as the many different types of cabbage.

Roots and tubers are vegetables which grow underground, such as carrots, potatoes, parsnips, turnips, swede, celeriac, Jerusalem artichokes, beetroot and the lesser-known salsify and eddoes.

Pods, peas and beans take in the many varieties of fresh beans, along with peas, mangetout, okra and sweetcorn.

Stalks and shoots encompass such prized delicacies as asparagus, globe artichokes and fennel, along with celery.

The onion family comprises red, white and brown skinned onions, as well as leeks, garlic, shallots and spring onions.

Mushrooms are a type of fungus. A number of cultivated varieties are available and seasonal fresh wild mushrooms, such as chanterelles and ceps, are now easier to obtain.

Leafy vegetables include the array of salad leaves – baby spinach, rocket, lamb's lettuce, frisée, radicchio, chicory and all kinds of lettuces.

Vegetable fruits is a diverse category in which the vegetables are more correctly the fruits of their plants. Aubergines, avocado, peppers, tomatoes, cucumbers, courgettes and the other varieties of squash are all included.

BUYING AND STORING

Look for bright, firm vegetables. Avoid any that look shrivelled or bruised. Resist buying the largest specimens, particularly when choosing roots. In general, the younger and smaller the vegetable, the sweeter and more tender it will be, although some of the baby vegetables may lack flavour because they are so immature.

To enjoy them at their best and most nutritious, vegetables should be eaten as soon as possible after picking or buying, but most will keep for a few days in a cool, dark place. Store green vegetables and salad ingredients in the salad drawer of the fridge. Root vegetables can be stored in a cool, dark place, such as a wire rack in a cool larder, for up to 1 week. Exposure to light turns potatoes green, so they must be kept in the dark.

PREPARATION AND COOKING

Clean all vegetables thoroughly before cooking. Brush or shake off any loose dirt, then wash thoroughly (except mushrooms which are best wiped with a damp cloth.) As soon as vegetables are peeled they begin to lose vitamins so, where possible, prepare at the last minute. If the produce is organic and the skins are edible, there is no need to peel. Non-organic produce is better peeled; washing alone is not enough to remove all traces of residual chemicals. Never prepare vegetables hours in advance and leave them immersed in cold water as water-soluble vitamins will be lost.

Vegetables can be cooked by a variety of methods, including steaming, boiling, sautéeing, stir-frying, roasting, braising and grilling. To minimise the loss of water-soluble vitamins, cook in the minimum amount of water (if boiling), and use the cooking water as vegetable stock or to make a sauce. Avoid overcooking, whichever method you are using. In general, vegetables are at their best cooked until *al dente*, tender but still retaining some bite.

GUIDE TO TYPES OF VEGETABLE

Artichoke, Globe

Related to the thistle family, artichokes have a delicious nutty flavour. Choose heavy heads with firm, tight leaves. Allow one globe per person if serving whole as a starter. If only the hearts are being served, allow 2–3 per person.

To prepare cut off the stalks and snip off any leaf spikes with scissors.

Cook in boiling salted water with a slice of lemon added for 35–40 minutes or until you can pull out a leaf easily.

Serve globe artichokes warm with melted butter or hollandaise (page 23), or cold with mayonnaise (page 351) or French dressing (page 351). Pull off the leaves one by one, dip in the dressing, then suck off the fleshy part. Once all the leaves have been removed, slice off and discard the hairy choke, which is easily visible and use a knife and fork to eat the delicate heart. Young, baby artichokes are delicious eaten whole.

Artichoke, Jerusalem

Unrelated to the globe artichoke, this is a knobbly tuber with a nutty flavour, which ranges in colour from beige to brownish-red. Choose the smoothest available as these will be easier to peel. Allow about 175g (6oz) per person.

To prepare scrub well and peel thinly. If they are very knobbly and difficult to peel, cook first and then peel. Like other tubers, Jerusalem artichokes can be cubed, diced, sliced or cut into julienne.

Cook in boiling salted water, acidulated with 1 tbsp lemon juice to prevent discolouration, for 10–15 minutes.

Serve as an accompaniment, purée or make into a creamy soup.

Asparagus

This wonderful vegetable has a distinctive flavour. There are several different varieties: thick green, thin green, fine sprue and white asparagus. Choose fresh-looking bundles, with tight buds and smooth stems; avoid any which look wilted or coarse and woody. Buy English asparagus when it's in season – for around 6 weeks from early May. Allow 6–8 medium spears each, depending on size.

To prepare bend the lower end of each stem until it snaps, which will be the point where it begins to toughen. Peel the ends of thicker stems.

Cook in a special asparagus pan or stand the spears upright in a deep pan of gently simmering salted water, ideally so the tips steam while the stems cook in the water. Simmer for about 3–5 minutes, until tender.

Serve hot with melted butter or hollandaise (page 23), or cold with mayonnaise (page 351) or French dressing (page 351).

Aubergine (Eggplant)

Apart from the familiar large, oval, dark purple-skinned aubergines, you can buy thin pinkish purple ones, small round purple aubergines and a variety with greenish white skins. Choose firm, shiny aubergines. Allow about 175g (6oz) per person.

To prepare cut off the stem, trim the ends and halve or slice. Aubergines are less bitter nowadays, so it isn't usually necessary to dégorge them. However, if they are very large, sprinkle with salt and leave for 30 minutes to extract the bitter juices. Rinse well, then dry with kitchen paper.

Cook aubergine slices by sautéeing or grilling for 5–8 minutes. Bake aubergine halves, with or without stuffing and serve as a starter or main dish.

Serve slices as an accompaniment; stuffed halves as a main dish or starter. Aubergine is an essential ingredient in ratatouille and moussaka.

Bamboo Shoot

Native to Asia, these are the conical-shaped shoots of the bamboo plant. They are sometimes obtainable fresh from Asian food stores. Canned ready-cooked bamboo shoots are available from supermarkets. Allow 50–75g (2–3oz) per person.

To prepare and cook fresh bamboo shoots, peel and cook in boiling water for about 40 minutes or until tender. Or par-boil and use in stir-fries.

Bean, Broad

Home-grown broad beans are in season from late May to the end of June and they have a delicious, slightly sweet, nutty flavour. Choose small pods as the beans will be young and have a better flavour than bigger, older beans. Very young broad beans, less than 7.5cm (3 inches) long, can be cooked in their pods and eaten whole. Older beans must be podded and are best skinned to remove the outer coat which toughens with age. The easiest way to do this is to slip the beans out of their skins after blanching. Allow about 250g (9oz) weight of whole beans in pods per person.

To prepare Unless tiny, remove the beans from their pods.

Cook in boiling salted water for 8–10 minutes or until tender. Skin if necessary.

Serve broad beans topped with melted butter and chopped herbs. Older beans can be made into soup or puréed.

Bean, French (Green Bean)

Varieties of this bean include the common slim green bean or snap bean; haricot vert or classic slender, French bean; and the shorter, dwarf (bobby) bean. Other related beans are the Chinese yard-long bean and yellow wax bean. Choose young, tender beans. Allow 125g (4oz) per person.

To prepare trim off the ends. Most varieties are stringless, but if not remove the strings from the seams of the pods.

Cook in boiling salted water or steam for 5–7 minutes until tender, depending on variety and age.

Serve hot as an accompaniment, or cold as a salad tossed in a herb-flavoured vinaigrette.

Bean, Runner

Native to South America, this fast-growing climber is popular with gardeners in this country. Runner beans are at their best when young; with age they toughen and become stringy. Choose beans that break with a crisp snap. Allow 125–150g (4–5oz) per person.

To prepare cut off the ends and remove the strings from the sides. Cut lengthways into fine slices using a bean slicer, or cut young beans into short lengths.

Cook in boiling salted water or steam for about 10 minutes, depending on age, until tender.

Serve hot, with a knob of butter.

Beansprout

These are the shoots of germinated dried beans, such as mung beans or aduki beans. Choose crisp, small, fresh shoots, or sprout your own but be sure to buy beans or seeds which are specifically produced for sprouting – from a healthfood shop or other reliable source. Mung beans take only 5–6 days to sprout. Allow about 125g (4oz) beansprouts per person. Cook as soon as possible after buying or cutting.

To prepare rinse beansprouts thoroughly in cold water, then drain.

Cook in boiling salted water or steam for about 30 seconds, or stir-fry for 1–2 minutes.

Serve beansprouts in stir-fries or salads to appreciate their crunchy texture and nutty taste.

Beetroot

This bulbous root vegetable, with its characteristic dark red colour, is available all year round. Small, tender baby beetroot are sold in bunches in early summer and have a wonderful earthy flavour. Maincrop beetroot are often sold cooked and vacuum packed. Cooked beetroot is also sold preserved in vinegar. Choose firm, smallish beetroot with crisp tops and skin that is intact. Allow 125–150g (4–5oz) per person.

To prepare cut off the leafy stalks about 2.5cm (1 inch) above the bulbous root and wash the beetroot carefully to avoid tearing the skin. Young beetroot can be grated, marinated and used raw in salads.

Cook in lightly salted boiling water until soft, allowing about 30–40 minutes. Or, better still, roast with thyme sprigs and a drizzle of olive oil at 180°C (160°C fan oven) mark 4 until tender, allowing about 20 minutes for baby beets, up to 1 hour for larger beetroot. After cooking, peel, slice or dice.

Serve beetroot hot as an accompaniment, or cold with a vinaigrette dressing.

Broccoli (Calabrese)

There are two types of broccoli: the compact, dark-green headed calabrese and sprouting broccoli which has clusters of smaller, loose green or purple florets. Purple-sprouting broccoli is slightly sweeter with a more intense flavour, but the two are interchangeable in recipes. Choose firm, tightly packed heads with strong stalks. Allow 125–150g (4–5oz) per person.

To prepare trim the stalks and leaves. Halve the shoots if large.

Cook upright in boiling salted water (to allow the heads to steam rather than cook in the water) for 5–6 minutes, or steam for 10–15 minutes. Or stir-fry small broccoli florets for 4–5 minutes.
Serve hot on its own, or sprinkled with toasted nuts or breadcrumbs.

Brussels Sprout

Named after the capital of their country of origin, these miniature cabbages are a popular winter vegetable. Choose small round sprouts with tightly packed heads and no wilted leaves. Allow 125–175g (4–6oz) per person.
To prepare remove damaged or wilted leaves and cut off the stem. Cut a cross on the stump to ensure the thick part cooks as quickly as the leaves.
Cook in boiling salted water for 7–10 minutes or steam for 10–15 minutes.
Serve hot as an accompaniment. Very young Brussels sprouts are also good shredded and served raw in salads.

Cabbage

There are many varieties, with different harvesting times, so you have several cabbages to choose from throughout the year. In spring the thinnings from the main crop of spring cabbages are sold as spring greens before the heart has formed.

Spring cabbages are available from March to May; these are generally pointed, green and have a small heart. Summer cabbages are firm and green. Winter cabbages include the heavy, round red and white cabbages, though the latter is now available all year round. The crinkly Savoy cabbage is considered to be one of the finest of the winter crops. Pak choi, also known as bok choy or Chinese cabbage, has broad green leaves which taper to white stalks.

Choose fresh-looking cabbage with firm leaves, without insect damage or wilted leaves. Winter varieties should feel heavy for their size. Allow 175–225g (6–8oz) per person.
To prepare remove the coarse outer leaves, then cut in half and remove the centre stalk. Shred or cut into wedges. White or red cabbage can be finely shredded for using raw in salads.
Cook in boiling salted water or steam for 3–5 minutes if shredded; 10 minutes for wedges. Cabbage can also be braised; red cabbage is best

cooked this way. Stir-frying is an ideal way to retain the colour and crispness of cabbage, especially pak choi. Blanched cabbage leaves can also be stuffed. Shredded green cabbage can be deep-fried to make 'Chinese seaweed'.
Serve cabbage as soon as it is cooked.

Cardoon

An edible thistle related to the artichoke, which grows in the Mediterranean. It resembles celery and the stalks can be eaten raw or cooked in the same way. Allow 225g (8oz) per person.
To prepare discard the tough outer stalks. Separate the inner stalks and remove any strings. Cut the stalks into lengths and thinly slice the heart. Immerse in cold water acidulated with lemon juice to prevent browning until ready to serve or cook.
Cook in boiling salted water with added lemon juice for 25–30 minutes until tender.
Serve cold with a vinaigrette, or hot with melted butter or a cheese or tomato sauce.

Carrot

Popular root vegetable, available all year round. Look out for home-grown new baby carrots – sold by the bunch in early summer. Choose brightly coloured, firm carrots with smooth skins. Allow 125–175g (4–6oz) per person.
To prepare scrub small new carrots, leaving them whole with a tuft of green stalks attached. Always peel older carrots and quarter lengthways or slice.
Cook in boiling salted water for 10–15 minutes or steam for 12–18 minutes.
Serve hot as an accompaniment or make into a purée or soup. Raw carrots, either grated or cut into julienne, are excellent in salads.

Cassava (Manioc, Yuca)

A tropical long, brown-skinned tuber with white starchy flesh. There are two varieties, bitter and sweet. The bitter variety is poisonous until cooked. Allow 125–175g (4–6oz) per person.
To prepare peel and cut into slices.
Cook in boiling salted water for about 20 minutes.
Serve as an alternative to potato.

Cauliflower

Common brassica, now also available as a dwarf vegetable, and as green and purple-headed varieties. Choose a cauliflower with a firm, compact creamy white (or green or purple) head surrounded by fresh-looking green leaves. This vegetable is usually cooked, but can be eaten raw in salads. A medium cauliflower serves 4–6.

To prepare cut away the outer leaves and chop off the stem. Cauliflower is then usually cut into florets. If cooking whole, cut a cross on the stump to help the thick part cook more quickly.

Cook cauliflower florets in boiling salted water for 5–8 minutes, keeping the stalks immersed, but the heads out of the water, so that the florets cook in the steam; alternatively, cook in a steamer. Allow about 15 minutes if cooking whole.

Serve plain, topped with toasted nuts, or with a cheese or béchamel sauce.

Celeriac

This versatile root vegetable has a pronounced celery flavour. Allow about 175g (6oz) per person. Choose small, firm bulbs that feel heavy for their size and are free from blemishes.

To prepare scrub well, cut off the roots and peel thickly. Grate or cut into julienne for salads; cut into slices or strips for cooking. Immerse in cold water with a little lemon juice added to prevent discolouration until ready to cook.

Cook in boiling salted water for about 15–20 minutes until tender, or steam allowing a little longer. Drain well.

Serve hot with melted butter or a sauce, or mash with seasoning and butter or cream. Use blanched or raw celeriac in salads.

Celery

Intensely flavoured, celery is excellent for flavouring soups and stews, but it is also delicious served as a vegetable in its own right. Pale green celery is available all year round; white (blanched) winter celery is usually available from October through to January. Choose celery with firm, crisp sticks and fresh leafy tops. Allow 3–4 sticks per person.

To prepare trim off the base, separate the stalks and scrub well. Leave whole or slice.

Cook to serve as a hot vegetable. Braise in stock for about 20 minutes, or stir-fry, steam or boil in stock until tender.

Serve raw in salads or with cheese, or cooked as an accompaniment.

Chayote (Christophene)

Also called 'vegetable pear', this pear-shaped pale green gourd has white to green flesh and a high water content. Young chayotes have a delicate flavour which becomes bland as they grow larger. Buy small, firm ones, allowing two per person.

To prepare peel and slice, unless stuffing to bake.

Cook small chayotes like courgettes. Peel larger ones and cook in boiling salted water for 15–20 minutes until tender, or stuff and bake.

Serve topped with a knob of butter.

Chicory

Compact, spear-shaped vegetable, which is grown in darkness to produce crisp white leaves. Red-leafed chicory is also available – as the long-leafed striped treviso variety and the more familiar, related round radicchio. Choose chicory heads with crisp white leaves – too much green indicates a bitter flavour. Allow ½ head per person in salads; one head if serving cooked.

To prepare trim off the root base and remove any damaged outer leaves. Leave whole, halve lengthways or slice.

Cook by blanching in boiling salted water for 3–4 minutes; or grill, braise or bake.

Serve chicory raw in salads, or cooked as an accompaniment.

Chinese Leaf

Crunchy vegetable, resembling an elongated cabbage, with a subtle flavour. Choose fresh-looking heads which feel heavy. Allow 125–175g (4–6oz) per person.

To prepare cut off the stem and shred, slice, chop or simply separate the leaves.

Cook as for cabbage; stir-frying is ideal.

Serve Chinese leaf raw in salads, or cooked as an accompaniment.

Courgette

This miniature marrow is available all year round. Most varieties are green, but there are also yellow courgettes. Baby courgettes are particularly tender and delicately flavoured. Courgette flowers can be eaten too. Choose small, firm courgettes with smooth, shiny skins. Large ones often lack flavour and are best stuffed and baked. Allow 125–150g (4–5oz) per person.

To prepare trim off the ends, then slice or dice, or halve lengthways for stuffing. Baby courgettes can be cooked whole.

Cook in the minimum of boiling salted water for 3–5 minutes, or steam or microwave. Alternatively, sauté in butter, or stuff and bake.

Serve hot topped with herbs, or raw in salads.

Cucumber

Salad vegetable, which can be served hot. Choose small ones with blemish-free skins.

To prepare slice or dice. To deseed, if required, halve the cucumber lengthways and scoop out the seeds using a teaspoon.

Cook by steaming or sautéeing in butter to serve hot, though cucumber is usually eaten raw in salads.

Serve cold in salads, or hot – tossed with chervil, dill or fennel – as an accompaniment.

Dudi

Pale green gourd with creamy mild-flavoured flesh. Choose smooth-skinned ones. One dudi serves 4.

To prepare simply top and tail, then cut into thick slices leaving the seeds in; there is no need to peel.

Cook in boiling salted water for about 10 minutes until tender, or shallow-fry.

Serve topped with melted butter.

Eddoe and Dasheen

These two root vegetables are used in Caribbean and West African cooking. They are related and can be treated in the same way. Eddoe is a small round tuber, resembling a potato. Dasheen is a large, irregularly shaped tuber. Both have white flesh with a potato-like flavour. Allow 175–225g (6–8oz) per person.

To prepare peel and cut into even pieces or slices (as for potatoes).

Cook and serve eddoes and dasheen as you would potatoes: boil, bake, fry, or add to curries or spicy casseroles.

Fennel

Also known as Florence fennel or sweet fennel to distinguish it from the herb, this looks like a bulbous celery heart, but it has a distinctive aniseed flavour. Choose well-rounded, white or pale green bulbs – a dark green indicates bitterness. Allow 125–150g (4–5oz) per person.

To prepare trim both root and stalk ends, reserving the feathery leaves for garnish if appropriate. Halve, quarter, slice or chop.

Cook in boiling salted water for about 15 minutes; or steam, sauté in butter, braise or bake.

Serve fennel raw in salads, or hot as an accompaniment. Use the feathery leaves as a garnish, or add to salads.

Kale

From the same family as cabbage, kale has a much more intense flavour. It has coarse-textured curly or flat leaves, dark green or sometimes purple in colour. Curly kale is the most common variety. Avoid kale that shows signs of wilting or turning yellow. Allow 125–150g (4–5oz) per person.

To prepare trim off tough stalks and tear leaves into pieces, or shred coarsely. Wash thoroughly.

Cook in boiling salted water for 6–8 minutes until tender but still crisp, or steam for a little longer. Or stir-fry finely sliced kale for 3 minutes.

Serve hot, topped with a knob of butter.

Karela (Bitter Gourd)

Long pod-like vegetable with knobbly skin and edible red seeds, which looks rather like a large okra. Choose karela with firm green pods. Allow 125g (4oz) per person.

To prepare top and tail, then scrape off the knobs. Slice the pods, place in a colander, sprinkle with salt and leave to dégorge for 1 hour, then rinse well, drain and pat dry.

Cook gently in butter until tender.

Serve with a little sugar added, as a curry side dish.

Kohlrabi

An unusual looking white or purple skinned vegetable, similar in size to a turnip and with a similar flavour. It may look like a root vegetable but kohlrabi is a swollen stalk, with protruding leaves. Choose small fresh-looking kohlrabi, no more than 5cm (2 inches) in diameter, as larger ones can be tough. Allow 125–150g (4–5oz) per person.

To prepare trim the base, cut off the leaves and stalks and peel thinly. Quarter or slice.

Cook kohlrabi in boiling salted water for 20–30 minutes; or steam for a little longer.

Serve hot, tossed in butter or with a sauce. Or grate or slice very thinly and eat raw in salads.

Leek

Popular vegetable with a distinctive flavour. Choose small, young firm leeks with white stalks and fresh green leaves that are blemish-free.

To prepare trim the root end and coarse tops; discard any tough outer leaves. The easiest way to clean leeks is to slit them lengthways and rinse under cold running water to remove any grit. (If serving whole, slit the top part only.) It may take several rinses to remove all the grit trapped between the layers. Allow 1–2 leeks per person.

Cook in boiling salted water for 8–10 minutes; steam for 12–15 minutes; braise in stock until tender; or sauté slices in butter until tender.

Serve hot, topped with herbs or a sauce. Or cool and serve with a herb dressing (page 351), or raw in salads. Also good in soups.

Lettuce

Although normally served raw in salads (see page 349), lettuce can be cooked as a vegetable. Allow 1 small lettuce per person if cooked, less in salads.

To prepare trim base and remove any damaged outer leaves. Separate the leaves, wash and dry gently. Tear into pieces, rather than cut with a knife.

Cook by braising in stock for 25–30 minutes, or stir-frying. Lettuce also makes a good soup.

Serve raw in salads, or cooked as an unusual accompaniment.

Marrow

A common variety of summer squash with a delicate flavour, provided it is eaten young. Choose a firm marrow, no longer than 30cm (12 inches) and weighing 900g (2lb) or less. Larger ones tend to be full of seeds, fibrous and lacking in flavour. Allow about 175g (6oz) per person.

To prepare young marrow, simply trim off the ends and cut into pieces. Peel larger marrow, halve lengthways and discard the seeds and central fibres, then cut into pieces and put into a colander. Sprinkle with salt and leave for 30 minutes to extract the bitter juices, then rinse and pat dry. If preferred the marrow can be cut into rings, then deseeded and dégorged.

Cook in boiling salted water for 5–10 minutes, steam for a little longer, or sauté for 5 minutes. Or stuff and bake marrow halves for about 45 minutes.

Serve topped with herbs and butter.

Mushroom

There are many edible mushroom species. The common cultivated mushroom is sold at various different stages of development: as young button mushrooms; as cup mushrooms when the cap has partially opened; and as flat mushrooms when the cap has opened out flat. More flavourful cultivated varieties are increasingly available, including chestnut mushrooms, small crimini and large portabello mushrooms. Cultivated oriental varieties include the pale fan-shaped oyster mushroom and darker velvety shiitake mushroom.

Wild mushrooms are now available from selected supermarkets as well as specialist shops and markets. Most are in the shops during late summer and autumn, but the delicately flavoured morel is in season during spring. Look out for golden chanterelles, ceps, horn of plenty and other varieties from late summer onwards. Truffles are the most highly prized of all edible fungi. Black Périgord truffles come from France, while the white Piedmontese truffle is Italian.

Only gather wild mushrooms yourself if you are certain you can identify poisonous species. Several wild mushrooms are available dried. When reconstituted, 25g (1oz) dried mushrooms is roughly equivalent to 150g (5oz) fresh ones.

Choose fresh mushrooms with firm caps and fresh-looking stalks. Wild mushrooms, in particular, should be used as soon as possible after purchase because they deteriorate quickly. Allow 125g (4oz) fresh mushrooms per person.

To prepare wipe with a clean, damp cloth. If very dirty, wash quickly but don't leave fresh mushrooms to soak. Leave whole, halve, quarter or slice, depending on size. Soak dried mushrooms in warm water for 15–20 minutes before use.

Cook quickly, by sautéeing in butter or oil, stir-frying, grilling or baking.

Serve immediately after cooking. Marinate young mushrooms and use raw in salads.

Okra

Also known as ladies' fingers, these green tapering pods are used in Caribbean and Indian dishes. Choose firm, bright green pods, about 7.5cm (3 inches) in length. Allow 125g (4oz) per person.

To prepare trim okra carefully, removing a tiny piece from each end without cutting into the seed pod, otherwise a sticky juice is released which lends a gelatinous texture.

Cook okra in boiling salted water for 5 minutes, or steam, sauté or stew.

Serve hot on its own, or in spicy stews.

Onion

An essential flavouring vegetable in many dishes. There are several different varieties, some more strongly flavoured than others. With the exception of spring onions, onions are allowed to dry after harvesting and are covered in a thin, papery skin.

Brown-skinned globe onions are the most commonly used variety. Spanish onions are larger and have a less pronounced flavour. Italian red onions are smaller and have a mild, almost sweet flavour. White onions are covered in a distinctive silvery white skin; these are mild in flavour too.

Shallots have papery-brown skins and resemble small onions, but they grow in clusters rather than singly. Their purple-tinged flesh has a more intense, sweeter flavour than onion.

Pickling onions, also referred to as button or pearl onions, are maincrop onions picked when only about 2.5cm (1 inch) in diameter; these have a strong flavour. Silverskin onions are another small variety with a silvery skin, used for pickling.

Spring onions, or scallions, are the popular salad onion. These are long, slender and tender – excellent in stir-fries as well as salads.

Allow 2–3 spring onions or shallots, or 1 onion per person if serving as a vegetable.

To prepare trim root and top, then peel (except spring onions). Slice, chop or leave whole.

Cook according to use. Onions can be sautéed, fried, baked, braised, grilled, blanched or steamed. Blanching onions in boiling water for 2–3 minutes prior to further cooking will reduce their pungency.

Serve spring onions in salads or add to stir-fried dishes. Serve other onions as an accompaniment or use in composite dishes.

Palm Heart

Palm hearts are the edible inner part of palm tree shoots. The firm, creamy-coloured flesh has a delicate flavour rather like artichoke or asparagus. They are rarely found fresh here, but are sold pre-cooked and canned.

Serve hot as a vegetable or add to salads.

Parsnip

A root vegetable with a nutty, sweet flavour which improves if harvested after several frosts. If possible, choose firm, small or medium parsnips – without side shoots or brown marks. Allow 175g (6oz) per person.

To prepare scrub well, trim the top and root ends and peel thinly. Leave young parsnips whole or slice. Quarter larger ones and remove the core.

Cook by steaming, or add to cold salted water and boil for 10–15 minutes; drain well. For optimum flavour, par-boil for 2 minutes, then roast around a joint of meat or sauté in butter or oil.

Serve hot sprinkled with herbs, or mashed with a knob of butter and plenty of seasoning.

Pea

This highly popular frozen vegetable is only in season for a few months during the summer. Fresh peas – especially home-grown – have a delicious sweet flavour. Tiny petit pois are particularly sweet and tender. Choose crisp, well-filled pods with some air space between the peas; very full pods are likely to contain tough peas. Allow 225g (8oz) in the pod, or 125g (4oz) shelled weight, per person.

To prepare shell the peas and discard any that are discoloured; rinse well and cook immediately for optimum flavour.

Cook in the minimum amount of boiling salted water for 5–7 minutes, depending on size.

Serve hot, tossed with butter and mint.

Pea, Mangetout

This popular flat podded pea is harvested very young when the peas are under-developed and the pods are still tender and succulent. It is therefore eaten whole – hence the name, mangetout which translates as 'eat all'. Choose pods in which the peas are very small and under-developed. Allow about 125g (4oz) per person.

To prepare simply trim the ends.

Cook in boiling salted water for 2–3 minutes, or stir-fry for 3–4 minutes.

Serve hot with a knob of butter if wished.

Pea, Sugar Snap

An American variety of edible-podded pea, which has become very popular. It has a crisp, stringless pod with well-developed seeds and a sweet flavour. Prepare, cook and serve sugar snap peas as for mangetout (see left).

Pepper, Sweet

Peppers belong to the capsicum family and come in a variety of colours as they are picked at different stages of development. The sharp, crisp green pepper is the young version; it turns yellow, then orange and finally red as it matures. White and purple varieties are also available. Red peppers are the sweetest and have the softest texture. Choose firm shiny peppers without soft spots or signs of shrivelling. They can be eaten cooked or raw.

To prepare cut off the stalk end. If serving whole, scoop out the core and seeds; otherwise halve lengthways, core and deseed. To skin peppers, grill skin-side up, until charred, then cover with a cloth or put into a covered bowl; the steam will help to lift the skins. When cool enough to handle, peel away the skin. Slice or dice as required.

Cook peppers by grilling, stir-frying or blanching, or stuff and bake whole.

Serve raw (skinned if preferred) in salads, or cooked (as above).

Pepper, Chilli

There are many different chillies, varying in shape, size, colour and potency, but they all have a hot, spicy flavour. Most start off green and ripen to red, but there are yellow and black ones too. Choose those free from wrinkles and brown patches.

To prepare wear rubber gloves or prepare in a bowl of cold water to protect your skin from the volatile oils in chillies, which can cause irritation. Take care to avoid touching your eyes and wash hands immediately afterwards. Use chillies whole, or finely slice or dice, discarding the seeds if a less hot flavour is required.

Cook in curries and stews as a spicy flavouring ingredient – use sparingly.

Plantain

This resembles the banana and belongs to the same family, but is cooked and eaten as a vegetable – especially in the West Indies.

Choose firm, undamaged plantains which are still green or partly green. Allow 175g (6oz) per person.

To prepare and cook peel, slice and fry gently in butter and oil.

Potato

The most familiar of all vegetables, this starchy underground tuber has long been a staple food in many countries. Potatoes vary considerably in size. They may be red or brown skinned, and the colour of the flesh also varies from white to yellow, depending on the variety. The many varieties of potatoes fall into two categories: early or new potatoes, and maincrop varieties. Home-grown new potatoes are available from May to August, though imported produce gives us year round new potatoes. Maincrop British potatoes or 'old potatoes' are lifted during September and October and stored for sale over the next 8 months.

Potato varieties can be categorised into two types: new and old. In general, new potatoes have a firm, waxy texture, which does not break up during cooking; these are therefore ideal for boiling, sautéeing and salads. Old potatoes have a floury texture, which softens on cooking; these are better for mashed potatoes, roasting and baking (in their jackets). Both types can be used to make chips.

Individual potato varieties have their own characteristics; some maincrop varieties, for example, are better for baking than boiling and vice versa. Refer to pack instructions or ask your supplier for advice. Good all-round maincrop varieties are King Edward, Maris Piper, Desirée, Romano, Cara and Pentland Hawk. The Pink Fir Apple variety is fine-flavoured with an unusual texture for a maincrop potato – being firm and waxy it is more like a new potato and is ideal for salads.

Jersey Royals with their creamy, tender flesh and fine flavour have long been regarded as the 'king' of new potatoes. Other varieties to look out for are Belle de Fontenay, Charlotte, Maris Bard and Pentland Javelin.

Choose potatoes with smooth, firm skins. Don't buy potatoes with a green tinge, as these are unfit for eating. Most new potatoes have skins that can be rubbed off fairly easily. Buy new potatoes in small quantities and use them up quickly. Allow 175–225g (6–8oz) per person.

To prepare scrub or scrape new potatoes. Peel old potatoes (unless baking in jackets).

Boiled potatoes Cut into even-sized pieces, unless small. Add to a pan of cold salted water and bring to the boil. Cook until tender, 12–15 minutes for new potatoes; about 20 minutes for maincrop.

Chipped potatoes Peel and cut into thick slices, then into sticks. Leave in a bowl of cold water for 30 minutes to remove excess starch, then drain thoroughly and dry in a tea-towel or on kitchen paper. Heat the oil in a deep frying pan or electric deep-fryer to 190°C, or until one chip dropped in rises to the surface immediately, surrounded by bubbles. Quarter-fill the frying basket with chips, lower into the oil and cook for 6–7 minutes, until beginning to colour. Raise the basket to drain the chips; repeat with the rest of the potatoes. Fry all the chips for a second time, for 3 minutes until golden and crisp. Drain and serve.

Game chips Cut peeled potatoes into very thin slices, then deep-fry until golden.

Jacket potatoes Wash baking potatoes, dry and prick with a fork. For crisp skins, brush with oil and sprinkle with salt. Bake at 190°C (170°C fan oven) mark 5 for 1–1½ hours until tender. Cut a cross in the top or halve and add a knob of butter.

Mashed and creamed potatoes Boil, then drain thoroughly and mash until smooth, using a potato masher, potato ricer or fork; season. For creamed potatoes, add a large knob of butter and a little warm milk and beat until fluffy.

Steamed potatoes Scrub new potatoes and steam for about 15–20 minutes until tender.

Sautéed potatoes Boil the potatoes for 10–15 minutes until barely tender. Drain, peel and cut into large chunks. Sauté gently in hot butter and oil until golden and crisp on all sides. Drain on kitchen paper and sprinkle with salt.

Roast potatoes Peel potatoes, halve or quarter if large, add to cold salted water and bring to the boil. Cook for 1 minute, then drain well. Heat a little oil in a roasting tin, add the potatoes, turn to coat and roast at 190°C (170°C fan oven) mark 5 for 45 minutes to 1 hour, basting regularly and turning once or twice. (Or roast potatoes around a joint).

Pumpkin

One of the largest winter squashes, pumpkin is available from October to December. Pumpkins on sale are generally about 4.5–6.8 kg (10–15lb), so they are often sold by the wedge. Choose firm pumpkins and, if the flesh is visible, check that it is not fibrous. Allow 175–225g (6–8oz) per person.

To prepare cut in half, scoop out seeds and cut into wedges. Peel and chop into even-sized pieces.

Cook until tender by steaming rather than boiling, which turns pumpkin mushy. Or drizzle with olive oil and roast at 200°C (180°C fan oven) mark 6 for 30 minutes or until tender. Pumpkin can also be stuffed and baked or used in soups or stews.

Serve topped with melted butter and herbs.

Radish

There are several quite different varieties of this peppery root vegetable. The familiar small, round red radish and similar small white variety are sold all year round; these are typically eaten raw in salads. The white Japanese radish, known as mooli or daikon, is larger and elongated in shape – rather like a long, white parsnip. It is milder than other types and is usually peeled, grated and used as a garnish, or pickled. The black-skinned round Spanish radish, which is about the size of a small turnip, has a stronger flavour; after peeling it can be eaten raw, or cooked. Choose radishes with fresh green tops or, if these have been cut off, look for ones with firm bright skins. Allow 75–125g (3–4oz) per person.

Salsify and Scorzonera

Closely related, these are both long, tapering root vegetables. Salsify has a white skin and a flavour reminiscent of oysters – hence it is also known as oyster plant or vegetable oyster. Scorzonera, also called black salsify, has a brownish black skin and a stronger flavour than salsify. Choose smooth, firm specimens. Allow 125–175g (4–6oz) per person.

To prepare top and tail, then scrub well under cold running water.

Cook in boiling salted water with a little added lemon juice for 25–30 minutes until tender but still crisp. Drain well.

Serve hot with lemon juice, melted butter and chopped herbs, or purée for soups; or use in casseroles or salads.

Seakale

This vegetable isn't often found in shops, but it looks like a cross between blanched forced rhubarb and celery. It has crisp white stalks topped with tiny green leaves. Choose firm, white stalks that show no sign of discolouration or wilting. Allow 125–175g (4–6oz) per person.

To prepare Trim the stalks and wash well.

Cook upright in bunches, as for asparagus, in a deep pan with a little lemon juice added to the water for 15–20 minutes. Or steam for 20–25 minutes. Drain well.

Serve hot, topped with melted butter, hollandaise (page 23) or cheese sauce (page 22).

Sorrel

Wild sorrel and French sorrel are the two main varieties of this sharp, acidic leafy vegetable. Sorrel is not widely available, but it is easily grown in a garden. It should be picked when young before it flowers. Choose small, bright green leaves which look fresh. Allow 50g (2oz) per person.

To prepare wash well and tear up any large leaves into smaller pieces.

Cook in butter for a few minutes until wilted.

Serve as an omelette or crêpe filling, or use in soups or sauces. Use raw, sparingly, in salads.

Spinach

Home-grown spinach is available from May to October and, with imported supplies at other times, this versatile, leafy vegetable is available all year round. Young, tender leaves are excellent raw in salads. Larger leaves need to be washed thoroughly and are best steamed or cooked in the minimum of water until just wilted. Spinach beet, also called perpetual spinach, looks like coarse spinach, but it is a type of beetroot grown solely for its leaves, which have a stronger flavour.

Choose bright green spinach, avoiding leaves that are turning yellow or show signs of wilting. Allow at least 225g (8oz) spinach per person.

To prepare wash spinach thoroughly as it collects dirt. Use several changes of water and handle the leaves gently as they bruise easily. Remove the tough stalks and central ribs from coarser spinach leaves.

Cook in a covered pan with just the water that clings to the leaves after washing until just wilted. Drain well and press out excess water from the leaves with the back of a wooden spoon.

Squash

There are many different varieties of squash, including the familiar pumpkin, marrow and courgette (see individual entries). Summer squash, such as courgettes, are generally thin-skinned,

immature and tender; other summer varieties include the patty pan and custard marrow. Winter squashes are larger, more mature and have hard skins. Winter varieties include the spaghetti squash and butternut squash.

Select firm blemish-free squash. Depending on the variety, allow 125–175g (4–6oz) per person.

Prepare and cook summer squash as for courgettes. Winter squash are often halved and baked with a tasty filling. Otherwise they are peeled, cut into chunks and steamed, or added to soups and stews. Spaghetti squash is boiled whole, then halved before serving so the fibres can be scooped out.

Swede

A heavy, coarse-skinned root vegetable with orange flesh. Choose small swede, as large ones can be tough. Avoid those with damaged skins. Allow about 175g (6oz) per person.

To prepare peel thickly to remove all skin and roots, then cut into chunks.

Cook by steaming, or add to cold salted water and boil for 15–20 minutes; drain well, return to the pan and dry over a low heat for a minute or two. Mash or purée with a knob of butter and seasoning. Alternatively, par-boil, then sauté in butter, or roast chunks of swede in hot fat around a joint of meat at 200°C (180°C fan oven) mark 6 for 1–1½ hours.

Sweetcorn

The sweet nutty flavour of this vegetable is at its best just after picking. Once the cob is cut from the plant the natural sugar in the kernel changes to starch and the cob starts to lose sweetness and flavour. Baby corn, which looks like miniature corn-on-the-cob, is popular; the whole cob is eaten.

Choose whole cobs with a pale green, tightly fitting husk, enclosing plump, creamy-coloured kernels that are not dry. Once these turn golden, some of the sweetness is lost and the corn becomes tougher. Allow one cob per person, or 75–125g (3–4oz) loose corn or baby corn.

To prepare remove the stem, leaves and silky fibres. If the corn is to be served off the cob, remove it by holding the cob upright on a board and cutting off the kernels with a sharp knife, working downwards.

Cook whole cobs in boiling water (without salt which toughens corn) for 5–15 minutes until a kernel comes away easily. Cook loose corn kernels in a little boiling water for 5–10 minutes; drain. Boil baby corn for a few minutes only, or stir-fry, or grill. **Serve** with melted butter. The easiest way to eat corn-on-the-cob is to hold it between two forks or special tiny skewers. Serve baby corn whole or halved, as an accompaniment, in stir-fries or salads.

Sweet Potato

In spite of its name this vegetable isn't related to the common potato, although it is similarly a tuber. Most sweet potatoes are elongated in shape, but there are some round varieties. The outer skin colour varies from tan to red, and the sweet, slightly perfumed flesh may be white or yellow. The red-skinned variety is most common in this country. Choose small, firm sweet potatoes; large ones tend to be fibrous. Allow 225g (8oz) per person.
To prepare scrub well. If boiling, peel afterwards.
Cook as for potatoes – boil, bake, fry or roast.

Swiss Chard

This is related to seakale beet and is grown mainly for its leaves, which resemble spinach. These have prominent white central ribs, which are also eaten. Choose fresh-looking chard, with unblemished ribs and crisp leaves. Allow 225g (8oz) leaves per person and 125–175g (4–6oz) ribs per person.
Prepare and cook the leaves in the same way as winter spinach. The central ribs are prepared and cooked as for seakale.

Tomato

Although strictly a fruit, the tomato is nearly always used as a vegetable. There are many varieties, ranging in colour from red to orange, yellow to green. Home-grown tomatoes are available from mid-spring and throughout the summer; imported tomatoes are available year round, but sometimes lack flavour. Italian plum tomatoes at their peak are excellent for soups, sauces and casseroles. Tiny cherry tomatoes and baby plum tomatoes are usually very sweet and delicious eaten raw. Beef tomatoes are very large, weighing up to 450g (1lb); they can be stuffed or used raw. Marmande tomatoes from Provence are also large and generally have a good flavour.

Choose firm unblemished tomatoes, ideally with the calyx still attached, and a hint of fragrance – a good indication of flavour. Allow 1–2 tomatoes per person if serving raw, 1 large tomato for stuffing.
To prepare first remove the calyx if appropriate. To skin tomatoes if required, cover with boiling water, leave for 20–30 seconds, then plunge into cold water, drain and peel away the skins. Or, hold on a fork over a gas flame for 15–30 seconds, turning until the skin blisters, then peel.

Slice or quarter tomatoes if using raw. If they are to be stuffed, cut a small sliver from the base to enable them to stand, then cut off the top and scoop out the seeds and flesh. Use over-ripe tomatoes in sauces.
Serve raw in salads. Stuffed tomatoes may be served hot or cold.

Turnip

The early and maincrop types of this root vegetable are quite different. Early young turnips, available from April to July, have a sweet flavour with a hint of mustard and are usually tender. These have purple or green-tinged white skins.

Maincrop turnips, which are on sale for the rest of the year have thicker skins and coarser flesh. Choose smooth, unblemished turnips. Allow 175g (6oz) per person.
To prepare peel young turnips thinly. Peel older ones thickly, then slice or cut into chunks.
Cook small young turnips whole, but older ones must be cut up. Add to cold salted water and boil for 20–30 minutes, or steam until tender.
Serve older turnips either in chunks or mashed with an equal part of mashed potato or carrot to mellow their flavour. Use older turnips sparingly, diced or thinly sliced, in soups and casseroles. Young turnips can be served raw, sliced thinly or grated into salads; or cooked as a vegetable.

Yam

A member of the tuber family, originating from Africa. Yams have a brownish-pink skin and white flesh. Allow 175g (6oz) per person.
To prepare wash and peel, then dice.
Cook in boiling salted water, with a little added lemon juice to avoid discolouration, for 20 minutes until tender; or steam. Yams can also be roasted, baked or fried – like potatoes.

Marinated Artichoke Hearts with Mint and Dill

8 medium globe artichokes
juice of 1½ lemons
100ml (3½fl oz) olive oil
2 garlic cloves, peeled and chopped
6 coriander seeds, bruised
1 rosemary sprig, bruised
50ml (2fl oz) dry white wine
salt and pepper
1 tbsp chopped mint
1 tbsp chopped dill

serves 4
preparation: 30 minutes, plus marinating
cooking time: 15 minutes
per serving: 220 cals; 22g fat;
   3g carbohydrate

1 First, prepare the artichokes. Hold one firmly and snap off the stalk, then peel away the tough outer leaves around the base until the pale inner heart remains. Cut across the top of the base and scrape away the prickly choke inside. Immerse in a bowl of cold water with the juice of 1 lemon added. Repeat with the rest of the artichokes, then drain and pat dry.
2 Heat half the olive oil in a large frying pan or flameproof casserole, add the artichoke bases and sauté over a high heat for 4–5 minutes until just turning golden. Add the garlic, coriander, rosemary, wine, 2 tbsp water and salt and pepper. Cover and braise over a low heat for 8–10 minutes until the artichoke hearts are tender. Remove from the heat.
3 Add the rest of the olive oil and juice from the other lemon half. Leave to cool. Scatter the chopped mint and dill over the artichoke hearts, cover and leave to marinate for 1 hour before serving.

note: *This is delicious served as part of an antipasto platter, with Parma ham, olives etc.*

Jerusalem Artichoke Dauphinoise

700g (1½lb) Jerusalem artichokes
juice of 1 lemon
175g (6oz) thinly sliced pancetta or rindless
   streaky bacon
50g (2oz) butter
225g (8oz) onions, peeled and finely sliced
2 garlic cloves, peeled and crushed
2 tsp chopped thyme
200ml (7fl oz) chicken stock
150ml (¼ pint) white wine
150ml (¼ pint) double cream
salt and pepper

serves 4–6
preparation: 15 minutes
cooking time: about 1½ hours
per serving: 540–360 cals; 46–31g fat;
   22–14g carbohydrate

1 Peel and roughly chop the artichokes and immerse in a bowl of cold water with the lemon juice added.
2 Grill the pancetta slices until golden and crisp; cut into pieces.
3 Melt the butter in a frying pan, add the onions, garlic and thyme and cook for 10 minutes or until soft. Add the artichokes, together with the stock and wine. Bring to the boil and simmer for 10 minutes. Stir in the cream, pancetta and seasoning.
4 Transfer to an ovenproof dish and cook at 190°C (170°C fan oven) mark 5 for 1–1¼ hours until tender, golden and bubbling; if the dish appears to be over-browning towards the end of the cooking time, cover with foil. Serve hot.

note: *Serve as an accompaniment, or with a salad and crusty bread as a lunch or supper.*

Roasted Asparagus Salad

700g (1½lb) asparagus spears
6 tbsp olive oil
handful of rocket leaves
3 tbsp lemon juice
coarse sea salt and pepper
lemon wedges, to serve

serves 4–6
preparation: 10 minutes, plus cooling
cooking time: about 20 minutes
per serving: 220–150 cals; 21–14g fat;
    4–2g carbohydrate

1 Trim the asparagus spears and peel the bottom 5cm (2 inches) of each stalk, using a potato peeler.
2 Put the asparagus into a shallow roasting tin and toss with 4 tbsp of the olive oil. Roast at 200°C (180°C fan oven) mark 6 for about 20 minutes until just tender, turning the asparagus once during cooking. Transfer to a serving dish and allow to cool.
3 To serve, add the rocket leaves, lemon juice and remaining olive oil. Season with coarse sea salt and pepper and toss lightly. Serve with lemon wedges.

note: *This cooking time applies to stalks of medium thickness; increase if using fatter asparagus stems.*

Stuffed Baby Aubergines

700g (1½lb) baby aubergines
salt and pepper
4 tbsp olive oil
1 large onion, peeled and chopped
4 garlic cloves, peeled and finely sliced
230g can chopped tomatoes
1 tbsp thyme leaves
1 tbsp oregano leaves, plus extra to garnish
4 tbsp roughly chopped parsley
2 tsp tomato purée

serves 6
preparation: 20 minutes, plus standing
cooking time: 1 hour 20 minutes
per serving: 110 cals; 9g fat;
    6g carbohydrate

1 To prepare the aubergines, slit each one lengthways to make a cavity, without cutting right through to the base or ends. Put into a bowl and sprinkle the cut surfaces with salt. Leave to dégorge the bitter juices for 20 minutes.
2 Meanwhile, heat 2 tbsp olive oil in a pan, add the chopped onion and fry gently for 10 minutes until softened. Add the sliced garlic, cook for 2 minutes, then stir in the tomatoes, thyme, oregano, parsley, tomato purée and seasoning. Bring to a simmer and cook for 15 minutes until reduced and thickened.
3 Rinse the aubergines well to remove the salt. Heat the remaining olive oil in a large frying pan and pan-fry the aubergines in batches for 10 minutes to soften slightly. Transfer to a baking dish.
4 Carefully spoon the tomato mixture into the aubergine cavities, cover the dish with foil and bake at 200°C (180°C fan oven) mark 6 for 45 minutes until the aubergines are really tender. Scatter with oregano leaves to serve.

Green Beans with Almonds

450g (1lb) green beans, trimmed
salt and pepper
25g (1oz) unsalted butter
25g (1oz) flaked almonds
2 tbsp balsamic vinegar

serves 8
preparation: 10 minutes
cooking time: 4 minutes
per serving: 50 cals; 5g fat; 2g carbohydrate

1 Add the beans to a pan of boiling salted water, bring back to the boil and cook for 2 minutes. Drain and refresh under cold running water.
2 Melt the butter in a frying pan, add the flaked almonds and fry for a minute or two until golden. Add the beans and toss to mix. Season with salt and pepper to taste.
3 Drizzle with balsamic vinegar just before serving.

French Beans with Tomatoes and Herbs

2 tbsp olive oil
1 onion, peeled and chopped
1 garlic clove, peeled and crushed
450g (1lb) tomatoes, skinned and roughly
    chopped
700g (1½lb) French beans, halved
salt and pepper
1 tbsp chopped parsley
1 tbsp chopped basil

serves 6
preparation: 15 minutes
cooking time: 20 minutes
per serving: 90 cals; 5g fat;
    8g carbohydrate

1 Heat the olive oil in a pan, add the onion and fry for about 10 minutes until softened and beginning to colour. Stir in the garlic and tomatoes. Cook, covered, for about 5 minutes.
2 Meanwhile, add the French beans to a pan of boiling salted water, return to the boil and cook for 2–3 minutes only.
3 Drain the beans and add to the tomato mixture. Cover and cook gently for about 10 minutes until the beans are tender and the sauce is reduced. Stir in the herbs and season with salt and pepper to taste.

Baked Baby Beetroot

1.25kg (2¾lb) baby beetroot
15g (½oz) butter
salt and pepper
chopped parsley or chives, to garnish

serves 6
preparation: 15 minutes
cooking time: 1¼–1½ hours
per serving: 90 cals; 2g fat;
    15g carbohydrate

1 Trim the beetroot and carefully rinse in cold water, making sure you do not tear the skins.
2 Rub the butter over the middle of a large piece of foil. Put the beetroot on the buttered foil and season with salt and pepper. Bring the edges of the foil up over the beetroot and fold together to seal and form a parcel. Put on a baking sheet.
3 Bake at 200°C (180°C fan oven) mark 6 for 1¼–1½ hours or until the beetroot are soft and the skin comes away easily.
4 Leave for a minute or two until cool enough to handle, then rub off the skins. Scatter chopped parsley over the beetroot to serve.

Stir-fried Purple-sprouting Broccoli

200g (7oz) purple-sprouting broccoli
1 tbsp sunflower oil
15g (½oz) unsalted butter
1 mild red chilli, deseeded and finely sliced
1 lemon grass stalk
2 garlic cloves, peeled and sliced
salt and pepper

serves 2
preparation: 5 minutes
cooking time: 7–12 minutes
per serving: 150 cals; 14g fat;
    3g carbohydrate

1 Trim the broccoli, slicing the chunky stems on the diagonal and halving any thick ones.
2 Heat the oil and butter in a wok, then add the chilli, lemon grass and garlic and cook for 1 minute. Add the purple-sprouting broccoli and stir-fry for 5–10 minutes or until tender. Season with salt and pepper to taste and serve straightaway.

Brussels Sprouts with Chestnuts and Shallots

900g (2lb) small Brussels sprouts, trimmed
salt and pepper
1 tbsp olive oil
8 shallots, peeled and finely chopped
200g pack peeled cooked chestnuts
15g (½oz) butter
pinch of freshly grated nutmeg

serves 8
preparation: 15 minutes
cooking time: 10 minutes
per serving: 140 cals; 5g fat;
   18g carbohydrate

1 Add the sprouts to a large pan of boiling salted water, return to the boil and blanch for 2 minutes. Drain the sprouts and refresh with cold water.
2 Heat the olive oil in a wok or sauté pan. Add the shallots and stir-fry for 5 minutes until almost tender.
3 Add the sprouts to the pan with the chestnuts and stir-fry for about 4 minutes to heat through.
4 Add the butter and nutmeg, and season generously with salt and pepper. Serve immediately.

note: *For convenience, blanch the Brussels sprouts ahead, then pan-fry just before serving. This helps to retain their colour and texture.*

Spicy Red Cabbage with Apples

½ red cabbage, about 500g (1lb 2oz)
1 tbsp olive oil
1 small red onion, peeled and sliced
2 garlic cloves, peeled and crushed
1 tbsp light muscovado sugar
1 tbsp red wine vinegar
4 juniper berries
¼ tsp freshly grated nutmeg
¼ tsp ground allspice
150ml (¼ pint) vegetable stock
salt and pepper
50g (2oz) sultanas
2 eating apples, cored and sliced

serves 8
preparation: 10 minutes
cooking time: 50 minutes
per serving: 270 cals; 2g fat;
   12g carbohydrate

1 Shred the red cabbage and set aside. Heat the olive oil in a large heavy-based pan, add the onion and cook gently for 3–4 minutes to soften.
2 Add the garlic, cabbage, sugar, wine vinegar, juniper berries, nutmeg, allspice and stock. Season well with salt and pepper. Bring to the boil, lower the heat, then cover the pan and simmer for 30 minutes.
3 Add the sultanas and apples and stir through. Cook for a further 15 minutes or until the cabbage is just tender and nearly all the liquid has evaporated.

note: *The flavour of this dish improves with keeping, so make it a day ahead and reheat to serve.*

Illustrated on page 312

Savoy Cabbage with Crème Fraîche

1 large Savoy cabbage, about 900g (2lb)
salt and pepper
25g (1oz) butter
200ml carton crème fraîche
2 tbsp chopped flat-leafed parsley

serves 6
preparation: 8 minutes
cooking time: 5 minutes
per serving: 200 cals; 17g fat;
   6g carbohydrate

1 Cut the Savoy cabbage into large wedges. Bring a pan of salted water to the boil. Add the cabbage wedges, return to the boil and boil for 1–2 minutes only. Drain thoroughly.
2 Heat the butter in a large frying pan, add the cabbage and stir-fry for 3–4 minutes. Add the crème fraîche and chopped parsley, toss briefly and season with pepper to taste. Serve straightaway.

Carrots with Cumin and Orange

450g (1lb) baby carrots, scraped and halved
   lengthways
200ml (7fl oz) hot chicken or vegetable stock
finely grated zest and juice of 1 orange
1 tbsp golden caster sugar
2 tsp cumin seeds
1 bay leaf
salt and pepper

serves 6
preparation: 10 minutes
cooking time: 10 minutes
per serving: 40 cals; trace of fat;
   10g carbohydrate

1 Put the carrots into a pan with the hot stock, orange zest and juice, sugar, cumin seeds and bay leaf. Cover the pan, bring to a simmer and cook for 5 minutes.

2 Remove the lid and cook for a further 5 minutes until the carrots are tender and the liquid has evaporated. Season with salt and pepper to taste and serve straightaway.

variation: *To vary the flavour, replace the cumin seeds with a cinnamon stick. Add a knob of butter at the beginning of stage 2.*

Caramelised Carrots

700g (1½lb) baby carrots, scraped
50g (2oz) butter
50g (2oz) light muscovado sugar
300ml·(½ pint) chicken or vegetable stock
salt and pepper
2 tbsp balsamic vinegar
2 tbsp chopped parsley, to serve

serves 8
preparation: 15 minutes
cooking time: 10–15 minutes
per serving: 100 cals; 5g fat;
   13g carbohydrate

1 Thinly slice the carrots lengthways, then put into a pan with the butter, sugar and stock. Season with salt and pepper, then cover and bring to the boil. Reduce the heat and simmer for 5 minutes.

2 Remove the lid, add the balsamic vinegar and cook for a further 5–10 minutes or until the carrots are tender and the liquid has reduced to form a glaze. Scatter with the chopped parsley to serve.

Cauliflower Cheese

1 large cauliflower
salt and pepper
40g (1½oz) butter
40g (1½oz) plain flour
600ml (1 pint) milk
125g (4oz) mature Cheddar cheese, grated
4 streaky bacon rashers
4 sun-dried tomatoes, drained and sliced

serves 4
preparation: 10 minutes
cooking time: 25–30 minutes
per serving: 480 cals; 31g fat;
   23g carbohydrate

1 Trim the cauliflower, removing the stem and retaining the green leaves. Cut into florets.

2 Put the cauliflower florets into a large pan of boiling salted water and cook for 10–12 minutes or until just tender, adding the green leaves for the last 2 minutes of the cooking time.

3 Meanwhile, melt the butter in a pan, then add the flour and cook, stirring, for 1 minute. Gradually stir in the milk and cook for a further 3–4 minutes until thickened. Stir in half of the cheese. Season the sauce well with salt and pepper. Grill the bacon under a high heat for 6–8 minutes, turning once, until crisp.

4 Drain the cauliflower, put into a warmed gratin dish and pour the sauce over. Sprinkle the remaining cheese on top and grill for 3–4 minutes until bubbling. Cut the bacon into pieces. Scatter the bacon and sun-dried tomatoes on top of the cauliflower cheese. Serve with baked potatoes.

Celeriac Mash

450g (1lb) potatoes, peeled
450g (1lb) celeriac, peeled
salt and pepper
25g (1oz) butter
2 tbsp double cream

serves 6
preparation: 10 minutes
cooking time: 20–25 minutes
per serving: 120 cals; 6g fat;
   14g carbohydrate

1 Cut the potatoes and celeriac into even-sized pieces. Add to a pan of cold salted water and bring to the boil. Lower the heat and cook for 15–20 minutes or until tender. Drain well, return to the pan and put back over the heat for 30 seconds–1 minute, shaking the pan, to remove excess moisture.

2 Mash the potatoes and celeriac well with plenty of salt and pepper, then add the butter and double cream and mash until smooth. Serve piping hot.

variations: *For a piquant flavour, replace the double cream with 1–2 tbsp wholegrain or Dijon mustard, or 1–2 tbsp creamed horseradish.*

Braised Celery with Pancetta and Cheese

1 head of celery, trimmed, about 450g (1lb)
   trimmed weight
125g (4oz) smoked pancetta or rindless
   streaky bacon, diced
25g (1oz) butter
1 large onion, peeled and chopped
2 garlic cloves, peeled and crushed
150ml (¼ pint) single cream
salt and pepper
125g (4oz) Gruyère cheese, grated

serves: 4–6
preparation: 10 minutes
cooking time: 25 minutes
per serving: 410–270 cals; 36–24g fat;
   6–4g carbohydrate

1 Separate the celery sticks and cut into 5cm (2 inch) lengths, on the diagonal.
2 Preheat a large sauté pan (suitable for use under the grill). Add the pancetta and stir-fry over a high heat until it releases its fat and browns. Remove with a slotted spoon and set aside.
3 Melt the butter in the pan, add the onion and garlic, and fry gently for 10 minutes until softened. Add the celery and cook for a further 5 minutes.
4 Return the pancetta to the pan, add the cream and bring to the boil. Cover and simmer for 5 minutes; season with salt and pepper to taste.
5 Scatter the cheese over the celery and put under a hot grill for 1–2 minutes until golden. Serve at once.

Braised Chicory in White Wine

50g (2oz) butter, softened
6 heads of chicory, trimmed
salt and pepper
100ml (3½fl oz) white wine
snipped chives, to serve

serves 6
preparation: 5 minutes
cooking time: about 1 hour
per serving: 80 cals; 7g fat;
   3g carbohydrate

1 Grease a 1.7 litre (3 pint) ovenproof dish with 15g (½oz) butter and lay the chicory in the dish.
2 Season with salt and pepper, add the wine and dot the remaining butter over the top. Cover with foil and cook at 190°C (170°C fan oven) mark 5 for 1 hour or until soft. Scatter with chives to serve.

Baby Courgettes with Pine Nuts

25g (1oz) pine nuts
1 tsp cumin seeds
2 tbsp olive oil
450g (1lb) baby courgettes, trimmed
   and halved
1 garlic clove, peeled and crushed
juice of ½ lemon
salt and pepper

serves 6
preparation: 10 minutes
cooking time: 5–10 minutes
per serving: 80 cals; 8g fat;
   2g carbohydrate

1 Heat a non-stick wok or frying pan and dry-fry the pine nuts for 1–2 minutes until golden. Remove and set aside.
2 Add the cumin seeds to the pan and dry-fry for a minute or until they release their aroma. Tip into a bowl and allow to cool.
3 Heat the olive oil in the same pan and add the courgettes and garlic. Stir-fry for 3–5 minutes or until golden. Add the lemon juice, cumin seeds and salt and pepper to taste. Scatter the pine nuts over the courgettes and serve.

Roasted Fennel and Red Onion with Orange

2 fennel bulbs, trimmed, halved and cored
2 red onions, peeled
2 tbsp olive oil
salt and pepper
2 oranges, peeled and segmented
50g (2oz) walnut halves, roughly chopped

serves 4
preparation: 20 minutes
cooking time: 50 minutes
per serving: 180 cals; 13g fat;
    13g carbohydrate

1 Cut the fennel and onions into wedges and put into a large roasting tin. Drizzle with the olive oil and season well with salt and pepper. Roast at 220°C (200°C fan oven) mark 7 for 45 minutes or until soft.
2 Meanwhile, peel the oranges and cut out the segments, discarding all white pith and pips.
3 Add the orange segments and chopped walnuts to the vegetables and return to the oven for 5 minutes. Serve immediately.

Fennel Gratin

3 fennel bulbs, trimmed
300ml (½ pint) vegetable stock
25g (1oz) butter
1 garlic clove, peeled and crushed
1 bunch of spring onions, trimmed and
    finely chopped
2 tbsp chopped fennel fronds or dill
300ml (½ pint) double cream
50g (2oz) Cheddar cheese, grated
pepper

serves 6
preparation: 10 minutes
cooking time: 15–20 minutes
per serving: 310 cals; 31g fat;
    4g carbohydrate

1 Cut the fennel lengthways into 5mm (¼ inch) thick slices and put into a large shallow pan with the stock and half of the butter. Bring to the boil, lower the heat, cover and simmer for 10–15 minutes until just tender.
2 Meanwhile, melt the remaining butter in another pan, add the garlic and spring onions and fry gently for 5 minutes until softened. Stir in the chopped fennel fronds or dill.
3 Lift out the poached fennel with a slotted spoon and place in a gratin dish. Add 150ml (¼ pint) of the cooking liquid to the spring onions. Pour in the cream, bring to the boil and simmer gently for 1 minute. Take off the heat and stir in the cheese and pepper to taste.
4 Pour the sauce over the fennel and grill under a high heat for 1–2 minutes until bubbling and golden.

Creamy Kale

450g (1lb) curly kale
25g (1oz) unsalted butter
5 tbsp double cream
salt and pepper
¼ tsp freshly grated nutmeg

serves 6
preparation: 10 minutes
cooking time: 7 minutes
per serving: 100 cals; 10g fat;
    1g carbohydrate

1 Remove and discard the tough central stem from each kale leaf, then wash thoroughly; drain. Put into a large pan with a drizzle of water and simmer, covered, for 5 minutes until bright green and almost cooked. Drain off any liquid.
2 Return the kale to the pan. Add the butter and cream and heat through, stirring, for 2 minutes. Add the grated nutmeg, season generously with salt and pepper and serve.

Creamy Leeks

900g (2lb) leeks, trimmed and cut into chunks
salt and pepper
25g (1oz) butter
150ml (¼ pint) crème fraîche
freshly grated nutmeg, to taste

serves 8–10
preparation: 15 minutes, plus cooling
cooking time: 20 minutes
per serving: 120–100 cals; 11–8g fat;
    4–3g carbohydrate

1 Cook the leeks in a pan of boiling salted water for 7–10 minutes until just tender. Drain and immediately plunge into a bowl of icy cold water to refresh. When cool, drain and pat dry with kitchen paper.

2 Roughly chop the leeks in a food processor. Take out half of them and set side. Whiz the remainder until smooth.

3 Melt the butter in a frying pan, add the chopped and puréed leeks and stir over a high heat for a minute or two. Add the crème fraîche, and season with salt and pepper. Stir over a medium heat until bubbling. Sprinkle with grated nutmeg to serve.

Marrow with Coriander and Chilli

1 medium marrow, about 800g (1¾lb)
2 tbsp olive oil
4 tbsp plain flour
2–3 tsp chilli powder
2–3 tsp ground coriander
2 tsp salt
2 tbsp chopped coriander
oil, to shallow-fry

serves 4
preparation: 10 minutes
cooking time: about 10 minutes
per serving: 260 cals; 22g fat;
   15g carbohydrate

1 Cut off the ends of the marrow, peel away the skin and cut the flesh into 1cm (½ inch) thick rings. Using a small pastry cutter, stamp out and discard the central seeded core. Brush the marrow rings lightly with olive oil.

2 Combine the flour, spices, salt and chopped coriander in a shallow dish, add the marrow rings and toss to coat lightly.

3 Heat a thin film of oil in a large non-stick frying pan. Fry the marrow rings in batches over a low heat for 3–4 minutes each side until tender and golden. Drain on kitchen paper and keep warm while frying the remainder, using clean oil as necessary.

4 Serve hot, with yogurt or soured cream if you like.

Grilled Mushrooms with Herb and Garlic Butter

125g (4oz) butter, softened
2 garlic cloves, peeled and crushed
2–3 tsp each chopped chives and parsley
1 tsp grated lemon zest
salt and pepper
12 field mushrooms, trimmed
1 tbsp olive oil

serves 4–6
preparation: 10 minutes, plus chilling
cooking time: 10 minutes
per serving: 300–200 cals; 30–20g fat;
   1g carbohydrate

1 Cream the butter, garlic, herbs, lemon zest and a little salt and pepper together in a bowl. Cover and chill in the fridge for at least 30 minutes.

2 Brush the mushrooms with oil, lay gill-side down on a grill pan and grill under a high heat for 5 minutes. Meanwhile, cut the flavoured butter into pieces.

3 Turn the mushrooms gill-side up. Dot with the butter and grill for a further 4–5 minutes tender and sizzling. Serve at once, as an accompaniment to grilled meat or vegetables.

variation: *Flavour the butter with chopped basil, garlic and chopped sun-dried tomatoes.*

Spiced Okra with Onion and Tomato

450g (1lb) okra
2.5cm (1 inch) piece fresh root ginger, peeled
1 onion, peeled and quartered
2 garlic cloves, peeled and roughly chopped
2 tsp ground coriander
½ tsp each ground cinnamon and turmeric
3 tbsp oil
3 tomatoes, skinned and chopped
salt and pepper
2 tbsp thick yogurt
2 tbsp chopped coriander

serves 4
preparation: 20 minutes
cooking time: 25 minutes
per serving: 150 cals; 12g fat;
   8g carbohydrate

1 Trim the okra, removing a small piece from each end; don't cut into the flesh or the dish will acquire an unpleasant glutinous texture during cooking.

2 Roughly chop the ginger and put into a blender with the onion, garlic and 1 tbsp water. Process until smooth. Add the spices and process again.

3 Heat the oil in a large frying pan, add the spicy onion paste and stir-fry over a high heat for 2 minutes. Lower the heat and cook for 5 minutes or until the onion paste is golden brown and loses its raw aroma.

4 Add the chopped tomatoes and season with salt and pepper. Cook for 5 minutes until the tomato has reduced down, then add the okra and stir to coat in the mixture. Cover and simmer gently for 5 minutes or until the okra is just tender.

5 Stir in the yogurt, then add the chopped coriander and heat through gently. Serve straightaway.

Minted Peas with Spring Onions and Courgettes

450g (1lb) shelled fresh peas
225g (8oz) French beans, trimmed
1 bunch of spring onions, trimmed
225g (8oz) courgettes, trimmed
25g (1oz) butter
200ml carton crème fraîche
1 tsp sugar (optional)
3 tbsp roughly chopped mint leaves
salt and pepper

serves 6
preparation: 15 minutes
cooking time: 10 minutes
per serving: 240 cals; 8g fat;
    13g carbohydrate

1 Cook the peas and French beans in a pan of boiling water for 5 minutes or until tender, then drain.
2 In the meantime, thickly slice the spring onions. Cut the courgettes lengthways into wedges.
3 Heat the butter in a frying pan and sauté the spring onions and courgette wedges for 3 minutes. Add the crème fraîche and bring to a simmer. Let bubble for 2 minutes.
4 Stir in the peas, French beans, sugar if using, and chopped mint. Season with salt and pepper to taste and serve at once.

Crisp Parsnip Cakes

700g (1½lb) parsnips, peeled, cored
   and diced
salt and pepper
25g (1oz) unsalted butter
3 tbsp plain flour, plus extra to dust
several pinches of ground mace
1 large egg, beaten
100g (3½oz) fresh white breadcrumbs
1 tbsp oil

serves 6
preparation: 10 minutes, plus chilling
cooking time: 25 minutes
per serving: 190 cals; 8g fat;
   26g carbohydrate

1 Put the parsnips into a pan of cold salted water. Bring to the boil and simmer for about 10 minutes until tender. Drain well and return to the pan. Add the butter and 1 tbsp flour. Mash well, adding the mace and seasoning to taste. Leave to cool for 10 minutes.

2 Put the remaining flour on a plate. Pour the beaten egg into a shallow bowl. Scatter the breadcrumbs on to another plate. With lightly floured hands, divide the parsnip mash into six and roll into balls. Flatten slightly to form cakes.

3 Take one parsnip cake and dust with a little flour, then dip in the beaten egg and finally roll in the breadcrumbs to coat, shaking off any excess. Repeat with the remaining cakes. Chill for 15 minutes (or overnight if preparing ahead).

4 To cook, heat the oil in a large non-stick frying pan. Add the parsnip cakes and fry for 15 minutes, turning halfway through, until crisp and golden all over.

Crisp-fried Onion Rings

4 red onions, peeled
2 tsp sea salt
oil, to deep-fry
plain flour, to coat
white pepper
lemon wedges, to serve

serves 4
preparation: 10 minutes, plus standing
cooking time: 10 minutes
per serving: 230 cals; 15g fat;
   22g carbohydrate

1 Slice the onions into thin rings and separate the rings out, placing them in a large bowl. Sprinkle with the salt and leave to stand for 20 minutes.

2 Heat a 5cm (2 inch) depth of oil in a deep heavy pan until it registers 180°C on a thermometer. Season the flour with white pepper.

3 Cook the onion rings in batches. Dip into the seasoned flour to coat lightly, then deep-fry in the hot oil for 2–3 minutes until crisp and golden. Drain on kitchen paper and keep warm in a low oven while cooking the rest.

4 Season with a little extra salt and pepper if liked. Serve as soon as possible, with the lemon wedges.

Honey-glazed Shallots

450g (1lb) shallots
25g (1oz) butter
1 tbsp thin honey
juice of ½ lemon
1 tbsp Worcestershire sauce
1 tbsp balsamic vinegar
salt and pepper

serves 4
preparation: 15 minutes, plus soaking
cooking time: 25 minutes
per serving: 100 cals; 5g fat;
   14g carbohydrate

1 Put the shallots in a bowl, add cold water to cover and leave to soak for 20 minutes. Drain and peel away the skins.

2 Tip the shallots into a pan and add just enough cold water to cover. Bring to the boil, lower the heat and simmer for 5 minutes. Drain well and return the shallots to the pan.

3 Add all of the remaining ingredients and stir until the shallots are well coated with the glaze. Cover and cook gently, stirring occasionally, until the shallots are tender. Remove the lid and bubble for 2–3 minutes until the liquid is reduced and syrupy. Serve hot.

Peperonata

4 red peppers
3 orange peppers
1 green pepper
100ml (3½fl oz) olive oil
2 garlic cloves, peeled and crushed
salt and pepper
2 tbsp capers in brine, rinsed
18 black olives
1 tbsp chopped flat-leafed parsley

serves 6–8
preparation: 15 minutes
cooking time: about 45 minutes
per serving: 130–180 cals; 12–16g fat;
   6–7g carbohydrate

1 Halve the peppers, remove the core and seeds, then slice lengthways. Heat the oil in a large pan, add the garlic and stir-fry over a medium heat for 1 minute.
2 Add the peppers, season well and toss to coat in the oil. Cover the pan with a lid and continue to cook over a low heat for 40 minutes.
3 Add the capers, olives and chopped parsley and stir to mix. Either serve straightaway or cool and chill until required.
4 Serve the peperonata warm or cold, with warm crusty bread.

note: *This Italian sweet pepper stew is best made 2–3 days ahead to allow time for the flavours to develop. Cover and chill, but bring to room temperature to serve.*

Jersey Royals with Mint and Petits Pois

3 tbsp olive oil
900g (2lb) Jersey Royals, scrubbed and
   thickly sliced
175g (6oz) frozen petits pois
3 tbsp chopped mint
salt and pepper

serves 6
preparation: 15 minutes
cooking time: 30 minutes
per serving: 180 cals; 7g fat;
   27g carbohydrate

1 Heat half the olive oil in a large non-stick frying pan, add half of the potatoes and cook for 5 minutes, turning, until browned on both sides. Remove with a slotted spoon and set aside. Add the remaining oil to the pan, then brown the rest of the potatoes in the same way.
2 Return all the potatoes to the pan and cook, partially covered, for a further 10–15 minutes.
3 Meanwhile, cook the petits pois in a pan of boiling water for 2 minutes, then drain well. Add them to the potatoes and cook through for 2–3 minutes.
4 Add the chopped mint, and salt and pepper to taste, then serve.

Pan-fried New Potatoes with Parmesan

700g (1½lb) small new potatoes
salt and pepper
3 tbsp olive oil
50g (2oz) Parmesan cheese, freshly grated

serves 4
preparation: 5 minutes
cooking time: 20 minutes
per serving: 270 cals; 14g fat;
   28g carbohydrate

1 Put the new potatoes into a pan, add cold salted water to cover and bring to the boil. Simmer for about 12 minutes until just tender.
2 Heat the olive oil in a large frying pan, add the new potatoes and cook, tossing occasionally, for 5 minutes. Stir in the grated Parmesan and cook for a further 2 minutes. Season with pepper to taste and serve straightaway.

Potato Croquettes

1kg (2¼lb) Desirée potatoes, scrubbed

salt and pepper

150g (5oz) fresh white breadcrumbs

50g (2oz) butter, softened, plus extra
   to grease

100g (3½oz) Parmesan cheese,
   freshly grated

2 tbsp chopped flat-leafed parsley

freshly grated nutmeg, to taste

2 medium eggs, beaten

olive oil, to drizzle

serves 6

preparation: 30 minutes, plus chilling

cooking time: 45 minutes

per serving: 370 cals; 17g fat;
   41g carbohydrate

1 Put the potatoes into a pan of cold salted water. Bring to the boil and simmer for about 20 minutes until tender.

2 Meanwhile, spread the breadcrumbs on a baking sheet and bake at 230°C (210°C fan oven) mark 8 for 15 minutes or until golden. Tip on to a plate.

3 Drain the potatoes well, leave to cool for 5 minutes then peel. Use a potato ricer or masher to mash them smoothly. Add the butter, grated Parmesan and parsley. Season well with nutmeg, salt and pepper, and mix thoroughly.

4 Put the beaten eggs into a shallow bowl. Take about 2 tbsp of the potato mixture and shape into a small sausage. Roll the croquette first in the beaten egg and then in the breadcrumbs to coat. Put into a greased roasting tin.

5 Repeat to use up all the potato mixture – you'll need two roasting tins. Cover with clingfilm and chill for 30 minutes.

6 Uncover the croquettes, drizzle with a little olive oil and bake for 25 minutes or until golden. Serve at once.

note: *Using a potato ricer gives a lovely fluffy texture – make sure the potatoes are still hot when you begin to mash them.*

Potato Gratin

450ml (¾ pint) milk

150ml (¼ pint) double cream

2 bay leaves, bruised

2 strips of lemon zest, bruised

pinch of saffron strands

900g (2lb) even-sized, small waxy potatoes

1 small onion, peeled and grated

2 garlic cloves, peeled and finely chopped

25g (1oz) butter, diced

salt and pepper

serves 4–6

preparation: 15–20 minutes

cooking time: 1¼ hours

per serving: 450–300 cals; 25–17g fat;
   49–33g carbohydrate

1 Put the milk, cream, bay leaves and lemon zest into a pan. Bring slowly to the boil, then remove from the heat, add the saffron and set aside to infuse for 10 minutes.

2 In the meantime, peel the potatoes, then cut into even, thin slices, preferably using a mandolin or food processor fitted with a fine slicing blade.

3 Arrange a layer of potato slices over the base of a 1.5 litre (2½ pint) gratin dish. Scatter over some of the onion, garlic and butter; season generously with salt and pepper. Repeat the layers, finishing with potatoes and a few pieces of butter.

4 Strain the infused cream over the potatoes, pressing the herbs and lemon to extract as much flavour as possible. Cover the dish with foil, put on a baking sheet and bake at 200°C (180°C fan oven) mark 6 for 1 hour.

5 Remove the foil and bake for a further 15–20 minutes until the potatoes are softened and golden brown on top.

Oven Chips

900g (2lb) Desirée potatoes
salt
2–3 tbsp olive oil
sea salt flakes

serves 4
preparation: 10 minutes
cooking time: 40 minutes
per serving: 220 cals; 6g fat;
39g carbohydrate

1 Peel the potatoes and cut into chips. Add to a pan of boiling salted water, cover and bring to the boil, then boil for 2 minutes. Drain well, then pat dry with kitchen paper.

2 Now tip the par-boiled potatoes into a large non-stick roasting tin, toss with the olive oil and season with sea salt. Roast at 240°C (220°C fan oven) mark 9 for 40 minutes or until golden and cooked, turning from time to time. Drain on kitchen paper and serve.

Spiced Potatoes and Spinach

900g (2lb) potatoes
2–3 tbsp oil
1 onion, peeled and finely sliced
2 garlic cloves, peeled and finely chopped
1 tbsp black mustard seeds
2 tsp ground turmeric
1 tsp salt
4 handfuls of baby spinach leaves

serves 4
preparation: 15 minutes
cooking time: 55 minutes
per serving: 260 cals; 9g fat;
43g carbohydrate

1 Peel the potatoes and cut them into 4cm (1½ inch) chunks. Heat the oil in a large pan, add the onion and fry over a medium heat for 10 minutes until soft and golden.

2 Add the garlic, mustard seeds and turmeric and cook for a further 1 minute.

3 Add the potatoes, salt and 150ml (¼ pint) water. Cover and bring to the boil, then lower the heat and cook gently for 35–40 minutes or until tender.

4 Add the spinach and cook until the leaves just wilt. Serve immediately, as an accompaniment to tandoori chicken (page 137) or a curry.

Rösti Potatoes

4 medium potatoes, such as Desirée,
    about 1kg (2¼lb) in total, scrubbed
salt and pepper
50g (2oz) butter, melted, plus extra
    to grease
4 slices Emmental cheese

serves 4
preparation: 20 minutes, plus cooling
cooking time: 40 minutes
per serving: 380 cals; 18g fat;
43g carbohydrate

1 Put the potatoes into a large pan of cold salted water, cover and bring to the boil. Cook for 5–8 minutes, then drain, transfer to a bowl and leave to cool for 10 minutes.

2 Peel the potatoes, then grate coarsely into long strands by rubbing each one lengthways along a coarse grater. Divide into four.

3 Shape each portion into a mound and put well apart on one or two large greased baking trays. Drizzle the melted butter over each mound, season generously and roast at 220°C (200°C fan oven) mark 7 for about 30 minutes until golden.

4 Put a slice of cheese on each rösti and return to the oven for 10 minutes or until golden and bubbling. Serve immediately.

Mustard Roast Potatoes and Parsnips

1.5kg (3¼lb) small even-sized potatoes
800g (1¾lb) small parsnips
salt
50g (2oz) goose fat
1–2 tbsp black mustard seeds
2–3 tsp sea salt flakes

serves 8
preparation: 25 minutes
cooking time: about 1 hour
per serving: 220 cals; 5g fat;
   41g carbohydrate

1 Peel the potatoes and parsnips and cut out a small wedge from one side (this will help make them extra crispy). Put them into a pan of cold salted water, bring to the boil and cook for 6 minutes. Drain thoroughly.

2 Heat the goose fat in a roasting tin at 200°C (180°C fan oven) mark 6 for 4 minutes until sizzling hot. Add the potatoes, toss in the hot melted fat and roast for 30 minutes.

3 Add the parsnips and sprinkle over the mustard seeds and sea salt. Roast for a further 30–35 minutes or until golden, turning halfway. Serve at once.

note: *For convenience, par-boil the potatoes and parsnips ahead, spread out on a baking tray and freeze, then bake from frozen in goose fat, allowing an extra 15–20 minutes.*

Saffron Roast Potatoes

1.5kg (3¼lb) Desirée potatoes
salt
2 large pinches of saffron strands
4 tbsp goose fat
2 tbsp coarse sea salt

serves 8
preparation: 15 minutes
cooking time: 1 hour
per serving: 140 cals; 5g fat;
   22g carbohydrate

1 Peel the potatoes and shape roughly into 7.5cm (3 inch) ovals. Put into a pan of cold salted water, add the saffron and bring to the boil. Cover and boil for 6 minutes, then drain and shake in a colander to roughen the surface.

2 Heat the goose fat in a roasting tin at 200°C (180°C fan oven) mark 6 for 4 minutes until sizzling. Add the potatoes, sprinkle with the sea salt and roast for about 1 hour until golden, shaking the pan after half an hour. Serve straightaway.

Baked Jacket Potatoes

6 large baking potatoes, each about
   275g (10oz)
salt and pepper
50–75g (2–3oz) butter

serves 6
preparation: 5 minutes
cooking time: about 1½ hours
per serving: 280 cals; 9g fat;
   47g carbohydrate

1 Scrub the potatoes and prick all over with a fork. Put them on a baking sheet and bake at 200°C (180°C fan oven) mark 6 for about 1½ hours or until the potatoes feel soft when gently squeezed, turning them over once.

2 When the potatoes are cooked, score a deep cross on each one, season with salt and pepper and top with a generous knob of butter to serve.

variations: *Top the jacket potatoes with grated cheese, or crème fraîche and chopped chives, or soured cream and chopped spring onions.*

Colcannon

900g (2lb) potatoes, cut into even-sized
   chunks
salt and pepper
50g (2oz) butter
¼ Savoy cabbage, shredded
100ml (3½fl oz) semi-skimmed milk

serves 4
preparation: 10 minutes
cooking time: 20 minutes
per serving: 310 cals; 12g fat;
   45g carbohydrate

1 Put the potatoes into a pan of cold salted water. Bring to the boil, then lower the heat and simmer, partially covered, for 15–20 minutes or until the potatoes are tender.

2 Meanwhile, melt the butter in a large frying pan. Add the cabbage and stir-fry for 3 minutes.

3 Drain the potatoes well, then tip back into the pan and put over a medium heat for 1 minute to drive off excess moisture. Turn into a colander and cover to keep warm.

4 Pour the milk into the potato pan and bring to the boil, then take off the heat. Add the potatoes and mash well until smooth.

5 Add the cabbage and any butter from the pan and mix together. Season with salt and pepper to taste and serve immediately.

Bubble and Squeak

1 tbsp oil
1 red onion, peeled and thinly sliced
4 streaky bacon rashers, derinded and cut
   into small pieces
550g (1¼lb) cooked mashed potatoes
300g (11oz) cooked Brussels sprouts, cut in
   half if large
salt and pepper
25g (1oz) Parmesan cheese, freshly grated
melted butter, to brush and grease

serves 6
preparation: 10 minutes
cooking time: 35 minutes
per serving: 220 cals; 12g fat;
   19g carbohydrate

1 Heat the oil in a large pan, add the onion and cook for 5 minutes or until softened. Add the bacon and cook for a further 3–4 minutes until it begins to brown. Transfer to a large bowl.

2 Add the mashed potatoes and cooked Brussels sprouts, and season generously with salt and pepper. Add the grated Parmesan and mix well.

3 Divide the mixture into six and shape each portion into a cake, using your hands. Put on to a greased baking tray and brush with a little melted butter. Bake at 200°C (180°C fan oven) mark 6 for 25 minutes until lightly golden. Serve hot.

Creamed Spinach

900g (2lb) spinach leaves, stalks removed
4 tbsp crème fraîche
salt and pepper

serves 6
preparation: 15 minutes
cooking time: 5 minutes
per serving: 80 cals; 5g fat;
   3g carbohydrate

1 Cook the spinach with just the water clinging to the leaves after washing in a covered pan for 3–4 minutes or until just wilted.

2 Stir in the crème fraîche and season with salt and pepper to taste. Serve at once.

Sweetcorn on-the-cob with Chilli Lime Butter

4 corn-on-the-cobs

CHILLI LIME BUTTER
125g (4oz) unsalted butter, slightly softened
1 tbsp sweet chilli sauce
2 tbsp lime juice
salt and pepper

serves 4
preparation: 15 minutes, plus chilling
cooking time: 6–8 minutes
per serving: 360 cals; 28g fat;
    23g carbohydrate

1 First prepare the chilli lime butter. In a bowl, mix the butter with the chilli sauce and lime juice, then season with salt and pepper. Put on a piece of clingfilm, roll into a log, wrap well and chill to firm up.

2 Strip the outer husks from the corn cobs and trim the bases. Bring a large pan of water to the boil, add the corn cobs and cook for 6–8 minutes until tender. (Don't add salt to the cooking water, or it will toughen the corn.)

3 Drain the corn cobs and serve, topped with slices of chilli lime butter.

Sesame-fried Swede

900g (2lb) swede
1 tbsp sunflower oil
1 tsp sesame oil
1 garlic clove, peeled and crushed
2 tsp grated fresh root ginger
1 red chilli, deseeded and finely chopped
4 ripe tomatoes, deseeded and diced
2 tbsp dark soy sauce
pinch of sugar
salt and pepper
1 tbsp sesame seeds, toasted
coriander leaves, roughly torn, to serve

serves 4
preparation: 15 minutes
cooking time: 20 minutes
per serving: 110 cals; 7g fat;
    9g carbohydrate

1 Cut the swede into 2.5cm (1 inch) cubes. Heat the sunflower and sesame oils in a frying pan. Add the swede and stir-fry for 5 minutes until beginning to brown on all sides.

2 Add the garlic, ginger and chilli and fry gently for a further 5 minutes.

3 Add the diced tomatoes, soy sauce, sugar and 2 tbsp water. Cover and cook for 10 minutes until the swede is tender. Season with salt and pepper to taste.

4 Sprinkle with the toasted sesame seeds and scatter over the coriander leaves to serve.

variation: *Sprinkle with chopped toasted almonds instead of sesame seeds.*

Roasted Sweet Potatoes with Sage

5 sweet potatoes, about 1.1kg (2½lb)
    in total, peeled
2 tbsp chopped sage
2 tsp yellow mustard seeds
3–4 tbsp olive oil
salt and pepper

serves 8
preparation: 10 minutes
cooking time: 50 minutes–1 hour
per serving: 140 cals; 4g fat;
    27g carbohydrate

1 Cut the sweet potatoes into wedges and put into a large roasting tin. Add the chopped sage, mustard seeds and olive oil, and season well with salt and pepper. Toss well to coat the sweet potatoes with the oil and flavourings.

2 Roast at 200°C (180°C fan oven) mark 6 for 50 minutes to 1 hour until golden and tender, turning twice during cooking.

Glazed Turnips

1kg (2¼lb) turnips, peeled
40g (1½oz) butter
2 tbsp golden caster sugar
300ml (½ pint) chicken stock

serves 6
preparation: 10 minutes
cooking time: 25 minutes
per serving: 100 cals; 6g fat;
  12g carbohydrate

1 Cut the turnips into wedges and put into a large pan with the butter, sugar and stock. Bring to the boil and simmer, covered, for 20 minutes or until the turnips are tender.
2 Remove the lid and cook for a further 5 minutes or until the liquid is reduced and the turnips are glazed. Serve straightaway.

Slow-roasted Tomatoes

12 large ripe tomatoes
2 garlic cloves, peeled and roughly chopped
2 thyme sprigs, bruised
pinch of sugar
salt and pepper
4 tbsp extra-virgin olive oil
squeeze of lemon juice
basil leaves, to garnish

serves 4
preparation: 10 minutes
cooking time: 2½–3 hours
per serving: 170 cals; 14g fat;
  9g carbohydrate

1 Halve the tomatoes and scoop out most of the seeds. Put the tomato halves into a baking dish in which they fit closely together and scatter over the garlic, thyme, sugar, salt and pepper.
2 Drizzle the olive oil over the tomatoes and add a good squeeze of lemon juice. Roast at 150°C (130°C fan oven) mark 2 for 2½–3 hours until the tomatoes are shrivelled (but not as dried as sun-dried tomatoes). Allow to cool.
3 Scatter basil leaves over the tomatoes and serve, as an accompaniment to cold meats and cheese.

Summer Vegetable Stir-fry

125g (4oz) baby carrots, trimmed
salt and pepper
125g (4oz) baby courgettes, trimmed
2 tbsp sunflower oil
2 garlic cloves, peeled and roughly chopped
1 large yellow pepper, halved, cored,
  deseeded and cut into broad strips
125g (4oz) patty pans (optional), halved
125g (4oz) thin asparagus spears, trimmed
125g (4oz) cherry tomatoes, halved
2 tbsp balsamic or sherry vinegar
1 tsp sesame oil
1 tbsp sesame seeds, toasted

serves 4–6
preparation: 15 minutes
cooking time: 7–8 minutes
per serving: 130–80 cals; 10–7g fat;
  6–4g carbohydrate

1 Blanch the baby carrots in boiling salted water for 2 minutes; drain and pat dry. Halve the courgettes lengthways.
2 Heat the sunflower oil in a preheated wok or deep frying pan until smoking. Add the chopped garlic and stir-fry for 20 seconds. Add the carrots, courgettes, yellow pepper, patty pans if using, and asparagus. Stir-fry over a high heat for 1 minute.
3 Add the cherry tomatoes and season with salt and pepper to taste. Stir-fry for 3–4 minutes until the vegetables are just tender. Add the balsamic vinegar and sesame oil, toss well and sprinkle with the sesame seeds. Serve immediately.

note: *Vary the vegetables as you like, but always blanch the harder ones first. For a winter vegetable stir-fry, use cauliflower and broccoli florets, carrot sticks, 2–3 spring onions, sliced, and a little chopped fresh root ginger.*

Ratatouille

4 tbsp olive oil

2 onions, peeled and thinly sliced

1 large garlic clove, peeled and crushed

350g (12oz) small aubergine, trimmed and
thinly sliced

450g (1lb) small courgettes, trimmed and
thinly sliced

450g (1lb) tomatoes, skinned, deseeded and
roughly chopped

1 green pepper, cored, deseeded and sliced

1 red pepper, cored, deseeded and sliced

1 tbsp chopped basil

2 tsp chopped thyme

2 tbsp chopped parsley

2 tbsp sun-dried tomato paste

salt and pepper

serves 4–6

preparation: 20 minutes

cooking time: about 45 minutes

per serving: 220–150 cals; 15–10g fat;
18–12g carbohydrate

1 Heat the olive oil in a large pan, add the onions and garlic and fry gently for 10 minutes or until softened and golden.

2 Add the aubergine, courgettes, tomatoes, peppers, herbs, tomato paste and seasoning. Fry, stirring, for 2–3 minutes.

3 Cover the pan tightly and simmer for 30 minutes or until all the vegetables are just tender. If necessary, uncover towards the end of the cooking time to evaporate some of the liquid.

4 Taste and adjust the seasoning. Serve the ratatouille hot or cold.

Roasted Root Vegetables

350g (12oz) carrots, peeled

350g (12oz) parsnips, peeled

350g (12oz) celeriac, peeled

350g (12oz) sweet potato, peeled

150ml (¼ pint) olive oil

4 cardamom pods, lightly crushed

1 tbsp muscovado sugar

coarse sea salt and pepper

serves 6–8

preparation: 20 minutes

cooking time: about 1 hour

per serving: 300–230 cals; 23–17g fat;
23–17g carbohydrate

1 Quarter the carrots and parsnips lengthways. Cut the celeriac and sweet potato into chunks.

2 Heat the olive oil in a roasting tin, add the vegetables and toss well. Roast at 200°C (180°C fan oven) mark 6 for 30 minutes, turning the vegetables twice during cooking.

3 Sprinkle the cardamom pods and sugar over the vegetables and turn them to coat evenly. Bake for a further 30 minutes until well browned and completely soft, but not disintegrating.

4 Season liberally with coarse sea salt and pepper, then serve.

SALADS

Endlessly versatile, quick and easy to prepare, and mouthwatering, salads may be served as starters, accompaniments, main courses, snacks, lunches or light suppers. A side salad needs to be carefully composed so that the colours, flavours and textures complement the main dish and don't overpower it. Substantial salads – served with some good bread – are excellent, healthy main dishes, especially in the summer. A satisfying complete meal salad is generally based around one or two high-protein foods with complementary flavouring ingredients, which offer a contrast in texture as well as taste. A tempting salad, served in moderate portions, is an ideal starter to stimulate the taste buds without taking the edge off the appetite. Warm salads, which are either tossed in a warm dressing or feature warm ingredients, are perfect starters.

SALAD LEAVES
The wonderful array of lettuces and other salad leaves on sale in most supermarkets, quality greengrocers and markets is inspiring. There are soft delicate leaves, such as the the familiar round lettuce, lamb's lettuce (also known as corn salad and mâche), russet-coloured oak leaf and frilly-leafed lollo rosso. Crisper lettuces include cos, iceberg and little gem or, for a crunchy texture, buy Chinese leaves. In addition, there are deliciously bitter leaves such as dark red radicchio, peppery rocket, crisp chicory, watercress, frisée (curly endive) and tender baby spinach.

Ready-prepared bags of mixed salad leaves are widely available and a convenient way of buying salad leaves if you want a selection but only require a small quantity. Leaf salads are simple, refreshing and easily enhanced by the addition of fresh herbs or edible flowers.

When you are choosing salad plants, look for fresh, crisp leaves and a tightly packed head if appropriate. Avoid any with wilted or bruised leaves. Store loosely wrapped in the salad drawer of the fridge.

To prepare, pull off and discard any coarse or damaged outer leaves, then divide the salad plant if appropriate. Wash the leaves thoroughly in cold water. Drain and dry well, using a clean tea-towel or a salad spinner.

OTHER SALAD VEGETABLES
Beetroot, carrots, celery, courgettes, cucumber, fennel, mushrooms, peppers, radishes and salad onions are just a few of the many vegetables which are eaten raw in salads. Beans and peas, such as broad beans, French beans and mangetout, are best blanched and refreshed first. Tomatoes and avocados are synonymous with salads, but they must be at their peak of ripeness and flavourful for optimum results. New potatoes are excellent in salads, especially if they are combined with the dressing while still warm.

SALAD HERBS
Fresh herbs will enhance most salads and it is well worth growing your own supply in the garden or in tubs or windowboxes. The flowers from herbs such as borage, chives, fennel and thyme can also be added to salads. Not all herbs are good in raw salads, but most work well.

Basil is almost indispensable in tomato salads; it complements leafy salads too. Chervil, chives and flat-leafed parsley will flatter most salads. Coriander is excellent with robust green leaves, bulgur wheat and couscous. Dill and fennel are particularly good in fish salads, while mint combines well with oranges and peas.

Oregano is a classic ingredient in traditional Greek salad and, like marjoram and thyme, it works well in cooked salads too. Strongly flavoured tarragon is great with chicken salads; it also enhances creamy salad dressings, particularly those containing mustard.

SALAD DRESSINGS

A salad is rarely complete without a dressing. Whether it's a piquant vinaigrette, a creamy mayonnaise or simply a squeeze of lemon or lime juice, it is invariably the dressing that pulls all the ingredients together.

There are two main types of salad dressings: oil and vinegar or citrus dressings, and creamy dressings, which are usually mayonnaise-based. The proportion of oil to vinegar in the former is largely a matter of personal taste. In general, about 6 parts oil to 1 part vinegar works best, but you may prefer a more acidic dressing, perhaps 4 parts oil to 1 part vinegar.

Oils and vinegars form the basis of most salad dressings. For best results, use the correct oil, and/or vinegar, for the particular dressing.

Olive Oil

Olive oil comes in a range of flavours and styles, from zingy, pungent extra-virgin to light, mild olive oil. Extra-virgin olive oil – cold pressed and from a single estate – is the premium type. A good extra-virgin olive oil can be used with great effect in salads. It is particularly good drizzled liberally over raw vegetables, tomatoes or salad leaves, with just a little lemon juice or balsamic vinegar. Light or mild olive oil is the best choice for making mayonnaise, where extra-virgin oil would be too overpowering.

Nut Oils

These are excellent in salads. Ranging from mild to strong, these include groundnut or peanut, hazelnut, walnut, almond and sesame oils. Sesame oil is used in very small amounts, often blended with groundnut or even vegetable oil. Nut oils combine particularly well with fruit-flavoured vinegars and sherry vinegar.

Flavoured Oils

These add character to salad dressings. You can buy ready-made flavoured oils or make your own. Try the following simple ideas:

Herb oil is easy to make. Simply take 4 sprigs of fresh rosemary or thyme and tap lightly with a rolling pin to release the flavour. Put them into a jug, add 600ml (1 pint) extra-virgin olive oil, cover and leave to infuse in a cool place for several days. Strain into a clean bottle and use as required.

Fresh herb oil needs to be used within a day. To make this, put 15g (½oz) mixed chopped fresh herbs – such as basil, chervil, chives and parsley – in a bowl, pour on 150ml (¼ pint) extra-virgin olive oil and set aside to infuse for 2–3 hours.

Chilli and garlic oil will spike up a salad. To prepare, put the peeled cloves from a whole head of garlic into a small pan with 300ml (½ pint) mild olive oil and 1 small red chilli, deseeded and very finely chopped. Heat gently for 5–6 minutes until the garlic is golden. Cool, then strain the oil into a clean bottle. Use as required.

Balsamic Vinegar

Dark and aromatic, this Italian vinegar has an exquisite mellow, sweet/sour flavour and lends a good depth and character to salad dressings. Traditionally matured in oak casks for anything between 5–20 years, balsamic vinegar is expensive, but a little goes a long way – a few drops can transform a salad.

Wine Vinegar

This is the strongest natural vinegar with an average acidity of 6.5% and no preservatives. Special varieties include pale yellow Champagne vinegar, Rioja red wine vinegar with a deep mellow flavour, and full-bodied, nutty brown sherry vinegar.

Cider Vinegar

This is milder than wine vinegar and works well in salad dressings where a subtle acidity is required.

Flavoured Vinegar

Like oils, wine vinegars can be flavoured with aromatic herbs, fruits, spices, and even flower petals. It is worth noting that the better wine vinegars, such as Champagne and sherry vinegars, need nothing to enhance their natural flavours. Of the fruit vinegars, raspberry vinegar is the most popular and is available from most good supermarkets. Strawberry, blackberry and peach vinegars are also obtainable.

To make your own herb vinegar, immerse a few herb sprigs, such as rosemary or thyme, in a bottle of good quality red or white wine vinegar, or cider vinegar. Leave in a cool, dark place to infuse for 2–3 weeks. Strain and re-bottle, adding a fresh herb sprig if desired.

Mayonnaise

2 egg yolks
2 tsp lemon juice or white wine vinegar
1 tsp Dijon mustard
salt and pepper
pinch of sugar
300ml (½ pint) light olive oil

makes 300ml (½ pint)
preparation: 10 minutes
per 15ml (1 tbsp): 110 cals; 12g fat;
    trace carbohydrate

1 Put all the ingredients except the oil into a food processor and blend briefly until pale and creamy.
2 With the blade motor running, pour in the olive oil through the feeder tube, in a steady stream, until the mayonnaise is thick. Thin to the required consistency, if necessary, with a little hot water.
3 Store the mayonnaise in a screw-topped jar in the fridge for up to 3 days.

notes
• The ingredients must be at room temperature. If eggs are used straight from the fridge the mayonnaise is liable to curdle.
• To make mayonnaise by hand, mix the egg yolks, mustard, sugar and seasoning in a bowl, then whisk in the oil, drop by drop to begin with, then in a slow, steady stream. Finally add the vinegar or lemon juice.

variations
herb mayonnaise: *Fold in 2 tbsp chopped herbs, such as chives, chervil, basil, tarragon or coriander.*
lemon mayonnaise: *Use lemon juice. Add 1 tsp grated lemon zest and an extra 1 tbsp lemon juice at the end.*
aïoli: *Put 4 crushed garlic cloves into the processor with 2 egg yolks, 1 tbsp lemon juice and ½ tsp salt; process as in stage 1, until evenly combined. Add 300ml (½ pint) light olive oil, as in stage 2.*
garlic and basil mayonnaise: *Add 1 crushed garlic clove at stage 1. Fold 2 tbsp shredded basil into the mayonnaise at the end.*
thousand island dressing: *Add 2 tsp tomato purée, 2 tbsp chopped stuffed olives, 2 tsp finely chopped onion, 1 chopped hard-boiled egg and 1 tbsp chopped parsley to the finished mayonnaise.*
tartare sauce: *Add 2 tsp chopped tarragon or chives, 4 tsp each chopped capers, gherkins and parsley, and 2 tbsp lemon juice to the prepared mayonnaise.*
blue cheese dressing: *Put 50g (2oz) diced Gorgonzola cheese into a food processor with 2 tbsp milk, 1 tbsp white wine vinegar, a little pepper and 6 tbsp olive oil. Whiz until smooth.*

French Dressing

1 tsp Dijon mustard
pinch of sugar
1 tbsp white or red wine vinegar
salt and pepper
90ml (6 tbsp) extra-virgin olive oil

makes 100ml (3½fl oz)
preparation: 10 minutes
per 15ml (1 tbsp): 110 cals; 11g fat;
    trace carbohydrate

1 Whisk the mustard, sugar, vinegar and seasoning together in a bowl, then gradually whisk in the olive oil until the dressing is amalgamated and thickened.

note: *Alternatively, put all the ingredients in a screw-topped jar and shake well to combine.*

variations
herb dressing: *Use ½ tsp mustard. Replace the vinegar with lemon juice and add 2 tbsp chopped mixed herbs, such as parsley, chervil and chives.*
balsamic dressing: *Omit the mustard and sugar. Use balsamic vinegar instead of wine vinegar.*
garlic dressing: *Whisk 1 crushed garlic clove into the dressing at stage 1.*
honey and lemon dressing: *Use lemon juice instead of vinegar, 1 tsp thin honey in place of the sugar, and wholegrain rather than Dijon mustard.*

Mixed Leaf Salad

1 small frisée
1 radicchio
70g bag lamb's lettuce
1 fennel bulb, trimmed

DRESSING
4 tbsp extra-virgin olive oil
2 tbsp white wine vinegar
1 tbsp Dijon mustard
salt and pepper

serves 6
preparation: 10 minutes
per serving: 90 cals, 9g fat; 1g carbohydrate

1 First make the dressing. Put the olive oil, wine vinegar and Dijon mustard into a screw-topped jar and season generously with salt and pepper. Shake well to combine.
2 Divide the frisée and radicchio into leaves. Wash and dry thoroughly and combine with the lamb's lettuce in a shallow serving bowl. Finely slice the fennel and add to the leaves. Toss to mix.
3 Drizzle the dressing over the salad and serve.

note: *Vary the salad leaves according to taste and availability. Try using treviso or red chicory in place of radicchio or baby spinach leaves instead of frisée.*

Courgette and Lemon Salad

900g (2lb) courgettes (see note)
grated zest and juice of 1 lemon
small handful of oregano leaves
1 large garlic clove, peeled and crushed
4 tbsp extra-virgin olive oil
salt and pepper

serves 6
preparation: 10 minutes, plus marinating
per serving: 110 cals; 9g fat;
   3g carbohydrate

1 Trim and thinly slice the courgettes. Put them into a large serving bowl.
2 Add the lemon zest and juice, oregano, garlic and olive oil. Season generously with salt and pepper. Cover and leave to marinate in the fridge for about 3 hours.
3 Toss the salad lightly, then taste and adjust the seasoning before serving.

note: *If available, use a combination of yellow and green courgettes.*

French Bean, Rocket and Pistachio Salad

200g (7oz) fine French beans, trimmed
salt
110g bag continental salad leaves
100g bag rocket leaves
2 x 250g punnets baby plum tomatoes, halved
25g (1oz) shelled pistachio nuts, roughly chopped

DRESSING
3 tbsp extra-virgin olive oil
3 tbsp balsamic vinegar
salt and pepper

serves 8
preparation: 5 minutes
cooking time: 4 minutes
per serving: 80 cals, 7g fat; 3g carbohydrate

1 Bring a pan of salted water to the boil, add the beans and cook for 3–4 minutes until just tender but still crisp. Drain and refresh under cold running water, then drain again and set aside.
2 For the dressing, whisk together the olive oil, balsamic vinegar and a little seasoning.
3 Tip the continental salad and rocket leaves into a bowl and toss together, then add the beans and tomatoes. Drizzle with the balsamic dressing, then scatter the pistachios over the salad and serve.

Broad Bean and Pancetta Salad

250g (9oz) podded broad beans
1 tbsp olive oil
1 shallot, peeled and finely chopped
125g (4oz) pancetta cubes
50g (2oz) rocket leaves
1 tbsp chopped mint
2 tbsp extra-virgin olive oil
juice of ½ lemon
salt and pepper

serves 4
preparation: 15 minutes
cooking time: 6 minutes
per serving: 2 cals, 23g fat; 6g carbohydrate

1 Add the broad beans to a pan of boiling water and cook for 2–3 minutes. Drain and refresh in cold water, then slip off the skins.
2 Heat the olive oil in a pan, add the shallot and pancetta, and stir-fry for 2–3 minutes or until golden. Tip into a bowl and add the broad beans. Toss to mix.
3 Add the rocket, chopped mint, extra-virgin olive oil and lemon juice. Season well with salt and pepper and toss all the ingredients together.

note: *For this quantity of broad beans, you will need to buy around 750g (1½lb) beans in pods. Choose small pods, as the beans will be young and will have a better flavour than bigger, older beans.*

Tomato and Onion Salad

500g (1lb 2oz) baby plum tomatoes, halved

1 bunch of spring onions, sliced

500g (1lb 2oz) plum tomatoes, sliced
   lengthways

handful of basil leaves, roughly torn, plus
   sprigs to garnish

2 beef tomatoes, about 450g (1lb) in total,
   sliced

100g (3½oz) pine nuts, toasted

250g (9oz) medium tomatoes, cut into
   wedges

salt and pepper

DRESSING

100ml (3½fl oz) extra-virgin olive oil

50ml (2fl oz) balsamic vinegar

pinch of golden caster sugar

serves 4
preparation: 15 minutes, plus standing
per serving: 450 cals, 40g fat;
   16g carbohydrate

1 First make the dressing. Put the olive oil, balsamic vinegar and sugar into a screw-topped jar, then season generously with salt and pepper. Shake well to combine.

2 Layer the baby plum tomatoes, spring onions, plum tomatoes, basil, beef tomatoes, pine nuts and finally the medium tomatoes in a shallow serving bowl, seasoning each layer with salt and pepper.

3 Drizzle the dressing over the salad and set aside to allow the flavours to mingle for 1 hour. Garnish with basil sprigs to serve.

variation: *For a simple tomato and basil salad, omit the spring onions and pine nuts, and reduce the quantity of dressing by one third.*

Warm Oyster Mushroom and Spinach Salad

4 slices focaccia bread, cut into cubes

225g (8oz) streaky bacon rashers, derinded
   and cut into short, thin strips

3 tbsp walnut oil

350g (12oz) oyster mushrooms

25g (1oz) walnut pieces

salt and pepper

450g (1lb) baby spinach leaves, washed
   and dried

DRESSING

2 tbsp balsamic vinegar

1 tsp Dijon mustard

3 tbsp sunflower oil

3 tbsp walnut oil

serves 4
preparation: 20 minutes
cooking time: 8 minutes
per serving: 840 cals, 71g fat;
   25g carbohydrate

1 Scatter the focaccia cubes on a baking sheet and bake at 200°C (180°C fan oven) mark 6 for 6–8 minutes or until lightly toasted.

2 To make the dressing, whisk the balsamic vinegar and mustard together in a small bowl with salt and pepper until combined, then whisk in the sunflower and walnut oils. Put to one side.

3 Cook the bacon strips in a non-stick frying pan for 2–3 minutes. Add the walnut oil and heat, then add the oyster mushrooms. Stir-fry over a brisk heat for 2–3 minutes or until the mushrooms are soft and the bacon is brown and crisp. Take the pan off the heat, stir in the walnut pieces and season to taste with salt and pepper.

4 Put the spinach leaves into a large bowl, add the bacon and mushrooms and toss together with the balsamic dressing. Pile into a serving dish and sprinkle with the focaccia croûtes. Serve immediately, as a starter or accompaniment.

Sweet and Sour Cucumber Salad

1 cucumber
½ onion, peeled and thinly sliced into rings
2 tbsp golden caster sugar
1 tsp salt
2 tbsp white wine vinegar
1–2 tbsp chopped dill or mint, plus sprigs
    to garnish

serves 4
preparation: 15 minutes, plus chilling
per serving: 40 cals, trace fat;
    10g carbohydrate

1 Peel the cucumber, halve lengthways and remove the seeds, then slice thinly. Place the cucumber slices between sheets of kitchen paper to absorb excess moisture and chill for 30 minutes.

2 Place the drained cucumber slices in a bowl with the onion, sugar, salt, wine vinegar and dill. Cover and chill in the refrigerator for 30 minutes.

3 Transfer to a serving dish and garnish with dill sprigs to serve.

Warm Pepper and Cherry Tomato Salad

4 red peppers
400g (14oz) cherry tomatoes
2 tbsp chilli oil, plus extra to oil
salt and pepper
1 tbsp light muscovado sugar
2 tbsp balsamic vinegar
3 tbsp olive oil
1 small red chilli, deseeded and chopped
basil leaves, to garnish

serves 4
preparation: 15 minutes
cooking time: 50 minutes
per serving: 210 cals, 17g fat;
    13g carbohydrate

1 Cut the red peppers in half lengthways. Remove the core and seeds, but leave the stalks intact. Lay on a lightly oiled baking tray and fill each half with the cherry tomatoes. Drizzle with the chilli oil and season with salt and pepper. Roast the peppers in the oven at 180°C (160°C fan oven) mark 4 for 45–50 minutes until lightly browned.

2 Meanwhile, put the sugar and balsamic vinegar into a bowl and whisk until the sugar has dissolved. Gradually whisk in the olive oil, stir in the chopped chilli and season with salt and pepper.

3 Put the peppers on individual plates, pour the roasting juices over and drizzle with the dressing. Scatter with basil leaves to serve.

Coleslaw

350g (12oz) white cabbage, cored
1 large carrot, peeled
1 onion, peeled and finely chopped
2–3 celery sticks, finely sliced
3 tbsp chopped parsley or chervil, plus
    leaves to garnish
150ml (¼ pint) mayonnaise, preferably
    homemade (see page 351)
salt and pepper
paprika, to sprinkle

serves 4–6
preparation: 20 minutes, plus standing
per serving: 270–180 cals; 26–17g fat;
    7–5g carbohydrate

1 Coarsely grate or shred the cabbage and carrot, using a food processor fitted with a coarse grater if possible.

2 Combine the cabbage and carrot in a large bowl with the onion, celery and chopped parsley. Add the mayonnaise and season generously. Toss well to mix. Cover and leave to stand for 2–3 hours before serving to allow the flavours to mingle.

3 Sprinkle the coleslaw with paprika and garnish with parsley to serve.

variation: *Add 50g (2oz) pecans or walnuts, toasted and roughly chopped, just before serving.*

Red Cabbage and Beetroot Salad

½ red cabbage, cored
500g (1lb 2oz) cooked beetroot (see note)
8 cornichons (baby gherkins), sliced
2 tbsp baby capers in vinegar, rinsed

DRESSING
6 tbsp extra-virgin olive oil
2 tbsp sherry vinegar
3 tbsp chopped dill
salt and pepper

serves 8
preparation: 15 minutes
per serving: 150 cals, 10g fat;
    11g carbohydrate

1 Finely slice the red cabbage and put it into a large bowl. Cut the beetroot into matchstick strips or grate coarsely and add to the cabbage with the cornichons and capers. Toss well to mix.

2 For the dressing, put the olive oil, sherry vinegar and chopped dill into a small bowl. Season well with salt and pepper, then add a splash of cold water to help emulsify the dressing. Whisk together thoroughly.

3 Pour the dressing over the salad and toss everything together well.

notes
• *Buy vacuum-packed cooked beetroot or cook it yourself. Beetroot pickled in vinegar is not suitable.*
• *This salad is particularly good with baked ham.*

Chicory, Fennel and Orange Salad

300g (11oz) fennel bulb, with fronds
250g (9oz) chicory bulbs, sliced
2 oranges
25g (1oz) hazelnuts, chopped and toasted

DRESSING
juice of ½ orange
2 tbsp hazelnut oil (preferably toasted)
salt and pepper

serves 4–6
preparation: 10 minutes
per serving: 125–85 cals, 9–6g fat;
    10–7g carbohydrate

1 Trim the fronds from the fennel, chop them roughly and put to one side.
2 Finely slice the fennel bulb lengthways and put into a bowl with the chicory.
3 Peel the oranges, removing all white pith and pips, then slice into rounds and add to the salad with the toasted hazelnuts.
4 For the dressing, put the orange juice and hazelnut oil into a small bowl and season well with salt and pepper. Whisk to combine.
5 Pour the dressing over the salad, add the reserved fennel fronds and toss well. Serve at once.

Carrot Salad with Toasted Sunflower Seeds

700g (1½lb) carrots, peeled
50g (2oz) sunflower seeds, toasted
2 tbsp sesame seeds
1 tbsp poppy seeds
4 tbsp chopped flat-leafed parsley

DRESSING
6 tbsp light olive oil
1 tbsp sesame oil
2 tbsp white wine vinegar
1 tbsp thin honey
salt and pepper

serves 8
preparation: 15 minutes, plus standing
per serving: 200 cals, 17g fat;
    10g carbohydrate

1 Shred the carrots, using a food processor, then tip them into a large bowl. Add the sunflower, sesame and poppy seeds, with the chopped parsley. Toss the ingredients together to mix well.
2 To make the dressing, put the olive and sesame oils, white wine vinegar and honey into a small bowl and season well with salt and pepper. Whisk together to combine.
3 Pour the dressing over the salad and toss well. Leave at room temperature for 30 minutes before serving to allow the flavours to mingle.

Fruity Couscous Salad

225g (8oz) couscous
600ml (1 pint) boiling vegetable stock
3 tbsp chopped mint
3 tbsp chopped parsley
75g (3oz) chopped ready-to-eat dried apricots
75g (3oz) sultanas
finely grated zest of 1 orange
3 tbsp olive oil
salt and pepper

serves 6
preparation: 10 minutes plus standing
per serving: 250 cals, 7g fat;
    40g carbohydrate

1 Put the couscous into a bowl, pour on the boiling stock and set aside to cool.
2 When cold, add the chopped mint and parsley, chopped dried apricots, sultanas, grated orange zest and olive oil. Season with salt and pepper to taste and toss to mix.

variation: Scatter a handful of toasted pine nuts over the salad before serving.

Herbed Bulgur Wheat Salad

175g (6oz) bulgur or cracked wheat
2 tomatoes, deseeded and diced
½ cucumber, deseeded and diced
2 shallots, peeled and chopped
4 tbsp chopped mint, plus leaves to garnish
4 tbsp chopped flat-leafed parsley
salt and pepper
3 tbsp olive oil
juice of 1 lemon

serves 8
preparation: 10 minutes plus standing
per serving: 130 cals, 5g fat;
   18g carbohydrate

1 Put the bulgur wheat into a bowl, pour on 300ml (½ pint) boiling water and cover. Leave to soak for 5–10 minutes until all the water is absorbed. Fork through, then set aside to cool.

2 Add the tomatoes, cucumber, shallots and chopped herbs. Mix well and season with salt and pepper to taste.

3 Add the olive oil and lemon juice and toss to mix. Leave to stand for a few hours if time, to allow the flavours to infuse. Garnish with mint leaves to serve.

Potato Salad with Basil

700g (1½lb) firm waxy potatoes, scrubbed
salt and pepper
90ml (3fl oz) extra-virgin olive oil
1 garlic clove, peeled and crushed
grated zest of 1 lemon
2–3 tbsp chopped basil
1 tbsp sherry vinegar
4 spring onions, finely chopped
25g (1oz) pine nuts, toasted

serves 4
preparation: 10 minutes, plus standing
cooking time: about 15 minutes
per serving: 350 cals, 24g fat;
   31g carbohydrate

1 Put the potatoes into a pan, add cold salted water to cover, bring to the boil and cook for about 12–15 minutes until just tender.

2 Meanwhile, heat 2 tbsp of the olive oil in a large frying pan, add the garlic and lemon zest and fry gently for 5 minutes until soft but not golden.

3 In a bowl, whisk the remaining olive oil with the chopped basil, sherry vinegar and seasoning.

4 Drain the potatoes and shake off excess water. Add to the frying pan and stir fry for 1 minute. Stir in the basil mixture and remove from the heat. Set aside to cool to room temperature.

5 Just before serving, add the spring onions and pine nuts and toss lightly; check the seasoning.

New Potato and Dill Salad

900g (2lb) baby new potatoes, scrubbed
salt and pepper
4 tbsp chopped dill

DRESSING
4 tbsp Greek-style yogurt
4 tbsp mayonnaise
4 tsp wholegrain mustard
1 tsp lemon juice

serves 6
preparation: 5 minutes
cooking time: about 15 minutes
per serving: 190 cals, 9g fat;
   24g carbohydrate

1 Put the new potatoes into a pan, add cold salted water to cover and bring to the boil. Simmer for about 15 minutes until just tender.

2 Meanwhile, put the ingredients for the dressing into a bowl, stir to combine and season with salt and pepper to taste.

3 Drain the potatoes and let cool slightly, then toss with the dressing and chopped dill while still warm. Serve warm or cool.

variation: Replace the dill with 4–6 chopped spring onions and 2–3 tbsp chopped parsley or chervil.

Chickpea Salad with Lemon and Parsley

2 x 410g cans chickpeas, drained and rinsed

1 small red onion, peeled and finely sliced

4 tbsp chopped flat-leafed parsley, plus
    extra sprigs to garnish

DRESSING

juice of ½ lemon

6 tbsp extra-virgin olive oil

salt and pepper

serves 4

preparation: 15 minutes, plus standing

per serving: 350 cals; 23g fat;
    25g carbohydrate

1 First make the dressing. Put the lemon juice and olive oil into a bowl and whisk together. Season generously with salt and pepper.

2 Tip the chickpeas into a large salad bowl, add the red onion and chopped parsley, then drizzle over the dressing. Mix together well and check the seasoning. Set aside for 5 minutes to allow the onion to soften slightly in the dressing.

3 Serve the salad garnished with parsley sprigs.

Pasta Salad with Sun-dried Tomatoes

175g (6oz) dried pasta shapes, such
    as penne

salt

1 tbsp extra-virgin olive oil

4 sun-dried tomatoes in oil, drained
    and sliced

225g (8oz) cherry tomatoes, halved

4–6 spring onions, shredded

8–12 black olives

8–12 basil leaves, torn

DRESSING

2 sun-dried tomatoes in oil, drained

2 tbsp oil (from sun-dried tomato jar)

2 tbsp red wine vinegar

1 garlic clove, peeled

1 tbsp sun-dried tomato paste

pinch of sugar (optional)

coarse sea salt and pepper

2 tbsp extra-virgin olive oil

serves 4

preparation: 15 minutes, plus standing

cooking time: 10 minutes

per serving: 360 cals, 21g fat;
    38g carbohydrate

1 Cook the pasta in a large pan of boiling salted water until *al dente*. Drain in a colander, refresh under cold running water, then drain thoroughly. Tip the pasta into a large bowl and toss with the olive oil to prevent sticking.

2 Add the sun-dried tomatoes, cherry tomatoes, spring onions, olives and torn basil leaves. Toss to mix with the pasta.

3 To make the dressing, put the sun-dried tomatoes and oil, wine vinegar, garlic and tomato paste into a blender or food processor. Add the sugar if using, and salt and pepper. With the motor running, pour the olive oil through the feeder tube and process briefly to make a fairly thick dressing.

4 Pour the dressing over the pasta and toss well. Cover and leave to stand for 1–2 hours before serving if possible, to allow the flavours to develop.

Bacon, Avocado and Walnut Salad

125g (4oz) bacon lardons
1 shallot, peeled and finely chopped
120g bag mixed baby salad leaves
1 medium avocado, sliced
50g (2oz) shelled walnuts, roughly
   chopped
4 tbsp olive oil
4 tbsp red wine vinegar
salt and pepper

serves 4
preparation: 5 minutes
cooking time: 7 minutes
per serving: 410 cals, 40g fat;
   3g carbohydrate

1 Put the bacon lardons in a frying pan over a medium heat for a minute or two until the fat starts to run. Add the chopped shallot and fry gently for about 5 minutes until golden.

2 Meanwhile, divide the salad leaves among four serving plates. Halve and stone the avocado, then peel and slice the flesh. Arrange on the salad leaves.

3 Add the walnuts, olive oil and wine vinegar to the frying pan and let bubble for 1 minute. Season with salt and pepper.

4 Tip the bacon, walnuts and dressing over the salad and serve straightaway, while still warm, as a starter.

note: *Use a combination of baby spinach leaves and lollo rosso or oak leaf lettuce if you prefer.*

Caesar Salad

450g (1lb) cos lettuce

CROÛTONS
125g (4oz) one day-old rustic white bread
3 tbsp olive oil
1 tsp paprika
pinch of cayenne pepper

DRESSING
200ml (7fl oz) olive oil
8 garlic cloves, peeled and crushed
8 anchovy fillets in oil, drained and chopped
1 tbsp balsamic vinegar
2 tbsp Dijon mustard
juice of 1 lemon
1 medium egg

TO FINISH
50g (2oz) Parmesan cheese, finely grated
crushed black peppercorns
snipped chives

serves 6
preparation: 10 minutes
cooking time: 16 minutes
per serving: 450 cals, 41g fat;
    12g carbohydrate

1 Divide the lettuce into leaves, wash and dry, then put into a large bowl.
2 To make the croûtons, cut the bread into 2.5cm (1 inch) cubes. Put the olive oil, paprika and cayenne pepper into a bowl and mix together. Add the bread cubes and toss until well coated in the spiced oil. Place the bread cubes on a baking sheet and bake at 220°C (200°C fan oven) mark 7 for 6–8 minutes until crisp and golden. Set aside.
3 To make the dressing, put the olive oil in a small pan with the garlic and anchovies and heat gently for 5–6 minutes until the anchovies have broken down. Transfer to a bowl and allow to cool. Add the balsamic vinegar, mustard and lemon juice and whisk together until thickened.
4 Cook the egg in boiling water for 2 minutes only, then cool under cold running water. Remove the shell and break open the egg. Drop the yolk directly into the cool dressing and whisk until smooth – don't worry if some of the white goes in too.
5 Scatter the croûtons and grated Parmesan over the lettuce leaves, drizzle the dressing over and toss together. Sprinkle with crushed pepper and chives, then serve immediately as a lunch or light supper.

Traditional Greek Salad

1 red onion, peeled and thinly sliced
½ cucumber, peeled and cut into chunks
1 green pepper, cored, deseeded and
    finely sliced
3 beef tomatoes, sliced
10 Kalamata olives packed in olive oil
    with oregano, drained
200g pack feta cheese, chopped
salt and pepper
juice of ½ lemon
4 tbsp extra-virgin olive oil

serves 4
preparation: 15 minutes, plus standing
per serving: 280 cals, 24g fat;
    6g carbohydrate

1 Put the red onion, cucumber, green pepper, tomatoes, olives and feta into a large bowl and toss to mix. Season very lightly with salt (as feta is quite salty) and generously with pepper.
2 Drizzle the lemon juice and olive oil over the salad and toss everything together. Leave to stand for about 10 minutes before serving to allow the flavours to mingle. Serve as a starter or light lunch.

variation: *Use plain black olives and add 1–2 tbsp chopped oregano to the salad dressing.*

Goat's Cheese and Walnut Salad

1 large radicchio
2 bunches of watercress, trimmed
1 red onion, peeled and finely sliced
2 x 100g packs mild goat's cheese
150g (5oz) walnut pieces

DRESSING
2 tbsp red wine vinegar
8 tbsp olive oil
large pinch of golden caster sugar
salt and pepper

serves 6
preparation: 10 minutes
per serving: 370 cals, 36g fat;
    4g carbohydrate

1 Tear the radicchio leaves into bite-sized pieces and put into a large salad bowl with the watercress and red onion.

2 To make the dressing, put the wine vinegar, olive oil, sugar, salt and pepper into a screw-topped jar and shake well to combine.

3 Pour the dressing over the salad and toss well. Crumble the goat's cheese on top and sprinkle with the walnuts. Serve with French bread as a starter, or light lunch.

note: *Mild Welsh goat's cheese is an ideal choice for this salad.*

Roasted Vegetable Salad with Fontina

2 aubergines, trimmed
2 courgettes, trimmed
salt and pepper
2 red peppers, halved, cored and deseeded
2 small red onions, peeled and cut into
    wedges
1 fennel bulb, quartered, cored and diced
1 tbsp chopped thyme
1 tbsp chopped sage
4 tbsp olive oil, plus extra to drizzle
1 small head of garlic
125g (4oz) fontina or mozzarella cheese,
    diced
2 tbsp chopped basil
25g (1oz) pitted black olives
25g (1oz) pine nuts, toasted

DRESSING
10ml (2 tsp) balsamic or sherry vinegar
60ml (4 tbsp) extra-virgin olive oil

serves 8
preparation: 20 minutes, plus standing
cooking time: 45–50 minutes
per serving: 240 cals, 20g fat;
    7g carbohydrate

1 Cut the aubergines and courgettes into 2.5cm (1 inch) cubes. Layer in a colander, sprinkling with 2 tsp salt. Set aside for 30 minutes to dégorge, then rinse well to remove the salt and dry on kitchen paper.

2 Cut the peppers into 2.5cm (1 inch) squares and place in a large bowl with the aubergines, courgettes, onions, fennel, thyme, sage and olive oil. Toss well, then place in a large roasting tin, in a single layer. (If necessary, use two roasting tins.)

3 Slice the top from the head of garlic and stand on a small sheet of foil. Drizzle over a little olive oil, season and seal the foil to form a parcel. Sit the parcel among the vegetables.

4 Roast at 230°C (210°C fan oven) mark 8 for 45–50 minutes, stirring from time to time to ensure even browning. Transfer the vegetables to a large bowl and stir in the cheese.

5 Unwrap the garlic and scoop the flesh into a bowl. Whisk in the dressing ingredients and season with salt and pepper.

6 Pour the dressing over the vegetables, add the basil, olives and pine nuts and toss lightly. Serve warm, as a starter or light lunch, with crusty bread.

Halloumi and Avocado Salad

250g pack halloumi cheese
1 tbsp plain flour
salt and pepper
200g bag mixed leaf salad
2 avocados
2 tbsp vegetable oil

DRESSING
3 tbsp lemon juice
8 tbsp olive oil
3 tbsp chopped mint

serves 4
preparation: 10 minutes
cooking time: 3 minutes
per serving: 600 cals, 57g fat;
    4g carbohydrate

1 First make the dressing. Whisk the lemon juice and olive oil together in a bowl, then add the chopped mint and season with salt and pepper.
2 Cut the halloumi into 8 slices. Season the flour with salt and pepper and use to coat the halloumi.
3 Put the salad leaves into a large bowl. Halve and stone the avocados, then peel and slice. Add to the salad leaves with half the dressing and toss together.
4 Heat the oil in a large frying pan, add the halloumi slices and fry for 1 minute on each side or until a golden crust forms. Arrange on top of the salad and drizzle over the remaining dressing.
5 Serve immediately, as a lunch or light supper, with warm bread.

Salade Niçoise

450g (1lb) fresh tuna steaks (see note)
1 garlic clove, peeled and crushed
grated zest of ½ lemon
salt and pepper
2 tbsp olive oil, plus extra to cook
1 thyme sprig
2 small red peppers, halved and deseeded
350g (12oz) vine-ripened tomatoes, skinned
2 large eggs
250g (9oz) podded broad beans
2 large basil sprigs, leaves only
½ cucumber, deseeded and cut into chunks
50g (2oz) small black olives
6 spring onions, trimmed and chopped
50g can anchovy fillets, drained and chopped
50g (2oz) rocket or other salad leaves

DRESSING
2 tbsp lemon juice
1 tsp Dijon mustard
6 tbsp extra-virgin olive oil

serves 4–6
preparation: 40 minutes, plus marinating
cooking time: 30 minutes
per serving: 570–380 cals, 41–27g fat;
    11–7g carbohydrate

1 Rub the tuna steaks with the garlic, lemon zest and pepper. Put into a dish, spoon over 2 tbsp oil, cover and leave to marinate in a cool place for 3–4 hours.

2 Transfer the tuna to a small pan, add the thyme and enough oil to barely cover the tuna. Bring slowly to the boil, turn the tuna over and remove the pan from the heat. Leave to stand for 5 minutes, then remove the fish with a slotted spoon and leave until cool.
3 Grill the peppers, skin-side up, under a hot grill until charred. Put in a bowl, cover with clingfilm and leave until cool. Thickly slice or quarter the tomatoes. Skin the peppers, cut into thick strips and put to one side.
4 Bring a small pan of water to the boil, add the eggs (making sure they're covered with water) and simmer for 8 minutes. Cool under cold running water, shell and quarter. Add the broad beans to a pan of boiling water and cook for 2–3 minutes. Drain and refresh in cold water, then slip off the skins.
5 For the dressing, put all the ingredients in a screw-topped jar, season and shake well until combined.
6 Break the cooked tuna into large flakes. Pound the basil leaves with 1 tsp salt in a wide salad bowl to release their flavour. Add the peppers, tomatoes, eggs, cucumber, olives, spring onions, anchovies and broad beans. Add just enough dressing to moisten the salad and toss gently. Check the seasoning.
7 Serve on a bed of rocket or other leaves as a main course. Hand the rest of the dressing separately.

Illustrated on page 348

variations
• *Instead of fresh tuna, use 2 x 200g cans tuna steak in olive oil. Drain well and add at stage 5.*
• *Add about 12 cooked small new potatoes.*

Tuna, Bean and Red Onion Salad

410g can cannellini beans, drained
  and rinsed
1 small red onion, peeled and very
  finely sliced
1 tbsp red wine vinegar
salt and pepper
225g can tuna steak in oil (see note)
2 tbsp chopped parsley

serves 4
preparation: 10 minutes
per serving: 340 cals, 19g fat;
  19g carbohydrate

1 Put the cannellini beans, onion slices and wine vinegar into a bowl, season with a little salt and mix well. Add the tuna with its oil, breaking the fish into large flakes.

2 Add half of the chopped parsley and season generously with pepper. Toss the salad, then scatter the remaining parsley over the top. Serve as a light lunch or supper, with a green salad and plenty of warm crusty bread.

note: *Buy tuna steak canned in extra-virgin olive oil, which flakes easily into large, meaty flakes and has a good flavour.*

Squid and Roasted Pepper Salad

3 large red peppers, cored, deseeded
   and cut into broad strips
16 small shallots, peeled
4 rosemary sprigs, bruised
4 thyme sprigs, bruised
4 tbsp olive oil
8 garlic cloves, peeled
600g (1¼lb) baby squid, cleaned (see
   pages 82–3)
finely pared zest of 2 lemons, in strips
vegetable oil, to fry
sea salt
1 tsp chopped thyme

DRESSING
5 tbsp extra-virgin olive oil
juice of ½ lemon
2 tbsp chopped parsley
pinch of sugar
salt and pepper

serves 4
preparation: 20 minutes, plus standing
cooking time: 45 minutes
per serving: 450 cals, 33g fat;
   12g carbohydrate

1 Put the red peppers into a small roasting tin with the shallots and herb sprigs. Add 3 tbsp of the olive oil and toss well. Roast at 220°C (200°C fan oven) mark 7 for 20 minutes.

2 Add the garlic cloves to the roasting tin, stir once and roast for a further 20 minutes or until all the vegetables are tender. Set aside to cool.

3 Meanwhile, slice open the squid pouches and lay flat them on a board, inside uppermost. Score a criss-cross pattern, using a sharp knife. Leave the tentacles whole. Rinse the squid pieces under cold running water and pat dry on kitchen paper.

4 Fry the lemon zest in a little hot oil for 30 seconds until crisp. Drain on kitchen paper and sprinkle with a little sea salt.

5 Shake all the dressing ingredients together in a screw-topped jar until combined. Pour over the cooled vegetables and toss well.

6 Heat the remaining 1 tbsp olive oil in a non-stick heavy-based frying pan until very hot. Add the squid and stir-fry for 1 minute. Stir in the chopped thyme, then add to the roasted vegetables. Leave to stand for 10 minutes.

7 Scatter the lemon zest on top of the salad and serve warm, as a lunch or light supper.

Chicory and Crab Salad with Lime Dressing

450g (1lb) fresh white crab meat (see note)
1 tbsp groundnut oil
2 tbsp chopped coriander, plus sprigs
   to garnish
1 red chilli, deseeded and finely chopped
1–2 tsp chopped Japanese pickled ginger
3 tbsp lime juice
½ tsp sea salt
white pepper, to taste
2 heads of chicory

serves 4
preparation: 10 minutes
per serving: 170 cals, 9g fat;
   1g carbohydrate

1 Pick over the crab meat, discarding any small pieces of cartilage that may remain, then put into a large bowl. Add the oil, coriander, chilli, ginger, lime juice, salt and pepper to taste. Toss gently to mix.

2 Separate out the chicory leaves and arrange on a large plate. Spoon the crab salad into the centre and serve immediately, garnished with coriander.

notes
• *Ideally, buy a fresh crab and prepare it yourself (see pages 80–1), or buy fresh dressed crab from your fishmonger or supermarket fresh fish counter.*
• *Japanese pickled ginger is available in jars from larger supermarkets and delicatessens.*

Smoked Mackerel Salad

450g (1lb) new potatoes, scrubbed
salt and pepper
4 tbsp extra-virgin olive oil
3 smoked mackerel fillets, skinned
250g (9oz) cherry tomatoes, halved
½ cucumber, cut into small cubes
85g bag watercress
2 tsp creamed horseradish
2 tbsp white wine vinegar

serves 4
preparation: 20 minutes
cooking time: 15 minutes
per serving: 420 cals, 32g fat;
    21g carbohydrate

1 Halve the potatoes lengthways and add them to a pan of cold salted water. Bring to the boil and cook for 10 minutes or until tender.

2 Drain the potatoes well. Tip back into the pan, add 1 tbsp olive oil and season well with salt and pepper. Put the lid on and shake the pan to coat the potatoes in the oil. Tip into a salad bowl.

3 Break the mackerel fillets into strips and add to the potatoes with the cherry tomatoes, cucumber and watercress leaves. Season well.

4 Put the horseradish, remaining olive oil and wine vinegar into a small bowl and season well. Whisk to combine, then pour the dressing over the salad. Toss to mix and serve.

Coronation Chicken

1 tbsp vegetable oil
1 onion, peeled and chopped
1 tbsp ground coriander
1 tbsp ground cumin
1½ tsp ground turmeric
1½ tsp paprika
150ml (¼ pint) dry white wine
500ml (16fl oz) chicken stock
6 boneless, skinless chicken breasts, thighs
    or suprêmes
salt and pepper
2 bay leaves
2 thyme sprigs
2 parsley sprigs

DRESSING
150ml (¼ pint) mayonnaise, preferably
    homemade (see page 351)
5 tbsp natural yogurt
2 tbsp mango chutney
125g ready-to-eat dried apricots, chopped
juice of ½ lemon

TO SERVE
3–4 tbsp roughly chopped flat-leafed parsley

serves 6
preparation: 20 minutes
cooking time: about 50 minutes
per serving: 530 cals, 28g fat;
    32g carbohydrate

1 Heat the oil in a large heavy-based pan, add the onion and fry for 5–10 minutes until softened and golden. Add the ground spices and cook, stirring, for 1–2 minutes.

2 Pour in the wine, bring to the boil and let bubble for 5 minutes to reduce right down. Add the stock and bring to the boil again.

3 Season the chicken with salt and pepper, then add to the pan with the bay leaves and herb sprigs. Cover and bring to the boil. Turn the heat down low and poach the chicken for 25 minutes until cooked. Cool quickly (by plunging the base of the pan into a sink of cold water, replacing the water as it warms up).

4 Meanwhile, for the dressing, mix the mayonnaise, yogurt and mango chutney together in a bowl. Drain the cooled stock from the chicken and whisk 200ml (7fl oz) into the mayonnaise mixture. Add the apricots and lemon juice and season well.

5 Stir the chicken into the curried mayonnaise, then cover and chill until required. Scatter over chopped parsley and serve with French bread.

Chicken Caesar Salad with Parmesan Croûtons

1 cos lettuce

about 700g (1½lb) cooked chicken breast,
  sliced

CROÛTONS

2 tbsp olive oil

1 garlic clove, peeled and crushed

2 thick slices country-style bread, cubed

6 tbsp freshly grated Parmesan cheese

DRESSING

4 tbsp mayonnaise

2 tbsp lemon juice

1 tsp Dijon mustard

2 canned anchovy fillets, drained and
  very finely chopped

salt and pepper

serves 4
preparation: 30 minutes
cooking time: 12 minutes
per serving: 580 cals, 34g fat;
  13g carbohydrate

1 Divide the lettuce into leaves, wash and dry, then put into a large bowl.

2 To make the croûtons, put the olive oil, garlic and bread cubes into a bowl and toss well. Tip on to a baking sheet and bake at 180°C (160°C fan oven) mark 4 for 10 minutes, turning halfway through. Sprinkle the Parmesan over the bread cubes and bake for a further 2 minutes or until the cheese has melted and the bread is golden.

3 Meanwhile, for the dressing, put the mayonnaise, lemon juice, mustard and anchovy fillets in a bowl. Season well with pepper and a little salt, and whisk to combine.

4 Slice the cooked chicken and add to the lettuce. Pour the dressing over the salad and toss to mix. Top with the Parmesan croûtons and serve.

note: *Alternatively, buy 4 fresh chicken breast fillets and poach in chicken stock flavoured with herbs, as for coronation chicken (see left).*

Beef and Roasted Vegetable Salad

600g (1¼lb) fillet of beef, trimmed

dash of mushroom ketchup or
  Worcestershire sauce, to taste

salt and pepper

150ml (¼ pint) olive oil

2 red onions

1 red pepper, cored, deseeded and cut
  into large pieces

1 yellow pepper, cored, deseeded and cut
  into large pieces

3 courgettes, about 450g (1lb), trimmed
  and cut into chunks

1 small aubergine, about 250g (9oz),
  trimmed and cut into chunks

2 thyme sprigs

2 tbsp balsamic vinegar, or to taste

garlic and basil mayonnaise (page 351),
  to serve

serves 6
preparation: 30 minutes, plus cooling
  and chilling
cooking time: 45 minutes
per serving: 360 cals, 27g fat;
  8g carbohydrate

1 Sprinkle the beef with mushroom ketchup and pepper. Heat 2 tbsp of the olive oil in a heavy roasting tin over a high heat, add the beef and turn to sear on all sides to seal in the juices and brown.

2 Transfer the meat to the oven and roast at 200°C (180°C fan oven) mark 6 for 15 minutes. Leave to cool, then cover and chill until required.

3 Quarter the onions vertically, keeping the roots on, then peel. Put the onion wedges into a large roasting tin with the peppers, courgettes and aubergine.

4 Pour the rest of the olive oil over the vegetables and toss well. Roast at 220°C (200°C fan oven) mark 7 for about 35 minutes until lightly coloured and tender, but not disintegrating, turning twice, and adding the thyme sprigs 10 minutes before the end of the cooking time. Season generously, transfer to a bowl and leave to cool.

5 Just before serving, cut the beef into strips. Drain the vegetables, reserving the liquor. Flavour the liquor with balsamic vinegar to taste, to make a dressing. Carefully toss the beef and vegetables with the dressing. Transfer to a large shallow bowl and serve with the flavoured mayonnaise.

FRUIT AND NUTS

An excellent variety of fresh fruit is available all year round in this country. Home-grown fruits, including fragrant berries and flavourful orchard fruits, are supplemented by imported produce throughout the year, including a host of exotic fruits from the tropics. The availability of organic fruits – grown without the use of chemicals – has improved significantly in recent years and most supermarkets now devote a section to organic fresh produce.

With the development of cross-hybrids, new fruit varieties appear on supermarket shelves from time to time. In their quest to develop sweet, seedless, easy-peel oranges, growers are constantly introducing new oranges, so apart from familiar jaffas, navels, clementines and satsumas, you will find shamoutis, minneolas and salustinas. Baby fruits have also become popular and you can now buy small, sweet pineapples and dwarf bananas, for example.

Nutritionally, fruit is important – both as a source of dietary fibre and of minerals and vitamins, especially vitamin C. Some varieties, especially apricots, mangoes and peaches, also provide vitamin A in the form of carotene. All fruits provide some energy, in the form of fructose (or fruit sugar), but most varieties are very low in fat and therefore low in calories.

Fruits can be classified into broad categories:–
Soft fruits include strawberries, raspberries, red, white and blackcurrants, blueberries, cherries, cranberries and gooseberries. Home-grown soft fruits have a superb flavour and fragrance, but a relatively short season. Imported varieties are available at other times of the year, but they often lack the flavour and aroma of home-grown fruit.
Orchard fruits are at their most plentiful and best during the autumn, especially home-grown apples, pears and plums. Peaches, nectarines and apricots are at their best during the summer.
Citrus fruits are imported, mainly from Mediterranean countries and South Africa. Popular varieties include lemons, limes, grapefruit, kumquats and the numerous different oranges. They are all rich in vitamin C. Citrus zest is used as a flavouring, especially lemon zest. If you are likely to use the zest, buy unwaxed fruit if possible.

Tropical fruits such as bananas, mangoes, guavas, persimmons and rambutans are imported throughout the year.
Vine fruits come mainly from the Mediterranean and South Africa. They include grapes, kiwi fruit, melons and passion fruit, and are available all year.

DRIED FRUITS

Dried fruits are very nutritious, as they provide a concentrated source of energy, protein, iron, calcium and vitamins A and B, as well as dietary fibre. Many different dried fruits are now available from healthfood shops and supermarkets. Apart from familiar raisins, sultanas, apricots, dates, figs, prunes and apple slices, you can also buy dried pear, peach, banana and mango slices, and dried cherries and cranberries, for example. Prunes are dried plums; sultanas, currants and raisins are different kinds of dried grapes. Both dried dates and figs are sold loose and in pressed blocks.

Dried fruits are sometimes treated with sulphur dioxide to prevent discolouration, and sprayed with mineral oils to enhance their appearance. Check pack labels for these additives and buy untreated fruit if possible. Alternatively, washing in warm water will help to remove these chemicals.

Dried vine fruits – raisins, sultanas and currants – don't need soaking, though macerating them in a little warm fruit juice or alcohol before adding to puddings or cakes will help to plump them up. Many other dried fruits, including apricots, dates and prunes, are now sold 'pre-soaked' or 'ready-to-eat', but some need soaking before use – check pack instructions. Soaking in fruit juice or alcohol rather than water gives a better flavour.

Dried fruits can be eaten as a nutritious snack; added to muesli and other breakfast cereals; used in winter fruit compotes, purées, pies and puddings; included in biscuits, teabreads and cakes; or used in sauces and stuffings, especially for poultry and game.

BUYING AND STORING FRESH FRUIT

Choose fruits which look bright and fresh, avoiding any with bruised or shrivelled skins. In general, fruit should feel heavy for its size, as this is an indication of adequate moisture. For the same reason, berries and other soft fruits should look plump; avoid any with signs of mould or seeping juices.

Some varieties of fruit are more delicate than others, but they all need to be handled carefully, to avoid bruising. Fully ripe fruit should be used as soon as possible.

Most unripe fruit will eventually ripen at home at room temperature but certain varieties, such as melons, will never do so if they have been picked too early. When choosing fragrant fruits, such as melons, mangoes, pineapple and peaches, make sure you can detect their distinctive aroma, as this is a good indication of ripeness. Melons and pineapples should yield to gentle pressure applied at the stem end.

Soft fruits are best eaten within a day or two of purchase; transfer to a shallow dish, cover loosely and chill. Most other ripe fruits, including peaches, apricots, plums and tropical fruits, are best kept in the fridge. Bananas and unripe fruits should be stored at room temperature. To speed up ripening – of pears, peaches and plums, for example – put them in a fruit bowl with ripening bananas.

Ethylene, given off by the bananas will accelerate the ripening process. Citrus fruits keep well at cool room temperature for up to a week.

PREPARATION AND COOKING

The majority of fresh, ripe fruits can be eaten raw. With the exception of soft berries, all fruit should be washed before eating. Delicate berries should only be washed immediately before eating if they are sandy, as water encourages them to rot.

Peel away inedible skins, and edible ones too, if the produce is non-organic and you are concerned about chemical residues. Fruits such as apples and pears quickly discolour when their flesh is exposed to air. Rubbing the cut surfaces with lemon or lime juice, or immersing in water acidulated with lemon or lime juice helps to prevent this.

Slightly under-ripe tree fruits, such as apricots and plums, and tart currants and berries, like gooseberries and blackcurrants are transformed by poaching in sugar syrup until tender. To make a sugar syrup, dissolve 125g (4oz) granulated sugar in 300ml (½ pint) water, then boil for 2 minutes. This quantity is sufficient for poaching 450g (1lb) apricots or plums.

GUIDE TO FRUIT VARIETIES

Apple

There are two types of apples: cooking and eating (or dessert). Cooking apples are too tart to eat on their own, and are therefore cooked with sugar. Bramley Seedling, usually termed simply 'Bramley' is the best cooking apple; other varieties include Lord Derby and Grenadier. Cooking apples can be stuffed and baked; used in pies and puddings; or cooked to a pulp and puréed to make a tart apple sauce (page 25) to cut the richness of fatty meats.

Eating apples may be soft-textured or crisp, sweet or tart, mild or distinctive. Cox's Orange Pippin, Spartan, Laxton Superb, Worcester Pearmain and Granny Smith are popular dessert varieties. Eating apples are good served with cheese; they are also used to make French-style tarts. Apple slices should be brushed with lemon juice to prevent browning.

Apricot

This sweet fruit should be firm to the touch, unwrinkled, and the skin should have a pink or orange tinge. Eat within a few days or keep in the fridge as apricots soften quickly in a fruit bowl. Once ripe, eat within 2–3 days.

Ripe apricots are best eaten raw. To peel apricots if required, immerse in boiling water for 30 seconds to loosen the skins, then peel. Sliced apricots should be brushed with lemon juice to prevent browning.

Poach slightly under-ripe fruit in sugar syrup or sweet wine until tender and serve with thick cream or yogurt, or halve, stone and use in puddings and tarts. Apricots also make very good jam and a glaze for celebration cakes. In the Middle East, apricots are a popular inclusion in meat dishes, especially with lamb as they offset the richness.

Avocado

This pear-shaped, sub-tropical fruit has either a shiny green or knobbly purple brown skin according to variety, enclosing pale green soft, oily flesh and a large stone. Avocados are prized for their delicate creamy texture and subtle flavour.

A ripe avocado will 'give' slightly when pressed at the pointed end. A hard, under-ripe avocado should ripen in a day or two at room temperature. Ripe fruit can be kept in the fridge for 2–3 days.

To open an avocado, cut in half lengthways and turn the halves in opposite directions until they come apart. Prise out the stone and brush cut surfaces with lemon juice to prevent browning.

Avocados are normally eaten as a savoury starter or in salads; they can also be made into dips and mousses.

Babaco

A large distinctively shaped fruit, about 25cm (10 inches) long, with an edible skin that is green, turning yellow when ripe, and pinkish-orange flesh. In flavour and texture it is a cross between strawberry, melon and pineapple. When sliced crossways, it gives attractive star-shaped slices. Babaco is usually eaten sliced and sprinkled with sugar, and sometimes in drinks and fruit salads.

Banana

Easily the most popular tropical fruit, the banana is a good source of instant energy. Bananas are picked in large bunches called 'hands' when they are still hard and green, but they have usually turned yellow by the time they reach the shops. Look for fruit with evenly coloured skins. Bananas are ready to eat when yellow and slightly flecked brown; black patches on the surface indicate the fruit is over-ripe. Unripe bananas will ripen quickly in the fruit bowl at room temperature. Once peeled and cut, bananas should be brushed with lemon juice to prevent browning.

Bananas are eaten raw, used in fruit salads, ice creams, cakes and various Asian dishes. They are delicious baked, barbecued or pan-fried in butter, or made into fritters. For cooking, choose slightly under-ripe fruit.

Red bananas have deep red skins and a soft, sweet flesh. Another variety is plantain; this is always cooked and eaten as a vegetable.

Bilberry

Bilberries are small dark blue berries, which grow wild on open moorland; they may also be called whortleberries or huckleberries. Blueberries (see below) are cultivated in preference to bilberries because they are easier to pick. To prepare bilberries, remove the stalks and any leaves, then rinse carefully and dry well.

Bilberries can be eaten raw, although their acidic flavour is better appreciated in tarts, pies, compotes or jam.

Blackberry

This small soft fruit, dark red to black in colour, is available wild and cultivated. The cultivated varieties tend to be larger and juicier. Once picked, blackberries lose their flavour rapidly and should be eaten on the day of purchase. To prepare, wash and remove stalks.

Blackberries can be eaten raw, stewed (especially good with apple), included in fruit puddings and pies, or made into jams and jellies.

Blueberry

Blueberries are small round, sweet and blue-black in colour. Most supplies come from the USA. They can be stored in the fridge for 3–4 days. To prepare, rinse and dry thoroughly.

Serve blueberries with cream or crème fraîche, or use in tarts, pies, summer puddings or crêpes.

Cherry

Cherries vary in colour from white, through red to very dark red. They are mainly eaten raw but some varieties have sour flesh and are used for pies and jams. Popular home-grown sweet cherries include Sweetheart, Bing and Stella. The tart Morello cherry is the best choice for cooking, and its intense, acidic flavour makes it perfect for sauces, tarts and preserves.

Avoid split or immature fruit. To prepare cherries, remove the stalks and rinse. If required, remove the stone with a cherry stoner or split the fruit and prise out the stone with the point of a knife.

Citron

Only the peel and pith of this large lemon-shaped fruit are used – for candying or other preserves; citron flesh is very sour.

Crab apple

This is the fruit of the original wild apple tree. Crab apples are small fruit, with shiny red or yellow skins and firm, sour flesh. Their high acidity makes them perfect for apple jelly and other preserves.

Cranberry

This small red berry has an intense sweet-sharp flavour. Originating from the USA, it is in season in autumn and early winter. To prepare, remove the stalks and rinse well, then simmer in a little fruit juice until the skins pop, or according to the recipe.

Cooked cranberries are delectable in puddings, tarts and muffins, but they are most commonly used to make a sauce or jelly to serve with poultry and game (see cranberry sauce, page 26).

Currant

Black, red and white varieties of this small home-grown berry fruit are available. Blackcurrants and redcurrants are more common than white ones. They are normally sold on their stems; use a fork to detach them. Choose those with a distinct gloss; avoid withered or dusty currants.

Blackcurrants have a rich, slightly sour flavour; they are best used in puddings and pies. Cassis, the blackcurrant liqueur, is used in drinks and desserts. Redcurrants are sweeter and can be eaten raw, but are mainly used in preserves, tarts and puddings. White currants are similar in flavour to redcurrants, although slightly less acidic; they are used in the same way.

Custard apple

The anona trees produce several tropical fruit, which are known collectively as custard apples. They include the cherimoya, sugar apple, sour sop and bullock's heart. They resemble apples with green, purple-green or yellow-brown skin and flesh that varies from sweet to acid. Cherimoya is the best known variety; it has pineapple-flavoured flesh, the colour and texture of custard.

To prepare, cut off the top and remove the flesh, discarding the seeds. Use in fruit salads, ice cream and creamy desserts.

Date

The fruit of the date palm tree, these have firm, sweet flesh and a long, slim stone. They are mainly cultivated in the deserts of Tunisia and Southern Algeria. Medjool dates are especially succulent.

Fresh dates should be plump and shiny, with smooth golden brown skins. Squeeze the stem end to remove the tough skin, then slit open the date and remove the stone with the point of a knife.

Dates are eaten raw, used in salads or sweets, or stuffed with cream cheese or nut pastes.

Durian

This very large fruit weighs up to 9kg (20lb). It has a thick, dull yellow skin covered with rough spines, and creamy-coloured flesh. Durian is an acquired taste as it has an unpleasant aroma.

To prepare, slit the fruit at the segment joints with a sharp knife and prise open, taking care of the sharp spines. Durian flesh can be eaten raw or added to Indonesian savoury dishes. The large seeds can be lightly roasted and eaten like nuts.

Elderberry

This is the fruit of the elder tree, which grows wild in hedgerows and similar places. The berries are small, round and shiny, almost black in colour, and ripen in late summer. Elderberries are mainly used to make elderberry wine and preserves.

Feijoa

Also called pineapple guava, this oval fruit has a tough reddish-green skin, scented flesh and a soft centre with edible seeds. The flavour is somewhere between pineapple, strawberry and guava. Feijoas are ripe when slightly soft and sweet smelling.

To prepare, peel off the thin outer skin. The rest of the fruit can be eaten, either raw, sliced into fruit salads or made into jams or jellies.

Fig

There are green, white, purple and black varieties of this prized ancient Mediterranean fruit. They all have soft, creamy-pink, juicy flesh full of tiny edible seeds. Most varieties have thin tender skins that are edible, although you may prefer to peel figs before eating.

Fresh figs should be soft to the touch and have skins with a distinct bloom. They are delicate and must be handled carefully. Also, they don't keep well and should be eaten soon after purchase. To prepare, simply rinse and remove the stalks.

Gooseberry

Cooking gooseberries are usually green with very sour, firm flesh and edible seeds. Sweeter dessert gooseberries are green, yellow-white or russet in colour, often with hairy skin and usually with soft pulpy flesh and large seeds.

Choose evenly coloured fruit, keep in the fridge and eat within 3 days. To prepare, wash, top and tail. Dessert varieties can be eaten raw. Cooking varieties can be used in pies, puddings and preserves, or lightly poached in sugar syrup, cooled and folded into whipped cream to make a fruit fool.

Granadilla

A larger, smooth orange-skinned member of the passion fruit family. The creamy-yellow pulp is full of edible seeds.

Grape

Grapes range from pale amber to deep blue in colour. Popular dessert varieties include white or golden Muscat grapes, Almeria, with golden-yellow or pale green berries, black or white Italia grapes and Alphonse Lavallée with purple-black berries. Common seedless varieties include white Thompson Seedless and red Flame Seedless.

Choose bunches of plump grapes with a distinct bloom. Keep in the fridge and use within 3 days. To remove pips, halve with a knife and flick out the pips with the point of a knife. Grapes can be used in fruit salads and other raw fruit dishes; they are rarely cooked.

Grapefruit

These large citrus fruit have thick yellow skins and either yellow or pink flesh. Pink-fleshed grapefruit are the sweeter kind. To prepare, cut in half and cut the flesh from the skin with a serrated knife, then cut the half-segments free from the membrane.

Grapefruit can be eaten raw on their own, sweetened with a little sugar if preferred; with other fruits; or used to make mixed fruit marmalades.

Guava

This tropical fruit of South American and Indian origin, may be round or pear-shaped, with green to whitish-yellow or dark red skins. The flesh is creamy-white to pink, sweet-tasting and contains edible seeds. Guavas have a strong distinctive aroma when ripe. They are particularly rich in vitamin C. To prepare, cut in half and peel. Guavas can be eaten raw.

Jackfruit

Widely cultivated in the tropical lowlands of Asia, Africa and America, jackfruit can grow up to 32kg (70lb) in weight. They have a rough, spiky green skin and yellow fibrous flesh, which contains juicy pulp surrounding walnut-sized seeds. The pulp tastes like a cross between banana and pineapple, with the texture of lychee.

To prepare, remove the skin and eat the pulp, discarding the seeds.

Japonica

The fruit of the japonica tree is the ornamental version of the quince. Japonicas do not always ripen on the tree but can be picked while still green and stored until they begin to turn slightly yellow. They have a distinctive flavour and are often cooked with apples, or made into a jelly.

Kiwi fruit (Chinese gooseberry)

These egg-shaped fruit with their brown, hairy skins and bright green flesh, pitted with edible black seeds, have good keeping qualities. They are grown mainly in New Zealand and the Canaries.

Choose firm fruit and keep at room temperature until just softened. Cut in half and eat with a teaspoon, or peel and slice to use in fruit salads, or as a decorative finish for desserts.

Kumquat

A close relative of the citrus family, this tiny oval fruit has a smooth, orange, edible skin and a sweet-sour flavour. Kumquats may be sliced and eaten raw, poached in sugar syrup, candied, or made into preserves.

A number of hybrids are produced, including the limequat and citrangequat.

Lemon

This common citrus fruit has many culinary uses, although it is too acidic to be eaten raw on its own. Look for lemons with a strong 'lemon yellow' skin, which looks moist; a shrivelled skin indicates that some of the juice has evaporated.

When grating lemon zest, do so thinly to make sure that none of the bitter-tasting white pith is included. To finely pare the zest, use a zester or swivel vegetable peeler, avoiding any white pith.

Lemon zest and juice is widely used in puddings, cakes, pies, fruit drinks and preserves such as lemon curd and marmalade, as well as in many savoury dishes and sauces.

Lime

This fruit looks like a small lemon, but with green skin and a distinctive, sharp flavour. Prepare in the same way as lemons. The juice and zest are used in ices and sorbets, other desserts, drinks, curries and preserves.

Loganberry and tayberry

The dark red loganberry is a hybrid of blackberry and raspberry, with a flavour similar to a raspberry but more intense. The tayberry is a hybrid of loganberry and blackberry. Both fruits can be used in the same way as raspberries.

Loquat (Japanese medlar)

Originally an oriental fruit, the loquat is now grown in Mediterranean countries and the USA. It resembles a small plum with sweet, scented, slightly tart flesh and yellow-orange skin. The seeds are within the large stone. Look for firm fruit with smooth golden skins.

To eat raw, cut crossways and remove the stone. The outer skin can be eaten. To cook loquats, stone, quarter and poach in a light syrup; skin if preferred, and serve chilled. Loquats can also be made into preserves.

Lychee

Originally a Chinese fruit, the lychee is a stone fruit the size of a plum, which grows in bunches. Lychees have hard skins, ranging from pink to brown, and sweet, juicy white flesh. Peel and eat raw, discarding the skin and stone, or poach in syrup and serve chilled on their own, with ice cream or a fruit salad.

Mango

The skin of this large tropical fruit may be green, golden-yellow, red or orange, depending on the variety. Similarly the shape varies, from round,

through pear-shaped, to long and narrow. The juicy orange-yellow flesh has a distinctive flavour and fragrance. Ripe mangoes are very juicy and 'give' if gently squeezed. Ripe mangoes are best used within 3 days.

To prepare, cut a large slice from one side of the fruit, close to the stone. Cut another slice from the opposite side. Cut the flesh in these pieces lengthways and crossways without breaking the skin, then push the skin inside out to expose the cubes of flesh. These can then be easily removed with a spoon or fork. Peel the remaining centre section and cut the flesh away from the stone.

Mangoes can be served with ice cream, in fruit salads, or puréed for mousses etc. Green, unripe mangoes are suitable for chutney.

Mangosteen

This tropical fruit has a deep purple, fibrous outer shell and juicy segments of creamy-white flesh with a sweet delicate flavour.

To prepare, cut the thick rind through the centre and remove the top part to reveal the fruit, which is best eaten raw.

Medlar

A small brown fruit, about the size of a crab apple, with sharp-flavoured flesh. Medlars are best eaten when very ripe and soft. To prepare, wash, halve and spoon out the flesh. Eat the fruit raw or use to make preserves.

Melon

Depending on the variety, melons can be smooth-skinned or have a light or heavy 'netting'. They vary in size and colour. All melons have perfumed, sweet flesh; usually the more fragrant the melon, the sweeter and juicier the flesh.

Melons should feel heavy for their size and slightly soft at the stalk end when ripe. Soft patches on the rind indicate bruising rather than ripeness. Melons should be stored in a cool place.

Melon is usually eaten raw, cut into wedges with the seeds removed. It can be served as a starter on its own or with Parma ham; as a dessert; or puréed for ice creams and sorbets. The following are the best-known varieties:

Charentais are small round melons with pale green skin and superb fragrant orange flesh.

Cantaloupe has a green to yellow rough, grooved skin and orange-yellow flesh with a peachy flavour.

Galia is a round melon with lightly netted green to yellow skin. The green flesh has a good flavour.

Honeydew is oval in shape, usually with bright yellow skin. The flesh is pale green, sweet and refreshing, although rather less flavoursome than other varieties.

Ogen is round, with yellow to orange skin marked with faint green stripes, and very sweet juicy flesh.

Watermelon is a very large, heavy, round or oblong melon with glossy dark green or striped green and yellow skin. The pink to deep red watery flesh, which contains black seeds, is sweet and very refreshing.

Mulberry

The most common variety is the black mulberry, which is dark red and has a sharp flavour. To prepare, wash carefully, then leave to dry in a colander. Mulberries are generally eaten raw or used to make jams and wines.

Nectarine

A smooth-skinned variety of peach with white-yellow to pinkish-red sweet flesh. White-fleshed nectarines have a particularly good flavour. Avoid buying fruit that is hard, extremely soft or shrivelled. Nectarines will ripen at room temperature, but once ripe should be kept in the fridge and used within a few days.

To prepare, simply wash and brush cut flesh with lemon juice to prevent browning. Eat on their own, in fruit salads or make into preserves.

Orange

This common citrus fruit is particularly rich in vitamin C. There are two main types: bitter and sweet. The two main bitter varieties, which are never eaten raw, are Seville, which is used to make marmalade and occasionally in meat and fish dishes; and Bergamot, which is prized for its oil. Sweet orange varieties include Shamouti, Navel, Blood and Valencia. They are very juicy and can be squeezed for their juice or sliced for fruit salads.

Choose firm fruit with a glossy skin. Avoid oranges with hard or dry skins. Oranges will keep for at least 4 days at cool room temperature.

To prepare oranges, remove the peel and white pith, and discard the seeds. To use orange zest in cooking, pare the zest with a zester or vegetable peeler avoiding any white pith, then blanch in boiling water for 3 minutes to remove bitterness; rinse under cold water and shred before using.

In addition to the bitter and sweet types there are several small varieties of oranges:

Mandarins and tangerines are smaller than oranges and have loose skin, which is easy to remove.

Satsumas are similar to tangerines with a sweet flesh, which is usually seedless.

Clementines are similar to satsumas and tangerines but smaller with stiffer skins and they usually contain pips.

Ortaniques are a cross between an orange and a tangerine. They have a thin orange-yellow skin and sweet juicy flesh.

Tangelos (**ugli fruit**) are a cross between tangerine and grapefruit.

Minneolas are a hybrid, like tangelos, but smaller with a sweeter taste.

Papaya (paw paw)

Large tropical fruit with smooth skin, which ripens from green to yellow or orange. Papayas have juicy, orange-pink flesh with black seeds in the centre. These seeds are usually removed because they have a peppery flavour. Papayas are ripe when the skin is yellow and the fruit feels soft. To prepare, cut in half, remove the seeds and serve in wedges; or cube and add to fruit salads.

Passion fruit

This tropical vine fruit look like a large wrinkled purple plum. The inedible skin is deeply wrinkled when ripe. Passion fruit flesh is pinkish-yellow in colour, fragrant, sweet and juicy. It is pitted with small edible black seeds. To eat raw, cut passion fruit in half and scoop out the flesh with a teaspoon. The pulp can be used to make drinks or to flavour ice cream and other desserts.

Peach

There are many varieties of this fruit, including yellow-fleshed, pink-fleshed and white-fleshed peaches, which have a particularly fine flavour. Peaches can be roughly divided into two main types, the 'freestone' type with a stone that separates easily from the flesh, and the 'clingstone' type, in which the stone adheres to the flesh.

Choose firm, but not hard, peaches with soft, velvety skins free from blemishes. The slightest bruise will cause rapid deterioration. Peaches are best eaten as soon as they are ripe, when they are just slightly soft – within a day or two if kept in the fruit bowl, or a little longer if chilled.

Peaches can be eaten raw or cooked. To skin, immerse in boiling water for 15 seconds, refresh in cold water, then peel. As scalding softens and slightly discolours the flesh, simply peel peaches with a sharp knife if they are to be eaten raw. Brush cut fruit with lemon juice to prevent browning.

Peaches can be eaten on their own as a dessert, added to fruit salads, poached in a light syrup, stuffed and baked Italian-style, or made into jams or chutneys.

Persimmon (sharon fruit)
Large tomato-like fruit with leathery skin which turns from yellow to bright orangey-red on ripening. The most common variety is the sharon fruit. Unlike other persimmons, it is seedless and both skin and flesh can be eaten. To prepare, wash the fruit and slice. The flesh can be spooned out and added to fruit salads or puréed and used in ice creams and mousses.

Pear
There are many varieties of pear, differing in shape, size and colour, and most are suitable for eating raw. Williams, Conference, Comice, Packham's and Red Bartlett are good dessert pears.

Choose fairly firm, slightly under-ripe pears and let them ripen in a fruit bowl. Once ripe, eat within a day or two.

To prepare, wash, peel, halve and scoop out the core; brush with lemon juice to prevent browning. A sweet juicy pear at the peak of ripeness, on its own, is sublime. Pears can also be eaten with cheese or added to fruit salads. Firm pears can be poached. Williams and Comice both hold their shape well when cooked.

Physalis fruit (Cape gooseberry)
This fruit acquired its alternative name, Chinese Lantern, from the lantern-shaped papery calyx that surrounds it. Physalis fruit are round and golden, with delicately scented, juicy flesh, which has many edible seeds. To prepare, peel back the papery skin and use as a decorative finish for desserts, eat raw or cook in pies or compotes.

Pineapple
This distinctive, large, oval fruit with hard knobbly skin grows in tropical and sub-tropical countries. The skin varies in colour from deep yellow to orange-brown.

When pineapples are fully ripe, they give off a sweet aroma and a leaf can easily be pulled from the crown. Avoid pineapples that are bruised, discoloured or have wilting leaves. Pineapples continue to ripen after picking and are often sold slightly under-ripe. An unripe fruit without any sign of an aroma will not ripen properly.

To prepare, cut off the leaf crown and base, then cut away the skin and brown 'eyes' from the flesh. Slice or cut into wedges and remove the central core. Pineapple flesh can be eaten raw, or used in sweet or savoury dishes.

Pineapple can also be halved lengthways, hollowed out, leaving the skin intact, and filled with a mixture of pineapple flesh and other fruits.

Plum
There are numerous different varieties, varying in size, colour of skin and flesh, and sweetness. For eating raw or using in fruit salads, choose a sweet dessert plum, such as Victoria, Red Rosa, Ruby Red, Autumn Red, Songold, Cassleman or Laetitia. Plums for cooking mostly have purple-black skin, with an almost juiceless flesh. Monarch and Marjorie's Seedling, Czar, Opal, Black Giant and Friar are all good cooking varieties. They can be stewed, used in pies, tarts, crumbles and fools, or made into preserves.

Avoid plums that are very soft. Ripe fruit should be eaten soon after purchase. To prepare, wash, halve and stone the plums.

Greengages are small sweet, green-amber coloured plums with a particularly good flavour. Delicious raw or poached, they also make an excellent jam.

Damsons are small dark blue to purple plums with yellow flesh. They must be cooked as they are sour, and are usually made into pies or preserves.

Pomegranate

This fruit has a thin, tough pink or red skin, and juicy red flesh packed with seeds. Buy pomegranates with hard, undamaged skins.

To prepare, simply cut the fruit in half vertically and carefully scoop out the seeds and juice, which is pleasantly sharp. Avoid the creamy yellow membrane, which tastes bitter. Pomegranates are used in desserts and Middle Eastern dishes. The seeds can be used as a decorative finish.

Prickly pear

Also known as Indian fig, this pear-shaped fruit with its greenish-orange skin covered with fine, needle-sharp prickles is a member of the cactus family. The sweet juicy pink flesh has edible seeds. This fruit needs to be handled carefully because of its prickles.

To prepare, wash and scrub off the prickles, cut a slice off each end, then score the skin downwards and peel back. Slice the flesh and serve with a squeeze of lemon juice.

Quince

Small, pear-shaped fruit with yellow skin and scented flesh. Avoid scabby, split or very small fruit. To prepare, simply peel and slice. Quince make good jams and jellies, or they can be stewed with apples and pears.

Rambutan

This dark red-brown Malaysian fruit has a brittle skin, which is covered with soft spines. Its white translucent flesh is similar in flavour to a lychee. To prepare a rambutan, simply peel away the skin. The fruit can be eaten on its own, or chopped and added to fruit salads.

Raspberry

Soft, juicy home-grown raspberries have a superb sweet, yet slightly acidic, flavour. Raspberries are usually sold hulled and clean. When buying, choose fragrant berries and avoid punnets that are stained with juice – indicating over-ripe or damaged fruit. Use soon after purchase or picking.

Raspberries are probably at their best sprinkled with a little sugar and served with cream. They are also used in all kinds of summer desserts, and make superb jam.

Rhubarb

Rhubarb is strictly a vegetable as it is the stem of a plant, but it is always eaten in sweet dishes. Forced rhubarb is pink, tender-looking and sweet-tasting; maincrop rhubarb has a stronger colour, a thicker stem and a more acidic flavour. Look for young pink rhubarb; once the stems are thick and green they are coarse and tart.

To prepare, cut off the leaves and root, then wash and chop the stems. Rhubarb is always cooked and is used for pies, crumbles and fools. The leaves are poisonous and must not be eaten.

To cook, simmer 450g (1lb) chopped rhubarb with 50g (2oz) light muscovado sugar, a pinch of ground cinnamon and the juice of ½ lemon for 5 minutes or until tender; drain. Serve hot or cold.

Sloe

Sloes are the small, round, bluish-black fruit of the blackthorn tree, which grows wild. They are used to make sloe gin, wine and preserves.

Star fruit (carambola)

Fluted yellow, waxy-looking fruit with a sweet and sour taste, which slices into star shapes. To prepare, peel off the skin and slice. Eat on its own or add to fruit salads.

Strawberry

The most popular of our summer fruits, strawberries are now available all year, with imported supplies during the colder months. Buy plump glossy strawberries with their green hulls still attached. Strawberries are usually sold clean, but if you wash them, do so carefully, just before hulling and eating.

Strawberries are best appreciated raw and at room temperature – on their own, or with cream and a little sugar. They are also excellent with other summer fruits, meringues, in tarts, and in various cold desserts. They can be also used to make jam.

Tamarillo

Originally from South America, this large egg-shaped fruit is now grown in other tropical and sub-tropical countries. Tamarillos have yellow or red hard skins, which must be peeled off. Their flesh is very acidic and contains edible seeds. Tamarillo flesh can be sweetened and eaten raw, but it is more often cooked.

NUTS

A nut is a seed or fruit with an edible kernel found inside a hard shell. Nuts are a highly concentrated food, rich in protein, vitamins, minerals, fats and fibre. As well as being popular snacks, they are widely used in baking, desserts, vegetarian dishes, salads and sweets. Some nuts are cultivated as much for their oil as their flesh, especially almonds, hazelnuts, walnuts and peanuts.

BUYING AND STORING

Certain varieties of nuts, such as walnuts, are sometimes available fresh or 'green' but they are most commonly sold dried – the form we are familiar with. Nuts can be bought in shells, shelled, or further processed into flakes, pieces or ground. If buying nuts in shells, make sure they feel heavy for their size; if light they are likely to be stale. Store in a cool, dark place and use within the 'use-by' date. Nuts do not keep well and turn rancid if stored for too long. Shelled, flaked, chopped and ground nuts are best bought loose in small quantities, or vacuum packed. Store them in airtight containers in a cool place and use quickly.

TOASTING NUTS

Toasting enhances the flavour of nuts, especially almonds, pine nuts and hazelnuts. To toast shelled whole, chopped or ground nuts, spread out on a baking sheet and put in the oven at 180°C (160°C fan oven) mark 4 for about 10 minutes, stirring once or twice. Alternatively, toast under a medium grill for 1–2 minutes, turning frequently.

GUIDE TO NUT VARIETIES

Almond

Almonds are the seeds of a tree belonging to the peach family. There are two varieties: bitter and sweet. Bitter almonds are not eaten raw; they are used mainly for making extracts and oils.

Sweet almonds are sold in their brown skins, or blanched (and skinned). Split, flaked, chopped and ground almonds are widely used in baking.

To blanch almonds, cover with boiling water for 10 seconds, then rinse and rub off the skins.

Brazil nut

Native to Brazil, this large, oval, creamy-coloured nut has a very hard brown shell, which is not easy to crack. Shelled Brazil nuts are available from most supermarkets. They are eaten raw, used in sweets, and popular in vegetarian dishes.

Cashew nut

The tropical cashew tree bears reddish pear-shaped fruit and one kidney-shaped nut grows from the base of each fruit. Cashew nuts are always sold shelled and skinned, to exclude the toxic acid found in the skins. They have a slightly crumbly texture and delicate sweet flavour. Salted or toasted cashew nuts are often served as an appetiser with drinks. Plain cashews are also used in salads, vegetarian dishes and Chinese stir-fries.

Chestnut

This is the fruit of the sweet chestnut tree, not to be confused with the horse chestnut. Sweet chestnuts must be cooked before they are eaten. They can be freshly roasted in their shells, but note that chestnuts gathered (or bought) in shells have a short shelf life as they are not dried at all. Dried chestnuts are available but rarely used; these need to be soaked in hot water for 30 minutes.

Cooked, peeled sweet chestnuts are sold in vacuum packs and cans. Chestnut purée is also available canned – sweetened and unsweetened. Chestnuts in their skins must be peeled and cooked before eating.

To peel chestnuts, make a tiny slit in the skin near the pointed end, then cover with boiling water and leave for 5 minutes. Take out one at a time and peel off the shell and thin inner skin while warm.

To cook, simmer peeled chestnuts in water for 30–40 minutes. Or bake in their skins at 200°C (180°C fan oven) mark 6 for 20 minutes, then peel.

Chestnuts are used to make soups and stuffings, served with vegetables such as Brussels sprouts, and preserved in sugar to make marrons glacés. Chestnut purée is used in desserts.

Coconut

Native to south-east Asia, the coconut palm now grows in other tropical areas. Where they grow, coconuts are harvested young and green, and their watery juice is served as a refreshing drink. It is the mature fruit that is familiar in Britain. It has a hard, hairy brown shell containing the sweet white coconut flesh and liquid.

When buying a coconut, shake it to test for freshness – to make sure it contains liquid. There should be no signs of mould around the three 'eyes' on the top of the nut.

To prepare, puncture two of the eyes with a hammer and screwdriver and drain out the milk. Open the coconut by cracking the shell all around at the widest part. Separate the halves and prise the flesh from the shell with a sharp knife.

Coconut flesh can be eaten raw, puréed in a blender with the liquid to make coconut cream, or shredded and used in baking. Freshly grated coconut can be toasted. Coconut flesh is also available flaked or shredded and dried (desiccated).

To prepare coconut milk, soak grated fresh coconut in boiling water, cool, then strain and squeeze through muslin. Creamed coconut is sold in blocks and can be sliced and mixed with hot water to make coconut milk for use in curries.

Hazelnut

Hazelnuts, filberts and cobs are all fruits of different kinds of hazel tree. Cobs are not as common as the other two. Hazelnuts are available in their shells, as shelled whole nuts (plain or roasted), flaked or ground. Remove the skins as for almonds (see left). Hazelnuts are often used in sweets, desserts, cakes and pastries; their flavour marries particularly well with chocolate.

Macadamia nut

Native to Australia, this wonderful creamy, soft-textured nut is encased in a hard brown shell, which is very difficult to crack. Macadamia nuts are therefore sold shelled – either raw or roasted in oil. They are eaten raw or used in baking.

Peanut (ground nut, monkey nut)

Strictly, this is not a nut at all but a type of underground bean, which grows in India, Africa and parts of America and the Far East. Peanuts consist of two kernels, which grow in a crinkly shell. They are available as whole nuts roasted in their shells, or as shelled nuts – which may be plain, dry roasted or roasted and salted. Ground peanuts are used to make peanut butter.

Peanuts are rich in protein and highly nutritious. They are commonly eaten as a snack, but may be added to salads or used in cooked dishes. Peanut butter is used in satay sauces.

Pecan nut

This member of the walnut family is grown in North America where it is also known as a hickory nut. Pecans are available in shells or shelled. They can be substituted for walnuts in any recipe.

Pine nut (pine kernel)

This small, pale seed of the Mediterranean pine tree has a mild, creamy flavour and soft texture. Pine nuts are always sold shelled and their flavour is greatly enhanced by toasting. They are popular in Middle Eastern cooking and Mediterranean dishes, including classic Italian pesto (page 28). Pine nuts can also be sprinkled over cooked vegetables or added to savoury or fruit salads.

Pistachio nut

Native to the Middle East, the pistachio nut is a vivid green kernel covered with a purple skin, within a beige shell. The oval shell splits when the kernel is ripe. Pistachios are available in their shells or shelled (plain or salted). Skin them as for almonds (see left). Typically eaten as a snack or used as a colourful garnish, pistachios also feature in sweets, ices, terrines and pâtés.

Walnut

Encased in a round, crinkly shell, the walnut is a wrinkled kernel with a mildly bitter, creamy flavour. Sold in their shells, shelled, chopped or ground, this nut is very popular in baking. Fresh unripe green walnuts are sometimes available pickled in jars. Walnuts have a moist, oily texture, which is used to good effect in cakes, breads, pies, tarts, other desserts, stuffings and salads.

DESSERTS

A perfect dessert is one that balances the rest of the meal perfectly. It's important to complement the other courses in terms of texture, colour and weight. If the starter or main course includes pastry, for example, avoid a tart or pie for dessert. Follow a rich or heavy main course with a light concoction or a refreshing fruity dessert. If the preceding courses are light, be extravagant and opt for an indulgent pudding.

With all year round availability of ingredients, the season no longer dictates your choice, though it is well worth making the most of home-grown fruits in season. Out-of-season imported fruits often lack the flavour of home-grown varieties, especially summer soft fruits, so they are generally better avoided. In autumn and winter, make comforting pies, fruit crumbles or a creamy bread and butter pudding instead. When you are entertaining, it makes sense to choose a dessert that can be prepared in advance. Refreshing homemade ice creams, parfaits and sorbets are excellent freezer standbys and, of course, they can be prepared several days ahead.

Fruits and nuts feature strongly in puddings and desserts and you'll find plenty of information on preparing these ingredients in the preceding section. Cream, eggs and chocolate are other important ingredients.

Cream is a versatile ingredient. When air is incorporated into it by whisking, the fat globules swell and thicken the cream, increasing the volume. Cream is classified according to its fat content and this determines its use. Single cream cannot be whipped because it doesn't contain enough fat, but it is an excellent pouring cream. Whipping cream and double cream can both be whipped until thick; whipping cream has the lower fat content of the two and gives a lighter result. Crème fraîche is slightly thickened and has a deliciously rich, slightly sharp taste. Half-fat crème fraîche is a lighter alternative to accompany puddings. Synthetic cream substitutes never taste like the real thing and are best avoided.

Eggs are essential in many classic desserts. Mousses, soufflés, ice creams and sorbets are prepared with raw eggs; others, such as egg custards, are based on lightly cooked eggs. There is a slight risk of salmonella if raw or undercooked eggs are eaten, which is generally ignored, but if you are in an at-risk group (see page 4) you should avoid these desserts.

Chocolate features in many desserts. It is important to use good quality chocolate. Generally, chocolate with a high proportion of cocoa solids – at least 50 per cent cocoa solids, preferably 70 per cent minimum – will give the best results. Most supermarkets offer a selection of 'luxury' dark chocolate bars – check the labels for cocoa solid content. Avoid chocolate-flavoured imitations of the real thing at all costs.

FINISHING TOUCHES

Always consider the finishing touches when you make a dessert. Elaborate decorations are a thing of the past, but a simple decorative touch can make an effortless dessert look stunning. A generous dusting of icing sugar, vanilla sugar or cocoa powder, chocolate curls (see page 503), or drizzled melted chocolate are all effective.

Fresh fruits can be relied on to give a touch of colour and interest. Strawberries and redcurrants always look mouth-watering; or try using physalis fruit – with their papery calyxes peeled back to reveal orange berries; or tiny bunches of seedless grapes – frosted by dipping into egg white and caster sugar. Fresh herb sprigs, such as mint, are appropriate on many ices and fruit desserts. Toasted nuts are another way to add texture and colour, as well as a decorative finish.

FRUIT DESSERTS

Fresh fruits at their seasonal best and peak of ripeness are a refreshing way to round off a meal, either eaten on their own or with yogurt, crème fraîche, cream or ice cream. They also lend themselves to simple, mouth-watering desserts that can be prepared with the minimum of effort.

Summer Fruit Salad in Vanilla Syrup

400g strawberries, hulled and halved
2 nectarines, stoned and sliced
125g (4oz) raspberries
½ vanilla pod, split lengthways
4 tbsp golden caster sugar

serves 4
preparation: 10 minutes, plus chilling
per serving: 83 cals; trace fat;
   20g carbohydrate

1 Put the strawberries, nectarine slices and raspberries into a bowl. Scrape out the seeds from the vanilla pod and mix them with the caster sugar and 2 tbsp water. Pour this vanilla syrup over the fruit, then mix gently.
2 Cover and chill for 2 hours, turning the fruit from time to time. Divide among serving glasses and serve with Greek-style yogurt or fromage frais.

Mixed Fruit Salad

2 oranges
5 plums, halved and stoned
4 apricots, halved and stoned
2 peaches or nectarines, halved
   and stoned
125g (4oz) redcurrants
125g (4oz) raspberries

SYRUP
25g (1oz) golden caster sugar
300ml (½ pint) orange juice
1–2 tbsp eau de framboise (raspberry
   liqueur), Grand Marnier or crème de
   cassis (optional)

serves 4
preparation: 20 minutes, plus chilling
cooking time: 5 minutes
per serving: 160 cals; 0g fat;
   38g carbohydrate

1 To make the syrup, dissolve the sugar in 100ml (3½fl oz) water in a heavy-based pan over a low heat, stirring occasionally. Increase the heat and bring the syrup to the boil. Boil rapidly for 2 minutes, then remove from the heat and stir in the orange juice. Add the liqueur if using.
2 Working on a plate to catch the juices, cut the peel and white pith from the oranges using a large sharp knife, then cut out the segments.
3 Cut the plums, apricots and peaches into thick wedges and put into a glass bowl with the orange segments and any juice. Pour over the warm syrup, then chill for up to 2 hours.
4 Just before serving, stir in the redcurrants and raspberries. Serve accompanied by crisp dessert biscuits, and thick pouring cream if you like.

variation: *You can vary the fruits according to taste and season – grapes, strawberries, mango, banana (added at the last minute), melon and papaya all work well.*

Tropical Fruit Salad

4 passion fruit, halved
100g (3½oz) golden caster sugar
50ml (2fl oz) white rum or Malibu
grated zest and juice of 1 lime
125g (4oz) cranberries
1 small pineapple
1 papaya
1 large ripe mango
1 large banana, sliced on the diagonal

serves 8
preparation: 20 minutes, plus standing
cooking time: 7 minutes
per serving: 120 cals; trace fat;
    28g carbohydrate

1 Scoop out the pulp from the passion fruit into a sieve over a small pan and press with the back of a wooden spoon to extract the juice. Discard the seeds.
2 Add the sugar, rum, lime zest and juice to the passion fruit juice in the pan and heat gently to make a syrup. Add the cranberries and cook over a medium heat for 5 minutes. Allow to cool.
3 Peel, halve and core the pineapple, then slice lengthways. Peel and halve the papaya, scoop out the seeds, then slice lengthways. Peel the mango, then cut the flesh from the stone and slice lengthways.
4 Put the pineapple, papaya, mango and banana into a large bowl, then add the cranberries and syrup. Leave to stand at room temperature for at least 30 minutes before serving to let the flavours develop.

Winter Fruit Compote

75g (3oz) ready-to-eat dried pears
75g (3oz) ready-to-eat dried figs
75g (3oz) ready-to-eat dried apricots
75g (3oz) ready-to-eat prunes
300ml (½ pint) apple juice (approximately)
300ml (½ pint) dry white wine
1 star anise
½ cinnamon stick
light muscovado sugar, to taste

serves 6
preparation: 10 minutes
cooking time: 50 minutes, plus cooling
per serving: 150 cals; trace fat;
    28g carbohydrate

1 Put the dried fruits into a pan with the apple juice, white wine, star anise and cinnamon stick. Slowly bring to the boil.
2 Cover and simmer for 45 minutes until the fruits are plump and tender. Check the liquid during cooking to ensure there is sufficient; add a little more apple juice if necessary.
3 Turn the compote into a bowl. Taste the cooking liquid for sweetness, adding a little sugar if necessary. Leave to cool to room temperature.
4 Serve the compote with crème fraîche or thick Greek-style yogurt.

variation: *Replace the figs with dried apple rings and the pears with raisins.*

Caramel Oranges with Vanilla Mascarpone

200g carton mascarpone
1 vanilla pod, split lengthways
150ml (¼ pint) Cointreau
6 oranges
175g (6oz) golden caster sugar

serves 6
preparation: 15 minutes
cooking time: 5 minutes, plus cooling
per serving: 380 cals; 16g fat;
    49g carbohydrate

1 Put the mascarpone into a bowl. Scrape the vanilla seeds from the pod and add to the mascarpone with 1 tbsp Cointreau. Stir to mix well, then cover and chill.
2 Working on a plate to catch the juices, cut the peel and white pith from the oranges using a large sharp knife, then slice the oranges crossways into rounds.
3 Put the sugar and remaining Cointreau into a heavy-based frying pan and heat gently to dissolve. Bring to the boil and cook to a light caramel.
4 Now add the oranges, together with any juice, and cook gently for 2–3 minutes. Allow to cool, then chill until ready to serve.
5 Either serve cold or warm through if preferred, and accompany with the vanilla mascarpone.

Peaches in Sauternes Syrup with Ricotta

175g (6oz) golden granulated sugar

3 vanilla pods, halved

200ml (7fl oz) Sauternes or other sweet
   dessert wine

6–8 ripe peaches, halved and stoned

250g carton ricotta cheese

25g (1oz) flaked almonds, toasted

serves 6

preparation: 15 minutes

cooking time: 20–25 minutes

per serving: 270 cals; 7g fat;
   43g carbohydrate

1 Put the granulated sugar into a pan, add the vanilla pods and 300ml (½ pint) water and heat gently to dissolve the sugar, then bring to the boil. Add the Sauternes and the peach halves and bring back to a simmer. Cover and cook for 15–20 minutes or until the peaches are tender.

2 Using a slotted spoon, transfer the peaches to a bowl; set aside. Boil the liquor for around 3 minutes until reduced and syrupy.

3 The peaches can be served warm or chilled. Divide among serving plates, top with a spoonful of ricotta, sprinkle with the toasted almonds and drizzle the syrup over.

Spicy Pears in Mulled Wine Syrup

6 tbsp thin honey

6 tbsp light muscovado sugar

300ml (½ pint) full-bodied, fruity red wine

1 cinnamon stick

pared zest and juice of 1 large orange

6 small pears, ripe but firm

serves 6

preparation: 15 minutes, plus
    overnight chilling

cooking time: 40–45 minutes

per serving: 200 cals; 0g fat;
    48g carbohydrate

1 Put the honey, sugar, wine, cinnamon stick, orange zest and juice into a medium pan and heat gently until the sugar dissolves. Bring to the boil, then reduce the heat to a simmer.

2 Meanwhile, peel the pears, leaving the stalks intact. Cut a thin slice from the base of each one so that it sits upright. Lower into the wine.

3 Add enough water just to cover the pears and set a heatproof plate on top to keep them immersed in the liquid. Poach the pears at a gentle simmer for 20–25 minutes until tender when pierced with a knife.

4 Lift the cooked pears from the pan and lie flat in a serving dish. Bring the syrup to the boil and bubble for 15–20 minutes or until it is well reduced and syrupy. Strain over the pears to colour them evenly, then cover with clingfilm and chill overnight (to intensify the flavour and colour).

5 Stand the pears upright in the syrup to serve.

Illustrated on page 370

Summer Pudding

175g (6oz) redcurrants

175g (6oz) blackcurrants

275g (10oz) blackberries

grated zest of ½ orange

175g (6oz) golden caster sugar

350g (12oz) raspberries

9–10 thin slices two-day-old white bread
    or brioche, crusts removed

2 tbsp cassis, plus extra to serve (optional)

serves 8

preparation: 20 minutes, plus overnight
    chilling

cooking time: 6–8 minutes, plus cooling

per serving: 200 cals; 1g fat;
    46g carbohydrate

1 Put the redcurrants, blackcurrants and blackberries into a large pan with the orange zest and sugar, and gently mix together. Cover the pan and cook for 3–4 minutes over a low heat, stirring from time to time.

2 Add the raspberries and cook for a further 2–3 minutes. Tip the fruit mixture into a bowl and leave to cool for 30 minutes.

3 Cut a round from one slice of bread to line the base of a 1.2 litre (2 pint) pudding basin. Put 4 slices of bread equally spaced around the inside of the basin. Cut triangles from 1 or 2 slices of bread and use to fill the spaces between the slices, overlapping as necessary to ensure there are no gaps.

4 Add the cassis if using, to the fruit. Set aside about 4 tbsp of the fruit juice in a jug. Spoon half of the fruit with its juice into the basin. Put another slice of bread on top, then add the rest of the fruit and juice. Cover completely with bread, trimming the slices to fit.

5 Put the basin on a large plate. Put a small plate on top and weigh it down. Chill overnight.

6 To serve, run a palette knife around the side of the pudding, then invert on to a serving plate. Pour the reserved juice over the pudding, to cover any white patches of bread. Drizzle with a little crème de cassis if you like, and serve with crème fraîche.

note: *Make this pudding at least a day ahead, to allow the juices to be fully absorbed.*

Baked Apricots with Almonds

12 apricots, halved and stoned
6 tbsp golden caster sugar
2 tbsp amaretto liqueur
25g (1oz) unsalted butter
25g (1oz) flaked almonds

serves 6
preparation: 10 minutes
cooking time: 20–25 minutes
per serving: 160 cals; 6g fat;
    26g carbohydrate

1 Put the apricot halves, cut-side up, in an ovenproof dish. Sprinkle with the sugar, drizzle with the liqueur, then dot each apricot half with a little butter. Scatter over the flaked almonds.
2 Bake at 200°C (180°C fan oven) mark 6 for 20–25 minutes until the apricots are soft and the juices are syrupy. Serve warm, with crème fraîche.

Illustrated on page 382

Baked Apples

4 Bramley cooking apples
grated zest and juice of 1 small orange
75g (3oz) light muscovado sugar
50g (2oz) dried cherries
25g (1oz) butter

serves 4
preparation: 10 minutes
cooking time: 30–35 minutes
per serving: 220 cals; 5g fat;
    45g carbohydrate

1 Using an apple corer, scoop out the core from each apple, working from the stalk end. Score the apples around the middle with a sharp knife, then stand them in a roasting pan or small ovenproof dish.
2 In a bowl, mix together the orange zest and juice, muscovado sugar and dried cherries. Divide the mixture into four and spoon one portion into the hollow centre of each apple.
3 Dot the apples with the butter and bake at 200°C (180°C fan oven) mark 6 for 30–35 minutes or until they are soft.
4 Serve the baked apples warm, with crème fraîche or double cream.

variation: *Replace the cherry and orange stuffing with mincemeat (page 543).*

Baked Bananas

5 cardamom pods, split
juice of 1 orange
juice of 1 lemon
2 tbsp muscovado sugar
4 tbsp apricot jam
25g (1oz) butter
4 tbsp rum or brandy
6 large bananas

serves 6
preparation: 5 minutes
cooking time: 15–20 minutes
per serving: 210 cals; 4g fat;
    37g carbohydrate

1 Extract the seeds from the cardamom pods and crush with a pestle and mortar.
2 Combine the crushed cardamom seeds, orange and lemon juices, sugar, apricot jam, butter and rum in a pan and warm gently over a low heat until the butter has melted.
3 Peel and halve the bananas. Put into a large, shallow ovenproof dish, add the fruit juice mixture and turn to coat. Bake at 200°C (180°C fan oven) mark 6 for 15–20 minutes or until the bananas are soft, basting occasionally. Serve immediately, with ice cream or crème fraîche.

Gooseberry Fool

450g (1lb) gooseberries, topped
    and tailed
125g (4oz) golden caster sugar
1 tbsp custard powder
150ml (¼ pint) milk
few drops of green food colouring
    (optional)
150ml (¼ pint) whipping cream
chopped toasted nuts, to decorate

serves 4
preparation: 20 minutes, plus chilling
cooking time: 10 minutes
per serving: 370 cals; 19g fat;
    50g carbohydrate

1 Put the gooseberries, sugar and 2 tbsp water into a pan, cover and cook for about 10 minutes until the fruit is soft. Allow to cool slightly.

2 Purée the fruit in a blender or food processor. Pass through a nylon sieve to remove the pips.

3 Blend the custard powder with a little of the milk; heat the remaining milk in a pan. Pour the hot milk on to the blended custard powder, stirring constantly, then return to the pan and stir over a gentle heat until the custard is thickened.

4 Beat the custard into the fruit pulp and allow to cool. Add the food colouring if using.

5 Whip the cream until soft peaks form, then fold into the gooseberry purée. Spoon into individual glasses and chill in the fridge until required. Decorate with toasted nuts to serve.

variation: *Use raspberries, strawberries or blackberries instead of gooseberries. Omit stage 1. Sweeten the fruit purée with golden caster sugar to taste at stage 2.*

Plum and Cardamom Fool

1kg (2¼lb) dessert plums, halved
    and stoned
125g (4oz) golden caster sugar
2 tbsp lemon juice
4 cardamom pods, split
150g ready-made fresh custard
200g carton Greek-style yogurt, plus
    extra to serve

serves 4
preparation: 15 minutes, plus chilling
cooking time: 25–30 minutes, plus cooling
per serving: 370 cals; 11g fat;
    64g carbohydrate

1 Roughly slice the plums and put into a pan with the sugar and lemon juice. Extract the seeds from the cardamom pods, crush with a pestle and mortar, then add to the plums. Cover and bring to the boil, then lower the heat and simmer for 20–25 minutes or until the plums are soft but still holding their shape. Pour into a cold bowl and leave for 30 minutes.

2 Drain the plums, reserving the juice, and set aside 4 good slices. Tip the rest into a food processor and whiz to a purée, then pour into a bowl.

3 Boil the reserved juice in a pan for 3–4 minutes until reduced to 3 tbsp, then stir into the plum purée with the custard and yogurt until smooth. Spoon into serving glasses and chill for up to 2 hours.

4 Top each portion with a spoonful of yogurt and a plum slice. Serve with amaretti biscuits.

STEAMED PUDDINGS

Steamed puddings are cooked in a heatproof bowl in a steamer or heavy-based pan of boiling water, then turned out to serve. If cooked correctly, they have a deliciously soft, moist texture. The following guidelines apply:

• Half-fill the bottom of the steamer with water and heat so that it is boiling by the time you have made the pudding. Alternatively, fill a large saucepan with enough water to come halfway up the pudding basin, cover and bring to the boil.

• Grease the base and side of the pudding basin thoroughly with softened butter.

• Cut a double thickness of greaseproof paper or a piece of foil to cover the pudding basin and grease well. Make a pleat in the paper or foil to allow the pudding to rise.

• Fill the basin no more than two-thirds full to allow room for expansion.

• Secure the paper or foil tightly under the rim with string to prevent water entering. Leave a length of string to act as a handle, making it easier to lift the basin out of the pan.

• If using a saucepan, put a trivet, or an old saucer or metal pastry cutter in the base to keep the basin off the bottom.

• Keep the water in the steamer or saucepan boiling steadily and have a kettle of boiling water ready to top it up regularly, or it will boil dry.

Steamed Syrup Sponge Pudding

125g (4oz) butter, softened, plus extra
   to grease
3 tbsp golden syrup
125g (4oz) golden caster sugar
few drops of vanilla extract
2 medium eggs, beaten
175g (6oz) self-raising flour, sifted
3 tbsp milk (approximately)

serves 4
preparation: 20 minutes
cooking time: 1½ hours
per serving: 580 cals; 29g fat;
   75g carbohydrate

1 Half-fill a steamer or large pan with water and put it on to boil. Grease a 900ml (1½ pint) pudding basin and spoon the golden syrup into the bottom.

2 Cream the butter and sugar together in a bowl until pale and fluffy. Stir in the vanilla extract. Add the eggs, a little at a time, beating well after each addition.

3 Using a metal spoon, fold in half of the flour, then fold in the rest with enough milk to give a dropping consistency. Spoon the mixture into the prepared pudding basin.

4 Cover with greased and pleated greaseproof paper and foil, and secure with string. Steam for 1½ hours, checking the water level from time to time and topping up with boiling water as necessary. Turn out on to a warmed plate and serve with custard.

variations
steamed jam sponge pudding: *Put 4 tbsp raspberry or blackberry jam into the bottom of the basin instead of the syrup.*
steamed chocolate sponge pudding: *Omit the golden syrup. Blend 4 tbsp cocoa powder with 2 tbsp hot water, then gradually beat into the creamed mixture before adding the eggs.*

Date and Walnut Pudding with Chocolate Sauce

125g (4oz) butter, softened, plus extra
   to grease
125g (4oz) golden caster sugar
3 medium eggs, beaten
175g (6oz) self-raising flour
3 tbsp milk
75g (3oz) walnuts, toasted and roughly
   chopped
175g (6oz) pitted dates, roughly chopped

CHOCOLATE FUDGE SAUCE
50g (2oz) unsalted butter
50g (2oz) light muscovado sugar
50g (2oz) plain dark chocolate, in pieces
100ml (3½fl oz) double cream

serves 8
preparation: 20 minutes, plus standing
cooking time: 2 hours
per serving: 550 cals; 33g fat;
   50g carbohydrate

1 Half-fill a steamer or large pan with water and put it on to boil. Grease a 1.2 litre (2 pint) pudding basin.
2 Put the butter, sugar, eggs, flour and milk in a bowl and beat with an electric beater until smooth. Fold in the nuts and dates.
3 Spoon the mixture into the prepared pudding basin and smooth the surface. Cover with greased and pleated greaseproof paper and foil, and secure under the rim with string.
3 Steam the pudding for 2 hours, checking the water level from time to time and topping up with boiling water as necessary. Lift the pudding out of the pan and leave to rest for 15 minutes.
4 Meanwhile, make the chocolate fudge sauce. Put the butter, muscovado sugar and chocolate into a pan and heat gently until the chocolate is melted. Add the cream, bring to a simmer and let bubble for 3 minutes until thickened.
5 To serve, unmould the pudding on to a warmed plate. Cut into wedges and serve with the chocolate fudge sauce poured over.

Steamed Chocolate Pudding

125g (4oz) butter, softened, plus extra
   to grease
50g (2oz) plain chocolate, in pieces
125g (4oz) golden caster sugar
2 medium eggs, beaten
125g (4oz) self-raising flour
1 tbsp cocoa powder
5 tbsp milk
50g (2oz) fresh white breadcrumbs

serves 4
preparation: 20 minutes
cooking time: 2 hours
per serving: 610 cals; 34g fat;
   72g carbohydrate

1 Half-fill a steamer or large pan with water and put it on to boil. Grease a 1.2 litre (2 pint) pudding basin. Melt the chocolate in a bowl set over a pan of hot water, stir until smooth and set aside to cool slightly.
2 Cream the butter and sugar together in a bowl until pale and fluffy. Add the eggs, a little at a time, beating well after each addition.
3 Sift the flour and cocoa powder together. Using a metal spoon, fold half into the creamed mixture, then fold in the rest together with the milk. Finally fold in the melted chocolate and breadcrumbs until evenly combined. Spoon the mixture into the prepared pudding basin.
4 Cover with greased and pleated greaseproof paper and foil, and secure under the rim with string. Steam for about 2 hours, checking the water level from time to time and topping up the pan with boiling water as necessary.
5 Turn the pudding out on to a warmed plate and serve with ice cream, chocolate fudge sauce (see recipe above) or custard.

Christmas Pudding

150g (5oz) currants

150g (5oz) raisins

150g (5oz) sultanas

150g (5oz) ready-to-eat dates, chopped

150g (5oz) ready-to-eat prunes, chopped

1 carrot, about 75g (3oz), peeled and grated

100ml (3½fl oz) Grand Marnier

100ml (3½fl oz) Guinness

finely grated zest and juice of 1 orange

175g (6oz) butter, softened, plus extra
    to grease

175g (6oz) molasses or dark muscovado
    sugar

3 medium eggs, beaten

75g (3oz) self-raising flour

1 tbsp ground mixed spice

150g (5oz) crustless fresh white bread

75g (3oz) blanched almonds, toasted

50g (2oz) pecan nuts, toasted

TO FLAMBÉ

2 tbsp Cognac

makes 2 puddings, each serves 6

preparation: 30 minutes, plus macerating
    and maturing

cooking time: 6–8 hours, plus 2 hours
    to reheat

per serving: 470 cals; 20g fat;
    65g carbohydrate

1 Put all the dried fruit into a bowl with the grated carrot, Grand Marnier, Guinness and orange juice. Stir to mix and leave to macerate for 1 hour. Meanwhile, grease two 1 litre (1¾ pint) pudding basins and line each with a 40cm (16 inch) muslin square.

2 Put the butter, sugar and orange zest into a large bowl and cream together, using a hand-held electric whisk or wooden spoon until pale and fluffy. Gradually beat in the eggs, adding a little flour if the mixture appears to be starting to curdle.

3 Sift together the flour and mixed spice. Put the bread into a food processor and pulse to make crumbs; remove and set aside. Put the nuts into the processor and pulse briefly to chop roughly.

4 Using a large metal spoon, fold the flour, breadcrumbs and nuts into the creamed mixture. Add the macerated fruit and alcohol and stir to combine.

5 Divide the mixture evenly between the two prepared pudding basins and smooth the surface. Gather the muslin up and over the top, then twist and secure with string.

6 To cook each pudding, put in the top of a steamer filled with simmering water and steam for 8 hours, topping up the water as necessary. Or stand the basin on a trivet in a large pan containing boiling water and boil for 6 hours, checking the water level from time to time and topping up as needed.

7 Leave the puddings to cool, then wrap tightly in foil and store in a cool, dark place for at least 1 month (or up to 6 months) to mature.

8 To reheat a pudding, steam as before for 2 hours, topping up the water twice. Once the heat is turned off, the pudding will keep hot for up to 1 hour. To serve, carefully lift out the pudding, cut the string and remove the muslin. Upturn the pudding on to a serving plate and decorate with a sprig of holly.

9 To flambé, warm the Cognac in a ladle, held over the hob until the alcohol ignites, then pour over the pudding. Serve immediately, with fresh vanilla custard (page 29) or brandy butter (page 31).

BAKED PUDDINGS

Most of these comforting puddings take very little time to prepare and you can make them well ahead. Make sure the oven is preheated to the correct temperature before baking.

Bread and Butter Pudding

50g (2oz) butter, softened
6 slices white bread
25g (1oz) currants
25g (1oz) sultanas
3 medium eggs
600ml (1 pint) whole milk
50g (2oz) light muscovado sugar
pinch of ground mixed spice

serves 6
preparation: 10 minutes, plus soaking
cooking time: 45–55 minutes
per serving: 300 cals; 14g fat;
   35g carbohydrate

1 Lightly grease a 1.2 litre (2 pint) ovenproof dish with a little of the softened butter.
2 Spread the rest of the butter evenly over the bread, then cut each slice in half diagonally. Arrange the buttered bread in the prepared dish, each slice slightly overlapping the last. Sprinkle the currants and sultanas over the top.
3 Beat the eggs, milk, sugar and mixed spice together in a bowl, then pour over the bread. Leave to soak for 30 minutes.
4 Bake in the middle of the oven at 180°C (160°C fan oven) mark 4 for 45–55 minutes or until the pudding is golden brown but still slightly moist in the centre. Serve with a drizzle of single cream.

Golden Croissant Pudding

4 large croissants (preferably one-day old)
75g (3oz) unsalted butter, softened, plus
  extra to grease
50g (2oz) sultanas

CUSTARD
300ml (½ pint) whole milk
300ml (½ pint) double cream
1 vanilla pod, split lengthways
6 medium egg yolks
125g (4oz) golden caster sugar

TO FINISH
icing sugar, to dust

serves 6
preparation: 15 minutes
cooking time: 40–50 minutes
per serving: 640 cals; 48g fat;
  47g carbohydrate

1 Slice the croissants thickly, then spread with the butter. Arrange the croissant slices, butter-side up and overlapping, in a buttered 1.7 litre (3 pint) shallow baking dish, scattering in the sultanas as you do so.
2 To make the custard, pour the milk and cream into a pan. Add the vanilla pod and put over a very low heat for about 5 minutes until the mixture is almost boiling and well flavoured with vanilla.
3 Meanwhile, in a large bowl, whisk together the egg yolks and caster sugar until light and foamy. Strain the flavoured milk on to the egg mixture, whisking all the time. Pour the egg mixture evenly over the croissants.
4 Stand the dish in a bain-marie or large roasting tin and pour in enough boiling water to come halfway up the sides of the dish. Bake at 180°C (160°C fan oven) mark 4 for 40–50 minutes until the custard is softly set and the top is crisp and golden.
5 Leave the pudding in the bain-marie to cool slightly. Serve warm, dusted with icing sugar and accompanied by cream or crème fraîche.

Rice Pudding

butter, to grease
125g (4oz) short-grain pudding rice
1.2 litres (2 pints) whole milk
50g (2oz) golden caster sugar
grated zest of 1 orange (optional)
1 tsp vanilla extract
freshly grated nutmeg, to taste

serves 6
preparation: 5 minutes
cooking time: 1½ hours
per serving: 220 cals; 8g fat;
  32g carbohydrate

1 Lightly butter a 1.8 litre (3 pint) ovenproof dish. Add the pudding rice, milk, sugar, orange zest if using, and vanilla extract and stir everything together. Grate the nutmeg over the top of the mixture.
2 Bake the pudding in the middle of the oven at 170°C (150°C fan oven) mark 3 for 1½ hours or until the top is golden brown.

note: *Orange zest gives the pudding a fruity tang, but you can leave it out for a more traditional flavour.*

Baked Egg Custard

600ml (1 pint) whole milk
3 large eggs
2 tbsp golden caster sugar
butter, to grease
freshly grated nutmeg, to taste

serves 4
preparation: 5 minutes
cooking time: 45 minutes
per serving: 210 cals; 13g fat;
  15g carbohydrate

1 Warm the milk in a pan, but do not boil. Whisk the eggs and sugar together lightly in a bowl, then pour on the hot milk, stirring.
2 Strain the mixture into a greased 900ml (1½ pint) ovenproof dish. Grate the nutmeg on top and bake in the middle of the oven at 170°C (150°C fan oven) mark 3 for about 45 minutes until set and firm to the touch. Serve hot or cold.

Rhubarb and Apple Cobbler

900g (2lb) rhubarb
450g (1lb) Bramleys or other
    cooking apples
6 tbsp golden caster sugar
4 tbsp plain flour
1 tbsp cornflour
½ tsp ground ginger
knob of butter
grated zest of 1 orange

COBBLER
150g (5oz) plain flour
2 tsp baking powder
pinch of salt
65g (2½oz) butter, diced
3 tbsp golden caster sugar
125ml (4fl oz) buttermilk (or whole milk
    plus a squeeze of lemon juice)

GLAZE
2 tbsp double cream
1 tsp demerara sugar

serves 6
preparation: 20 minutes
cooking time: 30–40 minutes, plus standing
per serving: 370 cals; 13g fat;
    63g carbohydrate

1 Cut the rhubarb into 2.5cm (1 inch) lengths. Peel, quarter, core and slice the apples. Put the fruit, sugar, flour, cornflour, ginger, butter and orange zest in a 25cm (10 inch) shallow ovenproof dish, toss to mix and set aside.

2 To make the cobbler dough, sift the flour, baking powder and salt together into a bowl. Rub in the butter until the mixture resembles fine breadcrumbs. Stir in the sugar, then add the milk and mix with a knife to a soft dough.

3 Spoon the dough on to the fruit in clumps, making sure it doesn't completely cover it. Mix the cream with the demerara sugar and drizzle over the top.

4 Stand the dish on a baking tray and bake at 220°C (200°C fan oven) mark 7 for 10 minutes. Lower the oven setting to 190°C (170°C fan oven) mark 5 and bake for a further 20–30 minutes or until the cobbler is puffed and brown and the fruit is just soft.

5 Leave the pudding to stand for 10 minutes before serving, with pouring cream or custard.

Blackberry and Apple Crumble

CRUMBLE TOPPING
50g (2oz) plain white flour
25g (1oz) plain wholemeal flour
75g (3oz) light muscovado sugar
50g (2oz) ground almonds
50g (2oz) unsalted butter

FILLING
700g (1½lb) eating apples
50g (2oz) unsalted butter
50g (2oz) golden caster sugar
225g (8oz) blackberries

serves 6
preparation: 45 minutes
cooking time: 25 minutes
per serving: 340 cals; 18g fat;
    43g carbohydrate

1 To make the crumble topping, sift the flours into a bowl, then tip in any bran from the sieve. Stir in the sugar and ground almonds, then work in the butter, using your fingertips, to make a very crumbly mixture.

2 Quarter the apples, then peel, core and cut into 2.5 cm (1 inch) chunks. Melt the butter in a large frying pan. Add the apples with the sugar, and cook, stirring, over a high heat for 3–5 minutes until golden brown and tender. Transfer to a 1.7 litre (3 pint) pie dish. Scatter the blackberries on top.

3 Spoon over the crumble topping and bake at 190°C (170°C fan oven) mark 5 for 25 minutes until the topping is golden brown. Serve warm, with custard, cream or ice cream.

variations
apple crumble: *Use cooking apples and an extra 25g (1oz) sugar at stage 2; cook gently until soft.*
red fruit crumble: *Replace the blackberries with 225g (8oz) mixed summer fruits, such as red and blackcurrants, raspberries and pitted cherries.*

Frangipane Baked Pears

25g (1oz) blanched almonds, chopped
25g (1oz) candied peel, chopped
25g (1oz) raisins
3 tbsp kirsch or rum
75g (3oz) flaked almonds
50g (2oz) plain flour
225g (8oz) golden caster sugar
6 pears
1 tbsp apricot jam
125g (4oz) butter
2 medium eggs, beaten
few drops of almond extract

serves 6
preparation: 40 minutes, plus macerating
cooking time: 50 minutes
per serving: 580 cals; 28g fat;
   75g carbohydrate

1 Put the chopped almonds, candied peel and raisins in a small bowl. Sprinkle with the kirsch, cover and leave to macerate for 6 hours or overnight. Drain, reserving the liquor.
2 Whiz the flaked almonds and flour in a food processor until the nuts are finely ground; set aside.
3 Dissolve half of the sugar in 900ml (1½ pints) water in a large pan over a low heat, then bring to the boil. Add the pears, cover with a disc of greaseproof paper and poach gently for 10–15 minutes or until tender. Remove the pears with a slotted spoon; set aside.
4 Add the apricot jam to the liquor and simmer for 30 minutes until reduced to a syrupy glaze; set aside.
5 Meanwhile, cream the butter and remaining sugar together in a bowl until light and fluffy. Beat in the eggs a little at a time. Then fold in the flour and almond mixture, reserved kirsch and almond extract.
6 Scoop out the base of each pear with a teaspoon. Stir a spoonful of the cake mix into the raisin mixture; use to fill the pears. Put in a 900ml (1½ pint) shallow ovenproof dish and spoon the rest of the cake mixture around them. Brush the pears with a little of the glaze.
7 Bake at 190°C (170°C fan oven) mark 5 for about 50 minutes until the sponge is golden brown and just firm to the touch; cover with foil during baking if it appears to be overbrowning. Brush with a little more glaze and serve with cream.

Lemon Layer Puddings

50g (2oz) butter, plus extra to grease
125g (4oz) golden caster sugar
finely grated zest and juice of 2 lemons
2 medium eggs, separated
50g (2oz) self-raising flour
300ml (½ pint) semi-skimmed milk

serves 4
preparation: 30 minutes
cooking time: 35 minutes
per serving: 340 cals; 15g fat;
   46g carbohydrate

1 Lightly grease four 200ml (7fl oz) ovenproof cups.
2 In a bowl, cream together the butter, sugar and lemon zest until the mixture is pale and fluffy. Beat in the egg yolks, and then the flour. Stir in the milk and lemon juice – the mixture will curdle at this stage so don't be alarmed.
3 In a clean, grease-free bowl, whisk the egg whites until soft peaks form, then fold them into the lemon mixture (which will still look curdled.) Divide the mixture among the prepared cups.
4 Stand the cups in a roasting tin and surround with boiling water to come halfway up the sides of the cups. Bake at 190°C (170°C fan oven) mark 5 for 35 minutes or until the puddings are spongy and light golden. When cooked, the puddings will have separated into a tangy lemon-custard layer beneath a light sponge topping. Serve immediately.

note: *If you prefer softer tops, cover the entire roasting tin with foil before baking the puddings.*

Gooey Chocolate Puddings

125g (4oz) unsalted butter, plus extra
   to grease
100g (3½oz) good quality plain dark
   chocolate, in small pieces
2 tbsp dark rum or Tia Maria
2 medium eggs, plus 1 egg yolk
50g (2oz) golden caster sugar
2 tbsp plain flour, sifted
icing sugar, to dust

serves 4
preparation: 20 minutes
cooking time: 12–14 minutes
per serving: 520 cals; 38g fat;
   35g carbohydrate

1 Lightly butter four 150ml (¼ pint) ramekins.
2 Melt the chocolate and butter in a heatproof bowl set over a pan of gently simmering water. Take off the heat, add the rum and stir until smooth.

3 Meanwhile, whisk the eggs, egg yolk and caster sugar together in a large heatproof bowl set over a pan of hot water, using a hand-held electric whisk, until the mixture is mousse-like and doubled in volume. This will take about 5 minutes – continue to whisk until the beaters leave a ribbon-like trail when they are lifted up over the mixture.
4 Pour the melted chocolate mixture into the egg mixture, then add the sifted flour. Carefully and thoroughly fold everything together, using a large metal spoon.
5 Divide the mixture equally among the ramekins. Bake the puddings at 200°C (180°C fan oven) mark 6 for 12–14 minutes or until just firm – they'll still have a gooey centre. Dust with icing sugar and serve with crème fraîche.

note: *For convenience, prepare ahead and cover the ramekins tightly with clingfilm. Freeze on a baking tray overnight (or for up to 1 month). Bake the puddings from frozen, allowing 16–17 minutes.*

Individual Chocolate Soufflés

125g (4oz) golden caster sugar
50g (2oz) cocoa powder
9 medium egg whites, at room
    temperature
pinch of cream of tartar
15g (½oz) plain dark chocolate,
    roughly grated
2 tsp dark rum
1 tsp vanilla extract

serves 8
preparation: 10 minutes
cooking time: 12–15 minutes
per serving: 110 cals; 2g fat;
    18g carbohydrate

1 Sift 100g (3½oz) caster sugar together with the cocoa powder; set aside.
2 Using an electric whisk, whisk the egg whites in a clean bowl with the cream of tartar until foamy. Continue whisking at high speed, gradually adding the remaining sugar, a spoonful at a time, until the meringue holds stiff peaks.
3 Using a large metal spoon, carefully fold the sugar and cocoa mixture into the meringue with the chocolate, rum and vanilla extract. The mixture should be evenly combined but still stiff.
4 Divide the soufflé mixture among eight 175ml (6fl oz) ovenproof cups. Stand the cups in a large roasting tin and pour enough boiling water into the tin to come at least halfway up their sides.
5 Immediately bake at 180°C (160°C fan oven) mark 4 for 12–15 minutes or until the soufflés are puffed and set round the edges but still soft in the centre. Serve at once.

Hot Orange Soufflé

65g (2½oz) unsalted butter
2 tbsp dried breadcrumbs
40g (1½oz) plain flour
grated zest and juice of 2 small
    (or 1 large) oranges
grated zest and juice of 1 lemon
200ml (7fl oz) milk
125g (4oz) golden caster sugar
3 tbsp Grand Marnier
4 large eggs, separated
icing sugar, to dust

serves 6
preparation: 20 minutes
cooking time: 25–30 minutes
per serving: 310 cals; 14g fat;
    38g carbohydrate

1 Melt 15g (½oz) of the butter and use to grease a 1.5 litre (2½ pint) soufflé dish. Coat the dish with the breadcrumbs; set aside.
2 Melt the remaining butter in a pan, add the flour, orange and lemon zest, and cook for 30 seconds. Off the heat, gradually beat in the milk until smooth. Cook, stirring, over a low heat until the sauce is thickened and smooth. Continue to cook for a further 2 minutes.
3 Remove from the heat and stir in the sugar, orange and lemon juices and Grand Marnier, then beat in the egg yolks.
4 Whisk the egg whites in another clean bowl until stiff, then carefully fold into the sauce until evenly incorporated. Spoon into the soufflé dish and run a knife around the outside of the mixture.
5 Immediately bake at 190°C (170°C fan oven) mark 5 for 25–30 minutes until the soufflé is risen and golden. Dust with icing sugar and serve at once.

SWEET PIES AND TARTS

Fruit-filled tarts and pies are an ideal way of making the most of fruits in season. Simple shortcrust pastry (page 269) is used for some of the classic fruit pies. Pâte sucrée (page 270) is the classic French rich short pastry used for sweet tarts; it is thin and crisp, yet melting in texture. Sweet tart pastry (page 269) is an enriched sweetened version of shortcrust, which is quick and easy to make. All of these pastries benefit from being left to rest in the fridge for at least 30 minutes before rolling out, to prevent shrinkage during baking. They are all suitable for freezing.

Double-crust Fruit Pie

shortcrust pastry (page 269), made with
   225g (8oz) flour
flour, to dust

FILLING
700g (1½lb) Bramleys or other cooking
   apples
finely grated zest and juice of ½ lemon
50g (2oz) granulated sugar
50g (2oz) dark muscovado sugar
1 tbsp plain flour
pinch of freshly grated nutmeg
¼ tsp ground cinnamon
finely grated zest and juice of ½ orange
50g (2oz) sultanas
15–25g (½–1oz) butter

TO FINISH
golden caster sugar, to dust

serves 6
preparation: 20 minutes, plus pastry
cooking time: 35–40 minutes
per serving: 430 cals; 27g fat;
   45g carbohydrate

1 Roll out two-thirds of the pastry on a lightly floured surface and use to line a 23cm (9 inch) pie plate. Chill for 30 minutes, along with the remaining dough wrapped in clingfilm.
2 Meanwhile to make the filling, peel, quarter and core the apples, then slice and sprinkle with the lemon juice to prevent discolouration.
3 Mix the sugars, flour, nutmeg, cinnamon, lemon and orange zests together and sprinkle a little of this mixture on to the pastry lining.
4 Cover with half the sliced apples, then sprinkle with half the sultanas and half the remaining sugar mixture. Repeat, using all the apples, sultanas and sugar. Sprinkle with the orange juice and dot with the butter.
5 Roll out the remaining pastry to make a lid and use to cover the pie, pressing the edges together well to seal. Slash the top twice to let steam escape.
6 Cut leaves and berries from the pastry trimmings. Brush the top of the pie with water and position the decorations. Dust with caster sugar. Bake at 190°C (170°C fan oven) mark 5 for 35–40 minutes until the fruit is tender and the top is golden brown. Serve warm, with custard or cream.

variation: *For the filling, use a mixture of summer fruits, such as blackcurrants, redcurrants, blueberries and raspberries.*

Traditional Apple Pie

shortcrust pastry (page 269), made with
  175g (6oz) flour
flour, to dust

FILLING
700g (1½lb) Bramleys or other cooking
  apples
75g (3oz) granulated sugar
¼ tsp freshly grated nutmeg
¼ tsp ground cinnamon

TO FINISH
golden caster sugar, to dust

serves 4
preparation: 15 minutes, plus pastry
cooking time: 35–40 minutes
per serving: 540 cals; 27g fat;
  72g carbohydrate

1 To make the filling, peel, quarter, core and slice the apples. Layer the apple slices in a 900ml (1½ pint) pie dish, sprinkling with the sugar and spices.
2 Roll out the pastry on a lightly floured surface and use to cover the pie dish (see pages 267–8), sealing the edges well, and make a hole in the top.
3 Cut leaves from the pastry trimmings, if you like. Brush the top of the pie with water and position the decorations. Dust with caster sugar. Bake at 190°C (170°C fan oven) mark 5 for 35–40 minutes until the fruit is tender and the pastry is golden brown. Serve warm, with custard or cream.

variations
bramble and apple pie: *Substitute 225g (8oz) of the apples with blackberries.*
gooseberry pie: *Replace apples with gooseberries, increasing the sugar to 125g (4oz), or to taste.*

French Apple Tart

PASTRY
175g (6oz) plain flour, plus extra to dust
125g (4oz) unsalted butter, diced
2 tsp golden caster sugar
1 large egg

FILLING
1.8kg (4lb) crisp tart eating apples
4 tbsp Calvados or brandy
grated zest and juice of 1 lemon
50–75g (2–3oz) golden caster sugar
  (depending on sweetness of apples)

GLAZE
15g (½oz) unsalted butter, melted
2 tbsp golden caster sugar
4 tbsp apricot jam

serves 10
preparation: 40 minutes, plus resting
  and cooling
cooking time: about 40 minutes
per serving: 310 cals; 12g fat;
  47g carbohydrate

1 To make the pastry, put the flour into a food processor, add the butter and process until the mixture resembles fine breadcrumbs. Add the sugar and egg and process briefly to a firm dough. Wrap in clingfilm and chill for 30 minutes.
2 Roll out the pastry on a lightly floured surface and use to line a 24cm (9½ inch) loose-based shallow tart tin. Line with greaseproof paper and baking beans and bake blind at 200°C (180°C fan oven) mark 6 for 15 minutes. Remove the beans and paper and bake for a further 5 minutes.
3 Set aside 4 eating apples. Roughly chop the rest, including the cores and unblemished skins. Put into a heavy-based pan with 1 tbsp water. Cover and cook very gently for 25–30 minutes, stirring occasionally, until the apples are soft. Press the pulp through a sieve into a clean pan. Add the Calvados, lemon zest and sugar to taste. Cook, uncovered, until slightly thickened; cool.
4 Peel, core and thinly slice the reserved apples; immerse in a bowl of cold water with 1 tbsp lemon juice added.
5 Spread the apple purée in the pastry case. Drain the apple slices, pat dry on kitchen paper and arrange in overlapping circles over the purée. Brush with the melted butter and sprinkle with the sugar. Bake at 220°C (200°C fan oven) mark 7 for 20 minutes or until the apples are golden.
6 Melt the jam with 1 tbsp water, sieve, then brush over the tart to glaze. Serve warm or cold.

Tarte Tatin

PASTRY

225g (8oz) plain flour, plus extra to dust

150g (5oz) unsalted butter, chilled and diced

¼ tsp salt

50g (2oz) golden icing sugar

1 medium egg

2–3 drops vanilla extract

TOPPING

200g (7oz) golden caster sugar

125g (4oz) unsalted butter, chilled

1.4–1.6kg (3–3½lb) eating apples,
    preferably Cox's

juice of ½ lemon

serves 6–8

preparation: 30 minutes, plus chilling

cooking time: 40–45 minutes

per serving: 760–570 cals; 39–30g fat;
    103–77g carbohydrate

1 To make the pastry, put the flour, butter and salt into a food processor and pulse briefly until the mixture resembles coarse crumbs. Add the icing sugar, egg and vanilla extract and pulse again until the mixture comes together. Gently knead the dough on a lightly floured surface until smooth. Wrap in clingfilm and chill for 20 minutes.

2 Take a 20cm (8 inch) tarte tatin tin or ovenproof frying pan. Sprinkle the caster sugar over the base. Cut the butter into slivers and scatter on top. Peel, half and core the apples and tightly pack, cut-side up, in the tin or pan.

3 Put the tin or pan directly on to the hob and cook over a medium heat for 30 minutes or until the apples are well caramelised, taking care that the caramel doesn't bubble over or catch on the bottom. Sprinkle with the lemon juice. Allow to cool for 15 minutes.

4 Roll out the pastry on a large sheet of baking parchment to a round, 2.5cm (1 inch) larger all round than the tarte tatin tin. Prick several times with a fork.

5 Lay the pastry over the top of the cooked apples, tucking the edges down the side of the tin. Bake at 220°C (200°C fan oven) mark 7 for 25–30 minutes until golden brown.

6 Leave in the tin for 10 minutes, then upturn on to a serving plate. Serve warm, cut into wedges with cream, custard or ice cream.

Bakewell Tart

sweet tart pastry (page 269), made with
    175g (6oz) flour

flour, to dust

4 tbsp strawberry or raspberry jam

FILLING

125g (4oz) ground almonds

125g (4oz) golden caster sugar

50g (2oz) butter, softened

3 medium eggs, beaten

¼ tsp almond extract

TO FINISH

icing sugar, to dust

serves 6

preparation: 15 minutes, plus pastry

cooking time: 30 minutes

per serving: 610 cals; 40g fat;
    55g carbohydrate

1 Roll out the pastry on a lightly floured surface and use to line a 23cm (9 inch) shallow pie plate.

2 Knock up the edge of the pastry with the back of a knife and mark the rim with the prongs of a fork. Spread the jam evenly over the base. Chill while you make the filling.

3 For the filling, beat the ground almonds, caster sugar, butter, beaten eggs and almond extract together in a bowl.

4 Pour the filling over the jam in the pastry case and spread evenly. Bake at 200°C (180°C fan oven) mark 6 for 10 minutes. Lower the oven setting to 190°C (170°C fan oven) mark 5 and bake for a further 20 minutes or until the filling is set.

5 Dust with icing sugar and serve warm or cold, with cream or custard.

Mince Pies

sweet tart pastry, made with 225g (8oz) flour
   (page 269)
flour, to dust

FILLING
225g (8oz) luxury mincemeat (preferably
   homemade, page 543)

TO FINISH
1 egg white, lightly beaten
caster sugar, to sprinkle

makes 12
preparation: 20 minutes, plus pastry
cooking time: 20–25 minutes
per pie: 220 cals; 12g fat; 28g carbohydrate

1 Line a patty tin with paper cases. On a lightly floured surface or sheet of baking parchment, roll out half of the pastry to a 3mm (⅛ inch) thickness. Using a 7.5cm (3 inch) fluted cutter, stamp out 12 rounds of pastry. Gently press these into the lined patty tins. Spoon 1 tbsp mincemeat into each pastry case.

2 Roll out remaining pastry and stamp out 12 rounds with a 6cm (2½ inch) fluted cutter. Dampen the edges of the pastry in the patty tins, then top with the smaller pastry circles. Press the edges together to seal.

3 Brush the tops with egg white, then sprinkle lightly with caster sugar. Bake at 190°C (170°C fan oven) mark 5 for 20–25 minutes until the pastry is golden. Leave in the tins for 5 minutes, then transfer to a wire rack to cool.

4 Serve warm, with brandy butter or pouring cream if you like.

note: *Mince pies can be glazed and baked from frozen as above, allowing an extra 10–15 minutes.*

variations
lattice mince pies: *At stage 2, dust a lattice roller with flour and run it over the rolled-out pastry before cutting out and positioning the pastry lids. Glaze and bake as above.* **Illustrated right**
holly mince pies: *At stage 2, cut remaining pastry into holly leaves, using a suitable cutter, and shape small berries. Arrange overlapping over the filling to form the pastry lids. Glaze and bake as above.*

Pear and Frangipane Tarts

375g pack ready-rolled puff pastry
75cl bottle dry red wine
125g (4oz) golden caster sugar
3 small pears, peeled

FRANGIPANE
50g (2oz) butter, softened
50g (2oz) golden caster sugar
3 tsp beaten egg
25g (1oz) plain flour, sifted
50g (2oz) ground almonds

TO FINISH
icing sugar, to dust

serves 6
preparation: 20 minutes, plus chilling
cooking time: 35–45 minutes
per serving: 580 cals; 27g fat;
   68g carbohydrate

1 Unroll the puff pastry and stamp out 6 rounds, using a 10cm (4 inch) cutter. Put them on a baking sheet, then rest in the fridge for 2 hours.

2 Put the red wine, sugar and 150ml (¼ pint) cold water in a large pan. Heat gently to dissolve the sugar, then bring to the boil. Add the pears, cover with greaseproof paper and a tight-fitting lid and poach for 15 minutes, turning the pears over halfway through. Leave to cool in the liquid.

3 For the frangipane, put the butter and sugar into a bowl and beat with an electric whisk until pale and creamy. Gradually mix in the egg, 1 tsp at a time, adding a little flour each time. Stir in the rest of the flour and the ground almonds to make a thick paste.

4 Spread a little frangipane over each pastry round, leaving a 1cm (½ inch) border. Lift out the pears and drain well, reserving the liquid. Cut the pears in half, remove the core, then thinly slice lengthways. Lay on top of the frangipane to cover it completely and push them down slightly. Bake the tarts at 220°C (200°C fan oven) mark 7 for 20–25 minutes.

5 Meanwhile, bring the reserved liquid to the boil and boil rapidly for 15–20 minutes to make a syrup. Pour a little on to each plate, carefully put the tart on top and dust with a little icing sugar to serve.

Pear, Cherry and Hazelnut Strudel

550g (1¼lb) Williams or Comice pears
125g (4oz) dried cherries
grated zest and juice of ½ small lemon
½ tsp ground cinnamon
1 tbsp cornflour
50g (2oz) hazelnuts, roughly chopped
    and toasted
2 tbsp golden caster sugar
4 sheets filo pastry, about 40g (1½oz)
25g (1oz) butter, melted, plus extra to grease

serves 4
preparation: 20 minutes
cooking time: 40 minutes
per serving: 270 cals; 10g fat;
    43g carbohydrate

1 Peel, quarter, core and slice the pears and put into a large bowl with the dried cherries. Mix in the lemon zest and juice, cinnamon, cornflour, hazelnuts and 1 tbsp of the sugar.
2 Lay two sheets of filo side by side on a clean tea-towel, so they overlap each other by 2.5cm (1 inch). Brush with a little melted butter. Cover with remaining sheets of filo, overlapping as before; brush with butter.
3 Spoon the pear filling along the nearest edge of filo and, lifting the nearest side of the tea-towel, roll up the pastry to enclose the filling. Trim the edges and carefully transfer the strudel to a greased baking sheet, keeping the seam underneath.
4 Brush the strudel with the remaining melted butter and sprinkle with the remaining sugar, then slash the pastry several times diagonally. Bake at 190°C (170°C fan oven) mark 5 for 40 minutes or until golden brown, covering loosely with foil if the top appears to be over-browning. Serve warm, with custard.

note: *The strudel can be frozen at the end of stage 3. Glaze and bake from frozen, as above, allowing an extra 10–15 minutes.*

Apple Strudel with Maple Fudge Sauce

grated zest and juice of 1 lemon
25g (1oz) fresh white breadcrumbs
2 tbsp golden caster sugar
700g (1½lb) Bramleys or other
    cooking apples
juice of ½ lemon
6 sheets filo pastry, about 50g (2oz)
40g (1½oz) butter, melted

MAPLE FUDGE SAUCE
75g (3oz) butter
150g (5oz) light muscovado sugar
2 tbsp maple syrup
90ml (3fl oz) double cream

TO FINISH
icing sugar, to dust

serves 6–8
preparation: 30 minutes
cooking time: 40 minutes
per serving: 420–310 cals; 23–17g fat;
    23–17g carbohydrate

1 Mix the lemon zest with the breadcrumbs and 1 tbsp of the caster sugar. Peel, quarter, core and thickly slice the apples; toss in lemon juice to prevent browning. Mix the apples with the breadcrumb mixture.
2 Lay 3 sheets of filo pastry side by side on a clean tea-towel, overlapping the longest edges by 5cm (2 inches). Brush with a little melted butter. Cover with the remaining sheets of filo, overlapping them as before; brush with butter.
3 Put the apple mixture on the filo pastry. Using the tea-towel to help, roll the filo from one longest edge to form a thick roll. Roll it on to a non-stick baking sheet, seam-side down, curling it slightly, if necessary, to fit the sheet. Brush with the remaining butter and sprinkle with the remaining caster sugar.
4 Bake the apple strudel at 190°C (170°C fan oven) mark 5 for 40 minutes or until the pastry is golden brown and the apples are soft. If necessary, cover the pastry loosely with foil to prevent over-browning.
5 Meanwhile, make the sauce. Melt the butter in a small heavy-based pan, add the sugar and maple syrup and cook gently until the sugar is dissolved. Stir in the cream and bring to the boil. Let cool slightly.
6 Dust the strudel with icing sugar, slice and serve with the maple sauce.

Brandied Prune Tart

PASTRY

175g (6oz) plain flour, plus extra to dust

75g (3oz) lightly salted butter, diced

75g (3oz) golden caster sugar

3 egg yolks

FILLING

250g (9oz) ready-to-eat pitted prunes

5 tbsp brandy

1 vanilla pod, split lengthways

150ml (¼ pint) double cream

150ml (¼ pint) single cream

25g (1oz) golden caster sugar

2 large eggs

GLAZE

4 tbsp apricot jam, sieved

2 tbsp brandy

serves 8

preparation: 25 minutes, plus macerating
and chilling

cooking time: 50 minutes

per serving: 460 cals; 24g fat;
49g carbohydrate

1 For the filling, put the prunes into a bowl, pour on the brandy and leave to soak overnight, or for several hours until the brandy is absorbed.

2 To make the pastry, whiz the flour and butter in a food processor until the mixture resembles fine breadcrumbs. Add the sugar and pulse to mix. Add the egg yolks and process briefly to a soft dough. Knead lightly, wrap in clingfilm and chill for 30 minutes.

3 Roll out the pastry on a lightly floured surface and use to line a 23–24cm (9–9½inch) loose-based tart tin, which is 2.5cm (1 inch) deep. Chill for 20 minutes.

4 Prick the pastry base with a fork, then line with greaseproof paper and baking beans. Stand the tin on a baking sheet and bake blind at 200°C (180°C fan oven) mark 6 for 15 minutes. Remove the beans and paper and bake for a further 5 minutes until the pastry is golden. Lower the oven setting to 180°C (160°C fan oven) mark 4.

5 Meanwhile, put the vanilla pod and double cream into a pan and bring just to the boil, then take off the heat and set aside to infuse for 20 minutes.

6 Strain the infused cream into a bowl, add the single cream, sugar and eggs, and beat well.

7 Scatter the prunes in the pastry case, then pour the cream around them. Bake for 30 minutes or until the custard is just set in the centre. Warm the apricot jam with the brandy, then brush this glaze over the warm tart. Serve warm or cold, with crème fraîche.

variation

apricot tart: *Use dried apricots instead of prunes; soak the fruit in half amaretto liqueur and half water.*

Treacle Tart

PASTRY

225g (8oz) plain flour, plus extra to dust

150g (5oz) unsalted butter, diced

1 egg yolk

15g (½oz) golden caster sugar

FILLING

700g (1½lb) golden syrup

175g (6oz) fresh white breadcrumbs

grated zest of 3 lemons

2 medium eggs, lightly beaten

serves 8–10

preparation: 25 minutes, plus chilling

cooking time: 45–50 minutes

per serving: 580–470 cals; 18–15g fat;
104–83g carbohydrate

1 To make the pastry, put the flour and butter into a food processor and whiz until the mixture resembles breadcrumbs. Add the egg yolk, sugar and about 2 tbsp cold water; process briefly to a firm dough. Turn on to a lightly floured surface and knead lightly, then wrap in clingfilm and chill for 30 minutes.

2 Roll out the pastry on a lightly floured surface and use to line a 25cm (10 inch) fluted loose-based tart tin, which is about 4cm (1½ inches) deep. Flute the edges and prick the base with a fork.

3 For the filling, lightly heat the golden syrup in a pan until thinned in consistency. Remove from the heat and mix in the breadcrumbs and lemon zest. Stir in the beaten eggs. Pour into the pastry case.

4 Bake at 180°C (160°C fan oven) mark 4 for about 45–50 minutes until the filling is lightly set and golden. Allow to cool slightly. Serve warm, with crème fraîche.

Chocolate Orange Tart

PASTRY

150g (5oz) plain flour, plus extra to dust

pinch of salt

75g (3oz) unsalted butter, chilled and
    diced

25g (1oz) golden icing sugar, plus extra
    to dust

grated zest of 1 orange

2 large egg yolks

FILLING

175g (6oz) good quality plain dark
    chocolate, in pieces

175ml (6fl oz) double cream

75g (3oz) light soft brown sugar

2 medium eggs

1 tbsp Grand Marnier or Cointreau

serves 8
preparation: 30 minutes, plus chilling
cooking time: 1 hour
per serving: 430 cals; 30g fat;
    33g carbohydrate

1 To make the pastry, whiz the flour, salt and butter in a food processor until the mixture resembles breadcrumbs. Add the icing sugar and orange zest, pulse to mix, then add the egg yolks and pulse until the mixture just comes together to form a soft dough.

2 Tip the dough out on to a lightly floured surface and knead gently into a ball, then flatten slightly. Wrap in clingfilm and chill for at least 30 minutes.

3 Roll out the pastry on a lightly floured surface, then use to line a 20cm (8 inch) loose-based tart tin. Prick the base all over with a fork, then put the tin on a baking sheet and chill for 30 minutes.

4 Line the tart with greaseproof paper and fill with baking beans. Bake blind at 190°C (170°C fan oven) mark 5 for 15 minutes. Remove beans and paper and bake for a further 5–10 minutes until the pastry is dry. Lower oven setting to 170°C (150°C fan oven) mark 3.

5 For the filling, melt the chocolate in a heatproof bowl set over a pan of hot water. Cool for 10 minutes.

6 Put the cream, sugar, eggs and liqueur into a bowl and mix well. Slowly stir in the chocolate, then pour the mixture into the pastry case. Bake for 30 minutes until just set. Serve warm or cold, cut into slices. Dust with icing sugar and serve with crème fraîche.

Maple Pecan Pie

PASTRY

250g (9oz) plain flour, plus extra to dust

pinch of salt

125g (4oz) unsalted butter, diced

FILLING

100g (3½oz) unsalted butter, softened

100g (3½oz) light muscovado sugar

125g (4oz) dates, pitted and roughly
    chopped

grated zest and juice of ½ lemon

100ml (3½fl oz) maple syrup, plus 4 tbsp
    extra to glaze

1 tsp vanilla extract

4 medium eggs

300g (11oz) pecan nut halves

serves 10–12
preparation: 40 minutes, plus chilling
cooking time: about 1 hour
per serving: 600–500 cals; 43–35g fat;
    50–41g carbohydrate

1 To make the pastry, put the flour and salt into a food processor. Add the butter, whiz until the mixture resembles fine breadcrumbs, then add 2 tbsp cold water and process briefly until the dough just comes together. Wrap in clingfilm and chill for 30 minutes.

2 Roll out the pastry on a lightly floured surface and use to line a 25cm (10 inch) fluted loose-based tart tin, about 4cm (1½ inches) deep. Chill for 30 minutes.

3 Prick the pastry base, line with greaseproof paper and fill with baking beans. Bake blind at 200°C (180°C fan oven) mark 6 for 15 minutes. Remove the beans and paper and bake for a further 5 minutes.

4 Meanwhile, make the filling. Put the butter, sugar and dates into the food processor and whiz to cream together. Add the lemon zest and juice, maple syrup, vanilla extract, eggs and 200g (7oz) nuts. Whiz until the nuts are finely chopped – the mixture will look curdled but don't worry. Pour into the pastry case and top with the rest of the nuts.

5 Bake for 40–45 minutes until almost set in the middle, covering with greaseproof paper for the last 10 minutes if the nuts turn very dark. Leave in the tin for 5 minutes, then remove and brush with maple syrup to glaze. Serve warm, with cream or ice cream.

Lemon Tart

PASTRY

150g (5oz) plain flour, plus extra to dust

pinch of salt

75g (3oz) unsalted butter, chilled and diced,
   plus extra to grease

50g (2oz) golden icing sugar

2 large egg yolks

FILLING

1 large egg, plus 4 large egg yolks

150g (5oz) golden caster sugar

grated zest of 4 medium lemons

150ml (5fl oz) freshly squeezed lemon juice
   (about 4 medium lemons)

142ml carton double cream

TO FINISH

raspberries

icing sugar, to dust

serves 8

preparation: 30 minutes, plus chilling

cooking time: 45–50 minutes, plus standing

per serving: 380 cals; 22g fat;
   42g carbohydrate

1 For the pastry, put the flour and salt into a food processor, add the butter and process briefly until the mixture resembles fine breadcrumbs. Add the icing sugar and pulse to mix. Add the 2 egg yolks, and pulse until the mixture just holds together but doesn't quite form a ball.

2 Tip the dough on to a lightly floured surface and knead gently into a ball. Wrap in clingfilm and chill for 30 minutes.

3 Roll out the pastry on a lightly floured surface to a 28cm (11 inch) round. Use to line a greased and floured 23cm (9 inch) deep loose-based tart tin, which is 2.5cm (1 inch) deep. Press the pastry into the edges of the tin and trim off the excess. Chill for 30 minutes.

4 Stand the tin on a baking sheet. Line the pastry case with greaseproof paper and baking beans, and bake blind at 190°C (170°C fan oven) mark 5 for 10 minutes. Remove the beans and paper and bake for a further 8–10 minutes until the base is dry and lightly cooked. Lower the oven setting to 170°C (150°C fan oven) mark 3.

5 Meanwhile, make the filling. Beat the whole egg, egg yolks and caster sugar together in a bowl until smooth. Carefully stir in the lemon zest, lemon juice and cream, and mix until evenly blended. Leave to stand for 5 minutes, then skim off the foam from the top of the mixture.

6 Carefully pour the filling into the pastry case. Bake the tart for 25–30 minutes or until the filling in the centre is just springy to the touch. Leave to stand for 15 minutes then serve warm, or cool completely and chill before serving. Decorate the tart with raspberries, and dust icing sugar over the top before serving.

note: *This tart has a refreshingly sharp, citrusy flavour. For a sweeter taste, add 1–2 tbsp icing sugar to the lemon filling at stage 5.*

Strawberry Tart

PASTRY

125g (4oz) plain flour, plus extra to dust

pinch of salt

50g (2oz) golden caster sugar

50g (2oz) butter, diced, at room
   temperature

2 medium egg yolks

CRÈME PÂTISSIÈRE

300ml (½ pint) whole milk

1 vanilla pod, split lengthways

2 medium egg yolks

50g (2oz) golden caster sugar

2 tbsp plain flour

2 tbsp cornflour

50ml (2fl oz) crème fraîche

TOPPING

450g (1lb) strawberries, hulled
   and halved

6 tbsp redcurrant jelly

serves 6

preparation: 40 minutes, plus cooling
   and chilling

cooking time: 35 minutes

per serving: 380 cals; 15g fat;
   58g carbohydrate

1 To make the pastry, put the flour, salt and sugar into a processor with the butter and egg yolks. Whiz until the mixture looks like loose breadcrumbs. Add 1–2 tsp cold water, then whiz again briefly to combine.

2 Tip on to a floured surface and knead gently to form a smooth dough. Shape into a ball, flatten lightly, then wrap in clingfilm and chill for 20 minutes.

3 To make the crème pâtissière, pour the milk into a heavy-based pan. Scrape the vanilla seeds from the pod and add them to the milk with the empty pod. Heat gently to just below boiling.

4 Meanwhile, beat the egg yolks and sugar together in a bowl until pale, then stir in the flour and cornflour. Discard the vanilla pod, then gradually pour the hot milk on to the mixture, whisking constantly. Return to the pan and bring slowly to the boil, stirring. Cook, stirring, for 3–4 minutes or until thickened and smooth. Transfer to a bowl and cover the surface with damp greaseproof paper. Leave to cool.

5 Roll out the pastry thinly between two sheets of baking parchment and use to line a 23cm (9 inch) loose-based tart tin. Prick the base with a fork, line with greaseproof paper and chill for 30 minutes. Fill with baking beans and bake blind at 190°C (170°C fan oven) mark 5 for 10–15 minutes. Remove the beans and paper, then bake for a further 10 minutes until firm and golden brown. Leave to cool.

6 Add the crème fraîche to the crème pâtissière and beat well until smooth. Spoon into the pastry case and spread evenly over the base. Arrange the strawberry halves on top of the cream mixture, starting from the outside edge and working into the centre. Heat the redcurrant jelly in a small pan, stirring, until syrupy, then brush over the strawberries to glaze. Serve within 2 hours of assembling.

Vanilla Egg Custard Tart

TART PASTRY

175g (6oz) plain flour, plus extra to dust

125g (4oz) butter, diced

25g (1oz) vanilla sugar (see page 16),
    plus extra to dust

1 tsp finely grated orange zest

1 egg yolk

VANILLA CUSTARD

2 large eggs

2 large egg yolks

40g (1½oz) golden caster sugar

450ml (¾ pint) single cream

½ vanilla pod, split lengthways

TO FINISH

175g (6oz) raspberries (optional)

serves 6

preparation: 40 minutes, plus chilling

cooking time: about 1 hour, plus cooling

per serving: 520 cals; 37g fat;
    41g carbohydrate

1 To make the pastry, put the flour into a food processor, add the butter and whiz until the mixture resembles breadcrumbs. Add the vanilla sugar and orange zest and pulse to mix. Add the egg yolk and 2–3 tsp water and process briefly to a firm dough. Knead lightly, wrap in clingfilm and chill for 20 minutes.

2 Roll out the dough on a lightly floured surface and use to line a 20cm (8 inch) loose-based fluted tart tin, which is 4cm (1½ inches) deep. Chill for 20 minutes. Line pastry case with greaseproof paper and baking beans and bake blind at 200°C (180°C fan oven) mark 6 for 15 minutes. Remove the beans and paper and return to the oven for 5–10 minutes to cook the base.

3 Meanwhile, make the custard filling. Put the whole eggs, egg yolks and sugar into a bowl and beat well. Put the cream and vanilla pod into a small pan over a very low heat until the cream is well flavoured and almost boiling. Pour on to the egg mixture, whisking constantly, then strain into the pastry case.

4 Lower the setting to 150°C (130°C fan oven) mark 2 and put the tart in the oven. Bake for 45 minutes or until the centre is softly set. Leave until cold, then carefully remove from the tin. Top with raspberries if you like, and dust with vanilla sugar to serve.

Banoffi Fudge Pie

shortcrust pastry (page 269), made with
    175g (6oz) flour

flour, to dust

FILLING

75g (3oz) butter

50g (2oz) light muscovado sugar

2 tbsp milk

220g can condensed milk

5 medium bananas, peeled

300ml (½ pint) double cream

juice of ½ lemon

50g (2oz) golden caster sugar

serves 6

preparation: 40 minutes, plus chilling

cooking time: 25 minutes, plus cooling

per serving: 820 cals; 53g fat;
    81g carbohydrate

1 Roll out the pastry on a lightly floured surface and use to line a 23cm (9 inch) loose-based tart tin, which is about 2.5cm (1 inch) deep.

2 Line the pastry case with greaseproof paper and baking beans. Bake blind at 200°C (180°C fan oven) mark 6 for 15 minutes, then remove beans and paper and bake for a further 8–10 minutes until golden. Cool.

3 For the filling, put the butter and muscovado sugar in a small heavy-based pan and heat gently until the butter melts and the sugar dissolves. Bring to the boil and bubble for 1 minute only, stirring frequently. Off the heat, add the milk and condensed milk. Return to the heat and bring to the boil. Bubble, stirring constantly, for 2 minutes or until the mixture is the consistency of a very thick sauce and turns golden. Keep warm.

4 Meanwhile, thickly slice 4 bananas and scatter in the pastry case. Spoon the warm fudge sauce evenly over the bananas to cover them completely. Leave to cool, then chill until set, about 45 minutes.

5 Whip the cream until it just holds its shape and pile on top of the pie. Chill for at least 1 hour.

6 Slice the remaining banana and toss in lemon juice. Pile on top of the cream. Melt the caster sugar in a small heavy-based pan over a low heat, then cook to a golden caramel colour. Cool for 1 minute or until the caramel thickens and darkens slightly, then spoon over the banana; it will run through the cream. Chill to set.

Profiteroles

CHOUX PASTE
65g (2½oz) white plain flour
pinch of salt
50g (2oz) butter, diced
2 large eggs, lightly beaten

CHOCOLATE SAUCE
225g (8oz) plain dark chocolate, in pieces
142ml carton double cream
1–2 tbsp Grand Marnier, to taste (optional)
1–2 tsp golden caster sugar, to taste
    (optional)

TO ASSEMBLE
284ml carton double cream
few drops of vanilla extract
1 tsp golden caster sugar

serves 6
preparation: 25 minutes, plus cooling
cooking time: 30 minutes
per serving: 660 cals; 54g fat;
    38g carbohydrate

1 Sift the flour with the salt on to a sheet of greaseproof paper. Put the butter into a medium heavy-based pan with 150ml (¼ pint) water. Heat gently until the butter melts, then bring to a rapid boil. Take off the heat and immediately tip in all the flour and beat thoroughly with a wooden spoon until the mixture is smooth and forms a ball. Turn into a bowl and leave to cool for about 10 minutes.

2 Gradually add the eggs to the mixture, beating well after each addition. Ensure that the mixture becomes thick and shiny before adding any more egg – if it's added too quickly, the choux paste will become runny and the cooked buns will be flat.

3 Sprinkle a large baking sheet with a little water. Using two damp teaspoons, spoon about 18 small mounds of the choux paste on to the baking sheet, spacing well apart to allow room for them to expand. Alternatively, spoon the choux paste into a piping bag fitted with a 1cm (½ inch) plain nozzle and pipe mounds on to the baking sheet.

4 Bake at 220°C (200°C fan oven) mark 7 for about 25 minutes or until well risen, crisp and golden brown. Make a small hole in the side of each bun to allow the steam to escape and then return to the oven for a further 5 minutes or until thoroughly dried out. Slide on to a large wire rack and set aside to cool.

5 To make the sauce, put the chocolate and cream into a medium pan with 4 tbsp water. Heat gently, stirring occasionally, until the chocolate melts to a smooth sauce; do not boil. Remove from the heat.

6 To assemble, lightly whip the cream with the vanilla extract and sugar until it just holds its shape. Pipe into the hole in each choux bun, or split the buns open and spoon in the cream. Chill for up to 2 hours.

7 Just before serving, gently reheat the chocolate sauce. Add Grand Marnier and caster sugar to taste, if you like. Divide the choux buns among serving bowls and pour over the warm chocolate sauce. Serve immediately.

CHEESECAKES

This sweet dessert is more of a deep tart than a cake. It has its roots in Europe, but America now boasts more cheesecake recipes than anywhere else. It is essentially a rich flavoured mixture of eggs, cream and full or low-fat soft cheese, curd cheese or cottage cheese – set on a buttery biscuit, sponge or pastry base. Cheesecakes are either baked to cook and set the filling, or uncooked and set with gelatine. Use a spring-release cake tin to make it easier to unmould.

Classic Baked Cheesecake

BASE
250g pack digestive biscuits
125g (4oz) unsalted butter, melted, plus
   extra to grease

FILLING
1 large unwaxed lemon
2 x 250g cartons curd cheese
142ml carton soured cream
2 medium eggs
175g (6oz) golden caster sugar
1½ tsp vanilla extract
1 tbsp cornflour
50g (2oz) sultanas

serves 12
preparation: 30 minutes, plus chilling
cooking time: 55 minutes, plus cooling
per serving: 350 cals; 21g fat;
   35g carbohydrate

1 For the base, put the biscuits into a food processor and whiz to fine crumbs. Add the melted butter and mix until well combined.

2 Tip the crumb mixture into a greased 20cm (8 inch) spring-release cake tin. Press evenly on to the base, using the back of a spoon. Chill for 1 hour until firm.

3 Grate the zest from the lemon and set aside. Halve the lemon, cut 3 very thin slices from one half and put to one side. Squeeze the juice from the rest of the lemon.

4 To make the filling, put the lemon zest, lemon juice, curd cheese, soured cream, eggs, sugar, vanilla extract and cornflour into a large bowl. Using an electric mixer, whisk together until thick and smooth, then fold in the sultanas.

5 Pour the mixture into the tin and shake gently to level the surface. Bake at 180°C (160°C fan oven) mark 4 for 30 minutes. Put the lemon slices, overlapping, on top. Bake for a further 20–25 minutes until the cheesecake is just set and golden brown. Turn off the oven and leave the cheesecake inside with the door ajar until it is cool, then chill for at least 2 hours or overnight.

6 Remove the cheesecake from the fridge about 30 minutes before serving. Run a knife around the edge, release the side of the tin and remove. Cut the cheesecake into slices to serve.

Orange and Chocolate Cheesecake

BASE

225g (8oz) butter, chilled, plus extra to grease

250g (9oz) plain flour, sifted

150g (5oz) light muscovado sugar

3 tbsp cocoa powder

FILLING

2 oranges

4 x 200g cartons cream cheese

250g carton mascarpone

4 large eggs

225g (8oz) golden caster sugar

2 tbsp cornflour

½ tsp vanilla extract

1 vanilla pod, split lengthways

TO FINISH (OPTIONAL)

chocolate curls (see page 503)

serves 12–14

preparation: 45 minutes

cooking time: 2–2¼ hours, plus cooling

per serving: 850–730 cals; 64–55g fat;

   63–54g carbohydrate

1 To make the base, cut 175g (6oz) of the butter into cubes; melt the rest and set aside. Put the flour and cubed butter into a food processor with the sugar and cocoa powder. Whiz together to the texture of fine breadcrumbs, then pour in the melted butter and pulse until the mixture comes together.

2 Spoon into a greased and base-lined 23cm (9 inch) spring-release cake tin and press with the back of a spoon to level the surface. Bake at 180°C (160°C fan oven) mark 4 for 35–40 minutes until lightly puffed; do not overbrown otherwise the biscuit base will have a bitter flavour. Allow to cool. Lower the oven setting to 150°C (130°C fan oven) mark 2.

3 Meanwhile, make the filling. Grate the zest from the oranges, then squeeze the juice – you'll need 150ml (¼ pint). Put the cream cheese, mascarpone, eggs, sugar, cornflour, orange zest and vanilla extract into a large bowl and beat together, using a hand-held electric whisk, until well combined. Scrape out the seeds from the vanilla pod and add to the cheese mixture. Beat in the orange juice and continue whisking until smooth.

4 Pour the mixture over the cooled biscuit base. Bake for about 1½ hours or until pale golden on top, slightly risen and just set around the edge. The cheesecake should still be slightly wobbly in the middle; it will set as it cools. Turn off the oven and leave the cheesecake inside to cool for 1 hour. Remove and allow to cool completely; this will take 2–3 hours.

5 Just before serving, unclip the tin and transfer the cheesecake to a plate. Scatter chocolate curls on top to decorate if you like.

note: *You can prepare this cheesecake up to a day ahead. Keep refrigerated but bring back to room temperature before serving.*

Warm Ginger and Ricotta Cheesecake

BASE

225g (8oz) digestive biscuits

75g (3oz) butter, melted

FILLING

200g (7oz) full-fat soft cheese

225g (8oz) ricotta cheese

4 tbsp double cream

3 medium eggs, separated

1 tbsp cornflour

1 stem ginger ball in syrup, finely chopped

15ml (1 tbsp) stem ginger syrup (from the jar)

125g (4oz) golden icing sugar, sifted

GINGER AND WHISKY SAUCE

300ml (½ pint) single cream

2 tsp stem ginger syrup

2 tsp whisky

serves 6–8

preparation: 25 minutes

cooking time: 1¼ hours, plus cooling

per serving: 760–570 cals; 56–42g fat;
    55–41g carbohydrate

1 For the base, put the biscuits into a food processor and whiz to fine crumbs. Add the melted butter and mix until well combined.

2 Line the base of a 20cm (8 inch) spring-release cake tin with baking parchment and cover the base with two-thirds of the crumb mixture; set aside.

3 For the filling, put the cheeses, cream, egg yolks, cornflour, ginger and ginger syrup in the cleaned processor bowl and whiz briefly until the mixture is evenly blended and the ginger is roughly chopped through it. Transfer to a large bowl.

4 Whisk the egg whites in a clean bowl until soft peaks form. Gradually whisk in the icing sugar, keeping the meringue very stiff and shiny. Fold into the ginger mixture and spoon into the tin. Sprinkle over the remaining biscuit crumbs.

5 Bake the cheesecake at 200°C (180°C fan oven) mark 6 for 30 minutes. Cover loosely with foil, lower the oven setting to 180°C (160°C fan oven) mark 4 and bake for a further 45 minutes or until the filling feels just set in the centre. Leave to cool on a wire rack for 15 minutes; the cheesecake will sink slightly.

6 For the sauce, heat all the ingredients together in a pan; do not boil.

7 Unmould the cheesecake and serve warm with the ginger and whisky sauce.

note: *If frozen, bake from the freezer; allow an extra 15 minutes at the lower oven setting.*

Chilled Lemon Cheesecake

BASE

75g (3oz) butter, melted, plus extra
    to grease

175g (6oz) digestive biscuits

FILLING

finely grated zest and juice of 2 lemons

1 tbsp powdered gelatine

225g (8oz) full-fat soft cheese

150ml (¼ pint) Greek-style yogurt or
    crème fraîche

4 tbsp thin honey

2 medium egg whites

serves 6

preparation: 25 minutes, plus chilling

per serving: 420 cals; 35g fat;
    22g carbohydrate

1 Grease a 20cm (8 inch) spring-release cake tin. Crush the biscuits in a food processor, then mix with the melted butter until evenly combined. Press over the base of the prepared tin.

2 To make the filling, make up the juice from the lemons to 150ml (¼ pint) with water. Sprinkle on the gelatine and leave to soften for 2–3 minutes. Stand the bowl over a pan of simmering water until the gelatine is dissolved. Leave to cool slightly.

3 Beat the soft cheese, yogurt and honey together in a bowl. Stir in the lemon zest and dissolved gelatine.

4 Whisk the egg whites in a clean bowl until stiff. Fold into the cheese mixture and spoon into the tin. Level the surface. Chill for at least 4 hours until set.

5 Carefully remove the cheesecake from the tin and transfer to a plate to serve.

CRÊPES AND BATTER PUDDINGS

Batter puddings include crêpes or pancakes, fritters and oven-baked clafoutis. Crêpes are made from a thin pouring batter, which has a consistency similar to single cream. A thicker coating batter is used for fritters; this must be thick enough to cling to the appropriate fruit, so it will form a protective coating during deep-frying.

If you have sufficient time, leave the batter to rest at room temperature for about 20 minutes before cooking to allow the starch grains time to swell and soften. This gives a lighter batter.

To freeze crêpes, interleave them with freezer tissue and wrap in foil. Defrost at room temperature, separating the crêpes, then reheat briefly.

Plain Crêpes

CREPE BATTER
125g (4oz) plain flour
pinch of salt
1 medium egg
300ml (½ pint) milk
a little oil, to fry

TO SERVE
golden caster sugar
lemon juice

makes 8
preparation: 10 minutes, plus
   optional standing
cooking time: about 15 minutes
per crêpe: 100 cals; 3g fat;
   16g carbohydrate

1 Sift the flour and salt into a bowl and make a well in the centre. Add the egg and whisk well with a balloon whisk. Gradually beat in the milk, drawing in the flour from the sides to make a smooth batter. Cover and leave to stand if possible, for 20 minutes.
2 Heat a few drops of oil in an 18cm (7 inch) heavy-based crêpe pan or non-stick frying pan. Pour in just enough batter to thinly coat the bottom of the pan. Cook over a medium-high heat for about 1 minute until golden brown. Turn or toss and cook the second side for ½–1 minute until golden.
3 Transfer the crêpe to a plate and keep hot. Repeat to cook the remaining batter, stacking the cooked crêpes on top of each other with greaseproof paper in between; keep warm in the oven while cooking the remaining crêpes.
4 Serve as soon as the crêpes are all cooked, sprinkled with sugar and lemon juice.

variations
buckwheat crêpes: *Replace half of the flour with buckwheat flour and add an extra egg white.*
orange, lemon or lime crêpes: *Add the finely grated zest of 1 lemon, ½ an orange or 1 lime, with the milk.*
chocolate crêpes: *Replace 15g (½oz) of the flour with sifted cocoa powder.*

Chocolate Crêpes with a Boozy Sauce

100g (3½oz) plain flour, sifted

pinch of salt

1 medium egg

300ml (½ pint) semi-skimmed milk

sunflower oil, to fry

100g (3½oz) unsalted butter

100g (3½oz) light muscovado sugar,
    plus extra to sprinkle

4 tbsp brandy

50g (2oz) good quality plain dark chocolate,
    roughly chopped

serves 4

preparation: 5 minutes, plus standing

cooking time: 10 minutes

per serving: 550 cals; 32g fat;
    52g carbohydrate

1 Put the flour and salt into a food processor. Add the egg and milk and process until smooth. Pour the batter into a jug, cover and leave to stand for about 20 minutes.

2 Heat 1 tsp oil in a 23cm (9 inch) non-stick crêpe pan or small frying pan. Pour 100ml (3½fl oz) batter into the centre and tilt the pan around so that the batter coats the bottom. Cook for 1–2 minutes until golden underneath. Use a palette knife to flip the crêpe over, and cook the other side.

3 Tip the crêpe on to a plate, cover with a piece of greaseproof paper and repeat with the remaining batter, using a little more oil as necessary, and stacking the crêpes as they are cooked.

4 Melt the butter and sugar together in a frying pan over a low heat. Add the brandy and stir.

5 Divide the chocolate among the crêpes. Fold each in half, then in half again. Slide each one into the frying pan and cook for 3–4 minutes to melt the chocolate, turning halfway through to coat with the sauce. Serve the crêpes drizzled with the sauce and sprinkled with extra sugar.

Crêpes Suzette

1 quantity crêpe batter (page 420)
1 tsp golden icing sugar
grated zest of ½ orange
knob of butter, plus extra to fry

ORANGE SAUCE
50g (2oz) golden caster sugar
50g (2oz) butter
juice of 2 oranges
grated zest of 1 lemon
3 tbsp Cointreau

TO FLAMBE
2 tbsp brandy

serves 4
preparation: 20 minutes, plus standing
cooking time: 15 minutes
per serving: 260 cals; 9g fat;
  39g carbohydrate

1 Flavour the crêpe batter with the icing sugar and orange zest, then leave to stand for 30 minutes. Just before cooking the crêpes, melt the knob of butter and stir it into the batter.

2 To cook the crêpes, heat a small amount of butter in a 15–18cm (6–7 inch) heavy-based frying pan. Pour in just enough batter to cover the bottom, swirling it to coat. Cook over a medium heat for about 1 minute, until the crêpe is golden underneath. Using a palette knife, flip it over and cook briefly on the other side. Lift on to a plate, cover with greaseproof paper and keep warm while you cook the others in the same way, interleaving each with a square of greaseproof paper to keep them separated.

3 To make the orange sauce, put the sugar into a large heavy-based frying pan and heat gently, shaking the pan occasionally, until the sugar has melted and turned golden brown. Remove from the heat and add the butter, orange juice and lemon zest. Return the pan to the heat, and stir the sauce until it begins to simmer. Add the Cointreau.

4 Fold each crêpe in half and then in half again. Put all the crêpes back into the pan and simmer for a few minutes to reheat, spooning the sauce over them.

5 To flambé, warm the brandy and pour it over the crêpes. Using a taper and standing well clear, ignite the brandy. When the flame dies down, serve at once.

Apple Fritters with Honey Cream

1 egg, separated
50g (2oz) plain flour
25g (1oz) golden caster sugar
½ tsp ground cloves
90ml (3fl oz) apple juice
4 large eating apples
oil, to deep-fry

HONEY CREAM
200ml (7fl oz) double cream
2 tbsp thin honey
1 tbsp lemon juice

TO FINISH
icing sugar, to dust

serves 4
preparation: 15 minutes, plus standing
cooking time: 3–4 minutes
per serving: 510 cals; 40g fat;
  35g carbohydrate

1 Put the egg yolk, flour, sugar, cloves and apple juice in a bowl and beat until smooth. Cover and leave to stand for 30 minutes.

2 For the honey cream, whip the cream in a bowl until it almost holds its shape, then fold in the honey and lemon juice. Chill until needed.

3 When ready to serve, heat a 10cm (4 inch) depth of oil in a deep heavy-based pan to 180°C as registered on a sugar thermometer, or until a cube of bread dropped in turns golden within 30 seconds.

4 Quarter, core and thickly slice the apples. Whisk the egg white until stiff and fold into the batter.

5 Dip a few apple slices into the batter to coat, then lower into the hot oil. Fry for up to 1 minute until crisp and golden brown. Drain on kitchen paper and keep warm, while cooking the remaining apple slices in the same way.

6 Dust the fritters with icing sugar and serve hot with the honey cream.

Lemon and Blueberry Pancakes

125g (4oz) plain flour
1 tsp baking powder
¼ tsp bicarbonate of soda
175g (6oz) caster sugar
grated zest of 1 lemon
125ml (4fl oz) yogurt
2 tbsp milk
2 medium eggs, beaten
250g (9oz) blueberries
2 tbsp lemon juice
a little sunflower oil, to fry
25g (1oz) butter, melted, plus extra to fry
finely pared lemon zest, to decorate
    (optional)

serves 4
preparation: 15 minutes
cooking time: about 10 minutes
per serving: 440 cals; 12g fat;
    77g carbohydrate

1 Sift the flour, baking powder and bicarbonate of soda together into a bowl. Add 3 tbsp caster sugar and the lemon zest. Pour in the yogurt, milk and eggs, and whisk together until smooth. Put the batter to one side.
2 For the blueberry syrup, dissolve the rest of the caster sugar in 100ml (3½fl oz) water in a pan over a low heat. Add 150g (5oz) blueberries, bring to the boil and bubble for 1 minute. Add the lemon juice and set aside while you cook the pancakes.
3 Heat a little drizzle of oil and a knob of butter in a frying pan over a medium heat. Stir the melted butter into the batter. Add a couple of spoonfuls of batter to the pan and scatter with a few blueberries. Cook for 1–2 minutes until golden underneath, then flip the pancake over and cook for a further 1 minute. Repeat to make 8 pancakes in total.
4 Spoon the blueberry syrup over the pancakes to serve. Top with a little lemon zest if you like and serve with crème fraîche.

Cherry Clafoutis

350g (12oz) pitted fresh cherries
3 tbsp kirsch
125g (4oz) caster sugar, plus extra to dust
150ml (¼ pint) milk
150ml (¼ pint) double cream
4 large eggs
25g (1oz) plain flour
1 tsp vanilla extract
butter, to grease
icing sugar, to dust

serves 6
preparation: 20 minutes, plus standing
cooking time: 50–55 minutes
per serving: 340 cals; 18g fat;
    37g carbohydrate

1 Put the cherries into a bowl and sprinkle with the kirsch and 1 tbsp caster sugar. Toss together, cover and set aside for 1 hour.
2 Pour the milk and double cream into a pan and slowly bring to the boil. Meanwhile, whisk together the eggs, remaining caster sugar and flour in a large bowl. Pour in the hot creamy milk, whisking as you do so. Add the vanilla extract and strain into a bowl, cover and set aside for 30 minutes.
3 Lightly butter a 1.7 litre (3 pint) shallow ovenproof dish and dust with caster sugar. Spoon the cherries into the dish, whisk the batter once more and pour over the fruit. Bake at 180°C (160°C fan oven) mark 4 for 50–55 minutes or until golden and just set.
4 Dust with icing sugar and serve warm, with cream.

note: *You will need to buy about 500g (1lb 2oz) fresh cherries to give this pitted weight.*

CREAMY DESSERTS

Classic rich, creamy custards, refreshing fruity whips and favourite desserts, such as tiramisu, zabaglione and panna cotta are featured here. Real egg custard forms the basis of many creamy desserts, including crème caramel and trifle. Always cook custard in a heavy-based pan or in the top of a double boiler over a very low heat to avoid curdling. The custard is ready when it is slightly thickened – just enough to thinly coat the back of the wooden spoon.

Crème Caramel

CARAMEL

175g (6oz) granulated sugar

CUSTARD

600ml (1 pint) whole or semi-skimmed milk

1 vanilla pod, split lengthways, or a few
drops of vanilla extract

4 large eggs, plus 4 egg yolks

50–65g (2–2½oz) golden caster sugar,
to taste

serves 6
preparation: 15 minutes
cooking time: 20–30 minutes, plus cooling
per serving: 300 cals; 10g fat;
45g carbohydrate

1 Warm 6 ramekins. To make the caramel, put the granulated sugar into a heavy-based pan and heat gently until melted, brushing any sugar down from the side of the pan. Increase the heat and boil rapidly for a few minutes until the syrup turns to a rich golden brown caramel, gently swirling the pan to ensure even browning. Immediately dip the base of the pan in cool water to prevent further cooking.

2 Pour a little caramel into each of the warmed ramekins and quickly rotate to coat the bottom and part way up the sides. Leave to cool.

3 To make the custard, put the milk and vanilla pod in a pan and heat until almost boiling; if using vanilla extract add after heating the milk.

4 Meanwhile, beat the eggs, egg yolks and caster sugar in a bowl until well mixed. Stir in the hot milk. Strain, then pour into the ramekins.

5 Stand the ramekins in a roasting tin containing enough hot water to come halfway up the sides. Bake at 170°C (150°C fan oven) mark 3 for 20–30 minutes until just set and a knife inserted in the centre comes out clean. Remove from the tin. Cool.

6 To turn out, free the edges by pressing with the fingertips then run a knife around the edge of each custard. Put a serving dish over the top, invert and lift off the ramekin; the caramel will have formed a sauce around the custard.

variation: *Make one large crème caramel in a 15cm (6 inch) soufflé dish; bake as above for 1 hour until just set. After cooling, chill for several hours. Transfer to room temperature 30 minutes before serving.*

Crème Brûlée

600ml (1 pint) double cream
1 vanilla pod, split lengthways
4 large egg yolks
125g (4oz) golden caster sugar

serves 6
preparation: 15 minutes, plus infusing
    and chilling
cooking time: 30–35 minutes
per serving: 580 cals; 52g fat;
    25g carbohydrate

1 Pour the cream into a pan, add the vanilla pod and bring slowly to the boil. Remove from the heat, cover and set aside to infuse for at least 30 minutes. Stand 6 ramekins in a roasting tin.

2 Beat the egg yolks with 1 tbsp caster sugar in a bowl. Pour in the vanilla-infused cream, stirring constantly. Strain into a jug, then pour into the ramekins. Surround with hand-hot water to come halfway up the sides of the ramekins. Bake at 150°C (130°C fan oven) mark 2 for 30–35 minutes. Cool, then chill for at least 4 hours, preferably overnight.

3 Sprinkle the remaining sugar evenly on top of the custards to form a thin layer. Put under a very hot grill for 2–3 minutes until it caramelises. (Alternatively, you can wave a cook's blow-torch over the surface to caramelise the sugar.) Allow to cool for 1 hour, but do not chill – the caramel will form a crisp layer on the surface. Serve within 2–3 hours.

Summer Fruit Brûlée

1 ripe nectarine, halved, stoned and
    thinly sliced
350g (12oz) mixed summer berries,
    such as strawberries, blackberries,
    raspberries and redcurrants
2 tbsp ruby port
150ml (¼ pint) double cream
125g (4oz) Greek-style yogurt
few drops of vanilla extract
25g (1oz) demerara sugar

serves 4
preparation: 15 minutes, plus macerating
    and standing
cooking time: 3–4 minutes
per serving: 270 cals; 21g fat;
    16g carbohydrate

1 Put the nectarine and summer berries into a bowl, add the port and stir to mix. Leave to macerate for 1–2 hours if possible. Transfer to a 900ml (1½ pint) gratin dish.

2 Whip the cream in a bowl until it holds its shape, then fold in the yogurt together with the vanilla extract. Spread the cream mixture evenly over the fruit, to cover completely.

3 Scatter the demerara sugar over the cream and grill under a high heat as close to the heat source as possible for 3–4 minutes until the sugar is golden brown and caramelised. (Alternatively, you can wave a cook's blow-torch over the surface to caramelise the sugar.) Leave to stand for 5 minutes, then serve.

variation: *Divide the fruit among 4–6 ramekins. Cover with the cream mixture, then the sugar and finish as above.*

Rich Chocolate Pots

300g (11oz) good quality plain chocolate,
    in pieces (see note)
284ml carton double cream
250g carton mascarpone
3 tbsp Cognac
1 tbsp vanilla extract

TO DECORATE
6 tbsp crème fraîche
chocolate curls (see page 503)

serves 6
preparation: 15 minutes, plus chilling
per serving: 780 cals; 65g fat;
    41g carbohydrate

1 Put the chocolate into a heatproof bowl over a pan of gently simmering water. Leave until melted, then stir until smooth. Remove the bowl from the heat.
2 Add the cream, mascarpone, Cognac and vanilla extract, and mix well – the hot chocolate will melt the mascarpone.
3 Divide the mixture among six 150ml (¼ pint) glasses and chill for about 20 minutes.
4 Spoon a dollop of crème fraîche on top of each dessert and decorate with chocolate curls. Serve with cigarettes russes or other dessert biscuits.

note: *Use a good quality plain chocolate, such as Bournville, but not a very dark variety, otherwise the flavour of the chocolate pots will be too bitter.*

Petits Pots de Crème au Chocolat

600ml (1 pint) single cream
½ tsp vanilla extract
225g (8oz) good quality plain chocolate,
   in pieces
1 large egg
5 large egg yolks
25g (1oz) golden caster sugar

TO DECORATE
100ml (3½fl oz) cream, whipped
cocoa powder, to dust

serves 6–8
preparation: 15 minutes, plus chilling
cooking time: 1 hour
per serving: 530–400 cals; 46–35g fat;
   18–14g carbohydrate

1 Put the cream, vanilla extract and chocolate into a heavy-based pan over a low heat and heat gently, stirring, until the chocolate has melted and the mixture is smooth.
2 Lightly mix together the whole egg, egg yolks and caster sugar in a bowl, then stir in the chocolate cream until smooth.
3 Strain the chocolate mixture into eight 90ml (3fl oz) custard pots, or six ramekins. Cover the containers with lids or foil.
4 Stand the custard pots or ramekins in a roasting tin and pour in enough hot water to come halfway up the sides of the dishes. Cook at 150°C (130°C fan oven) mark 2 for about 1 hour until lightly set; the centres should still be slightly soft. Do not overcook or the texture will be spoilt.
5 Remove the pots or ramekins from the tin and leave to cool, then chill well. Serve topped with a spoonful of cream and a dusting of cocoa powder.

variation: *For a less rich version, use half single cream and half milk.*

Lemon Syllabub

grated zest and juice of 1 lemon
150ml (¼ pint) medium dry white wine
75g (3oz) golden caster sugar
284ml carton double cream
2 medium egg whites

serves 4
preparation: 15 minutes, plus cooling
   and chilling
per serving: 420 cals; 34g fat;
   22g carbohydrate

1 Put the lemon zest and juice into a pan with the white wine and sugar. Warm over a low heat until the sugar dissolves, then remove the pan from the heat. Strain the liquid, reserving the lemon zest, and set aside to cool.
2 In a large bowl, whip the cream until just holding its shape, then slowly add the cooled wine syrup, whisking continuously.
3 In a clean bowl, whisk the egg whites until soft peaks form. Fold into the cream mixture.
4 Divide the syllabub among serving glasses and sprinkle the reserved lemon zest on top to decorate. Chill for 1 hour before serving.

Zabaglione

8 medium egg yolks
200g (7oz) golden caster sugar
225ml (7½fl oz) sweet Marsala

serves 6
preparation: 5 minutes
cooking time: 20 minutes
per serving: 270 cals; 8g fat;
    37g carbohydrate

1 Using a hand-held electric whisk, whisk the egg yolks and sugar together in a large heatproof bowl set over a pan of gently simmering water or in the top of a double boiler for 15 minutes until pale, thick and foaming. The base of the bowl shouldn't be in contact with the water.

2 With the bowl or pan still over the heat, gradually pour in the Marsala, whisking all the time.

3 Pour the zabaglione into warmed glasses or small coffee cups. Serve immediately, with savoiardi (sponge fingers).

Atholl Brose

125g (4oz) raspberries, plus extra to decorate
pinch of ground cinnamon
1 tsp lemon juice
25g (1oz) golden caster sugar
300ml (½ pint) double cream
3 tbsp thin honey
25–50ml (1–2fl oz) whisky, to taste
50g (2oz) coarse oatmeal, toasted

serves 4
preparation: 10 minutes, plus chilling
cooking time: 2 minutes
per serving: 470 cals; 37g fat;
    28g carbohydrate

1 Put the raspberries, cinnamon, lemon juice, caster sugar and 2 tbsp water into a small pan. Heat gently for 1–2 minutes until the raspberries just soften. Remove from the heat and set aside to cool.

2 Whip the cream in a bowl with the honey until it just begins to hold its shape, then beat in the whisky. Fold in the toasted oatmeal.

3 Divide the raspberries among serving glasses and spoon the oatmeal cream on top. Chill in the fridge for 30 minutes before serving.

4 Decorate each serving with a few raspberries and serve with crisp dessert biscuits if you like.

Summer Fruit Whip

225g (8oz) strawberries
225g (8oz) raspberries
125g (4oz) redcurrants
1 tbsp kirsch
50g (2oz) golden caster sugar
300ml (½ pint) double cream
2 large egg whites

serves 6
preparation: 15 minutes, plus chilling
cooking time: 5 minutes
per serving: 290 cals; 24g fat;
    16g carbohydrate

1 Put all the fruits into a pan with the kirsch, sugar and 2 tbsp water. Slowly bring to a simmer and cook for 5 minutes until the fruits are softened. Strain off and reserve half of the juice. Set aside until cold.

2 Whip the cream in a bowl until it just holds its shape. Fold in the cooled fruit, reserving a few spoonfuls for decoration.

3 Whisk the egg whites in a clean bowl until soft peaks form, then lightly fold into the fruit mixture until evenly incorporated. Spoon into glasses and chill until ready to serve.

4 Top each serving with the reserved fruit and a little juice. Serve with crisp biscuits.

note: *If fresh fruit isn't available use 575g (1¼lb) frozen mixed summer fruits, thawed.*

Crème Fraîche Pots with Red Fruit

300ml (½ pint) crème fraîche
225g (8oz) mascarpone
2 tbsp golden caster sugar
2 large egg whites

RED FRUIT SAUCE
25g (1oz) blackcurrants
50g (2oz) redcurrants
50g (2oz) golden caster sugar
125g (4oz) raspberries

TO DECORATE
4 mint sprigs
icing sugar, to dust (optional)

serves 6
preparation: 20 minutes, plus
    overnight draining
cooking time: 3–5 minutes
per serving: 430 cals; 37g fat;
    22g carbohydrate

1 Line six 150ml (¼ pint) perforated moulds with muslin. Put the crème fraîche, mascarpone and sugar into a large bowl and beat until smooth and light.
2 In a clean bowl, whisk the egg whites until holding soft peaks, then fold into the crème fraîche mixture.
3 Spoon the mixture into the muslin-lined moulds; stand on a tray. Leave to drain in a cool place for at least 8 hours, or overnight.
4 To make the sauce, put the black- and redcurrants in a small pan with the sugar, and cook over a low heat for 3–5 minutes until just soft. Press the raspberries through a fine sieve into a bowl, then stir in the cooked fruit mixture. Leave to cool.
5 To serve, turn out the crèmets on to plates and surround with the fruit sauce. Top with mint sprigs and dust with icing sugar, if you like. Serve at once.

note: *Special heart-shaped moulds with draining holes are available from kitchen shops. Shallow 200ml (7fl oz) crème fraîche pots make good substitutes; puncture 8 holes in the base of each one with a skewer.*

Panna Cotta

2 sheets of leaf gelatine
vegetable oil, to oil
568ml carton double cream
125ml (4fl oz) whole or semi-skimmed milk
1 tsp vanilla extract
150g (5oz) golden caster sugar
2 oranges
2 tbsp Cointreau or orange liqueur

serves 6
preparation: 15 minutes, plus chilling
cooking time: 12 minutes
per serving: 570 cals; 47g fat;
    35g carbohydrate

1 Put the gelatine sheets in a shallow dish, cover with 600ml (1pint) cold water and leave to soak for 5 minutes. Lightly oil six 150ml (¼ pint) dariole moulds and set aside.
2 Put the cream, milk, vanilla extract and 100g (3½oz) sugar in a pan and slowly bring to the boil, then take off the heat. Lift the gelatine sheets out of the water and squeeze out excess liquid. Add to the cream mixture and stir well to dissolve the gelatine.
3 Pour the mixture into the dariole moulds, then cool and chill for 4–6 hours.
4 Using a swivel vegetable peeler, pare the zest from the oranges and cut into fine strips. Squeeze the juice from the oranges and strain into a pan. Add the rest of the sugar, the Cointreau and orange zest. Bring to the boil and simmer for 10 minutes. Cool.
5 To serve, run a palette knife round the edge of each panna cotta and invert on to a dessert plate. Spoon some of the orange sauce and zest over the panna cotta and serve.

note: *The name of this classic Italian dessert literally means cooked cream. Set with just a little gelatine, it has a lovely soft consistency.*

Raspberry Trifle

4 large egg yolks

100g (3½oz) golden caster sugar

2 tbsp cornflour

300ml (½ pint) whole or semi-
    skimmed milk

1 vanilla pod, split lengthways, or
    1 tsp vanilla extract

8 trifle sponges

4 tbsp raspberry conserve

50ml (2fl oz) sweet sherry or
    framboise (raspberry liqueur)

250g (9oz) raspberries

142ml carton double cream

284ml carton double cream

TO DECORATE

few ratafias

silver balls (optional)

serves 8
preparation: 30 minutes, plus cooling
cooking time: 10 minutes
per serving: 460 cals; 30g fat;
    45g carbohydrate

1 To make the custard, put the egg yolks, sugar, cornflour and 2 tbsp milk into a bowl and mix well. Put the rest of the milk in a pan. Scrape the seeds from the vanilla pod and add them to the milk with the empty pod. Slowly bring to the boil. Turn off the heat and remove the vanilla pod. (Alternatively, add the vanilla extract at this stage.)

2 Pour the hot milk on to the egg mixture, stirring constantly. Pour back into pan and cook over a medium heat, stirring constantly, for 5–8 minutes until the custard is thick and smooth. Pour into a bowl and cover the surface with wet greaseproof paper to prevent a skin forming. Leave to cool for 30 minutes.

3 Slice the trifle sponges in half and spread with the raspberry conserve. Use to cover the base of a large serving bowl and drizzle with the sherry. Scatter the raspberries on top.

4 Pour the smaller carton of cream into a bowl and whisk until thickened. Whisk the custard to loosen it, then whisk in the whipped cream. Pour on top of the raspberries.

5 Empty the other carton of cream into a clean bowl and whisk until soft peaks form. Using a large metal spoon, dollop the cream decoratively on top of the trifle. Crumble the ratafias over the top. Finish with silver balls if you like.

Lemon Crunch

50g (2oz) butter, melted, plus extra to grease

175g (6oz) ginger or lemon crunch biscuits

75g (3oz) blanched almonds, toasted

2 x 400g cans condensed milk

600ml (1 pint) double cream

grated zest and juice of 4 large lemons,
    about 200ml (7fl oz)

toasted flaked almonds, to decorate
    (optional)

serves 6–8
preparation: 20 minutes, plus chilling
per serving: 1070–805 cals; 66–50g fat;
    107–81g carbohydrate

1 Lightly grease an 18–20cm (7–8 inch) spring-release cake tin and base-line with baking parchment.

2 Put the biscuits and toasted almonds in a food processor and whiz for about 1 minute until roughly chopped. Mix with the melted butter until evenly combined. Press on to the base of the prepared cake tin and chill for at least 30 minutes.

3 Pour the condensed milk into a bowl and stir in the cream. Stirring constantly, add the lemon zest and juice a little at a time; the mixture will thicken dramatically. Pour it over the biscuit base and chill overnight to set.

4 Carefully remove from the tin and cut into wedges. Serve decorated with toasted almonds if you like.

Vanilla Tiramisu

200g carton mascarpone
1 vanilla pod, split lengthways
450ml (¾ pint) warm strong black coffee
4 medium egg yolks
75g (3oz) golden caster sugar
284ml carton double cream
100ml (3½fl oz) grappa
200g pack savoiardi or sponge fingers
cocoa powder, to dust

serves 10
preparation: 20 minutes, plus chilling
per serving: 380 cals; 27g fat;
   27g carbohydrate

1 Put the mascarpone into a bowl with the seeds from the vanilla pod.
2 Pour the coffee into a shallow dish, add the empty vanilla pod and set aside to infuse.
3 In a large bowl, whisk the egg yolks and sugar together until pale and thick, then whisk in the mascarpone until smooth.
4 Whip the cream in another bowl to soft peaks, then fold into the mascarpone mixture with the grappa.
5 Take half of the sponge fingers and dip each in turn into the coffee mixture, then arrange over the base of a 2.4 litre (4 pint) shallow dish. Spread a layer of mascarpone mixture over the sponge fingers, then dip the remaining sponge fingers into the coffee and arrange on top. Finish with a top layer of mascarpone. Cover and chill for at least 2 hours.
6 Dust with cocoa and cut into portions with a sharp knife. Use a spatula to lift them neatly on to plates.

note: *For optimum flavour, prepare a day ahead.*

Pistachio Praline Floating Islands

PRALINE
50g (2oz) unskinned pistachio nuts
50g (2oz) golden caster sugar
vegetable oil, to oil

FLOATING ISLANDS
2 large eggs, separated
150g (5oz) golden caster sugar
300ml (½ pint) single cream
300ml (½ pint) milk

serves 4–6
preparation: 30 minutes, plus cooling
   and chilling
cooking time: 18–20 minutes
per serving: 500–340 cals; 25–17g fat;
   61–41g carbohydrate

1 To make the praline, put the pistachios and sugar into a small heavy-based pan over a low heat and stir until the sugar melts and begins to caramelise. Cook to a deep brown colour, then immediately pour on to an oiled baking sheet. Leave to cool completely, then whiz to a coarse powder in a food processor.
2 To make the meringue, whisk the egg whites in a clean bowl to soft peaks. Gradually whisk in 75g (3oz) caster sugar until the mixture is very stiff and shiny. Quickly and lightly fold in all but 2 tbsp of the praline.
3 Put the cream, milk and remaining sugar into a medium pan and bring to a gentle simmer. Spoon 5–6 small rounds of meringue mixture into the pan and cook gently for 2–3 minutes or until doubled in size and firm to the touch. Carefully remove with a slotted spoon and drain on kitchen paper. Repeat with the remaining mixture to make 12–18 poached meringues depending on size.
4 Whisk the egg yolks into the poaching liquid. Heat gently, stirring all the time, until the custard thickens slightly to the consistency of double cream; don't boil.
5 Strain the custard into a serving dish, or individual dishes, and position the meringues on top. Cool, then chill for 30 minutes, or up to 2–3 hours.
6 Serve sprinkled with the reserved pistachio praline.

Apricot and Pistachio Creams

700g (1½lb) ripe apricots, halved and stoned
1 stem ginger ball in syrup, roughly chopped
1 tbsp stem ginger syrup (from the jar)
4 tbsp maple syrup
25g (1oz) ground rice
1 tbsp cornflour
25g (1oz) golden caster sugar
600ml (1 pint) milk
1 tbsp orange flower or rose water
25g (1oz) ground almonds
25g (1oz) pistachio nuts, roughly chopped
   and lightly toasted

serves 6
preparation: 15 minutes, plus cooling
   and chilling
cooking time: 45 minutes
per serving: 200 cals; 6g fat;
   31g carbohydrate

1 Put the apricots into a large shallow, ovenproof dish with the chopped ginger, ginger syrup and maple syrup. Bake, uncovered, at 200°C (180°C fan oven) mark 6 for 30 minutes or until tender and slightly caramelised, basting occasionally. Lightly crush the apricots, then leave to cool.
2 In a small bowl, blend the ground rice, cornflour and sugar to a smooth paste with 4 tbsp of the milk. Pour the remaining milk into a heavy-based pan, bring to the boil, then pour half on to the flour paste, stirring until well combined.
3 Return to the pan and bring to the boil, stirring. Simmer, stirring constantly, for 10 minutes or until the mixture has thickened. Stir in the orange flower water and ground almonds. Simmer for a further 5 minutes, then remove from the heat and leave to cool.
4 To serve, spoon half the apricot mixture into glass serving dishes, top with half the almond cream, then sprinkle with half the chopped pistachios. Cover with the rest of the fruit and almond cream. Sprinkle with the remaining pistachio nuts. Cover and chill for at least 2–3 hours before serving.

SOUFFLÉS, MOUSSES AND JELLIES

Jellies, cold soufflés and most mousses are set with gelatine. Both soufflés and mousses acquire their light, airy texture from whisked egg whites. A cold soufflé is really a mousse set high above the rim of the soufflé dish within a collar as an imitation of a hot soufflé. It's important to use the correct size of dish, to ensure the mixture sets above the rim.

PREPARING A SOUFFLÉ DISH

Cut a double strip of greaseproof paper long enough to go around the soufflé dish with the ends overlapping slightly, and deep enough to reach from the bottom of the dish to about 7cm (2¾ inch) above the rim. Wrap the greaseproof paper around the dish and secure under the rim with string or an elastic band, so that it fits closely and smoothly to the rim of the dish.

USING GELATINE

Powdered gelatine is commonly specified in recipes, although leaf gelatine is increasingly available and easy to use. Both forms should be softened in a liquid before adding to the mixture. Sprinkle powdered gelatine on to the liquid (rather than add the liquid to the gelatine). Leave to soften for 5–10 minutes until spongy, then stand the bowl over a pan of simmering water until fully dissolved and translucent. Leaf gelatine is soaked in cold water to soften, then squeezed to remove excess water and dissolved in warm liquid. Always add dissolved gelatine to a mixture that is warm or at room temperature. If added to a cold mixture, it will set on contact in fine threads and spoil the texture of the dish.

WHISKING EGG WHITES

Whisk egg whites in a clean dry bowl – any trace of fat, egg yolk or water will adversely affect the volume achieved. The egg whites should be whisked until they form soft peaks, the tips of which should just flop over gently when the whisk is lifted. Avoid over-whisking, otherwise you will find it difficult to incorporate the whisked egg whites into a mousse or soufflé evenly, without losing volume.

Cold Lemon Soufflé

3 large lemons
2 tsp powdered gelatine
4 large eggs, separated
125g (4oz) golden caster sugar
300ml (½ pint) double cream

TO DECORATE
chopped pistachio nuts, toasted

serves 6
preparation: 1 hour, plus chilling
cooking time: 2 minutes
per serving: 390 cals; 30g fat;
   24g carbohydrate

1 Prepare a 1.2 litre (2 pint) soufflé dish with a paper collar (see above).
2 Finely grate the zest of 2 lemons and squeeze the juice from all three; you need 125ml (4fl oz) juice. Spoon 3 tbsp cold water into a bowl, sprinkle on the gelatine and set aside to soften for 10 minutes.

3 Meanwhile, whisk the egg yolks and sugar together in a heatproof bowl set over a pan of hot water until the mixture is pale and thick enough to leave a trail when the beaters are lifted. Add the lemon juice and whisk for 2–3 minutes. Take off the heat and continue whisking from time to time until cool.
4 Stand the bowl of gelatine over a pan of simmering water until dissolved. Stir the dissolved gelatine into the lemon mixture. Lightly whip the cream in another bowl until it just holds its shape; set aside.
5 Stand the bowl of lemon mixture in a large bowl of ice-cold water. Stir very gently until it begins to thicken creamily. Lift the bowl out of the water and fold in the cream with the lemon zest, until just combined.
6 Whisk the egg whites in a clean bowl until they form soft peaks. Stir a spoonful into the lemon mixture to loosen it, then gently fold in the remainder. Pour the mixture into the prepared soufflé dish. Chill for 2–3 hours or overnight until set.
7 To serve, remove the paper collar from the dish. Press the toasted nuts around the edge to decorate.

Chilled Chocolate Soufflé

3 large eggs, separated
75g (3oz) golden caster sugar
75g (3oz) good quality plain dark chocolate
    (60–70% cocoa solids), in pieces
1 tbsp powdered gelatine
1 tbsp brandy
284ml carton double cream

TO FINISH
chocolate curls (see page 503) or
    grated chocolate

serves 4
preparation: 20 minutes, plus chilling
per serving: 650 cals; 51g fat;
    36g carbohydrate

1 Prepare a 600ml (1 pint) soufflé dish, 12cm (5 inch) diameter, with a paper collar (see left).
2 Whisk the egg yolks and sugar together in a heatproof bowl set over a pan of hot water, until thick and creamy. Remove from the heat and continue whisking from time to time until cool.
3 Meanwhile, melt the chocolate in a heatproof bowl set over a pan of simmering water; stir until smooth and allow to cool slightly.
4 Put 2 tbsp water in a small bowl, sprinkle the gelatine over the surface and set aside to soften for 10 minutes. Stand this bowl over a small pan of simmering water until the gelatine is dissolved. Allow to cool slightly, then pour it into the egg mixture in a steady stream, stirring constantly.
5 Stir in the melted chocolate and brandy. Leave the mixture to cool until it is almost at the point of setting.
6 Lightly whip half the cream and fold it into the chocolate mixture. Whisk the egg whites in a clean bowl until stiff but not dry, then quickly and lightly fold them into the mixture, using a large metal spoon, until evenly incorporated. Immediately pour into the prepared soufflé dish and chill for 2–3 hours until set.
7 To serve, once the soufflé has set, remove the string or elastic band and ease the paper away from the soufflé with a knife dipped in hot water. Whip the rest of the cream until thick and put 6–8 neat dollops around the top edge of the soufflé. Top with chocolate curls or grated chocolate.

Chocolate Mousse

350g (12oz) good quality plain chocolate,
    in pieces
6 tbsp rum, brandy or cold black coffee
6 large eggs, separated
pinch of salt
chocolate curls (see page 503) or grated
    chocolate, to decorate

serves 8
preparation: 20 minutes, plus chilling
per serving: 380 cals; 21g fat;
    36g carbohydrate

1 Put the chocolate into a bowl set over a pan of barely simmering water with the rum. Leave to melt, stirring occasionally. Remove from the heat and leave to cool slightly for 3–4 minutes, stirring frequently.
2 Beat the egg yolks with 2 tbsp water, then beat into the chocolate mixture until evenly blended.
3 Whisk the egg whites with the salt in a clean bowl until firm peaks form, then carefully fold into the chocolate mixture.
4 Pour the mixture into a 1.5–1.7 litre (2½–3 pint) soufflé dish or divide between eight 150ml (¼ pint) ramekins. Chill in the fridge for at least 4 hours, or overnight, until set. Decorate with chocolate curls or grated chocolate to serve.

note: *This rich mousse is best made with a good quality plain chocolate, such as Bournville. Avoid using a very dark chocolate with a high percentage of cocoa solids, as this would make it too bitter.*

Mango and Lime Mousse

2 very ripe mangoes, peeled
100ml (3½fl oz) double cream
finely grated zest and juice of 2 limes
11g sachet powdered gelatine
3 large eggs, plus 2 large yolks
50g (2oz) golden caster sugar

TO DECORATE
whipped cream
finely pared lime zest, shredded

serves 6
preparation: 20 minutes, plus chilling
per serving: 250 cals; 17g fat;
    18g carbohydrate

1 Cut the mango flesh away from the stone and whiz in a blender or food processor to give 300ml (½ pint) purée. Lightly whip the cream in a bowl and set aside.
2 Put 3 tbsp lime juice into a small heatproof bowl, then sprinkle over the powdered gelatine and leave to soak for 10 minutes.
3 In a large bowl, whisk the eggs, egg yolks and sugar together, using an electric beater, until thick and mousse-like; this will take about 4–5 minutes. Gently fold in the mango purée, cream and grated lime zest.
4 Set the bowl of softened gelatine over a pan of boiling water and leave until dissolved, then carefully fold into the mango mixture, making sure everything is evenly combined. Pour the mousse into glasses and chill for 2–3 hours until set.
5 Decorate each mousse with a dollop of whipped cream and a little shredded lime zest.

Chocolate Marquise

BISCUIT BASE

175g (6oz) bourbon or chocolate
    wholemeal biscuits

50g (2oz) butter, melted, plus extra to grease

CHOCOLATE MOUSSE

175g (6oz) good quality plain chocolate,
    in pieces

3 tbsp cooled strong black coffee

50g (2oz) unsalted butter

1 tbsp whisky

3 large eggs, separated

125g (4oz) golden caster sugar

TO FINISH

chocolate curls (see page 503, optional)

cocoa powder, to dust

serves 8

preparation: 25 minutes, plus overnight
    chilling

per serving: 430 cals; 25g fat;
    47g carbohydrate

1 Crush the biscuits coarsely with a rolling pin, or using a food processor. Stir in the melted butter until evenly blended. Spoon into a greased and lined 23cm (9 inch) spring-release cake tin and press into an even layer with the back of a spoon.

2 For the mousse topping, put the chocolate into a heatproof bowl with the black coffee, butter and whisky. Stand the bowl over a pan of hot water and leave to melt.

3 Whisk the egg yolks and sugar in a large bowl set over a pan of barely simmering water, using a hand-held electric whisk, until the mixture is thick and foamy and will hold a trail when the beaters are lifted.

4 Whisk the egg whites in a clean bowl until holding soft peaks. Fold the chocolate mixture into the whisked egg yolk mixture, then lightly stir in a large spoonful of the egg white. Carefully fold in the rest of the egg whites and pour into the prepared tin. Spread evenly, then cover and chill in the fridge overnight.

5 To serve, unclip the tin and peel away the lining paper. Carefully transfer the marquise to a serving plate and decorate with chocolate curls, if you like. Dust liberally with cocoa powder to serve.

Lemon Honeycomb Jelly

grated zest of 3 lemons

900ml (1½ pints) milk

3 medium eggs, separated

50g (2oz) golden caster sugar

2 drops of yellow food colouring
    (optional)

4 tbsp lemon curd

2 tbsp powdered gelatine

200ml carton crème fraîche, to finish

serves 6

preparation: 10 minutes, plus cooling
    and chilling

cooking time: 15–20 minutes

per serving: 310 cals; 20g fat;
    23g carbohydrate

1 Put the lemon zest and milk into a pan and bring to the boil, then remove from the heat and leave to infuse for 10 minutes.

2 Put the egg yolks and sugar into a bowl and beat with a hand hold electric whisk until pale and foamy. Stir in the milk and food colouring if using, followed by the lemon curd. Return to the pan and cook over a low heat, stirring, until slightly thickened. Remove from the heat and immediately pour into a cold bowl to prevent further cooking.

3 Put 6 tbsp hot water in a small pan, sprinkle the gelatine over and leave to soak for 5 minutes until spongy. Dissolve the gelatine mixture over a very low heat, then stir into the custard. Allow to cool.

4 Whisk the egg whites in a clean bowl until stiff but not dry, then fold into the cooled lemon mixture. Pour into a 1.8 litre (3¼ pint) bowl; cover and chill for about 2 hours until set.

5 To serve, decorate the mousse with spoonfuls of crème fraîche.

note: *This pudding separates into two layers: a clear jelly on the bottom and a fluffy mousse on top.*

Passion Fruit and Strawberry Terrine

225g (8oz) ripe strawberries
5 large oranges
5 pink grapefruit
8 passion fruit
2 tbsp powdered gelatine
150g (5oz) golden caster sugar

TO FINISH
strawberries
mint leaves

serves 8
preparation: 50 minutes, plus chilling
cooking time: 2–3 minutes
per serving: 140 cals; 0g fat;
   34g carbohydrate

1 Halve the strawberries or quarter if large. Squeeze the juice from three of the oranges. Using a sharp knife, cut the peel and pith from the grapefruit and remaining oranges, then cut into segments. Squeeze the juice from the membranes and add to the orange juice. Put the segments in a colander on a plate to catch the juice and leave to stand for 30 minutes. Halve the passion fruit and scoop out the pulp.
2 Pour 5 tbsp cold water into a small heatproof bowl, sprinkle on the gelatine and set aside to soak for 5 minutes.
3 Put the passion fruit pulp and 2 tbsp of the orange juice in a food processor and pulse for 1 minute. Strain into a measuring jug and make up to 600ml (1 pint) with the remaining juice. Pour into a pan, then add the sugar. Heat gently to dissolve, then bring to the boil. Remove from the heat, add the soaked gelatine and stir until dissolved.
4 Line a 1.5 litre (2½ pint) terrine or loaf tin with clingfilm. Mix the grapefruit and orange segments together with the strawberries and spoon into the mould. Strain over enough warm juice mixture to cover the fruit completely, then gently tap the mould to expel any air bubbles. Cover with clingfilm and chill for at least 6 hours, preferably overnight, until set.
5 To serve, turn the terrine out on to a board and cut into slices with a hot serrated knife. Decorate with strawberries and mint.

Sparkling Fruit Jellies

75cl bottle demi-sec or dry sparkling wine
300ml (½ pint) red grape juice
5 tsp powdered gelatine
125g (4oz) small seedless grapes, halved
225g (8oz) raspberries or small strawberries

serves 8
preparation: 10 minutes, plus chilling
per serving: 110 cals; trace fat;
   10g carbohydrate

1 Pour the sparkling wine into a bowl. Put 4 tbsp of the grape juice into a small pan, sprinkle over the gelatine and leave to soak for 5 minutes, then heat very gently until the gelatine is completely dissolved. Stir in the remaining grape juice, then stir this mixture into the wine.
2 Divide the grapes and raspberries among serving glasses, pour in enough of the wine mixture to cover them and chill until just set.
3 Pour on the remaining wine mixture and chill for a further 3–4 hours until set.

variation: *Use cranberry rather than grape juice.*

Port and Orange Jellies

125g (4oz) golden granulated sugar
450ml (¾ pint) ruby port
2 tbsp powdered gelatine
8 oranges

serves 8
preparation: 25 minutes, plus setting
cooking time: 15 minutes
per serving: 200 cals; 0g fat;
    34g carbohydrate

1 Line eight 150ml (¼ pint) individual fluted moulds with clingfilm and chill.
2 Put the sugar in a large pan with 600ml (1 pint) cold water. Heat gently to dissolve, then bring to the boil and bubble until the liquid has reduced by half; this will take about 15 minutes.

3 Meanwhile, pour 6 tbsp port into a bowl and sprinkle over the gelatine. Set aside until spongy.
4 In the meantime, cut away the peel and white pith from the oranges, using a large sharp knife, then carefully cut the segments free from the membrane. Discard any pips.
5 Add the rest of the port to the sugar syrup and bring to a simmer. Remove from the heat, add the soaked gelatine mixture and stir until completely dissolved.
6 Stand the orange segments in the flutes of the moulds so they are upright and rest against the edge of the mould. Pour in enough liquid to come halfway up the sides. Chill to set, then pour in the rest of the liquid and chill again.
7 To serve, dip each mould briefly in a bowl of hot water to loosen the surface. Upturn on to individual plates and carefully remove the moulds. Serve at once, with pouring cream.

MERINGUES

Meringues should be light and crisp on the surface, while still soft inside. They can be made up to a week in advance and stored in an airtight container.

To make classic French meringue, egg whites are whisked until very stiff, then the sugar is added a little at a time to make a thick glossy meringue – if added too quickly, the meringue will become thin. It is essential to use a clean, dry, grease-free bowl and a clean whisk. For best results, egg whites must be at room temperature.

To make classic Italian meringue, a boiling sugar syrup is whisked into the whisked egg whites to make a stable meringue. For a simplified version (see below), the egg whites and caster sugar can be whisked together in a bowl set over a pan of simmering water until thick, shiny and silky smooth.

Classic Meringues

3 medium egg whites, at room temperature
175g (6oz) golden caster sugar

TO SERVE
200ml (7fl oz) double cream, whipped
icing sugar, to dust (optional)

serves 6
preparation: 20 minutes
cooking time: 2–3 hours, plus cooling
per serving: 270 cals; 16g fat;
   32g carbohydrate

1 Whisk the egg whites in a large clean bowl until the mixture stands in stiff peaks, using an electric whisk. Gradually add the caster sugar, a tablespoonful at a time, whisking well after each addition. Continue whisking until the meringue is very stiff and shiny.
2 Line two baking sheets with baking parchment or a Teflon non-stick liner. Using two large spoons, shape the meringue into 12–15 ovals or rounds, spacing them well apart on the lined baking sheets.
3 Bake at 110°C (100°C fan oven) mark ¼ for 2–3 hours until the meringues are crisp and well-dried out, but still white; switch the baking sheets around halfway through cooking. Carefully peel the meringues off the paper and transfer to a wire rack to cool.
4 Sandwich the meringues together in pairs with cream and serve, dusted with icing sugar if you like.

Italian Meringues

3 medium egg whites, at room temperature
175g (6oz) golden caster sugar

TO SERVE
strawberries, raspberries or sliced peaches
whipped cream, crème fraîche or Greek-style
   yogurt
vanilla sugar (see page 16), to dust

serves 6
preparation: 20 minutes
cooking time: 2–3 hours, plus cooling
per serving (without cream or fruit):
   120 cals; 0g fat; 31g carbohydrate

1 Using an electric whisk on high speed, whisk the egg whites and caster sugar together in a large clean heatproof bowl set over a pan of gently simmering water. Whisk until the mixture is very thick and leaves a very thick 'trail' across the surface when the beaters are lifted. Immediately remove the bowl from the heat and continue whisking for 2 minutes until cooled.
2 Line two baking sheets with baking parchment or a Teflon non-stick liner. Using two large spoons, shape the meringue into 12–15 ovals or rounds, spacing them well apart on the lined baking sheets.
3 Bake at 110°C (100°C fan oven) mark ¼ for 2–3 hours until the meringues are crisp and firm, but still white; switch the baking sheets around halfway through baking. Carefully peel the meringues off the paper and transfer to a wire rack to cool.
4 Serve the meringues with the fruit, cream or yogurt, and a dusting of vanilla sugar.

Golden Hazelnut Meringues

4 medium egg whites, at room temperature
150g (5oz) golden caster sugar
75g (3oz) light muscovado sugar, sifted
25g (1oz) chopped hazelnuts

TO SERVE
284ml carton double cream
1–2 tbsp hazelnuts, toasted and ground
icing sugar, to taste (optional)

makes 12
preparation: 15 minutes
cooking time: 1 hour 30 minutes,
    plus cooling
per meringue: 90 cals; 1g fat;
    20g carbohydrate

1 Whisk the egg whites in a large clean bowl, using an electric whisk, until they stand in stiff peaks.
2 Mix the caster and muscovado sugars together in a separate bowl. Gradually whisk the sugar into the egg whites, a tablespoonful at a time.
3 Line two baking sheets with baking parchment or Teflon non-stick liners. Using a large metal spoon, dollop the mixture on to the lined baking sheets to make 12 meringues, spacing them well apart. Sprinkle with the chopped hazelnuts.
4 Bake the meringues at 130°C (110°C fan oven) mark ½ for 1½ hours or until they can be lifted from the paper without sticking; swap the baking sheets around after 45 minutes to ensure even cooking.
5 Turn off the oven and leave the meringues to cool inside with the door ajar, until they're completely cold.
6 To serve, whip the cream to soft peaks, then fold in the toasted ground hazelnuts, with icing sugar to taste if you like. Serve with the meringues.

Strawberry Pavlova

4 medium egg whites, at room temperature
225g (8oz) golden caster sugar
1 tbsp cornflour, sifted
1 tsp vanilla extract
2 tsp white wine vinegar
450g (1lb) strawberries, hulled and halved
    if large
3 tbsp framboise (raspberry liqueur) or
    1–2 tbsp kirsch
284ml carton double cream
200g carton half-fat crème fraîche

serves 6
preparation: 20 minutes
cooking time: 1¼–1½ hours, plus cooling
per serving: 480 cals; 28g fat;
    51g carbohydrate

1 Line a baking sheet with baking parchment and draw a 23cm (9 inch) circle on the paper; turn the paper over.
2 For the meringue, whisk the egg whites in a clean bowl, using an electric whisk, until stiff. Gradually add the sugar, a tablespoonful at a time, whisking well between each addition. Continue to whisk until the meringue is very stiff and glossy. Carefully fold in the cornflour, vanilla extract and wine vinegar.
3 Pile the meringue on to the marked circle. Using a palette knife, flatten the centre and push the meringue up around the edge, peaking as you do so.
4 Bake at 130°C (110°C fan oven) mark ½ for 1¼–1½ hours or until firm around the edges and slightly soft inside. Leave to cool; the meringue will probably crack and sink a little.
5 Meanwhile, put the strawberries in a bowl, sprinkle with the liqueur and leave to macerate for 1 hour.
6 To assemble, whip the cream in a clean bowl until softly peaking. Add the crème fraîche and fold together. Use a palette knife to lift the pavlova from the baking parchment and slide on to a serving plate.
7 Fold three-quarters of the strawberries into the cream mixture. Pile into the pavlova, then top with the remaining strawberries and any juice.

Baked Alaska

SPONGE FLAN
butter, to grease
50g (2oz) golden caster sugar, plus extra
    to dust
50g (2oz) plain flour, sifted, plus extra
    to dust
2 medium eggs
finely grated zest of 1 orange

FILLING
225g (8oz) raspberries
2 tbsp Grand Marnier or framboise
450ml (¾ pint) vanilla ice cream (preferably
    homemade, page 448)

MERINGUE
4 egg whites
175g (6oz) golden caster sugar

serves 6–8
preparation: 30 minutes, plus soaking
cooking time: about 25 minutes
per serving: 330–250 cals; 6–4g fat;
    60–45g carbohydrate

1 For the sponge, grease a 20cm (8 inch) non-stick flan tin and dust with sugar, then flour.
2 Whisk the eggs and sugar together in a bowl, using an electric whisk, until pale and thick. Carefully fold in the orange zest and flour. Pour the mixture into the flan tin and gently level the surface. Bake at 180°C (160°C fan oven) mark 4 for 20–25 minutes until golden. Turn out on to a wire rack to cool.
3 Meanwhile, put the raspberries into a bowl and sprinkle with the liqueur. Leave to stand for 2 hours.
4 Put the sponge flan on an ovenproof plate. Fill with the raspberries and juice.
5 For the meringue, whisk the egg whites in a clean bowl, using an electric whisk, until stiff. Whisk in half of the sugar, then carefully fold in the rest.
6 Spoon the ice cream on top of the raspberries, then spread the meringue over the top to cover the ice cream completely. Immediately bake at 230°C (210°C fan oven) mark 8 for 3–4 minutes until the meringue is tinged brown; watch carefully as it will quickly scorch. Serve immediately.

Orange Meringue Terrine

MERINGUE

5 large egg whites, at room temperature

275g (10oz) golden caster sugar

1 tsp orange juice

1 tsp cornflour, sifted

ORANGE FILLING

2 tbsp cornflour, sifted

4 large egg yolks

100g (3½oz) golden caster sugar

finely grated zest and juice of 2 oranges

125ml (4fl oz) milk

142ml carton double cream

ORANGE ZESTED SYRUP

finely pared zest and juice of 1 orange

125g (4oz) golden caster sugar

serves 8–10

preparation: 40 minutes

cooking time: 1 hour 35 minutes,
  plus cooling

per serving: 380–300 cals; 11–9g fat;
  71–57g carbohydrate

1 Draw three 25 x 10cm (10 x 4 inch) rectangles on baking parchment. Cut around the rectangles, leaving a 10cm (4 inch) border. Turn the paper over and put each rectangle on a baking sheet.

2 For the meringue, whisk the egg whites in a clean bowl until softly peaking. Whisk in the sugar, a tablespoonful at a time. Continue to beat until the meringue is glossy and firm. Fold in the orange juice and cornflour.

3 Put the meringue into a large piping bag fitted with a large star nozzle. Pipe widthways along each piece of parchment to create 3 oblongs. Pipe 4 stars on to another baking sheet lined with parchment.

4 Bake the meringue at 140°C (120°C fan oven) mark 1 for 20 minutes, then turn the oven down to 110°C (100°C fan oven) mark ¼ and bake for a further 1¼ hours. Turn the oven off and leave the meringue inside for 30 minutes to 1 hour to cool and dry out.

5 For the filling, mix the cornflour with 1 tbsp water in a bowl, then stir in the egg yolks, sugar, orange zest and juice. Bring the milk to the boil in a pan, then gradually stir into the cornflour mixture. Return to the pan and cook, stirring constantly with a whisk, over a gentle heat, until the custard is very thick. Tip into a bowl, cover the surface with wet greaseproof paper to prevent a skin forming, and allow to cool. Whip the cream until softly peaking, then fold into the custard.

6 For the orange syrup, put the orange juice and sugar into a pan over a low heat until the sugar has dissolved, then simmer for 8 minutes to make a syrup. Add the pared strips of orange zest and cook for 2–3 minutes. Leave to cool.

7 Carefully lift the meringue shapes off the parchment. Use the orange cream to sandwich the 3 meringue layers together and place on a serving plate. Spoon 4 blobs of orange cream on the top layer and position the meringue stars on top.

8 Just before serving, drizzle the zested orange syrup over the meringue. Cut into slices to serve.

note: For convenience, make the terrine up to a week ahead and freeze. To serve, defrost at room temperature for 3 hours and make the orange syrup.

Strawberry Meringue Crush

150ml (¼ pint) double cream
200g carton thick Greek-style yogurt
500g (1lb 2oz) strawberries, hulled
2 tbsp crème de cassis
5 ready-made meringue nests

serves 6
preparation: 15 minutes, plus chilling
per serving: 270 cals; 15g fat;
    28g carbohydrate

1 Lightly whip the cream until softly peaking, then fold in the yogurt and chill for 30 minutes. Put half the strawberries into a food processor, whiz to a purée, then stir in the crème de cassis. Set aside 6 tbsp of the purée for decoration.
2 Slice the remaining strawberries, reserving six for decoration, and put into a bowl. Pour the strawberry purée over them, cover and leave to macerate in the fridge for 20 minutes.
3 Break up the meringue nests and carefully fold into the cream mixture, with the strawberry mixture. Divide among glass serving bowls. Drizzle 1 tbsp of reserved strawberry purée over each serving and top with a halved strawberry.

Lemon Meringue Pie

sweet tart pastry (page 269), made with
    225g (8oz) flour
flour, to dust
a little beaten egg

FILLING
7 medium eggs, 4 separated, at room
    temperature
finely grated zest of 3 lemons
175ml (6fl oz) freshly squeezed lemon juice
    (about 4 lemons), strained
400g can condensed milk
150ml (¼ pint) double cream
225g (8oz) golden icing sugar

serves 8
preparation: 30 minutes, plus standing
cooking time: about 1 hour, plus cooling
per serving: 660 cals; 31g fat;
    86g carbohydrate

1 Roll out the pastry on a lightly floured surface and use to line a 23cm (9 inch) loose-based fluted tart tin, which is 4cm (1½ inches) deep. Prick the base with a fork. Chill for 30 minutes.
2 Line the pastry case with greaseproof paper and baking beans and bake blind at 190°C (170°C fan oven) mark 5 for 10 minutes. Remove the beans and paper and bake for a further 10 minutes or until golden and cooked. Brush the inside with beaten egg and return to the oven for 1 minute to seal.
3 Meanwhile to make the filling, put 4 egg yolks in a bowl with the 3 whole eggs. Add the lemon zest and juice; whisk lightly to combine. Mix in the condensed milk and cream.
4 Pour the lemon filling into the pastry case and bake at 180°C (160°C fan oven) mark 4 for 30 minutes or until just set in the centre. Set aside to cool while you prepare the meringue.
5 For the meringue, whisk the egg whites and icing sugar together in a heatproof bowl set over a pan of gently simmering water, using a hand-held electric whisk, for 10 minutes or until very shiny and thick. Take off the heat and continue to whisk at low speed for a further 5–10 minutes until the bowl is cool.
6 Pile the meringue on top of the lemon filling and swirl with a palette knife to form soft peaks. Bake at 200°C (180°C fan oven) mark 6 for 5–10 minutes until the meringue is tinged browned. Leave to stand for about 1 hour, then serve.

Chestnut and Chocolate Macaroon

MERINGUE

300g (11oz) golden icing sugar

½ tsp bicarbonate of soda

4 large egg whites

175g (6oz) hazelnuts, toasted and ground

FILLING

125g (4oz) chestnut purée

1 tbsp maple syrup

200ml (7fl oz) double cream

225g (8oz) mascarpone

50g (2oz) good quality plain dark chocolate, melted and cooled

TO DECORATE

chocolate curls (page 503)

icing sugar, to dust

serves 6

preparation: 45 minutes, plus chilling

cooking time: 1 hour 20 minutes

per serving: 740 cals; 48g fat;
   74g carbohydrate

1 Line three baking sheets with baking parchment and draw a 20cm (8 inch) circle on each; turn the paper over. Sift the icing sugar and bicarbonate of soda together on to a piece of paper.

2 Whisk the egg whites in a large bowl until very stiff but not dry. Gradually whisk in 50g (2oz) of the icing sugar, then carefully fold in the remaining icing sugar and ground hazelnuts.

3 Divide the meringue mixture among the marked circles on the parchment, spreading it evenly. Bake at 140°C (120°C fan oven) mark 1 for 5 minutes. Lower the oven setting to 130°C (110°C fan oven) mark ½ and bake for a further 1¼ hours. Switch the baking sheets around during baking to ensure even cooking.

4 Leave on the baking sheets for 5 minutes, then transfer to wire racks to cool. Peel away the paper.

5 For the filling, beat the chestnut purée and maple syrup together in a bowl until smooth.

6 Whip the cream in another bowl until it just holds its shape, then fold into the mascarpone. Stir half into the cooled melted chocolate; fold the rest into the chestnut purée.

7 Put a meringue round on a serving plate. Spread with the chestnut mixture. Put a second meringue on top; press down lightly. Cover with the chocolate cream. Position the final meringue on top.

8 Chill for at least 4 hours. Decorate with chocolate curls and dust with icing sugar to serve.

Hazelnut Meringue Gâteau

MERINGUE

5 medium egg whites

250g (9oz) golden caster sugar

½ tsp ground mixed spice

125g (4oz) hazelnuts, toasted and chopped

75g (3oz) plain dark chocolate, roughly chopped

75g (3oz) white chocolate, roughly chopped

TO ASSEMBLE

300ml (½ pint) double cream, lightly whipped

hazelnut praline (see page 499), coarsely crushed

cocoa powder, to dust

serves 8–10

preparation: 40 minutes, plus cooling

cooking time: about 1½ hours

per serving: 510–410 cals; 32–25g fat;
   53–43g carbohydrate

1 Line two baking sheets with baking parchment. Draw a 23cm (9 inch) circle on one, and an 18cm (7 inch) circle on the other sheet. Turn the paper over.

2 To make the meringue, whisk the egg whites in a bowl until stiff but not dry. Gradually whisk in the sugar, a spoonful at a time, whisking well between each addition until the meringue is stiff and shiny. Add the spice with the last of the sugar. Carefully fold in the chopped nuts and chocolate.

3 Spread the meringue over the drawn circles on the baking sheets. Swirl the surface of the smaller round and the edges of the larger one, with a palette knife.

4 Bake at 140°C (120°C fan oven) mark 1 for about 1½ hours until dry and the undersides are firm when tapped; switch the baking sheets halfway through cooking. Leave to cool in the switched-off oven.

5 Carefully transfer the largest meringue round to a serving plate. Spread with the cream and scatter the praline on top. Cover with the smaller meringue round and dust with cocoa powder to serve.

ICE CREAMS, SORBETS AND ICED DESSERTS

There is nothing quite like the rich, creamy flavour of a homemade ice cream, or the refreshing tang of a real fruit sorbet. A smooth-textured result is the key to success, so it is important to ensure that no large ice crystals form during freezing. An ice-cream maker will freeze and churn a mixture at the same time to give a smooth even-textured ice. If you do not own an ice-cream maker, you will need to whisk most ice cream and sorbet mixtures a few times during freezing to break down the ice crystals.

USING AN ICE-CREAM MAKER

Follow the manufacturer's instructions carefully and clean the machine thoroughly after every use.
• When making a sorbet, add the lightly whisked egg white at the start of the churning process.
• Freezing time is usually 20–30 minutes. The ice cream or sorbet is then usually transferred to the

freezer for 1–2 hours to let the flavours to develop. Soften slightly at room temperature before serving.

TO FREEZE ICE CREAM BY HAND

• Set the freezer to fast-freeze 1 hour ahead.
• Pour the ice cream mixture into a shallow freezerproof container, cover and freeze for 2–3 hours until partially frozen to a mushy consistency.
• Spoon into a bowl and mash with a fork or whisk to break down the ice crystals, working quickly to ensure that the ice cream does not melt completely. Return to the container and freeze, covered, for 2 hours or until mushy again.
• Mash again, folding in any ingredients, such as chocolate chips or nuts, at this stage. Freeze for about 3 hours until firm.
• Transfer to room temperature (or the fridge on a hot day) about 20 minutes before serving to soften.

Vanilla Ice Cream

300ml (½ pint) milk
1 vanilla pod, split lengthways
3 medium egg yolks
50–75g (2–3oz) golden caster sugar
300ml (½ pint) double cream

serves 4–6
preparation: 20 minutes, plus infusing
   and freezing
cooking time: 15 minutes
per serving: 480–320 cals; 41–28g fat;
   22–14g carbohydrate

1 Pour the milk into a heavy-based pan, add the vanilla pod and heat slowly until almost boiling. Take off the heat and leave to infuse for about 20 minutes. Remove the vanilla pod.
2 Whisk the egg yolks and sugar together in a bowl until thick and creamy. Gradually whisk in the hot milk, then strain back into the pan. Cook over a low heat, stirring constantly, until the custard has thickened enough to coat the back of the wooden spoon; do not boil. Pour into a chilled bowl and allow to cool.

3 Whisk the double cream into the cold custard until evenly blended.
4 Pour the mixture into an ice-cream maker and churn until frozen. Alternatively, freeze in a shallow container, whisking 2 or 3 times during freezing to break down the ice crystals and ensure an even-textured result.
5 Allow the ice cream to soften slightly at cool room temperature before serving. Scoop into balls and serve in individual bowls.

variations
strawberry ice cream: *Sweeten 300ml (½ pint) strawberry purée with sugar to taste, then add the cooled custard. (Other fruit ice creams can be made in the same way.)*
chocolate ice cream: *Omit the vanilla pod. Add 125g (4oz) plain dark chocolate to the milk and heat gently until melted, then bring almost to the boil and continue as above.*
coffee ice cream: *Omit the vanilla pod. Add 150ml (¼ pint) freshly made strong cooled coffee to the cooled custard, or 2 tsp instant coffee granules to the hot milk, stirring to dissolve.*

Rum and Raisin Ice Cream

250g (9oz) lexia (Australian muscat) raisins
100ml (3½fl oz) dark rum
4 large egg yolks
3 tbsp golden syrup
1 tbsp treacle
568ml carton double cream

serves 8
preparation: 40 minutes, plus freezing
cooking time: 3 minutes
per serving: 470 cals; 37g fat;
   28g carbohydrate

1 Put the raisins in a pan, add the rum and bring to a simmer. Turn off the heat and set aside to soak and plump up while you make the ice cream.

2 Put the egg yolks, golden syrup and treacle into a small bowl and whisk, using an electric whisk, for 2–3 minutes to a mousse-like consistency.

3 Whip the cream in another bowl until it forms soft ribbons when the beaters are lifted. Add the syrup mixture and whisk for 3–4 minutes until thick.

4 Pour the mixture into an ice-cream maker and churn until half-frozen. Alternatively, half-freeze in a shallow container, whisking twice during freezing to break down the ice crystals.

5 Add the soaked fruit and any remaining liquid to the ice cream and mix well. Put into a 1.7 litre (3 pint) freezerproof container and freeze for 45 minutes. Stir, then freeze for at least 2 hours until solid.

6 Scoop the ice cream into balls and serve in individual bowls.

Brown Bread Ice Cream

125g (4oz) fresh fine brown breadcrumbs
50g (2oz) light muscovado sugar
300ml (½ pint) double cream
150ml (¼ pint) single cream
1 tbsp dark rum
50g (2oz) golden icing sugar, sifted

serves 4–6
preparation: 20 minutes, plus freezing
cooking time: 10 minutes
per serving: 590–390 cals; 44–29g fat;
   44–29g carbohydrate

1 Spread the brown breadcrumbs on a baking sheet and sprinkle evenly with the brown sugar. Bake at 200°C (180°C fan oven) mark 6 for about 10 minutes, stirring occasionally, until the sugar caramelises and the crumbs are crisp. Allow to cool completely, then break up into pieces.

2 Whisk the creams together in a bowl until thick. Gently fold in the rum and icing sugar.

3 Pour the mixture into a freezerproof container and freeze for 2 hours until mushy.

4 Turn into a chilled bowl and beat with a fork or whisk to break down the ice crystals. Stir in the breadcrumbs. Return to the freezer container and freeze until firm.

5 Transfer the ice cream to the fridge to soften about 30 minutes before serving.

Banana Ice Cream

2 bananas, about 375g (13oz), peeled and
   roughly chopped
4 tbsp Tia Maria or other coffee liqueur
2 medium eggs, separated
75g (3oz) golden caster sugar
250g carton mascarpone
1 tsp vanilla extract
25g (1oz) coffee sugar crystals (optional),
   to serve

serves 8
preparation: 20 minutes, plus freezing
per serving: 280 cals; 17g fat;
   24g carbohydrate

1 Line eight 125ml (4fl oz) timbales or similar-sized moulds with clingfilm.
2 Put the bananas into a bowl, add the liqueur and toss to coat. Leave to macerate.
3 Whisk the egg whites in a clean bowl until they form stiff peaks. Gradually whisk in the sugar, a tablespoonful at a time, until the meringue stands in stiff peaks.
4 Put the mascarpone, egg yolks and vanilla extract in a separate bowl and beat until smooth. Stir in a large spoonful of the meringue to loosen the mixture, then fold in the rest. Stir in the macerated bananas.
5 Spoon into the prepared timbales, wrap in clingfilm and freeze for at least 4 hours.
6 About 15 minutes before serving, remove from the freezer to soften slightly. To serve, unwrap and turn out on to plates. Top with a sprinkling of coffee sugar crystals if you like.

Tiramisu Ice Cream

2 tsp instant espresso coffee powder
4 tbsp Tia Maria or other coffee liqueur
12–16 savoiardi or sponge fingers
2 medium eggs, separated
75g (3oz) golden caster sugar
250g carton mascarpone
4 tbsp Marsala
1 tsp vanilla extract
25g (1oz) plain dark chocolate, grated

serves 6
preparation: 20 minutes, plus freezing
per serving: 370 cals; 23g fat;
   32g carbohydrate

1 Double-line a 900g (2lb) loaf tin with clingfilm. Dissolve the coffee in 4 tbsp boiling water, add the liqueur and set aside.
2 Line the base of the loaf tin with half of the sponge fingers, placing them widthways and sugared-side down, trimming them as necessary; set aside.
3 Whisk the egg whites in a clean bowl until stiff. Whisk in the sugar, a tablespoonful at a time, and continue to whisk until the meringue holds stiff peaks.
4 In another bowl, beat together the mascarpone, egg yolks, Marsala and vanilla extract. Stir in a large spoonful of the meringue to loosen the mixture, then carefully fold in the rest.
5 Drizzle two-thirds of the coffee liqueur mixture over the sponge fingers and sprinkle with the grated chocolate. Spoon the mascarpone mixture into the tin and smooth the surface. Arrange the rest of the sponge fingers widthways on top and drizzle over the remaining coffee mixture. Cover and freeze until firm, about 5 hours.
6 To serve, invert on to a large serving plate, then lift off the loaf tin and remove the clingfilm. Cut into slices, using a knife dipped in warm water.

Orange Sorbet

10 juicy oranges
200g (7oz) golden caster sugar
2 tbsp orange flower water
1 large egg white

serves 4–6
preparation: 20 minutes, plus chilling
    and freezing
per serving: 300–200 cals; 0g fat;
    76–51g carbohydrate

1 Finely pare the zest from the oranges, using a citrus zester, then squeeze the juice. Put the zest and juice into a pan with the sugar and 200ml (7fl oz) water, and heat gently to dissolve the sugar. Increase the heat and boil for 1 minute. Set aside to cool.
2 Stir the orange flower water into the cooled sugar syrup. Cover and chill in the fridge for 30 minutes.
3 Strain the orange syrup into a bowl. In another bowl, beat the egg white until just frothy, then whisk into the orange mixture.
4 For best results, freeze in an ice-cream maker. Otherwise, pour into a shallow freezerproof container and freeze until almost frozen; mash well with a fork and freeze until solid. Transfer the sorbet to the fridge 30 minutes before serving to soften slightly.

Lemon Sorbet

3 juicy lemons
125g (4oz) golden caster sugar
1 large egg white

serves 3–4
preparation: 10 minutes, plus chilling
    and freezing
per serving: 170–130 cals; 0g fat;
    45–34g carbohydrate

1 Finely pare the lemon zest, using a zester, then squeeze the juice. Put the zest in a pan with the sugar and 350ml (12fl oz) water and heat gently to dissolve. Increase heat and boil for 10 minutes. Leave to cool.
2 Stir the lemon juice into the cooled sugar syrup. Cover and chill in the fridge for 30 minutes.
3 Strain the syrup through a fine sieve into a bowl. In another bowl, beat the egg white until just frothy, then whisk into the lemon mixture.
4 For best results, freeze in an ice-cream maker. Otherwise, pour into a shallow freezerproof container and freeze until almost frozen; mash well with a fork and freeze until solid. Transfer the sorbet to the fridge 30 minutes before serving to soften slightly.

Strawberry Sorbet

250g (9oz) golden caster sugar
450g (1lb) sweet ripe strawberries
1 tbsp balsamic vinegar
1 large egg white

serves 4–6
preparation: 20 minutes, plus chilling
    and freezing
per serving: 280–190 cals; 0g fat;
    73–48g carbohydrate

1 Put the sugar and 250ml (8fl oz) water in a pan and heat gently to dissolve the sugar. Increase the heat and boil for 1 minute. Cool, then chill for 30 minutes.
2 Meanwhile, purée the strawberries in a blender or food processor, then pass through a sieve to remove the seeds. Cover and chill for 30 minutes.
3 Stir the sugar syrup and balsamic vinegar into the strawberry purée.
4 In another bowl, beat the egg white until just frothy, then whisk into the strawberry mixture.
5 For best results, freeze in an ice-cream maker. Otherwise, pour into a shallow freezerproof container and freeze until almost frozen; mash well with a fork and freeze until solid. Transfer the sorbet to the fridge 30 minutes before serving to soften slightly.

Chocolate Cinnamon Sorbet

200g (7oz) golden granulated sugar
50g (2oz) cocoa powder
pinch of salt
1 tsp instant espresso coffee powder
1 cinnamon stick
6 tsp crème de cacao (chocolate liqueur)
   to serve

serves 6
preparation: 5 minutes, plus chilling
   and freezing
cooking time: 15 minutes
per serving: 170 cals; 2g fat;
   37g carbohydrate

1 Put the sugar, cocoa powder, salt, coffee and cinnamon stick into a large pan with 600ml (1 pint) water. Bring to the boil, stirring until the sugar has completely dissolved. Boil for 5 minutes, then remove from the heat. Leave to cool. Remove the cinnamon stick, then chill.

2 If you have an ice-cream maker, put the mixture into it and churn for about 30 minutes until firm. Otherwise, pour into a freezerproof container and put in the coldest part of the freezer until firmly frozen, then transfer the frozen mixture to a blender or food processor and blend until smooth. Quickly put the mixture back in the container and return to the freezer for at least 1 hour.

3 To serve, scoop the sorbet into individual cups and drizzle 1 tsp chocolate liqueur over each portion. Serve immediately.

Coffee Semifreddo

2 tbsp instant espresso coffee
2 tbsp sambucca or amaretto liqueur, plus
   extra to serve
75g (3oz) golden caster sugar
3 large egg yolks
284ml carton double cream
40g (1½oz) ground almonds, lightly toasted
   and cooled

serves 6
preparation: 20 minutes, plus freezing
per serving: 340 cals; 29g fat;
   15g carbohydrate

1 Line the bases of six individual 150ml (¼ pint) pudding moulds with greaseproof paper.

2 Dissolve the coffee in 100ml (3½fl oz) boiling hot water, then stir in the liqueur.

3 In a large bowl, whisk together the sugar and egg yolks until light and fluffy. Gradually whisk the coffee into the egg mixture.

4 Whip the cream in another bowl to soft peaks, then gently fold into the coffee mixture with the ground almonds until all the ingredients are combined.

5 Divide the mixture among the prepared moulds and freeze for at least 6 hours.

6 To serve, upturn the moulds on to individual plates and remove the paper. Drizzle a little liqueur around each ice cream and eat immediately, before they melt.

note: *This naturally soft iced dessert has a texture halfway between a mousse and an ice cream.*

Ginger Parfait

150g (5oz) ginger nut biscuits
15g (½oz) unsalted butter, melted
2 large eggs
175g (6oz) golden icing sugar
1 tbsp ground ginger
568ml carton double cream

serves 10
preparation: 20 minutes, plus freezing
per slice: 420 cals; 32g fat;
    32g carbohydrate

1 Put the biscuits into a food processor and whiz for 10 seconds to make crumbs.

2 Brush a 900g (2lb) loaf tin with melted butter, then line the tin with clingfilm and brush with the rest of the butter. Spoon about 3 tbsp of the biscuit crumbs into the tin and tip the tin around to give an even coating of crumbs. Put in the freezer.

3 Whisk the eggs, icing sugar and ginger together in a bowl, using an electric whisk, for 5–10 minutes until the mixture has a mousse-like consistency and is thick enough to leave a ribbon-like trail when the beaters are lifted.

4 Whisk the cream in another bowl until soft peaks form, then fold into the egg mixture. Set aside 3 tbsp biscuit crumbs, then fold the rest into the mixture. Pour into the prepared loaf tin and sprinkle with the remaining biscuit crumbs. Cover with clingfilm, then freeze for 6 hours.

5 To serve, dip the tin into hot water for 10 seconds, then turn out the parfait on to a board and remove the clingfilm. Cut into 2cm (¾ inch) slices and serve.

Christmas Pudding Parfait

finely grated zest and juice of 1 orange
2 tbsp brandy
125g (4oz) sultanas
125g (4oz) ready-to-eat prunes
1 tsp ground mixed spice
568ml carton double cream
4 large eggs, separated
125g (4oz) dark muscovado sugar, plus
    1 tbsp extra
½ tsp vanilla extract

TO FINISH
holly sprig (optional)
icing sugar, to dust

serves 12
preparation: 30 minutes, plus freezing
cooking time: 3–5 minutes
per serving: 340 cals; 25g fat;
    26g carbohydrate

1 Line a 2.3 litre (4 pint) pudding basin with clingfilm. Put the orange zest and juice, brandy, sultanas, prunes and mixed spice into a pan. Heat gently for 3–5 minutes until the liquid is absorbed and the fruit has plumped up. Tip into a food processor and whiz to a purée.

2 Whip the cream in a bowl until just thickened.

3 Whisk the egg yolks, 125g (4oz) of the sugar and the vanilla extract together in another bowl, using an electric whisk, for 5 minutes until creamy and the sugar has dissolved. Using a metal spoon, fold in the whipped cream.

4 Whisk the egg whites in a clean bowl until soft peaks form. Beat in the 1 tbsp sugar. Stir a large spoonful into the egg and cream mixture, then fold in the rest with a metal spoon. Fold in the puréed fruit. Pour the mixture into the prepared pudding basin and freeze for 6 hours.

5 To serve, run the base of the bowl under a warm tap, turn out on to a serving plate and remove the clingfilm. Wrap the end of a holly sprig in clingfilm and insert into the parfait to decorate if you like. Dust with icing sugar and slice to serve.

CAKES AND BISCUITS

The key to successful cake-making lies in using good quality ingredients at the right temperature, measuring them accurately – using scales and measuring spoons – and following recipes carefully. Weigh out all of the ingredients before you start, using either metric or imperial measures, never a combination of the two. Make sure that you have the correct cake tin – the tin size quoted in the recipes refers to the base measurement – and take care to line the tin properly where necessary. Allow at least 15 minutes to heat the oven to the correct oven temperature.

INGREDIENTS

Unsalted butter, rich and creamy in flavour, gives the best results in most recipes. Margarine can be substituted in many recipes although it doesn't lend such a good flavour, but low-fat 'spreads' with their high water content are not suitable. For most cake recipes, you need to use the fat at room temperature. If necessary you can soften it, cautiously, in the microwave.

Eggs should also be used at room temperature; if taken straight from the fridge they are more likely to curdle a cake mixture. Make sure you use the correct size too – unless otherwise stated medium eggs should be used in all of these recipes.

Golden caster sugar is generally used for cakes, but light or dark muscovado sugars can be substituted for a richer colour and flavour.

Self-raising white flour is used in most cake recipes as it provides a raising agent, whereas plain white flour is generally used for biscuits and cookies. Plain or self-raising wholemeal flour can be substituted although the results will be darker, denser and nuttier in flavour. Half white and half wholemeal makes a good compromise if you want to incorporate extra fibre. If you sieve it before use, tip the bran left in the sieve into the bowl.

Check that other storecupboard ingredients to be included – such as nuts, dried fruits, extracts and spices – are well within their 'use-by' date.

EQUIPMENT

Little is needed in the way of special cake-making equipment for these recipes, other than scales, bowls, spoons, etc. However, a hand-held electric whisk is most useful as it takes all the effort out of creaming and whisking, and if you bake frequently, you will find that a free-standing electric mixer is a good investment. A food processor is perfect for rubbing fat into flour – for scones, biscuits, etc.

Good quality cake tins are essential, and non-stick tins are particularly useful. Sturdy baking sheets are important too. Choose ones that are large (but fit comfortably into your oven) to avoid baking in several batches.

BAKING

Bake the cake mixture as soon as you have made it, as the raising agents will start to react straightaway. Once the cake is in the oven, resist the temptation to open the door – a sudden gush of cold air will make a part-baked cake sink. Instead wait until the cooking time is almost up before testing. If your cake appears to be browning too quickly, cover the top loosely with greaseproof paper towards the end of cooking.

Apart from very light sponges, all cakes are best left to stand in their tin for 5–10 minutes after baking to firm up slightly. Biscuits, with their high sugar content, will seem very soft after baking. These too, should be left on the baking sheet for a few minutes before transferring to a wire rack.

WHAT IF IT ISN'T A SUCCESS?

Unfortunately it's not always easy to determine why a cake hasn't turned out as expected. Here are some possible reasons:

A close, dense texture may be the result of using too much liquid, too little raising agent, or an ineffective raising agent that is past its 'use-by date'. It may also be the outcome if the mixture curdled during creaming, or if the flour was folded in too vigorously.

A peaked, cracked top often occurs if the oven was too hot, or the cake was too near the top of the oven. Or it may be due to insufficient liquid, or using a tin which is too small.

If a cake sinks in the middle it is most likely to be because the oven door was opened too soon. Alternatively, it may be because ingredients haven't been measured accurately, or the wrong size cake tin may have been used.

Sunken fruit in a fruit cake occurs if the mixture is too soft to support the weight of the fruit. This is liable to happen if the fruit was too sticky or wet.

If the cake is heavy there may be too much liquid or not enough raising agent, or you haven't creamed the fat and sugar together sufficiently.

STORAGE

With the exception of rich fruit cakes and gingerbread, most cakes and biscuits are best enjoyed freshly baked. If storing is necessary, use a cake tin or large plastic container. Make sure that the cake is completely cold before you put it into the container. If you haven't a large enough container, wrap in a double layer of greaseproof paper and overwrap with foil. Avoid putting rich fruit cakes in direct contact with foil; the fruit may react with it. Biscuits should never be stored in the same tin as a cake, and preferably not with other types of biscuits, as they quickly soften and absorb other flavours.

Most cakes, particularly sponges, freeze well, but they are generally best frozen before filling and decorating. If freezing a finished gâteau, open-freeze first, then pack in a rigid container.

PREPARATION TECHNIQUES

Successful baking is at least partly dependant on the use of good basic techniques, such as lining and filling tins, whisking, folding in, etc. The following step-by-step guides apply to many of the recipes.

PREPARING TINS

For most cakes it is necessary to line the tin with greaseproof paper, or non-stick baking parchment. Cakes that are particularly liable to stick, such as roulades and meringues, are best protected with baking parchment.

note: *If in addition to greasing, a cake tin needs a coating of flour to prevent sticking, sprinkle a little flour into the lined and greased tin, tap and tilt to coat the base and sides evenly, then tip out excess.*

LINING A SQUARE TIN

Cut a square of greaseproof paper fractionally smaller than the base of the tin. For the sides, cut strips about 2cm (¾ inch) wider than the depth of the tin. Fold up the bottom edge by 1cm (½ inch). Grease the tin. Make a cut from the edge of the paper to the fold and press into one corner. Continue fitting the paper around the cake tin, cutting it to fit at each corner. Lay the square of paper in the base, then grease all the paper.

LINING A ROUND TIN

Put the cake tin on a piece of greaseproof paper and draw around it. Cut out, just inside the line. Cut strip(s) of paper, about 2cm (¾ inch) wider than the depth of the tin. Fold up the bottom edge by 1cm (½ inch), then make cuts, 2.5cm (1 inch) apart, from the edge to the fold. Grease the tin. Position the paper strip(s) around the side of the tin so the snipped edge sits on the base. Lay the paper circle on top. Grease all the paper.

LINING A SWISS ROLL TIN OR SHALLOW BAKING TIN

Grease the base and sides. Cut a rectangle of baking parchment, 7.5cm (3 inches) wider and longer than the tin. Press into the tin and cut the paper at the corners, then fold to fit neatly. Grease the paper.

LINING A LOAF TIN

Grease the tin. Cut a baking parchment strip, the length of the base and wide enough to cover it and the long sides. Press into position. Cut another strip, the width of the tin base and long enough to cover the base and ends; position. Grease the paper.

OVERWRAPPING A TIN

This prevents the outside of a fruit cake overcooking. First line the inside, then cut a double thick strip of brown paper, the circumference of the tin and 2.5cm (1 inch) deeper. Wrap around the tin; tie with string.

CAKE TECHNIQUES

CREAMING METHOD

1 Beat together the softened butter and sugar until pale and fluffy, and very light in consistency. Use an electric whisk, or beat vigorously with a wooden spoon.

2 Using an electric whisk or wooden spoon, beat in the eggs, a little at a time, beating well after each addition. To prevent curdling, a little of the measured flour can be added with the eggs.

3 Sift the flour over the creamed mixture, sifting high so that plenty of air is incorporated. Use a large metal spoon or spatula to gently fold in the flour, cutting and folding into the mixture using a figure-of-eight movement.

note: If the mixture is too firm to fold in the flour, add a dash of milk. Once the flour is incorporated the mixture should drop easily from the spoon when tapped against the side of the bowl.

WHISKING METHOD

1 Put the eggs and sugar into a large heatproof bowl set over a pan of hot water. Whisk until the mixture is thick enough to leave a trail when the whisk is lifted from the bowl. Remove the bowl from the heat and continue whisking for about 5 minutes or until cool.

2 Sift half the flour over the mixture. Using a large metal spoon, gently cut and fold the flour into the whisked mixture. Sift the remaining flour on to the mixture and lightly fold in, until only just incorporated. Do not over-mix or the sponge mixture will reduce in volume.

GENOESE SPONGE

This is made by the whisking method, but melted butter is added with the flour. The butter must be cooled and beginning to thicken otherwise it will be difficult to incorporate.

1 Once half the flour has been folded into the whisked mixture (see previous page), gradually pour in the cooled butter around the edge. Sift the remaining flour over the bowl and gently cut and fold it in as lightly as possible.

note: *When mixing any type of cake, scrape down the sides of the bowl from time to time to ensure the ingredients are evenly incorporated.*

TURNING CAKE MIXTURE INTO TIN

Spoon the mixture into the tin, dividing it evenly between the tins if making a sandwich cake. Use a palette knife to spread the cake mixture lightly and in an even layer, right to the edges.

TURNING WHISKED SPONGE MIXTURE INTO TIN

Pour the whisked mixture into the tin and tilt the tin so that the mixture spreads to the edges. If necessary, use a plastic spatula to gently spread it into the corners. Avoid over-spreading as this will crush the air bubbles.

TESTING BAKED SPONGES

Carefully remove the cake from the oven and touch the centre with one hand. It should feel spongy and give very slightly. Whisked cakes should just be shrinking from the sides of the tin. If necessary return the cake to the oven for a few minutes, closing the door very gently so that vibration does not cause the cake to sink in the centre.

TESTING FRUIT CAKES

Take the cake out of the oven, insert a skewer into the centre and remove: it should come away cleanly. If any mixture is sticking to the skewer, return to the oven for a little longer.

TURNING OUT CAKES

Remove the sponge cakes from the tins immediately after baking. Loosen the edges, then invert on to a wire cooling rack. If preferred, put a sheet of baking parchment dusted with sugar on the rack before inverting, to stop the soft sponge sticking to the rack.

note: *Semi-rich fruit cakes should be left to cool in the tin for about 15 minutes, while rich fruit cakes are left to cool completely in the tin as they tend to break up if removed while still warm.*

BISCUITS AND COOKIES

Biscuits are quick, easy and inexpensive to make, and you can buy cutters from cookshops to shape festive and novelty biscuits. Don't be alarmed if the mixture still seems soft on removing from the oven; most cookies and biscuits firm up on cooling. Homemade biscuits freeze well and thaw in a matter of minutes, so it's a good idea to make a sizeable batch and freeze some for later use.

Shortbread

225g (8oz) butter, at room temperature
125g (4oz) golden caster sugar
225g (8oz) plain flour
125g (4oz) rice flour
pinch of salt
golden or coloured granulated sugar,
    to coat
caster sugar, to sprinkle

makes 18–20
preparation: 20 minutes, plus chilling
cooking time: 15–20 minutes, plus cooling
per piece: 190–170 cals; 10–9g fat;
    23–21g carbohydrate

1 Cream the butter and sugar together in a bowl until pale and fluffy. Sift the flour, rice flour and salt together on to the creamed mixture and stir in, using a wooden spoon, until the mixture resembles breadcrumbs.
2 Gather the dough together with your hand and turn on to a clean surface. Knead very lightly until it forms a ball, then lightly roll into a sausage, about 5cm (2 inches) thick. Wrap in clingfilm and chill in the fridge until firm.
3 Remove the clingfilm and slice the dough into discs, about 7–10mm ($\frac{1}{3}$–$\frac{1}{2}$ inch) thick. Pour some granulated sugar on to a plate and roll the edge of each disc in the sugar. Put the shortbread, cut-side up, on two baking sheets lined with greaseproof paper.
4 Bake the shortbread at 190°C (170°C fan oven) mark 5 for 15–20 minutes, depending on thickness, until very pale golden. On removing from the oven, sprinkle with caster sugar. Leave on the baking sheet for 10 minutes, then transfer to a wire rack to cool.

Shortbread Biscuits

175g (6oz) unsalted butter, softened
75g (3oz) golden caster sugar
200g (7oz) plain flour, sifted, plus extra
    to dust
50g (2oz) cornflour
white caster sugar, to sprinkle

makes 12
preparation: 15 minutes, plus chilling
cooking time: 15 minutes, plus cooling
per biscuit: 200 cals; 12g fat;
    23g carbohydrate

1 Whiz the butter and sugar together in a food processor for 1 minute until pale and fluffy. Add the flour and cornflour, and process briefly until the mixture just comes together. Wrap in clingfilm and chill for 30 minutes.
2 Roll out the dough on a lightly floured surface to a 1cm ($\frac{1}{2}$ inch) thickness. Cut out 12 rounds, using a 7cm ($2\frac{3}{4}$ inch) fluted cutter, and put on a baking sheet lined with baking parchment. Gently press a 4cm ($1\frac{1}{2}$ inch) plain cutter into the centre of each to mark a circle and prick the dough within the circle, using a fork.
3 Bake at 190°C (170°C fan oven) mark 5 for about 15 minutes until pale golden. Sprinkle with caster sugar and transfer to a wire rack to cool. Store in an airtight tin for up to 5 days.

Spiced Star Biscuits

2 tbsp thin honey

25g (1oz) unsalted butter

50g (2oz) light muscovado sugar

finely grated zest of ½ lemon

finely grated zest of ½ orange

225g (8oz) self-raising flour

1 tsp ground cinnamon

1 tsp ground ginger

½ tsp freshly grated nutmeg

pinch of ground cloves

pinch of salt

1 tbsp finely chopped candied peel

50g (2oz) ground almonds

1 large egg, beaten

1½ tbsp milk

TO DECORATE

150g (5oz) icing sugar

silver sugar balls

makes about 35
preparation: 15 minutes, plus chilling
cooking time: 15–20 minutes, plus cooling
per biscuit: 50 cals; 2g fat; 7g carbohydrate

1 Put the honey, butter, sugar and citrus zests into a small pan and stir over a low heat until the butter has melted and the ingredients are well combined.

2 Sift the flour, spices and salt together into a bowl, then add the chopped candied peel and ground almonds. Add the melted mixture, beaten egg and milk, and mix until the dough comes together.

3 Knead the dough briefly until smooth, then wrap in clingfilm and chill for at least 4 hours, or overnight.

4 Roll out the dough on a lightly floured surface to a 5mm (¼ inch) thickness. Stamp out stars, using a 5cm (2 inch) cutter, and put on baking sheets.

5 Bake at 180°C (160°C fan oven) mark 4 for 15–20 minutes or until just beginning to brown at the edges. Transfer the biscuits to a wire rack to cool. Store in an airtight tin for up to 1 week.

6 To decorate, mix the icing sugar with 1½ tbsp warm water to make a smooth icing. Coat some of the biscuits with icing and finish with a piped edging if you like, then decorate with silver balls. Pipe dots of icing on the plain biscuits and attach silver balls (as illustrated). Allow the icing to set, then store the biscuits in an airtight container for up to a week.

Ginger Biscuits

125g (4oz) golden syrup

50g (2oz) dark muscovado sugar

50g (2oz) butter, plus extra to grease

finely grated zest of 1 orange

2 tbsp orange juice

175g (6oz) self-raising flour

1 tsp ground ginger

makes 24
preparation: 15 minutes
cooking time: about 12 minutes,
   plus cooling
per biscuit: 55 cals; 2g fat;
   10g carbohydrate

1 Put the golden syrup, butter, sugar, orange zest and juice into a heavy-based pan and heat very gently until melted and evenly blended.

2 Leave the mixture to cool slightly, then sift in the flour with the ginger. Mix thoroughly until smooth.

3 Put small spoonfuls of the mixture on two lightly greased large baking sheets, spacing them well apart to allow room for spreading. Bake at 180°C (160°C fan oven) mark 4 for 12 minutes or until the biscuits are golden brown.

4 Leave on the baking sheets for 1 minute, then carefully transfer to a wire rack to cool. Store in an airtight tin for up to 5 days.

Gingerbread Men

350g (12oz) plain flour, plus extra to dust

1 tsp bicarbonate of soda

2 tsp ground ginger

125g (4oz) butter

175g (6oz) light muscovado sugar

1 medium egg, beaten

4 tbsp golden syrup

currants, to decorate

makes 12

preparation: 20 minutes

cooking time: 12–15 minutes, plus cooling

per biscuit: 250 cals; 8g fat;

   43g carbohydrate

1 Sift the flour, bicarbonate of soda and ginger together into a bowl. Rub in the butter until the mixture resembles fine crumbs. Stir in the sugar and make a well in the centre.

2 In another bowl, beat the egg and golden syrup together until evenly blended.

3 Pour the syrup mixture into the well and mix to a fairly firm dough; knead until smooth.

4 Divide in half and roll out, one portion at a time, on a lightly floured surface to a 5mm (¼ inch) thickness. Using a gingerbread man cutter, cut out figures and put them on lightly greased baking sheets. Press on currants to represent eyes and buttons. Bake at 190°C (170°C fan oven) mark 5 for 12–15 minutes until golden.

5 Leave on the baking sheets for 1 minute, then carefully transfer to a wire rack to cool.

Spiced Sultana and Lemon Cookies

225g (8oz) butter, at room temperature,

   plus extra to grease

175g (6oz) golden caster sugar

2 medium eggs, lightly beaten

350g (12oz) self-raising flour

¼ tsp baking powder

pinch of bicarbonate of soda

1 tsp ground mixed spice

150g (5oz) sultanas

finely grated zest of 2 lemons

makes 20

preparation: 15 minutes

cooking time: 15 minutes, plus cooling

per cookie: 200 cals; 10g fat;

   27g carbohydrate

1 Cream the butter and sugar together in a bowl, using a hand-held electric whisk, until pale and fluffy.

2 Add the eggs, one at a time, beating well to make sure the mixture is thoroughly combined.

3 Sift the flour, baking powder, bicarbonate of soda and mixed spice together on to the mixture. Add the sultanas and grated lemon zest to the bowl and fold everything together.

4 Take dessertspoonfuls of the mixture and roll into small balls. Put on two or three large greased baking sheets, spacing well apart, and flatten slightly, using a palette knife dipped in water. Bake in batches as necessary at 190°C (170°C fan oven) mark 5 for about 15 minutes until golden.

5 Leave on the baking sheets for a minute or two, then transfer the cookies to a wire rack to cool. Store in an airtight tin and eat within 2 days.

Cherry Chip Cookies

75g (3oz) unsalted butter, plus extra
   to grease
25g (1oz) golden caster sugar
50g (2oz) light muscovado sugar
few drops of vanilla extract
1 large egg, lightly beaten
175g (6oz) self-raising flour, sifted
finely grated zest of 1 orange
125g (4oz) white chocolate, roughly
   chopped
125g (4oz) natural glacé cherries, roughly
   chopped
icing sugar, to dust

makes 12
preparation: 20 minutes
cooking time: 10–12 minutes, plus cooling
per cookie: 210 cals; 9g fat;
   31g carbohydrate

1 Cream the butter, caster sugar, muscovado sugar and vanilla extract together in a bowl, using an electric whisk, until well combined. Gradually beat in the egg until the mixture is light and fluffy.

2 Using a metal spoon, lightly fold in the flour, orange zest, chopped chocolate and glacé cherries. Put tablespoonfuls of the mixture on to greased baking sheets and bake at 180°C (160°C fan oven) mark 4 for 10–12 minutes. The cookies should be soft under a crisp crust.

3 Leave the cookies on the baking sheet for a minute or two, then transfer them to a wire rack to cool. Store in an airtight tin for up to 3 days. Dust with icing sugar to serve.

note: *Natural glacé cherries (free from artificial colouring and additives) are available from selected supermarkets and delicatessens. They are dark red in colour.*

White and Dark Chocolate Cookies

125g (4oz) unsalted butter, softened,
   plus extra to grease
125g (4oz) golden caster sugar
2 medium eggs, beaten
2 tsp vanilla extract
250g (9oz) self-raising flour, sifted
finely grated zest of 1 orange
100g (3½oz) white chocolate,
   roughly chopped
100g (3½oz) plain dark chocolate,
   roughly chopped

makes 26
preparation: 15 minutes, plus chilling
cooking time: 10–12 minutes
per cookie: 140 cals; 7g fat;
   17g carbohydrate

1 Cream the butter and sugar together in a bowl until pale and creamy. Gradually beat in the eggs and vanilla extract.

2 Sift in the flour, add the orange zest, then sprinkle in the white and dark chocolate pieces. Mix the dough together with your hands.

3 Knead lightly, then wrap in clingfilm and chill for at least 30 minutes.

4 Divide the dough into 26 pieces, roll each into a ball and flatten slightly to make a disc. Using a palette knife, transfer to two or three large greased baking sheets, spacing the discs well apart. Bake at 180°C (160°C fan oven) mark 4 for 10–12 minutes or until golden, but still fairly soft.

5 Leave on the baking sheets for 5 minutes, then transfer to a wire rack to cool completely.

note: *Make a batch of these cookies and freeze any that are unlikely to be eaten within a couple of days, taking them out and allowing to defrost at room temperature as you need them.*

Macaroons

2 medium egg whites
225g (8oz) caster sugar
125g (4oz) ground almonds
¼ tsp almond extract
25 blanched almonds

makes 25
preparation: 10 minutes
cooking time: 12–15 minutes, plus cooling
per biscuit: 80 cals; 4g fat;
 10g carbohydrate

1 Whisk the egg whites in a clean bowl until stiff peaks form. Gradually fold in the sugar, then gently stir in the ground almonds and almond extract to make a firm paste.
2 Spoon teaspoonfuls of the mixture on to baking trays lined with baking parchment, spacing them slightly apart. Press an almond into the centre of each one and bake at 180°C (fan oven 160°C) mark 4 for 12–15 minutes until just golden and firm to the touch.
3 Leave on the baking sheets for 10 minutes, then transfer to wire racks to cool completely. Store in airtight containers or wrap in cellophane for a gift.

note: *On cooling, these biscuits have a soft, chewy centre and harden up after a few days. Once made, eat within 1 week.*

Brandy Snaps

vegetable oil, to oil
75g (3oz) butter
75g (3oz) golden caster sugar
3 tbsp golden syrup
75g (3oz) plain flour
1 tsp ground ginger
2 tbsp brandy
1 tbsp lemon juice
150ml (¼ pint) double cream, whipped,
 to serve (optional)

makes 12–16
preparation: 25 minutes
cooking time: 8–10 minutes, plus cooling
per brandy snap (with cream): 170–120 cals;
 11–8g fat; 16–12g carbohydrate
per brandy snap (no cream): 110–80 cals;
 5–4g fat; 15–11g carbohydrate

1 Lightly oil the handles of several wooden spoons.
2 Put the butter, sugar and golden syrup in a heavy-based pan and warm gently until evenly blended. Let cool for 2–3 minutes. Sift in the flour and ginger, and add the brandy and lemon juice. Mix until smooth.
3 Taking 1 tbsp of mixture at a time, spoon on to baking sheets lined with baking parchment, allowing plenty of room for spreading and putting no more than three on each baking sheet.
4 Bake, one sheet at a time, at 190°C (170°C fan oven) mark 5 for about 8–10 minutes or until golden brown – the texture will be open and lacy.
5 Remove from the oven and leave on the baking sheet for about 15 seconds to firm up slightly. Loosen with a palette knife and roll them around the spoon handles. Put on a wire rack and leave until set.
6 Twist the brandy snaps gently to remove and leave to cool completely and crisp up. Just before serving, fill with whipped cream, if you like, using a piping bag fitted with a 1cm (½ inch) nozzle.

note: *If the biscuits set too hard to roll while on the baking sheet, return to the oven for a few moments to soften.*

variations
tuiles: *Instead of using wooden spoon handles, curve the brandy snap rounds over a lightly oiled large rolling pin.*
brandy snap baskets: *Bake heaped tablespoonfuls of the mixture to make larger rounds. Once cooked, mould over upturned ramekins to form baskets. Lift off once set.*

Cigarettes Russes

25g (1oz) butter, melted and cooled, plus
   extra to grease
1 medium egg white
50g (2oz) golden caster sugar
25g (1oz) plain flour, sifted

makes 8
preparation: 20 minutes
cooking time: 6–7 minutes, plus cooling
per biscuit: 60 cals; 3g fat;
   9g carbohydrate

1 Lightly grease the handles of several wooden spoons.
2 Whisk the egg white in a bowl until stiff, then fold in the sugar. Gently stir in the melted butter, together with the flour.
3 Spread small spoonfuls of the mixture into oblongs, about 7.5 x 5cm (3 x 2 inches), on baking sheets lined with baking parchment, not more than two per baking sheet. Bake one sheet at a time at 190°C (170°C fan oven) mark 5 for 6–7 minutes.
4 Allow to stand for 1–2 seconds, then carefully lift off, using a spatula, and put upside down on a flat surface. Wind each biscuit tightly around a greased wooden spoon handle. Cool slightly until firm.
5 Ease the biscuits off the handles and finish cooling on a wire rack.

Florentines

65g (2½oz) unsalted butter, plus extra
   to grease
50g (2oz) golden caster sugar
2 tbsp double cream
25g (1oz) sunflower seeds
20g (¾oz) chopped mixed candied peel
20g (¾oz) sultanas
25g (1oz) glacé cherries, roughly chopped
40g (1½oz) flaked almonds, lightly crushed
15g (½oz) plain flour
125g (4oz) plain dark chocolate, in pieces,
   to finish

makes 12
preparation: 15 minutes
cooking time: 8–10 minutes, plus cooling
per biscuit: 170 cals; 11g fat;
   16g carbohydrate

1 Melt the butter in a small heavy-based pan. Add the sugar and heat gently until dissolved, then bring to the boil. Take off the heat and stir in the cream, sunflower seeds, peel, sultanas, cherries, almonds and flour. Mix well until evenly combined.
2 Put heaped teaspoonfuls of the mixture on two lightly greased baking sheets, spacing them well apart to allow room for spreading.
3 Bake, one sheet at a time, at 180°C (160°C fan oven) mark 4 for about 6–8 minutes until the biscuits have spread considerably and the edges are golden brown. Using a large round metal cutter, push the edges into the centre to create neat rounds. Bake for a further 2 minutes or until deep golden.
4 Leave on the baking sheet for 2 minutes, then transfer to a wire rack to cool.
5 Melt the chocolate in a heatproof bowl set over a pan of simmering water; stir until smooth. Roll the edges of the biscuits in the chocolate and put on a sheet of baking parchment until set.

note: *If the biscuits solidify before you have time to use the cutter, return to the oven for 30 seconds.*

SMALL CAKES AND PASTRIES

Small cakes are quick and easy to make, and most of them are based on a handful of storecupboard ingredients. Ideas in this section include traditional fairy cakes, sponge fingers and Madeleines, ever-popular no-bake children's favourites, moreish fruity muffins and tempting choux buns.

Queen Cakes

125g (4oz) butter, at room temperature
125g (4oz) golden caster sugar
2 medium eggs, beaten
125g (4oz) self-raising flour, sifted
50g (2oz) sultanas

makes 16
preparation: 15 minutes
cooking time: 15–18 minutes, plus cooling
per cake: 130 cals; 7g fat;
   16g carbohydrate

1 Line a bun tin tray with 16 paper cases (or use two trays if necessary).
2 Cream the butter and sugar together in a bowl until pale and fluffy. Gradually beat in the eggs, a little at a time, beating well after each addition. Carefully fold in the flour, then the sultanas.
3 Half-fill the paper cases with the mixture. Bake at 190°C (170°C fan oven) mark 5 for 15–18 minutes until golden. Transfer to a wire rack to cool.

variations
glacé cherry cakes: *Replace the sultanas with chopped glacé cherries.*
fairy cakes: *Omit the sultanas. Ice the cakes with glacé icing (page 513).*

Sponge Fingers

2 medium eggs, beaten
50g (2oz) golden caster sugar
50g (2oz) plain flour, sifted
icing sugar, to dust

makes 16
preparation: 15 minutes
cooking time: 10–15 minutes, plus cooling
per sponge finger: 40 cals; 1g fat;
   7g carbohydrate

1 Whisk the eggs and sugar together in a bowl, using an electric whisk, until the mixture is pale and creamy, and thick enough to leave a trail when the whisk is lifted.
2 Lightly fold in half of the flour, using a large metal spoon, then carefully fold in the remaining flour in the same way.
3 Spoon the mixture into a piping bag fitted with a 1cm (½ inch) plain nozzle. Pipe 7.5cm (3 inch) lengths on a baking sheet lined with baking parchment, allowing room for spreading. Dust with icing sugar.
4 Bake the sponge fingers at 190°C (170°C fan oven) mark 5 for 10–15 minutes until golden. Carefully transfer to a wire rack to cool.

Cherry Cup Cakes

175g (6oz) butter, at room temperature
175g (6oz) golden caster sugar
3 medium eggs
175g (6oz) self-raising flour, sifted
75g pack dried cherries
2 tbsp milk

ICING
225g (8oz) golden icing sugar
3 tbsp lemon juice

makes 12
preparation: 30 minutes
cooking time: 15–20 minutes, plus cooling
per cake: 330 cals; 14g fat;
  50g carbohydrate

1 Line a 12-hole muffin tin with paper muffin cases.
2 Put the butter and sugar into a bowl and cream together until pale, light and fluffy. Beat in the eggs, one at a time, folding in 1 tbsp flour with the last egg if the mixture appears to be starting to curdle.
3 Set aside 12 dried cherries for decoration. Fold the remaining flour and cherries into the mixture, together with the milk, until evenly combined.
4 Spoon into the cases and bake at 190°C (170°C fan oven) mark 5 for 15–20 minutes until pale golden, risen and springy to the touch. Transfer to a wire rack to cool.
5 To make the icing, sift the icing sugar into a bowl and mix in the lemon juice to give a smooth icing with a dropping consistency. Spoon on to the cakes and decorate each one with a dried cherry.

note: *These are deep, muffin-style cup cakes.*

Madeleines

125g (4oz) unsalted butter, melted and
    cooled until tepid
125g (4oz) plain flour, plus extra to dust
4 medium eggs
125g (4oz) golden caster sugar
finely grated zest of 1 lemon
1 tsp baking powder
pinch of salt
icing sugar, to dust

makes 24
preparation: 20 minutes, plus chilling
cooking time: 10–12 minutes, plus cooling
per cake: 90 cals; 5g fat;
    10g carbohydrate

1 Brush two Madeleine trays with a little of the melted butter. Allow to set, then dust with flour, shaking out any excess.

2 Whisk the eggs, sugar and lemon zest together in a bowl, using an electric whisk, until the mixture is pale, creamy and thick enough to leave a trail when the whisk is lifted.

3 Sift in half of the flour, together with the baking powder and salt. Carefully pour in half of the melted butter around the edge of the bowl and gently fold in until evenly incorporated. Repeat with the remaining flour and butter. Cover and chill the mixture in the fridge for 45 minutes.

4 Two-thirds fill the Madeleine moulds with the mixture and bake at 220°C (200°C fan oven) mark 7 for 10–12 minutes or until well risen and golden. Ease out of the tins and cool on a wire rack. Serve dusted with icing sugar.

notes
• *Resting the sponge mixture before baking gives the Madeleines their characteristic dense texture.*
• *If you have only one Madeleine tray, bake in two batches.*

No-Bake Chocolate Slices

225g (8oz) butter, plus extra to grease
300g pack digestive biscuits
3 tbsp golden syrup
50g (2oz) cocoa powder, sifted
400g (14oz) plain chocolate, in pieces,
    to serve

makes 20 slices
preparation: 10 minutes, plus chilling and
    cooling
per slice: 270 cals; 19g fat;
    25g carbohydrate

1 Grease a 25 x 16cm (10 x 6½ inch) shallow baking tin. Roughly crush the biscuits or break them into small pieces.

2 Put the butter, golden syrup and cocoa powder into a heavy-based pan over a low heat until melted. Take off the heat and stir until evenly combined.

3 Add the crushed biscuits and mix thoroughly until the pieces are well coated, crushing any larger pieces as you do so. Spoon into the prepared tin. Allow to cool, then cover and chill for 30 minutes.

4 Melt the chocolate in a heatproof bowl set over a pan of simmering water. Take off the heat, stir until smooth and leave to cool slightly.

5 Pour the melted chocolate over the biscuit base, then put the tin in the fridge for 30 minutes or until the topping has set.

6 Using a sharp knife, cut the refrigerator cake in half lengthways in the tin, then cut each section into 10 slices and remove with a palette knife.

Chocolate Crackles

225g (8oz) milk chocolate, in pieces
1 tbsp golden syrup
50g (2oz) butter
50g (2oz) Corn Flakes or Rice Krispies

makes 12
preparation: 10 minutes, plus chilling
per crackle: 150 cals; 9g fat;
   17g carbohydrate

1 Put 12 paper cake cases in a bun tin tray.
2 Put the chocolate, golden syrup and butter into a heavy-based pan over a low heat until melted; stir until smooth.
3 Fold in the cereal until evenly mixed, then divide the mixture evenly among the paper cases. Chill in the fridge until set.

note: *These no-bake treats are popular with children and easy for them to make.*

Fruity Energy Bars

250g pack ready-to-eat dried apricots
250g pack ready-to-eat dried papaya
50g (2oz) ready-to-eat dried mango
50g (2oz) plain chocolate, chopped
50g (2oz) pecan nuts, chopped and toasted
50g (2oz) brazil nuts, chopped and toasted
1 tbsp pumpkin seeds
1 tbsp sesame seeds
1 tbsp sunflower seeds
¼ tsp ground nutmeg
2 tbsp Malibu (coconut liqueur) or
   orange juice

makes 12
preparation: 10 minutes, plus standing
per bar: 180 cals; 9g fat; 21g carbohydrate

1 Line a 23 x 18cm (9 x 7 inch) shallow baking tin with rice paper. Put the dried apricots, papaya and mango into a food processor and whiz for 15 seconds to mince the fruit. Tip into a bowl.
2 Add the chopped chocolate, toasted nuts, pumpkin, sunflower and sesame seeds, nutmeg and liqueur or orange juice to the bowl. Mix everything together well, using your hands.
3 Turn the mixture into the prepared tin, spread level and press to flatten with the back of a spoon. Leave to firm up, then cut into 12 bars and wrap each one in rice paper.

note: *These little healthy treats are perfect for lunchboxes. You will need rice paper to line the baking tin and wrap the bars.*

Sticky Toffee Crunchies

125g (4oz) butter, plus extra to grease
227g pack dairy toffees
200g pack marshmallows
200g (7oz) Rice Krispies

makes 24
preparation: 10 minutes
cooking time: 5 minutes, plus cooling
per piece: 140 cals; 6g fat;
   21g carbohydrate

1 Grease a 30 x 20cm (12 x 8 inch) shallow baking tin with butter.
2 Unwrap the toffees and put them in a bowl. Melt in a 900W microwave on High for 2 minutes. Stir, then add the butter and marshmallows and continue to cook in the microwave for 1½ minutes. Stir with a wooden spoon for 30 seconds until the mixture is smooth. (Alternatively, melt the toffees with the butter in a heavy-based pan over a very low heat, then add the marshmallows and stir until melted and smooth.)
3 Add the Rice Krispies and mix until well coated in the toffee mixture. Spoon into the prepared tin and push into the corners, using the back of a wet spatula. Leave to cool.
4 Cut in half lengthways, then cut each section into 6 rectangles. Cut each rectangle in half diagonally to make 24 triangles and take out of the tin.

Chocolate Brownies

200g (7oz) butter, plus extra to grease
400g (14oz) good quality plain dark chocolate
  (minimum 70% cocoa solids), in pieces
225g (8oz) light muscovado sugar
1 tsp vanilla extract
150g (5oz) pecan nuts, roughly chopped
25g (1oz) cocoa powder, sifted
75g (3oz) self-raising flour, sifted
3 large eggs, beaten

makes 16
preparation: 20 minutes
cooking time: 1¼ hours, plus cooling
per brownie: 380 cals; 28g fat;
  25g carbohydrate

1 Line a 20cm (8 inch) square baking tin, which is 5cm (2 inch) deep, with baking parchment and grease the paper.
2 Melt the chocolate together with the butter in a heatproof bowl set over a pan of gently simmering water; stir until smooth. Remove from the heat and leave to cool slightly.
3 Stir the sugar, vanilla extract, chopped nuts, cocoa powder, flour and eggs into the melted chocolate.
4 Turn the mixture into the prepared tin and level with the back of a spoon. Bake at 170°C (150°C fan oven) mark 3 for about 1¼ hours until set to the centre on the surface but still soft underneath. Do not overcook or the soft, gooey texture will be spoilt.
5 Leave to cool in the tin for 2 hours. Turn the cake out on to a board and trim the edges. Dust with sifted cocoa powder and cut into squares. Serve cold, or slightly warm with ice cream if you like.

Blueberry Muffins

300g (11oz) plain flour
2 tsp baking powder
150g (5oz) golden caster sugar
finely grated zest of 1 lemon
125g (4oz) dried blueberries
1 medium egg
1 tsp vanilla extract
225ml (7½fl oz) milk
50g (2oz) unsalted butter, melted
  and cooled
icing sugar, to dust

makes 10
preparation: 15 minutes
cooking time: 20–25 minutes, plus cooling
per muffin: 250 cals; 6g fat;
  50g carbohydrate

1 Line a muffin tin with 10 paper muffin cases.
2 Sift the flour and baking powder together into a bowl. Stir in the caster sugar, lemon zest and dried blueberries.
3 Put the egg, vanilla extract, milk and melted butter into a jug and mix together with a fork. Pour this liquid into the dry ingredients and lightly fold together – don't over-mix.
4 Spoon the mixture into the muffin cases to three-quarters fill them. Bake at 200°C (180°C fan) mark 6 for 20–25 minutes until the muffins are risen, pale golden and just firm.
5 Transfer to a wire rack and leave to cool slightly. Dust with icing sugar to serve.

variation
cranberry muffins: *Replace the blueberries with dried cranberries.*

Banana and Pecan Muffins

275g (10oz) self-raising flour

1 tsp bicarbonate of soda

½ tsp salt

3 large ripe bananas, about 450g
    (1lb), peeled

125g (4oz) golden caster sugar

1 large egg, beaten

50ml (2fl oz) milk

75g (3oz) butter, melted and cooled

50g (2oz) pecan nuts, toasted and
    roughly chopped

makes 12

preparation: 15 minutes

cooking time: 20 minutes, plus cooling

per muffin: 220 cals; 9g fat;
    33g carbohydrate

1 Line a muffin tin with 12 muffin paper cases. Sift the flour, bicarbonate of soda and salt together into a large mixing bowl and put to one side.

2 Mash the bananas in a bowl, using a fork. Add the caster sugar, beaten egg, milk and melted butter and mix together until well combined. Add this to the flour mixture, along with the pecan nuts and stir briefly; the mixture will be lumpy and rather like a batter in consistency.

3 Spoon the mixture into the muffin cases, half-filling them, then bake at 180°C (160°C fan oven) mark 4 for 20 minutes or until they are golden and well risen.

4 Transfer to a wire rack to cool a little. Serve while still warm.

note: *This recipe is a great way to use up over-ripe bananas.*

Citrus Eccles Cakes

rough puff pastry, made with 225g (8oz) flour
    (page 271)

flour, to dust

FILLING

175g (6oz) currants

50g (2oz) chopped mixed candied peel

50g (2oz) muscovado sugar

finely grated zest of 2 lemons

TO FINISH

50g (2oz) unsalted butter, melted, plus
    extra to grease

beaten egg, to glaze

caster sugar, to sprinkle

makes 20

preparation: 35 minutes

cooking time: 12–15 minutes, plus cooling

per cake: 170 cals; 10g fat;
    20g carbohydrate

1 For the filling, mix the currants, candied peel, muscovado sugar and lemon zest together in a bowl.

2 Roll out half of the rough puff pastry on a lightly floured surface to a 50 x 20cm (20 x 8 inch) rectangle, then cut in half lengthways. Cut each strip crossways into 5 equal pieces.

3 With the tip of a sharp knife, make rows of 2cm (¾ inch) slits on each piece of pastry, spacing them 5mm (¼ inch) apart and staggering alternate rows so that the pastry forms a lattice when pulled apart slightly. Brush the edges with beaten egg.

4 Divide half of the filling among the latticed pastries, placing it in the centre of each one. Bring the edges of the pastry up over the filling, pinching them together to seal. Invert on to a lightly greased baking sheet, so that the neat lattice sides are uppermost.

5 Repeat with the remaining pastry and filling to make 20 in total. Brush with beaten egg and sprinkle lightly with sugar. Bake at 220°C (200°C fan oven) mark 7 for 12–15 minutes until puffed and golden.

6 Pour a little melted butter into each eccles cake, through the lattice. Serve warm.

Chocolate Choux Buns

65g (2½oz) plain flour
pinch of salt
50g (2oz) butter, cut into cubes
150ml (¼ pint) sparkling spring water
1 tbsp golden caster sugar
2 medium eggs, lightly beaten

FILLING
284ml carton double cream
1 tsp vanilla extract
1 tsp golden caster sugar

TOPPING
200g (7oz) plain chocolate, in pieces
75g (3oz) butter, at room temperature

makes 8
preparation: 25 minutes
cooking time: 40–45 minutes, plus cooling
per bun: 470 cals; 39g fat; 26g carbohydrate

1 Sift the flour with the salt on to a sheet of greaseproof paper. Put the butter, sparkling water and caster sugar into a medium heavy-based pan. Heat gently until the butter is melted and the sugar dissolved, then bring to a rapid boil.

2 Take off the heat and immediately tip in all the flour. Beat thoroughly with a wooden spoon until the mixture forms a smooth ball in the centre of the pan. Turn into a bowl and leave to cool for 15 minutes.

3 Add the eggs to the mixture, a little at a time, beating well after each addition. Make sure the mixture is thick and shiny before adding any more egg – if it's added too quickly, the choux paste will become thin. Add just enough egg to give a smooth, dropping consistency (you may not need all of it).

4 Sprinkle a non-stick baking sheet with a little water. Using two dampened tablespoons, spoon the choux paste into 8 large mounds on the baking sheet, spacing them well apart to allow room for expansion.

5 Bake at 220°C (200°C fan oven) mark 7 for about 30 minutes until risen and golden brown. Make a small hole in the side of each bun, then put in the switched-off oven for 10–15 minutes to dry out. Transfer to a wire rack and set aside to cool.

6 For the filling, whip the cream with the vanilla extract and sugar to soft peaks. Split the choux buns and fill them with the flavoured cream.

7 For the topping, melt the chocolate with the butter in a heatproof bowl set over a pan of simmering water. Leave to cool until beginning to thicken. Top the choux buns with the warm melted chocolate to serve.

SCONES, TEABREADS AND TRAYBAKES

Homemade scones and fruity teabreads – served warm from the oven – are irresistible. Light handling is the key to success with scones. Remember that the raising agent begins to work as soon as it is mixed with liquid, so for best results, always put scones into a hot oven as soon as you have shaped them. Traybakes and most teabreads keep well for several days, or longer, in an airtight tin. Scones are best eaten on the day they are made – preferably fresh from the oven, or griddle.

Oven Scones

225g (8oz) self-raising flour, plus
    extra to dust
pinch of salt
1 tsp baking powder
40g (1½oz) butter, diced, plus extra
    to grease
about 150ml (¼ pint) milk
beaten egg or milk, to glaze
whipped cream, or butter and jam,
    to serve

makes 8
preparation: 15 minutes
cooking time: 10 minutes, plus cooling
per scone: 150 cals; 6g fat;
    22g carbohydrate

1 Sift the flour, salt and baking powder together into a bowl. Rub in the butter until the mixture resembles fine breadcrumbs. Stir in enough milk to give a fairly soft dough, using a knife.
2 Gently roll or pat out the dough on a lightly floured surface to a 2cm (¾ inch) thickness and cut out rounds with a 6cm (2½ inch) plain cutter.
3 Put on a greased baking sheet and brush the tops with beaten egg or milk. Bake at 220°C (200°C fan oven) mark 7 for about 10 minutes until golden brown and well risen. Transfer to a wire rack to cool.
4 Serve warm, split and filled with cream, or butter and jam.

note: *To ensure a good rise, avoid heavy handling, and make sure the rolled-out dough is at least 2cm (¾ inch) thick.*

variations
wholemeal scones: *Replace half of the white flour with wholemeal flour.*
fruit scones: *Add 50g (2oz) currants, sultanas, raisins or chopped dates (or a mixture) to the dry ingredients.*
cheese and herb scones: *Sift 1 tsp mustard powder with the dry ingredients. Stir 50g (2oz) finely grated Cheddar cheese into the mixture before adding the milk. After glazing, sprinkle the tops with a little cheese.*

Buttermilk Scones

300g (11oz) self-raising flour, sifted, plus
   extra to dust
1 tsp baking powder
pinch of salt
50g (2oz) butter, diced and chilled, plus
   extra to grease
25g (1oz) golden caster sugar
284ml carton buttermilk
milk, to glaze
blueberry jam to serve

VANILLA MASCARPONE
250g (9oz) mascarpone
1 vanilla pod, split lengthways

makes 8
preparation: 15 minutes
cooking time: 12–15 minutes, plus cooling
per scone: 200 cals; 6g fat;
   33g carbohydrate

1 Sift the flour, baking powder and salt together and put into a food processor with the diced butter. Whiz for 30 seconds until the mixture resembles fine breadcrumbs. Tip the mixture into a large bowl.
2 Add the sugar and buttermilk, and use a knife to mix everything together quickly. Knead the dough lightly on a floured board and shape it into a round.
3 Lightly roll or pat out the dough to a 2.5cm (1 inch) thickness. Using a floured 6cm (2½ inch) plain cutter, stamp out rounds. Put these on two greased baking sheets, brush the tops with milk and bake at 220°C (200°C fan oven) mark 7 for 12–15 minutes or until the scones are golden and risen.
4 Meanwhile, make the vanilla mascarpone. Beat the mascarpone in a bowl with a wooden spoon to soften it. Scrape out the seeds from the vanilla pod and add them to the bowl. Beat well to mix everything together.
5 Cool the scones on a wire rack. Serve them while still warm, split and sandwiched together with the vanilla mascarpone and blueberry jam.

Griddle Scones

225g (8oz) self-raising flour, plus extra
    to dust
pinch of salt
½ tsp freshly grated nutmeg
50g (2oz) butter, diced
50g (2oz) golden caster sugar
1 medium egg, beaten
3–4 tbsp milk
vegetable oil, to oil
butter, to serve

makes 8–10
preparation: 10 minutes
cooking time: 10 minutes, plus cooling
per scone: 180–140 cals; 6–5g fat;
    28–22g carbohydrate

1 Sift the flour, salt and nutmeg together into a bowl and rub in the butter until the mixture resembles fine breadcrumbs. Stir in the sugar and make a well in the centre. Add the beaten egg and sufficient milk to mix to a firm dough.

2 Gently roll or pat out out the dough on a lightly floured surface to a 1cm (½ inch) thickness and cut into triangles or rounds.

3 Cook on a medium-hot, oiled griddle or heavy-based frying pan for about 5 minutes on each side until the scones are browned and cooked through.

4 Serve the scones warm, split in half and spread with butter.

Drop Scones (Scotch Pancakes)

125g (4oz) self-raising flour
2 tbsp caster sugar
1 medium egg, beaten
150ml (¼ pint) milk
vegetable oil, to oil
butter, or whipped cream and jam,
    to serve

makes 15–18
preparation: 10 minutes
cooking time: 12–18 minutes
per scone: 50–40 cals; 1g fat;
    9–7g carbohydrate

1 Mix the flour and sugar together in a bowl. Make a well in the centre and mix in the egg, with enough of the milk to make a batter the consistency of thick cream – working as quickly and lightly as possible.

2 Cook the mixture in batches: drop spoonfuls on to an oiled hot griddle or heavy-based frying pan. Keep the griddle at a steady heat and when bubbles rise to the surface of the scone and burst, after 2–3 minutes, turn over with a palette knife.

3 Cook for a further 2–3 minutes until golden brown on the other side.

4 Put the cooked drop scones on a clean tea-towel and cover with another tea-towel to keep them moist. Serve warm, with butter, or cream and jam.

Sticky Gingerbread

175g (6oz) unsalted butter, in pieces, plus
   extra to grease
1 large cooking apple, about 225g (8oz)
1 tbsp lemon juice
125g (4oz) black treacle
125g (4oz) golden syrup
175g (6oz) molasses or dark muscovado
   sugar
225g (8oz) plain flour
125g (4oz) plain wholemeal flour
1 tsp ground mixed spice
1½ tsp bicarbonate of soda
2 medium eggs
150g (5oz) preserved stem ginger in syrup,
   thinly sliced
3 tbsp ginger syrup (from ginger jar)

makes 12
preparation: 20 minutes
cooking time: 1 hour 20 minutes,
   plus cooling
per slice: 350 cals; 14g fat;
   56g carbohydrate

1 Grease and line a deep 18cm (7 inch) square cake tin. Peel, core and quarter the apple; immerse in a bowl of water with the lemon juice added to prevent discolouration.

2 Put the treacle, golden syrup, sugar and butter in a heavy-based pan. Heat gently until the butter melts; leave to cool slightly.

3 Sift the flours, spice and bicarbonate of soda into a bowl. Grate three-quarters of the apple into the bowl and toss lightly to mix. Add the melted mixture, eggs and three quarters of the ginger pieces. Beat well until thoroughly combined.

4 Turn the mixture into the prepared tin, spreading it into the corners. Using a potato peeler, pare the remaining apple into thin slices. Scatter the apple slices and remaining ginger over the surface of the gingerbread and press down lightly into the mixture with the tip of a knife. Bake at 170°C (150°C fan oven) mark 3 for 1 hour 20 minutes or until firm to the touch. Leave to cool in the tin.

5 Turn out the cake and drizzle the ginger syrup over the surface. Cut into slices to serve.

note: *Gingerbread will keep in an airtight tin for up to 1 week. The flavour is improved if it is stored for several days before eating.*

variation: *For a more pronounced flavour add 2 tsp ground ginger with the mixed spice.*

American Banana Loaf

225g (8oz) plain flour
1 tsp bicarbonate of soda
½ tsp cream of tartar
100g (3½oz) butter, plus extra to grease
175g (6oz) golden caster sugar
1 tsp lemon juice
3 tbsp milk
2 bananas, about 300g (11oz), peeled
finely grated zest of 1 lemon
2 medium eggs, beaten
½ tsp vanilla extract
golden granulated sugar, to dredge

makes 10 slices
preparation: 20 minutes
cooking time: 1¼ hours, plus cooling
per slice: 280 cals; 11g fat;
   43g carbohydrate

1 Put the flour, bicarbonate of soda and cream of tartar into a food processor and pulse to mix. Add the butter and whiz until the mixture resembles breadcrumbs. Add the sugar and whiz briefly.

2 Mix the lemon juice and milk together in a jug and leave to stand for 1 minute. Grease and base-line a 900g (2lb) loaf tin.

3 Mash the bananas in a bowl, then stir in the lemon zest, eggs, milk mixture and vanilla extract. Add to the food processor and whiz until combined.

4 Put the mixture into the loaf tin, dredge with granulated sugar and bake at 180°C (160°C fan oven) mark 4 for 1¼ hours or until risen and golden, and a skewer inserted into the centre comes out clean.

5 Leave in the tin for 5 minutes, then turn out on to a wire rack to cool. Cut into slices to serve.

Fruity Teabread

1 Earl Grey or Darjeeling tea bag

75g (3oz) ready-to-eat dried figs,
   roughly chopped

75g (3oz) ready-to-eat dried pears,
   roughly chopped

225g (8oz) sultanas

grated zest and juice of 1 orange

125g (4oz) butter, softened, plus extra
   to grease

175g (6oz) dark muscovado sugar

2 medium eggs, beaten

225g (8oz) self-raising flour

1 tsp ground mixed spice

demerara sugar, to sprinkle

butter, to serve

serves 12
preparation: 30 minutes, plus soaking
cooking time: about 1¼ hours, plus cooling
per serving: 290 cals; 10g fat;
   49g carbohydrate

1 Put the tea bag in a jug, add 150ml (¼ pint) boiling water and infuse for 3 minutes. Discard the tea bag.

2 Put the figs, pears, sultanas, orange zest and juice into a bowl, then pour in the tea. Cover the bowl and leave the fruit to soak for at least 6 hours, or overnight.

3 Grease and line a 900g (2lb) loaf tin.

4 Cream the butter and sugar together in a large bowl. Gradually add the eggs and beat well. Sift the flour and spice together over the mixture and add the soaked fruit. Mix together until thoroughly combined.

5 Spoon the mixture into the prepared tin and bake in the middle of the oven at 180°C (160°C fan oven) mark 4 for 50 minutes. Take out, sprinkle the top with demerara sugar and cover loosely with foil. Bake for a further 25–35 minutes or until a skewer inserted in the centre comes out clean.

6 Leave in the tin for 10 minutes, then turn out on to a wire rack to cool. Serve sliced and buttered.

note: *This teabread will keep for up to 2 weeks wrapped in clingfilm and stored in an airtight tin.*

Coconut and Cherry Loaf

150g (5oz) unsalted butter, softened, plus
   extra to grease
75g (3oz) golden caster sugar
3 medium eggs, separated
75g (3oz) desiccated coconut
125g (4oz) self-raising flour, sifted
125g (4oz) glacé cherries, roughly
   chopped

TOPPING
75g (3oz) strawberry jam, warmed
   and sieved
75g (3oz) glacé cherries, roughly chopped
50g (2oz) desiccated coconut

makes 8 slices
preparation: 20 minutes
cooking time: 50 minutes, plus cooling
per slice: 440 cals; 28g fat;
   43g carbohydrate

1 Grease and base-line a 900g (2lb) loaf tin with greaseproof paper.
2 Using an electric whisk, cream the butter and caster sugar together in a bowl until light and fluffy. Add the egg yolks slowly, beating well between each addition. Fold in the desiccated coconut, flour and glacé cherries.
3 Whisk the egg whites in a clean bowl to soft peaks and beat one spoonful into the cake mixture to lighten it. Using a large metal spoon, lightly fold in the rest.
4 Pour the mixture into the prepared loaf tin. Bake at 170°C (150°C fan oven) mark 3 for 45–50 minutes, covering the top with foil if it begins to brown too quickly. To test, insert a skewer into the centre of the loaf – it should come out clean.
5 Leave the loaf to cool completely in the tin; this will take about 3 hours.
6 For the topping, brush the top of the loaf with the jam to glaze, then top with the glacé cherries and sprinkle with the coconut. Leave to cool and set. Cut into slices to serve.

note: *Use natural colour glacé cherries, available from most supermarkets.*

Blackberry and Cinnamon Loaf

125ml (4fl oz) sunflower oil, plus
   extra to oil
175g (6oz) plain flour
1½ tsp baking powder
1½ tsp ground cinnamon
200g (7oz) frozen blackberries
125g (4oz) golden caster sugar
grated zest and juice of 1 lemon
125ml (4fl oz) Greek-style yogurt
3 medium eggs
golden icing sugar, to dust

makes 8 slices
preparation: 15 minutes
cooking time: 55 minutes, plus cooling
per slice: 320 cals; 18g fat;
   35g carbohydrate

1 Grease and base-line a 900g (2lb) loaf tin with greaseproof paper.
2 Sift the flour, baking powder and ground cinnamon into a bowl, add the frozen blackberries and turn to coat. Make a well in the centre.
3 In another bowl, whisk together the sugar, oil, lemon zest and juice, yogurt and eggs. Pour into the well in the flour mixture and stir to combine.
4 Spoon the mixture into the prepared loaf tin and level the surface. Bake at 170°C (150°C fan oven) mark 3 for 55 minutes, covering the top with foil if it begins to brown too quickly. To test, insert a skewer into the centre of the loaf – it should come out clean.
5 Leave in the tin for 10 minutes, then turn out on to a wire rack to cool completely.
6 When cool, dust the loaf with icing sugar. Cut into slices to serve.

variation: *Use frozen raspberries or a mixture of frozen berry fruits in place of blackberries.*

Apricot and Almond Traybake

250g (9oz) butter, at room temperature,
   plus extra to grease
225g (8oz) golden caster sugar
275g (10oz) self-raising flour
2 tsp baking powder
finely grated zest of 1 orange
2 tbsp orange juice
75g (3oz) ground almonds
5 medium eggs, lightly beaten
225g (8oz) ready-to-eat dried apricots,
   roughly chopped
25g (1oz) flaked almonds

makes 18 bars
preparation: 10 minutes
cooking time: 30–40 minutes, plus cooling
per bar: 280 cals; 16g fat; 30g carbohydrate

1 Grease and base-line a 33 x 20cm (13 x 8 inch) baking tin.
2 Put the butter, caster sugar, flour, baking powder, orange zest and juice, ground almonds and beaten eggs into a large bowl (or a free-standing mixer if you have one). Mix with an electric beater on a low setting for 30 seconds, then increase the speed and mix for 1 minute until thoroughly combined.
3 Using a large metal spoon, fold in the dried apricots. Spoon the mixture into the baking tin and smooth the surface with a palette knife. Scatter the flaked almonds over the top.
4 Bake at 180°C (160°C fan oven) mark 4 for 30–40 minutes or until risen and golden brown, and when a skewer inserted into the centre comes out clean.
5 Leave the traybake to cool in the tin, then cut into 18 bars and lift out with a palette knife.

Flapjacks

75g (3oz) butter, plus extra to grease
175g (6oz) rolled oats
50g (2oz) light muscovado sugar
30ml (2 tbsp) golden syrup

makes 8–10
preparation: 15 minutes
cooking time: 20 minutes, plus cooling
per flapjack: 190–150 cals; 10–8g fat;
   26–20g carbohydrate

1 Grease a shallow 18cm (7 inch) square cake tin. Put the rolled oats into a large bowl and set aside.
2 Put the butter, sugar and golden syrup into a heavy-based pan over a low heat until the butter has melted and the mixture is smooth.
3 Pour the syrup mixture on to the rolled oats and mix thoroughly. Turn into the prepared tin and press well down with the back of a spoon.
4 Bake at 180°C (160°C fan oven) mark 4 for about 20 minutes until golden brown. Leave to cool slightly in the tin, then mark into fingers with a sharp knife and loosen the edges.
5 When firm, remove from the tin and transfer to a wire rack to cool, then break into fingers.

note: *The flapjacks will keep for up to 1 week in an airtight container.*

Muesli Bars

175g (6oz) unsalted butter, in pieces
150g (5oz) light muscovado sugar
2 tbsp golden syrup
375g (13oz) porridge oats
100g (3½oz) ready-to-eat dried papaya,
    roughly chopped
50g (2oz) sultanas
50g (2oz) pecan nuts, roughly chopped
25g (1oz) pine nuts
25g (1oz) pumpkin seeds
1 tbsp plain flour
1 tsp ground cinnamon

makes 12
preparation: 10 minutes
cooking time: 25-30 minutes, plus cooling
per bar: 260 cals; 18g fat; 25g carbohydrate

1 Melt the butter, sugar and golden syrup together in a heavy-based pan over a low heat.
2 Meanwhile, put the oats, dried fruit, nuts, seeds, flour and cinnamon into a large bowl and stir to mix. Pour in the melted mixture and mix together until thoroughly combined.
3 Spoon the mixture into a 30 x 20cm (12 x 8 inch) non-stick baking tin and press down into the corners.
4 Bake at 180°C (160°C fan oven) mark 4 for 25–30 minutes or until golden.
5 Press the mixture down again if necessary, then use a palette knife to mark into 12 bars. Leave to cool completely. Use a palette knife to lift the bars out of the tin and store in an airtight container.

Date Crunchies

175g (6oz) butter, plus extra to grease
175g (6oz) self-raising flour
175g (6oz) semolina
75g (3oz) golden caster sugar
225g (8oz) pitted dates, chopped
1 tbsp thin honey
1 tbsp lemon juice
pinch of ground cinnamon

makes 12
preparation: 20 minutes
cooking time: 30–35 minutes, plus cooling
per slice: 280 cals; 12g fat;
    42g carbohydrate

1 Grease a shallow 18cm (7 inch) square baking tin.
2 Mix the flour and semolina together in a bowl and make a well in the centre. Put the butter and sugar into a pan over a low heat until the butter has melted and the sugar dissolved, then stir into the flour mixture. Press half of this mixture into the prepared tin.
3 Meanwhile, put the dates into a pan with the honey, 4 tbsp water, the lemon juice and cinnamon. Stir over a low heat until soft and fairly smooth.
4 Spread the date filling over the mixture in the tin, then cover with the remaining semolina mixture and press down lightly. Bake at 190°C (170°C fan oven) mark 5 for 30–35 minutes until golden.
5 Cut into bars, then leave in the tin until cold. Lift out the bars and store in an airtight container.

variation
apricot crunchies: *Use chopped ready-to-eat dried apricots instead of the dates. Purée the apricot filling if preferred in a blender or food processor.*

LARGE CAKES AND GÂTEAUX

Classic, everyday sandwich cakes, whisked sponges and simple fruit cakes are included here, as well as elegant gâteaux for special occasions.

Refer to the step-by-step guide on pages 458–460 for specific cake-making techniques, including lining cake tins and testing cakes.

Victoria Jam Sandwich with Mascarpone

175g (6oz) butter, at room temperature,
    plus extra to grease
175g (6oz) golden caster sugar
3 medium eggs, beaten
175g (6oz) self-raising flour, sifted

TO ASSEMBLE
150g (5oz) mascarpone
1 tsp milk (optional)
1 tsp icing sugar (optional), plus extra to dust
4 tbsp raspberry conserve

makes 6–8 slices
preparation: 20 minutes
cooking time: 25 minutes, plus cooling
per slice: 610–460 cals; 39–30g fat;
    61–46g carbohydrate

1 Grease and base-line two 18cm (7 inch) sandwich cake tins (see page 458).
2 Put the butter and caster sugar into a large bowl and cream together with a hand-held electric beater (or a free-standing electric mixer) until light and fluffy.
3 Gradually beat in the eggs until the mixture is smooth, then gently fold in the flour, using a large metal spoon or spatula.
4 Divide the mixture between the prepared tins and gently level the surface with a palette knife. Bake at 180°C (160°C fan oven) mark 4 for about 25 minutes until golden, firm to the touch and beginning to shrink away from the sides of the tin.
5 Leave the cakes to cool in the tins for 5 minutes, then turn out each layer on to a wire rack and leave to cool completely.
6 For the filling, beat the mascarpone to loosen, adding the milk if it is too thick to spread. Sweeten with icing sugar if you like.
7 Spread the mascarpone on top of one cake layer, then cover with the raspberry conserve. Put the other layer on top and lightly press the two together. Using a fine sieve, dust the top liberally with icing sugar.

variations
basic Victoria sandwich: *Omit the mascarpone and simply sandwich the cake layers together with raspberry or strawberry conserve. Dredge the top with caster sugar.*
chocolate sandwich cake: *Replace 3 tbsp flour with cocoa powder. Sandwich the cakes with vanilla or chocolate buttercream (page 514).*
coffee sandwich cake: *Blend 2 tsp instant coffee granules with 1 tbsp boiling water. Cool and add to the creamed mixture with the eggs. Sandwich the cakes with vanilla or coffee buttercream (page 514).*
citrus sandwich cake: *Add the finely grated zest of 1 orange, lime or lemon to the mixture. Sandwich the cakes together with orange, lime or lemon buttercream (page 514).*

One-Stage Quick Mix Cake

175g (6oz) soft margarine, plus extra
   to grease
175g (6oz) self-raising flour
1 tsp baking powder
175g (6oz) golden caster sugar
3 medium eggs, beaten

TO ASSEMBLE
3–4 tbsp jam
caster sugar, to sprinkle

makes 8 slices
preparation: 20 minutes
cooking time: 25 minutes, plus cooling
per slice: 390 cals; 21g fat;
   47g carbohydrate

1 Grease and base-line two 18cm (7 inch) sandwich tins (see page 458).
2 Sift the flour and baking powder into a bowl. Add the sugar, margarine and eggs. Mix together with a wooden spoon, then beat with an electric mixer for 1–2 minutes until smooth and glossy, or mix in a food processor until smooth.
3 Divide the mixture evenly between the prepared tins and level with a palette knife. Bake at 180°C (160°C fan oven) mark 4 for 25 minutes or until well risen and the cakes spring back when lightly pressed in the centre. Loosen the edges of the cakes with a palette knife and leave to cool in the tins for 5 minutes.
4 Turn out and cool on a wire rack. Sandwich the cakes together with jam and sprinkle the top with caster sugar to serve.

Whisked Sponge

butter, to grease
90g (3oz) plain flour, plus extra to dust
3 large eggs
125g (4oz) golden caster sugar

TO ASSEMBLE
3–4 tbsp strawberry, raspberry or apricot jam
125ml (4fl oz) whipping cream, whipped
   (optional)
caster or icing sugar, to dust

makes 6–8 slices
preparation: 25 minutes
cooking time: 20–25 minutes, plus cooling
per slice (without cream): 215–160 cals;
   4–3g fat; 30–24g carbohydrate

1 Grease and base-line two 18cm (7 inch) sandwich tins and dust with a little flour or with a mixture of flour and caster sugar (see pages 458–9).
2 Put the eggs and sugar in a large heatproof bowl and whisk until well blended, using an electric whisk. Put the bowl over a pan of hot water and whisk until pale and creamy, and thick enough to leave a trail on the surface when the whisk is lifted. Remove the bowl from the pan and whisk until cool and thick.
3 Sift half the flour over the mixture and fold it in very lightly, using a large metal spoon or plastic-bladed spatula. Sift in the remaining flour and fold in gently until evenly incorporated.
4 Pour the mixture into the prepared tins, tilting the tins to spread the mixture evenly. Bake in the middle of the oven at 190°C (170°C fan oven) mark 5 for 20–25 minutes until well risen and the cakes spring back when lightly pressed in the centre. Turn out and cool on a wire rack.
5 Sandwich the cakes together with jam, and cream if using. Dust with caster or icing sugar to serve.

note: *This classic fatless sponge does not keep well and is best eaten on the day it is made.*

variation
chocolate whisked sponge: *Replace 1½ tbsp of the flour with 1½ tbsp cocoa powder. Sandwich the cake layers together with vanilla or chocolate buttercream (page 514). Dust with icing sugar.*

Swiss Roll

butter, to grease
125g (4oz) golden caster sugar, plus extra
   to dust
125g (4oz) plain flour, plus extra to dust
3 large eggs

TO ASSEMBLE
caster sugar, to sprinkle
125g (4oz) jam, warmed

makes 8 slices
preparation: 25 minutes
cooking time: 10–12 minutes, plus cooling
per slice: 200 cals; 3g fat;
   41g carbohydrate

1 Grease and line a 33 x 23cm (13 x 9 inch) Swiss roll tin (see page 459); grease the paper. Dust with caster sugar and flour.
2 Put the eggs and sugar into a large heatproof bowl and whisk until well blended using a hand-held electric whisk. Put the bowl over a pan of hot water and whisk until the mixture is pale and creamy, and thick enough to leave a trail on the surface when the whisk is lifted. Remove bowl from pan and whisk until cool and thick.

3 Sift half the flour over the mixture and fold it in very lightly, using a large metal spoon or spatula. Sift in the remaining flour and gently fold in until evenly incorporated. Carefully fold in 1 tbsp hot water.
4 Pour into the prepared tin and tilt the tin backwards and forwards to spread the mixture evenly. Bake at 200°C (180°C fan oven) mark 6 for 10–12 minutes until pale golden, risen and springy to the touch.
5 Meanwhile, put a sheet of greaseproof paper on a damp tea-towel. Dredge the paper with caster sugar.
6 Quickly turn out the cake on to the paper and remove the lining paper. Trim off the crusty edges and spread the cake with jam.
7 Roll up the cake from a short side, with the aid of the paper. Make the first turn firmly so that the cake will roll evenly and have a good shape when finished, but roll more lightly after this turn. Put seam-side down on a wire rack and sprinkle with sugar to serve.

variation

chocolate Swiss roll: *Replace 1 tbsp flour with cocoa powder. Turn out and trim sponge as above, then cover with a sheet of greaseproof paper and roll with the paper inside. When cold, unroll and remove paper. Spread with whipped cream or buttercream (page 514) and re-roll. Dust with icing sugar.*

Genoese Sponge

40g (1½oz) unsalted butter, plus extra
   to grease
65g (2½oz) plain flour, plus extra to dust
75g (3oz) golden caster sugar, plus extra
   to dust
3 large eggs
1 tbsp cornflour

TO ASSEMBLE
soft fruit and whipped cream, or jam
icing sugar, to dust

makes 6–8 slices
preparation: 25 minutes
cooking time: 25–40 minutes, plus cooling
per slice (without cream): 220–160 cals;
   9–7g fat; 31–23g carbohydrate

1 Grease and base-line two 18cm (7 inch) sandwich tins, or one 18cm (7 inch) deep round cake tin; dust with a little flour and caster sugar (see pages 458–9).
2 Put the butter into a pan and heat gently until melted, then remove from the heat and leave to cool slightly for a few minutes until beginning to thicken.
3 Put the eggs and sugar into a large heatproof bowl and whisk until evenly blended, using an electric whisk. Put the bowl over a pan of hot water and whisk until pale and creamy, and thick enough to leave a trail on the surface when the whisk is lifted. Remove the bowl from the pan and whisk until cool and thick.
4 Sift the flour and cornflour together. Fold half into the whisked mixture with a large metal spoon or plastic spatula. Pour the cooled butter around the edge of the mixture, leaving the sediment behind. Gradually fold it in very lightly, cutting through the mixture until it is all incorporated. Carefully fold in the remaining flour as lightly as possible. Pour into the prepared tins.
5 Bake in the centre of the oven at 180°C (160°C fan oven) mark 4 for 25–30 minutes, or the deep cake for 35–40 minutes, until well risen and the cakes spring back when lightly pressed. Loosen the cake edge and leave in the tin for 5 minutes. Turn out, remove the lining paper and cool on a wire rack.
6 Serve filled with fruit and cream, or jam. Dust the top with icing sugar to serve.

Carrot Cake

250ml (8fl oz) sunflower oil, plus extra to oil
225g (8oz) light muscovado sugar
3 large eggs
225g (8oz) self-raising flour
large pinch of salt
½ tsp ground mixed spice
½ tsp ground nutmeg
I tsp ground cinnamon
250g (9oz) carrots, peeled and coarsely
    grated

FROSTING
50g (2oz) butter, preferably unsalted, at
    room temperature
225g pack Philadelphia cream cheese
25g (1oz) golden icing sugar
½ tsp vanilla extract

TO FINISH
8 pecan halves, roughly chopped

makes 12 slices
preparation: 15 minutes
cooking time: 40 minutes, plus cooling
per slice: 450 cals; 32g fat;
    38g carbohydrate

1 Oil and base-line two 18cm (7 inch) sandwich tins (see page 458).
2 Using a hand-held electric whisk, whisk the oil and muscovado sugar together to combine, then whisk in the eggs, one at a time.
3 Sift the flour, salt and spices together over the mixture, then gently fold in, using a large metal spoon. Tip the grated carrots into the bowl and fold in.
4 Divide the cake mixture between the prepared tins and bake at 180°C (160°C fan oven) mark 4 for 30–40 minutes or until golden and a skewer inserted into the centre comes out clean. Leave in the tins for 10 minutes, then turn out on to a wire rack to cool.
5 To make the frosting, beat the butter and cream cheese together in a bowl until light and fluffy. Sift in the icing sugar, add the vanilla extract and beat well until smooth.
6 Spread one third of the frosting over one cake and sandwich together with the other cake. Spread the remaining frosting on top and sprinkle with the pecans. Store the cake in an airtight container and eat within 2 days.

note: *The cake will keep for up to a week in an airtight tin if it is stored before the frosting is applied.*

Madeira Cake

175g (6oz) butter, softened, plus extra
    to grease
125g (4oz) plain flour
125g (4oz) self-raising flour
175g (6oz) golden caster sugar
1 tsp vanilla extract
3 large eggs, beaten
1–2 tbsp milk (optional)
2–3 thin slices citron peel

makes 12 slices
preparation: 20 minutes
cooking time: about 50 minutes,
    plus cooling
per slice: 260 cals; 14g fat;
    31g carbohydrate

1 Grease and line a deep 18cm (7 inch) round cake tin. Sift the plain and self-raising flours together.
2 Cream the butter and sugar together in a bowl until pale and fluffy, then beat in the vanilla extract. Add the eggs, a little at a time, beating well after each addition.
3 Fold in the sifted flours using a metal spoon, adding a little milk if necessary to give a dropping consistency.
4 Spoon the mixture into the prepared tin and level the surface. Bake at 180°C (160°C fan oven) mark 4 for 20 minutes. Lay the citron peel on the cake and bake for a further 30 minutes or until a skewer inserted into the centre comes out clean. Turn out and cool on a wire rack.

variation: *Add the grated zest of 1 lemon at stage 2. Add the juice of the lemon instead of the milk at stage 3.*

Almond and Orange Torte

vegetable oil, to oil
flour, to dust
1 medium orange
3 medium eggs
225g (8oz) golden caster sugar
250g (9oz) ground almonds
½ tsp baking powder
icing sugar, to dust

makes 10 slices
preparation: 30 minutes
cooking time: 1 hour 50 minutes,
    plus cooling
per slice: 265 cals; 16g fat;
    25g carbohydrate

1 Grease and line, then oil and flour a 20cm (8 inch) spring-release cake tin.
2 Put the whole orange into a small pan and cover with water. Bring to the boil. Cover and simmer for at least 1 hour until tender. Drain and cool.
3 Cut the orange in half and remove the pips. Whiz in a food processor to make a smooth purée.
4 Put the eggs and sugar into a bowl and whisk together until thick and pale. Fold in the ground almonds, baking powder and orange purée.
5 Pour the mixture into the prepared tin. Bake at 180°C (160°C fan oven) mark 4 for 40–50 minutes or until a skewer inserted into the centre comes out clean. Leave to cool in the tin.
6 Unclip the tin and remove the lining paper from the cake. Dust with icing sugar and serve cut into slices, with crème fraîche if you like.

note: *A whole orange, boiled and then puréed, is the secret ingredient in this moist, tangy cake.*

Chocolate Roulade

175g (6oz) good quality plain dark chocolate
    (with 60–70% cocoa solids), in pieces
6 large eggs, separated
175g (6oz) golden caster sugar

FILLING
284ml carton whipping cream
1 tsp golden caster sugar, plus extra to dust
½ tsp vanilla extract

TO FINISH
cocoa powder, to sprinkle
chocolate curls (see page 503), to decorate

makes 10 slices
preparation: 30 minutes, plus chilling
cooking time: 25 minutes, plus cooling
per serving: 330 cals; 23g fat;
    35g carbohydrate

1 Line a 38 x 28cm (15 x 11 inch) non-stick Swiss roll tin with baking parchment.
2 Put the chocolate into a heatproof bowl with 150ml (¼ pint) water. Melt over a pan of gently simmering water. Stir until smooth off the heat and cool slightly.
3 Put the egg yolks and caster sugar into a bowl and beat with an electric whisk until light in colour and thick. Beat in the chocolate until thoroughly blended.
4 In a clean bowl, whisk the egg whites until they just hold soft peaks. Beat one quarter of the egg white into the chocolate mixture to loosen it, then carefully fold in the remainder using a large metal spoon, until evenly combined; do not over-fold. Pour immediately into the prepared tin.
5 Bake at 180°C (160°C fan oven) mark 4 for about 25 minutes (see note). Leave the roulade to cool a little in the tin, then cover with a clean, warm damp tea-towel. Once cold, cover the cloth with clingfilm; chill for at least 6 hours or overnight.
6 Whip the cream in a bowl until it is just beginning to thicken. Add the caster sugar and vanilla extract. Continue to whip until the cream just holds its shape.
7 Lightly dust a large sheet of greaseproof paper with caster sugar. Remove the clingfilm and cloth from the roulade and carefully turn out on to the greaseproof paper. Trim 5mm (¼ inch) off the two short sides to neaten. Spread the cream over the roulade and roll up tightly from the long side, using the greaseproof paper to help – don't worry if the sponge cracks, this is a characteristic of a roulade.
8 Transfer to a serving dish, sprinkle with cocoa powder and decorate with chocolate curls to serve.

note: *A crust will form during baking, making it tricky to tell if the roulade is cooked. Press the centre lightly with your fingertips – it should spring back.*

Lemon Drizzle Loaf

2 large lemons, preferably unwaxed
225g (8oz) self-raising flour
pinch of salt
125g (4oz) butter, diced
225g (8oz) caster sugar
2 large eggs
2 tbsp lemon curd

makes 10 slices
preparation: 15 minutes, plus soaking
cooking time: 1¼ hours, plus cooling
per slice: 280 cals; 12g fat;
    43g carbohydrate

1 Line a 900g (2lb) loaf tin with a loaf tin liner or baking parchment. Grate the zest and squeeze the juice from 1 lemon.
2 Sift the flour and salt into a large bowl, rub in the butter until the mixture resembles breadcrumbs, then stir in half the sugar. Add the eggs, grated lemon zest and juice and 1 tbsp lemon curd. Mix until smooth.

3 Spoon the soft mixture into the prepared loaf tin and bake at 180°C (160°C fan oven) mark 4 for 45–55 minutes until well risen and golden, and a skewer inserted in the centre comes out clean. (The top may crack during baking.) Leave in the tin for 10 minutes then lift out, keeping the cake in the lining paper.
4 Finely pare the zest from the remaining lemon, using a vegetable peeler, and soak it in 450ml (¾ pint) hot water for at least 30 minutes. Put the water and lemon zest into a pan, bring to the boil and simmer for 10 minutes. Add the remaining caster sugar and let bubble for 10 minutes or until reduced by one third. Remove from the heat and stir in the remaining lemon curd and 1 tbsp lemon juice. Allow the lemon syrup to cool a little.
5 Pierce the cake several times with a skewer and drizzle the lemon syrup over the cake while it is still warm. Decorate with the lemon zest. Store in an airtight container and eat within 1 week.

note: *The light lemon syrup that is poured over at the end gives this cake an intense citrus flavour.*

Almond and Apricot Roulade

butter, to grease
25g (1oz) flaked almonds
5 medium eggs, separated
150g (5oz) golden caster sugar, plus extra
    to sprinkle
1 tsp vanilla extract
125g (4oz) ready-made white almond paste,
    grated
3 tbsp plain flour
3 tbsp amaretto liqueur

TO ASSEMBLE
300ml (½ pint) crème fraîche
6 ripe apricots, halved, stoned and chopped
caster or icing sugar, to dust

makes 8 slices
preparation: 20 minutes
cooking time: 20 minutes, plus cooling
per slice: 420 cals; 25g fat;
    40g carbohydrate

1 Grease a 33 x 23cm (13 x 9 inch) Swiss roll tin and line with greased baking parchment. Scatter the flaked almonds evenly over the paper.

2 Put the egg yolks and 125g (4oz) of the sugar in a bowl and whisk until pale and fluffy.
3 Stir in the vanilla extract and grated almond paste. Sift the flour over the mixture, then lightly fold in.
4 Whisk the egg whites in a clean bowl until stiff but not dry. Gradually whisk in the remaining sugar. Using a large metal spoon, fold a quarter of the egg whites into the almond mixture to loosen it, then carefully fold in the remainder.
5 Turn the mixture into the prepared tin and gently ease it into the corners. Bake at 180°C (160°C fan oven) mark 4 for about 20 minutes or until well risen and just firm to the touch. Cover with baking parchment and a damp tea-towel and leave until cool.
6 Remove the tea-towel and invert the roulade (and paper) on to a board. Peel off the lining paper. Sprinkle another piece of baking parchment with caster sugar and flip the roulade on to it. Drizzle with the liqueur.
7 Spread the roulade with the crème fraîche and scatter with the apricots. Starting from one of the narrow ends, carefully roll up the roulade, using the paper to help. Transfer to a plate and dust with caster or icing sugar to serve.

note: *The sponge will probably crack during rolling – this is a characteristic of roulades.*

Iced Ginger Cake

175g (6oz) butter, diced, plus extra to grease
150g (5oz) dark muscovado sugar
3 tbsp black treacle
150ml (¼ pint) semi-skimmed milk
2 preserved stem ginger balls in syrup,
    drained and grated
225g (8oz) plain flour
1 tbsp ground ginger
1½ tsp ground cinnamon
1½ tsp bicarbonate of soda
2 medium eggs, beaten

TO FINISH
150g (5oz) golden icing sugar
2 tbsp ginger syrup from the jar
1 preserved stem ginger ball in syrup,
    drained and roughly chopped

makes 15 slices
preparation: 20 minutes
cooking time: 30 minutes, plus cooling
per slice: 250 cals; 11g fat;
    37g carbohydrate

1 Grease and line a 20cm (8 inch) square cake tin with greaseproof paper.
2 Put the butter, sugar and treacle into a large pan with the milk and grated ginger, and heat gently until melted, stirring to mix well.
3 Sift the flour, spices and bicarbonate of soda together over the mixture, then add the eggs and quickly mix together.
4 Spoon the mixture into the prepared tin. Bake at 200°C (180°C fan oven) mark 6 for 30 minutes or until a skewer inserted into the centre comes out clean. Leave in the tin for a few minutes, then remove and transfer to a wire rack to cool, still in the paper.
5 For the icing, sift the icing sugar into a bowl, add the ginger syrup and 1 tbsp cold water and mix until smooth. Pour the icing over the cooled cake, then scatter the chopped ginger on top.

note: *This cake will keep for up to 1 week, wrapped in foil and stored in an airtight container.*

Apple Cake with Cinnamon

250g (9oz) unsalted butter, softened,
    plus extra to grease
4 sharp eating apples, such as
    Granny Smiths
250g (9oz) golden caster sugar
grated zest of 1 lemon
3 medium eggs, beaten
150g (5oz) self-raising flour
1 tsp ground cinnamon
½ tsp baking powder
50g (2oz) ground almonds

makes 6 slices
preparation: 45 minutes
cooking time: 1 hour 10 minutes,
    plus cooling
per slice: 680 cals; 42g fat;
    71g carbohydrate

1 Grease and base-line a 23cm (9 inch) spring-release cake tin.
2 Peel, quarter and core the apples, then cut each quarter in half. Melt 50g (2oz) butter in a pan, add the apples and 50g (2oz) sugar. Fry until the apples are caramelised, then add the lemon zest. Transfer to the prepared tin and leave to cool.
3 Put the remaining butter and sugar into a bowl and beat until light and fluffy, then gradually beat in the eggs. Sift the flour, cinnamon and baking powder together over the mixture, then add the ground almonds. Fold in gently, using a large metal spoon, until evenly incorporated.
4 Spoon the mixture on top of the apples and smooth the surface. Bake at 180°C (160°C fan oven) mark 4 for 50–60 minutes or until a skewer inserted into the centre comes out clean.
5 Leave in the tin for 15 minutes, then turn out on to a wire rack to cool. Serve cut into wedges, with crème fraîche or yogurt if you like.

note: *This moist cake improves in flavour and texture with keeping – you can store it in an airtight container in a cool place for up to 1 week.*

Espresso Coffee Cake

175g (6oz) unsalted butter, softened, plus
   extra to grease
175g (6oz) golden caster sugar
3 medium eggs
175g (6oz) self-raising flour
1 tsp baking powder
1 tbsp coffee liqueur, such as Tia Maria
   or Kahlua
3 tbsp instant espresso coffee

ICING
175g (6oz) golden icing sugar, sifted
2 tsp instant espresso coffee, dissolved in
   1 tbsp boiling water

TO FINISH
18 dark chocolate-coated coffee beans

serves 12
preparation: 30 minutes
cooking time: 45–50 minutes, plus cooling
per serving: 340 cals; 16g fat;
   47g carbohydrate

1 Grease and line a 900g (2lb) loaf tin with a loaf tin liner or baking parchment.
2 Cream the butter and sugar together in a large bowl with an electric whisk until pale and fluffy. Beat in the eggs one at a time. Add 1 tbsp flour with the last egg to prevent curdling.
3 Sift remaining flour and baking powder together on to the mixture, add the liqueur and fold in carefully, using a large metal spoon. Put half the mixture into another bowl and mix the coffee into that portion.
4 Spoon some of each mixture alternately into the prepared tin, and then repeat to create layers. Shake the tin once to distribute the mixture, then drag a skewer back and forth a few times through the mixture to create a marbled effect.
5 Bake at 190°C (170°C fan oven) mark 5 for 45–50 minutes or until a skewer inserted into the centre comes out clean. Turn the cake out on to a wire rack and leave to cool. Remove the lining paper.
6 For the icing, put the icing sugar in a bowl. Dissolve the coffee in 2 tbsp plus 1 tsp boiling water and mix with the icing sugar until smooth. Pour on top of the cake and finish with the mocha beans.

Dundee Cake

225g (8oz) butter or margarine, softened,
    plus extra to grease
125g (4oz) currants
125g (4oz) raisins
50g (2oz) blanched almonds, chopped
125g (4oz) chopped mixed candied peel
300g (11oz) plain flour
225g (8oz) light muscovado sugar
finely grated zest of 1 lemon
4 large eggs, beaten
75g (3oz) split almonds, to finish

makes 16 slices
preparation: 20 minutes
cooking time: about 2 hours, plus cooling
per slice: 350 cals; 18g fat;
    45g carbohydrate

1 Grease and line a deep 20cm (8 inch) round cake tin. Wrap a double thickness of brown paper around the outside and secure with string (see page 459).
2 Combine the dried fruit, chopped nuts and peel in a bowl. Sift in a little flour and stir to coat the fruit.
3 Cream the butter and sugar together in a bowl until pale and fluffy, then beat in the lemon zest. Add the eggs a little at a time, beating well after each addition.
4 Sift in the remaining flour and fold in lightly, using a metal spoon, then fold in the fruit and nut mixture.
5 Turn the mixture into the prepared tin and make a slight hollow in the centre with the back of a metal spoon. Arrange the split almonds on top.
6 Bake at 170°C (150°C fan oven) mark 3 on the centre shelf for 2 hours, or until a skewer inserted into the centre comes out clean. Cover the top of the cake with foil if it appears to be browning too quickly. Leave in the tin for 15 minutes, then turn out on to a wire rack to cool. Wrap in greaseproof paper and foil. Leave to mature for at least a week before cutting.

Spiced Fruit Cake

250g (9oz) mixed dried fruit
15g (½oz) preserved stem ginger in syrup,
    drained and chopped
100g (3½oz) ready-to-eat pitted prunes,
    chopped
1 tsp grated lemon zest
1 tbsp lemon juice
100ml (3½fl oz) brandy, plus 1 tsp to sprinkle
1 tbsp ginger wine
150g (5oz) butter, softened, plus extra to grease
150g (5oz) dark muscovado sugar
2 medium eggs, beaten
150g (5oz) self-raising flour
1 tsp ground mixed spice
½ tsp ground cinnamon
½ tsp ground ginger
50g (2oz) ground almonds

makes 16 slices
preparation: 45 minutes, plus 2 days
    soaking
cooking time: 2 hours, plus cooling
per slice: 230 cals; 10g fat;
    25g carbohydrate

1 Put the dried fruit, stem ginger, prunes, lemon zest and juice in a bowl and pour on the brandy and ginger wine. Cover and leave to soak for at least 48 hours.
2 Grease and line a 15cm (6 inch) round cake tin, using a double thickness of baking parchment. Wrap a double thickness of brown paper around the outside of the tin and secure with string (see page 459).
3 Cream the butter and sugar together in a large bowl until light and fluffy. Add the eggs a little at a time, beating well after each addition, adding a little of the flour to stop the mixture curdling.
4 Sift the flour and spices together. Carefully fold into the mixture with the ground almonds.
5 Put half the soaked fruit in a food processor, and whiz to a purée. Fold this into the cake mixture, together with the remaining whole fruit.
6 Spoon into the prepared tin and smooth the surface. Bake at 170°C (150°C fan oven) mark 3 on the centre shelf for 2 hours or until a skewer inserted into the centre comes out clean. Cover the top of the cake with foil if it appears to be browning too quickly.
7 Leave the cake in the tin for 10 minutes, then make a few holes in the surface with a skewer and spoon the 1 tsp brandy on top, allowing it to soak through. Turn the cake out on to a wire rack to cool completely.
8 Remove the lining paper. Wrap the cake in greaseproof paper, then in foil. Store in an airtight tin in a cool, dark place for up to 1 month.

Italian Sponge with Prunes in Marsala

olive oil, to oil
5 medium eggs
100g (3½oz) caster sugar
50ml (2fl oz) extra-virgin olive oil
75g (3oz) self-raising flour
1 tsp baking powder
250g (9oz) ready-to-eat prunes
50g (2oz) light muscovado sugar
1 cinnamon stick
450ml (¾ pint) sweet Marsala
icing sugar, to dust

makes 9 slices
preparation: 25 minutes
cooking time: 45 minutes, plus cooling
per slice: 300 cals; 8g fat; 40g carbohydrate

1 Oil and line a 23cm (9 inch) spring-release cake tin. Whisk the eggs in a large bowl for 2–3 minutes (using a free-standing electric mixer if you have one).

2 Add the caster sugar and whisk until the mixture is increased in volume, thick, foaming and leaves a trail when the beaters are lifted. Continue to whisk on a high speed while adding the olive oil drop by drop.

3 Sift the flour and baking powder over the mixture and fold in gently. Turn into the prepared tin.

4 Bake at 170°C (150°C fan oven) mark 3 for 40–45 minutes or until springy to the touch, firm in the centre and shrinking away from the sides.

5 Meanwhile, put the prunes, sugar, cinnamon and Marsala into a pan, bring to the boil and simmer for 20 minutes until the fruit is tender; discard cinnamon.

6 Leave the cake in the tin for 10 minutes, then turn out and cool on a wire rack. Dust with icing sugar, cut into wedges and serve with the warm prunes in syrup.

Creamy Coffee and Praline Gâteau

50g (2oz) butter, melted, plus extra to grease
125g (4oz) plain flour, plus extra to dust
4 large eggs, separated
125g (4oz) golden caster sugar
1 tbsp rich coffee granules, dissolved in
   2 tsp boiling water

HAZELNUT PRALINE
50g (2oz) whole blanched hazelnuts
150g (5oz) white caster sugar

FILLING
2 x 250g cartons mascarpone
250g (9oz) golden icing sugar, sifted
2 tbsp rich coffee granules dissolved in
   1 tbsp boiling water

serves 8
preparation: 45 minutes
cooking time: 25 minutes, plus cooling
per serving: 700 cals; 40g fat;
   84g carbohydrate

1 Grease two loose-based 18cm (7 inch) sandwich tins with butter. Dust the tins lightly with flour and tip out excess.

2 Whisk the egg whites in a large bowl (using a free-standing electric mixer if you have one) until soft peaks form. Add 1 egg yolk and carefully whisk in; repeat with the other 3 yolks. Whisk in the sugar, 1 tbsp at a time, and continue to whisk until the mixture is thick enough to leave a trail when the beaters are lifted.

3 Sift half of the flour over the mixture and carefully fold in, using a large metal spoon. Mix the dissolved coffee with the melted butter and pour around the edge of the mixture. Sift in the remaining flour and gradually fold in.

4 Divide the mixture between the tins and bake at 190°C (170°C fan oven) mark 5 for 25 minutes until risen and firm to the touch. Ease a small palette knife round the side of each sponge, then turn out on to wire racks and leave to cool.

5 Meanwhile, make the hazelnut praline. Scatter the hazelnuts on a baking sheet lined with baking parchment. Melt the sugar in a heavy-based pan over a low heat, shaking the pan once or twice to help the sugar melt evenly, then increase the heat to medium and cook until it forms a dark golden brown caramel. Immediately pour the hot caramel over the nuts. Leave to cool and harden.

6 To make the filling, whisk the mascarpone, icing sugar and dissolved coffee together in a large bowl until smooth.

7 Slice each cake in half horizontally to give 4 layers. Put one cake layer on a plate and spread with a quarter of the filling. Continue layering to sandwich the whole cake together, finishing with a topping of mascarpone icing.

8 Break up the praline and put between sheets of greaseproof paper. With a rolling pin, smash into small pieces. Use to decorate the top of the cake.

Sachertorte

175g (6oz) unsalted butter, at room
    temperature, plus extra to grease
225g (8oz) good quality plain dark chocolate
    (with 70% cocoa solids), in pieces
175g (6oz) golden caster sugar
5 medium eggs, lightly beaten
3 tbsp cocoa powder
125g (4oz) self-raising flour
4 tbsp brandy

CHOCOLATE GANACHE
175g (6oz) good quality plain chocolate,
    in pieces
75g (3oz) butter, in pieces
4 tbsp double cream, warmed

TO FINISH
12 lilac sugar-coated almonds, or 50g
    (2oz) milk chocolate, melted

makes 12–16 slices
preparation: 35 minutes
cooking time: 45–55 minutes, plus cooling
per slice: 540–410 cals; 37–28g fat;
    43–32g carbohydrate

1 Grease and line a 20cm (8 inch) spring-release cake tin with baking parchment. Melt the chocolate in a heatproof bowl set over a pan of simmering water. Take off the heat, stir until smooth and leave to cool slightly for 5 minutes.

2 Cream the butter and sugar together (using a free-standing electric mixer if you have one) until pale and fluffy. Gradually beat in two thirds of the beaten eggs – don't worry if the mixture curdles.

3 Sift in the cocoa powder together with 3 tbsp of the flour, then gradually beat in the remaining eggs. Fold in the rest of the flour. Pour in the melted chocolate and fold in, using a large metal spoon, until evenly incorporated. Add 2 tbsp of the brandy and stir to combine.

4 Spoon the mixture into the prepared tin, spread evenly and bake at 190°C (170°C fan oven) mark 5 for 45 minutes, covering the tin loosely with foil if the cake appears to be browning too quickly. To test, insert a skewer into the centre of the cake; it should come out clean; if necessary, cook for an extra 5–10 minutes. Leave the cake to cool in the tin for 30 minutes.

5 Remove the cake from the tin and put on to a wire rack. Leave until cold, then drizzle with the rest of the brandy.

6 For the chocolate ganache, melt the chocolate in a heatproof bowl set over a pan of simmering water. Add the butter and warm cream and stir until smooth.

7 Position the wire rack over a tray and ladle the warm chocolate ganache over the top of the cake, letting it trickle down the sides. Use a palette knife to spread the ganache evenly over the cake.

8 Finish with sugar-coated almonds or a zig-zag drizzle of melted chocolate. Allow to set, then store in an airtight container for up to a week.

Devil's Food Cake

100g (3½oz) butter, softened, plus extra
   to grease
225ml (7½fl oz) milk
1 tbsp lemon juice or vinegar
225g (8oz) plain flour
1 tsp bicarbonate of soda
50g (2oz) cocoa powder
250g (9oz) golden caster sugar
3 medium eggs, beaten

FROSTING
250g (9oz) good quality plain dark chocolate
3 t bsp golden caster sugar
2 x 150ml cartons soured cream

serves 12
preparation: 30 minutes
cooking time: 30 minutes, plus cooling
per serving: 430 cals; 21g fat;
   56g carbohydrate

1 Grease and base-line two 20cm (8 inch) sandwich tins with greaseproof paper, then grease the paper.
2 Pour the milk into a jug, then add the lemon juice and put to one side to sour. Sift the flour, bicarbonate of soda and cocoa powder together.
3 Cream the butter and half the sugar together in a large bowl until light. Gradually beat in the eggs, then the remaining sugar. Mix in the soured milk alternately with the flour mixture, about 2 tbsp at a time.
4 Divide the mixture between the prepared tins and spread level. Bake in the centre of the oven at 180°C (160°C fan oven) mark 4 for 30 minutes. Leave in tins for 10 minutes, then turn out and cool on a wire rack.
5 For the frosting, break up the chocolate and melt in a heatproof bowl set over a pan of gently simmering water. Leave to cool slightly, then whisk in the sugar and soured cream.
6 Slice each cake in half to make 4 layers. Put one on a plate, then spread with a quarter of the frosting. Repeat to layer the cake up, finishing with frosting.

Chocolate Brandy Torte

125g (4oz) butter, diced, plus extra to grease
225g (8oz) good quality plain dark chocolate
    (with 60–70% cocoa solids), in pieces
3 large eggs, separated
125g (4oz) light muscovado sugar
50ml (2fl oz) brandy
75g (3oz) self-raising flour, sifted
50g (2oz) ground almonds
icing sugar, to dust

makes 6–8 slices
preparation: 20 minutes
cooking time: 45 minutes, plus cooling
per slice: 580–440 cals; 40–30g fat;
    43–32g carbohydrate

1 Grease and line a 20cm (8 inch) spring-release cake tin.

2 Melt the butter and chocolate in a bowl set over a pan of simmering water. Stir until smooth; cool slightly.
3 Whisk the egg yolks and muscovado sugar together until pale and creamy, then whisk in the brandy and melted chocolate on a low speed. Carefully fold in the flour and ground almonds, using a large metal spoon.
4 Whisk the egg whites in a clean bowl to the soft peak stage. Beat a large spoonful of the egg white into the chocolate mixture to lighten it, then carefully fold in the remainder, using a large metal spoon.
5 Pour the mixture into the prepared tin and bake at 180°C (160°C fan oven) mark 4 for 45 minutes or until a skewer inserted into the centre comes out clean. The surface will be crusted and cracked, concealing a soft, moist cake beneath. Leave to cool in the tin for 10 minutes, then turn out on to a wire rack. Remove the lining paper when the cake is cold.
6 To serve, dust the top of the cake with icing sugar.

Chocolate Mousse Cake

125g (4oz) butter, in pieces, plus extra
    to grease
200g (7oz) good quality plain chocolate,
    such as Bournville, in pieces
8 medium eggs, separated
200g (7oz) golden caster sugar

CHOCOLATE GANACHE
100g (3½oz) plain chocolate, such as
    Bournville, in pieces
90ml (3fl oz) double cream
25g (1oz) butter

TO DECORATE
chocolate curls (see right)

makes 16 slices
preparation: 20 minutes
cooking time: 1¼ hours, plus cooling
per slice: 310 cals; 20g fat;
    29g carbohydrate

1 Grease and line a 23cm (9 inch) spring-release cake tin.
2 Melt the chocolate and butter in a heatproof bowl set over a pan of simmering water. Cool slightly.
3 Whisk the egg yolks and sugar together (using a free-standing electric mixer if you have one) until pale, thick and mousse-like. Whisk in the melted chocolate.

4 Whisk the egg whites in a clean bowl to soft peaks. Add a third to the chocolate mixture and fold in, using a large metal spoon. Add the rest and fold in carefully.
5 Immediately pour into the prepared tin and bake at 180°C (160°C fan oven) mark 4 for 1¼ hours. Turn off the oven. Cover the cake with a damp tea-towel and leave to cool in the oven; it will sink a little in the centre.
6 For the ganache, melt the chocolate with the cream and butter in a heatproof bowl set over a pan of simmering water. Remove the bowl from the pan and set aside to cool for 5 minutes or until thickened.
7 Take the cake out of the tin and peel off the lining paper. Put on a serving plate, then ladle the ganache over the cake, so it covers the top and drizzles down the sides. Leave until just set. Using a palette knife, scatter the chocolate curls on top to finish.

chocolate curls (caraque): Melt about 75g (3oz) plain or white chocolate in a bowl set over a pan of hot water. Spread out thinly on a marble slab or clean surface and leave to set until no longer sticky to the touch. Holding a large knife at a slight angle to the surface, push the blade across the chocolate to shave off long thin curls. Adjust the angle of the blade to obtain the best curls.

variation: *For a simple finish, omit the chocolate curls and dust the top of the cake liberally with 2 tbsp each of cocoa powder and icing sugar.*

CELEBRATION CAKES

Cakes for Christmas, birthdays, weddings and other special occasions generally require a richer, more substantial cake than a simple sponge, as they are usually covered with almond paste and sugar paste or royal icing, then decorated to suit the event. The advantage of a rich fruit cake is its keeping qualities. A light fruit cake or Madeira cake may be used instead if preferred.

Rich Fruit Cake

This moist, rich cake is suitable for any celebration cake. It can be made in stages, which is convenient if time is short or if you are making more than one cake. Most dried fruit is sold ready cleaned and dried so it does not need to be washed before use. The fruit can be weighed and mixed a day ahead, the cake tins prepared and lined in advance, and other ingredients weighed ready to mix. On the day of baking, simply make the cake and bake.

The quantities have been carefully worked out so that the depth of each cake is the same. This is very important when making several tiers for a wedding cake, as they must all be the same depth to look aesthetically correct.

For sizes and quantities, refer to the Rich Fruit Cake Chart (see opposite). Use the same amount of brandy stated for the cake to 'feed' the cake after baking. Spoon half this amount over the surface after baking and the remainder over about a week later.

METHOD

1 Grease and line the appropriate cake tin for the size of cake you wish to make, using a double thickness of greaseproof paper. Tie a double band of brown paper round the outside and secure with string (see page 459). Stand the tin on a baking sheet, double lined with brown paper.

2 Prepare the ingredients for the appropriate size of cake according to the chart (see opposite). Put the currants, sultanas, raisins, glacé cherries, mixed peel and flaked almonds into a large mixing bowl. Stir these ingredients together, then cover the bowl with clingfilm. Leave for several hours or overnight in a cool place if required.

3 Sift the flour, mixed spice and cinnamon together into another mixing bowl.

4 Put the butter, muscovado sugar and grated lemon zest into a bowl and cream together until pale and fluffy. Add the beaten eggs gradually, beating well after each addition.

5 Gradually and lightly fold the flour into the creamed mixture with a plastic-bladed spatula, then fold in the brandy. Finally fold in the fruit and nuts until evenly distributed throughout the mixture.

6 Spoon the mixture into the prepared tin and spread evenly. Give the tin a few sharp taps to level the mixture and to remove any air pockets. Smooth the surface with the back of a metal spoon, making a slight depression in the centre.

7 Bake in the centre of the oven at 150°C (130°C fan oven) mark 2, using the time suggested in the chart as an approximate guide (see note at the end of page 505). Test the cake to see if it is cooked 15 minutes before the end of the baking time. If cooked, it will feel firm and a fine skewer inserted into the centre should come out cleanly (see page 460). If the cake is not cooked, return it to the oven, re-testing at 15-minute intervals. Remove the cake from the oven and leave it to cool in the tin.

8 Turn the cake out of the tin but do not remove the lining paper as this helps to keep the cake moist. Prick the top all over with a fine skewer and spoon over half the quantity of brandy, listed in the recipe. Wrap in a double thickness of foil.

9 Store the cake, the right way up, in a cool dry place for 1 week. Unwrap and spoon over the remaining brandy. Re-wrap and store the cake upside down, so the brandy moistens the top of the cake and helps to keep it flat. The cake keeps well for up to 2–3 months. For longer storage, freeze the cake, making sure it is completely thawed before applying the almond paste (or ready-made marzipan) and icing.

RICH FRUIT CAKE CHART

CAKE TIN	12cm (5in) square 15cm (6in) round	15cm (6in) square 18cm (7in) round	18cm (7in) square 20cm (8in) round	20cm (8in) square 23cm (9in) round
Currants	225g (8oz)	350g (12oz)	450g (1lb)	625g (1lb 6oz)
Sultanas	100g (4oz)	125g (4½oz)	200g (7oz)	225g (8oz)
Raisins	100g (4oz)	125g (4½oz)	200g (7oz)	225g (8oz)
Glacé cherries	50g (2oz)	75g (3oz)	150g (5oz)	175g (6oz)
Mixed peel	25g (1oz)	50g (2oz)	75g (3oz)	100g (3½oz)
Flaked almonds	25g (1oz)	50g (2oz)	75g (3oz)	100g (3½oz)
Plain flour	175g (6oz)	215g (7½oz)	350g (12oz)	400g (14oz)
Mixed spice	¼ tsp	½ tsp	½ tsp	1 tsp
Cinnamon	¼ tsp	½ tsp	½ tsp	1 tsp
Butter	150g (5oz)	175g (6oz)	275g (10oz)	350g (12oz)
Muscovado sugar	150g (5oz)	175g (6oz)	275g (10oz)	350g (12oz)
Lemon zest	a little	a little	a little	¼ lemon
Eggs, beaten	2½	3	5	6
Brandy	1 tbsp	1 tbsp	1–2 tbsp	2 tbsp
Baking time	2½–3 hours	3½ hours	3½ hours	4 hours
Cooked weight	1.1kg (2½lb)	1.5kg (3¼lb)	2.1kg (4¾lb)	2.7kg (6lb)

CAKE TIN	23cm (9in) square 25cm (10in) round	25cm (10in) square 28cm (11in) round	28cm (11in) square 30cm (12in) round	30cm (12in) square 33cm (13in) round
Currants	775g (1¾lb)	1.1kg (2½lb)	1.5kg (3lb 2oz)	1.7kg (3¾lb)
Sultanas	375g (13oz)	400g (14oz)	525g (1lb 3oz)	625g (1lb 6oz)
Raisins	375g (13oz)	400g (14oz)	525g (1lb 3oz)	625g (1lb 6oz)
Glacé cherries	250g (9oz)	275g (10oz)	350g (12oz)	425g (15oz)
Mixed peel	150g (5oz)	200g (7oz)	250g (9oz)	275g (10oz)
Flaked almonds	150g (5oz)	200g (7oz)	250g (9oz)	275g (10oz)
Plain flour	600g (1lb 5oz)	700g (1½lb)	825g (1lb 13oz)	1kg (2lb 6oz)
Mixed spice	1 tsp	2 tsp	2½ tsp	2½ tsp
Cinnamon	1 tsp	2 tsp	2½ tsp	2½ tsp
Butter	500g (1lb 2oz)	600g (1lb 5oz)	800g (1¾lb)	950g (2lb 2oz)
Muscovado sugar	500g (1lb 2oz)	600g (1lb 5oz)	800g (1¾lb)	950g (2lb 2oz)
Lemon zest	¼ lemon	½ lemon	½ lemon	1 lemon
Eggs, beaten	9	11	14	17
Brandy	2–3 tbsp	3 tbsp	4 tbsp	6 tbsp
Baking time	4½ hours	6 hours	6–6½ hours	6½ hours
Cooked weight	3.8kg (8½lb)	4.8kg (10¾lb)	6.1kg (13½lb)	7.4kg (16½lb)

note: When baking large cakes, 25cm (10 inch) and upwards, it is advisable to lower the oven temperature to 130°C (110°C fan oven) mark ½ after two-thirds of the baking time.

Apricot Glaze

125g (4oz) apricot jam

makes 150ml (¼ pint)
preparation: 5 minutes
cooking time: 2 minutes
per 25g (1oz): 60 cals; 0g fat;
   16g carbohydrate

1 Put the jam and 2 tbsp water into a small pan. Heat gently, stirring, until the jam begins to melt. Bring to the boil and simmer for 1 minute.
2 Strain the jam through a nylon sieve. Use the apricot glaze while it is still warm.

Almond Paste

225g (8oz) ground almonds
125g (4oz) golden caster sugar
125g (4oz) golden icing sugar
1 large egg
1 tsp lemon juice
1 tsp sherry
1–2 drops of vanilla extract

makes 450g (1lb)
preparation: 10 minutes
per 25g (1oz): 130 cals; 7g fat;
   15g carbohydrate

1 Put the ground almonds, caster sugar and icing sugar into a bowl and mix together. In a separate bowl, whisk the egg with the remaining ingredients and add to the dry mixture.
2 Stir well to mix, pounding gently to release some of the oil from the almonds. Knead with your hands until smooth. Cover until ready to use.

note: *If you wish to avoid using raw egg to bind the almond paste, mix the other liquid ingredients with a little water instead.*

Royal Icing

2 large egg whites, or 1 tbsp egg
   albumen powder
2 tsp liquid glycerine (optional, see note)
450g (1lb) icing sugar, sifted

makes 450g (1lb)
preparation: 20 minutes
per 25g (1oz): 100 cals; 0g fat;
   26g carbohydrate

1 If using the egg whites and the glycerine, put them in a bowl and stir just enough to break up the egg whites. If using albumen powder, mix according to manufacturer's instructions.
2 Add a little icing sugar and mix gently with a wooden spoon to incorporate as little air as possible.
3 Add a little more icing sugar as the mixture becomes lighter. Continue to add the icing sugar, stirring gently but thoroughly until the mixture is stiff and stands in soft peaks. For coating it should form soft peaks; for piping it should be a little stiffer.
4 Transfer to an airtight container, cover the surface closely with clingfilm to prevent it drying out, then seal. When required, stir the icing slowly.

notes
• *Glycerine keeps the icing from becoming hard. Omit it if the icing is required to cover a tiered cake, as a very hard surface is required to support the tiers.*
• *The chart opposite indicates the amount of royal icing needed to cover different sized, almond paste covered cakes. Multiply the recipe as appropriate, but note that it is better not to make up more than 900g (2lb) at a time. The quantities in the chart opposite will give you enough icing for 2–3 coats.*

QUANTITY GUIDE FOR ALMOND PASTE, SUGAR PASTE (READY-TO-ROLL ICING) OR ROYAL ICING

SQUARE TIN	ROUND TIN	ALMOND PASTE	SUGAR PASTE	ROYAL ICING
12cm (5 inch)	15cm (6 inch)	350g (12oz)	350g (12oz)	450g (1lb)
15cm (6 inch)	18cm (7 inch)	450g (1lb)	450g (1lb)	550g (1¼lb)
18cm (7 inch)	20cm (8 inch)	550g (1¼lb)	700g (1½lb)	700g (1½lb)
20cm (8 inch)	23cm (9 inch)	800g (1¾lb)	800g (1¾lb)	900g (2lb)
23cm (9 inch)	25cm (10 inch)	900g (2lb)	900g (2lb)	1kg (2¼lb)
25cm (10 inch)	28cm (11 inch)	1kg (2¼lb)	1kg (2¼lb)	1.1kg (2½lb)
28cm (11 inch)	30cm (12 inch)	1.1kg (2½lb)	1.1kg (2½lb)	1.4kg (3lb)
30cm (12 inch)	33cm (13 inch)	1.4kg (3lb)	1.4kg (3lb)	1.6kg (3½lb)
33cm (13 inch)	35cm (14 inch)	1.6kg (3½lb)	1.6kg (3½lb)	1.8kg (4lb)

COVERING A CAKE WITH ALMOND PASTE

Almond paste or marzipan is applied to rich fruit cakes to create a smooth foundation for the icing, so it must be positioned neatly. You can either make your own almond paste (see left), or buy ready-made marzipan. Opt for white, rather than yellow ready-made marzipan, as it is less likely to discolour the icing. The flavour of homemade almond paste is, of course, superior. Allow time for the almond paste to dry before covering with icing. Homemade almond paste takes longer to dry out than the ready-made variety.

2 Roll out half the almond paste on a surface dusted with icing sugar to fit the top of the cake. Brush the top of the cake with apricot glaze.

4 Cut a piece of string the height of the almond paste topped cake, and another the circumference of the cake. Roll out the remaining almond paste and using the string as a guide, trim to size. Brush the sides of the cake and the almond paste rim with apricot glaze.

1 Trim the top of the cake level. Turn the cake over so that the flat bottom becomes the top.

3 Lift the almond paste round (or square) on a rolling pin and position on top of the cake. Smooth over, neatening the edges. Place on a cake board, which is at least 5cm (2 inches) larger than the cake.

5 Roll up the almond paste strip loosely. Put one end against the side of the cake and unroll to wrap round the cake. Smooth the sides and joins with a palette knife.

6 Flatten the top lightly with a rolling pin. Leave the cake in a cool, dry place to dry out thoroughly for at least 2 days before applying smooth royal icing. Ready-to-roll icing can be applied after 24 hours.

COVERING A CAKE WITH READY-TO-ROLL ICING (SUGAR PASTE)

1 Dust the surface and rolling pin lightly with cornflour. Knead the ready-to-roll icing until pliable, then roll out to a round or square, 5–7.5cm (2–3 inches) larger all round than the cake.

2 With the help of a rolling pin, lift the icing on top of the cake and allow it to drape over the edges. Dust your hands with a little cornflour and press the icing on to the sides of the cake, easing it down to the board.

3 Trim off the excess icing at the base to neaten.

4 Using your fingers dusted with a little cornflour, gently rub the surface in a circular movement to buff the icing and make it smooth.

COVERING A CAKE WITH ROYAL ICING

1 Put a large spoonful of icing on to the centre of the almond paste coated cake and spread out with a palette knife and paddling action.

2 Draw an icing ruler across the top of the cake towards you,

applying an even pressure and keeping the ruler at an angle of about 30°. Remove surplus icing by running a palette knife around the edge, at right angles to the surface of the cake.

3 To cover the sides, for best results, put a round cake on a turntable. Spread icing on to the sides using the same paddling motion. Hold a cake scraper at an angle of about 45° and draw it around the side, then pull it off quickly to leave only a slight mark. Leave to dry in a cool place for 24 hours. Keep the remaining icing well covered and sealed.

4 The next day, scrape away any rough icing from the top edge with a small sharp knife. Clean fine sandpaper can be used to achieve a very smooth finish. Brush off loose icing with a clean pastry brush. Apply two or three more coats, allowing each coat to dry overnight before applying the next. Leave to dry overnight before applying decorations.

Classic Christmas Cake

150g (5oz) organic currants

150g (5oz) organic sultanas

150g (5oz) organic raisins

100g (3½oz) natural glacé cherries, halved

50g (2oz) preserved stem ginger in syrup,
  drained and chopped

grated zest and juice of 1 unwaxed lemon

juice of ½ lemon

1 tsp vanilla extract

75ml (2½fl oz) ginger wine

75ml (2½fl oz) Cognac, plus extra to drizzle

175g (6oz) butter, at room temperature, plus
  extra to grease

175g (6oz) dark muscovado sugar

2 medium eggs, beaten

175g (6oz) self-raising flour

1 tsp ground mixed spice

½ tsp ground cinnamon

½ tsp ground ginger

50g (2oz) mixed nuts, such as almonds,
  walnuts and brazils, roughly chopped

50g (2oz) carrots, peeled and coarsely grated

TO DECORATE

700g (1½lb) almond paste (page 506)

800g (1¾lb) royal icing (page 506)

green and red food colourings

edible glitter flakes (optional)

makes 16 slices

preparation: 45 minutes, plus macerating

cooking time: 2 hours, plus cooling

per slice: 240 cals; 12g fat;
  30g carbohydrate

1 Put the dried fruit, glacé cherries, stem ginger, lemon zest and juice, and vanilla extract into a bowl. Pour the ginger wine and Cognac over, stir, then cover and leave to macerate in a cool place for 1–5 days.

2 Grease a 20cm (8 inch) round, 7.5cm (3 inch) deep cake tin and line with baking parchment. Wrap a double layer of brown paper around the outside of the tin (see page 459) and secure with string.

3 Cream the butter and sugar together in a large bowl (using a free-standing mixer if you have one) for 5 minutes until light and fluffy. Add the eggs, one at a time, mixing well between each addition. If the mixture looks like curdling, add 2 tbsp of the flour with the second egg.

4 Sift the flour and spices together, then fold half into the creamed mixture.

5 Put half of the soaked fruit mixture into a food processor with some of the soaking liquid and whiz to a purée. Fold this into the cake mixture together with the remaining soaked fruit and liquor, nuts, carrots and the rest of the flour.

6 Turn the mixture into the prepared cake tin and spread evenly, then make a dip in the middle. Bake at 170°C (150°C fan oven) mark 3 for 2 hours or until a skewer inserted into the centre for 30 seconds comes out clean. Leave the cake to cool in the tin for 20 minutes, then turn out on to a wire rack and drizzle with 2 tsp Cognac. Leave to cool completely.

7 Wrap the cake in greaseproof paper and foil and store in an airtight tin for up to 1 month.

8 About 5 days before Christmas, unwrap the cake and put on a 25cm (10 inch) board. Cut off a quarter of the almond paste and wrap in clingfilm. Use the rest of the almond paste to cover the top and sides of the cake (see page 507), adding the trimmings to the wrapped portion. Leave the cake to dry for a day or two before applying the royal icing.

9 Spread half the royal icing over the top and sides of the cake with a palette knife. Either pipe the rest of the icing in wavy lines on top of the cake or apply with the palette knife and flick up to create peaks, resembling snow.

10 Colour two-thirds of the reserved almond paste green by kneading in a little colouring. Roll out between sheets of baking parchment, then stamp out holly leaves with a cutter and mark veins with a knife. Colour the rest of the almond paste red, break into pieces and roll into balls for holly berries. For added effect, brush the leaves and balls with cooled, boiled water and dip in glitter. Arrange the holly leaves and berries around the edge of the cake. Leave to set.

Illustrated on page 456

Simnel Cake

250g (9oz) unsalted butter, softened, plus
   extra to grease
grated zest of 2 unwaxed lemons
250g (9oz) golden caster sugar
4 large eggs, beaten
250g (9oz) plain flour
½ tsp ground mixed spice
75g (3oz) ground almonds
50g (2oz) candied citrus peel, finely chopped
150g (5oz) organic currants
300g (11oz) organic sultanas
75g (3oz) natural glacé cherries, halved
100g (3½oz) icing sugar, plus extra to dust
600g (1lb 5oz) almond paste (page 506) or
   ready-made white marzipan
2 tbsp thin honey, warmed
1 egg, beaten, to glaze

makes 12–16 slices
preparation: 1½ hours, plus setting
cooking time: 2¾ hours, plus cooling
per slice: 750–565 cals; 36–27g fat;
   104–78g carbohydrate

1 Grease a 20cm (8 inch) round, 7.5cm (3 inch) deep cake tin and line with greaseproof paper.
2 Beat the butter and lemon zest together, using a free-standing mixer or hand-held electric whisk, until very soft. Add the sugar gradually and continue beating until light and fluffy. Slowly beat in the eggs until evenly incorporated.
3 Sift in the flour with the mixed spice, and add the ground almonds, candied peel, currants, sultanas and glacé cherries. Fold the ingredients together, using a large metal spoon, until evenly combined. Set aside.
4 Spoon just over half of the cake mixture into the prepared tin and smooth the surface. Roll out 200g (7oz) of the almond paste on a surface dusted with icing sugar to an 18cm (7 inch) round.
5 Put the almond paste round on top of the mixture in the tin, then cover with the remaining cake mixture. Smooth the surface and make a slight hollow in the centre, then brush lightly with cold water. Wrap a double layer of brown paper around the outside of the tin (see page 459) and secure with string. Bake at 170°C (150°C fan oven) mark 3 for 1¼ hours. Cover with greaseproof paper, lower the oven setting to 150°C (130°C fan oven) mark 2 and bake for a further 1½ hours or until cooked to the centre.
6 Leave to cool in the tin for 1 hour, then transfer to a wire rack to finish cooling. Wrap in greaseproof paper and foil and store in an airtight container for up to 2 weeks.
7 When ready to decorate, roll out 200g (7oz) almond paste to a 20cm (8 inch) round. Cut a 7.5cm (3 inch) round from the centre and add this piece to the remaining almond paste. Brush the top of the cake with honey, cover with the almond paste ring and press down. Crimp the edge with your fingers.
8 Divide the rest of the almond paste into 11 or 12 pieces and shape into oval balls. Brush the ring with the beaten egg, position the balls on top and brush them with egg. Put a disc of foil over the exposed centre of the cake, then put under a hot grill for 1–2 minutes to brown the almond paste.
9 Mix the icing sugar with 2–3 tbsp warm water to make a smooth icing. Remove the foil disc, then pour the icing on to the exposed centre and smooth it with a palette knife. Leave the icing to set. To finish, secure a yellow ribbon around the side of the cake.

note: *Simnel cake is the classic Easter celebration cake, its marzipan balls representing the disciples – either 11 or 12 – depending on whether you think Judas should be included.*

Madeira Celebration Cake

350g (12oz) unsalted butter, at room
  temperature, plus extra to grease
350g (12oz) golden caster sugar
6 medium eggs, at room temperature,
  beaten
350g (12oz) self-raising flour, sifted
2 tbsp vanilla extract
¼ tsp salt
175g (6oz) plain flour, sifted

GLAZE AND FONDANT ICING
4–6 tbsp apricot glaze, or warm
  sieved jam
500g (1lb 2oz) golden icing sugar, plus
  extra to dust
1 medium egg white
2 tbsp liquid glucose, warmed
1 tsp vanilla extract

makes 30 slices
preparation: 1 hour 30 minutes, plus setting
cooking time: 1¼–1½ hours, plus cooling
per slice: 280 cals; 11g fat;
  45g carbohydrate

1 Grease a 23cm (9 inch) square, 7.5cm (3 inch) deep cake tin and line it with a double layer of baking parchment. Wrap a double layer of brown paper around the outside of the tin and secure with string (see page 459).

2 Cream the butter and sugar together, using a free-standing mixer or hand-held electric whisk, for 5 minutes until light and fluffy. Add the eggs, one at a time, mixing well between each addition. If the mixture looks like curdling, add 2 tbsp of the self-raising flour with the last of the egg. Mix in the vanilla extract.

3 Add 1 tbsp water, the salt, plain and self-raising flours, then fold everything together, using a large metal spoon. Transfer the mixture to the tin and spread evenly, smoothing it into the corners, then make a dip in the middle. Bake at 170°C (150°C fan oven) mark 3 for 1¼–1½ hours or until a skewer inserted into the centre of the cake for 30 seconds comes out clean.

4 Leave the cake to cool in the tin for 20 minutes, then turn it out on to a wire rack and leave to cool completely. Carefully peel off the lining paper and turn the cake again. If necessary, trim the top of the cake level. Brush the apricot glaze evenly over the top and leave to set.

5 To make the fondant icing, whiz the icing sugar in a food processor for 30 seconds, then add the egg white, glucose and vanilla extract, and whiz for 2–3 minutes, until the mixture forms a ball.

6 Roll out the icing to a 25cm (10 inch) square on a sheet of baking parchment dusted with icing sugar. If it starts to stick, ease a palette knife underneath. With a ravioli cutter, cut out a 23cm (9 inch) square of icing, using the cake tin as a guide. Upturn the icing on to clean parchment and peel off the top paper.

7 Put the cake on the icing, glazed side down. Position a cake board on the cake and turn the cake the right way up. Remove the paper, then rub the icing gently with clean fingers to make it shine.

note: *Decorate this cake to suit any occasion, with fresh or frosted flowers, or other decorations.*

ICINGS AND FROSTINGS

Icings and frostings are used to fill, cover and decorate cakes. Some icings are poured over the cake to give a smooth glossy finish, others need to be spread or swirled to give a textured finish. Fresh whipped cream and buttercream may be smoothed flat, textured with a palette knife or piped. Sometimes the same mixture is used to fill and cover the cake, or it may be different – a jam-filled sponge, for example, can be topped with buttercream or glacé icing.

The filling must have the right consistency for spreading: if too firm it will pull the crumbs from the cake, making an untidy layer; if too soft it will cause the cake layers to slip and move around, and ooze out of the side of the cake. Use a palette knife dipped in hot water for spreading the filling. Jam should be warmed gently until thinned to a spreading consistency.

To cover a cake with buttercream or crème au beurre icing, use a small palette knife dipped in hot water to spread the icing smoothly and evenly. For a textured effect, paddle the palette knife backwards and forwards, or swirl the icing decoratively. For a more formal finish, pipe a design directly on to the surface of the cake, such as a piped scroll, shell or swirl edging.

If you are covering a cake with frosting, make sure it is the correct consistency – thick enough to coat the back of a spoon. Frostings are often warm at this stage; if too thick, the bowl will need to be placed over hot water, or the frosting may be thinned with a little water. On the other hand, if the frosting is too slack, leave it to cool and thicken slightly. Pour all of the frosting over the top of the cake and allow it to fall over the sides, gently tapping the cake to encourage it to flow; don't be tempted to use a knife, which would leave marks. When the frosting has stopped falling, neaten the bottom edge and allow to dry.

Once a cake has been covered with icing or frosting, the sides may be coated with crushed praline, grated chocolate or toasted chopped or flaked nuts; pistachio nuts, in particular, add colour as well as texture. Simple finishing touches are often the most effective – a drizzle of melted chocolate or caramel, fresh or frosted herbs and flowers, fresh fruit, toasted nuts and chocolate curls all work well.

Glacé Icing

225g (8oz) icing sugar
few drops of vanilla extract (optional)
few drops of food colouring (optional)

makes 225g (8oz)
preparation: 5 minutes
per 25g (1oz): 100 cals; 0g fat;
   26g carbohydrate

1 Sift the icing sugar into a bowl. Add a few drops of vanilla extract if you like.
2 Using a wooden spoon, gradually stir in 2–3 tbsp hot water until the mixture is the consistency of thick cream. Beat until white and smooth and the icing is thick enough to coat the back of the spoon. Add colouring if you like, and use straightaway.

note: *This quantity is sufficient to cover the top of one large sandwich cake, or about 16 small cakes.*

variations
orange or lemon glacé icing: *Replace the water with strained orange or lemon juice.*
chocolate glacé icing: *Sift 2 tsp cocoa powder with the icing sugar.*
coffee glacé icing: *Flavour the icing with 1 tsp coffee essence or 2 tsp instant coffee granules dissolved in 1 tbsp of the hot water.*

Buttercream

75g (3oz) unsalted butter, softened
175g (6oz) icing sugar, sifted
few drops of vanilla extract
1–2 tbsp milk or water

makes 250g (9oz)
preparation: 5 minutes
per 25g (1oz): 130 cals; 6g fat;
   18g carbohydrate

1 Put the butter into a bowl and beat with a wooden spoon until it is light and fluffy.
2 Gradually stir in the icing sugar, vanilla extract and milk. Beat well until light and smooth.

note: *This quantity is sufficient to cover the top of a 20cm (8 inch) cake. To make enough to cover the top and sides, increase the quantities by one third.*

variations
orange, lime or lemon buttercream: *Replace the vanilla extract with a little finely grated orange, lime or lemon zest. Add 1–2 tbsp juice from the fruit instead of the milk, beating well to avoid curdling the mixture. If the mixture is to be piped, omit the zest.*
chocolate buttercream: *Blend 1 tbsp cocoa powder with 2 tbsp boiling water and cool before adding to the mixture.*
coffee buttercream: *Replace the vanilla extract with 2 tsp instant coffee granules dissolved in 1 tbsp boiling water; cool before adding to the mixture.*

Crème au Beurre

75g (3oz) golden caster sugar
2 medium egg yolks, beaten
175g (6oz) unsalted butter, softened

makes 275g (10oz)
preparation: 15 minutes
cooking time: 5 minutes
per 25g (1oz): 160 cals; 14g fat;
   7g carbohydrate

1 Put the caster sugar and 4 tbsp water into a heavy-based pan and heat gently to dissolve the sugar, without boiling.
2 When the sugar has completely dissolved, bring to the boil and boil steadily for 2–3 minutes until the syrup registers 107°C on a sugar thermometer (ie the thread stage – when a little syrup placed between two dry teaspoons and pulled apart forms a fine thread).
3 Put the egg yolks into a bowl and pour on the syrup in a thin stream, whisking all the time with a hand-held electric whisk. Continue to whisk until the mixture is thick and cold.
4 In another bowl, cream the butter until light and fluffy. Gradually add the egg yolk mixture, whisking well after each addition.

variations
orange or lemon crème au beurre: *Add the finely grated zest and a little orange or lemon juice to taste at stage 4.*
chocolate crème au beurre: *Melt 50g (2oz) plain chocolate, cool slightly, then beat into the crème au beurre mixture at stage 4.*
coffee crème au beurre: *Dissolve 1–2 tbsp coffee granules in 1 tbsp boiling water. Cool, then beat into the crème au beurre mixture at stage 4.*

Coffee Fudge Frosting

50g (2oz) butter
125g (4oz) light muscovado sugar
2 tbsp single cream or milk
1 tbsp coffee granules
200g (7oz) golden icing sugar, sifted

makes 400g (14oz)
preparation: 5 minutes
cooking time: 5 minutes
per 25g (1oz): 110 cals; 3g fat;
    21g carbohydrate

1 Put the butter, muscovado sugar and cream into a pan. Dissolve the coffee in 2 tbsp boiling water and add to the pan. Heat gently until the sugar dissolves, then bring to the boil and boil briskly for 3 minutes.
2 Remove from the heat and gradually stir in the icing sugar. Beat well with a wooden spoon for 1 minute until smooth.
3 Use the frosting immediately, spreading it over the cake with a wet palette knife, or dilute with a little water to use as a smooth coating.

variation
chocolate fudge frosting: *Omit the coffee. Add 75g (3oz) plain chocolate, in pieces, to the pan with the butter at the beginning of stage 1.*

American Frosting

1 large egg white
225g (8oz) golden caster or granulated sugar
pinch of cream of tartar

makes 225g (8oz)
preparation: 15 minutes
cooking time: 5 minutes
per 25g (1oz): 100 cals; 0g fat;
    26g carbohydrate

1 Whisk the egg white in a clean bowl until stiff. Put the sugar, 4 tbsp water and the cream of tartar into a heavy-based pan. Heat gently, stirring, until the sugar has dissolved. Bring to the boil, without stirring, and boil until the sugar syrup registers 115°C on a sugar thermometer.
2 Remove from the heat and, as soon as the bubbles subside, pour the syrup on to the egg white in a thin stream, whisking constantly until thick and white. Leave to cool slightly.
3 When the frosting begins to turn dull around the edges and is almost cold, pour quickly over the cake and spread evenly with a palette knife.

Chocolate Ganache

225g (8oz) good quality plain dark chocolate
    (with 60–70% cocoa solids), chopped into
    small pieces
250ml (8fl oz) double cream

serves 8
preparation: 10 minutes
cooking time: 1 minute, plus cooling
per serving: 280 cals; 28g fat;
    8g carbohydrate

1 Put the chocolate into a medium heatproof bowl. Pour the cream into a small heavy-based pan and bring to the boil.
2 Immediately pour the cream on to the chocolate and stir gently in one direction until the chocolate has melted and the mixture is smooth. Set aside to cool for 5 minutes.
3 Whisk the ganache until it begins to hold its shape. Used at room temperature, the mixture should be the consistency of softened butter.

note: *Use ganache at room temperature as a smooth coating for special cakes, or chill it lightly until thickened and use to fill meringues, choux buns or sandwich cakes.*

BREADS AND YEAST BAKING

There's nothing quite like the aroma of fresh, hot bread in the kitchen and once you've mastered the basic techniques you will be able to make speciality savoury and sweet breads, as well as everyday loaves. Use the recipes in this chapter as your basis and experiment with flavourings. Savoury doughs can be enhanced with cheese, fresh herbs, olives or sun-dried tomatoes, for example; while sweet doughs are enriched with dried fruits, nuts, vanilla sugar, or scented spices like cinnamon and nutmeg.

YEAST

Yeast is available in a number of different forms, which are interchangeable in recipes providing that the method is adjusted accordingly. As a rough guide, 15g (½oz) fresh yeast, a 7g sachet (2 tsp) fast-action (easy-blend) dried yeast, or 1 tbsp ordinary dried yeast is enough to rise 700g (1½lb) flour. In general, if you add more than this, the dough will not rise any higher and the bread is likely to have an unpleasant yeasty taste. However, if the dough is enriched with fruit, sugar, butter or nuts, the rise is more difficult and you will usually need more yeast – be guided by the recipes.

As fast-action dried yeast is now the most readily available dried form, it is used in most of the recipes in this chapter; should you wish to use 'ordinary' dried yeast simply adjust the quantity and method accordingly.

Fresh yeast is a living organism and must be handled in the right way in order to work effectively. It is available from good healthfood shops, some bakers and selected supermarkets. It should be firm, moist and creamy coloured with a good 'yeasty' smell. If it is dry and crumbly with discoloured brown patches then it is probably stale and won't work effectively. When you buy fresh yeast it is alive, but inactive. Only when it is mixed with a warm liquid does it become active and release the gases that make the dough rise.

Fresh yeast is easy to use: simply blend with a little of the liquid specified in the recipe, add the remaining liquid, then mix into the flour. Fresh yeast will stay fresh for about 3 days if stored in the fridge, or it can be frozen for up to 3 months.

Fast-action dried yeast also called easy-blend dried yeast, has revolutionised bread-making. It is sprinkled directly into the flour and the liquid is mixed in afterwards. After kneading, the dough can be shaped straightaway and only requires one rising. However, for enriched doughs – particularly heavily fruited ones – better results are obtained if the dough is given the traditional two rises. Always make sure you adhere to the 'use-by' date on the pack; fast-action dried yeast won't work if it is stale.

Ordinary dried yeast needs sugar to activate it. If using milk as the liquid, the natural sugars present in the milk will be enough; if using water, you will need to add a pinch of sugar. To use 'ordinary' dried yeast, simply blend it with the warm liquid (see overleaf), adding a pinch of sugar if needed, and leave it in a warm place for about 15 minutes or until a frothy head (similar to the head on a pint of Guinness) develops. This shows that the yeast is active. If it refuses to froth, then it is probably past its 'use-by date'; discard and begin again with a fresh pack of yeast.

Sourdough starter is a traditional method that has regained popularity. A mixture of yeast, flour and water is left to ferment for several days before it is added to the dough. A sourdough starter produces a close-textured loaf with a distinctive flavour. If you make bread regularly, a sourdough starter is a convenient way of leavening.

Simply blend 15g (½oz) fresh yeast (or its equivalent) with 450ml (¾ pint) warm water and about 225g (8oz) strong plain white flour or enough to make a thick pourable batter. Cover the bowl with a damp cloth and leave at room temperature for 3–5 days to ferment and develop the sourdough flavour. Use 125ml (4fl oz) of the starter to replace each 15g (½oz) fresh yeast called for in a recipe, then make the bread in the usual way. If you do not use it for a few days, store it in the fridge and use within 1 week.

LIQUID

No matter which variety of yeast you are using, the liquid should be just warm or tepid, that is at a temperature of 43°C, which will feel slightly warm to the fingertips. If it is too hot it could kill the yeast; if too cold the yeast will not begin to work.

Milk gives bread a slightly softer texture than water. You should always regard any quantity of liquid specified in a recipe as a guide because flour absorbency varies according to the type of flour, and from brand to brand.

FLOUR

Various flours are used for bread-making. Strong flours give better results because they have a higher proportion of protein, which promotes the formation of gluten – the substance that stretches the dough and traps in air as it cooks, to give bread its characteristic airy texture. Ordinary plain flour produces a close-textured crumbly loaf.

Strong white bread flour is ideal. If possible, use unbleached white flour, which has not been chemically treated to whiten it.

Strong wholemeal bread flour is ground from the whole wheat kernel and has a coarser texture than white flour, with a fuller flavour and more nutrients; it is also an excellent source of fibre. This flour is widely available and lends a distinctive flavour, but it is best used with a proportion of strong white flour to obtain a good textured loaf. Bread made with 100% wholemeal flour has a heavy, dense texture.

Strong brown bread flour has a percentage of the bran removed and therefore has a finer texture than wholemeal flour.

Stoneground flour takes its name from the specific grinding process – between stones – which heats the flour and gives it a slightly roasted, nutty flavour. Both stoneground wholemeal and brown flours are available.

Granary flour is a strong brown flour, with added malted wheat flakes, which give it a distinctive flavour.

Rye flour makes a dark, close-textured bread with plenty of flavour. As it is low in gluten, it must be mixed with a strong white flour for best results.

OTHER INGREDIENTS

Salt is an important ingredient in breads because it controls fermentation, strengthens gluten and improves the flavour. However, it also slows down the action of yeast, so don't add too much. Be guided by the amount specified in the recipe.

Some recipes call for a little fat to be rubbed into the flour before the yeast is added. This improves the keeping quality of the bread and imparts extra flavour, but too much fat will slow down the action of the yeast.

MIXING AND KNEADING THE DOUGH

Some recipes recommend warming the flour and mixing bowl in advance. If using fresh or 'ordinary' dried yeast, or if you are working in a cold room, this helps to speed things up a little, but otherwise it isn't necessary.

After mixing the yeast and liquid into the dry ingredients, the dough must be kneaded. Vigorous kneading is required to strengthen the gluten in the flour, make the dough elastic and ultimately to achieve a good rise. If you omit this stage, the dough will not rise. There is nothing difficult about kneading and, contrary to popular belief, it doesn't take long – 10 minutes should be enough.

Turn the dough on to a floured surface, fold it firmly towards you, then quickly and firmly push it down and away from you with the heel of your hand. Give it a quarter turn and continue kneading until the dough feels elastic and smooth: it shouldn't be sticky.

As an alternative to kneading by hand, you can use a large mixer with a dough hook attachment. Alternatively, if you enjoy homemade bread, you might consider inverting in a bread-maker. These machines produce very good crusty bread, but you cannot easily convert conventional recipes for use in a bread machine. If you decide to buy one of these appliances, we recommend you use the recipes in Good Housekeeping's 'Great Recipes for your Bread Machine' cookbook.

RISING

Put the kneaded dough into a clean bowl and cover with a clean tea-towel, an oiled plastic bag or oiled clingfilm to prevent a skin forming. Leave in a warm place until the dough has doubled in size and springs back when pressed.

The time it takes for the dough to rise will depend on the ambient temperature. If you put the bowl near a warm oven or in an airing cupboard, rising can take as little as 30 minutes, while at cooler temperatures it may take well over an hour. Don't be tempted to put it somewhere hot to speed things up; you will end up with a badly shaped, uneven-textured loaf, or you could even kill the yeast.

For a slower rise, leave the dough in the fridge overnight, then bring it to room temperature in the morning before shaping.

KNOCKING BACK AND PROVING

The risen dough is 'knocked back' to smooth out any large pockets of air. A brief kneading is sufficient, just 2–3 minutes, before shaping as required. Leave the shaped dough once again in a warm place until it has doubled in size and springs back when pressed. This proving stage is quicker than the first rising.

SHAPING BREAD

The simplest way to shape a loaf is to roll the dough into a ball, flatten it slightly and put on a baking sheet. Or to make a baton, form into a long roll with tapering ends. Alternatively, shape the dough as follows:

Traditional tin loaf is made by flattening the dough to an oblong, the length of the dough, but three times as wide. Fold this in three, then put into the tin, to two-thirds fill it.

Cottage loaf always looks attractive. To shape, cut off one third of the dough. Shape both pieces into rounds and put the smaller one on top of the larger round. Push the handle of a wooden spoon down through the middle.

Plait requires the dough to be divided into three equal pieces. Roll each piece into a long sausage, then pinch these together at one end and plait loosely. Pinch the other ends together firmly.

Rolls can be formed into any of the above shapes, from small pieces of dough.

GLAZING

Glazing bread before baking gives an attractive finish. For a golden, shiny effect, brush with beaten egg or egg beaten with a little water or milk.

For a crusty finish, brush with salted water, made by dissolving 2 tsp salt in 2 tbsp water. For a soft golden crust, brush with milk. Some breads and yeast buns are glazed after baking with warm honey or syrup.

BAKING

Bread is baked in a hot oven to kill the yeast and halt its action. If the bread shows signs of browning too quickly, cover with foil. When cooked, the bread should be well risen, firm to the touch and golden brown; if you turn it over and tap it on the bottom the loaf should sound hollow. To crisp the crust of large loaves all over, return them to the oven upside down for about 10 minutes. Always remove bread from the tins before transferring to wire racks to cool.

STORING BREAD

Bread with a high fat or sugar content should keep well for 3–4 days, but other homemade bread stales quite quickly. It is best stored in a dry, well-ventilated bread bin, not the fridge, and eaten the day it is made.

Bread freezes well for a relatively short time, up to 1 month, after which the crust begins to deteriorate and lift off. Frozen or slightly stale bread can be freshened in a warm oven.

Quick yeastless breads, leavened with baking powder or bicarbonate of soda rather than yeast, tend to stale quickly. They are invariably at their best eaten fresh and warm from the oven.

Brown Loaf

300g (11oz) strong plain white flour, sifted,
plus extra to dust
200g (7oz) strong plain wholemeal flour
15g (½oz) fresh yeast, or 1 tsp ordinary
dried yeast
2 tsp salt
vegetable oil, to oil

makes 16 slices
preparation: 25 minutes, plus sponging
and rising
cooking time: 45–50 minutes, plus cooling
per slice: 100 cals; 1g fat; 22g carbohydrate

1 Put both flours into a large bowl, make a well in the middle and pour in 325ml (11fl oz) tepid water. Crumble the fresh yeast into the water (if using dried yeast, just sprinkle it over). Draw a little of the flour into the water and yeast, and mix to form a batter. Sprinkle the salt over the remaining dry flour, so that it doesn't come into contact with the yeast. Cover with a clean tea-towel and leave to 'sponge' for 20 minutes.

2 Combine the flour and salt with the batter to make a soft dough and knead for at least 10 minutes until the dough feels smooth and elastic. Shape into a ball, put into an oiled bowl, cover with the tea-towel and leave to rise at warm room temperature until doubled in size, about 2–3 hours.

3 Knock back the dough, knead briefly and shape into a round on a lightly floured baking sheet. Slash the top with a sharp knife and dust with flour. Cover and leave to rise for 45 minutes–1½ hours or until doubled in size and spongy.

4 Bake at 200°C (180°C fan oven) mark 6 for 45–50 minutes or until the loaf sounds hollow when tapped underneath. Transfer to a wire rack and leave to cool.

note: *The 'sponging' process in step 1 adds a fermentation stage, which gives a slightly lighter loaf.*

White Farmhouse Loaf

575g (1¼lb) strong plain white flour, plus
extra to dust
125g (4oz) strong plain wholemeal flour
1 tbsp salt
1 tsp golden caster sugar
1½ tsp fast-action dried yeast
(see note)
25g (1oz) butter, diced
vegetable oil, to oil

makes 16 slices
preparation: 20 minutes, plus rising
cooking time: 30–35 minutes, plus cooling
per slice: 160 cals; 2g fat;
32g carbohydrate

1 Sift the white flour into a large bowl and stir in the wholemeal flour, salt, sugar and yeast. Rub in the butter with your fingertips. Make a well in the middle and add about 450ml (¾ pint) warm water. Work to a smooth soft dough, adding a little extra water if necessary.

2 Knead for 10 minutes until smooth, then shape the dough into a ball and put into an oiled bowl. Cover and leave to rise in a warm place for 1–2 hours until doubled in size.

3 Knock back the dough on a lightly floured surface and shape into a large oval loaf. Transfer the dough to a floured baking sheet, cover loosely and leave to rise for a further 30 minutes.

4 Slash the top of the loaf with a sharp knife, dust with flour and bake at 230°C (210°C fan oven) mark 8 for 15 minutes. Lower the oven setting to 200°C (180°C fan oven) mark 6 and bake for a further 15–20 minutes or until the bread is risen and sounds hollow when tapped underneath. Cool on a wire rack.

note: *If available, use 25g (1oz) fresh yeast instead of dried. Crumble into a bowl, add the sugar, 150ml (¼ pint) of the warmed water and 4 tbsp of the white flour. Stir well to dissolve the yeast, then leave in a warm place for 20 minutes until very frothy. Continue as above, adding the frothy yeast to the dry ingredients with the rest of the water.*

Wholemeal Loaf

225g (8oz) strong plain white flour, plus
   extra to dust
450g (1lb) strong plain wholemeal flour
2 tsp salt
1 tsp golden caster sugar
2 tsp fast-action dried yeast (see note)
vegetable oil, to oil

makes 16 slices
preparation: 15 minutes, plus rising
cooking time: 30–35 minutes, plus cooling
per slice: 140 cals; 1g fat;
   29g carbohydrate

1 Sift the white flour into a large bowl and stir in the wholemeal flour, salt, sugar and yeast. Make a well in the middle and add about 450ml (¾ pint) warm water. Work to a smooth, soft dough, adding a little extra water if necessary.

2 Knead for 10 minutes until smooth, then shape the dough into a ball and put into an oiled bowl. Cover and leave to rise in a warm place for about 2 hours until doubled in size.

3 Knock back the dough on a lightly floured surface and shape into an oblong. Press into an oiled 900g (2lb) loaf tin, cover and leave to rise for a further 30 minutes.

4 Bake the loaf at 230°C (210°C fan oven) mark 8 for 15 minutes. Lower the oven setting to 200°C (180°C fan oven) mark 6 and bake for a further 15–20 minutes or until the bread is risen and sounds hollow when tapped underneath. Leave in the tin for 10 minutes, then turn out and cool on a wire rack.

note: *If available, use 40g (1½oz) fresh yeast instead of dried. Proceed as for white farmhouse loaf (see note, page 520).*

Granary Bread

125g (4oz) strong plain wholemeal flour,
   plus extra to dust
450g (1lb) malted strong Granary flour
2 tsp salt
15g (½oz) butter, diced
125g (4oz) rolled oats, plus extra to dust
2 tsp fast-action dried yeast (see note)
150ml (¼ pint) warm milk
1 tbsp malt extract
vegetable oil, to oil

makes 16 slices
preparation: 20 minutes, plus rising
cooking time: 30–35 minutes, plus cooling
per slice: 160 cals; 2g fat;
   30g carbohydrate

1 Put the flours into a bowl and stir in the salt. Rub in the butter, then stir in the rolled oats and yeast. Make a well in the middle and add the warm milk, malt extract and 300ml (½ pint) warm water. Work to a smooth soft dough, adding a little extra water if necessary.

2 Knead for 10 minutes until smooth, then shape the dough into a ball and put into an oiled bowl. Cover and leave to rise in a warm place for 1–2 hours until doubled in size.

3 Knock back the dough on a lightly floured surface and shape into a large round. Put on a baking sheet, cover and leave to rise for a further 30 minutes.

4 Using a sharp knife, cut a cross on the top of the loaf and sprinkle over a few more oats. Bake at 230°C (210°C fan oven) mark 8 for 15 minutes. Lower the oven setting to 200°C (180°C fan oven) mark 6 and bake for a further 15–20 minutes or until the bread is risen and sounds hollow when tapped underneath. Cool on a wire rack.

note: *If available, use 40g (1½oz) fresh yeast instead of dried. Proceed as for white farmhouse loaf (see note, page 520).*

Apricot and Hazelnut Bread

450g (1lb) strong Granary flour
225g (8oz) strong plain white flour, plus
    extra to dust
2 tsp salt
25g (1oz) butter, diced, plus extra to grease
75g (3oz) hazelnuts, toasted and chopped
75g (3oz) ready-to-eat dried apricots,
    chopped
1½ tsp fast-action dried yeast
2 tbsp molasses
milk, to glaze

makes 2 loaves; 12 slices each
preparation: 20 minutes, plus rising
cooking time: 30–35 minutes, plus cooling
per slice: 120 cals; 2g fat;
    23g carbohydrate

1 Put the flours into a large bowl. Add the salt, then rub in the butter. Stir in the hazelnuts, dried apricots and dried yeast.
2 Make a well in the middle and gradually work in the molasses and 350ml (12fl oz) warm water to form a soft dough.
3 Knead for 8–10 minutes until smooth, then transfer the dough to a greased bowl. Cover and leave to rise in a warm place for 1–1½ hours until doubled in size.
4 Preheat a large baking sheet on the top shelf of the oven set at 220°C (200°C fan oven) mark 7. Knock back the dough, then divide in half. Shape each portion into a small flattish round and put on a well floured baking sheet. Cover loosely and leave to rise for a further 30 minutes.
5 Using a sharp knife, cut several slashes on each round, brush with a little milk and transfer to the heated baking sheet. Bake for 15 minutes, then lower the oven setting to 190°C (170°C fan oven) mark 5 and bake for a further 15–20 minutes or until the bread is risen and sounds hollow when tapped underneath. Cool on a wire rack.

Multigrain Loaf

225g (8oz) strong plain wholemeal flour,
    plus extra to dust
350g (12oz) strong Granary flour
125g (4oz) rye flour
25g (1oz) butter, diced, plus extra to grease
2 tsp salt
2 tsp fast-action dried yeast (see note)
1 tsp golden caster sugar
40g (1½oz) rolled oats or barley, or millet
    flakes
2 tbsp each sesame seeds, poppy seeds,
    sunflower seeds and linseed
2 tbsp malt extract
vegetable oil, to oil

TO FINISH
egg beaten with a little water, to glaze
few extra sesame, poppy and sunflower
    seeds

makes 2; each 12 slices
preparation: 20 minutes, plus rising
cooking time: 30–35 minutes, plus cooling
per slice: 130 cals; 3g fat;
    23g carbohydrate

1 Mix the wholemeal, Granary and rye flours together in a large bowl. Rub in the butter, then stir in all the remaining dry ingredients. Make a well in the middle and gradually work in 450ml (¾ pint) warm water and the malt extract to form a soft dough.
2 Knead the dough for 10 minutes, then transfer to a greased bowl, cover and leave to rise in a warm place for 2 hours or until doubled in size.
3 Lightly oil two 900g (2lb) loaf tins. Knock back the dough, then divide it in half and shape each portion into an oblong.
4 Press into the prepared tins, cover loosely and leave to rise for 30 minutes until the dough reaches the top of the tins.
5 Carefully brush each loaf with the egg glaze and scatter over some extra seeds. Bake at 220°C (200°C fan oven) mark 7 for 30–35 minutes until the loaves are risen and golden brown. Leave them in the tins for 10 minutes, then transfer to a wire rack to cool.

note: *If available, use 25g (1oz) fresh yeast instead of dried. Proceed as for white farmhouse loaf (see note, page 520).*

Cornbread

225g (8oz) coarse cornmeal
225g (8oz) strong plain white flour
1½ tsp fast-action dried yeast
1 tsp salt
½ tsp golden caster sugar
400ml (14fl oz) milk
15g (½oz) butter or margarine
vegetable oil, to oil

makes 16 slices
preparation: 15 minutes, plus rising
cooking time: 25–30 minutes, plus cooling
per slice: 120 cals; 1g fat;
    23g carbohydrate

1 Combine all of the dry ingredients in a large bowl. Heat the milk and butter in a small pan until the butter is melted, cool until tepid, then work into the dry ingredients to form a soft dough.
2 Knead for 8–10 minutes until smooth, then transfer the dough to an oiled bowl. Cover and leave to rise in a warm place for 1–1½ hours until doubled in size.
3 Oil a 20cm (8 inch) square cake tin. Knock back the dough and shape into a square a little smaller than the prepared tin. Press into the tin, cover loosely and leave to rise for a further 30 minutes.
4 Bake at 220°C (200°C fan oven) mark 7 for 25–30 minutes until risen and golden. Leave the cornbread in the tin for 10 minutes, then transfer to a wire rack to cool. Serve cold, cut into fingers.

Soda Bread

350g (12oz) plain wholemeal flour
125g (4oz) coarse oatmeal
2 tsp bicarbonate of soda
1 tsp salt
1 tsp thin honey
300ml (½ pint) buttermilk
2–3 tbsp milk
vegetable oil, to oil

makes 14 slices
preparation: 15 minutes
cooking time: 30–35 minutes, plus cooling
per slice: 120 cals; 1g fat; 24g carbohydrate

1 Combine the flour with the other dry ingredients in a large bowl. Make a well in the middle and gradually beat in the honey, buttermilk and enough milk to form a soft dough.
2 Knead for 5 minutes until smooth. Shape the dough into a 20cm (8 inch) round and put on a lightly oiled baking sheet.
3 Using a sharp knife, cut a deep cross on top of the dough. Brush with a little milk and bake at 200°C (180°C fan oven) mark 6 for 30–35 minutes until the bread is slightly risen and sounds hollow when tapped underneath. Cool on a wire rack; eat the same day.

Parmesan and Chive Rolls

450g (1lb) strong plain white flour
1 tsp salt
2 tsp fast-action dried yeast
pinch of sugar
4 tbsp chopped chives
65g (2½oz) Parmesan cheese, freshly
    grated
300ml (½ pint) milk
25g (1oz) butter, plus extra to grease
vegetable oil, to oil

makes 8
preparation: 20 minutes, plus rising
cooking time: 10–15 minutes, plus cooling
per roll: 270 cals; 6g fat; 44g carbohydrate

1 Sift the flour and salt into a bowl and stir in the yeast, sugar, chives, and all but 15g (½oz) of the Parmesan.
2 Heat the milk and butter in a small pan until the butter is melted; cool slightly until tepid. Gradually add this warm liquid to the dry ingredients and work together to form a soft dough.
3 Knead for 8–10 minutes until smooth, then transfer to a greased bowl. Cover and leave to rise in a warm place for 1 hour.
4 Knock back the dough and divide into 8 pieces. Shape into balls, flatten slightly and put on an oiled large baking sheet. Cover loosely and leave to rise for 30 minutes.
5 Sprinkle the remaining Parmesan over the rolls and bake at 220°C (200°C fan oven) mark 7 for 15–20 minutes until risen and golden. Cool on a wire rack.

Pepper and Pancetta Buns

2 tbsp chilli oil

2 red peppers, cored, deseeded and diced

75g (3oz) sliced pancetta, torn into pieces

500g (1lb 2oz) strong plain white flour,
plus extra to dust

1 tsp salt

1¼ tsp fast-action dried yeast

2 tsp golden caster sugar

few tarragon or flat-leafed parsley sprigs,
roughly chopped

3 tbsp sun-dried tomato paste

vegetable oil, to oil

makes 12
preparation: 20 minutes, plus rising
cooking time: 10–15 minutes, plus cooling
per roll: 190 cals; 4g fat; 34g carbohydrate

1 Heat the chilli oil in a frying pan and fry the peppers and pancetta for 4–5 minutes until soft. Cool slightly.

2 Sift the flour and salt into a large bowl and stir in the yeast, sugar and tarragon or parsley. Make a well in the centre and add 275ml (9fl oz) warm water and the sun-dried tomato paste. Mix thoroughly to form a soft, smooth dough, adding a little more water if necessary.

3 Knead for 10 minutes until smooth and elastic, then put in a lightly oiled bowl. Cover and leave to rise in a warm place for 1½–2 hours or until doubled in size.

4 Cut twelve 14cm (5½ inch) baking parchment squares and have ready a 12-hole muffin tin.

5 Knock back the dough and knead on a lightly floured surface for 1 minute. Add the the pancetta and peppers and knead until evenly incorporated.

6 Divide the dough into 12 even-sized pieces. Push a square of parchment into one of the tin sections and drop a piece of dough into the centre. Repeat with the remainder. Cover loosely with a tea-towel and leave in a warm place for about 30 minutes until well risen.

7 Bake at 220°C (fan oven 200°C) mark 7 for 15–18 minutes until risen and golden. Lift out the paper cases holding the buns and put on a wire rack to cool.

Crumpets

350g (12oz) strong plain white flour
½ tsp salt
½ tsp bicarbonate of soda
1½ tsp fast-action dried yeast
250ml (8fl oz) warm milk
a little vegetable oil, to fry
butter, to serve

makes about 24
preparation: 20 minutes, plus rising
cooking time: about 35 minutes
per crumpet: 60 cals; 1g fat;
   12g carbohydrate

1 Sift the flour, salt and bicarbonate of soda into a large bowl and stir in the yeast. Make a well in the centre, then pour in 300ml (½ pint) warm water and the milk. Mix to a thick batter.

2 Using a wooden spoon, beat the batter vigorously for about 5 minutes. Cover and leave in a warm place for about 1 hour until sponge-like in texture. Beat the batter for a further 2 minutes; transfer to a jug.

3 Put a large non-stick frying pan over a high heat and brush a little oil over the surface. Oil the insides of 4 crumpet rings or 7.5cm (3 inch) plain metal cutters. Put the rings, blunt-edge down, on to the hot pan surface and leave for about 2 minutes, or until very hot.

4 Pour a little batter into each ring to a depth of 1cm (½ inch). Cook the crumpets for 5–7 minutes until the surface is set and appears honeycombed with holes.

5 Carefully remove each metal ring. Flip the crumpets over and cook the other side for 1 minute only. Transfer to a wire rack. Repeat to use all of the batter.

6 To serve, toast the crumpets on both sides and serve with butter.

note: *The pan and metal rings must be well oiled each time, and heated between frying each batch.*

Griddled Spicy Flatbreads

300g (11oz) strong plain white flour,
   plus extra to dust
175g (6oz) gram flour
1 tsp salt
2 tsp fast-action dried yeast
2 tsp ground cumin
½ tsp golden caster sugar
vegetable oil, to oil

makes 12
preparation: 15 minutes, plus rising
cooking time: 2–3 minutes per batch
per bread: 140 cals; 1g fat;
   30g carbohydrate

1 Mix the flours together in a large bowl. Stir in the salt, yeast, cumin and sugar. Make a well in the middle and gradually work in 250–300ml (8–10fl oz) warm water to form a soft dough.

2 Knead for 8–10 minutes until smooth and elastic, transfer to an oiled bowl, cover and leave to rise in a warm place for 1–1½ hours until doubled in size.

3 Knock back the dough and divide into 12 equal pieces. Roll each piece out to a small oval about 7.5 x 15cm (3 x 6 inches) and put on well floured baking sheets. Spray with a little water, cover loosely and leave to rise for a further 15 minutes.

4 Preheat a lightly oiled griddle, or the grill. Cook the breads, a few at a time, for 1–2 minutes or until puffed up and golden (see note). Flip the breads over and cook the underside for 30 seconds–1 minute.

5 Transfer to a basket, cover with a tea-towel and keep warm while cooking the rest. Serve the breads as soon as possible.

notes
• *If grilling the breads, position the grill rack 8–10cm (3–4 inches) below the heat to allow room for the breads to puff up.*
• *Unless serving immediately, put the breads into a plastic bag as they are cooked to keep them soft.*

Focaccia

700g (1½lb) strong plain white flour, plus
    extra to dust
2 tsp salt
1 tbsp fast-action dried yeast
3 tbsp extra-virgin olive oil, plus extra to oil

TO FINISH
4 tbsp extra-virgin olive oil
coarse sea salt or crystal salt, to sprinkle

makes 2; each serves 6
preparation: 30 minutes, plus rising
cooking time: 20–25 minutes, plus cooling
per serving: 270 cals; 8g fat; 45g
    carbohydrate

1 Sift the flour and salt into a large bowl, stir in the yeast and make a well in the middle. Work in 450ml (¾ pint) warm water and the olive oil to form a soft smooth dough.
2 Knead for 10 minutes until smooth and elastic, then put in a lightly oiled bowl. Cover and leave to rise in a warm place for 1½–2 hours until doubled in size.
3 Lightly oil two shallow 25cm (10 inch) metal pizza tins or pie plates. Knock back the dough and divide in half. Roll out each piece to a 25cm (10 inch) round. Put in the oiled tins. Cover with a damp tea-towel and leave to rise for 30 minutes.
4 Using your fingertips, make deep dimples all over the surface of the dough. Drizzle with the olive oil, sprinkle generously with salt and spray with water. Bake at 200°C (180°C fan oven) mark 6 for 20–25 minutes, spraying with water twice during cooking.
5 Transfer the focaccia to a wire rack to cool slightly. Serve warm, on the same day.

variations
sun-dried tomato focaccia: *Drain 50g (2oz) sun-dried tomatoes in oil, slice and knead into the dough at stage 2.*
sage and onion focaccia: *Knead 15–20 chopped sage leaves into the dough at stage 2. Sprinkle the focaccia with extra sage leaves and 2 peeled thinly sliced red onions at stage 4 before baking.*

Olive Focaccia

25g (1oz) fresh yeast, or 2 tsp ordinary
    dried yeast
500g (1lb 2oz) strong plain white flour,
    plus extra to dust
2 tsp salt
2 tbsp extra-virgin olive oil, plus extra to oil
100g (3½oz) black olives, pitted and
    roughly chopped

TO FINISH
4 tbsp extra-virgin olive oil
coarse sea salt or crystal salt, to sprinkle

makes 2; each serves 6
preparation: 30 minutes, plus rising
cooking time: 25–30 minutes, plus cooling
per serving: 210 cals; 8g fat;
    31g carbohydrate

1 Pour 150ml (¼ pint) tepid water into a jug, crumble in the fresh yeast (if using dried yeast, just sprinkle it over) and leave for 10 minutes until foamy.
2 Sift the flour and salt into a large bowl and make a well in the middle. Add the yeast liquid, olive oil and 200ml (7fl oz) warm water. Mix to a soft smooth dough.
3 Knead for 10 minutes until smooth and elastic, then put into a lightly oiled bowl. Cover and leave to rise in a warm place for 1½–2 hours or until doubled in size.
4 Lightly oil two shallow baking tins, each 25 x 15cm (10 x 6 inches) and 4cm (1½ inches) deep. Knock back the dough and knead on a lightly floured surface for 1 minute. Add the chopped olives and knead until evenly combined.
5 Divide the dough in half, shape into rectangles and put into the oiled tins. Cover with a damp tea-towel and leave to rise in a warm place for 1 hour or until the dough is puffy.
6 Using your fingertips, make dimples all over the surface of the dough. Drizzle with 2 tbsp olive oil, sprinkle generously with salt and spray with water. Bake at 200°C (180°C fan oven) mark 6 for 25–30 minutes or until golden.
7 Transfer the focaccia to a wire rack and sprinkle with the remaining oil. Leave to cool slightly, covered with a cloth if you prefer a softer crust. Serve while still warm, cut into slices.

Illustrated on page 516

Malt Bread

25g (1oz) fresh yeast, or 1½ tsp fast-action
    dried yeast
450g (1lb) strong plain white flour, plus
    extra to dust
1 tsp salt
4 tbsp malt extract
1 tbsp black treacle
25g (1oz) butter, plus extra to grease
1 tbsp sugar, dissolved in 1 tbsp water,
    to glaze

makes 2; each 8–10 slices
preparation: 20 minutes, plus rising
cooking time: 30–40 minutes, plus cooling
per slice: 120–100 cals; 2–1g fat;
    26–21g carbohydrate

1 If using fresh yeast, blend with 150ml (¼ pint) warm water.

2 Sift the flour and salt into a large bowl. Warm the malt extract, treacle and butter together in a pan until just melted.

3 Stir the yeast liquid (or fast-action dried yeast and 150ml (¼ pint) warm water) and malt mixture into the dry ingredients and mix to a fairly soft, sticky dough, adding a little more water if necessary.

4 Turn on to a floured board and knead well for about 10 minutes until the dough is smooth and elastic. Divide in half. Shape both pieces into oblongs and put in two greased 450g (1lb) loaf tins.

5 Leave to rise in a warm place until the dough fills the tins; this may take up to 1½ hours.

6 Bake at 200°C (180°C fan oven) mark 6 for 30–40 minutes until well risen and golden brown. Brush the top of the loaves with the sugar glaze and leave in the tins for 10 minutes. Turn out and cool on a wire rack.

Hot Cross Buns

100ml (3½fl oz) warm milk, plus extra
    to glaze
15g (½oz) fresh yeast or 7g sachet (2 tsp)
    ordinary dried yeast
50g (2oz) golden caster sugar, plus extra
    to glaze
350g (12oz) strong plain white flour, sifted,
    plus extra to dust
pinch of salt
pinch of ground cinnamon
pinch of freshly grated nutmeg
25g (1oz) chopped mixed candied peel
125g (4oz) mixed raisins, sultanas and
    currants
25g (1oz) butter, melted and cooled until
    tepid
1 medium egg, beaten
vegetable oil, to oil

makes 15 buns
preparation: 30 minutes, plus sponging
    and rising
cooking time: 15–18 minutes, plus cooling
per bun: 120 cals; 2g fat; 22g carbohydrate

1 Mix the warm milk with an equal quantity of warm water. Put the yeast in a small bowl with 1 tbsp of the warm liquid and 1 tsp sugar; set aside for 5 minutes.

2 Put 225g (8oz) flour and the salt into a large bowl, make a well in the middle and pour in the yeast mixture. Cover with a clean tea-towel and leave in a warm place for 20 minutes to sponge.

3 Mix the remaining flour and sugar together with the spices, peel and dried fruit. Add to the yeast mixture with the melted butter and egg. Mix thoroughly to form a soft dough, adding a little more liquid if needed.

4 Put the dough in a lightly oiled bowl, cover and leave to rise in a warm place for 1–1½ hours or until doubled in size.

5 Knock back the dough and knead lightly on a lightly floured surface for 1–2 minutes. Divide the dough into 15 equal-sized pieces and shape into buns. Put well apart on a large oiled baking sheet. Make a deep cross on the top of each one with a sharp knife, then cover with a tea-towel and leave in a warm place for about 30 minutes until doubled in size.

6 Brush with milk and sprinkle with sugar, then bake at 220°C (200°C fan oven) mark 7 for 15–18 minutes or until the buns sound hollow when tapped underneath. Transfer to a wire rack to cool. Serve warm.

variation: *Rather than mark crosses on the buns, brush with beaten egg to glaze, then top each with a pastry cross and glaze again. Bake as above.*

Chelsea Buns

15g (½oz) fresh yeast, or 1½ tsp fast-action
    dried yeast
125ml (4fl oz) warm milk
225g (8oz) strong plain white flour, plus
    extra to dust
½ tsp salt
40g (1½oz) butter, diced, plus extra
    to grease
1 egg, beaten
125g (4oz) mixed currants, sultanas and
    raisins
50g (2oz) light muscovado sugar
thin honey, to glaze

makes 12
preparation: 30 minutes, plus rising
cooking time: 30 minutes, plus cooling
per bun: 140 cals; 4g fat; 27g carbohydrate

1 If using fresh yeast, blend with the milk.

2 Sift the flour and salt into a large bowl, then rub in 25g (1oz) of the butter. Make a well in the middle, then pour in the yeast liquid (or fast-action dried yeast and milk), with the egg. Mix to a soft dough.

3 Turn on to a lightly floured surface and knead for 10 minutes until smooth and elastic. Cover and leave in a warm place for 1 hour or until doubled in size.

4 Knead the dough lightly on a floured surface, then pat out to a large rectangle, 30 x 23cm (12 x 9 inches).

5 Melt remaining butter and brush over the dough. Mix the dried fruit with the sugar and scatter over the dough, leaving a 2.5cm (1 inch) border at the edges.

6 Roll up tightly like a Swiss roll, starting at a long edge. Press the edges together to seal, then cut into 12 slices. Put the rolls, cut-side up, in a greased 18cm (7 inch) square tin. Cover and leave in a warm place for 30 minutes or until doubled in size.

7 Bake at 190°C (170°C fan oven) mark 5 for about 30 minutes until well risen and golden brown. Brush with honey while still hot. Leave to cool slightly in the tin before turning out. Serve warm.

Brioche

15g (½oz) fresh yeast, or 1½ tsp fast-action
    dried yeast
225g (8oz) strong plain white flour, plus extra
    to dust
pinch of salt
1 tbsp golden caster sugar
2 extra large eggs, beaten
50g (2oz) butter, melted and cooled until
    tepid
vegetable oil, to oil
beaten egg, to glaze

serves 10
preparation: 20 minutes, plus rising
cooking time: 15–20 minutes, plus cooling
per serving: 140 cals; 6g fat;
    19g carbohydrate

1 If using fresh yeast, blend with 2 tbsp tepid water. Mix the flour, salt and sugar together in a large bowl. (Stir in fast-action dried yeast if using.)

2 Make a well in the middle and pour in the yeast liquid (or 2 tbsp tepid water if using fast-action dried yeast) plus the eggs and melted butter. Work the ingredients together to a soft dough.

3 Turn out on to a floured surface and knead for about 5 minutes until smooth and elastic. Put the dough in a large oiled bowl, cover and leave in a warm place for about 1 hour until doubled in size.

4 Knock back the dough on a lightly floured surface. Shape three quarters of it into a ball and put into an oiled 1.2 litre (2 pint) brioche mould. Press a hole through the centre. Shape the remaining dough into a round, put on top of the brioche and press down lightly.

5 Cover and leave in a warm place until the dough is puffy and nearly risen to the top of the mould. Brush lightly with beaten egg and bake at 230°C (210°C fan oven) mark 8 for 15–20 minutes until golden.

6 Turn out and transfer to a wire rack to cool. Serve warm or cold.

note: *For individual brioches, divide the dough into 10 pieces. Shape as above. Bake in individual tins, for 10 minutes.*

Stollen

75g (3oz) fresh yeast, crumbled, or
40g (1½oz) ordinary dried yeast
700g (1½lb) strong plain white flour, warmed,
plus extra to dust
½ tsp ground coriander
¼ tsp freshly grated nutmeg
100g (3½oz) caster sugar
2 mediums egg, beaten
250g pack butter, very soft
vegetable oil, to oil
300g (11oz) raisins
125g (4oz) currants
150g (5oz) mixed candied peel, finely
chopped
4 tbsp rum
grated zest of 1 large lemon
150g (5oz) blanched almonds, roughly
chopped
1 tsp salt
250g (9oz) almond paste (page 506), or
250g pack ready-made white marzipan

TO FINISH
250g pack unsalted butter, melted, to brush
50g (2oz) icing sugar, sifted

makes 2, each 12 slices
preparation: 30 minutes, plus rising
cooking time: 35-45 minutes
per slice: 390 cals; 20g fat;
49g carbohydrate

1 Mix the yeast with 150ml (¼ pint) warm water. Sift the flour and spices into a warmed bowl, make a well in the middle, pour in the yeast mixture and sprinkle with a little flour from the sides. Leave for 15 minutes or until the yeast bubbles.

2 Mix the sugar and eggs together in another bowl, then pour into the flour. Add the butter and mix everything together until a rough dough forms. Turn on to a lightly floured surface and knead for about 5 minutes until smooth.

3 Put the dough into a lightly oiled bowl, cover with clingfilm and leave in a warm place for about 2 hours or until doubled in size. In the meantime, put the raisins, currants and mixed peel in a bowl, add the rum, cover and put to one side to macerate.

4 Turn the dough out on to a lightly floured surface and stretch into a rough rectangle, about 35 x 25cm (14 x 10 inches). Tip the macerated fruit into the middle, add the lemon zest, chopped almonds and salt, then knead until the fruit and nuts are incorporated. Cut the dough in half.

5 Cut the almond paste in half and roll each piece to a sausage, 25cm (10 inches) long.

6 Shape the dough into two ovals, each about 30cm (12 inches) long. Press a rolling pin lengthways down the middle of each to make a trough and lay the almond paste in the trough. Fold the dough over the almond paste, then put both stollens on a baking sheet. Cover with clingfilm and a clean tea-towel, and leave to rise for 1 hour.

7 Bake at 180°C (160°C fan oven) mark 4 for 35–45 minutes or until the stollens sound hollow when tapped on the base. Transfer to a wire rack to cool. After 15 minutes, brush generously with the melted butter, using it all up. Dust heavily with the icing sugar just before serving.

note: *This authentic German Christmas bread will keep in an airtight container for up to a week; it also freezes well. The quantities are sufficient to make two stollen – one to keep and one to give away.*

PRESERVES

Homemade jams, jellies, chutneys and pickles are easy and satisfying to prepare, free from artificial colourings and preservatives, and taste infinitely better than their commercially produced equivalents. They are also a good way of using a glut of fruit – or vegetables – from the garden. Preserves also make ideal food gifts, especially if you use attractive jars and add decorative labels.

EQUIPMENT

Although not essential, a few items of equipment are very useful for making preserves. You will need a large preserving pan or a large, wide saucepan to allow maximum evaporation. If you make a lot of preserves, it is well worth investing in a proper preserving pan: the sloping sides help maintain a fast boil and reduce the chance of everything boiling over. Stainless steel or lined aluminium pans are best. Don't use unlined aluminium, particularly when cooking acidic fruits or pickles. Make sure the pan is never more than half-full. If necessary, divide the mixture in half before adding the sugar and cook in two batches.

If you do not have a preserving pan, use a large, wide heavy-based saucepan instead. Note that if using a saucepan rather than a preserving pan the preserve will take much longer to reach the setting point owing to the reduced surface area.

You'll also need a long-handled wooden spoon for stirring, a slotted spoon for skimming and, ideally, a sugar thermometer for testing for a set.

For jelly-making, you really need a jelly bag for straining the juice from the cooked fruit. Although you can improvise with a large piece of muslin, it is much easier to use a jelly bag. Before straining, the jelly bag or muslin should be scalded with boiling water to sterilise it. If the jelly bag doesn't have a stand, suspend it from the legs of an upturned chair or stool. Leave undisturbed until the juice has stopped dripping through – don't squeeze the bag, if you do the finished jelly will be cloudy.

INGREDIENTS

Pectin is naturally present in fruit, and reacts with sugar and acid to set jams, jellies, marmalades and conserves. Some fruits, such as cooking apples, lemons, Seville oranges, gooseberries and damsons, are high in natural pectin and acid. Eating apples, raspberries, blackberries, apricots and plums have a medium pectin and acid content, while cherries, grapes, peaches, rhubarb and strawberries score low on both counts.

Fruits with a low or medium pectin content should be cooked together with a fruit that is high in pectin to achieve a satisfactory set. Lemon juice is most commonly used since it is rich in both pectin and acid; 2 tbsp lemon juice to 1.8kg (4lb) fruit should be enough. Alternatively use 'sugar with pectin' (see below) or commercially produced bottled pectin to ensure a good set.

Sugar acts as a preservative as well as helping to achieve a set, so it is important to use the amount stated in the recipe. Granulated sugar is fine for jams and most preserves, though preserving sugar will give a clearer finish and is the best choice for jellies. Caster sugar or muscovado sugar can also be used. Muscovado sugar lends a distinctive flavour and darker colour and is more suited to chutneys and pickles. 'Sugar with pectin' or 'jam sugar' is granulated sugar with added pectin and citric acid, and is used for jams made with fruit that is low in pectin. Preserves made with this should reach setting point in just 4 minutes.

Vinegar acts as a preservative in pickles and some chutneys. Virtually any vinegar is suitable – red, white or flavoured vinegar – providing that the acetic acid content is 5 per cent or more, as is generally the case.

YIELDS

It is difficult to predict the exact yield from a given quantity of fruit, since this will depend on its juice content, which will vary from batch to batch. Jelly yields are particularly hard to estimate since so much depends on the time allowed for dripping and the quality and ripeness of the fruit.

TESTING FOR A SET

Jams, jellies, marmalades and conserves are cooked sufficiently when setting point is reached. It is important to test regularly for a set; if boiled for too long preserves darken and caramelise. There are various tests to determine setting point. Remove the pan from the heat while you are testing, to prevent overcooking.

Temperature test The preserve is ready when it registers 105°C on a sugar thermometer.

Saucer test For this, you will need one or two chilled saucers. Spoon a little of the jam or marmalade on to a cold saucer. Push a finger across the preserve: if the surface wrinkles and it is beginning to set, it has reached 'setting point'. If not, boil for another 5 minutes and repeat the test.

Flake test Using a wooden spoon, lift a little of the preserve out of the pan. Let it cool slightly then tip the spoon so that the preserve drops back into the pan. If the drips run together and fall from the spoon in a 'flake' rather than as drips, it is ready.

There is no accurate test for chutneys and pickles, as they are not cooked to a setting point. Instead, be guided by the consistency and cooking time specified. Chutneys and pickles are ready when no excess liquid remains and the mixture is very thick.

POTTING PRESERVES

All preserves must be potted in scrupulously clean, sterilised containers. Wash the jars or bottles in very hot soapy water, rinse thoroughly, then put upturned on a baking sheet in the oven at 140°C (120°C fan oven) mark 1 for 10–15 minutes until completely dry. Stand the jars upside down on a clean tea-towel until the preserve is ready.

Once setting point is reached, leave the hot jam or marmalade to stand for 15 minutes. Pour into the jars while they are still warm, to reduce the chances of the glass cracking, and fill them almost to the top. If potting jam, jelly, marmalade or conserve, immediately cover with a waxed disc while the preserve is warm. Leave to go cold, then cover the jars with dampened cellophane and secure with an elastic band. If you seal while the preserve is warm, mould will grow on the surface. Chutneys and pickles are covered in the same way. For long-term storage, cover the jar with a screw top as well. Label and store in a cool, dry place for up to 6 months. Once opened, preserves should be stored in the fridge or a cool larder.

JAMS

Jams are basically a cooked mixture of fruit and sugar. The high concentration of sugar used in jam-making effectively preserves the fruit and retards the growth of micro-organisms, allowing the jam to be kept in a cool place for many months without deterioration.

Raspberry Jam

1.8kg (4lb) raspberries
1.8kg (4lb) golden caster sugar
knob of butter

makes about 2.4kg (5¼lb)
preparation: 10 minutes, plus standing
cooking time: about 45 minutes
per tbsp: 50 cals; trace fat;
    12g carbohydrate

1 Put the raspberries into a preserving pan and simmer very gently in their own juice for 15–20 minutes, stirring carefully from time to time, until soft.
2 Remove the pan from the heat and add the sugar, stirring until dissolved, then add the butter and boil rapidly for 20 minutes or until setting point is reached.
3 Take the pan off the heat, remove any scum with a slotted spoon, then leave to stand for 15 minutes. Pot and cover (see above).

Illustrated on page 532

Apricot Jam

1.8kg (4lb) apricots, halved and stoned
juice of 1 lemon
1.8kg (4lb) sugar
knob of butter

makes about 3kg (6½lb)
preparation: 20 minutes, plus standing
cooking time: about 40 minutes
per tbsp: 40 cals; trace fat;
    10g carbohydrate

1 Crack a few of the apricot stones with a nutcracker; take out the kernels and blanch them in boiling water for 1 minute; drain.
2 Put the apricots, lemon juice, apricot kernels and 450ml (¾ pint) water into a preserving pan and simmer for about 15 minutes or until well reduced and the fruit is soft.
3 Off the heat, add the sugar and stir until dissolved. Add the butter and boil rapidly for 15 minutes or until setting point is reached.
4 Take the pan off the heat, remove any scum with a slotted spoon, then leave to stand for 15 minutes. Pot and cover in the usual way (see left).

Blackcurrant Jam

1.8kg (4lb) blackcurrants
2.7kg (6lb) sugar
knob of butter

makes about 4.5kg (10lb)
preparation: 10 minutes, plus standing
cooking time: 55 minutes
per tbsp: 40 cals; trace fat;
    20g carbohydrate

1 Put the blackcurrants into a preserving pan with 1.7 litres (3 pints) water. Simmer gently for about 45 minutes until the fruit is soft and the liquid is well reduced, stirring from time to time to prevent sticking.
2 Remove the pan from the heat, add the sugar, stir until dissolved, then add the knob of butter. Bring to the boil and boil rapidly for about 10 minutes, stirring frequently, or until setting point is reached.
3 Take the pan off the heat, remove any scum with a slotted spoon, then leave to stand for 15 minutes. Pot and cover (see left).

Plum Jam

2.7kg (6lb) plums
2.7kg (6lb) sugar
knob of butter

makes about 4.5kg (10lb)
preparation: 15 minutes, plus standing
cooking time: 45 minutes
per tbsp: 40 cals; trace fat;
    10g carbohydrate

1 Put the plums and 900ml (1½ pints) water into a preserving pan. Simmer gently for 30 minutes or until well reduced and the fruit is very soft.
2 Remove the pan from the heat, add the sugar, stirring until dissolved, then add the knob of butter. Bring to the boil and boil rapidly for 10–15 minutes or until setting point is reached, stirring frequently.
3 Take the pan off the heat. Using a slotted spoon, remove the plum stones and skim off any scum from the surface of the jam, then leave to stand for about 15 minutes. Pot and cover in the usual way (see left).

note: *If dessert plums are used rather than a cooking variety, add the juice of 1 large lemon.*

variations
greengage jam: *Use greengages instead of plums and reduce the water to 600ml (1 pint).*
damson jam: *Use 2.3kg (5lb) damsons instead of plums. After adding sugar, boil for 10 minutes only.*

Blackberry and Apple Jam

900g (2lb) Bramleys or other cooking
    apples, peeled, cored and diced
juice of 1 large lemon
900g (2lb) blackberries
1.2kg (2¾lb) granulated sugar
5 tbsp crème de mûre (blackberry
    liqueur)
15g (½oz) butter

makes 2.7kg (6lb)
preparation: 10 minutes, plus standing
cooking time: 50 minutes
per tbsp: 30 cals; trace fat; 9g carbohydrate

1 Put the apples and 300ml (½ pint) water into a preserving pan and bring to the boil. Lower the heat and cook gently for 10–12 minutes or until soft.
2 Add the lemon juice and blackberries and return to the boil, then simmer for 12–15 minutes or until the blackberries begin to break up.
3 Add the sugar to the pan and heat slowly until it has dissolved, stirring occasionally. Increase the heat and cook at a rolling boil for 10–12 minutes. Add the liqueur and test for a set (see page 534).
4 Once setting point is reached, stir in the butter and leave to settle. Take off the heat, remove the scum with a slotted spoon and leave to stand for 15 minutes, then pot and cover in the usual way (see page 534).

Gooseberry and Elderflower Jam

2.7kg (6lb) slightly under-ripe gooseberries,
    topped and tailed
20 elderflower heads, cut close to the
    stem (see note)
2.7kg (6lb) sugar
knob of butter

makes about 4.5kg (10lb)
preparation: 20 minutes, plus standing
cooking time: 50 minutes
per tbsp: 40 cals; trace fat;
    10g carbohydrate

1 Put the gooseberries into a preserving pan with 1.2 litres (2 pints) water. Tie the elderflowers in a piece of muslin and add to the pan. Simmer gently for about 30 minutes or until the fruit is very soft and reduced, mashing to a pulp with a wooden spoon and stirring from time to time to prevent sticking.

2 Remove the pan from the heat, add the sugar and stir until dissolved, then add the butter. Bring to the boil and boil rapidly for about 10 minutes or until setting point is reached.

3 Take the pan off the heat and remove any scum with a slotted spoon. Remove the muslin bag, then leave to stand for 15 minutes. Pot and cover in the usual way (see page 534).

note: *Elderflowers impart a delicious flavour but they may be omitted if unavailable.*

Strawberry Jam

900g (2lb) strawberries, hulled
1kg (2¼lb) 'sugar with pectin'
juice of ½ lemon

makes about 1.8kg (4lb)
preparation: 10 minutes, plus standing
cooking time: about 10 minutes
per tbsp: 35 cals; 0g fat; 9g carbohydrate

1 Put the strawberries into a preserving pan with the sugar and lemon juice. Heat gently, stirring until the sugar has dissolved.

2 Bring to the boil and boil steadily for 4 minutes or until setting point is reached.

3 Take the pan off the heat and remove any scum from the surface with a slotted spoon. Leave to stand for 15–20 minutes.

4 Stir the jam gently, then pot and cover in the usual way (see page 534).

Strawberry Conserve

1.4kg (3lb) strawberries, hulled
1.4kg (3lb) sugar

makes about 1.4kg (3lb)
preparation: 15 minutes, plus 3 days
    standing
cooking time: about 20 minutes
per tbsp: 60 cals; 0g fat; 17g carbohydrate

1 Put the strawberries into a large bowl, sprinkling evenly with the sugar. Cover and leave to stand in a cool place for 24 hours.

2 Put the strawberries and sugar into a preserving pan. Heat gently, stirring until the sugar dissolves. Bring to the boil and boil rapidly for 5 minutes.

3 Return to the bowl, cover and leave in a cool place for a further 2 days.

4 Return to the pan, bring to the boil and boil rapidly for 10 minutes. Remove from the heat and leave to stand for 15 minutes. Pot and cover in the usual way (see page 534).

Uncooked Freezer Jam

1.4kg (3lb) raspberries or strawberries, hulled
1.8kg (4lb) golden caster sugar
4 tbsp lemon juice
225ml (7½fl oz) commercial pectin

makes about 3.2kg (7lb)
preparation: 15 minutes, plus overnight
    standing
per tbsp: 35 cals; 0g fat; 9g carbohydrate

1 Put the fruit into a large bowl and very lightly mash with a fork. Stir in the sugar and lemon juice and leave at room temperature, stirring occasionally, for about 1 hour until the sugar has dissolved.
2 Gently stir in the pectin and continue stirring for a further 2 minutes.
3 Pour the jam into small freezerproof containers, leaving a little space at the top to allow for expansion. Cover and leave at room temperature for a further 24 hours.
4 Label and freeze for up to 6 months.
5 To serve, defrost the jam at room temperature for about 1 hour.

JELLIES

Jellies differ from jams in that only the juice from the fruit is used in the end product. They are a little more difficult to make and the yield is not as high, but they taste delicious and are well worth the effort. Homemade jellies can be served with roast meats to counteract the richness, used as a glaze for flans, and spread on scones or bread in the same way as jam. It isn't practicable to state the exact yield in jelly recipes because the ripeness of the fruit and time allowed for dripping both affect the quantity of juice obtained. As a rough guide, for each 450g (1lb) sugar added, a yield of about 700g (1½lb) will result. It is also difficult to give precise nutritional information for the same reasons, but you can assume that for each of the following recipes 1 tbsp jelly provides roughly 40 calories.

Apple and Mint Jelly

2.3kg (5lb) cooking apples, such as Bramleys
few large mint sprigs
1.2 litres (2 pints) distilled white vinegar
sugar (see method)
6–8 tbsp chopped mint
few drops of green food colouring (optional)

preparation: 30 minutes, plus standing
cooking time: about 1¼ hours

1 Remove any bruised parts from the apples, then cut into chunks without peeling or coring. Put the apples into a preserving pan with 1.2 litres (2 pints) water and the mint sprigs.

2 Bring to the boil, then simmer gently for about 45 minutes or until soft and pulpy, stirring from time to time to prevent sticking. Add the vinegar and boil for a further 5 minutes.
3 Spoon the pulp into a jelly bag suspended over a large bowl. Leave to drip through for at least 12 hours.
4 Discard the pulp left in the jelly bag. Measure the extract and return to the preserving pan, adding 450g (1lb) sugar for each 600ml (1 pint) extract.
5 Heat gently, stirring, until the sugar has dissolved, then bring to the boil and boil rapidly for 10 minutes or until setting point is reached.
6 Take off the heat and remove any scum with a slotted spoon. Stir in the chopped mint, and colouring if using. Cool slightly, stir well to distribute the mint, then pot and cover in the usual way (see page 534).

note: *This jelly is excellent with roast lamb or pork.*

Bramble Jelly

1.8kg (4lb) slightly under-ripe blackberries
juice of 2 lemons
sugar (see method)

preparation: 30 minutes, plus standing
cooking time: about 1¼ hours

1 Put the blackberries into a preserving pan with the lemon juice and 450ml (¾ pint) water. Simmer gently for about 1 hour until the fruit is very soft and pulpy, stirring from time to time.

2 Spoon the blackberry pulp into a jelly bag suspended over a large bowl and leave to drip through for at least 12 hours.

3 Discard the fruit pulp remaining in the jelly bag. Measure the juice extract and return it to the pan, adding 350g (12oz) sugar for each 600ml (1 pint) extract. Heat gently, stirring, until the sugar has dissolved, then bring to the boil and boil rapidly for about 10 minutes until setting point is reached.

4 Take the pan off the heat and remove any scum with a slotted spoon. Pot and cover in the usual way (see page 534).

Elderberry Jelly

900g (2lb) cooking apples, such
    as Bramleys
900g (2lb) elderberries, washed
sugar (see method)

preparation: 30 minutes, plus standing
cooking time: about 1¼ hours

1 Cut away any bruised or damaged parts from the apples, then roughly chop the fruit into chunks, without peeling or coring. Put the chopped apples into a preserving pan with just enough water to cover and simmer gently for about 1 hour until the fruit is very soft and pulpy.

2 At the same time, put the elderberries into another pan with just enough water to cover and simmer gently for about 1 hour until very soft.

3 Combine the cooked apples and elderberries in a bowl. Stir well, then spoon the fruit pulp into a jelly bag suspended over a large bowl and leave to drip through for at least 12 hours.

4 Discard the pulp remaining in the jelly bag. Measure the juice extract and put it into a preserving pan, adding 350g (12oz) sugar for each 600ml (1 pint) extract. Heat gently, stirring, until the sugar has dissolved, then bring to the boil and boil rapidly for about 10 minutes or until setting point is reached.

5 Take the pan off the heat and remove any scum with a slotted spoon. Pot and cover (see page 534).

Redcurrant Jelly

1.4kg (3lb) redcurrants
sugar (see method)
3 tbsp port (optional)

preparation: 30 minutes, plus standing
cooking time: about 1 hour

1 Put the redcurrants into a preserving pan with 600ml (1 pint) water and simmer gently for about 30 minutes until the fruit is very soft and pulpy, stirring from time to time to prevent sticking.

2 Spoon the fruit pulp into a jelly bag suspended over a large bowl and leave to drip through for at least 12 hours.

3 Discard the pulp remaining in the jelly bag. Measure the juice extract and return it to the pan, adding 450g (1lb) sugar for each 600ml (1 pint) extract.

4 Heat gently, stirring, until the sugar has dissolved, then bring to the boil and boil rapidly for about 15 minutes or until setting point is reached.

5 Take the pan off the heat and remove any scum with a slotted spoon. Stir in the port if using. Pot and cover in the usual way (see page 534).

MARMALADE

Seville or bitter oranges make the best marmalade, with a good flavour and clear set, though other citrus fruits, such as limes and grapefruit, can be used. The best time to make marmalade is during January and February when Seville oranges are in season. Buy unwaxed fruit if you possibly can, otherwise wash thoroughly in water with washing-up liquid added, then rinse well.

Seville Orange Marmalade

1.4kg (3lb) Seville oranges
juice of 2 lemons
2.7kg (6lb) sugar, warmed

makes about 4.5kg (10lb)
preparation: 30 minutes, plus standing
cooking time: about 2½ hours
per tbsp: 40 cals; 0g fat; 10g carbohydrate

1 Halve the oranges and squeeze out the juice and pips. Tie the pips, and any membrane that has come away during squeezing, in a piece of muslin. Slice the orange peel thinly or thickly, as preferred, and put it into a preserving pan with the orange and lemon juices, muslin bag and 3.4 litres (6 pints) water.
2 Simmer gently for about 2 hours or until the peel is very soft and the liquid has reduced by about half.

3 Remove the muslin bag, squeezing it well and allowing the juice to run back into the pan. Add the sugar and heat gently, stirring until it has dissolved. Bring to the boil and boil rapidly for about 15 minutes until setting point is reached. Use the saucer test (see page 534).
4 Take the pan off the heat and remove any scum with a slotted spoon. Leave to stand for 15 minutes, then stir to distribute the peel. Pot and cover in the usual way (see page 534).

note: *It is important to add all the pips and excess pith to the muslin bag as they contain pectin, which helps to set the marmalade.*

variation
dark chunky marmalade: *Thickly slice the peel. At stage 2, simmer for a further 1½ hours until the marmalade has darkened. Finish as above.*

Mixed Fruit Marmalade

2 Seville oranges
2 yellow grapefruit
2 limes
4 large unwaxed lemons
3kg (6½lb) sugar, warmed

makes about 4kg (9lb)
preparation: 30 minutes, plus standing
cooking time: about 2¼ hours
per tbsp: 45 cals; 0g fat; 12g carbohydrate

1 Wash any unwaxed fruit thoroughly, rinse well and dry. Weigh the fruit – you need around 1.6kg (3½lb) in total. Cut in half and squeeze to extract as much juice as possible, then pour through a sieve into a jug, reserving any pips in the sieve.
2 Cut the spent fruit halves into quarters. Cut away the membrane and a thin layer of pith and tie these and the pips in a piece of muslin.

3 Cut the peel into thin strips and tip into a preserving pan.
4 Add all of the citrus fruit juices to the preserving pan, together with 3 litres (5¼ pints) cold water and the muslin bag. Bring to the boil, then simmer for 2 hours or until the peel is very, very tender and the liquid has reduced by about half. Skim off any scum during cooking and discard.
5 Remove the muslin bag from the pan, squeezing well and allowing the juice to run back into the pan. Add the warmed sugar to the pan and stir until dissolved. Bring to the boil, then reduce the heat and bubble until the temperature registers 104°C on a sugar thermometer. Cook at this temperature for about 10 minutes or until setting point is reached. Use the saucer test (see page 534).
6 Take the pan off the heat and remove any scum with a slotted spoon. Leave to stand for 15 minutes, then stir to distribute the peel. Pot and cover in the usual way (see page 534).

FRUIT CURDS

Made with eggs and butter as well as sugar and fruit, these are not true 'preserves' as they do not keep for long, but they are eaten in the same way as jams, taste delicious and are well worth making. All fruit curds should be made in small quantities, kept in the fridge and eaten within 2 weeks.

Lemon Curd

grated zest and juice of 4 medium ripe,
   juicy lemons
4 medium eggs, beaten
125g (4oz) butter, cut into small pieces
350g (12oz) golden caster sugar

makes about 700g (1½lb)
preparation: 20 minutes
cooking time: about 25 minutes
per tbsp: 60 cals; 3g fat; 8g carbohydrate

1 Put all the ingredients into a double boiler or a large heatproof bowl set over a pan of simmering water. Stir the mixture until the sugar has dissolved. Continue to heat gently, stirring frequently, for about 20 minutes until thick enough to coat the back of the spoon; do not allow to boil or it will curdle.

2 Strain the lemon curd through a fine sieve. Pot and cover in the usual way (see page 534). Store in the fridge and use within 2 weeks.

variation
lime curd: *Replace the lemons with the grated zest and juice of 5 large ripe, juicy limes.*

Orange Curd

grated zest and juice of 2 large oranges
juice of ½ lemon
225g (8oz) golden caster sugar
125g (4oz) unsalted butter
3 large egg yolks, beaten

makes about 500g (1lb 2oz)
preparation: 20 minutes
cooking time: about 25 minutes
per tbsp: 60 cals; 4g fat; 8g carbohydrate

1 Put all the ingredients into a double boiler or a large heatproof bowl set over a pan of simmering water. Stir the mixture until the sugar has dissolved. Continue to heat gently, stirring frequently, for 20 minutes or until the curd is thick enough to coat the back of a spoon; don't allow it to boil or it will curdle.

2 Strain the curd through a fine sieve, then pot and cover in the usual way (see page 534). Store in the fridge and use within 2 weeks.

note: *This orange curd has a zingy flavour and a spreading consistency similar to thin honey.*

Luxury Mincemeat

350g (12oz) seedless raisins
350g (12oz) currants
350g (12oz) sultanas
150g (5oz) candied peel, finely chopped
250g pack shredded vegetable suet
100g (3½oz) blanched almonds, finely
    chopped
350g (12oz) demerara sugar
125g (4oz) natural glacé cherries, chopped
2 medium Bramley apples, peeled, cored
    and grated
3 tsp ground mixed spice
grated zest and juice of 1 lemon
grated zest and juice of 1 orange
150ml (¼ pint) brandy
150ml (¼ pint) Drambuie

makes 2.6kg (6lb)
preparation: 20 minutes, plus standing
per 25g (1oz): 80 cals; 3g fat;
    13g carbohydrate

1 Put all of the ingredients into a large mixing bowl and mix thoroughly to combine, then cover and set aside in a cool place for 24 hours, stirring from time to time.
2 Either use the mincemeat immediately or spoon into sterilised jars, cover and seal in the usual way (see page 534). Store in a cool, dark place and use within 3 months.

note: *This Christmas preserve was originally made over 400 years ago from a mixture of meat and eggs enriched with dried fruit and spices, hence the name. Beef suet is traditionally used now, but this recipe is made with vegetable suet, which is lower in fat and suitable for vegetarians.*

FRUITS IN ALCOHOL

Clementines in Grand Marnier Syrup

10 clementines
175g (6oz) golden caster sugar
1 cinnamon stick
6 cloves
300ml (½ pint) Grand Marnier
juice of ½ lemon

makes 10
preparation: 20 minutes, plus cooling
   and maturing
cooking time: 20–25 minutes
per clementine: 200 cals; 0g fat;
   37g carbohydrate

1 Score a cross on the top and bottom of each clementine, then put into a bowl and cover with boiling water. Set aside for 1 minute, then drain and peel.

2 Put the sugar in a large heavy-based pan with the cinnamon stick, cloves and 300ml (½ pint) water. Heat gently to dissolve the sugar, then increase the heat and bring the syrup to the boil. Simmer for 5 minutes.

3 Add the clementines and Grand Marnier and cook for 15–20 minutes. Off the heat, add the lemon juice.

4 Lift out the fruit with a slotted spoon and spoon into a 1 litre (1¾ pint) sterilised jar. Pour the syrup over the fruit, cover and cool. Leave to mature in the fridge for up to 1 month. Once opened, use within 1 week.

Peaches in Grand Marnier

450g (1lb) peaches
225g (8oz) sugar
150ml (¼ pint) Grand Marnier
   or brandy

makes about 450g (1lb)
preparation: 20 minutes, plus cooling
   and maturing
cooking time: about 10 minutes
per 25g (1oz): 80 cals; 0g fat;
   15g carbohydrate

1 Put the peaches into boiling water for 30 seconds. Remove and peel off the skins, then halve and stone.

2 Put half the sugar and 300ml (½ pint) water into a large heavy-based pan. Dissolve over a low heat, then bring to a simmer. Add the peaches and poach gently for 4–5 minutes. Remove from the heat, lift out the fruit with a slotted spoon and put into sterilised jars.

3 Add remaining sugar to the syrup and heat slowly until dissolved. Bring to the boil and boil until the syrup registers 110°C on a sugar thermometer. Allow to cool, then measure the sugar syrup and add an equal quantity of Grand Marnier. Pour over the peaches.

4 Cover and leave to mature in a cool, dark place for 2–3 months. Once opened, use within 2–3 weeks.

Cherries in Brandy

450g (1lb) cherries
225g (8oz) sugar
1 cinnamon stick
about 150ml (¼ pint) brandy

makes about 450g (1lb)
preparation: 15 minutes, plus cooling
   and maturing
cooking time: about 15 minutes
per 25g (1oz): 80 cals; 0g fat;
   16g carbohydrate

1 Prick the cherries all over with a sterilised fine skewer. Put half the sugar in a heavy-based pan with 300ml (½ pint) water and dissolve over a low heat.

2 Add the cherries and cinnamon stick to the light sugar syrup and poach gently for 4–5 minutes. Drain, reserving the syrup; discard the cinnamon. Allow to cool, then put the cherries into small sterilised jars.

3 Add the remaining sugar to the poaching syrup. Heat slowly until dissolved, then boil until the syrup registers 110°C on a sugar thermometer. Allow to cool.

4 Measure the volume of syrup and add an equal quantity of brandy. Pour over the cherries. Cover and leave to mature in a cool, dark place for 1 month.

PICKLES

Pickles are a traditional way of preserving fruit and vegetables with vinegar, spices and flavourings. They can be either sweet or sharp, or an interesting blend of both. Fruits for pickling are usually lightly cooked first. For sharp pickles, the vegetables are generally brined first in a salt solution for up to 24 hours, or sometimes longer.

Large, wide-necked bottles are recommended for pickling, though smaller jam jars can be used. Screw-topped jars with tops that have plastic-coated linings, such as those used for coffee jars and bought pickles, are ideal. Metal tops should not be placed in direct contact with the pickle because the vinegar will react with the metal.

Summer Pickle

225g (8oz) red onions, peeled
225g (8oz) celery, thickly sliced
225g (8oz) carrots, peeled and thinly sliced
600ml (1 pint) distilled vinegar
6 allspice berries
6 black peppercorns
1 mace blade
1 bay leaf
2 cloves
pinch of powdered saffron or ground
    turmeric
125g (4oz) light muscovado sugar
1 tsp salt
225g (8oz) cucumber
225g (8oz) red peppers, halved, cored
    and deseeded
125g (4oz) green beans, trimmed
125g (4oz) baby corn cobs, trimmed
125g (4oz) button mushrooms, trimmed
125g (4oz) cherry tomatoes
6 tbsp walnut oil
2 tbsp chopped dill

makes about 1.8kg (4lb)
preparation: 25 minutes, plus marinating
    and maturing
cooking time: 5 minutes
per tbsp: 15 cals; 1g fat; 2g carbohydrate

1 Cut each onion into 8 wedges. Put in a large pan with the celery and carrots. Add the vinegar, spices, sugar and salt. Bring slowly to the boil.
2 Meanwhile, halve the cucumber lengthways and slice thickly; cut the red peppers into similar-sized pieces. Add to the pan with the green beans, baby corn and mushrooms. Simmer for 5 minutes.
3 Stir in the cherry tomatoes, walnut oil and dill. Transfer to a non-metallic bowl and allow to cool. Cover with a plate and leave to marinate overnight.
4 Taste the pickle and add a little more sugar if required. Pack into sterilised jars, cover and seal in the usual way with vinegar-proof tops. Store in a cool, dark place for at least 1 month before using. Serve with cheese and cold meats.

note: *You may prefer to remove the whole spices before potting the pickle. If so, crush them lightly and tie in muslin, before adding to the pan. Remove the muslin bag after marinating the pickle overnight.*

Piccalilli

1.8kg (4lb) mixed marrow, cucumber,
  French beans, small onions and
  cauliflower (prepared weight, see recipe)
225g (8oz) salt
175g (6oz) sugar
2 tsp mustard powder
1 tsp ground ginger
2 garlic cloves, peeled and crushed
1 litre (1¾ pints) distilled vinegar
25g (1oz) plain flour
4 tsp ground turmeric

makes 1.8kg (4lb)
preparation: 25 minutes, plus standing
  and maturing
cooking time: 25 minutes
per tbsp: 10 cals; trace fat; 2g carbohydrate

1 Deseed and finely dice the marrow and cucumber; top, tail and slice the French beans; peel and halve the onions; divide the cauliflower into florets.

2 Layer the vegetables in a large bowl, sprinkling each layer with salt. Add 2.4 litres (4 pints) water, cover and leave to stand for 24 hours.

3 The following day, drain the vegetables, rinse well and drain thoroughly.

4 Combine the sugar, mustard powder, ginger, garlic and 900ml (1½ pints) of the vinegar in a preserving pan. Add the vegetables, bring to the boil, lower the heat and simmer, uncovered, for 20 minutes until the vegetables are cooked but still crisp.

5 Blend the flour and turmeric with the remaining vinegar and stir into the vegetables. Bring to the boil and cook for 2 minutes.

6 Spoon into sterilised jars, then cover and seal in the usual way with vinegar-proof tops. Store in a cool, dark place for at least 1 month before using.

Pickled Onions

1.8kg (4lb) pickling onions
450g (1lb) salt

SPICED VINEGAR
1.2 litres (2 pints) distilled vinegar
2–3 mace blades
1 tbsp whole allspice
1 tbsp cloves
2 cinnamon sticks
6 black peppercorns
1 bay leaf

makes 1.8kg (4lb)
preparation: 25 minutes, plus 2 days
  marinating and maturing
per 25g (1oz): 10 cals; 0g fat;
  1g carbohydrate

1 First make the spiced vinegar. Put the vinegar, spices and bay leaf into a pan, bring to the boil, then allow to cool. Cover and leave to marinate for about 2 hours. Strain the vinegar through a muslin-lined sieve into a jug. Pour into sterilised bottles and seal with airtight and vinegar-proof tops until ready to use.

2 Put the (unpeeled) onions in a large bowl. Dissolve half of the salt in 2.3 litres (4 pints) water. Pour this brine solution over the onions and leave to marinate for 12 hours.

3 Drain the onions, peel away the skins, then put in a clean bowl. Dissolve the rest of the salt in 2.3 litres (4 pints) water. Pour this fresh brine over the peeled onions and leave for a further 24–36 hours.

4 Drain the onions and rinse well, then pack into sterilised jars. Pour enough spiced vinegar over the onions to cover them completely. Cover in the usual way and seal with vinegar-proof tops. Store in a cool, dark place for at least 1 month before using.

Pickled Red Cabbage

1.4kg (3lb) firm red cabbage, cored and
  finely shredded
2 large onions, peeled and sliced
4 tbsp salt
2.3 litres (4 pints) spiced vinegar
  (see pickled onions, page 547)
1 tbsp light muscovado sugar

makes about 1.4kg (3lb)
preparation: 20 minutes, plus
  overnight standing
per tbsp: 10 cals; trace; 1g carbohydrate

1 Layer the red cabbage and onions in a large bowl, sprinkling each layer with salt, then cover and leave to stand overnight.
2 The following day, drain the cabbage and onions, rinse off the surplus salt and drain thoroughly.
3 Pack the cabbage mixture into sterilised jars. Pour the spiced vinegar into a pan and heat gently. Add the sugar and stir until dissolved. Leave to cool.
4 Pour the cooled vinegar over the cabbage and onion and cover immediately with vinegar-proof tops. Use within 2–3 weeks; thereafter the cabbage tends to lose its crispness.

Pickled Pears

900g (2lb) ripe but firm William pears
300ml (½ pint) distilled malt vinegar, plus
  a dash
300ml (½ pint) white wine vinegar
450g (1lb) golden granulated sugar
2.5cm (1 inch) piece fresh root ginger,
  peeled and thinly sliced
finely pared zest of 1 lemon
1 tbsp allspice berries
1 tbsp cloves
1 cinnamon stick or few pieces of
  cassia bark

makes 900g (2lb)
preparation: 20 minutes
cooking time: about 30 minutes
per 25g (1oz): 60 cals; 0g fat;
  16g carbohydrate

1 Carefully peel the pears. Halve or quarter them, then remove the cores. Put into a bowl of water with a dash of vinegar added to prevent discolouration.
2 Put the vinegars and sugar into a pan and dissolve over a gentle heat. Add the ginger, lemon zest, spices and drained pears. Slowly bring to the boil and simmer gently for about 20 minutes or until the pears are just tender, but still whole.
3 Lift out the pears with a slotted spoon and pack into sterilised jars, with an even distribution of the cooked spices.
4 Bring the syrup to the boil and boil for 10 minutes or until syrupy. Pour over the pears, making sure they are all covered. Seal with vinegar-proof lids and store in a cool dark place for at least 2 weeks. Use within 6 months. Serve the pickled pears with hot or cold baked gammon or ham.

variation

pickled peaches or nectarines: *Prepare as above, but skin, halve and stone the fruit. Use orange instead of lemon zest, and omit the ginger.*

CHUTNEYS

Chutneys are easy to make – you simply put all the ingredients in a large pan and cook until thick. The fruit and, or vegetables are first chopped or sliced, then cooked slowly for several hours with vinegar and spices to produce a sweet-sour mixture, with the texture of a chunky jam. Never leave chutney unattended while it is simmering as it can easily burn, especially towards the end of cooking.

Spiced Plum Chutney

450g (1lb) plums
1 tbsp olive oil
1 onion, peeled and finely chopped
1 garlic clove, peeled and crushed
½ tsp ground mixed spice
½ tsp ground cumin
2 tbsp light muscovado sugar
2 tbsp white wine vinegar
salt and pepper

makes 450g (1lb)
preparation: 15 minutes
cooking time: about 40 minutes
per tbsp: 25 cals; 1g fat; 5g carbohydrate

1 Halve the plums, remove the stones, then cut into chunks and set aside.
2 Heat the olive oil in a large heavy-based pan, add the onion and cook for 5 minutes or until softened. Add the garlic and spices, and cook for 2 minutes.
3 Add the sugar, wine vinegar, plums and 1–2 tbsp water. Bring to the boil, lower the heat and simmer for 30 minutes or until the fruit has softened. Season to taste with salt and pepper.
4 Pour into a warmed sterilised jar, cover and allow to cool. Keep in the fridge and use within 1 month. Serve the plum chutney with a sour, crumbly cheese, such as Lancashire or Cheshire.

Sweet Mango Chutney

1.8kg (4lb) ripe yellow mangoes
2 small cooking apples
2 onions, peeled and chopped
125g (4oz) seedless raisins
600ml (1 pint) distilled malt vinegar
350g (12oz) demerara sugar
1 tbsp ground ginger
3 garlic cloves, peeled and crushed
1 tsp freshly grated nutmeg
½ tsp salt

makes 2kg (4½lb)
preparation: 30 minutes
cooking time: about 1½ hours
per tbsp: 20 cals; trace fat; 6g carbohydrate

1 Halve, peel and thinly slice the mangoes, cutting the flesh away from the stone. Peel, quarter, core and chop the apples. Put the fruits into a preserving pan together with all the remaining ingredients.
2 Bring to the boil, then reduce the heat and simmer gently, uncovered, stirring occasionally, for about 1½ hours until no excess liquid remains and the mixture is thick and pulpy.
3 Spoon the chutney into warmed sterilised jars and allow to cool. Cover and seal in the usual way, with vinegar-proof tops. Once opened, store in the fridge and use within 1 month. Serve with curries, cheese and cold meats.

Spiced Tomato Chutney

1kg (2¼lb) ripe tomatoes, chopped

2 onions, peeled and finely chopped

3 garlic cloves, peeled and crushed

2 red peppers, cored, deseeded and
    finely chopped

1 red chilli, deseeded and diced

450ml (¾ pint) distilled malt vinegar or
    white wine vinegar

350g (12oz) soft light brown sugar

100g (3½oz) raisins

1 tsp black mustard seeds

1 tsp salt

2 tsp smoked paprika

1 cinnamon stick

¼ tsp ground cloves

makes about 1.2kg (2¾lb)
preparation: 15 minutes, plus maturing
cooking time: about 2 hours
per tbsp: 25 cals; trace fat; 6g carbohydrate

1 Put the tomatoes into a large preserving pan, add all the remaining ingredients and stir together. Bring slowly to the boil, stirring from time to time to make sure the sugar has dissolved.

2 Cook the tomato chutney at a medium simmer for 1–1½ hours, stirring occasionally, until it is reduced to a thick, jammy consistency, and no excess liquid remains. It's ready when a wooden spoon drawn through the chutney leaves a clear channel with just a little juice.

3 Spoon the chutney into warmed sterilised jars and allow to cool. Cover and seal in the usual way, with vinegar-proof tops.

4 Store in a cool, dark place and allow to mature for at least 1 month, or up to 3 months, before eating. Once opened, store the chutney in the fridge and use within 1 month. Serve with cheese and cold meats, especially turkey.

note: *This tangy chutney is a great way to use a glut of tomatoes in the garden.*

Green Tomato Chutney

450g (1lb) Bramley or other cooking apples

2 onions, peeled and grated

1.4kg (3lb) under-ripe green tomatoes,
    thinly sliced

225g (8oz) sultanas

225g (8oz) demerara sugar

2 tsp salt

450ml (¾ pint) malt vinegar

4 small pieces dried root ginger

½ tsp cayenne pepper

1 tsp mustard powder

makes 1.4kg (3lb)
preparation: 20 minutes, plus maturing
cooking time: about 2 hours
per tbsp: 20 cals; trace fat; 5g carbohydrate

1 Peel, quarter and core the apples, then grate the flesh finely. Put into a large preserving pan together with all the remaining ingredients. Bring the mixture slowly to the boil, stirring occasionally to make sure the sugar dissolves.

2 Simmer the chutney gently for about 2 hours, stirring occasionally, until the mixture is reduced to a thick consistency, and no excess liquid remains. Discard the ginger.

3 Spoon the chutney into warmed sterilised jars and allow to cool. Cover and seal in the usual way, with vinegar-proof tops.

4 Store in a cool, dark place and allow to mature for 2–3 months before eating. Once opened, store in the fridge and use within 1 month. Serve this chutney with cheese and cold meats.

Chilli Tomato Chutney

900g (2lb) very ripe tomatoes, roughly
    chopped
8 medium red chillies, deseeded
    and roughly chopped
6 garlic cloves, peeled and crushed
5cm (2 inch) piece fresh root ginger, grated
1 lemon grass stalk, trimmed with outer
    layer removed
1 star anise
550g (1¼lb) golden caster sugar
200ml (7fl oz) red wine vinegar

makes about 900g (2lb)
preparation: 25 minutes
cooking time: 50–55 minutes
per 25g (1oz): 60 cals; 0g fat;
    16g carbohydrate

1 Put half the tomatoes into a food processor or blender with the chillies, garlic and ginger. Whiz to a purée, then transfer to a heavy-based pan.

2 Crush or bruise the lemon grass and cut in half. Tie the cut halves together with string, then add to the pan with the star anise, sugar and wine vinegar.

3 Bring the mixture to the boil, add the remaining tomatoes, then reduce the heat. Cook gently for 45–50 minutes until the mixture is thickened and slightly reduced, stirring occasionally and skimming off any scum from the surface.

4 Discard the star anise and lemon grass. Spoon the chutney into warmed sterilised jars and allow to cool. Cover and seal in the usual way, with vinegar-proof tops. Store the chutney in the fridge and use within 1 month. Serve with cheese or cold meats, such as turkey and baked ham.

Pumpkin, Apricot and Almond Chutney

450g (1lb) wedge of pumpkin
600ml (1 pint) cider vinegar
450g (1lb) light muscovado sugar
225g (8oz) sultanas
2 large onions, peeled and sliced
225g (8oz) ready-to-eat dried apricots,
    cut into chunks
finely grated zest and juice of 1 orange
2 tbsp salt
½ tsp ground turmeric
2 cardamom pods, crushed
1 tsp mild chilli seasoning
2 tsp coriander seeds
125g (4oz) blanched almonds

makes 1.8kg (4lb)
preparation: 30 minutes, plus maturing
cooking time: 1–1¼ hours
per 25g (1oz): 50 cals; 1g fat;
    11g carbohydrate

1 Remove any seeds from the pumpkin and cut off the skin. Cut the flesh into 2.5cm (1 inch) cubes.

2 Put the vinegar and sugar into a large heavy-based pan and heat gently, stirring until the sugar has dissolved. Slowly bring to the boil.

3 Add the pumpkin, together with all the remaining ingredients, except the almonds. Stir well and bring to the boil. Lower the heat and cook gently for about 1 hour until soft and thick, stirring occasionally while the mixture is still runny, but more frequently as the chutney thickens; do not let it catch and burn. To test, draw a wooden spoon through the mixture – it should leave a clear trail at the bottom of the pan, which fills up slowly.

4 Stir in the almonds and pack the chutney into warmed sterilised jars. Allow to cool. Cover and seal in the usual way, with vinegar-proof tops. Store in a cool dark place for at least 1 month before using. Once opened, store in the fridge and use within 1 month. Serve with cheese and cold meats.

variation

prune and apple chutney: *Use 450g (1lb) cooking apples and 225g (8oz) pitted prunes in place of the pumpkin and apricots. Substitute lemon, raisins and walnuts for the orange, sultanas and almonds. Instead of the spices listed, use 2 tsp mustard seeds, 1 cinnamon stick and 3 cloves.*

Cranberry and Apple Chutney

1 cinnamon stick
1 tsp allspice berries, crushed
1 tsp cumin seeds
1kg (2¼lb) cranberries
1kg (2¼lb) Granny Smith apples, peeled,
    cored and diced
450g (1lb) onions, peeled and chopped
500g (1lb 2oz) light muscovado sugar
284ml bottle distilled malt vinegar

makes 1.5kg (3¼lb)
preparation: 30 minutes, plus maturing
cooking time: about 1¾ hours
per 25g (1oz): 45 cals; trace fat;
    12g carbohydrate

1 Put the cinnamon stick, allspice berries and cumin seeds in a piece of muslin and tie with string.
2 Put the cranberries, apples, onions, sugar and vinegar into a preserving pan, add the muslin bag and bring to the boil. Reduce heat and simmer very slowly, uncovered, stirring occasionally, for about 1½ hours until the mixture is thick and pulpy. To test, draw a wooden spoon through the mixture – it should leave a clear trail at the bottom of the pan and there should be hardly any liquid left. Remove the bag of spices.
3 Spoon the chutney into warmed sterilised jars. Cool, then cover and seal in the usual way with vinegar-proof tops. Store in a cool, dark place for up to 3 months. Once opened, keep in the fridge and use within 1 month. Serve with cheese or cold turkey.

SWEETS

Homemade sweets are very special, and make delightful gifts if you pack them in pretty boxes or wrap them in cellophane and tie with ribbon. Most sweets are easy to make and don't require much in the way of special equipment, but for those which involve sugar-boiling you really need a sugar thermometer and a strong, wide, heavy-based pan, which is large enough to allow room for the boiling sugar to rise in the pan without spilling over.

SUGAR BOILING

This is the essential technique in many kinds of sweets, including toffee, butterscotch and fudge. The sugar is first completely dissolved in liquid over a low heat, then brought to the boil and boiled until the syrup reaches the correct stage. As it boils, water evaporates and the syrup thickens and gradually darkens. The temperature continues to rise as this happens. A sugar thermometer is the most reliable way of checking sugar boiling stages. The thermometer must be warmed before putting into hot sugar syrup, otherwise the heat might cause the tube to crack.

There are also simple tests that determine the different stages, as described below. Don't stir the syrup during boiling unless the recipe instructs you to do so. If sugar crystals form on the side of the pan, brush them away with a pastry brush dipped in cold water. As soon as the syrup reaches the required stage, take the pan off the heat and briefly dip the base into cold water to stop the heating process (unless you are immediately pouring the syrup from it).

Thread stage at 110°C is used for crystallising purposes. At this stage the mixture still looks syrupy. To test, dip a teaspoon into the boiling syrup, take a little and dip it into very cold water. Knead the syrup between your fingers. It will slide smoothly, but should form a fine thread between the thumb and forefinger when they are slowly pulled apart.

Soft ball stage at 115°C is used for fudge. To test, drop a little syrup into very cold water, then roll between your fingers. It should form a soft ball.

Hard ball stage at 120°C is used for caramel. To test, drop a little syrup into very cold water, then roll between your fingers. It should form a ball that is firm enough to hold its shape but still pliable.

Soft crack stage at 129°C is used for toffee. To test, drop a little of the syrup into cold water. It should separate into hard, but not brittle threads.

Hard crack stage at 143°C is used for hard toffee. To test, drop a little of the syrup into cold water. It should separate into hard, brittle threads.

Light caramel stage at 160°C is used for pralines and caramel. To test for a light caramel, drop a little of the syrup into cold water. The syrup will turn a deep golden brown. When it reaches 165–175°C the syrup turns golden brown in the pan to form a medium caramel. A dark, bitter caramel will result if you continue to boil.

MELTING CHOCOLATE

Chocolate can be melted over a pan of gently simmering water, or in a microwave. Either way, you must avoid overheating, or water coming into contact with the chocolate, otherwise it is liable to become grainy, or 'seize' into a solid mass. Even condensation can cause the chocolate to seize. Particular care must be taken when melting white chocolate, which is very sensitive to heat.

To melt chocolate break into pieces and put into a heatproof bowl set over a pan of gently simmering water, making sure that the bowl does not touch the water otherwise the chocolate will get too hot. Leave undisturbed until melted, then stir until smooth and remove the bowl from the pan.

To melt chocolate in a microwave break into pieces, put into a bowl and microwave on high allowing about 2 minutes for 125g (4oz) chocolate. It is safer to melt white or milk chocolate on a low setting, allowing about 4 minutes for 125g (4oz).

Peppermint Creams

450g (1lb) icing sugar, sifted, plus extra
    to dust
½ tsp cream of tartar
4–5 tbsp evaporated milk
2 tsp peppermint essence
red food colouring

makes 50
preparation: 45 minutes
per peppermint cream: 40 cals; trace fat;
    12g carbohydrate

1 Put the icing sugar and cream of tartar into a bowl. Add the evaporated milk and peppermint essence and stir together until evenly combined. Use your hands to bring the mixture together into a ball.

2 Knead on a surface dusted with icing sugar to make a smooth fondant. Cut the fondant in half; wrap one piece in clingfilm and set aside.

3 Dust the surface with more icing sugar. Roll out the other half of the fondant to a round, about 5mm (¼ inch) thick. Stamp out 4cm (1½ inch) rounds, with a plain cutter. Transfer the fondant discs to a tray lined with baking parchment.

4 Unwrap the other portion of fondant. Dip a skewer into the food colouring, press on to the fondant to apply a little colouring, then knead until it is evenly pink in colour. Roll out to a 5mm (¼ inch) thickness, stamp out 4cm (1½ inch) rounds and then put on a lined tray, as above. Cover the mints loosely with baking parchment and leave to dry overnight.

5 Store in airtight containers for up to 3 weeks and serve as after-dinner mints, or put into paper sweet cases and pack into boxes to offer as a gift.

Illustrated on page 554

Marzipan Fruits

225g (8oz) golden icing sugar, sifted
225g (8oz) golden caster sugar
450g (1lb) ground almonds
1 tsp vanilla extract
squeeze of lemon juice
2 medium eggs, lightly beaten

TO FINISH
food colourings
cloves

makes 900g (2lb)
preparation: 40 minutes
per 25g (1oz): 120 cals; 7g fat;
    14g carbohydrate

1 Mix the icing sugar, caster sugar and ground almonds together in a bowl.

2 Add the vanilla extract, lemon juice and sufficient beaten egg to mix to a stiff dough. Form into a ball and knead lightly.

3 Take small balls of marzipan and mould into shapes to resemble fruits.

4 Using a small paintbrush and food colourings, tint them all over or add shading. Finish as follows:

oranges and lemons: To obtain a pitted surface, roll the fruit lightly on the finest part of a grater. Press a clove into one end.

strawberries and raspberries: Roll in caster sugar to give them a bumpy surface. Colour a little marzipan green for the hull and press into the tops.

apples and pears: Press a clove into the top to resemble the stalk, and one into the base for the stem.

Pecan Praline

200g (7oz) granulated sugar
125ml (4fl oz) golden syrup
150g (5oz) pecan halves
½ tsp vanilla extract
50g (2oz) unsalted butter, plus extra
    to grease
¾ tsp bicarbonate of soda
pinch of salt

makes about 450g (1lb)
preparation: 10 minutes
cooking time: 15 minutes, plus cooling
per 25g (1oz): 140 cals; 08g fat;
    18g carbohydrate

1 Put the sugar and golden syrup into a large heavy-based pan and heat gently, stirring constantly until the sugar dissolves in the syrup.

2 Increase the heat and boil until the syrup registers 110°C on a sugar thermometer.

3 Add the pecan halves to the pan and continue to boil until the mixture reaches 150°C. Immediately remove the pan from the heat and stir in the vanilla extract, butter, bicarbonate of soda and salt. Make sure the ingredients are thoroughly combined.

4 Tip the mixture on to a greased large baking sheet, spreading it thinly. Set aside until completely cooled and hardened.

5 Break the pecan praline into pieces and store in an airtight container, layered between baking parchment, for up to 10 days, or gift wrap in cellophane.

Butterscotch

450g (1lb) demerara sugar
50–75g (2–3oz) unsalted butter
vegetable oil, to oil

makes about 450g (1lb)
preparation: 15 minutes
cooking time: about 15 minutes,
    plus cooling
per 25g (1oz): 120 cals; 3g fat;
    26g carbohydrate

1 Put the sugar and 150ml (¼ pint) water in a heavy-based pan and heat gently until dissolved.
2 Bring to the boil and boil steadily until the syrup registers 138°C on a sugar thermometer (ie the medium crack stage – when a little of the mixture dropped into a cup of cold water separates into hard, but not brittle threads). As the syrup is boiling, brush down the sides of the pan occasionally with a damp pastry brush.
3 Add the butter a little at a time, stirring until each addition is incorporated before adding more. Pour the mixture into a lightly oiled 15cm (6 inch) shallow square tin. Leave until almost set, then mark into pieces.
4 Leave until completely cold, then break into pieces. Store in an airtight container.

Toffee Apples

450g (1lb) demerara sugar
50g (2oz) butter or margarine, plus extra
    to grease
2 tsp distilled malt vinegar
1 tbsp golden syrup
6–8 medium eating apples

makes 6–8
preparation: 15 minutes, plus cooling
cooking time: about 10 minutes
per apple: 410–320 cals; 7–5g fat;
    92–72g carbohydrate

1 Put the sugar, butter, vinegar, 150ml (¼ pint) water and the golden syrup into a heavy-based pan and heat gently until the sugar is dissolved and the butter is melted.
2 Bring to the boil and boil steadily until the syrup registers 143°C on a sugar thermometer (ie the hard crack stage – when a little of the mixture dropped into a cup of cold water separates into hard, but not brittle threads). While the syrup is boiling, brush down the sides of the pan occasionally with a damp pastry brush.
3 Wipe the apples, dry well and push a wooden stick through the base of each one into the cores, making sure they are secure.
4 Dip the apples into the toffee to coat all over, twirl around for a few seconds to allow excess toffee to drip off, then leave to cool and set on a buttered baking tray or waxed paper.

Clotted Cream Vanilla Fudge

50g (2oz) butter, plus extra to grease
450g (1lb) granulated sugar
170g can evaporated milk
113g carton clotted cream
1 tsp vanilla extract

makes 700g (1½lb)
preparation: 15 minutes, plus overnight
    chilling
cooking time: 20–30 minutes, plus cooling
per 25g (1oz): 120 cals; 4g fat;
    20g carbohydrate

1 Lightly grease a shallow 18cm (7 inch) square tin.
2 Put the sugar, evaporated milk, clotted cream and butter into a large heavy-based pan and heat gently to dissolve the sugar.
3 Bring to the boil and boil steadily, stirring frequently to prevent sticking. The mixture is ready when it reaches the soft ball stage (see page 555) and registers 115°C on a sugar thermometer. Immediately plunge the base of the pan into a sink of cold water to stop the cooking process, then remove.
4 Add the vanilla extract and beat with a hand-held electric whisk, scraping down the sides from time to time, until the mixture is thick, paste-like and no longer glossy; this will take about 5 minutes.
5 Pour the fudge into the prepared tin, patting it into the corners with the back of a spoon. Cover and chill overnight until completely set.
6 Cut into squares and pack into boxes, or store in an airtight container in the fridge for up to 2 weeks.

variations
ginger fudge: *Add 75g (3oz) chopped stem ginger (drained of syrup) at the end of stage 4.*
coffee and pecan fudge: *Add 3–4 tbsp coffee essence in stage 2 and 75g (3oz) chopped pecans at the end of stage 4. Omit the vanilla extract.*

Chocolate Fudge

50g (2oz) unsalted butter, plus extra
    to grease
225g (8oz) granulated sugar
400g can sweetened condensed milk
1 tbsp thin honey
1 tsp vanilla extract
100g (3½oz) good quality plain chocolate,
    grated

makes 700g (1½lb)
preparation: 15 minutes
cooking time: about 10 minutes,
    plus cooling
per 25g (1oz): 110 cals; 3g fat;
    19g carbohydrate

1 Lightly grease a shallow 20cm (8 inch) square tin and line with baking parchment.
2 Put the sugar, condensed milk, butter, honey and vanilla extract into a medium heavy-based pan and heat gently until the sugar dissolves. Bring to the boil, stirring, and boil for 6–8 minutes, stirring frequently to prevent sticking. The mixture is ready when it reaches the soft ball stage (see page 555) and registers 115°C on a sugar thermometer.
3 Take off the heat, add the grated chocolate and beat until the mixture is smooth and glossy.
4 Pour the fudge into the prepared tin, spreading it into the corners. Leave for 2 hours or until set.
5 Remove the fudge from the tin and cut into squares. Store in an airtight container.

variations
chocolate nut fudge: *Stir in 50g (2oz) chopped walnuts at the end of stage 3.*
chocolate rum and raisin fudge: *Stir in 25g (1oz) chopped raisins and 1 tbsp rum at stage 3.*

Nutty Chocolate Truffles

100g (3½oz) skinned hazelnuts
200g (7oz) good quality plain dark chocolate
    with 60–70% cocoa solids, in pieces
25g (1oz) butter
142ml carton double cream
3 tbsp cocoa powder, sifted
3 tbsp icing sugar, sifted

makes about 30
preparation: 20 minutes, plus chilling
cooking time: about 10 minutes
per truffle: 80 cals; 6g fat; 6g carbohydrate

1 Toast the hazelnuts in a dry frying pan over a low heat for 3–4 minutes, shaking the pan occasionally, to colour the nuts evenly. Put 30 whole nuts into a bowl and set aside to cool.

2 Whiz the remaining hazelnuts in a food processor until finely chopped. Put the chopped nuts into a shallow dish and set aside.

3 Melt the chocolate in a heatproof bowl set over a pan of gently simmering water.

4 Put the butter and cream into a separate pan and heat gently until the butter has melted, then bring just to the boil and remove from the heat. Carefully stir in the melted chocolate and whisk until cool and thick. Cover and chill for 1–2 hours.

5 Put the cocoa powder and icing sugar into separate shallow dishes. Scoop up a teaspoonful of truffle mix and push a hazelnut into the centre. Working quickly, shape into a ball, then roll in cocoa, icing sugar or chopped nuts and put on a baking sheet lined with baking parchment. Repeat with the remaining truffle mixture.

6 Chill overnight, then pack into boxes or an airtight container. Keep in the fridge and eat within 1 week.

Brandy Truffles

142ml carton thick double cream
½ vanilla pod
200g (7oz) good quality plain dark chocolate
    with 60–70% cocoa solids, in pieces
25g (1oz) unsalted butter, in pieces
2 tbsp brandy
25g (1oz) cocoa powder, to dust

makes about 20–25
preparation: 35 minutes, plus overnight
    chilling
per truffle: 90 cals; 8g fat; 3g carbohydrate

1 Pour the cream into a heavy-based pan. Split the vanilla pod and scrape the vanilla seeds into the pan; add the pod, too. Slowly bring to the boil, take off the heat and set aside to infuse for 20 minutes.

2 Meanwhile, melt the chocolate in a heatproof bowl set over a pan of gently simmering water. Take off the heat and beat in the butter.

3 Remove the vanilla pod from the cream and discard. Stir the infused cream into the chocolate mixture, with the brandy. Pour into a shallow tin, cover and chill overnight until firm.

4 Dust your hands with cocoa powder and shape the truffle mixture into balls. Roll in cocoa to coat and put on a baking sheet lined with baking parchment.

5 Chill overnight, then pack into boxes or an airtight container and keep in the fridge for up to 1 week.

note: *These velvety smooth truffles are best removed from the fridge 1 hour before serving.*

Tiffin

125g (4oz) butter, plus extra to grease
50g (2oz) raisins
75g (3oz) pitted dates, chopped
4 tbsp brandy
200g (7oz) good quality plain chocolate,
    in pieces
3 tbsp golden syrup
250g (9oz) digestive biscuits, roughly
    crushed
grated zest of ½ large orange

TOPPING
150g (5oz) good quality plain chocolate,
    in pieces
25g (1oz) butter

makes 8 wedges
preparation: 40 minutes, plus
    overnight chilling
cooking time: 5 minutes, plus cooling
per wedge: 570 cals; 36g fat;
    54g carbohydrate

1 Lightly grease and base-line a 20cm (8 inch) round shallow tin, about 4cm (1½ inch) deep.
2 Put the raisins and dates into a bowl. Pour on the brandy and leave to soak for 30 minutes.
3 Melt the chocolate with the butter and golden syrup in a heavy-based pan over a gentle heat. Remove from the heat.
4 Add the crushed biscuits, orange zest, raisins and dates, together with any remaining brandy. Mix well, pour into the prepared tin and spread evenly. Allow to cool, then chill for 1 hour.
5 For the topping, melt the chocolate with the butter in a heatproof bowl set over a pan of simmering water. Stir until smooth, allow to cool, then pour over the biscuit layer. Chill in the fridge overnight. Cut into wedges to serve.

note: *This tempting 'refrigerator cake' can be stored in the fridge for up to 1 week.*

Chocolate Peanut Butter Chunks

butter, to grease
400g (14oz) good quality white chocolate,
    in pieces
400g (14oz) good quality plain chocolate,
    in pieces
150g (5oz) crunchy peanut butter

makes 80 chunks
preparation: 30 minutes, plus chilling
cooking time: 10–15 minutes
per chunk: 70 cals; 4g fat; 6g carbohydrate

1 Grease and line a shallow 30 x 20cm (12 x 8 inch) tin with baking parchment.
2 Melt the white chocolate in a heatproof bowl set over a pan of simmering water, making sure the base of the bowl doesn't touch the water. Stir until smooth and remove the bowl from the pan. Melt the plain chocolate in the same way and remove from the heat.
3 Add the peanut butter to the white chocolate and stir well until smooth.
4 Drop alternate spoonfuls of each chocolate into the prepared tin, then tap the tin to level the mixture. Drag a skewer through both mixtures to create a marbled effect. Tap the tin again to level the mixture, then chill for 2–3 hours until firm.
5 Turn out on to a board and cut into 10 fingers, then cut each finger into 8 chunks. Pack into boxes or an airtight container, separating layers with baking parchment. Store in the fridge for up to 1 month.

Chocolate Dipped Fruit and Nuts

225g (8oz) strawberries
125g (4oz) physalis fruit
125g (4oz) kumquats
125g (4oz) red cherries
125g (4oz) grapes
50g (2oz) skinned Brazil nuts
150g (5oz) good quality plain chocolate with
   50–60% cocoa solids, in pieces, to dip

serves: 8
preparation: 20 minutes, plus setting
per serving: 170 cals; 11g fat;
   15g carbohydrate

1 Wash the fruit if necessary and pat dry thoroughly on kitchen paper, but don't remove the stems from the cherries or strawberries. Peel back the papery petals from the physalis fruit. Set aside with the nuts.
2 Put the chocolate in a heatproof bowl set over a pan of simmering water to melt. Stir until smooth and leave to cool until thickened to a coating consistency.
3 Partially dip the fruits and nuts in the chocolate to half-coat, allowing excess chocolate to drip back into the bowl. Put on a tray lined with baking parchment and leave in a cool place or chill until set.

note: *Use these as a decorative finish for cold desserts and smart cakes, or serve a selection in a glass serving bowl to round off a special meal.*

variation: *Use good quality white or milk chocolate for dipping.*

Chocolate Easter Egg

275–300g (10–11oz) good quality plain or milk
   chocolate, in pieces
melted chocolate, to assemble

makes 1
preparation: 1 hour, plus setting
per egg: 1600 cals; 88g fat;
   194g carbohydrate

1 Polish the inside of each half of a 15cm (6 inch) plastic Easter egg mould with cotton wool or a soft cloth. Put on a tray lined with baking parchment.
2 Melt the chocolate in a heatproof bowl set over a pan of simmering mater. Cool slightly.
3 Pour the melted chocolate into each half-mould, tilting gently until evenly coated. Pour any excess chocolate back into the bowl.
4 Invert the moulds on to the baking parchment, then chill until set. Apply a second coat of chocolate; chill again. Repeat once more and chill for 1 hour or until set – the egg will crack if removed too soon.
5 To turn out the egg halves, trim the excess chocolate from the outer edges of the moulds, then run the point of a knife around the edge to loosen. Carefully pull each mould away from the chocolate and press firmly – the chocolate egg halves should slip out easily. Cover loosely, then chill.
6 Spread a little melted chocolate on the egg rims and, holding the other egg half in baking parchment, press on to the melted chocolate to complete the egg. Chill to set, then decorate with ribbons, chicks and sugar flowers.

note: *Easter egg moulds are available from selected cookshops and cake decorating suppliers. The finished egg can be kept chilled for up to 24 hours.*

KITCHEN EQUIPMENT

In most homes, the kitchen is the focus of the house. More than simply a space in which to cook and prepare food, it often doubles up as a dining area, sitting room, perhaps even a study. More often than not, it is the place where everyone tends to gather and, as such, it's worth investing a little time and money to ensure the room is as practical and as comfortable as possible.

Equipping your kitchen requires both discipline and imagination; discipline to select those things you really do need, rejecting items you might use only rarely; imagination to create the sort of kitchen that will work best for you and your family. Above all, think simple. Browse through magazines and brochures and look around stores for inspiration, but don't be lured by sales jargon or over-complicated product descriptions. When it comes to labour-saving devices, it's worth remembering that the time taken to clean the intricate parts of some machines might take longer than it would have done to do the task by hand.

Simplicity is the key in a multi-tasking kitchen but it has as much to do with aesthetics as it has to do with practicality. An attractive pestle and mortar, a rack of shiny utensils, some basic cooking and serving wooden spoons and a set of good quality stainless steel pans will justify their position in your kitchen and will also look good.

Of course, how you choose to equip your kitchen will depend on the kind of cook you are. If cooking is a real passion, you will probably look to buy a more extensive – and expensive – range of items than if you are simply catering for a young family on a limited budget. Balance out your needs and aspirations, making sure that you cover your needs first. Remember that kitchen equipment is subject to a great deal of wear and tear, and look for good quality items. To a large extent, you will get what you pay for, though you will not necessarily pay more for quality products in the long run. Cheap, flimsy baking sheets, for example, will buckle in no time and need replacing. More expensive, sturdy baking sheets will last a lifetime.

Finally, take into account the amount of space you have to work with. If you're working in a galley kitchen, you'll have to think hard about storage and accessibility – there's no point housing items of equipment in another room because you are unlikely to use them. Anything you use regularly should be within reach, and not involve stretching on tip-toe from a kitchen chair.

COOKERS

The most basic cooking appliance you can buy will have four rings on top, an oven below and a grill. Free-standing cookers are cheaper to install than a separate oven and hob, which will require their own carcasses. If you prefer the grill at eye-level, there are a few models still available but they are basic with limited features. If you have very limited space, you can buy a compact model – widths range from as little as 50cm (20 inches); table-top two-ring hobs are also available.

Cookers can have either one or two separate compartments: single ovens are less versatile because they incorporate the grill, so you can't grill and bake at the same time. Cookers with two cavities have either two ovens with the grill in the top of one, or a large main oven with separate grill compartment. The same applies to built-in ovens, but these have a standard width and depth to fit into kitchen units. Built-under double ovens are designed to fit under the work surface so the ovens can be quite small.

In recent years, there has been an increased demand for bigger, better and more professional kitchen appliances. Industrial-look ranges of professional calibre have started to flood the market, with a wide variety of accompanying features. A top-of-the-range range will equip you for more ambitious cookery and is an attractive option if you take your cooking seriously, or if you are after the best the market has to offer. Choose among sleek cast-iron or stainless steel machines with very high heat capacity, mixed fuel and a choice of hobs with accessories, such as a griddle, steamer, trivet and wok ring. Some of the more sophisticated ranges offer a barbecue, five or six gas burners and separate roasting and baking ovens. If you opt for a French make, take note that the gas marks on French appliances may be hotter than their British equivalents.

A dual fuel range combines gas-powered burners with one or more fan and/or conventional electric ovens. Gas is traditionally the fuel of choice for the hob, as it is so much easier to control than electricity. Gas burners will hardly ever need replacing. For ovens, however, electricity provides a more even temperature, which is preferable for accurate baking.

Agas and Rayburns are enamelled cast-iron stoves powered by oil, gas, electricity or solid fuel, with hot plates or burners on top and two to four ovens below. Traditionally seen in country farmhouse kitchens, they are also popular in larger urban kitchens. The great advantage to owning one, in a cool climate at least, is that they are always on and ready for use, and provide general warmth and comfort.

The temperature in an Aga or Rayburn varies from the top of the hob to the bottom oven, so you can cook a number of dishes at different temperatures at the same time and use the bottom oven to warm plates or for slow cooking. One of these stoves will also make your kitchen an efficient drying and airing room for laundry. Be aware that your floor must be solid and strong enough to take the weight of the Aga, and may even need to be specially strengthened. You might also want a stand-by conventional oven and hob if you want to turn off the Aga in the hottest summer months, to keep your kitchen cool.

Aga now manufactures a series of cookers that look like traditional ranges but feature a convectional electric oven with integral grill and a fan electric oven. Available with a choice of hot plate, the gas or electric unit can be either attached to the main cooker or left free-standing.

OVENS

There are three main types of oven: convection, fan and multi-function, all described in this section. Microwave ovens operate very differently (see pages 571–3). Conventional ovens can be built at a height to suit you and, if the hob will be separate, your oven can be fitted into a wall cabinet at eye-level. This reduces the strain on the back because you will not be bending down to lift dishes out of the oven.

Most ovens have transparent doors so that you can check how food is cooking without letting in a blast of cold air. This is particularly useful when you are baking cakes or Yorkshire puddings, when a sudden influx of cool air can cause the rising mixture to flop. Check that doors do not overheat while the oven is on, as this can be dangerous to unsuspecting children. Some models are fitted with a child-locking facility to prevent the oven door being opened by accident.

Cleaning is an important consideration when you are buying a cooker. Basic ovens have enamel linings that feel smooth to the touch but are difficult to keep clean. Oven sides with self-clean or catalytic linings are treated with a special vitreous enamel that absorbs cooking spills. The linings feel rough to the touch and should not be cleaned with detergents. For best results, run the oven on a high temperature for around 30 minutes once a week to burn off any grease residue.

Ovens that have a pyrolytic cleaning cycle are the most convenient and easy to keep clean. They work by heating the oven to around 500°C for 1–3 hours to turn any food residue into ash. After cooling, the ash can be swept off the floor of the oven. Hydroclean systems are messier and less effective, but more economical on fuel. This system involves pouring water and detergent on to the oven floor – the steam loosens dirt so you can wipe it off when the oven has cooled down.

Gas ovens are temperature designated by gas marks. The temperature in the middle of the oven relates to the selected gas mark. The temperature on the top shelf will be slightly higher and the base shelf will be a little cooler. 'Zoned heat' is ideal for complete meals, where dishes need to be cooked at different temperatures. Gas is a much more moist form of heat than electric, which is particularly noticeable in baking. It results in food with a glossy appearance on the outside and a moist texture inside.

Convection ovens use radiant heat and have heating elements positioned on the top and base (or sides) of the oven. When these heat up, they 'radiate' heat to the centre of the oven to cook the food. Convection ovens may take a little longer to cook food than fan ovens, but they are good for browning and crisping.

Fan ovens use a method called 'forced-air' cooking, where heating elements combine with the motion of a fan to heat and circulate air. This ensures a more even distribution of heat, which penetrates the food faster and quicker, so lower temperatures can be used. However, they can have a drying effect on foods. Cooking time is generally shorter than with convection ovens. Consequently, fan ovens are also more energy-efficient. As with all other appliances, choose a fan oven with a low noise level if possible.

Multi-function ovens combine both the convection and fan methods of heating. Each option can be used separately or together depending on the type of food you are cooking. In a multi-function oven, the grill can be used with the fan, giving a similar effect to a rotisserie. These ovens are ideal for batch baking, as well as traditional cooking.

Double ovens are good for cooks who entertain regularly or prepare large family meals on a regular basis. These usually comprise a main fan oven and a smaller conventional oven with a grill element. Double ovens can be built-in at eye-level, into existing kitchen cabinets.

Grills are usually located in the roof of the oven – some can be operated with the door closed. Split-grill ovens are useful in one or two-person households, where small quantities of food are being cooked, as only 50 per cent of a large grilling area needs to be used. Infra-red electric grills are free-standing and produce a higher temperature than most built-in oven grills.

Steam ovens can be connected to the water supply and built into wall cabinets, but they are expensive and relatively uncommon.

Other Oven Features
Defrost setting is available on some fan ovens, and is used for defrosting meat, fish and poultry. Some models have special settings for bread baking and hot-air grilling, too.

Interior light usually comes on automatically when the oven is on. Generally this can be switched on and off at any time to check on food while it's cooking.

Timer is a standard feature on most cookers. This is provided by a digital clock and allows you to set the start and stop time for cooking. If you are baking, you can set the timer to alarm to remind you when the time is up. Digital displays can also tell you the temperature of the oven as it heats up.

HOBS
As you will spend a lot of time standing at the hob, you need to make sure it is at a comfortable height – you should be able to see into pans and stir without bending over. Hobs can now be built to your requirements and can be made up of a combination of different fuel types, rings, burners, steamers, griddles and simmer plates.

Some models have touch-sensitive controls and two-ring cooking zones for energy efficiency – if using a small pan, you only need to use the smaller zone. 'Pan recognition' hobs automatically select the right area for heating, depending on the size of the pan. The pan grids over gas rings should be stable and heavy-duty (made from stainless steel or vitreous enamel).

Ceramic or glass hob surfaces with electric or halogen rings that work by induction heat are easy to keep clean. Electric induction hobs are fast becoming more affordable. They heat the pan directly via a spiral copper coil beneath the glass surface, which transfers energy straight to the pan. The coil is only activated when an iron-based magnetic pan is placed on it, so the glass itself does not heat up before cooking starts, although it will be warm immediately after use. They are fast to heat and nearly as responsive as gas. Some models have a cooling fan, which operates after cooking is complete.

Halogen works by converting light energy into heat, which is reflected upwards and glows when the hob is switched on. Halogen gives an immediate response and is very controllable.

Traditional sealed plates, found on lower priced cookers, are less easy to keep clean. Some have autotherm facilities for more accurate heat control.

Other Hob Features
Many models have extra features to extend the versatility of the hob. Accessories, such as griddles and wok rings, are usually optional so you will need to order them, if required, when you buy your hob.

Contact grill or 'gourmet grill', for fast grilling of fish, meat and vegetables.

Cast-iron griddle plate designed to fit over a gas burner – good for sealing meat, vegetables and fish, and for creating a char-grilled look.

Elongated burner for using a fish kettle or oval flameproof casserole.

Simmer plate operates at a low temperature and is ideal for making sauces.

Tepan plate for stir-frying ingredients with little oil, and for flash-frying.

Wok ring is perfect for supporting a wok securely over the high heat of a burner. Small and large wok rings are available.

COOKER HOODS

A hood with an extractor fan positioned over your cooker and/or hob is important for stopping strong smells from penetrating too far into your living area, and for keeping any smoke and steam under control. Extractors also deter mould by reducing condensation caused by steam.

Cooker hoods can be either ducting or recirculating. Ducted hoods remove grease, steam and cooking smells through a grease filter and to the outside via a pipe. Recirculating cooker hoods are easier to install but not as efficient as the filtered air is returned to the kitchen. Two filters are required – a charcoal one to absorb cooking smells and a grease filter. Always make sure permanent filters are cleaned regularly and disposable ones are replaced every 3–4 months.

The cooker hood must be powerful enough to cope with the size of your cooker and kitchen. You really need a minimum of twelve air changes per hour to work in the kitchen comfortably, but the higher the extraction or recirculating rate, the more efficient the cooker hood. Ideally, the hood should be fitted with a backsplash, which sits behind the hob to collect spills and drips that can then be wiped away easily. Some have pan racks with hooks for convenient storage of shallow pans. Halogen spotlights are now a standard fitting underneath modern cooker hoods. These light up the hob effectively, and are most useful when you are cooking.

Extractors can be noisy, so try to choose one with a low noise level and ask for a test if possible, before you buy. The distance between the extractor and the hob is very important for efficient air extraction, so make sure the manufacturer's instructions are followed carefully when one is installed. Extractors should be fitted away from windows and draughts, so flames do not wander. They can be fixed to the wall, to the ceiling over island units, or built in.

FRIDGES AND FREEZERS

The size of your fridge or fridge-freezer is naturally determined by your priorities and the number of people in your household. If, for example, you buy in bulk once a month, you will need a large-capacity freezer as well as a separate fridge. On the other hand, if your household is small and you buy fresh food little and often, a small fridge-freezer may suffice.

A large fridge with a medium-sized freezer is often the solution, as a small fridge-freezer may just be too small, and overloading a refrigerator can damage the appliance; it may also have a detrimental effect on the food because the temperature may be raised above the correct operating level.

When it comes to size, you will need to decide whether you want a free-standing fridge that asserts its presence, stylishly or otherwise, in the kitchen, or a built-in appliance that can be housed discreetly behind cabinet doors. You may want your fridge and freezer in separate parts of the house, or side by side in the kitchen. American-style side by side fridge-freezers with separate doors provide plenty of storage, but at a cost; they also take up more space. These often have special features, including water and ice dispensers on the freezer door.

As the fridge is one of the most frequently used appliances in the kitchen, durability is important. Sturdy shelves and salad drawers are a must. Shelving inside any refrigerator should be adjustable so that tall items, such as bottles and tall cartons of milk and fruit juice can be accommodated. Door space should be deep, with plenty of different compartments so that food can be kept separate to avoid transferring odours. All drawers should be easy to remove and clean.

Appliances that offer different temperature zones (a standard refrigerated section, a freezer and a cool cabinet) enable different foods to be kept at their optimum storage temperature. The latest fridges and freezers are much more environmentally friendly, containing refrigerants that are CFC and HFC free, so they have lower ozone depleting and global warming potential.

The latest technology has dispensed with the tedious task of defrosting the fridge and freezer – automatic defrost systems collect water from melted ice and allow it to evaporate. Frost-free freezers contain a small fan that circulates the cold air, so reducing the build-up of ice. However, these can be noisier than standard freezers.

All refrigerators carry a climate rating on their rating plate. This refers to the optimum ambient temperature for best performance:

SN = extended temperate 10–32°C

N = temperate 16–32°C

ST = sub-tropical 16–38°C

T= tropical 18–43°C

Every refrigeration product is required by law to carry an energy label displaying its minimum energy efficiency. Ratings are A++ to C, plus D and E for chest freezers, where A++ is the most energy efficient.

FOOD PREPARATION MACHINES

Food processor is a versatile machine that will blend, chop, mince, slice and grate. You can buy processors with a wide range of attachments for slicing and grating to different thicknesses, kneading, even whisking. However, the processor's main functions – blending and liquidising – do not need any extra fittings. Think hard about which attachments you are likely to use – a few grating and slicing discs will certainly come in useful; a second bowl is likely to be more handy than a wide range of cutting blades.

Free-standing mixer copes with larger quantities of mixtures than an electric hand-whisk. These powerful machines are particularly useful for bread-making and lengthy whisking, but they take up quite a lot of space on the work surface.

Blender has less functions than a food processor but blends mixtures more smoothly, and gives better results for puréed soups and baby foods in particular. Most blenders have two speeds. A large capacity blender means that you do not need to blend in batches and you're not tempted to overfill. Alternatively, a small, hand-held blender is useful for working small quantities.

Electric hand whisk is more flexible than a free-standing electric whisk, as it allows you to work over pans as well as bowls. Choose one with a metal shaft if you intend to use it for hot mixtures.

Deep-fat fryer is worth buying if you deep-fry food often, as it is far safer to use than a large pan of oil on the hob, especially if you have young children. Deep-fat fryers are available with various features, such as an electronic timer, thermostatic control, lights and viewing windows.

Electric ice-cream maker is a worthwhile investment if you make your own ice creams and sorbets as it churns the mixture for you and gives excellent results. Available in capacities from 750ml–1.5 litres (1¼-2½ pints).

Pasta machine is invaluable, if not essential, for pasta-making. It rolls out the dough thinly and evenly between metal rollers, then passes it through perforated discs to cut into the required shape. Change the disc to change the shape of pasta you produce.

Pressure cooker is a less popular appliance nowadays, but you may find one useful if you cook casseroles, stocks and preserves regularly, as a pressure cooker reduces cooking time by about two-thirds.

Slow cooker is an effortless way of creating flavourful meat and vegetable stews. The ingredients are placed in the free-standing electric casserole, which is then covered and left to cook at a very low heat for up to 8 hours. It is a good way of cooking the less expensive cuts of meat.

OTHER ELECTRICAL APPLIANCES

Bread-maker is a useful item if you regularly bake your own bread.

Coffee grinder gives you freshly ground coffee. The best ones are swift and easy to clean.

Electric steamer is used for steaming whole meals at once, in trays placed on different levels. It can also be used for steaming puddings.

Espresso machine is available in a wide range of options. Most are equipped with a hot steam generator to froth milk for cappuccinos. You can also buy traditional stove-top appliances, which should be placed on a trivet over a gas flame.

Filter coffee-maker models vary in price and the functions offered. Buy one that is essentially easy to use and easy to clean. Multi-function coffee-makers can produce espresso as well as filter coffee and are equipped with a nozzle to froth up milk.

Juice extractor is excellent for preparing fresh fruit and vegetable juices. There are quite a number on the market and most are fairly expensive, so choose carefully.

Kettle has moved on from being an appliance in which to boil water. The latest models are cordless with powerful elements for rapid boiling. Most have a hidden element beneath a limescale-resistant metal disc to reduce damage by scaling up. All electric kettles should have a safety cut-out mechanism to prevent overheating.

Toaster with pull-out crumb trays or hinged crumb doors for easy cleaning. If you want a multi-slot toaster, buy one with a switch to control which slots are heated, so energy isn't wasted when toasting one slice of bread.

POTS AND PANS

You should have at least three good quality saucepans in the kitchen with thick, sturdy bases, tall sides and tight-fitting lids. Ideally one or two of these should have steamer inserts for steaming vegetables. In addition to these, you will need two frying pans – one large and one small, both with heavy bases, a non-stick sauté pan, a small milk pan with high sides to prevent milk boiling over, a gratin dish and a non-stick roasting pan. A wok is also useful if you do a lot of stir-frying. A large flameproof casserole (such as an enamelled cast-iron one) is a must for dishes that start on the hob and finish in the oven; you may require two or three of these in different sizes.

Ensure that all your pans have handles that stay cool over the hob and, to prevent sticking, follow the manufacturer's instructions on 'seasoning' new pots and pans before using them.

Stainless steel pans look good and are extremely hard-wearing and easy to clean. Stainless steel itself is not a good conductor of heat, so pans must have a thick base, either of aluminium sealed with a protective coating of stainless steel, or of copper and silver alloy for even, energy-efficient heating.

Enamelled cast-iron pans are very heavy to lift and take time to heat up, but they retain heat very well and are energy-efficient as they do not need high temperatures to be effective. They are hard-wearing, easy to clean and durable. However, these pans need to be handled carefully, as they can chip or crack if dropped on a hard surface.

Heavy-gauge anodized aluminium pans are relatively easy to care for; they also conduct and retain heat well. Do not let food stand too long in aluminium pans, as the metal can react with the food. Aluminium non-stick cookware is popular but care must be taken not to scratch the non-stick surface while cleaning, and metal spoons should not be used for stirring.

Copper pans are expensive and often the preserve of the professional kitchen. A copper pan should be lined with stainless steel and the copper should not be allowed to come into contact with acids such as lemon juice. They should not be used on induction hobs.

Other pans you may wish to buy include a cast-iron flat griddle for searing foods and cooking drop scones, and a cast-iron ridged grill pan for char-grilling fish and meat. Both can be heated to high temperatures and the food or pan just needs to be lightly brushed with oil before cooking.

A multi-cooker is good for ambitious cooks. It comprises a large-capacity stockpot with different inserts: a bain-marie, steamer, deep steamer and pasta holder. You may also wish to invest in a steaming set, with a large pot, a shallow steaming pan and lid.

KNIVES

You will need at least three basic chopping and utility knives in different sizes. As a guide, blade measurements should be around 7.5cm (3 inches), 12cm (5 inches) and 20cm (8 inches). You'll also need a carving knife (and two-pronged carving fork), a palette knife and a bread knife with a serrated edge. Knives should be well-balanced in weight and, ideally, have blades made of strong, high grade stainless steel or carbon steel and good handles to provide a solid grip.

Knives with wooden handles should usually be hand-washed; most are not dishwasher-proof. Sharpen knives regularly with a steel or an electric knife sharpener.

SMALL EQUIPMENT CHECKLIST

UTENSILS
Apple corer
Basting spoon
Bottle opener
Can opener
Ceramic baking beans
Cherry/olive stoner
Chopping boards
Citrus press
Corkscrew
Fish slice
Flour dredger
Funnel
Garlic press
Grapefruit knife
Grater
Ice cream scoop
Ice cube trays
Kitchen scissors
Kitchen tongs
Knives (see page 569)
Knife sharpener
Ladle
Mandolin
Mincer
Melon baller
Nutcrackers
Nutmeg grater
Palette knives, small and
   large
Pastry brush
Pastry cutters
Pepper and salt mills
Pastry wheel
Pestle and mortar
Poultry shears
Rolling pin
Pie funnel
Potato masher
Salad spinner
Sieves
Skewers
Skimmer
Slotted spoon
Spatula
Trivet
Trussing needle
Vegetable peeler
Water filter
Whisks, balloon

Wire cooling racks
Wooden spoons
Zester

COOKING EQUIPMENT
Asparagus steamer
Bain-marie
Baking sheets
Baking trays
Cafetière
Casseroles with lids
Cake tins
Dariole moulds
Double boiler
Egg poacher
Fish kettle
Flan rings
Flan tins
Frying pans and lids
Gratin dishes
Griddle
Jelly mould
Loaf tins
Madeleine sheet
Mixing bowls
Omelette pan
Patty tin
Pie dishes
Pudding basins
Pyrex dishes
Ramekins
Roasting tin
Saucepans and lids
Sauté pan
Springform cake tins
Steamer/steamer
   baskets
Stockpot
Swiss roll tin
Terrine
Wok, non-stick
Yorkshire pudding tin

WEIGHTS AND MEASURES
Kitchen timer
Kitchen scales
Measuring jug
Measuring spoons
Frying thermometer
Meat thermometer

Sugar thermometer
Spaghetti measure

SMALL APPLIANCES
Blender
Bread-maker
Coffee grinder
Coffee maker
Deep-fat fryer
Electric hand whisk
Electric stick blender
Ice-cream maker
Juice extractor
Kettle
Food processor
Free-standing mixer
Pressure cooker
Sandwich toaster
Slow cooker
Toaster

STORAGE CONTAINERS
Airtight containers for
   fridge/freezer
Airtight containers for
   dried goods
Bread bin
Cake tins
Salt box
Vegetable rack

CAKE DECORATING
Piping bags and nozzles
Icing turntable
Icing ruler
Serrated scraper

FOR PRESERVING
Preserving pan
Jam funnel
Jelly bag and stand
Jam jars

MICROWAVE COOKING

A basic microwave oven is an inexpensive buy and most useful for reheating frozen foods and speeding up conventional cooking. It is particularly good for cooking vegetables and fish because the food remains moist and keeps its flavour, texture and colour. Microwave cooking is fast, efficient and clean, because foods don't get burned on to the interior of the oven. All that is required is an occasional wipe round with a damp cloth.

Unless your cooking is very limited, you will want a microwave oven to supplement your conventional cooker, rather than replace it. A combination oven, which combines the efficiency of a microwave with the traditional browning and roasting from a conventional oven and grill is more versatile, and can function as a sole cooker if required. You can also buy microwave ovens with a browner, which functions like a grill. All domestic microwave ovens run off a 13 amp socket outlet; they may be free-standing or built-in.

HOW A MICROWAVE OVEN WORKS

Microwave energy is produced by the magnetron, which is housed inside the microwave cooker but not visible to the user. Microwaves are absorbed by food and liquid but they only penetrate food to a depth of 4–5cm (1½–2 inches). Heat is transmitted to the centre of larger containers and joints of meat by conduction.

SAFETY

Microwaves are short wavelengths similar to radio waves. They are quite safe, but as an added precaution microwave ovens only operate when the door is closed and the door is fitted with seals and safety cut-out switches. Most manufacturers recommend that your model is checked on a regular basis (usually every 1–2 years) by a qualified engineer. Never switch on the microwave cooker when there is nothing inside. The waves will bounce around the empty cavity and could damage the magnetron.

USING A MICROWAVE OVEN

Microwave ovens are becoming more powerful and it's now impossible to buy the 650W or 750W models that were standard a decade or so ago. Most range from 800W to 900W with a medium setting of 600W. Most ovens also have auto-cook and auto-defrost programmes, which give short bursts of power at lower levels, producing food that's evenly heated.

Good Housekeeping recipes are tested in a 900W oven, with a 600–650W medium setting. If your model has a different wattage you can calculate how much time you need to allow: Multiply the power output in a recipe or pack instructions by the cooking time (in seconds), then divide by the power output of your oven. If in any doubt, refer to your manufacturer's handbook.

Cooking by microwave is much faster than conventional cooking. The length of time food takes to cook is determined by the wattage of your oven and its capacity, the density of the food, its starting temperature (frozen, fridge or room) and the quantity – the more food you are cooking, the longer it will take. When doubling a microwave recipe, increase the cooking time by about one-third to one-half. If you're halving the amount, reduce the cooking time by around two-thirds.

Keep food moist during cooking by covering it with a lid, plate or microwave film. Pierce film or leave a gap at one side to allow steam to escape. Minimise fat splattering from foods like sausages and bacon by covering them with kitchen paper.

Where a recipe specifies standing time, don't ignore it, as it helps to distribute the heat evenly. Food still continues to cook in the residual heat after the microwave is switched off.

MICROWAVE FROM THE FREEZER

Since reheating is so quick, a microwave cooker is the ideal complement to your freezer. Many dishes, such as casseroles, which need long, slow cooking are best cooked conventionally but reheat perfectly in the microwave. Freeze food in containers that can be put into the microwave to reheat, in convenient portions.

With the exception of vegetables, frozen foods are generally best defrosted at room temperature or in the fridge before reheating in the microwave. Only defrost food in the microwave if time is short, making sure the ice is melted slowly, otherwise the food will begin to cook on the outside before it is thawed through. Allow food to rest between bursts of microwave energy or use an auto-defrost setting, which pulses the energy on and off. It is quicker to defrost several small portions one after the other, than one large frozen lump.

MICROWAVE COOKWARE

Round, large, shallow containers with straight sides are the best choice for microwave cooking. They need to be made from a material that allows microwaves to pass straight through to the food. Metal deflects microwaves and must not be used. It results in arcing (seen as a flare of light), which can damage the magnetron. You also need to avoid glass or china containers decorated with metal paint (gilding).

Ovenproof glass and ceramic dishes are ideal for microwave cooking. Paper plates, kitchen paper and straw baskets can all be used for short reheating tasks. Plastics vary in their capacity to cope with microwaves, but in general most rigid plastics are suitable, whereas flexible plastics tend not to be. Roasting bags are useful for cooking joints and poultry without splattering. Use string or plastic ties to secure them, not metal twist ties which could cause arcing. Pierce the bags before cooking to allow steam to escape.

The size of container is important. Use a larger container for microwave cooking than you would for conventional cooking, and never fill a dish more than two-thirds full. This allows liquids to boil up and provides space for stirring. Containers which transmit microwaves quickly and efficiently have straight sides and are round, large and shallow. Other shapes concentrate microwaves in the corners, which means food cooks unevenly and parts may burn.

To check if a container is suitable for the microwave, half-fill it with water and cook on the highest setting for about 1 minute. If the water is hot and the top of the container cool, the microwaves are passing through the material effectively. If both the water and container are warm, the dish can be used safely but cooking will be less efficient. If the container is hot and the water cool, the microwaves are being trapped in the container and it isn't suitable to use.

MICROWAVE ACCESSORIES

A browning dish or skillet, for searing and colouring foods that would otherwise be grilled or fried is most useful, unless you have a grill or combination cooker. Some microwave ovens are supplied with a useful probe that plugs into the inside of the oven and can be inserted into joints, for example, to determine the internal temperature of the meat.

ARRANGING FOOD

In a microwave oven, food cooks more rapidly at the edge of the dish, so whenever possible it should be stirred into the middle to give an even result. Rotate dishes of food that cannot be stirred. Even if the cooker has a turntable, it is advisable to stir or turn foods to ensure even cooking. Irregular items cook unevenly, as the thinner parts take less time. Put thicker parts towards the outside of the dish and thinner parts towards the middle to ensure even cooking.

Where possible, try to arrange food so that there is an empty space in the middle, then microwaves can penetrate it from both sides. Stand ramekins or individual dishes in a circle. Use a ring mould (or glass tumbler in a round dish) for cooking large cakes.

TEN BEST MICROWAVE USES

- Reheating cooked food
- Defrosting small portions of frozen food
- Ready-prepared meals
- Melting butter and chocolate
- Making milky drinks
- Defrosting and refreshing bread and cakes
- Making sauces, including custard
- Sterilising bottles and jars
- Cooking vegetables
- Cooking fish

COOKING VEGETABLES AND FRUIT

Cooking vegetables in the microwave ensures they keep their colour and have a good bite. Cut them into uniform-sized pieces so that they cook evenly, put them in a shallow microwave-proof dish and add 4 tbsp water. Cover the dish with clingfilm and pierce in a few places. Stir or shake during cooking and don't add salt until afterwards, otherwise the skins may toughen. Note that frozen vegetables need no added liquid.

COOKING MEAT, POULTRY AND FISH

In general, meat and poultry are better cooked in a conventional oven than in a microwave oven. Should you intend to cook joints of meat in the microwave, you'll need a non-metal microwave meat thermometer to check when the 'roast' is ready. Joints cook more evenly if they are symmetrically shaped, ie boned and rolled. Do not salt meat before cooking. Improve the browning of meat and poultry by microwaving in a covered glass dish.

Fish fillets and steaks can be cooked by microwave very successfully. To prevent drying out, brush the skin with melted butter or oil before cooking. Breaded and battered fish is not suitable for microwave cooking.

EGGS AND CHEESE

Eggs and cheese are very easily overcooked in a microwave oven, quickly becoming tough and rubbery. For a smooth result, hard cheese should be grated finely before cooking. Eggs can be poached in ramekins or teacups; prick the yolk before cooking to prevent it exploding. Do not boil eggs in their shells in a microwave oven, as they are liable to explode.

Many sauces, including custard, can be cooked by microwave – in their serving jugs to cut down on washing-up.

CAKES AND PUDDINGS

In general, these are best cooked conventionally, but the following guidelines apply if you want to try microwaving them. Use larger containers, making sure they are no more than half-full, to allow for the extra rise during microwave cooking. Line containers with greaseproof paper, rather than grease and flour them as this gives an unattractive coating. Mixtures should be of a softer consistency than when baking in a conventional oven: add an extra 1 tbsp milk for each egg used. Underbake a mixture if you're not sure about timing; if necessary, you can put it back for a few seconds without spoiling. If a mixture seems to be rising unevenly, give it a partial turn.

Remove cakes and sponge puddings from the microwave after the time recommended even if the mixture looks wet; standing time will complete the cooking process.

REHEATING FOODS

When reheating food in the microwave, you must ensure that it is piping hot. The liquid may be bubbling at the edge of the dish but the food in the middle can still be cold. For best results follow these guidelines:

- Put the food in a shallow microwave container in the middle of the oven.
- Three-quarters cover food before reheating. The steam trapped in the dish will help the heating process.
- Stir foods once or twice during reheating. Dishes that cannot be stirred (eg cannelloni) should be gently shaken.
- Don't try to reheat large pieces of meat, chicken or fish in the microwave. To get them hot enough in the middle, the edges will begin to disintegrate.
- Ensure that the food is initially too hot to eat. If in any doubt, microwave for a little longer. A useful check is to touch the base of the cooking dish in the middle on removing from the oven; if it is cold, the food will not be hot enough.
- Fat and sugar attract microwaves and tend to cook before other ingredients. For example, beware of fillings in sweet pies, as these can be considerably hotter than the pastry.
- Special attention must be paid to cooked pastry and breads. Place on kitchen paper to absorb moisture during reheating, and to prevent the base from becoming soggy. Alternatively, place on a microwave roasting rack so that air can circulate freely underneath.

READY MEALS

Only microwave ready-meals that have pack instructions recommending this reheating method. Follow the instructions carefully, not cutting back on time because a dish is bubbling. If in any doubt about the temperature reached, return the product to the microwave for further reheating.

FOOD STORAGE AND HYGIENE

Storing food correctly and preparing food in a hygienic way is important to ensure that food remains as nutritious and flavourful as possible, and to reduce the risk of food poisoning. When you are preparing food, follow these guidelines:
• Always wash your hands thoroughly before handling food and again between handling different types of food, such as raw and cooked meat and poultry. Keep any cuts or grazes covered with a waterproof plaster.
• Wash down work surfaces regularly with a mild detergent solution or multi-surface cleaner.
• Use a dishwasher if available. Otherwise, wear rubber gloves for washing-up, so that the water can be hotter than hands can bear. Change drying-up cloths and cleaning cloths regularly. Note that leaving dishes to drain is more hygienic than drying them with a tea-towel.
• Keep raw and cooked foods separate, especially meat, fish and poultry. Wash kitchen utensils in between preparing raw and cooked foods. Never put cooked or ready-to-eat foods directly on to a surface which has just had raw fish, meat or poultry on it.
• Keep pets out of the kitchen if possible; at least make sure they stay away off work surfaces.

SHOPPING

Most of us need to limit the time spent food shopping. It makes sense to do a weekly supermarket shop (or use the internet option), choosing a time to suit your schedule. Keep a checklist to hand through the week, jotting down items as you run out of them. Pick up fresh ingredients during the week, from your local market, greengrocer, butcher and fishmonger – if you are lucky enough to have good quality suppliers nearby.

Plan your meals for the week ahead, especially if you have a family, then finalise your shopping list accordingly. You don't necessarily have to cook every night – use the freezer and fridge to save things for later.

Always choose fresh ingredients in prime condition from stores and markets that have a regular turnover of stock.

To ensure food safety, stick to the following guidelines:
• Foods with a longer shelf life have a best-before date; more perishable items have a 'use-by' date. Make sure items are within either date.
• When supermarket shopping, pack frozen and chilled items in an insulated cool bag at the check-out and put them into the freezer or fridge as soon as you get home.
• During warm weather in particular, buy perishable foods just before you return home. As you pack items at the supermarket check-out, sort them according to where you will store them when you get home – the fridge, freezer, storecupboard, vegetable rack, fruit bowl etc. This will make unpacking easier – and quicker.

THE STORECUPBOARD

Having a storecupboard well stocked with the basic essentials will save repeated visits to the shops to pick up missing items. Although storecupboard ingredients will generally last a long time, correct storage is important.

The following guidelines apply:
• Always check packaging for storage advice – even with familiar foods as storage requirements may have changed if additives, sugar or salt have been reduced.
• Never keep storecupboard foods beyond their 'use-by' date.
• Keep all food cupboards scrupulously clean.
• Once opened, treat canned foods as though fresh. Transfer the contents to a clean container, cover and keep in the fridge. Similarly, jars, sauce bottles and cartons should be kept chilled after opening.
• Transfer dry goods such as sugar, rice and pasta to moisture-proof containers. When supplies are used up, wash out and thoroughly dry containers before refilling with fresh stock.

Tailor the following guidelines for a well-equipped cupboard to your own needs and likes:
Cans, bottles and condiments offer endless possibilities. The following items are most useful: canned tomatoes, cartons of passata, tomato

paste and sun-dried tomatoes in oil; jars of pesto; canned coconut milk; tomato ketchup, English, wholegrain and Dijon mustard; Worcestershire sauce, Tabasco, chilli, hoisin, oyster and soy sauces; cans of fruits in natural juice; cartons or cans of ready-made custard; canned chickpeas, red kidney beans and haricot beans; and, of course, baked beans.

Rice, grains and pulses are available in many different varieties. Keep a stock of the following: long-grain rice, pudding rice, mixed wild rice, brown rice and arborio rice for creamy risottos; couscous, bulgur wheat, rolled oats, oatmeal and polenta; dried kidney beans, haricot beans and flageolets; red, green and Puy lentils.

Pasta is the ultimate fast food. Keep at least one long dried pasta such as spaghetti, a box of dried ribbon pasta like tagliatelle, several dried pasta shapes, such as penne, spirals and macaroni, plus a box of lasagne sheets. A bag of tiny soup pasta is also useful.

Dried fruit and nuts are excellent nutritious snacks, and add interest to many sweet and savoury dishes. Store them in airtight containers in a cool, dry cupboard. Nuts, in particular, stale quickly if they are kept in a humid atmosphere. Vacuum-packed chestnuts are a handy time-saver; shelled walnuts, hazelnuts, almonds (and ground almonds), pistachio nuts and pine nuts are worth buying; currants, raisins, sultanas, dried apricots and prunes are most useful for winter fruit compotes, cakes and biscuits.

Dried mushrooms make tasty additions to soups and stews. You can now buy several different varieties of dried wild mushrooms, including ceps, porcini and morels.

Oils are best stored in a dark cupboard away from any heat source, as heat and light can make them turn rancid and affect the colour. For the same reason, buy olive oil in dark green bottles. Keep a stock of the following: vegetable oil for deep-frying; sunflower oil for frying and salads; light olive oil for cooking; good quality extra-virgin olive oil for salad dressings; sesame oil for Chinese cooking; walnut or hazelnut oil for dressings.

Vinegars last a long time, but they must be kept cool or they can turn bad. White and red wine vinegars have a range of uses; balsamic and sherry vinegars are invaluable for sauces and dressings; cider vinegar and flavoured vinegars lift ordinary dressings and mayonnaise. Distilled malt vinegar is used for pickles and chutneys; malt vinegar is traditional with fish 'n' chips.

Dried herbs, spices and flavourings are indispensable. Stock a good selection from those detailed on pages 8–17. Whole spices keep their flavour better than ready-ground ones, but all spices need to be replaced afrter a while, as they lose their pungency. Store them in a cool, dark cupboard or in dark jars.

The following items are especially useful: sea salt, black and green peppercorns; Indian curry and tandoori pastes (better than powders and keep their flavour longer); Thai green and red curry pastes; vanilla and almond extracts; vanilla pods, whole nutmegs, cloves and cinnamon sticks.

Baking ingredients worth keeping include baking powder, bicarbonate of soda and cream of tartar; thin honey and golden syrup; gelatine; fast-action dried yeast; cocoa powder; instant coffee granules; good quality chocolate (keep firmly wrapped and cool); UHT or dried milk (in case you run out of fresh milk).

Flours, sugars etc., should be stored in airtight containers, which are easy to access with a spoon or measure. For a basic store you need plain white flour; self-raising white flour; wholemeal flour; cornflour; golden caster sugar; unrefined granulated sugar; light and dark muscovado sugars and golden icing sugar. Other ingredients can be bought as required in small quantities.

FRIDGE STORAGE

Fresh food needs to be kept in the cool climate of the fridge to keep it in good condition and deter the growth of harmful bacteria. Store day-to-day perishable items, such as opened jams and jellies, mayonnaise and bottled sauces, in the fridge along with eggs and dairy products, fruit juices, bacon, fresh and cooked meat (on separate shelves), and salads and vegetables (except potatoes which don't like the cold).

A fridge should be kept at an operating temperature of 4–5°C. It is worth investing in a fridge thermometer to ensure the correct temperature is maintained.

To ensure your fridge is functioning effectively for safe food storage, follow these guidelines:

• Store cooked and raw foods on separate shelves to avoid bacterial cross-contamination, putting cooked foods on the top shelf. Ensure that all items are well wrapped.

• Never put hot food into the fridge as this will cause the internal temperature to rise.

• Avoid overfilling the fridge as this restricts the circulation of air and prevents the appliance from working properly.

• It can take some time for the fridge to return to the correct operating temperature once the door has been opened, so don't leave it open any longer than is necessary.

• Clean the fridge regularly, using one of the specially formulated germicidal 'fridge cleaners'. Alternatively, use a weak solution of bicarbonate of soda: 1 tbsp to 1 litre (1¾ pints) water.

• If your fridge doesn't have an automatic defrost facility, make sure you defrost it regularly.

MAXIMUM FRIDGE STORAGE TIMES

For pre-packed foods, adhere to the 'use-by' date. For other foods the following storage times should apply, providing the food is in prime condition when it goes into the fridge and that your fridge is in good working order:

Raw Fish and Meat

fish	1 day
shellfish	1 day
joints	3 days
poultry	2 days
game	2 days
raw sliced meat	2 days
minced meat	1 day
offal	1 day
sausages	3 days
bacon	7 days

Cooked Meat

joints	3 days
casseroles/stews	2 days
pies	2 days
sliced meat	2 days
ham	2 days
vacuum-packed	1–2 weeks (or according to pack instructions)

Vegetables and Fruit

salad leaves	2–3 days
green vegetables	3–4 days
soft fruit	1–2 days
hard and stone fruit	3–7 days

Dairy Food

milk	4–5 days
cheese, soft	2–3 days
cheese, hard	1 week
eggs	1 week

FREEZER STORAGE

Freezing is an excellent way of preserving food. Those foods which are suitable for freezing retain their colour, texture, taste and nutritional value, while remaining safe to eat. Many of the recipes in this book are suitable for freezing and, of course, freezing is ideal for preserving seasonal fresh fruit and vegetables.

When you have some time to spare, cook meals in bulk and freeze portions to be eaten later. You can also freeze concentrated reduced fresh stock in small containers. The following prepared items freeze well: bread and scones; pastries and part-baked bread from the supermarket; soups and pizzas. Keep some good quality ice cream and a few frozen vegetables, especially petits pois, broad beans and sweetcorn; keep a supply of ice in the freezer, too. The correct operating temperature for a freezer is -18°C.

The following guidelines apply:

• Only freeze food that is very fresh and in prime condition.

• Handle the food as little as possible.

• Never put any foods that are still slightly warm into the freezer, as this will cause a rise in temperature and may result in deterioration of other frozen items.

• Never freeze more than one tenth of your freezer's capacity in any 24 hours, as this will also cause the internal temperature to rise.

• When freezing large quantities, use the fast-freeze option.

• Pack and seal items well before freezing, especially non-packaged foods. If moisture or cold air comes into contact with the food it will begin to deteriorate. Cross-flavouring might also occur. Wrap awkward-shaped items in foil or freezer film (ordinary clingfilm is not suitable for the freezer), then seal in a bag. Freezer film can also be used as a lining for acidic foods.

- Where possible use square containers to store food in the freezer; they stack better than round ones and take up less space.
- Interleave any items of food that might otherwise stick together with pieces of greaseproof paper, polythene, foil or freezer film.
- When freezing liquids, allow some room for expansion, as a liquid expands by about one-tenth of its volume during freezing and will push off the lid if the container has been overfilled. Remember to do this when you are freezing stocks and soups.
- Freeze single and double portions rather than whole recipe quantities, for versatility and faster defrosting.
- Do not re-freeze food once it has thawed.
- Keep your freezer as full as possible. Empty spaces require more energy to keep cool.
- Label and date freezer containers clearly. This helps ensure items are used in rotation – within recommended maximum storage times.

FREEZING VEGETABLES

If you have your own vegetable garden or local farm shop, freezing is the ideal way to preserve vegetables in peak condition. Always freeze vegetables as soon as possible after picking. Most vegetables keep better for longer if they are blanched before freezing. Blanching impedes enzyme action, which causes loss of colour, flavour and vitamins. Vegetables that are to be eaten within a few weeks of freezing do not need to be blanched. Before blanching (or putting straight into the freezer), trim, shell, peel and/or slice the vegetable as appropriate, then weigh and divide into 450g (1lb) quantities.

To blanch vegetables place the prepared vegetable in a blanching basket and lower into a large pan of fast-boiling water. Time from the moment the water returns to the boil: 1 minute for most varieties; 2–3 minutes for hard vegetables, such as carrots and corn-on-the-cob; 10 seconds for soft vegetables, such as courgettes, mangetout and spinach. Lift out the basket at the end of the blanching time and plunge straight into a bowl of ice-cold water to refresh. Drain thoroughly and pack in containers or freezer bags.

FREEZING FRUIT

As with vegetables, if you have a glut of ripe home-grown fruit in the garden or a nearby pick-your-own fruit farm, it is well worth freezing some for later use. Not all seasonal fruits freeze well; most berry fruits lose some quality of texture if frozen whole, but they can be puréed before freezing if preferred. Lemon and lime slices are worth freezing for drinks. If you only need half a lemon or lime for a recipe for example, thinly slice the other half and freeze. Fruit that is to be frozen must be perfectly ripe and in very good condition.

Open-freezing is the ideal way to freeze small berry fruits, such as raspberries, blackcurrants and redcurrants, which freeze quite successfully. Spread the fruit out on a tray lined with non-stick baking parchment and put into the freezer. 'Open-freeze' on the tray until solid, then pack in freezer bags. Frozen in this manner, the berries will not stick together and you can easily take out the required quantity.

Fruit purée is a convenient method for storing many fruits in the freezer, including cooking apples, apricots, blackcurrants, gooseberries and rhubarb. Fruits which don't freeze well because their texture is spoiled – strawberries, for example – are only really suitable for freezing as a purée, to be used in sauces etc. Fruits that need to be cooked before eating, such as blackcurrants and gooseberries, should be cooked first. Purée the fresh or cooked fruit in a food processor or blender, then pass through a sieve to remove pips, skins etc. Sweeten the purée with sugar to taste if necessary, then freeze in rigid containers.

Freezing fruit in sugar syrup with added lemon juice is the best way to treat halved and stoned, or sliced firm-textured fruits, which are liable to discolouration. Suitable varieties include apricots, damsons, greengages, plums, cooking apples and rhubarb.

To make up a quantity of sugar syrup, dissolve 450g (1lb) sugar in 1 litre (1¾ pints) water over a low heat. Bring to the boil and boil for 1 minute, then take off the heat. Leave the sugar syrup to cool, then add the juice of 1 lemon.

Pack the halved and stoned or sliced fruit in rigid plastic containers, add sufficient cold sugar syrup to cover, leaving room for expansion, then seal with an airtight lid and freeze.

FREEZER STORAGE TIMES

Where applicable, follow the manufacturer's instructions. Otherwise use the following recommended maximum times:

Vegetables

blanched vegetables	10–12 months
unblanched vegetables	3–4 weeks
tomatoes	6–8 months
vegetable purées	6–8 months

Fruit

fruit in syrup	9–12 months
open frozen fruit	6–8 months
fruit purées	6–8 months
fruit juice	4–6 months

Fish

white fish	6–8 months
oily fish	3–4 months
fish portions	3–4 months
shellfish	2–3 months

Meat and Poultry

beef and veal	4–6 months
lamb	4–6 months
pork	4–6 months
offal	3–4 months
sliced bacon	2–3 months
cured meat	2–3 months
ham/bacon joints	3–4 months
chicken/turkey	4–6 months
duck and goose	4–6 months
venison	4–6 months
rabbit	4–6 months
sausages	2–3 months
minced beef	3–4 months

Prepared Foods

soups and sauces	3 months
stocks	6 months
prepared meals	4–6 months
cakes	4–6 months
bread	2–3 months
sandwiches	2–3 months
bread dough	2–3 months
pastries	3–4 months

Dairy Produce

butter, salted	3–4 months
butter, unsalted	6–8 months
ice cream	3–4 months

DEFROSTING FROZEN FOOD

This must be done thoroughly and efficiently to ensure food is safe to eat.

- Never leave food to defrost in a warm place; this is the ideal breeding ground for harmful bacteria. Instead, leave the food to defrost gradually in the fridge or in a cool larder.
- Cover food loosely while defrosting.
- Make sure large items, in particular, are thoroughly defrosted before cooking.
- Cook food as soon as possible after it has thawed.
- If defrosting ready-prepared frozen meals in a microwave, follow the pack instructions.

FREEZER EMERGENCIES

The most common freezer emergency is loss of power. This can be as a result of a power cut or someone inadvertently turning the freezer off. If there is a power cut, don't panic; if you leave the freezer door closed the food should stay frozen for about 30 hours (48 hours in a chest freezer).

- If possible, wrap the freezer with a blanket to increase insulation, but do not cover the condenser or pipes.
- If you have advance warning of a power cut, turn on the fast-freeze switch, making sure the freezer is full to capacity. Towels or rolled newspaper can be used to fill any gaps.
- Do not re-freeze any food you suspect may have begun to defrost.

BALANCED NUTRITION

A diet that is healthy and varied, interesting and tasty, yet familiar and comforting should be everyone's aim. A sound diet, combined with regular exercise, will help you to keep healthy and full of energy, even with the demands of a modern hectic lifestyle. Diet can not only affect weight, but mental well-being too. A balanced diet is the answer, but what exactly does that mean?

Food gives us energy – in the form of calories – which is burnt up naturally with everyday living, but if we consume more calories than the body can use, even with increased exercise, excess calories are stored in the body as fat and the result is weight gain.

A basic understanding of food values will help you towards a healthy diet. It is important to eat as wide a variety of foods as possible, taking care not to over-eat, while cutting down to some extent on our intake of saturated fats. To maintain a healthy body, everyone needs protein, vitamins, minerals, fibre, carbohydrate and a little fat.

Protein is made up of smaller units called amino acids, which are an important part of every cell in the body and therefore necessary for healthy skin, teeth, internal organs and other tissues. The body can manufacture some of these amino acids itself, but the 'essential amino acids' must be derived from food. Animal protein and soya protein contain almost all of these and are regarded as 'complete'. The best sources of protein are meat, poultry, fish, eggs, dairy products such as yogurt, milk and cheese, and soya products. Other vegetable proteins are lacking in one or more of the essential amino acids, not that this need be a problem for vegetarians (see page 580).

Vitamins are vital for a variety of body processes; a deficiency will result in illness. The fat-soluble vitamins A, D, E and K – as their name suggests – are largely derived from foods which contain fat, though the body acquires most of its vitamin D from the action of sunlight on the skin. These vitamins are stored in the liver. Water-soluble vitamins B and C cannot be stored so a regular intake is important.

Minerals are needed in minute quantities to maintain a healthy body. Iron, calcium and zinc are especially important. A deficiency of iron will lead to anaemia. Meat and leafy green vegetables are good sources of iron, and the absorption of this mineral is greatly increased if some vitamin C rich food – even a glass of orange juice – is consumed at the same meal.

Carbohydrates provide the body with the most readily accessible form of energy. Carbohydrates in the form of sugars are found in fruit, milk and sugar; starch carbohydrates are familiar in cereals, pasta, rice, potatoes, bread and pulses. In a healthy diet, starch carbohydrates supply a higher proportion of energy than fats or sugar carbohydrates.

Fat is important in small quantities in a healthy diet, for heat, energy and to aid the absorption of fat-soluble vitamins A and D, which are present in fatty foods. All fats are made up of smaller units, called fatty acids. There are three types: saturated, monosaturated and polyunsaturated fatty acids, which occur in different proportions in foods. Saturated fatty acids are linked to higher blood cholesterol, which can lead to heart disease.

Saturated fats are mainly found in dairy products, especially butter and cream, as well as meat and poultry; monosaturated fats are present in olive oil; and polyunsaturated fats are found in vegetable oils extracted from nuts, beans and seeds. Oily fish, such as mackerel, sardines and herring, are high in unsaturated fat.

Fibre isn't really a nutrient, but it is necessary for the proper functioning of the digestive system. Fibre abounds in unrefined cereals, wholegrain breads, the skins of fruit and vegetables and, of course, bran-related products. If you start the day with a wholegrain cereal and eat plenty of fresh fruit and vegetables, you will easily have enough fibre in your diet.

Salt contains minerals, but should be added to food in moderation; remember that convenience and processed foods are often high in salt.

Water is essential to life because it is the main constituent of all cells, but it is all too easily overlooked. Most of us do not drink nearly enough water. Ideally, we should consume at least 1.5 litres (2½ pints) every day.

BALANCING YOUR DIET

Eating a variety of foods is essential to ensure that your body receives all the nutrients it needs, but a balanced intake is also important. Supplements should not be necessary, except when there are excessive losses of certain nutrients – due to pregnancy, illness or infirmity, or a poor diet. Your diet should be nutritionally sound provided that you eat some foods from each of the following food categories every day:

Cereals and grains – bread, pasta, rice and breakfast cereals – for energy, fibre, B vitamins, calcium and iron.

Fruit and vegetables – excellent sources of vitamins, especially C, vitamin A (in the form of beta-carotene), and minerals, notably iron and calcium. Fruit and vegetables are also valuable sources of antioxidants, which boost the immune system and may help to provide some protection from certain forms of cancer and other diseases. It is recommended that you have at least five fruit and vegetable portions every day.

Meat, poultry and fish – for those valuable amino acids that make up protein, plus energy and iron. Unless of course you are vegetarian, eat a little red meat once or twice a week, balanced with chicken or turkey and fish throughout the rest of the week (not necessarily every day). If possible, eat some oily fish, such as anchovies, sardines, mackerel or tuna, once a week, as these are very good sources of beneficial omega-3 fatty acids.

Pulses, nuts and seeds – for protein, energy, fibre, calcium, iron and zinc.

Dairy products – valuable sources of protein, energy, calcium, minerals, vitamin D and B12.

Water – at least five glasses a day, including fruit juices, milk etc., will help flush out impurities in the system and balance water loss at night. This does not include the intake of tea and coffee, both of which have a diuretic effect (encouraging the body to lose water) and should therefore be consumed in moderation.

CONVENIENCE FOODS

It is all too easy to rely on ready-meals, popping them into the microwave at a minute's notice, but a meal quickly prepared and cooked from fresh natural ingredients is likely have a better nutritional balance. Chilled ready-meals are acceptable from time to time, but do try to serve them with freshly cooked vegetables or a salad – and follow with fresh fruit if possible. If you always have standby ingredients in the fridge or storecupboard, which can be made into a healthy meal in a matter of minutes, then you are much less likely to resort to convenience foods.

A VEGETARIAN DIET

A vegetarian diet is one that excludes meat, poultry and fish. Many vegetarians also avoid other animal products, such as gelatine, animal fats such as lard and suet, and animal rennet in non-vegetarian cheeses. However, the majority of vegetarians do eat dairy produce, including milk, vegetarian cheeses and free-range eggs. Vegans follow a more restrictive diet, which also excludes all dairy products, eggs, and even foods like honey.

Provided a wide range of foods is eaten, a vegetarian diet is unlikely to be lacking nutritionally, but variety is important to ensure a good intake of protein. Vegetable proteins are lacking in one or more of the essential amino acids, but by eating certain foods together, this problem is overcome. Certain combinations provide complete protein: cereals with milk or other dairy products; pulses with rice or pasta; pulses or nuts with dairy produce; nuts with grains, for example. This isn't as complicated as it sounds and tends to happen naturally in most vegetarian meals.

A vegan diet can be deficient in vitamin B12, which is only present in animal and dairy foods. To make up for this, fortified breakfast cereals, yeast extract and/or soya milk should be consumed. Soya products are particularly valuable sources of protein, energy, calcium, minerals, vitamin B12, vitamin D and beneficial omega-3 fatty acids.

ENTERTAINING

Entertaining friends should be fun and relaxing, not only for your guests, but for yourself. Plan ahead and you are much more likely to enjoy the occasion – there's nothing worse than being ill-prepared.

The first golden rule is to avoid planning a meal that is too complicated. Do not tackle a recipe that is totally unfamiliar – as long as you are happy and confident with the dishes you are cooking, they should turn out well. A disaster could snowball and ruin the whole event. If you are determined to try something new, have a small practice run on the family beforehand.

When deciding on a menu, plan to keep it as well balanced as possible. Think about the colours, flavours and textures of the foods – rich and light, sweet and savoury, crunchy and smooth, hot and cold. There aren't really any hard or fast rules, but don't have cream in all the courses, or fruit featuring in every course, or an all-brown menu. Above all, keep it simple.

Select produce in season wherever possible, when it is invariably at its peak for flavour and best value for money. Out-of-season imported strawberries, for example, are very expensive and lacking in flavour. Avoid shopping around for elusive exotic ingredients shortly beforehand – that's time-consuming and potentially stressful.

Always check whether any of your guests are vegetarian or have special dietary needs. In this day and age we cannot assume that everyone eats meat. You will certainly want to avoid a situation where your guest only eats the vegetables! So as not to cause any embarrassment, try to cook an entirely meatless meal if you know that there is going to be just one vegetarian – not as difficult as it sounds, and rarely does anybody notice!

It is certainly an advantage to choose a menu featuring dishes that can be prepared well ahead of time or prepared up to a certain point and held, only needing a little last minute finishing in the kitchen. But don't waste time on elaborate garnishes or decorations – simple presentation is usually more appealing. Advance preparation will leave you time to concentrate on setting the table, last-minute cleaning and hopefully to have a shower and change at leisure!

PLANNING THE EVENT

Once the menu has been decided, make a master shopping list and separate lists of dishes to be prepared ahead, with a note of when to make them. This applies whatever the size of the occasion. Plan fridge and freezer space well ahead of time. For a large party, you may need to ask your neighbour to keep some foods in their fridge, or put bulky items into cool boxes – make sure you have plenty of cool blocks at the ready in the freezer. Check that you have candles if you plan to use them.

Invitations to a dinner party are best made over the phone about 10–12 days in advance. Always mention the type of occasion, whether formal or informal, the date and time, address if necessary, and say if there are any special dress requirements – this avoids embarrassing situations! If you are sending written invitations, post these 2–3 weeks in advance to give people plenty of warning. Keep a list of the guests you have invited and tick them off as they reply. Don't forget to include yourself in the numbers!

Check that table linen is laundered and ironed in advance, and that glasses and cutlery are clean. Clean the house a day or two before the event – not on the day or you will not be able to relax! Buy or order wine and drinks well in advance and avoid doing all the heavy shopping at once – it will seem like less of a chore.

COOKING IN QUANTITY

First of all, decide on the type of party you want to have and whether your plans are feasible in the space available. A buffet party is ideal if you are entertaining a large number and wish to serve a full meal. Decide on the menu well in advance, making sure that starters and main courses can be eaten with a fork. Choose some recipes that can be prepared and frozen ahead, leaving plenty of time on the day to deal with perishable salads, fruit etc. Many of the recipes in this book can be doubled up very easily. However, it isn't usually feasible to prepare a quantity that will serve more than 12 people in one go. Instead, make up the dishes in batches. On the day allow plenty of time to reheat dishes and/or arrange platters of cold food, enlisting help from friends. Make sure you have enough people to pass food around – at least one per 20 guests.

HANDY HINTS FOR ENTERTAINING

• Try to strike a balance between hot and cold items, light and substantial ones.

• Most supermarkets have a good selection of ready-to-eat or ready-to-cook appetisers to munch before the meal if you haven't time to make some. Similarly, you can use good quality bought ingredients, such as mayonnaise and fresh sauces, to save time.

• A freezer is invaluable when entertaining whether on a grand scale or just dinner for two. Make it work for you.

• Buy fresh stocks from the supermarket chilled cabinet and freeze.

• Keep a supply of ready-to-bake bread on hand in the fridge or freezer for quick fresh bread. Freeze packs of half-baked breads to pop in the oven as and when needed.

• Keep a supply of luxury ice cream in the freezer: real vanilla dairy ice cream, one or two tempting flavoured ices and maybe a good sorbet – these are invaluable last-minute standbys, especially in the summer.

• Don't neglect the cheeseboard. For advice on selecting cheeses, see page 241. Remember to unwrap cheeses and bring them to room temperature at least an hour before serving, keeping them lightly covered to prevent drying out until the last minute.

• Make ice well in advance, and store in large plastic bags in your freezer. Alternatively, you can buy large bags of ready-made ice from the supermarket. For large parties, fill cool boxes or the bath with ice and water to keep champagne and white wine well-chilled.

• During the winter, if you run out of fridge space, use a greenhouse or garage to keep drinks and other perishables cold; in warmer weather use cool boxes and ice blocks, or bags of bought ice.

• Use the microwave to reheat pre-cooked vegetables, sauces and gravy in moments.

• Stock up on rubbish bags and drying-up cloths for the aftermath of the party, and decide in advance where you are going to stack dirty plates.

A kitchen overflowing with washing-up looks unsightly, so consider paying someone to do this for you on the day.

WINES AND OTHER PARTY DRINKS

For large gatherings, offer one white and one red wine and plenty of different soft drinks. Keep to the same type of wine and make sure the alcohol content isn't too high – stick to around 12.5 per cent. Provide beer and lager if you like, but avoid spirits. Wines, sparkling wines, and hot or cold punches are ideal party drinks, and easy to serve.

For those who are driving or who prefer not to drink, have some low-alcohol alternatives and a good selection of non-alcoholic drinks. Non-drinkers should be well catered for.

For very large numbers, buy wines and champagne on a sale-or-return basis from a wine merchant. Mineral water, fruit juices and soft drinks can also be bought in this way. Wine merchants and warehouses usually provide this service. Most supermarkets will also allow this, provided the returned bottles are undamaged – check first. Buying sale-or-return means that – in theory anyway – you shouldn't run out of drink as you can order more than you think you will need, but only pay for what is consumed.

Wine boxes are good value and it is worth asking your local wine merchant for his advice – some are better than others. If you prefer to serve wine from the bottle, look at the cost-saving potential of buying by the case, or mixed case, as supermarkets and wine merchants usually have special offers on these.

When it comes to choosing wine it makes sense to find a supplier you can trust, whether it be a supermarket, wine merchant or warehouse. If you opt for something different, just buy one bottle and see if you enjoy it. In most cases you will find point-of-sale information about the wine – its origin, characteristics, and sometimes suggestions as to what it is best served with.

Generally red wine goes best with red meats, and white wine is the better complement to fish, chicken and light meats, but there really are no hard and fast rules any more. It is quite acceptable to serve a light red wine with fish, for example – it is what you enjoy and what goes best with the food that matters.

For an aperitif it is nice to serve a glass of chilled champagne or sparkling wine, or perhaps dry sherry. Avoid sweet drinks, or spirits with a high alcohol content, unless your guests request them, as these tend to take the edge off the appetite, rather than stimulate it. Wine or sherry can be served with a soup course. A full-bodied red wine is an excellent accompaniment to the cheeseboard though some people prefer to drink port with their cheese. Along with the dessert, you may wish to serve a dessert wine, such as Sauternes, or a glass of fruity demi-sec champagne. Coffee follows, with brandy and liqueurs if you like.

HOW MUCH TO BUY?

Obviously the amount of alcohol you will need depends on how much your guests will drink. If you allow one 75cl bottle of wine per head you should have more than enough. One standard 75cl bottle of wine, champagne or sparkling wine will give 6 glasses. A litre bottle will provide 8 glasses. For a dinner party, allow 1 or 2 glasses of wine as an aperitif, 1 or 2 glasses with the first course, 2 glasses with the main course and another with the dessert or cheese.

Remember to buy plenty of mineral water – sparkling and still – and fresh fruit juices. For every 10 guests, buy two 1.5 litre bottles of sparkling water and three similar-sized bottles of still water. Don't forget to buy mixers if you are offering spirits.

SERVING WINE

Wine and champagne are so much more enjoyable to drink if served at the right temperature. Warm white wine and champagne is inexcusable, and chilled red wine (unless young and intended for serving cold) is not at all pleasant.

Party food will probably take up most, if not all, of your available fridge space. In any case it is a good idea to keep drinks out of the fridge, as frequent opening and shutting of the door will only raise the internal temperature at the expense of the food inside. You will, therefore, need plenty of ice to keep drinks cool.

If you have a lot of wine to chill, use the bath, or a large deep sink if you have one. About an hour before the party, half-fill the bath with ice, pour in some cold water and add the bottles standing them upright and making sure the ice and water come up to their necks. Alternatively, use a clean plastic dustbin or cool boxes as containers. (Some hire companies will loan special plastic bins for cooling wines.)

A large block of ice, which can be added to chilled water to melt slowly and maintain the chilled temperature, is a good idea. Make this well in advance of the party: fill a large strong plastic bag with water, seal securely and place in the freezer until frozen.

Many people serve white wine too cold and red wine too warm. The ideal temperature for red is around 15–18°C, with the more tannic wines benefiting from the higher temperature. On a warm day, a brief spell in the fridge will help red wine. For whites, the more powerful wines, like Chardonnay, should be served cool rather than cold, at around 11–15°C, while other whites should be properly cold, at around 6–10°C. The golden rule is it's better too cold than too warm.

WINE AND PARTY DRINK CHECKLIST

- Champagne and sparkling wine
- Red wine
- White wine
- Beer and lager
- Mineral water, sparkling and natural
- Real fruit juices
- Other soft drinks and squashes for non-drinkers, children, punches and mixers
- Dessert wine or sweet sparkling wine
- Low-alcohol/alcohol-free wines, beer and lager
- Liqueurs, brandies etc., for cocktails
- Mixers
- Fail-safe screwpull corkscrews and wine bottle stoppers – to 're-cork' opened wine bottles
- Plenty of ice and re-usable ice packs.

GLOSSARY

Acidulated water Water to which lemon juice or vinegar has been added in which fruit or vegetables, such as pears or Jerusalem artichokes, are immersed to prevent discolouration.

Al dente Italian term commonly used to describe food, especially pasta and vegetables, which are cooked until tender but still firm to the bite.

Antipasto Italian selection of cold meats, fish, salads etc., served as a starter.

Au gratin Describes a dish that has been coated with sauce, sprinkled with breadcrumbs or cheese and browned under the grill or in the oven. Low-sided gratin dishes are used.

Bain-marie Literally, a water bath, used to keep foods, such as delicate custards and sauces, at a constant low temperature during cooking. On the hob a double saucepan or bowl over a pan of simmering water is used; for oven cooking, the baking dish(es) is placed in a roasting tin containing enough hot water to come halfway up the sides.

Baking blind Pre-baking a pastry case before filling. The pastry case is lined with greaseproof paper and weighted down with dried beans or ceramic baking beans.

Baking powder A raising agent consisting of an acid, usually cream of tartar and an alkali, such as bicarbonate of soda, which react to produce carbon dioxide. This expands during baking and makes cakes and breads rise.

Bard To cover the breast of game birds or poultry, or lean meat with fat to prevent the meat from drying out during roasting.

Baste To spoon the juices and melted fat over meat, poultry, game or vegetables during roasting to keep them moist. The term is also used to describe spooning over a marinade.

Beat To incorporate air into an ingredient or mixture by agitating it vigorously with a spoon, fork, whisk or electric mixer. The technique is also used to soften ingredients.

Béchamel Classic French white sauce, used as the basis for other sauces and savoury dishes.

Beurre manié Equal parts of flour and butter kneaded together to make a paste. Used to thicken soups, stews and casseroles. It is whisked into the hot liquid a little at a time at the end of cooking.

Bind To mix beaten egg or other liquid into a dry mixture to hold it together.

Blanch To immerse food briefly in fast-boiling water to loosen skins, such as peaches or tomatoes, or to remove bitterness, or to destroy enzymes and preserve the colour, flavour and texture of vegetables (especially prior to freezing).

Bone To remove the bones from meat, poultry, game or fish, so that it can be stuffed or simply rolled before cooking.

Bottle To preserve fruit, jams, pickles or other preserves in sterile glass jars.

Bouquet garni Small bunch of herbs – usually a mixture of parsley stems, thyme and a bay leaf – tied in muslin and used to flavour stocks, soups and stews.

Braise To cook meat, poultry, game or vegetables slowly in a small amount of liquid in a pan or casserole with a tight-fitting lid. The food is usually first browned in oil or fat.

Brochette Food cooked on a skewer or spit.

Brûlée A French term, literally meaning 'burnt' used to refer to a dish with a crisp coating of caramelised sugar.

Butterfly To split a food, such as a large prawn or poussin, almost in half and open out flat, so that it will cook more quickly.

Calorie Strictly a kilocalorie, this is used in dietetics to measure the energy value of foods.

Canapé Small appetiser, served with drinks.

Candying Method of preserving fruit or peel by impregnating with sugar.

Caramelise To heat sugar or sugar syrup slowly until it is brown in colour; ie forms a caramel.

Carbonade Rich stew or braise of meat, which includes beer.

Casserole A dish with a tight-fitting lid used for slow-cooking meat, poultry and vegetables, now used to describe food cooked in this way.

Charcuterie French term for cooked pork products, including hams, sausages and terrines.

Chill To cool food in the fridge.

Chine To sever the rib bones from the backbone, close to the spine. This is done to meat joints, such as loin of pork or lamb, to make them easier to carve into chops after cooking.

Clarify To remove sediment or impurities from a liquid. Stock is clarified by heating with egg white, while butter is clarified by melting and skimming. Butter that has been clarified will withstand a higher frying temperature.

To clarify butter heat until melted and all bubbling stops. Take off the heat and let stand until the sediment has sunk to the bottom, then gently pour off the fat, straining it through muslin.

Compote Mixture of fresh or dried fruit stewed in sugar syrup. Served hot or cold.

Concassé Diced fresh ingredient, used as a garnish. The term is most often applied to skinned, deseeded tomatoes.

Coulis A smooth fruit or vegetable purée, thinned if necessary to a pouring consistency.

Court bouillon Aromatic cooking liquid containing wine, vinegar or lemon juice, used for poaching delicate fish, poultry or vegetables.

Consistency Term used to describe the texture of a mixture, eg firm, dropping or soft.

Cream To beat together fat and sugar until the mixture is pale and fluffy, and resembles whipped cream in texture and colour. The method is used in cakes and puddings which contain a high proportion of fat and require the incorporation of a lot of air.

Crêpe French term for a pancake.

Crimp To decorate the edge of a pie, tart or shortbread by pinching it at regular intervals to give a fluted effect.

Croquette Seasoned mixture of cooked potato and fish, meat, poultry or vegetables shaped into a small roll, coated with egg and breadcrumbs and shallow-fried.

Croûte Circle or other shaped piece of fried bread, typically used as a base for serving small game birds.

Croûtons Small pieces of fried or toasted bread, served with soups and salads.

Crudités Raw vegetables, usually cut into slices or sticks, typically served with a dipping sauce as an appetiser.

Crystallise To preserve fruit in sugar syrup.

Curdle To cause sauces or creamed mixtures to separate once the egg is added, usually by overheating or over-beating.

Cure To preserve fish, meat or poultry by smoking, drying or salting.

Daube Braising meat and vegetables with stock, often with wine and herbs added.

Deglaze To heat stock, wine or other liquid with the cooking juices left in the pan after roasting or sautéeing, scraping and stirring vigorously to dissolve the sediment on the bottom of the pan.

Dégorge To draw out moisture from a food, eg salting aubergines to remove bitter juices.

Dice To cut food into small cubes.

Draw To remove the entrails from poultry or game.

Dredge To sprinkle food generously with flour, sugar, icing sugar etc.

Dress To pluck, draw and truss poultry or game. The term is also used to describe tossing a salad in vinaigrette or other dressing.

Dry To preserve food, such as fruit, pasta and pulses by dehydration.

Dust To sprinkle lightly with flour, cornflour, icing sugar etc.

Emulsion A mixture of two liquids, which do not dissolve into one another, such as oil and vinegar. Vigorous shaking or heating will emulsify them, as for a vinaigrette.

En croûte Term used to describe food that is wrapped in pastry before cooking.

En papillote Term used to describe food that is baked in a greaseproof paper or baking parchment parcel and served from the paper.

Enzyme Organic substance in food that causes chemical changes. Enzymes are a complex group. Their action is usually halted during cooking.

Escalope Thin slice of meat, such as pork, veal or turkey, from the top of the leg, usually pan-fried.

Extract Concentrated flavouring, which is used in small quantities, eg yeast extract, vanilla extract.

Ferment Chemical change deliberately or accidentally brought about by fermenting agents, such as yeast or bacteria. Fermentation is utilised for making bread, yogurt, beer and wine.

Fillet Term used to describe boned breasts of birds, boned sides of fish, and the undercut of a loin of beef, lamb, pork or veal.

Flake To separate food, such as cooked fish, into natural pieces.

Flambé Flavouring a dish with alcohol, usually brandy or rum, which is then ignited so that the actual alcohol content is burned off.

Folding in Method of combining a whisked or creamed mixture with other ingredients by cutting and folding so that it retains its lightness. A large metal spoon or plastic-bladed spatula is used.

Frosting To coat leaves and flowers with a fine layer of sugar to use as a decoration. Also an American term for icing cakes.

Fry To cook food in hot fat or oil. There are various methods: shallow-frying in a little fat in a shallow pan; deep-frying where the food is totally immersed in oil; dry-frying in which fatty foods are cooked in a non-stick pan without extra fat; *see also* Stir-frying.

Galette Cooked savoury or sweet mixture shaped into a round.

Garnish A decoration, usually edible, such as parsley or lemon, which is used to enhance the appearance of a savoury dish.

Glaze A glossy coating given to sweet and savoury dishes to improve their appearance and sometimes flavour. Ingredients for glazes include beaten egg, egg white, milk and syrup.

Gluten A protein constituent of grains, such as wheat and rye, which develops when the flour is mixed with water to give the dough elasticity.

Grate To shred hard food, such as cheese and carrots, with a grater or food processor attachment.

Griddle A flat, heavy, metal plate used on the hob for cooking scones or for searing savoury ingredients.

Grind To reduce foods such as coffee beans, nuts and whole spices to small particles using a food mill, pestle and mortar, electric grinder or food processor.

Gut To clean out the entrails from fish.

Hang To suspend meat or game in a cool, dry place for a number of days to tenderise the flesh and develop flavour.

Hull To remove the stalk and calyx from soft fruits, such as strawberries.

Infuse To immerse flavourings, such as aromatic vegetables, herbs, spices and vanilla, in a liquid to impart flavour. Usually the infused liquid is brought to the boil, then left to stand for a while.

Julienne Fine 'matchstick' strips of vegetables or citrus zest, sometimes used as a garnish.

Knead To work dough by pummelling with the heel of the hand.

Knock back To knead a yeast dough for a second time after rising, to ensure an even texture.

Lard To insert small strips of fat or streaky bacon into the flesh of game birds and dry meat before cooking. A special larding needle is used.

Liaison A thickening or binding agent based on a combination of ingredients, such as flour and water, or oil and egg.

Macerate To soften and flavour raw or dried foods by soaking in a liquid, eg soaking fruit in alcohol.

Mandolin A flat wooden or metal frame with adjustable cutting blades for slicing vegetables.

Marinate To soak raw meat, poultry or game – usually in a mixture of oil, wine, vinegar and flavourings – to soften and impart flavour. The mixture, which is known as a marinade, may also be used to baste the food during cooking.

Medallion Small round piece of meat, usually beef or veal.

Mince To cut food into very fine pieces, using a mincer, food processor or knife.

Mocha Term which has come to mean a blend of chocolate and coffee.

Parboil To boil a vegetable or other food for part of its cooking time before finishing it by another method.

Pare To finely peel the skin or zest from vegetables or fruit.

Pâte The French word for pastry, familiar in pâte sucrée, a sweet flan pastry.

Pâté A savoury mixture of finely chopped or minced meat, fish and/or vegetables, usually served as a starter with bread or toast.

Patty tin Tray of cup-shaped moulds for cooking small cakes and deep tartlets. Also called a bun tin.

Pectin A naturally occurring substance found in most varieties of fruit and some vegetables, which is necessary for setting jams and jellies. Commercial pectin and sugar with pectin are also available for preserve-making.

Pickle To preserve meat or vegetables in brine or vinegar.

Pith The bitter white skin under the thin zest of citrus fruit.

Pluck To remove the feathers from poultry and game birds.

Poach To cook food gently in liquid at simmering point; the surface should be just trembling.

Pot roast To cook meat in a covered pan with some fat and a little liquid.

Prove To leave bread dough to rise (usually for a second time) after shaping.

Purée To pound, sieve or liquidise vegetables, fish or fruit to a smooth pulp. Purées often form the basis for soups and sauces.

Reduce To fast-boil stock or other liquid in an uncovered pan to evaporate water and concentrate the flavour.

Refresh To cool hot vegetables very quickly by plunging into ice-cold water or holding under cold running water in order to stop the cooking process and preserve the colour.

Render To melt fat slowly to a liquid, either by heating meat trimmings, or to release the fat from fatty meat, such as duck or goose, during roasting.

Rennet An animal-derived enzyme used to coagulate milk in cheese-making. A vegetarian alternative is available.

Roast To cook meat by dry heat in the oven.

Roulade Soufflé or sponge mixture rolled around a savoury or sweet filling.

Roux A mixture of equal quantities of butter (or other fat) and flour cooked together to form the basis of many sauces.

Rub-in Method of incorporating fat into flour by rubbing between the fingertips, used when a short texture is required. Used for pastry, cakes, scones and biscuits.

Salsa Piquant sauce made from chopped fresh vegetables and sometimes fruit.

Sauté To cook food in a small quantity of fat over a high heat, shaking the pan constantly – usually in a sauté pan (a frying pan with straight sides and a wide base).

Scald To pour boiling water over food to clean it, or loosen skin, eg tomatoes. Also used to describe heating milk to just below boiling point.

Score To cut parallel lines in the surface of food, such as fish (or the fat layer on meat), to improve its appearance or help it cook more quickly.

Sear To brown meat quickly in a little hot fat before grilling or roasting.

Seasoned flour Flour mixed with a little salt and pepper, used for dusting meat, fish etc., before frying.

Shred To grate cheese or slice vegetables into very fine pieces or strips.

Sieve To press food through a perforated sieve to obtain a smooth texture.

Sift To shake dry ingredients through a sieve to remove lumps.

Simmer To keep a liquid just below boiling point.

Skim To remove froth, scum or fat from the surface of stock, gravy, stews, jam etc. Use either a skimmer, a spoon or kitchen paper.

Smoke To cure meat, poultry and fish by exposure to wood smoke.

Souse To pickle food, especially fish, in vinegar flavoured with spices.

Steam To cook food in steam, usually in a steamer over rapidly boiling water.

Steep To immerse food in warm or cold liquid to soften it, and sometimes to draw out strong flavours.

Sterilise To destroy bacteria in foods by heating.

Stew To cook food, such as tougher cuts of meat, in flavoured liquid which is kept at simmering point.

Stir-fry To cook small even-sized pieces of food rapidly in a little fat, tossing constantly over a high heat, usually in a wok.

Suet Hard fat of animal origin used in pastry and steamed puddings. A vegetarian alternative is readily available.

Sugar syrup A concentrated solution of sugar in water used to poach fruit and make sorbets, granitas, fruit juices etc.

Sweat To cook chopped or sliced vegetables in a little fat without liquid in a covered pan over a low heat to soften.

Tepid The term used to describe temperature at approximately blood heat, ie 37°C (98.7°F).

Thermometer, Sugar/Fat Used for accurately checking the temperature of boiling sugar syrups, and fat for deep-frying respectively. Dual purpose thermometers are obtainable.

Truss To tie or skewer poultry or game into shape prior to roasting.

Unleavened Flat bread, such as pitta, made without a raising agent.

Vanilla sugar Sugar in which a vanilla pod has been stored to impart its flavour.

Whipping (whisking) Beating air rapidly into a mixture either with a manual or electric whisk. Whipping usually refers to cream.

Zest The thin coloured outer layer of citrus fruit, which can be removed in fine strips with a zester.

INDEX

PHOTOGRAPHER CREDITS